UNTHINKING EUROCENTRISM

Seeing multiculturalism and the critique of Eurocentrism as inseparable concepts, *Unthinking Eurocentrism* links the often ghettoized debates concerning race and identity politics, on the one hand, and Third World nationalism and (post)colonial discourse on the other. The central role of the media in shaping communities and affiliations, the book further argues, places popular culture at the very kernel of these postmodern debates. The first comprehensive study of its kind, *Unthinking Eurocentrism* configures an emerging field that the authors call "multicultural media studies." It proposes a theoretical model both for looking at Hollywood and the mass-media (the musical, the western, the imperial film, TV News) and for highlighting alternative cultural practices (critical mainstream movies, "Third Cinema," rap video, "diasporic" and "indigenous" media). A reconceptualized media pedagogy, the authors assert, can catalyze altered paradigms of historical consciousness. With extraordinary interdisciplinary range, *Unthinking Eurocentrism* "multiculturalizes" cultural studies, exploring such topics as the contemporary resonances of the Columbus debate, the aporias of stereotype analysis, the ambiguities of postcolonial hybridity, the potentialities of media jujitsu, and the coalitionary ramifications of multicultural spectatorship, seeing all these issues as surface manifestations of a deeper seismological shift: the struggle to decolonize global culture.

Robert Stam is Professor of Cinema Studies at New York University, where he is also on the board of the Center for Media, Culture and History. He is author of *Reflexivity in Film and Literature* (Columbia), *Subversive Pleasures: Bakhtin, Cultural Criticism, and Film* (Johns Hopkins) and co-author (with Randal Johnson) of *Brazilian Cinema* (Columbia) and (with Robert Burgoyne and Sandy Flitterman-Lewis) of *New Vocabularies in Film Semiotics* (Routledge). He has won Guggenheim, Rockefeller, and Fulbright awards, and has taught and lived in Africa (Tunisia) and Latin America (Brazil).

Ella Shohat is Professor of Cultural and Women's Studies at the City University of New York–Graduate Center and the Coordinator of the Cinema Studies Program at Cuny-College of Staten Island. She is the author of *Israeli Cinema: East/West and the Politics of Representation* (Texas). Co-editor of *Social Text*, her work has appeared in *Screen, Public Culture, Transition, Third Text* and has been anthologized in a number of film, cultural, and feminist collections. Recently a fellow at the Society for the Humanities at Cornell, she has curated a number of film/video series and cultural events, including a conference on multicultural feminism at the New Museum in New York, to be published by MIT.

Color Schemes by Shu Lea Cheang

SIGHTLINES

Edited by Edward Buscombe, The British Film Institute and Phil Rossen, Center for Modern Culture and Media, Brown University, USA

Cinema Studies has made extraordinary strides in the past two decades. Our capacity for understanding both how and what the cinema signifies has been developed through new methodologies, and hugely enriched in interaction with a wide variety of other disciplines, including literary studies, anthropology, linguistics, history, economics and psychology. As fertile and important as these new theoretical foundations are, their very complexity has made it increasingly difficult to track the main lines of conceptualization. Furthermore, they have made Cinema Studies an ever more daunting prospect for those coming new to the field.

This new series of books will map out the ground of major conceptual areas within Cinema Studies. Each volume is written by a recognized authority to provide a clear and detailed synopsis of current debates within a particular topic. Each will make an original contribution to advancing the state of knowledge within the area. Key arguments and terms will be clearly identified and explained, seminal thinkers will be assessed, and issues for further research will be laid out. Taken together the series will constitute an indispensable chart of the terrain which Cinema Studies now occupies.

Books in the series include:

CINEMA AND SPECTATORSHIP
Judith Mayne

GENRE AND HOLLYWOOD
Steve Neale

NARRATIVE COMPREHENSION AND FILM
Edward Branigan

NEW VOCABULARIES IN FILM SEMIOTICS
Structuralism, Post-structuralism and Beyond
Robert Stam, Robert Burgoyne and Sandy Flitterman-Lewis

UNTHINKING EUROCENTRISM

Multiculturalism and the media

Ella Shohat/Robert Stam

Routledge
Taylor & Francis Group

LONDON AND NEW YORK

First published 1994
by Routledge
2 Park Square, Milton Park, Abingdon, Oxon, OX14 4RN

Simultaneously published in the USA and Canada
by Routledge
270 Madison Avenue, New York, NY 10016

Reprinted 1995, 1996, 1997, 2000, 2001, 2002, 2003, 2004, 2005, 2006, 2007 (three times)

Routledge is an imprint of the Taylor & Francis Group, an informa business

© 1994 Ella Shohat and Robert Stam

Typeset in Times by Solidus (Bristol) Limited
Printed and bound in Great Britain by
MPG Books Ltd, Bodmin, Cornwall

British Library Cataloguing in Publication Data
A catalogue record for this book is available from the British Library

Library of Congress Cataloging in Publication Data
Shohat, Ella
Unthinking Eurocentrism : multiculturalism and the media / Ella
Shohat and Robert Stam.
p. cm. – (Sightlines)
Includes bibliographical references and index.
1. Motion pictures–Developing countries. 2. Racism in motion
pictures. 3. Developing countries–Civilization–Western
influences. 4. Intercultural communication in motion pictures.
5. Culture diffusion. I. Stam, Robert. II. Title.
III. Series: Sightlines (London, England)
PN1993.5.D44S56 1994
302.23´43–dc20 93-41501

ISBN 10: 0–415–06324–8 (hbk)
ISBN 10: 0–415–06325–6 (pbk)
ISBN 13: 978–0–415–06324–1 (hbk)
ISBN 13: 978–0–415–06325–8 (pbk)

To our families in
Latin America and the Middle East

CONTENTS

CONTENTS

CONTENTS

PLATES

ACKNOWLEDGMENTS

Unthinking Eurocentrism is the culmination of a long period of research, teaching, curating, and activism on the part of two people. It is also the culmination of a long period of animated dialog concerning the issues treated here. The book first took public academic form as a course, entitled "European Colonialism in Literature and Film," taught by Robert Stam at the University of California, Berkeley in the mid-1970s. The ideas were further elaborated in an essay (co-signed by Stam and Louise Spence) entitled "Racism, Colonialism and Representation," published in *Screen* (1983). That essay was itself inflected by the work of a "Racism in the Media" study group at New York University, in which Ella Shohat and Robert Stam both participated, and whose work led to a special issue on "Third World Cinema" in the journal *Critical Arts* (1983), which included essays by Shohat on Egyptian Cinema and by Stam on Brazilian Cinema. Subsequently, we joined forces again to write either together ("Cinema After Babel: Language, Difference, and Power," published in *Screen* in 1985 and "*Zelig* and Contemporary Theory: Meditation on the Chameleon Text," *Enclitic*, 1987), or in tandem (parallel essays both for the Lester Friedman anthology *Unspeakable Images* and for the Robert Sklar/Charles Musser anthology *Resisting Images*). Given our affinities and common desire to critique Eurocentrism and racism and to disseminate Third World culture and cinema, then, we were eager to collaborate on *Unthinking Eurocentrism*.

Although most of the material in this book is new, certain sections were published, in preliminary and usually quite different form, in various journals. The material on Postcoloniality in Chapter 1 first appeared as Shohat, "Notes on the 'Post-Colonial'," *Social Text*, Vols 31–2 (Spring 1992). The material on the Columbus Debate and on Revisionist film in Chapter 2 first appeared as Stam, "Rewriting 1492: Cinema and the Columbus Debate," in *Cineaste*, Vol. 19, No. 4 (March 1993) and Shohat, "Staging the Quincentenary: The Middle East and the Americas," *Third Text*, No. 21 (Winter 1992–3). The section on "Cinema as Science and Spectacle" in Chapter 3 first appeared as Shohat, "Imaging *Terra Incognita*: The Disciplinary Gaze of Empire," *Public Culture*, Vol. 3, No. 2 (Spring 1991). The material on *Wild Geese* in Chapter 3 first appeared as Stam,

"The Wild Geese" in *Cineaste*, Vol. 9, No. 2 (1982), while the section on "Postmodern War" first appeared as Stam, "Mobilizing Fictions: The Gulf War, the Media, and the Recruitment of the Spectator," *Public Culture*, Vol. 4, No. 2 (Spring 1992), and as Shohat, "The Media's War," *Social Text* 28 (Spring 1991). Parts of Chapter 4, "Tropes of Empire," first appeared as Shohat, "Gender and the Culture of Empire: Toward a Feminist Ethnography of the Cinema," *Quarterly Review of Film and Video*, 131: 1–2 (Spring 1991) and "Gender in Hollywood's Orient," *Middle East Report*, 162 (January–February 1990). Parts of Chapter 5 appeared as Stam, "From Stereotype to Discourse: Some Methodological Reflexions on Realism in the Media," in *Cineaction*, No. 32 (Fall 1993), and Shohat, "Master Narrative/Counter Readings," in Sklar and Musser, eds, *Resisting Images: Essays on Cinema and History* (Philadelphia: Temple University Press, 1990). Parts of the section on "The Linguistics of Domination" appeared in Shohat/Stam, "The Cinema After Babel: Language, Difference, Power," *Screen* 26: 3–4 (May–August 1985). Parts of Chapter 6 appeared in very different form in two essays included in Lester Friedman, ed., *Unspeakable Images: Ethnicity and the American Cinema* (Champaign: University of Illinois Press, 1991): Shohat, "Ethnicities-in-Relation: Toward a Multi-Cultural Reading of American Cinema," and Stam, "Bakhtin, Polyphony and Ethnic/Racial Representation." The section on "Renegade Auteurs" first appeared as Stam, "Orson Welles, Brazil and the Power of Blackness," *Persistence of Vision*, No. 7 (1989). The material on *The Battle of Algiers* in Chapter 7 first appeared as Stam, "Film Study Extract" for Macmillan Films in 1975, while some of the material on militant documentaries first appeared as Stam, *"Hour of the Furnaces* and the Two Avant-Gardes," *Millenium Film Journal*, Nos 7–9 (Fall/Winter 1980–1). Parts of the sections on "Rewriting Colonial History," "Allegories of Impotence," and "Third World Reflexivity" first appeared as Stam/Xavier, "Recent Brazilian Cinema: Allegory, Metacinema, Carnival," *Film Quarterly*, Vol. XLI, No. 3 (Spring 1988), and Shohat, "Egypt: Cinema and Revolution," *Critical Arts*, Vol. 2, No. 4 (1983) and *"Wedding in Galilee,"* *Middle East Report*, 154 (September–October 1988). Parts of Chapter 9 appeared as contributions by both of us to a MLA symposium organized by Andrew Ross, "Can Popular Culture Be Politically Correct?" in *Social Text*, No. 36 (Fall 1993).

A word about the nature of our collaboration in relation to the various chapters. A number of the chapters, notably "The Introduction," "Stereotype, Realism, and the Struggle over Representation," "Ethnicities-in-Relation," and "The Politics of Multiculturalism in the Postmodern Age," were written, as it were, with four hands, melding our two voices from the outset. Other chapters (setting aside the previously published materials mentioned above), "From Eurocentrism to Polycentrism," "Formations of Colonialist Discourse," "The Imperial Imaginary," "The Third Worldist Film," and "Esthetics of Resistance," were largely written first by Stam, and then revised and supplemented by Shohat. Chapter 4, "Tropes of Empire," was written by Shohat and revised by Stam. In another sense, however, every word here is "shared territory" in that virtually all of it emerges from our ongoing conversations about the issues engaged, and because of the seemingly endless process of rewriting in which we both have participated. The entire text is imbued with our constant intellectual dialogue, and animated by a common vision, since while our socially constructed identities are distinct, our identifications, our goals and affiliations, are the same.

Unthinking Eurocentrism interweaves many voices. Our intellectual debts are made explicit in our copious footnotes and in our extended bibliography. However, we would especially like to thank the people who read our manuscript, in part or in its entirety, and who made useful suggestions: Manthia Diawara, David Frankel, Qadri Ismail, Caren Kaplan, Ernest Larsen, Joseph Massad, Richard Peña, Richard Porton, Bruce Robbins, João Luiz Vieira, Ismail Xavier, and our editors Ed Buscombe and Phil Rosen. We would also like to acknowledge the help of our various Routledge editors: Rebecca Barden, Sue Bilton, and Diana Russell.

The following foundations and institutions facilitated our work by providing grants: the Society for the Humanities at Cornell University fellowship (1991–2); Professional Staff Congress-City University of New York for Research Award (1990–1) and the CUNY-College of Staten Island's Incentive Award (1991–2) for Ella Shohat, and the Rockefeller Foundation for a fellowship for Robert Stam at SUNY Buffalo (1992–3). During the tenure of these grants, various people were helpful to us: in Buffalo, Michael Frisch, Patrizio Nisserio, Gerald O'Grady, Lynn Taylor, Nah Dove, Larry Chisholm, and Jolene Ricard; and at Cornell, Jonathan Culler, Dominic LaCapra, Annette Jaimes, Terence Turner, Selwyn Cudjoe, Richard Herskowitz, Cecily Marcus, Mary Ahl, Aggie Sirrine, and Linda Allen.

We are grateful to the following individuals and institutions for stills: Craig Baldwin (*O No Coronado!*); British Film Institute (*Alexandria Why ...?, The Battle of Algiers, Lawrence of Arabia, Sahara*); California Newsreel (*Touki Bouki*); Catherine Benamou and Paramount (*It's All True*); Shu Lea Cheang (*Color Schemes*); Gary Crowdus and *Cineaste* (*1492: The Conquest of Paradise*); the Cinemateca Brasileira (*Iracema, The Discovery of Brazil, How Tasty Was My Frenchman*); Cine-World (*Land in Anguish*), Monica Frota (Kayapo media); Coco Fusco (Inigo Manglano-Ovalle's "Green Card" (1992), a laminated Iris print with Plexiglas and mirror case, courtesy Randolph Street Gallery, Chicago, included in Guillermo Gomez-Peña and Coco Fusco's multi-media project "The Year of the White Bear," "Two Undiscovered Amerindians Visit Madrid," and *Border Brujo*); Faye Ginsburg (*Barbakiueria*); Renee Greene and the Pat Hearn gallery, NY (the "Hottentot Venus" layout); Kino International (*Daughters of the Dust* and *Zou Zou*); Milestone (*Simba*); Museum of Modern Art (*The Band Wagon, Cleopatra, Harem Scarum, The Mummy/Night of Counting the Years, The Sheik*); Mypheduh (*Sankofa*); New Yorker films (*The Other Francisco* and *Hour of the Furnaces*); PBS (*Surviving Columbus*); Richard Peña and the Film Society at Lincoln Center (*In Search of Famine, Sanders of the River, The Searchers, Thunderheart, Xala,* and *Wiping the Tears of Seven Generations*); Lourdes Portillo (*Columbus on Trial*); Gilberto Stam (ABC's *Lines in the Sand*); Elia

xvii

Suleiman (*Homage by Assassination* and *Introduction to the End of an Argument*); Women Make Movies (*Illusions, Measures of Distance, Slaying the Dragon*). Michael Marcinelli, who we learned about through Faye Ginsburg, generously helped us reproduce vídeo stills. Ernest Larsen, Sherry Millner, and Irit Rogoff offered advice on the selection of stills. We would also like to call attention to the US companies which distribute some of the alternative films discussed in this book: Arab Film Distributors, California Newsreel, Cinema Guild, First Run Features, Icarus, Kino International, Mypheduh, New Line Cinema, New Yorker Films, Third World Newsreel, Video Data Bank, Women Make Movies. We are enormously grateful to Nancy Lytle for generously allowing us to use her (and Jane Devon's) evocative collage for the cover.

We would also like to acknowledge a number of the participants in the recent Conferences and Film series we organized related to the themes of this book: first, those who participated in the "Goodbye Columbus: Media and Representation" Conference at Cornell University (Spring 1992, co-organized by Ella Shohat, Annette Jaimes and Terence Turner), notably José Barreiro, Ward Churchill, Donald Grinde, Jr., Harryette Mullen, José Piedra, Shirley Samuels, and Robert Venables; and second, for the "Rewriting 1492: Images of Conquest, Colonialism, and Resistance" Film Lecture Series at New York University (Fall 1992), notably Alex Ewen, Manthia Diawara, Jorge Klor de Alva, Mick Taussig, Edward Kamau Braithwaite, and Elizabeth Weatherford. Special gratitude goes to Ella Shohat's co-teachers on multiculturalism at the CUNY-Graduate Center: Electa Arenal and Juan Flores, along with all our colleagues both at NYU and CUNY. We are also immensely indebted to the many vibrant, articulate students in our multiculturalism-related seminars ("Third World Cinema," "Gender and the Culture of Empire," "Issues in Ethnic Representation," "Emergent Discourses," "Gender and the Discourses of Discovery," "Issues in Multicultural Feminism," "African Cinema," "Brazilian Cinema," "Eurocentrism and Multiculturalism," and "Rewriting 1492"), courses taught at the City University of New York, at New York University, at Cornell University and at the University of São Paulo.

One of the pleasures of working in the field of multicultural studies is the company of marvelous friends and allies. In this spirit, we would like to single out a few people who have been especially supportive: Rabab Abdul Hadi, Onsi Abuseif, Mirella Affron, Parag Anladi, Pat Auferheide, Karen Backstein, Janake Bakhle, Catherine Benamou, Julianne Burton, Jonathan Bucksbaum, Mary Schmidt Campbell, Jan Carew, Arlindo Castro, Sumita Chakravarty, Mbye Cham, Cheryl Chisholm, Jim Clifford, Luiz Antonio Coelho, Mark Crawford, George Custen, Dan Dawson, Daphne Depollo, Sandy Flitterman-Lewis, Ayse Franko, Coco Fusco, Jane Gaines, Faye Ginsburg, Brian Goldfarb, William Greaves, Inderpal Grewal, Heskel Helali, John Hess, Marina Heung, Patricia Hofbauer, Lynne Jackson, Randal Johnson, Jacquie Jones, Connie Katon, Parvaiz Khan, Michael Kepp, Chuck Kleinhans, Agostin Lao, Mary Lawlor, Paul Lenti, Julia Lesage, Ana Lopez, Wahneema Lubiano, Anne McClintock, John McClure, Lloyd MacNiell, Ivone Margulies, Waldo Martin, Sherry Millner, Chandra

Talpade Mohanty, Aamir Mufti, Hamid Naficy, James Naremore, Vinicius Navarro, Rob Nixon, Lourdes Portillo, Bérénice Reynaud, Ruby Rich, Mark Ried, Edward Said, Eric Smoodin, Viola Shafik, David Stam, Jim Stam, Juan Stam, Elia Suleiman, Clyde Taylor, David Traboulay, Jyotsna Uppal, Michele Wallace, Cornel West, and the entire *Social Text* collective. And finally our deep love to Rima, Amal, and Ya'aqub.

INTRODUCTION

Both in the media and in the academy, recent years have witnessed energetic debates about the interrelated issues of Eurocentrism, racism, and multiculturalism. Visible in the historical polemics about Columbus, in the academic quarrels about the canon, and in the pedagogical controversies about Afrocentric schools, these debates have invoked many buzzwords: "political correctness," "identity politics," "postcoloniality."

Unthinking Eurocentrism focusses on Eurocentrism and multiculturalism in popular culture. It is written in the passionate belief that an awareness of the intellectually debilitating effects of the Eurocentric legacy is indispensable for comprehending not only contemporary media representations but even contemporary subjectivities. Endemic in present-day thought and education, Eurocentrism is naturalized as "common sense." Philosophy and literature are assumed to be **European** philosophy and literature. The "best that is thought and written" is assumed to have been thought and written by Europeans. (By Europeans, we refer not only to Europe *per se* but also to the "neo-Europeans" of the Americas, Australia, and elsewhere.) History is assumed to be European history, everything else being reduced to what historian Hugh Trevor-Roper (in 1965!) patronizingly called the "unrewarding gyrations of barbarous tribes in picturesque but irrelevant corners of the globe."[1] Standard core courses in universities stress the history of "Western" civilization, with the more liberal universities insisting on token study of "other" civilizations. And even "Western" civilization is usually taught without reference to the central role of European colonialism within capitalist modernity. So embedded is Eurocentrism in everyday life, so pervasive, that it often goes unnoticed. The residual traces of centuries of axiomatic European domination inform the general culture, the everyday language, and the media, engendering a fictitious sense of the innate superiority of European-derived cultures and peoples.

Although neoconservatives caricature multiculturalism as calling for the violent jettisoning of European classics and of "western civilization as an area of study,"[2] multiculturalism is actually an assault not on Europe or Europeans but on Eurocentrism – on the procrustean forcing of cultural heterogeneity into a single paradigmatic perspective in which Europe is seen as the unique source of

1

meaning, as the world's center of gravity, as ontological "reality" to the rest of the world's shadow. Eurocentric thinking attributes to the "West" an almost providential sense of historical destiny. Eurocentrism, like Renaissance perspectives in painting, envisions the world from a single privileged point. It maps the world in a cartography that centralizes and augments Europe while literally "belittling" Africa.[3] The "East" is divided into "Near," "Middle," and "Far," making Europe the arbiter of spatial evaluation, just as the establishment of Greenwich Mean Time produces England as the regulating center of temporal measurement. Eurocentrism bifurcates the world into the "West and the Rest"[4] and organizes everyday language into binaristic hierarchies implicitly flattering to Europe: *our* "nations," *their* "tribes"; *our* "religions," *their* "superstitions"; *our* "culture," *their* "folklore"; *our* "art," *their* "artifacts"; *our* "demonstrations," *their* "riots"; *our* "defense," *their* "terrorism."

Eurocentrism first emerged as a discursive rationale for colonialism, the process by which the European powers reached positions of hegemony in much of the world. Indeed, J.M. Blaut calls Eurocentrism "the colonizer's model of the world."[5] As an ideological substratum common to colonialist, imperialist, and racist discourse, Eurocentrism is a form of vestigial thinking which permeates and structures *contemporary* practices and representations even after the formal end of colonialism. Although colonialist discourse and Eurocentric discourse are intimately intertwined, the terms have a distinct emphasis. While the former explicitly justifies colonialist practices, the latter embeds, takes for granted, and "normalizes" the hierarchical power relations generated by colonialism and imperialism, without necessarily even thematizing those issues directly. Although generated by the colonizing process, Eurocentrism's links to that process are obscured in a kind of buried epistemology.

Eurocentric discourse is complex, contradictory, historically unstable. But in a kind of composite portrait, Eurocentrism as a mode of thought might be seen as engaging in a number of mutually reinforcing intellectual tendencies or operations:

1. Eurocentric discourse projects a linear historical trajectory leading from classical Greece (constructed as "pure," "Western," and "democratic") to imperial Rome and then to the metropolitan capitals of Europe and the US. It renders history as a sequence of empires: Pax Romana, Pax Hispanica, Pax Britannica, Pax Americana. In all cases, Europe, alone and unaided, is seen as the "motor" for progressive historical change: it invents class society, feudalism, capitalism, the industrial revolution.

2. Eurocentrism attributes to the "West" an inherent progress toward democratic institutions (Torquemada, Mussolini, and Hitler must be seen as aberrations within this logic of historical amnesia and selective legitimation).

3. Eurocentrism elides non-European democratic traditions, while obscuring the manipulations embedded in Western formal democracy and masking the West's part in subverting democracies abroad.

2

4. Eurocentrism minimizes the West's oppressive practices by regarding them as contingent, accidental, exceptional. Colonialism, slave-trading, and imperialism are not seen as fundamental catalysts of the West's disproportionate power.

5. Eurocentrism appropriates the cultural and material production of non-Europeans while denying both their achievements and its own appropriation, thus consolidating its sense of self and glorifying its own cultural anthropophagy. The West, as Barbara Kirshenblatt-Gimblett puts it, "separates forms from their performers, converts those forms into influences, brings those influences into the center, leaves the living sources on the margin, and pats itself on the back for being so cosmopolitan."[6]

In sum, Eurocentrism sanitizes Western history while patronizing and even demonizing the non-West; it thinks of itself in terms of its noblest achievements – science, progress, humanism – but of the non-West in terms of its deficiencies, real or imagined.

As a work of adversary scholarship, *Unthinking Eurocentrism* critiques the universalization of Eurocentric norms, the idea that any race, in Aimé Césaire's words, "holds a monopoly on beauty, intelligence, and strength." Our critique of Eurocentrism is addressed not to Europeans as individuals but rather to dominant Europe's historically oppressive relation to its internal and external "others." We are in no way suggesting, obviously, that non-European people are somehow "better" than Europeans, or that Third World and minoritarian cultures are inherently superior. There is no inborn tendency among Europeans to commit genocide, as some "ice people" theorists would suggest – such theories merely invert colonialist demonizations – nor are indigenous or Third World peoples innately noble and generous. Nor do we believe in the inverted European narcissism that posits Europe as the source of all social evils in the world. Such an approach remains Eurocentric ("Europe exhibiting its own unacceptability in front of an anti-ethnocentric mirror," in Derrida's words) and also exempts Third World patriarchal elites from all responsibility.[7] Such "victimology" reduces non-European life to a pathological response to Western penetration. It merely turns colonialist claims upside down. Rather than saying that "we" (that is, the West) have brought "them" civilization, it claims instead that everywhere "we" have brought diabolical evil, and everywhere "their" enfeebled societies have succumbed to "our" insidious influence. The vision remains Promethean, but here Prometheus has brought not fire but the Holocaust, reproducing what Barbara Christian calls the "West's outlandish claim to have invented everything, including Evil."[8] Our focus here, in any case, is less on intentions than on institutional discourses, less on "goodness" and "badness" than on historically configured relations of power. The question, as Talal Asad puts it, is not "how far Europeans have been guilty and Third World inhabitants innocent but, rather, how far the criteria by which guilt and innocence are determined have been historically constituted."[9]

3

The word "Eurocentric" sometimes provokes apoplectic reactions because it is taken as a synonym for "racist." But although Eurocentrism and racism are historically intertwined – for example, the erasure of Africa as historical subject reinforces racism against African-Americans – they are in no way equatable, for the simple reason that Eurocentrism is the "normal" consensus view of history that most First Worlders and even many Third Worlders learn at school and imbibe from the media. As a result of this normalizing operation, it is quite possible to be antiracist at both a conscious and a practical level, and still be Eurocentric. Eurocentrism is an implicit positioning rather than a conscious political stance; people do not announce themselves as Eurocentric any more than sexist men go around saying: "Hi. I'm Joe. I'm a phallocrat." This point is often misunderstood, as in David Rieff's breathless claim that "there is no business establishment any more that is committed ... to notions of European superiority."[10] But corporate executives are the last people who need consciously to worry about European superiority; it is enough that they inherit the structures and perspectives bequeathed by centuries of European domination.

Rather than attacking Europe *per se*, an anti-Eurocentric multiculturalism, in our view, relativizes Europe, seeing it as a geographical fiction that flattens the cultural diversity even of Europe itself. Europe has always had its own peripheralized regions and stigmatized communities (Jews, Irish, Gypsies, Huguenots, Muslims, peasants, women, gays/lesbians). Nor do we endorse a Europhobic attitude; our own text invokes European thinkers and concepts. That we emphasize the "underside" of European history does not mean we do not recognize an "overside" of scientific, artistic, and political achievement. And since Eurocentrism is a historically situated discourse and not a genetic inheritance, Europeans can be anti-Eurocentric, just as non-Europeans can be Eurocentric. Europe has always spawned its own critics of empire. Some of the European cultural figures most revered by today's neoconservatives, ironically, themselves condemned colonialism. Samuel Johnson, the very archetype of the neoclassical conservative, wrote in 1759 that "Europeans have scarcely visited any coast but to gratify avarice, and extend corruption; to arrogate dominion without right and practice cruelty without incentive."[11] Even Adam Smith, the patron saint of capitalism, wrote in his *Wealth of Nations* (1776) that for the natives of the East and West Indies, all the commercial benefits resulting from the discovery of America "have been sunk and lost in the dreadful misfortunes which they have occasioned."[12] Yet when contemporary multiculturalists make the same points, they are accused of "Europe-bashing."[13] Or the critiques are acknowledged, but then turned into a compliment to Europe, in a kind of "fallback position" for Euro-narcissism: "Yes, Europe did all those cruel things, but then, only Europe has the virtue of being self-critical."

Eurocentric thinking, in our view, is fundamentally unrepresentative of a world which has long been multicultural. At times, even multiculturalists glimpse the issues through a narrowly national and exceptionalist grid, as when well-meaning curriculum committees call for courses about the "contributions" of the world's diverse cultures to the "development of *American* society," unaware of the nationalistic teleology underlying such a formulation. "Multiculturedness" is not a "United Statesian" monopoly, nor is multiculturalism the "handmaiden" of US identity politics.[14] Virtually all countries and regions are multicultural in a purely descriptive sense. Egypt melds Pharaonic, Arab, Muslim, Jewish, Christian/ Coptic, and Mediterranean influences; India is riotously plural in language and religion; and Mexico's "cosmic race" mingles at least three major constellations of cultures. Nor is North American multiculturalism of recent date. "America" began as polyglot and multicultural, speaking a myriad of languages: European, African, and Native American.

While the fashionability of the word multiculturalism might soon pass, the issues to which it points will not soon fade, for these contemporary quarrels are but the surface manifestations of a deeper "seismological shift" – the decoloniza- tion of global culture – whose implications we have barely begun to register. Only an awareness of the inertia of the colonialist legacy, and of the crucial role of the media in prolonging it, can clarify the deep-seated justice of the call for multiculturalism. For us, multiculturalism means seeing world history and contemporary social life from the perspective of the radical equality of peoples in status, potential, and rights. Multiculturalism decolonizes representation not only in terms of cultural artifacts – literary canons, museum exhibits, film series – but also in terms of power relations between communities.

Our purpose here is, above all, to make connections. We make connections, first, in temporal terms. While the media treat multiculturalism as a recent bandwagon phenomenon unrelated to colonialism, we ground our discussion in a longer history of multiply located oppressions. And where many literary studies of culture and empire privilege the nineteenth and twentieth centuries, we trace colonialist discourse back to 1492, linking representations of "ancient history" with contemporary representations, moving from discourses about classical Greece or Africa, for example, to present-day TV commercials. We make connections, second, in spatial/geographical terms, placing debates about repre- sentation in a broader context which embraces the Americas, Asia, and Africa. Third, we make connections in disciplinary terms, forging links between usually compartmentalized fields (media studies, literary theory, reflexive and experi- mental ethnography, Third World feminism, postcolonial studies, the diverse ethnic and "area studies"); and fourth, in intertextual terms, envisioning the media as part of a broader discursive network ranging from the erudite (poems, novels, history, performance art, cultural theory) to the popular (commercial television, pop music, journalism, theme parks, tourist ads). Although progressive literary intellectuals sometimes disdain the lower reaches of popular culture, it is precisely at the popular level that Eurocentrism generates its mass base in everyday feeling. Fifth, in conceptual terms, we link issues of colonialism, imperialism, and Third World nationalism on the one hand, and of race, ethnicity, and multiculturalism on the other, attempting to place often ghettoized histories and discourses in productive relation. (For example, we do not follow the conventional practice of delinking issues of racism from issues of anti-Semitism.)

Rather than segregating historical periods and geographical regions into neatly fenced-off areas of expertise, we explore their interconnectedness. Rather than speaking of cultural/racial groups in isolation, we speak of them "in relation," without ever suggesting that their positionings are identical. Rather than pitting a rotating chain of oppositional communities against a White European dominant (a strategy that privileges Whiteness if only as constant antagonist), we stress the horizontal and vertical links threading communities together in a conflictual network. Rather than recreating neat binarisms (Black/White, Native American/White) that ironically recenter Whiteness, while the "rest" who fit only awkwardly into such neat categories stand by as mere spectators, we try to address overlapping multiplicities of identity and affiliation.

Our larger goal is to "multiculturalize" a cultural studies field often devoid of substantive multicultural content. While many authors defend multiculturalism against neoconservative attack, the work itself is often not multicultural at all. While innumerable essays reshuffle or augment the "mantra" (Kobena Mercer's term) of race, class, gender, and sexuality, or explore dizzyingly abstract notions of "difference" and "alterity" in virtuoso flights of poststructuralese, few offer a participatory knowledge of non-European cultures. While foregrounding minor-itarian "star" intellectuals, the texts largely ignore the work carried on decades or even centuries earlier by anticolonialist thinkers, along with that of non-"stars" and of non-English-speaking Third World scholars. The privileging of the Anglo-American cultural world, and the tracing of cultural studies' pedigree only to London or Birmingham, prevents dialog with Latin American, Asian, and African studies; whatever does not belong to the Anglo-Western world is peripheralized as "area studies."

The global nature of the colonizing process, and the global reach of the contemporary media, virtually oblige the cultural critic to move beyond the restrictive framework of the nation-state. But although we try to set multicultural issues in a global context, we make no claim to "cover" the globe in a lordly imperial sweep. Our call to "think globally" is not a demand that individual scholars become omniscient polymaths, but rather the designation of a collective project. Indeed, *Unthinking Eurocentrism* configures an interdisciplinary field which has been gaining momentum but has barely been named, and which we would call "multicultural media studies." Various subcurrents mingle in the larger stream of multicultural media studies: the analysis of "minority" representation; the critique of imperialist media; the work on colonial and postcolonial discourse; the theorizing of "Third World" and "Third Cinema"; the histories and analyses of African, Asian, Latin American, First World "minority," "diasporic," and "indigenous" media; the work on antiracist and multicultural media pedagogy.

Since all political struggle in the postmodern era necessarily passes through the simulacral realm of a mass culture, the media are absolutely central to any discussion of multiculturalism. The contemporary media shape identity; indeed,

6

many argue that they now exist close to the very core of identity production. In a transnational world typified by the global circulation of images and sounds, goods and peoples, media spectatorship impacts complexly on national identity and communal belonging. By facilitating an engagement with distant peoples, the media "deterritorialize" the process of imagining communities. And while the media can destroy community and fashion solitude by turning spectators into atomized consumers or self-entertaining monads, they can also fashion community and alternative affiliations. Just as the media can "otherize" cultures (the emphasis in our earlier chapters), they can also promote multicultural coalitions (the emphasis in our later chapters). And if dominant cinema has historically caricatured distant civilizations, the media today are more multicentered, with the power not only to offer countervailing representations but also to open up parallel spaces for symbiotic multicultural transformation.

We are proposing a theorized and historicized discussion of Eurocentrism as shaped and challenged by the media. What narrative and cinematic strategies have privileged Eurocentric perspectives, and how have these perspectives been interrogated? Although we emphasize alternative texts and practices, *Unthinking Eurocentrism* does not take a monolithically hostile attitude toward dominant media. We do not make a blanket indictment of Hollywood – like every cultural praxis, Hollywood is the site of tensions and contradictions – nor do we see the avant-garde as a refuge from Eurocentrism. We do suggest, however, that there is "more in heaven and earth" than is dreamed of in the world of Hollywoodcentrism. (Needless to say, we use the term "Hollywood" not to convey a kneejerk rejection of all commercial cinema, but rather as a kind of shorthand for a massively industrial, ideologically reactionary, and stylistically conservative form of "dominant" cinema.) Our goal is not only to look at Hollywood through multicultural eyes but also to decenter the discussion by calling attention to other traditions, other cinemas, other audio-visual forms. Although the word "multiculturalism" sometimes provokes professional anxiety in privileged educators because they think they are being asked to "begin from scratch," in fact we are less interested in "throwing everything out" than in seeing everything anew.

Although we speak of films of diverse types (from Hollywood entertainment to militant avant-garde) and of very diverse national origins, it is not our goal to survey world cinema. (The prolific and innovative cinemas of East Asia, for example, are not a major presence here.) We focus on those films which engage with multiculturalism, not with those which bypass, ignore, or transcend it. We explore progressive audio-visual popular culture along a wide spectrum which includes critical Hollywood films, Third World and minoritarian films, rap music video, the politicized avant-garde, didactic documentaries, and the camcorder militancy of community activists. But rather than scanning the world's media as a whole, we invoke cultural practices and textual examples for their methodological, theoretical, or political value.

Mingling discursive history with textual analysis, speculative theoretical essay with critical survey, *Unthinking Eurocentrism* addresses diverse disciplinary

7

constituencies. While recognizing the specificity of film/media, we also grant ourselves a "cultural studies"-style freedom to wander among diverse disciplines, texts, and discourses, ancient and contemporary, low and high. As a disciplinary hybrid, the book develops a syncretic, even cannibalistic methodology. Its overall architectonics move from past to future, from didacticism to speculation, from hegemony to resistance, and from critique to affirmation. (Within "critique," we would add, there is also "celebration," just as within "celebration" there is buried a "critique.") Our purpose is not globally to endorse, or globally condemn, any specific body of texts; the point is only to become more historically informed and artistically nuanced readers of cultural practices. *Unthinking Eurocentrism* is therefore not structured as an inexorable linear movement toward a proscriptive conclusion. The overall "argument" concerning Eurocentrism is not stated baldly and explicitly, but worked out slowly, over the course of the book. Diverse leitmotifs are woven into the various chapters, creating a kind of musical echo effect whereby the same theme emerges in different contexts. If "The Imperial Imaginary" (chapter 3) stresses the colonialist writing of history, "The Third Worldist Film" (chapter 7) stresses the "writing back" performed by the ex-colonized. Such themes as the critique of Eurocentric paradigms, the elaboration of a relational methodology, the search for alternative esthetics, and the interrogation of the diverse "posts," meanwhile, structure the text throughout. Some themes that appear first in a colonialist register – hybridity, syncretism, *mestizaje*, cannibalism, magic – later reappear in a liberatory, anticolonialist register, so that the diverse sections reverberate together thematically.

The introductory chapter of *Unthinking Eurocentrism*, "From Eurocentrism to Polycentrism," synthesizes the crucial debates concerning "Eurocentrism," "racism," the "Third" and "Fourth" Worlds, and "postcoloniality" in order to provide conceptual groundwork for subsequent discussion. Here we propose the concept of "polycentric multiculturalism" as an alternative to liberal pluralism.

The second chapter, "Formations of Colonialist Discourse," examines, in a telescoped fashion, the nature, origins, and ramifications of colonialist-Eurocentric discourse, seen as an informing intertext for present-day representations. The media, we argue, absorb and retool the same colonialist discourse that permeates such widely divergent fields as philosophy, literature, and history. Rather than surveying an impossibly long history, we focus on landmark struggles over the inscription of "Greece/Egypt," the "voyages of discovery," the discourses of progress and the antinomies of "the Enlightenment," emphasizing less the historical events themselves than their discursive fallout. By way of illustration, we call attention to the media texts that take positions on these debates, for example the many films about Columbus and the conquistadors.

The third chapter, "The Imperial Imaginary," explores the shadow cast by empire over the cinema as an institution whose very origins coincided with the giddy heights of imperialism. What was the role of cinema vis-à-vis the novel and print media in creating a masculinist imperial imaginary? After addressing the early imperialist productions of the US, Britain, and France, including in the proto-cinematic form of colonial exhibitions, we examine the Hollywood western as a paradigm for Hollywood treatments of First World/Third World encounters. That the colonizing intertext of the imperial adventure film and the western subliminally structures even contemporary representations, we suggest, becomes obvious in films like the *Indiana Jones* series of the 1980s, in "colonial nostalgia" films like *Out of Africa* (1985) or *Passage to India* (1984), and even in the media coverage of the Persian Gulf war of 1991. Throughout the chapter we emphasize not only the content of these stories/histories but also their mediation through genre and through specifically cinematic and televisual means of manipulating point-of-view, focalization, identification.

The fourth chapter, "Tropes of Empire," concentrates on the tropological operations of Eurocentrism as a figurative substratum within the discourse of empire. Eurocentric discourse, we suggest, often operates through metaphors, tropes, and figures such as animalization, infantilization, and so forth. Here we focus specifically on the visual embodiments of gendered and eroticized tropes of "virgin lands" and "dark" continents, of "veiled" territories and imaginary harems, and of fantasies of rape and rescue. These embedded topoi, we argue, convey Eurocentric attitudes toward land, ecology, and non-European cultures, and exercise worldly effectivity through institutional discourses such as those of archeology and psychoanalysis.

The fifth chapter, "Stereotype, Realism, and the Struggle over Representation," intervenes in the debates about "realism" and "positive images," critically assessing the methodological field known as "image studies." To what extent has "stereotypes-and-distortions" analysis been useful in relation to a medium still massively associated with the real, and to what extent has it led us into theoretical blind alleys? While such work has been fundamental for identity mobilization and for the critique of the dominant media, we argue, it is also important to move from character-based approaches to more multidimensional methods that take into account such issues as institutional setting, the politics of language and casting, generic mediation, and cultural variation.

The sixth chapter, "Ethnicities-in-Relation," argues for a relational approach to media representation, one that operates at once within, between, and beyond the nation-state framework. A relational methodology, we argue, enables the excavation of a submerged racial presence even in films, such as "lily-white" Hollywood musicals, that do not thematize race *per se*. The complex relational presence of indigenous and Afro-diasporic peoples in all the Americas, we further suggest, requires a transnational approach that foregrounds the conflictual interplay of cultural communities and identities within and across borders.

The seventh chapter, "The Third Worldist Film," discusses the cinematic counter-telling of the history of colonialism and neocolonialism within Third World cinema. Here we "sample" specific films, largely from the 1960s and 1970s, in order to demonstrate a spectrum of revolutionary nationalist strategies: "Third Cinema," "esthetics of hunger," "allegories of underdevelopment." The films discussed exemplify a two-fronted struggle to fuse revisionist historiography with formal innovation. *Battaglia de Algeria* (Battle of Algiers, 1966) kidnaps the techniques associated with TV reportage to tell the story of Algerian independence. *Vidas Secas* (Barren Lives, 1963) embodies an "esthetic of hunger" by filming hunger in a style and production method appropriate to a Third World country. *La Hora de los Hornos* (Hour of the Furnaces, 1968) fuses formal and political avant-gardism in an incendiary fashion, while such films as *Terra em Transe* (Land in Anguish, 1967), *Xala* (1974), and *Urs bilGalil* (Wedding in Galilee, 1987) offer modernist "allegories of impotence." Reflexive films such as *Iskandariya Leh...?* (Alexandria Why ...?, 1979), *Aakaler Sandhane* (In Search of Famine, 1980), and *Cabra Marcado para Morrer* (Twenty Years After, 1984), finally, focalize the specificities of the filmmaking process in the Third World.

Chapter 8, "Esthetics of Resistance," focusses on the attempts to synthesize radical politics with alternative esthetics, in a double and complementary movement embracing both form and content. The films discussed here go "beyond" many of the films discussed in the previous chapter, first in that they reject realist esthetics in favor of anthropophagic, parodic-carnivalesque, and media-jujitsu strategies; and second, in that they transcend an exclusive concern with nation, interrogating nationalist discourse also from the standpoint of class, gender, sexuality, and diasporic identity. In what we call "post-Third Worldist" films, paramodern "archaic" cultural traditions such as orality and carnival become the trampolin for modernizing or postmodernizing esthetics. Rather than proposing a monolithically correct esthetic, here we evoke a varied constellation of oppositional strategies, which taken together have the potential of revolutionizing audio-visual production and pedagogy.

The ninth and final chapter, "The Politics of Multiculturalism in the Postmodern Age," theorizes media pedagogy, reception, and spectatorship. Here we examine issues of "political correctness," cross-cultural spectatorship, intercommunal coalitions, and the politics of popular culture in the postmodern age. How does spectatorship impact on communal belonging and political affiliation in an increasingly transnational world? We develop notions of "racially resistant readings," "analogical structures of feeling," and "multicultural spectatorship." We explore, finally, the opportunities opened up by anti-Eurocentric, multicultural, audio-visual pedagogy.

Our title, *Unthinking Eurocentrism*, has a double thrust that structures the book as a whole. On the one hand, we aim to expose the unthinking, taken-for-granted quality of Eurocentrism as an unacknowledged current, a kind of bad epistemic habit, both in mass-mediated culture and in intellectual reflection on that culture. In this sense, we want to clear Eurocentric rubble from the collective brain. On the other, we want to "unthink" Eurocentric discourse, to move beyond it toward a relational theory and practice. Rather than striving for "balance," we hope to "right the balance." Eurocentric criticism, we will argue, is not only politically retrograde but also esthetically stale, flat, and unprofitable. There are many cognitive, political, and esthetic alternatives to Eurocentrism; our hope is to define and illuminate them.

10

Unthinking Eurocentrism is not a politically correct book. The very word "correctness," in our view, comes with a bad odor. On the one (right) hand, it smells of Crusoe's ledger book, of manuals of etiquette and table manners, and even of the bookkeeping of the Inquisition and the Holocaust. On the other (left) hand, it has the odor of Stalinist purism, now transferred to a largely verbal register. The phrase "political correctness" (PC) evokes not only the neoconservative caricature of socialist, feminist, gay, lesbian, and multiculturalist politics but also a real tendency within the left – whence its effectiveness. Amplifying the preexisting association of the left with moralistic self-righteousness and puritanical antisensuality, the right wing has portrayed all politicized critique as the neurotic effluvium of whiny malcontents, the product of an uptight subculture of morbid guilt-tripping. But if "political correctness" evokes a preachy, humorless austerity, the phrase "popular culture" evokes a sense of pleasure. Thus an underlying question in *Unthinking Eurocentrism* is the following: given the eclipse of revolutionary metanarratives in the postmodern era, how do we critique the dominant Eurocentric media while harnessing its undeniable pleasures? For our part, we are not interested in impeccably correct texts produced by irreproachable revolutionary subjects. Indeed, a deep quasi-religious substratum underlies the search for perfectly correct political texts. In this sense, we would worry less about incorrectness (a word suggesting a positivist updating of "sin"), stop searching for perfectly correct texts (patterned after the model of the canonical sacred word), stop looking for perfect characters (modeled on impeccable divinities and infallible popes), and assume instead imperfection and contradiction.

Congruent with our double thrust, we will deploy a double operation of critique and celebration, of dismantling and rebuilding, of critiquing Eurocentric tendencies within dominant discourse while celebrating the transgressive utopianism of multicultural texts and practices. We do not mean "utopia" in the sense of scientistic "blueprint" utopias or totalizing metanarratives of progress, but rather in the sense of "critical utopias" which seek what Tom Moylan calls "seditious expression of social change" carried on in a "permanently open process of envisioning what is not yet."[15] Rather than constructing a purist notion of correct texts or immaculate sites of resistance, we would propose a positively predatory attitude which seizes esthetic and pedagogic potentialities in a wide variety of cultural practices, finding in them germs of subversion that can "sprout" in an altered context. Rather than engaging in a moralistic, hectoring critique, our hope is to point to the exuberant possibilities opened up by critical and polycentric multiculturalism.

NOTES

1 Hugh Trevor-Roper, *The Rise of Christian Europe* (New York: Harcourt Brace Jovanovich, 1965), p. 9.
2 For Roger Kimball, multiculturalism implies:

an attack on the ... idea that, despite our many differences, we hold in common an intellectual, artistic, and moral legacy, descending largely from the Greeks and the Bible [which] preserves us from chaos and barbarism. And it is precisely this legacy that the multiculturalist wishes to dispense with.

See Roger Kimball, *Tenured Radicals: How Politics Has Corrupted Higher Education* (New York: HarperCollins, 1990), postscript.

3 The world map designed by German historian Arno Peters corrects the distortions of traditional maps. The text on the map, distributed by the UN Development Programme, Friendship Press, New York, points out that traditional maps privilege the northern hemisphere (which occupies two-thirds of the map), that they make Alaska look larger than Mexico (when in fact Mexico is bigger), Greenland larger than China (although China is four times the size), Scandinavia larger than India (which is three times as big as Scandinavia).

4 The phrase "the West and the Rest," to the best of our knowledge, goes back to Chinweizu's *The West and the Rest of Us: White Predators, Black Slaves and the African Elite* (New York: Random House, 1975). It is also used in Stuart Hall and Bram Gieben, eds, *Formations of Modernity* (Cambridge: Polity Press, 1992).

5 J.M. Blaut, *The Colonizer's Model of the World: Geographical Diffusionism and Eurocentric History* (New York: Guilford Press, 1993), p. 10.

6 See Barbara Kirshenblatt-Gimblett, "Making Difference: Mapping the Discursive Terrain of Multiculturalism," draft of a paper given us by the author.

7 See Jacques Derrida, *De la Grammatologie* (Paris: Minuit, 1967), p. 168.

8 Barbara Christian, from a paper presented at the Gender and Colonialism Conference at the University of California, Berkeley (October 1989).

9 Talad Asad, "A Comment on Aijaz Ahmad's *In Theory*," *Public Culture*, Vol. 6, No. 1 (Fall 1993).

10 See David Rieff, "Multiculturalism's Silent Partner," *Harper's*, Vol. 287, No. 1719 (August 1993).

11 Samuel Johnson, *The World Displayed*, quoted in the Yale edition of *The Works of Samuel Johnson*, Vol. 10: *The Political Writings*, ed. Donald J. Greene (New Haven, Conn.: Yale University Press, 1977), p. 421.

12 Adam Smith, *The Wealth of Nations* (New York: Random House, 1937), p. 590.

13 Thomas Jefferson, similarly, called in his own time for the study of Native American culture and languages in schools, yet the multiculturalist call for a "curriculum of inclusion" is caricatured as "therapy for minorities." On Jefferson's interest in Native Americans, see Donald A. Grinde Jr and Bruce E. Johansen, *Exemplar of Liberty: Native America and the Evolution of Democracy* (Los Angeles: American Indian Studies Center, 1991).

14 For a critique of ethnocentric multiculturalism, see George Yudice, "We Are *Not* the World," *Social Text*, No. 31/32 (1992).

15 Tom Moylan, *Demand the Impossible: Science Fiction and the Utopian Imagination* (New York: Methuen, 1986), p. 213.

1

FROM EUROCENTRISM TO POLYCENTRISM

THE MYTH OF THE WEST

When Captain Mac, in King Vidor's *Bird of Paradise* (1932), repeats Kipling's nostrum that "East is East, and West is West, and never the twain shall meet," he receives the joking response: "Hey, Mac, what's the dope on the North and South?" This apparently frivolous exchange calls attention to the geographical imaginary that imposes neat divisions, along a double axis (East/West, North/South), on a globe inhospitable to such rigidities. Like its orientalizing counterpart the "East," the "West" is a fictional construct embroidered with myths and fantasies. In a geographical sense, the concept is relative. What the West calls the "Middle East" is from a Chinese perspective "Western Asia." In Arabic, the word for West (*Maghreb*) refers to North Africa, the westernmost part of the Arab world, in contrast to the *Mashreq*, the eastern part. (In Arabic, "West" and "foreign" share the same root – *gh.r.b.*) The South Seas, to the west of the US, are often posited as cultural "East."

Furthermore, the term "West" comes overlaid, as Raymond Williams has pointed out in *Keywords*, with a long sedimented history of ambiguous usage.[1] For Williams, this history goes back to the West/East division of the Roman Empire, the East/West division of the Christian Church, the definition of the West as Judeo-Christian and of the East as Muslim, Hindu, and Buddhist, and finally to the postwar division of Europe into the capitalist West and the communist East. Thus politics overdetermines cultural geography. In contemporary parlance, Israel is seen as a "Western" country while Turkey (much of which lies to the west of Israel), Egypt, Libya, and Morocco are all "Eastern." At times the "West" excludes Latin America, which is surprising since most Latin Americans, whatever their ethnic heritage, are geographically located in the western hemisphere, often speak a European tongue as their first language, and live in societies where European modes remain hegemonic. Our point is not to recover Latin America – the name itself is a nineteenth-century French coinage – for the "West," but only to call attention to the arbitrariness of the standard cartographies of identity for irrevocably hybrid places like Latin America, sites at once Western and non-Western, simultaneously African, indigenous and European.

13

Although the triumphalist discourse of Plato-to-NATO Eurocentrism makes history synonymous with the onward march of Western Reason, Europe itself is in fact a synthesis of many cultures, Western and non-Western. The notion of a "pure" Europe originating in classical Greece is premised on crucial exclusions, from the African and Semitic influences that shaped classical Greece itself to the osmotic Sephardic-Judeo-Islamic culture that played such a crucial role in the Europe of the so-called Dark Ages (a Eurocentric designation for a period of oriental ascendancy) and even in the Middle Ages and the Renaissance. As Jon Pieterse points out, all the celebrated "stations" of European progress – Greece, Rome, Christianity, Renaissance, Enlightenment – are "moments of cultural mixing."[2] Western art has always been indebted to and transformed by non-Western art, whence the Moorish influence on the poetry of courtly love, the African influence on modernist painting, the impact of Asian forms (Kabuki, Noh drama, Balinese theater, ideographic writing) on European theater and film, and the influence of Africanized dance forms on such choreographers as Martha Graham and George Balanchine.[3] The "West," then, is itself a collective heritage, an omnivorous mélange of cultures; it did not simply "take in" non-European influences, "it was constituted by them."[4]

An idealized notion of the West organizes knowledge in ways flattering to the Eurocentric imaginary. Science and technology, for example, are often seen as "Western." The correlative of this attitude in the realm of theory is to assume that all theory is "Western," or that movements such as feminism and deconstruction, wherever they appear, are "Western"; a view that projects the West as "mind" and theoretical refinement and the non-West as "body" and unrefined raw material. But until recent centuries Europe was largely a borrower of science and technology: the alphabet, algebra, and astronomy all came from outside Europe. Indeed, for some historians the first item of technology exported from Europe was a clock, in 1338.[5] Even the caravels used by Henry the Navigator were modeled after lateen-sailed Arab dhows.[6] From China and East Asia Europe borrowed printing, gunpowder, the magnetic compass, mechanical clockwork, segmental-arch bridges, and quantitative cartography.[7] But quite apart from the historical existence of non-European sciences and technologies (ancient Egyptian science; African agriculture; Dogon astronomy; Mayan mathematics; Aztec architecture, irrigation, and vulcanization), we should not ignore the interdependence of the diverse worlds. While the cutting edge of technological development over recent centuries has undoubtedly centered on Western Europe and North America, this development has been very much a "joint venture" (in which the First World owned most of the shares) facilitated by colonial exploitation then and neocolonial "brain draining" of the "Third World" now. If the industrial revolutions of Europe were made possible by the control of the resources of colonized lands and the exploitation of slave labor – Britain's industrial revolution, for example, was partly financed by infusions of wealth generated by Latin American mines and plantations – then in what sense is it meaningful to speak only of "Western" technology, industry, and science? The "West" and the "non-West" cannot, in sum, be posited as antonyms, for in fact the two worlds interpenetrate in an unstable space of creolization and syncretism. In this sense, the "myth of the West" and the "myth of the East" form the verso and recto of the same colonial sign. If Edward Said in *Orientalism* points to the Eurocentric construction of the East within Western writing, others, such as Martin Bernal in *Black Athena*, point to the complementary Eurocentric construction of the West via the "writing out" of the East (and Africa).

The fact is that virtually the entire world is now a mixed formation. Colonialism emerged from a situation that was "always already" syncretic (for example among Jews, Christians, and Muslims in Moorish Spain, among African nations before colonialism, among indigenous "Americans" before 1492), and the post-independence era has projected its own diasporas and crisscrossing migrations into a fluid cultural mix. Within this flux, "majorities" and "minorities" can easily exchange places, especially since internal "minorities" are almost always the dispersed fragments of what were once "majorities" elsewhere, whence the various "pan"-movements. The expanding field of "comparative intercultural studies" (North/South border studies, pan-American studies, Afro-diasporic studies, postcolonial studies) recognizes these dispersals, moving beyond the nation-state to explore the palimpsestic transnationalisms left in colonialism's wake.

THE LEGACY OF COLONIALISM

As we suggested earlier, contemporary Eurocentrism is the discursive residue or precipitate of *colonialism*, the process by which the European powers reached positions of economic, military, political, and cultural hegemony in much of Asia, Africa, and the Americas. Colonialism took the form both of distant control of resources (French Indochina, the Belgian Congo, the Philippines), and of direct European settlement (Algeria, South Africa, Australia, the Americas). We will use the term *imperialism* to refer to a specific phase or form of colonialism, running roughly from 1870 to 1914, when conquest of territory became linked to a systematic search for markets and an expansionist exporting of capital, and also, in an extended sense, to First World interventionist politics in the post-independence era.

Colonization *per se* preexisted latter-day European colonialism, having been practiced by Greece, Rome, the Aztecs, the Incas, and many other groups. The words "colonization," "culture," and "cult" (that is, religion) all derive from the same Latin verb *colo*, whose past participle is *cultus* and whose future participle is *culturus*, thus placing in play a constellation of values and practices which include occupying the land, cultivating the earth, the affirmation of origins and ancestors, and the transmission of inherited values to new generations.[8] While nations had previously often annexed adjacent territories, what was new in European colonialism was its planetary reach, its affiliation with global institutional power, and its imperative mode, its attempted submission of the world to a single "universal" regime of truth and power. Colonialism is ethnocentrism armed, institutionalized, and gone global. The colonial process had its origins in internal European expansions (the Crusades, England's move into Ireland, the Spanish *reconquista*), made a quantum leap with the "voyages of discovery" and the institution of New World slavery, and reached its apogee with turn-of-the-century imperialism, when the proportion of the earth's surface controlled by European powers rose from 67 per cent (in 1884) to 84.4 per cent (in 1914), a situation that began to be reversed only with the disintegration of the European colonial empires after World War II.[9] Some of the major corollaries of colonialism were: the expropriation of territory on a massive scale; the destruction of indigenous peoples and cultures; the enslavement of Africans and Native Americans; the colonization of Africa and Asia; and racism not only within the colonized world but also within Europe itself.

Colonialist thinking, unfortunately, is not a phenomenon of the past. A 1993 *New York Times Magazine* article by Paul Johnson ("Colonialism's Back – and Not a Moment Too Soon") explicitly calls for a return to colonialism. Excoriating social ills in contemporary Africa, the essay systematically elides the West's role in engendering the situations that provoked these ills. Thus it denounces Somalia as unfit to govern itself, but says nothing about the role of superpower rivalries in nourishing armed conflict there, denounces Angola but ignores US and South African complicity in Angola's civil war, denounces Haiti but remains silent about past US invasions and support for dictatorial regimes. Meanwhile, the essay praises the West's "high-mindedness," for providing a "superb infrastructure of roads and ports," and for "meticulously preparing" the colonies for their freedom, all as part of what for the colonizers was a "reluctant and involuntary process." Some peoples, the essay concludes, "are not yet fit to govern themselves."[10] Johnson's absolutionist discourse asserts the West's disinterested generosity, as if control of land, resources, and forced labor could ever be "unprofitable" or "disinterested."

Colonialism has never been disinterested even on a cultural level. A sequence in Safi Faye's film *Fadjal* (1979) powerfully evokes the experience of *cultural colonialism* from the standpoint of its victims. The scene shows a village classroom in Senegal, where barefoot pupils recite the phrases of their history lesson: "Louis XIV was the greatest king of France. He is called the Sun King." Faye's film stages the theft and substitution of cultural identity. "Real" history, these pupils are told, resides in Europe; only Europeans constitute historical subjects living in progressive time. "Our ancestors, the Gauls," according to French high-school history books for colonial pupils in Vietnam and Senegal, "had blond hair and blue eyes." The Guinean film *Blanc/Ebène* (White Ebony, 1991) has a character correct the French teacher, telling the students: "Your ancestors were Mandinke, and they were heroes." Colonialism, in Ngũgĩ wa Thiong'o's words, annihilated the "people's belief in their names, in their language, in their capacities and ultimately in themselves" and made them see their past as a "wasteland of non-achievement."[11] Colonialism exalted European

16

culture and defamed indigenous culture. The religions of the colonized were institutionally denounced as superstition and "devil-worship." Thus the "spirit dances" of the Native Americans were forbidden, and African diasporic religions such as Santeria and Candomblé were suppressed, partly because medicine men and women, prophets, and visionary-priests – the *papaloi* of the Haitian revolution, the *obeahs* of the Caribbean rebellions – often played key roles in resistance. Colonialist institutions attempted to denude peoples of the richly textured cultural attributes that shaped communal identity and belonging, leaving a legacy of both trauma and resistance.

Although direct colonial rule has largely come to an end, much of the world remains entangled in *neocolonialism*; that is, a conjuncture in which direct political and military control has given way to abstract, semi-indirect, largely economic forms of control whose linchpin is a close alliance between foreign capital and the indigenous elite. Partly as a result of colonialism, the contemporary global scene is now dominated by a coterie of powerful nation-states, consisting basically of Western Europe, the US, and Japan. This domination is economic ("the Group of Seven," the IMF, the World Bank, GATT); political (the five veto-holding members of the UN Security Council); military (the new "unipolar" NATO); and techno-informational-cultural (Hollywood, UPI, Reuters, France Presse, CNN).[12] Neocolonial domination is enforced through deteriorating terms of trade and the "austerity programs" by which the World Bank and the IMF, often with the self-serving complicity of Third World elites, impose rules that First World countries would never tolerate themselves.[13] The corollaries of neocolonialism have been: widespread poverty (even in countries rich in natural resources); burgeoning famine (even in countries that once fed themselves); the paralyzing "debt trap"; the opening up of resources for foreign interests; and, not infrequently, internal political oppression.

"Dependency theory" (Latin America), "underdevelopment theory" (Africa), and "world systems theory" argue that a hierarchical global system controled by metropolitan capitalist countries and their multinational corporations simultaneously generates both the wealth of the First World and the poverty of the Third World as the opposite faces of the same coin.[14] "Our [Latin American] defeat," as Eduardo Galeano puts it, "was always implicit in the victory of others; our wealth has always generated our poverty by nourishing the prosperity of others, the empires and their native overseers."[15] Dependency theory rejected the Eurocentric premises of "modernization" theories which blamed Third World underdevelopment on cultural traditions and assumed that the Third World need only follow in the footsteps of the West to achieve economic "takeoff." Dependency theory has been critiqued for its "metrocentrism," for its adherence to an unreformed version of Marxist base–superstructure theory, for its incapacity to conceptualize the interplay of global and local dynamics, for its failure to acknowledge the "residue" of precapitalist formations, for its blindness to the modernizing powers even of reactionary regimes, and for its insensitivity not only to class and gender issues but also to the "relative autonomy" of the cultural sphere.[16] Dependency theory was at times guilty of a kind of left Prometheanism, seeing the First World as an all-powerful mover and shaker, and the Third World as a homogenous block passively accepting the economic and ideological imprint of the First World.[17] Given these inadequacies, we are not suggesting here that neocolonial dependency constitutes a total explanation for the disadvantaged position of the Third World, only that any adequate account of that condition requires at least partial recourse to it.

Our concern here goes beyond political economy per se to the role of discourses in shaping colonialist practices. We mean *discourse*, in the Foucauldian sense of a transindividual and multi-institutional archive of images and statements providing a common language for representing knowledge about a given theme. As "regimes of truth," discourses are encased in institutional structures that exclude specific voices, esthetics, and representations. Peter Hulme defines *colonial discourse* as "an ensemble of linguistically-based practices unified by their common deployment of colonial relationships."[18] This discursive ensemble, which for Hulme includes everything from bureaucratic documents to romantic novels, produces the non-European world for Europe. We would distinguish, however, between colonial discourse as the historical product of colonial institutions, and *colonialist/imperialist discourse* as the linguistic and ideological apparatus that justifies, contemporaneously or even retroactively, colonial/imperial practices.

RACE AND RACISM

Racism, although hardly unique to the West, and while not limited to the colonial situation (anti-Semitism being a case in point), has historically been both an ally and the partial product of colonialism. The most obvious victims of racism are those whose identity was forged within the colonial cauldron: Africans, Asians, and the indigenous peoples of the Americas as well as those displaced by colonialism, such as Asians and West Indians in Great Britain, Arabs in France. Colonialist culture constructed a sense of ontological European superiority to "lesser breeds without the law." The "basic legitimation of conquest over native peoples," writes Jules Harmand, "is the conviction of our superiority, not merely our mechanical, economic, and military superiority, but our moral superiority."[19] Such imperial *pronunciamentos* exemplify Albert Memmi's definition of racism as "the generalized and final assigning of values to real or imaginary differences, to the accuser's benefit and at his victim's expense, in order to justify the former's own privilege or aggression."[20] Although racism can be irrational and even self-destructive, racism usually comes "in the wake" of concrete oppressions. Thus Native Americans were called "beasts" and "savages" because White Europeans were expropriating their land; Mexicans were derided as "bandidos" and "greasers" because Anglos were seizing Mexican territory; and the colonized generally were ridiculed as lacking in culture and history because colonialism, in the name of profit, was destroying the material basis of their culture and the archival memory of their history. Racism invokes a double movement of aggression and narcissism; the insult to the accused is doubled by a compliment to the accuser. Racist thinking is tautological and circular; we are powerful because we are right, and we are right because we are powerful. It is also essentializing, ahistorical, and metaphysical, projecting difference across historical time: "They are all that way, and they will always be that way."

Racial categories are not natural but constructs, not absolutes but relative, situational, even narrative categories, engendered by historical processes of differentiation. The categorization of the same person can vary with time, location, and context. Subjective self-definition and political mobilization also sabotage rigid definitions. Africans, prior to colonialism, did not think of themselves as Black but only as members of specific groups – Bantu, Fon, Hausa, Igbo – just as Europeans, prior to the invention of "Whiteness," thought of themselves as Welsh, Sicilians, and so forth. At times, the categories become mobilized as a form of solidarity. In contemporary Great Britain, politically active Asians, Caribbeans, and Africans have at times referred to themselves as "Black." In Israel, Sephardic Jews (who largely originate from Asia and Africa) are called and often call themselves "Black," and their militant 1970s movement was called "the Black Panthers" in honor of the American Black liberationist group of that name.[21]

Racism, similarly, does not "move tidily and unchanged through time and history."[22] That racism is positional, relational, means that diverse groups have occupied the functional slot of the oppressed.[23] Racism is above all a social relation – "systematized hierarchization implacably pursued," in Fanon's words[24] – anchored in material structures and embedded in historical configurations of power. In fact Memmi's definition, premised on a kind of one-on-one encounter between racist and victim, does not fully account for more abstract, indirect, submerged, even "democratic" forms of racism. Since racism is a complex hierarchical system, a structured ensemble of social and institutional practices and discourses, individuals do not have actively to express or practice racism to be its beneficiaries. Racism cannot be reduced, as it is in Samuel Fuller's *White Dog* (1982), to the canine ravings of pathological maniacs. It is not, as Whitney Young puts it, simply "a desire to wake up every morning and lynch a black man from a tall tree," but rather the "subtle humiliations" and "gross arrogance" that accompany taken-for-granted privilege.[25]

In a systemically racist society, no one is exempt from a hegemonic racist discourse, including the victims of racism. Racism thus "trickles down" and circulates laterally; oppressed people can perpetuate the hegemonic system by scapegoating one another "sideways," in a manner ultimately benefiting those at the top of the hierarchy. Since racism is a discourse as well as a praxis, a member of an oppressed community can also adopt an oppressive discourse: the anti-Black Black, the self-hating Jew. Samuel Fuller's *Shock Corridor* (1963) stages ethnic self-hatred in the form of a Black character who fancies himself the leader of the Ku Klux Klan. The German film *Weininger's Night* (1989), based on a play (*Soul*

19

of a Jew) by Yehoshua Sobol, similarly anatomizes European-Jewish self-hatred in its study of a historical German Jew who regarded Jews as the incarnation of evil. Thus discourse and ethnic affiliation can split apart under the extreme pressures of a racist or anti-Semitic society. Manning Marable distinguishes between race as a *passive affiliation*, a category into which one happens to be born, and ethnicity as an *active affiliation*, citing Judge Clarence Thomas as someone who is racially but not ethnically Black, in that he may be regarded as having ceased to function as a member of the Black community.[26] Dinesh de Souza, similarly, technically qualifies as a "Third World person of color," but his discourse is of a piece with that of many WASPish incarnations of privilege.

If racism generates contradictions in the victims of racism, it is no less contradictory on its own terms, often masking an attraction to its own hated object. Obsessive denigration can thus mask a perverse identification; repulsion can overlay desire. Ernest Renan, a passionate anti-Semite, devoted his life to studying the same Jewish religious culture that he supposedly despised.[27] The colonialist racist, likewise, feels endangered by an almost overwhelming attraction. Here is an anonymous British writer speaking of the seductions of India:

> It is in the religious atmosphere above all of India that the Englishman feels himself to be moving in a mysterious, unrealised world, and this feeling is the essence of romance. He does well to resist the seduction which this atmosphere exercises upon those too curious about it ... The English in India are wise to surround themselves, as far as they can, with English atmosphere, and to defend themselves from the magic of the land by sport, games, clubs and the chatter of fresh-imported girls, and by fairly regular attendance at church.[28]

These almost comic proposals for maintaining one's Englishness in the face of alien temptation, reminiscent of a headmaster's advice to masturbation-prone youngsters, betrays terror in the face of what is imagined as an exotic lure, even though here the explicit object of fear is religion.

The notion of ambivalence within racism, first broached by Fanon and today often discussed in psychoanalytic terms, needs to be historicized. At times, racism can constitute a disguised form of genealogical self-rejection. By identifying with imperial Rome, Native American scholars point out, the US founding fathers rejected the tribal and communal pasts of their own Northern European ancestors who were conquered by Rome.[29] In a later period, White European-American workers came to construct the African-American population as "otherized" incarnations of a permissive, erotic, pre-industrial past that Whites themselves both scorned and desired. "Englishmen and profit-minded settlers in America," as George Rawick puts it, "met the West African as a reformed sinner meets a comrade of his previous debaucheries."[30] The practice of "blacking up" before taking part in rebellious or riotous actions (directed both against authority and, sometimes, against Blacks) encodes this ambivalence; blacked-up maskers "both admired what they imagined blackness to symbolize and hated themselves for doing so."[31] The smearing of soot over the body was the height of "polymorphous perversity, an infantile playing with excrement or dirt . . . the polar opposite of the anal retentiveness usually associated with accumulating capitalist and protestant cultures."[32]

It is sometimes more revealing, then, to analyze the stereotyper than to deconstruct the stereotype. When anti-Black stereotypes (repulsive bestiality, say) are recoded as positive (libidinal freedom, presumably), it tells us more about the White erotic imaginary than about the objects of its fascination. The adulation of Black physical agility has as its tacit corollary a presumed mental incapacity. The lauding of "natural" talent in performance implies that Black achievements have nothing to do with work or discipline. The adoption by Euro-Americans of Native American words and symbols as names for cars, sports teams (the Braves), and so on surely marks a bizarrely mediated form of admiration, a form of "ambivalence" quite unwelcome to those invoked (whence the Native American protests over the football audience's "tomahawk chop", seen as a white projection of the symbolically endorsed but historically problematic violence of "scalping").

Racism is thus adept at the art of the false or boomerang compliment, two forms of which are primitivism and exoticism. A primitivist film like *The Emerald Forest* (1985) lauds the "natural ways" of the "Invisible People," but in a romanticizing manner that has little relevance to the concrete struggles of indigenous people. Exoticism solipsizes its object for the exoticist's pleasure, using the colonized "other" as an erotic fiction in order to reenchant the world. Phyllis Rose contrasts racism with exoticism:

> While racists are threatened by difference, the exoticist finds it amusing . . . Racism is like a poor kid who grew up needing someone to hurt. Exoticism grew up rich, and a little bored. The racist is hedged around by dangers, the exoticist by used-up toys."[33]

Racial attitudes are multiform, fissured, even schizophrenic. Multicultural bellies, full of tacos, felafel, and chow mein, are sometimes accompanied by monocultural minds. Ellison describes a White youngster, his transistor radio playing a Stevie Wonder song, shouting racial epithets at Blacks trying to swim at a public beach. Third World immigrants of color to the US, pressured by the reigning Black/White binarism, may adopt ambivalent attitudes, identifying with fellow minorities but also tempted to affirm their precarious sense of national belonging by themselves rejecting Blacks. When immigrants got off the boat, Toni Morrison suggests, the "second word they learned was 'nigger.'"[34] Racism also provokes another kind of schizophrenia: the same dominant society that adores African-American celebrities expresses rampant paranoia toward the so-called underclass of inner-city youth. In Latin America, the same Europeanized elites that proudly invoke their *mestizo* culture steadfastly refuse to empower the *mestizo* majority. Thus very real cultural "victories" – and it does indeed make a difference that millions of people adore "minority" celebrities – mask political defeats. Racial categories, in sum, are contradictory, and while these contradictions offer no solace for the victims of racism, any complex analysis must take them into account.

Racism often travels in gangs, accompanied by its buddies sexism, classism, and homophobia. Systems of social stratification thus get superimposed on one another, in ways that are both contradictory and mutually reinforcing. As a historical product, the causes of racism are at once economic (as a scapegoating mechanism linked to economic resentment or opportunism), psychological (having to do with the projections of insecure, ambivalent, or panicked identities), and discursive. (But although racism has a discursive dimension, it is not just a discourse; a police prod is not a discourse, even though discourses impinge on public perceptions of why and how police prods are used.) Racism offers its own perverse "pleasures": an easy, unearned feeling of superiority, the facile cementing of group identity on the fragile basis of arbitrary antipathy. These "pleasures" explain the racism of the weak, the racism that goes against the racist's own self-interest, as when working-class Euro-Americans reject programs beneficial to them because they might also help African-Americans.

Racism traces its deep psychic roots to fear of the "other" (associated with a suppressed animalic "shadowy" self) and to phobic atttitudes toward nature and the body. It was the "negro misfortune," writes Ralph Ellison, "to be caught up associatively on the negative side of [the] basic dualism of the white folk mind and to be shackled to almost everything it would repress from conscience and consciousness."[35] Lillian Smith describes the sexual education of southern Whites as homologically "segregating" the body into those parts that are dark and untouchable and those that are not.[36] The paired terms "Black" and "White" easily lend themselves to the Manicheanisms of good/evil; matter/spirit; devil/angel.[37] And since everyday speech posits blackness as negative ("black sheep," "black day"), and black and white as opposites ("it's not a black and white issue") rather than as nuances on a spectrum, Blacks have almost always been cast on the side of evil.[38] It is resistance to this Manichean temptation that has led many – from Franz Boaz in the 1920s to Jesse Jackson in the 1980s – to call for a move from a terminology based on color and race to one based on culture; to speak not of Blacks and Whites, for example, but rather of African-Americans and European-Americans.

Any analysis of racism calls for certain distinctions. First, *racism* differs from *ethnocentrism*. Any group can be ethnocentric, in that it sees the world through the lenses provided by its own culture. But to see the world through the lenses provided by one's own culture is not necessarily racist, nor is it racist simply to notice physical or cultural differences, or to detest specific members of a group, or even to dislike the cultural traits of specific groups. What is racist is the stigmatizing of difference in order to justify unfair advantage or the abuse of power, whether that advantage or abuse be economic, political, cultural, or psychological. Although people of all groups can entertain racist opinions – there

22

is no genetic immunity to racism – not every group enjoys the power to practice racism; that is, to translate a racial attitude into social oppression. Analysts also distinguish between *exclusive racisms* of extermination, or *inclusive racisms* of exploitation;[39] between *overt* racism, expressed in hostile actions, and *covert* racism, where hostility is not obvious or explicit. Racism can also be *inferential* (in Stuart Hall's words), in other words consisting in "those apparently naturalized representations of events and situations ... which have racist premises and propositions inscribed in them as a set of unquestioned assumptions."[40] The conventional distinction between *individual* and *institutional* racism, finally, is problematic, since racism is by definition "the expression or activation of group power."[41] Racism, then, is both individual and systemic, interwoven into the fabric both of the psyche and of the social system, at once grindingly quotidian and maddeningly abstract. It is not a merely attitudinal issue, but a historically contingent institutional and discursive apparatus linked to the drastically unequal distribution of resources and opportunities, the unfair apportioning of justice, wealth, pleasure, and pain. It is less an error in logic than an abuse of power, less about "attitudes" than about the deferring of hopes and the destruction of lives.

Within the transformational grammar of colonial-style racism, several key mechanisms stand out: (1) *the positing of lack*; that is, the projection of the racially stigmatized as deficient in terms of European norms, as lacking in order, intelligence, sexual modesty, material civilization, even history. Thus the colonialist ideolog Georges Hardy posits the "African mind" as a series of absences: of memory, a sense of truth, a capacity for abstraction, and so forth.[42] Through this same kind of negative alchemy French colonizers transformed the hospitality for which Arab culture has always been celebrated into a sign of backwardness. Arabs, like the New World indigenes, were seen as giving away things not out of cultural codes of generosity but because they were too stupid to recognize their value. The assumption of lack leads to what might be called the racism of surprise: "You mean that *you*'re the doctor!" "So there are universities in Africa!" Racism also involves (2) *the mania for hierarchy*, for ranking not only peoples (placing Europeans above non-Europeans, Zulus over Bushmen) but also artifacts and cultural practices (farming over nomadism, brick over thatch, melody over percussion). Racism also entails the interrelated processes of (3) *blaming the victim* and (4) *the refusal of empathy*, the withholding of sympathy for people caught up in the struggle for survival within the existing social order, the maintenance of a cool, skeptical distance in the face of claims of oppression. Racism involves (5) *the systematic devalorization of life*, which sometimes takes the extreme form of open calls for murder. Thus L. Frank Baum (the author of *The Wizard of Oz*), in 1891, casually recommends genocide: "the best safety of the frontier settlements will be secured by the total annihilation of the few remaining Indians. Why not annihilation? ... better that they should die than live the miserable wretches that they are."[43] The devalorization of life was classically and satirically expressed by Mark Twain, in Huck Finn's response to the question whether anyone was hurt in a steamboat accident: "No Maam, killed a nigger."

Racism in this sense operates less on the cerebral level of opinion than on the visceral level of ethnic solidarity and us/them antipathy, the pronomial level of an assumed "we."

The dominant media constantly devalorize the lives of people of color while regarding Euro-American life as sacrosanct, as when massive fratricidal killing in Miami's inner city is seen as less serious than the murders of a few European tourists, or when the talismanic phrase "saving American lives" is invoked as a pretext for murderous incursions in Third World countries. The same regime that devalorizes life then projects this devalorization on to those whose lives it has devalorized. In the film *Hearts and Minds* (1975), General Westmoreland, the chief administrator of the killing fields of the Vietnam war, sums up oriental philosophy in the phrase "life has no value." (His words are juxtaposed with Vietnamese parents weeping inconsolably over their lost children.)[44] The devalorization of life has as its corollary the media penchant for associating the Third World with violent, unnecessary, random death, or with disease and natural disaster, whereby "the dead or dying body has become in itself the visual sign of human reality in the Third World."[45]

By focussing on the moral dilemmas of the dominant group rather than on structures of oppression, even liberal discourse devalorizes the lives of people of color. Thus the PBS documentary *Dear America: Letters from Home* (1990) laments the "tragedy" of the Vietnam war, but only in relation to Americans.[46] The final intertitle registers the more than 50,000 American dead, but passes over the 2 million Vietnamese dead. Coppola's *Apocalypse Now* (1979), similarly, addresses the "madness" of the war without ever lending human depth to the Vietnamese themselves. Many Vietnam films, such as *Coming Home* (1978), *The Deer Hunter* (1978), *Platoon* (1986), and *Born on the Fourth of July* (1989), treat the war as a domestic tragedy; the real battle takes place within the (White) American soul, a logomachy within imperial culture. During the Gulf war, the mass media constantly framed debates and channeled empathy through a geopolitical grid. When Ted Koppel, at the height of the aerial bombardment of Iraq, spoke of a "quiet day in the Middle East," he did not mean that no Iraqis were being killed, only that no "important" people were getting hurt. And while the Gulf war was not a directly colonial war, the euphoria over "victory" was very much premised on a colonialist devalorization of non-Western life.

Finally, racism has its double binds and Catch 22s: if you are too unlike us, you are inferior; if you are too like us, you are no longer a "real" Black or Indian or Asian. Racism thus juggles two complementary procedures: *the denial of difference* and *the denial of sameness*. While obfuscating differences in historical experience, it denies the sameness of human aspiration. Confronted with demands for the "affirmative" correction of historical injustices, the dominant group becomes the partisan of equality (let everyone be treated just the same), forgetting its own inherited advantages and denying differences in location and experience. *A Dry White Season* (1989) crystallizes this issue by having the Black activist reject the liberal White South African lawyer's claim of a common life experience: "So you too knew passbooks, imprisonment, humiliation?" The liberal ideal of "color-blindness" which sees progress as "transcending" race, similarly, equates White racism and Black cultural nationalism as equally "race-conscious." But Black nationalism sees integrationist rationality simply as a "particular discourse of power" used by White Europeans to justify their own privileged status.[47] Indeed, some social theorists see liberalism as a constitutively exclusionary, sublimated form of Social Darwinism, in that liberal claims about equality and rights actually hide another unacknowledged set of social credentials (Whiteness, maleness, Americanness, propertiedness) that constitute the real bases of inclusion.[48] It is the failure to acknowledge this jungle law "off the books" that authorizes (6) a *discourse of reverse discrimination*; that is, a situation in which those who have long benefited from institutional favoritism resort to a meritocratic language of individual achievement and counter-victimization. This discourse goes at least as far back as the days of slavery, when a Frenchman warned that abolition " would ruin France, and by seeking to liberate 500,000 blacks . . . will have enslaved 25 million whites."[49]

THE THIRD WORLD

The definition of the "Third World" flows logically out of our discussion of colonialism and racism, for the "Third World" refers to the colonized, neocolonized, or decolonized nations and "minorities" whose structural disadvantages have been shaped by the colonial process and by the unequal division of international labor. The term itself was formed against the backdrop of the patronizing vocabulary which posited these nations as "backward," "underdeveloped," and "primitive." As a political coalition, the "Third World" coalesced around the enthusiasm generated by anticolonial struggles in Vietnam and Algeria, and specifically emerged from the 1955 Bandung Conference of "non-aligned" African and Asian nations. Coined by French demographer Alfred Sauvy in the 1950s by analogy to the revolutionary "third estate" of France – that is, the commoners, in contrast with the first estate (the nobility) and the second (the clergy) – the term posited three worlds: the capitalist First World of Europe, the US, Australia, and Japan; the "Second World" of the socialist block (China's place in the schema was the object of much debate); and the Third World proper. The fundamental definition of the "Third World" has more to do with protracted structural domination than with crude economic categories ("the poor"), developmental categories (the "non-industrialized"), racial categories ("the non-White"), cultural categories ("the backward"), or geographical categories ("the East," "the South"). These other categorizations are imprecise because the Third World is not necessarily poor in resources (Venezuela and Iraq are rich in oil), nor simply non-White (Argentina and Ireland are predominantly White), nor non-industrialized (Brazil, Argentina, and India are all highly industrialized), nor culturally "backward" even in "high art" terms (a fact recently recognized by the international prestige granted writers like

Rushdie, Fuentes, Brathwait, Ngũgĩ, Walcott, Soyinka, Mahfouz, and Morrison).

Our work intervenes at a precise juncture in the history of the Third World. On the one hand, recent years have seen ongoing revolutionary and anticolonial struggles. On the other, the period of "Third World euphoria," when it seemed that First World leftists and Third World guerillas would walk arm-in-arm toward global revolution, has given way to the collapse of communism, the indefinite postponement of the devoutly wished-for "tricontinental revolution," the realization that the "wretched of the earth" are not unanimously revolutionary (nor necessarily allies to one another), the appearance of an array of Third World despots, and the recognition that international geopolitics and the global economic system have obliged even socialist regimes to make a sort of peace with transnational capitalism.

Recent years have also witnessed a terminological crisis swirling around the term "Third World" itself, now seen as an inconvenient relic of a more militant period. For Shiva Naipaul, the term is symptomatic of a "bloodless universality that robs individuals and their societies of their particularity."[50] Echoing Naipaul, but from a Marxist perspective, Aijaz Ahmad argues that Third World theory is an "open-ended ideological interpellation" that papers over class oppression in all three worlds, while limiting socialism to the (now non-existent) "Second World."[51] Third World feminist writers such as Nawal El Saadawi, Assia Djebar, Gayatri Spivak, and Lelia Gonzales have shown the gendered limitations of Third World nationalism. Apart from the problem of local Third World imperialisms (Indonesia's over Timor, for example), moreover, countries such as Iran and Turkey fit uneasily into the tripartite scheme, in that they were never directly colonized, even though they form part of the economically "peripheral" countries subject to indirect European domination.[52] Three-worlds theory not only flattens heterogeneities, masks contradictions, and elides differences, it also obscures similarities (for example, the common presence of "Fourth World" indigenous peoples in both "Third World" and "First World" countries).

Third World nationalist discourse often assumes an unquestioned national identity, but most contemporary nation-states are "mixed" formations. A country like Brazil, arguably Third World in both racial terms (a *mestizo* majority) and economic ones (given its economically dependent status), is still dominated by a Europeanized elite. The US, a "First World" country which always had its Native American and African-American minorities, is now becoming even more "Third Worldized" by waves of post-independence migrations. Contemporary US life intertwines First and Third World destinies. The song "Are My Hands Clean?," by Sweet Honey in the Rock, traces the origins of a blouse on sale at Sears to cotton in El Salvador, oil in Venezuela, refineries in Trinidad, factories in Haiti and South Carolina. Thus there is no Third World, in Trinh T. Minh-ha's pithy formulation, without its First World, and no First World without its Third. The First World/Third World struggle takes place not only *between* nations but also *within* them.

But even within the current situation of "dispersed hegemonies" (in the words

26

of Arjun Appadurai)[53] the historical thread or inertia of Western domination remains a powerful presence. Despite its problems, the term "Third World" does retain heuristic value as a label for the "imperialized formations" (including some within the First World), thus conferring majority status on a group which constitutes three-fourths of the world's population. The countries of Latin America, Asia, and Africa do have in common an "exclusion from decision-making power and an oppressive experience of global development and industrialization, leading to economies obliged to be complementary to those of the advanced capitalist countries."[54] According to UN statistics, the First World, although it comprises only one-fifth of the world's population, enjoys 60 per cent of a global wealth drawn in substantial measure from the Third World.[55]

In geopolitical and economic terms, furthermore, the term "Third World" has certain advantages over alternative expressions. While the polarity "North–South" usefully describes the world as divided into rich and poor, whereby the industrial market economies (First World) and the formerly non-market economies (Second World) form the major consumers of the raw materials produced by a Third World largely located in the southern hemisphere, it is also misleading, not only because some wealthy countries (such as Australia) are located in the South, but also because of the current "Third Worldization" of a Second World increasingly dependent on the West. The North–South polarity also ignores the fact that it was the First World and not the Second World that exploited the Third World most egregiously. Finally, the idea of the "proletarian" versus the "bourgeois" nations obscures the patriarchal and classed nature of all three worlds. All these terms, like that of the "Third World," then, are only schematically useful; they must be placed "under erasure," seen as provisional and only partly illuminating. We will retain the expression "Third World," therefore, to signal both the dumb inertia of neocolonialism and the energizing collectivity of radical critique, but with the caveat that the term obscures fundamental issues of race, class, gender, and culture. At the same time, we would call for a more flexible conceptual framework to accommodate different and even contradictory dynamics in diverse world zones.

THIRD WORLD CINEMA

In relation to cinema, the term "Third World" is empowering in that it calls attention to the collectively vast cinematic productions of Asia, Africa, and Latin America and of minoritarian cinema in the First World. Just as peoples of color form the global majority, so the cinemas of people of color form the majority cinema, and it is only the notion of Hollywood as the only "real" cinema that obscures this fact. While some, such as Roy Armes (in 1987), define "Third World cinema" broadly as the ensemble of films produced by Third World countries, others, such as Paul Willemen (in 1989), prefer to speak of "Third Cinema" as an ideological project, that is as a body of films adhering to a certain political and esthetic program, whether or not they are produced by Third World peoples themselves. The notion of "Third Cinema" emerged from the Cuban revolution, from Peronism and Perón's "third way" in Argentina, and from such film movements as Cinema Novo in Brazil. Esthetically, the movement drew on currents as diverse as Soviet montage, Brechtian epic theater, Italian neorealism, and even the Griersonian "social documentary." The term was launched as a rallying cry in the late 1960s by Fernando Solanas and Octavio Getino, who define Third Cinema as "the cinema that recognizes in [the anti-imperialist struggle in the Third World and its equivalents within the imperialist countries] ... the most gigantic cultural, scientific, and artistic manifestation of our time ... in a word, the decolonization of culture."[56] As long as they are taken not as "essential" preconstituted entities, but rather as collective projects to be forged, it seems to us, both "Third World cinema" and "Third Cinema" retain important tactical and polemical uses for a politically inflected cultural practice.

In purely classificatory terms, we might envision overlapping circles of denotation:

1. A core circle of "Third Worldist" films produced by and for Third World peoples (no matter where those people happen to be) and adhering to the principles of "Third Cinema";
2. a wider circle of the cinematic productions of Third World peoples (retroactively defined as such), whether or not the films adhere to the principles of Third Cinema and irrespective of the period of their making;
3. another circle consisting of films made by First or Second World people in support of Third World peoples and adhering to the principles of Third Cinema; and
4. a final circle, somewhat anomolous in status, at once "inside" and "outside," comprising recent diasporic hybrid films, for example those of Mona Hatoum or Hanif Kureishi, which both build on and interrogate the conventions of "Third Cinema."

By far the largest category would be the second: the cinematic productions of countries now designated as "Third World." This group would include the major traditional film industries of countries like India, Egypt, Mexico, Argentina, and China, as well as the more recent post-independence or post-revolution industries of countries such as Cuba, Algeria, Senegal, Indonesia, and scores of others. What we now call "Third World cinema" did not begin in the 1960s, as is often assumed. Even before the beginning of the twentieth century, cinema was a world-wide phenomenon, at least in terms of consumption. The Lumière *cinématographe*, for example, went not only to London and New York but also to Buenos Aires, Mexico City, and Shanghai. Brazil's cinematic *bela epoca* occurred between 1908 and 1911, before the country was infiltrated by North American distribution companies in the wake of World War I. In the 1920s, India was producing more films than Great Britain. Countries like the Philippines were producing over fifty films a year by the 1930s, Hong Kong was making more than 200 films annually by the 1950s, and Turkey almost 300 films a year in the early

1970s. (One interesting feature of early Third World production is the presence of women directors and producers: Aziza Amir and Assia Daghir in Egypt; Carmen Santos and Gilda de Abreu in Brazil; Emilia Saleny in Argentina; and Adela Sequeyro, Matilda Landeta, Candida Beltran Rondon, and Eva Liminano in Mexico.) "Third World cinema," taken in a broad sense, far from being a marginal appendage to First World cinema, actually produces most of the world's feature films. If one excludes made-for-TV films, India is the leading producer of fiction films in the world, releasing between 700 and 1,000 feature films a year. Asian countries, taken together, make over half of the annual world total. Burma, Pakistan, South Korea, Thailand, the Philippines, Indonesia, and Bangladesh each produce over fifty feature films a year. Unfortunately, "standard" film histories, and the media generally, not to mention local cineplexes and video stores, rarely call attention to this filmic cornucopia.

Among the salient trends of recent years have been: a notable increase in Asian film production; the emergence of audio-visual media giants in Mexico and Brazil (Brazil's Rede Globo is now the fourth largest network in the world); the rise (and occasionally the decline) of centralized, state-sponsored film production in both socialist and capitalist countries (Cuba, Algeria, Mexico, Brazil); and the appearance of First World nations and institutions (notably in Britain, Japan, Canada, France, Holland, Italy, and Germany) as funding sources for Third World filmmakers. Severe IMF-provoked "austerity" crises and the collapse of the old developmentalist models, meanwhile, have led to the "dollarization" of film production and consequently to the rise of international co-productions or to a search for alternative forms such as video. Moreover, the forced or voluntary exile of Third World filmmakers has led to a kind of diasporic Third World cinema within the First World. At the same time, the diversification of esthetic models has meant that filmmakers have in part discarded the didactic Third Worldist model predominant in the 1960s in favor of a postmodern "politics of pleasure" incorporating music, humor, and sexuality. This diversification is evident even in the trajectories of individual filmmakers, between dos Santos' austere *Vidas Secas* (Barren Lives, 1963) and his exuberant *Na Estrada da Vida* (Road of Life, 1980), or between Solanas' militant *La Hora de los Hornos* (Hour of the Furnaces, 1968) and his playful *Tangos: Exilios de Gardel* (Tangos: Exiles of Gardel, 1983).

In film studies, one name for Eurocentrism is Hollywoodcentrism. "Because of the world-wide imitation of Hollywood's successful mode of production," we are told in a standard text on classical cinema, "oppositional practices have generally not been launched on an industry-wide basis. No absolute, pure alternative to Hollywood exists."[57] The somewhat tautological formulation – since all industries imitate Hollywood, no alternative exists – embeds a sequencing which makes Hollywood the *primum mobile* of film history, when in fact capitalist-based film production appeared roughly simultaneously in many countries, including in what are now called "Third World" countries. The Hollywoodcentric formulation would reduce India's giant film industry, which produces more films than Hollywood and whose hybrid esthetics mingle Hollywood continuity codes and production values with the anti-illusionist values of Hindu mythology, to a mere "mimicry" of Hollywood. Even that branch of cinema studies critical of Hollywood often centralizes Hollywood as a kind of *langue* in relation to which all other forms are but dialectal variants; thus the avant-garde becomes a carnival of negations of dominant cinema.

Despite its hegemonic position, then, Hollywood still contributes only a fraction of the annual world-wide production of feature films. Although arguably the majority cinema, Third World cinema is rarely featured in cinemas, video stores, or even in academic film courses, and when it is taught it is usually ghettoized. We would propose, therefore, the multiculturalization of the film studies curriculum. Even under the current rubrics of cinema studies (national cinemas, auteurs, genre, theory), one could easily devise national courses on the cinemas of India, China, Egypt, Mexico, Senegal; auteur courses on Ray, Sembene, Chahine, Rocha; genre courses on the melodrama that would include not only American but also Egyptian, Indian, Filipino, and Argentinian examples (along with Mexican or Brazilian *telenovelas*); musical courses which would feature Brazilian *chanchadas*, Argentinian tango films, Mexican cabaret films, Egyptian belly-dancing films, and Hindu "mythologicals" alongside the usual Hollywood productions; feminist theory courses that would feature the work of Sara Maldoror, Maria Novarro, Farida Ben Lyazid, Tracey Moffatt, Sara Gomez, Pratibha Parmar, Laleen Jayamanne; courses on "postcolonial" cinema that would treat the work of exile or diasporic filmmakers such as Raul Ruiz, Parvaz Sayad, Mona Hatoum, Indu Krishnan, Hanif Kureishi, Haile Gerima, and of movements such as "Black British" and French "Beur" cinema.

Despite the imbrication of "First" and "Third" Worlds, the global distribution of power still tends to make the First World countries cultural "transmitters" and to reduce most Third World countries to the status of "receivers." (One byproduct of this situation is that First World minorities have the power to project their cultural productions around the globe.) In this sense, the cinema inherits the structures laid down by the communication infrastructure of empire, the networks of telegraph and telephone lines and information apparatuses which literally wired colonial territories to the metropole, enabling the imperialist countries to monitor global communications and shape the image of world events. In the cinema, this hegemonizing process intensified shortly after World War I, when US film distribution companies (and, secondarily, European companies) began to dominate Third World markets, and was further accelerated after World War II, with the growth of transnational media corporations. The continuing economic dependency of Third World cinemas makes them vulnerable to neocolonial pressures. When dependent countries try to strengthen their own film industries by setting up trade barriers to foreign films, for example, First World countries can threaten retaliation in some other economic area such as the pricing or purchase of raw materials. Hollywood films, furthermore, often cover their costs in the domestic market, and can therefore be profitably "dumped" on Third World markets at very low prices.

While the Third World is inundated with North American films, TV series, popular music, and news programs, the First World receives precious little of the vast cultural production of the Third World, and what it does receive is usually mediated by transnational corporations. One telling index of this global Americanization is that even Third World airlines program Hollywood comedies, so that a Thai Air jet en route to India, packed with Muslims, Hindus, and Sikhs, screens *Honey, I Shrunk the Kids* (1989) as its idea of "universal" fare. These processes are not entirely negative, of course. The same multinational corporations that disseminate inane blockbusters and canned sitcoms also spread Afrodiasporic music such as reggae and rap around the globe. The problem lies not in the exchange but in the unequal terms on which the exchange takes place.

At the same time, the media imperialism thesis needs drastic retooling in the contemporary era. First, it is simplistic to imagine an active First World unilaterally forcing its products on a passive Third World. Second, global mass culture does not so much replace local culture as coexist with it, providing a cultural lingua franca with a "local" accent. Third, there are powerful reverse currents as a number of Third World countries (Mexico, Brazil, India, Egypt) dominate their own markets and even become cultural exporters. The Indian TV version of the *Mahabharata* won a 90 per cent domestic viewer share during a three-year run,[58] and Brazil's Rede Globo now exports its *telenovelas* to more than eighty countries around the world. One of the biggest TV hits in the new Russia is a venerable Mexican soap opera called *Los Ricos Tambien Lloran* (The Rich Also Cry). We must distinguish, furthermore, between the ownership and control of the media – an issue of political economy – and the specifically cultural issue of the implications of this domination for the people on the receiving end. The "hypodermic needle" theory is as inadequate for the Third World as it is for the First: everywhere spectators actively engage with texts, and specific communities both incorporate and transform foreign influences. For Arjun Appadurai, the global cultural situation is now more interactive; the US is no longer the puppeteer of a world system of images, but only one mode of a complex transnational construction of "imaginary landscapes." In this new conjuncture, he argues, the invention of tradition, ethnicity and other identity-markers becomes "slippery, as the search for certainties is regularly frustrated by the fluidities of transnational communication."[59] Now the central problem becomes one of tension between cultural homogenization and cultural heterogenization, in which hegemonic tendencies, well documented by Marxist analysts like Mattelart and Schiller, are simultaneously "indigenized" within a complex, disjunctive global cultural economy. At the same time, we would add, discernible patterns of domination channel the "fluidities" even of a "multipolar" world; the same hegemony that unifies the world through global networks of circulating goods and information also distributes them according to hierarchical structures of power, even if those hegemonies are now more subtle and dispersed.

FOURTH WORLD AND INDIGENOUS MEDIA

The concept of the "Third World" also elides the presence of a "Fourth World" existing within all of the other worlds; to wit, those peoples variously called "indigenous," "tribal," or "first nations"; in sum, the still-residing descendants of the original inhabitants of territories subsequently taken over or circumscribed by alien conquest or settlement.[60] As many as 3,000 native nations, representing some 250 million people, according to some estimates, function within the 200 states that assert sovereignty over them.[61] (In a larger sense, of course, all peoples go back to some indigenous communitas, all depend on the earth, and all are linked to a planetary destiny.) As non nation-state communities, native peoples rarely "scan" on the global screen and are often not even identified through their self-chosen names; rather, they are called "rebels," "guerillas," or "separatists," involved in "civil wars."[62] As small-scale, sometimes sovereign, nations, Fourth World peoples tend to practice communal and custodial ownership of land, community-based childcare, cooperative production. Unlike cultures of consumption geared to accumulation and expansion, Fourth World societies are geared to subsistence needs, using a variety of cultural mechanisms to disperse wealth and limit material acquisitiveness.

As late as 1820, indigenous peoples still controled half of the globe, but they have declined under the onslaught of both European and non-European nation-states.[63] "Wherever the European has trod," Charles Darwin wrote, "death seems to pursue the aboriginal."[64] Although the Indian wars, registered in Hollywood westerns and misrecognized as "manifest destiny," are the best known of European wars against tribal peoples, similar wars took place in Latin America (for example, the military campaigns against the Araucanian and Tehuelche Indians in Chile and Argentina), in Africa (the German campaign against the Herero), and in Asia (where campaigns against tribal peoples were conducted by the Japanese in Formosa, by the French in Indochina, and by the British in Burma and Assam). Unlike conventional wars, these wars were essentially "ethnocidal"; they aimed at the destruction of a way of life and the subjugation if not decimation of entire populations. The moral rationale for such policies was often formulated in Social Darwinist terms of "survival of the fittest" and inevitable "development."[65] Indigenous peoples were expected simply to wither away under the hot breath of European progress. Nor were indigenous peoples always "saved" by decolonization. Third World governments have themselves brutalized Fourth World peoples, as when the Uganda government in the late 1960s virtually "abolished" the hunting-and-gathering Ik population by gathering them up in trucks and driving them out of their homeland.[66] This process is not inevitable, however, and has occasionally been reversed by political activism. The Brazilian government, after long allowing Euro-Brazilian encroachments on indigenous land, has recently declared huge territories "out of bounds," ceding territory the size of Switzerland to the Amazonian Kayapo and land the size of Portugal to the Yanomami. Ecuador too has granted indigenous stewardship over a swath of rainforest roughly the size of Connecticut.

Plate 1 Commodification in
the Amazon: *Iracema*

Recently, First World people have become sensitized to the situation of Fourth World peoples, as the diverse campaigns mobilized around the global ecological crisis have shown that indigenous peoples have often been superior custodians of natural resources. (The monuments of such civilizations, in the words of Daryl Posey, are not cities and temples, but rather the natural environment itself.)[67] Filmmakers have translated this awareness, for better or worse, in such ecologically minded fiction films as *The Emerald Forest* (1985), *Iracema* (1975), *Quarup* (1989), *At Play in the Fields of the Lord* (1989), and even *The Forbidden Dance* (1990). Fourth World peoples have played a role in First World documentaries (such as, *When the Mountains Tremble*, 1983, an account of Rigoberta Menchu and the indigenous peoples of Guatemala) and in Third World films. In the 1950s and 1960s the Cuzco School in Peru made mixed-mode documentary fictions such as *Kukuli* (1961) and *Jarawu* (1966) in the Quechua language. In Bolivia, Jorge Sanjines made feature films such as *Yawar Mallku* (Blood of the Condor, 1969) in Quechua, and *Ukumau* (1966) in Aymara, with the collaboration of the indigenous people themselves. The former film, for example, speaks of popular indigenous revolts against US-supported policies of sterilization. Fourth World peoples more usually appear in "ethnographic films," which of late have attempted to divest themselves of vestigial colonialist attitudes.

33

While in the old ethnographic films self-confident "scientific" voice-overs delivered the "truth" about subject peoples unable to answer back (while sometimes prodding the "natives" to perform practices long abandoned), the new ethnographic films strive for "shared filmmaking," "participatory filmmaking," "dialogical anthropology," "reflexive distance," and "interactive filmmaking."[68] This new "modesty" on the part of filmmakers has been evidenced in a number of documentary and experimental films which discard the covert elitism of the pedagogical or ethnographic model in favor of an acquiescence in the relative, the plural, and the contingent, as artists experience a salutary self-doubt about their own capacity to speak "for" the other.

The reflexive challenge to representation typical of more recent films like *Reassemblage* (1982) was anticipated in *Petit à Petit* (Little by Little, 1969), where Jean Rouch has his African protagonist Damoure "do anthropology" among the "strange tribe" known as Parisians, measuring their skulls and interrogating them about their bizarre folkways. Some Brazilian films from the 1970s, such as Artur Omar's *Congo* (1977), mocked the idea of Euro-Brazilian filmmakers saying anything of value about indigenous or Afro-Brazilian culture, while others, for instance those of Andrea Tonacci, simply handed over the camera to the "other" in order to facilitate a two-way "conversation" between urban Brazilians and indigenous groups. At times the dialog turned against the filmmakers themselves. In *Raoni* (1978), the Indians ponder the advisability of killing the filmmakers – for them just another group of potentially murderous White men – ultimately deciding to spare them so "they can bring our message to other Whites." In Sergio Bianchi's *Mato Eles?* (Should I Kill Them?, 1983), a venerable Indian asks the director exactly how much money he made on the film, the kind of inconvenient question which would normally make its way to the editing-room trashcan. Thus the filmmaker assumes some of the risks of a real dialog, of potential challenge from interlocutors. The question changes from how one represents "the other" to how one collaborates with "the other" in a shared space. The goal, rarely realized, becomes to guarantee the effective participation of "the other" in all phases of production.

The most remarkable recent development has been the emergence of "indigenous media," that is to say the use of audio-visual technology (camcorders, VCRs) for the cultural and political purposes of indigenous peoples. The phrase itself, as Faye Ginsburg points out, is oxymoronic, evoking both the self-understanding of aboriginal groups and the vast institutional structures of TV and cinema.[69] Within "indigenous media," the producers are themselves the receivers, along with neighboring communities and, occasionally, distant cultural institutions or festivals such as the Native American film festivals held in New York and San Francisco. The three most active centers of indigenous media production are Native North American (Inuit, Yup'ik), Indians of the Amazon Basin (Nambiquara, Kayapo), and Aboriginal Australians (Warlpiri, Pitjanjajari). In 1982, the Inuit Broadcasting Corporation (IBC) began broadcasting regularly scheduled TV programs in order to strengthen the culture of the Inuit spread across northern

Canada. In Kate Madden's account, Inuit programming reflects Inuit cultural values. The news/public affairs program *Qagik* (Coming Together), for example, departs dramatically from Western norms and conventions by avoiding stories that might cause a family pain or intrude on its privacy, and by eschewing any hierarchy between correspondents and anchors.[70]

"Indigenous media" comprise an empowering vehicle for communities struggling against geographical displacement, ecological and economic deterioration, and cultural annihilation.[71] Although occasionally sponsored by liberal governments or international support groups, these efforts are generally small-scale, low-budget and locally based. Indigenous film and video-makers confront what Ginsburg calls a "Faustian dilemma": on the one hand, they use new technologies for cultural self-assertion, on the other they spread a technology that might ultimately only foster their own disintegration. The leading analysts of indigenous media, such as Ginsburg and Terence Turner, see such work not as locked into a bound traditional world but rather as concerned with "mediating across boundaries, mediating ruptures of time and history," and advancing the process of identity construction by negotiating "powerful relationships to land, myth and ritual."[72] At times, the work goes beyond merely asserting an existing identity to become "a means of cultural invention that refracts and recombines elements from both the dominant and minority societies."[73] Indigenous media thus bypass the usual anthropological hierarchy between scientist/anthropologist/filmmaker, on the one hand, and object of study and spectacle on the other. At the same time, "indigenous media" should not be seen as a magical panacea either for the concrete problems faced by indigenous peoples or for the aporias of anthropology. Such work can foster factional divisions within indigenous communities, and can be appropriated by international media as facile symbols of the ironies of the postmodern age.[74] Widely disseminated images of the Kayapo wielding video-cameras, appearing in *Time* and the *New York Times Magazine*, derive their power to shock from the premise that "natives" must be quaint and allochronic; "real" Indians don't carry camcorders.

In Brazil, the *Centro de Trabalho Indigenista* (Center for Work with Indigenous Peoples) and Mekaron Opoi D'joi (They Who Create Images) have been collaborating with indigenous groups, teaching video-making and editing, and offering technologies and facilities in order to protect indigenous land and consolidate resistance. In Vincent Carelli's *The Spirit of TV* (1991), the members of the Waiapi tribe, newly introduced to TV, reflect on ways that video can be used to make contact with other tribes and defend themselves against the encroachments of federal agents, goldminers, and loggers. Taking an eminently pragmatic approach, the Waiapi ask the filmmakers to hide their weakness from the outside world; "exaggerate our strength," they say, "so whites won't occupy our land." In *Arco de Zo'e* (Meeting Ancestors, 1993), Chief Wai-Wai recounts his visit to the Zo'e, a recently contacted group whom the Waiapi had known only through video images. The two groups compare hunting and weaving techniques, food, rituals, myths, and history. The film communicates the diversity of indigenous

35

cultures – Chief Wai-Wai has difficulty adjusting to the total nudity of his hosts, for example. *Like Brothers* (1993), finally, recounts the cultural exchange between the Parakateje of Para and their relatives the Kraho of Tocantins. The two groups exchange information and strategies for maintaining their language and identity and for resisting Euro-Brazilian domination. In all these films/videos, the "outside" spectator is no longer the privileged interlocutor; video is primarily a facilitator for exchange between indigenous groups. On a secondary level, "outsiders" are welcome to view these exchanges and even to support the cause in financial or other ways, but there is no romantic narrative of redemption whereby the raising of spectatorial consciousness will somehow "save the world." In these videos, the non-Indian spectator must become accustomed to "Indians" who laugh, who are ironical, and who are quite prepared to speak of the absolute necessity of killing non-Indian invaders.

Among the most media-savvy of the indigenous groups are the Kayapo, a Go-speaking people of central Brazil who live in fourteen communities scattered over an area roughly the size of Great Britain. When a documentary crew from Granada Television went to Brazil to film the Kayapo in 1987, the Kayapo demanded video-cameras, VCRs, monitors, and videotapes as the *quid pro quo* for their cooperation. They have subsequently used video to record their own traditional ceremonies, demonstrations, and encounters with officials (so as to have the equivalent of a legal transcript). They have documented their traditional knowledge of the forest environment, and plan to record the transmission of myths and oral history. For the Kayapo, as Turner puts it, video media have become "not merely a means of representing culture ... but themselves the ends of social action and objectification in consciousness."[75] The Kayapo not only sent a delegation to the Brazilian Constitutional Convention to lobby delegates debating indigenous rights, they also videotaped themselves in the process,

Plate 2 Indigenous media: the Kayapo

winning international attention for their cause.

In the Granada Television documentary *Kayapo: Out of the Forest* (1989), we see the Kayapo and other native peoples stage a mass ritual performance to protest the planned construction of a hydroelectric dam. (If the engineer in *The Emerald Forest* destroys the dam that he himself has designed, the Kayapo try to prevent such dams from ever being built.) One of the leaders, Chief Pombo, points out that the dam's name (*Kararao*) is taken from a Kayapo war-cry. Another, Chief Raoni, appears with the rock star Sting in a successful attempt to capture international media attention. At one point a woman presses a machete against the company spokesman's face as she scolds him in Kayapo. Another woman, in a remarkable reversal of colonialist *écriture*, tells the spokesman to write down her name, reminding him that she is one of those who will die because of the dam. The spectator enamored of "modernity" comes to question the reflex association of hydroelectric dams with an axiomatically good "progress."

In other films, not necessarily forming part of the "indigenous media" movement, native peoples "talk back" to the anthropologists. Hopi artist Victor Masayesva's *Ritual Clowns* (1988) deploys animated versions of Hopi clowns to mock anthropologists' misinterpretations of Hopi rituals. In the case of *Two Laws* (1981), members of the Australian Aboriginal Borroloola community commissioned a film to express their cultural and political goals. They invited two political-activist filmmakers, Caroline Strachan and Alessandro Cavadini, to work with them on a film about issues of law, kinship, and visual representation. *Two Laws* was subject to Aboriginal control. The community collectively decided all conditions of production, from the lenses used to the editing, ultimately enacting a four-part account of the community's history: "Police Times" focusses on police brutality; "Welfare Times" deals with assimilation policies; "Struggle for Our Land" explores Borroloola conceptions of land; and "Living with Two Laws" reenacts the community's forced resettlement by the government, which subsequently leased traditional lands to a mining operation. Given their communal landownership and collective decision-making, the Aboriginals called for wide-angle perspectives to avoid privileging any individual presence. The central theme is that the Aboriginal system of law regulating property rights and behavior should be respected, a point made necessary because of the White tendency to discount Aboriginal land claims whenever they conflicted with European notions of contracts and deeds. In such works, Fourth World peoples present themselves not as naive primitives but as ecologically and politically sophisticated antagonists ranged against imperialist civilization.

THE POSTCOLONIAL AND THE HYBRID

The cases of the Kayapo and the Borroloola throw into sharp focus some of the theoretical ambiguities of the currently fashionable term "postcoloniality." While Fourth World peoples emphasize an indigenizing discourse of territorial claims, symbiotic links to nature, and active resistance to colonial incursions,

37

postcolonial thought stresses deterritorialization, the constructed nature of nationalism and national borders, and the obsolescence of anticolonialist discourse. Despite the dizzying multiplicities invoked by the term "postcolonial," postcolonial theory has curiously failed to address the politics of location of the term "postcolonial" itself. The wide adoption of the term in the late 1980s, to designate work thematizing issues emerging from colonial relations and their aftermath, clearly coincided with the eclipse of the older "Third World" paradigm. The new term arrived with a magnetic aura of theoretical prestige, in contrast to the more activist aura once enjoyed by the phrase "Third World" within progressive academic circles. Largely emerging in the Anglo-American academe in the form of discursive analyses inflected by poststructuralism, the "postcolonial" is often buttressed by the theoretically connoted substantive "postcoloniality," a term marking a contemporary state, situation, condition, or epoch. The prefix "post" in this sense aligns "postcolonialism" with "postmodernism,"[76] "postfeminism," and, most important, "poststructuralism" – all sharing the notion of a "movement beyond" obsolescent discourses. Within the logic of these alignments, the textual disseminations of poststructuralism become easily conflated with the diasporic dispersals of postcoloniality. Yet while these other "posts" refer to the supersession of outmoded philosophical, esthetic, and political paradigms, "postcolonial" implies both going beyond anticolonial nationalist theory and a movement beyond a specific point in history. This latter sense aligns "postcolonial" with other "posts" – "post-cold war," "post-independence," "postrevolution" – all of which underline a closure of one historical period and the passage into another. The two "posts" are therefore referentially distinct, the first pointing to the disciplinary "advances" of intellectual history, the latter to the chronologies of history *tout court*, resulting in a tension between philosophical and historical teleologies.

Since the "post" in "postcolonial" on one level suggests a stage "after" the demise of colonialism, it is imbued, quite apart from its users' intentions, with an ambiguous spatiotemporality. "Postcolonial" tends to be associated with "Third World" countries that gained independence after World War II, yet it also refers to the "Third World" diasporic presence within "First World" metropolises. In some postcolonial literary theory, the term expands exponentially to include literary productions from all societies "affected" by colonialism, including Great Britain and the US.[77] But given that virtually all countries have been affected by colonialism, whether as colonizer, colonized, or both at the same time, the all-inclusive formulation homogenizes very different national and racial formations. Positioning Australia and India in a similar "colonial" relation to an imperial center, for example, equates the situation of European settlers with that of indigenous populations colonized by Europeans, as if both groups broke away from the "center" in the same way. The crucial differences between Europe's genocidal oppression of indigenous peoples, on the one hand, and Europe's domination of European "creole" elites on the other, are leveled with an easy stroke of the "post."

The term "postcolonial" also blurs the assignment of perspectives. Given that the colonial experience is shared, albeit asymmetrically, by (ex-)colonizer and (ex-)colonized, does the "post" indicate the perspective of the ex-colonized (Algerian, for example), the ex-colonizer (in this case French), the ex-colonial settler (*pied noir*), or the displaced immigrant in the metropole (Algerian in France)? Since most of the world is now living in the aftermath of colonialism, the "post" neutralizes salient differences between France and Algeria, Britain and Iraq, the US and Brazil. This effacement of perspectives generates a curious ambiguity. While "colonial discourse" refers to the discourse produced by colonizers, "postcolonial discourse" refers not to colonialist discourse after the end of colonialism but rather to left-inflected theoretical writings that attempt to transcend the (presumed) binarisms of Third Worldist militancy. The simultaneous privileging and distancing of the colonial narrative in the "postcolonial" become evident through a kind of commutation test. While one can posit a duality between colonizer and colonized and even between neocolonizer and neocolonized, it makes little sense to speak of "postcolonizer" and "postcolonized." While "colonialism" and "neocolonialism" imply both oppression and the possibility of resistance, "postcolonial" posits no clear domination and calls for no clear opposition. This structured ambivalence, while appealing in a post-structuralist academic context, also makes "postcolonial" a fragile instrument for critiquing the unequal distribution of global power and resources.

Apart from its dubious spatiality, the "postcolonial" also collapses diverse chronologies. The colonial settler-states of the Americas gained their independence, for the most part, during the eighteenth and nineteenth centuries. Most countries in Africa and Asia, in contrast, achieved independence during the twentieth century; some in the 1930s (Iraq), others in the 1940s (India, Lebanon), and still others in the 1960s (Algeria, Senegal) and the 1970s (Angola, Mozambique). Others have yet to achieve it. When exactly, then, does the "postcolonial" begin, and what are the relationships between these diverse beginnings? If the "post" refers to the nationalist struggles of the 1950s and 1960s, what time-frame would apply for *contemporary* anticolonial struggles? What is the status of Palestinian writers and filmmakers like Sahar Khalifeh, Mahmoud Darwish, Emil Habiby, and Michel Khleifi who work contemporaneously with "postcolonial" writers? Are they *pre-"postcolonial"*? The homogenizing temporality of "postcoloniality" risks reproducing the colonial discourse of an allochronic other lagging behind the genuinely postcolonial West. The term's globalizing gesture downplays multiplicities of location, as well as the discursive and political linkages between postcolonial theories and contemporary anti-colonial (or anti-neocolonial) struggles and discourses in Central America, in the Middle East, in Southern Africa and the Philippines, struggles that cannot be dismissed as mere epigonic repetitions of obsolescent discourses.[78]

Considering the term "postcolonial" in relation to other terms such as "neocolonial" and "post-independence" helps illuminate all the concepts. Since "post" signifies "after" it potentially inhibits forceful articulations of "neocoloniality." For previously colonized countries, formal independence has rarely meant an end to hegemony. Egypt's formal independence in 1923 did not prevent the British domination that provoked the 1952 revolution. Formal "creole" independence in Latin America, similarly, has not prevented either Anglo-American "free trade" hegemony or Monroe Doctrine-style military interventions. (The term "revolution" assumed a post-independence whose content was a suffocating hegemony.) Such processes distinguish the history of Central and South America from many other colonial settler-states, for despite shared historical origins with North America (European conquest, genocide, slavery), these regions have been subjected to a structural domination on some levels more severe, paradoxically, than that of more recently independent Third World countries such as Libya and even India.

The hegemonic structures and conceptual frameworks generated over the last 500 years cannot be easily vaporized with a "post." By implying that colonialism is over, "postcolonial" obscures the deformative traces of colonialism in the present. It lacks a political analysis of contemporary power relations, for example of recent US militaristic involvements in Grenada, Panama, Kuwait, and Iraq, or of the symbiotic links forged between US political and economic interests and those of local elites. For whatever the connotations of "post" as the locus of continuities and discontinuities,[79] its teleological lure evokes a celebratory clearing of a conceptual space.[80] While "neocolonial" also implies a passage, it emphasizes a repetition with difference, a regeneration of colonialism through other means. "Neocolonialism" usefully designates geo-ecomomic hegemony, while "postcolonial" subtly downplays contemporary domination. "Post-independence," meanwhile, evokes an achieved history of resistance. It shifts the focus to the emergent nation-state itself, opening up analytical space for such explosive "internal" issues as religion, gender, and sexual orientation, none of which are reducible to epiphenomena of colonialism or neocolonialism. "Post-independence" celebrates the nation-state; but by assuming these states' power and responsibility it also makes Third World regimes accountable.

The theoretical circulation of "postcolonial" suggests a supersession of "neocolonialism" and the "Third World" as unfashionable, even irrelevant categories. Yet the terms displaced do remain partly meaningful in broad political and economic terms, and become blurred when one addresses the differently modulated politics of culture. Replacing "Third World" with "postcolonial" has drawbacks as well as advantages. "Third World" still evokes a common project of (linked) resistances, and has served to empower intercommunal coalitions of peoples of color in the First World. Perhaps it is this sense of a common mobilizing project that is missing in the "postcolonial." If "postcolonial" and "post-independence" stress a rupture in relation to colonialism, and "neocolonial" emphasizes structural continuities, "Third World" implies that the shared history of neocolonialism and "internal" racism form a sufficient ground for alliance. If no such commonalities are envisioned, then "Third World" should indeed be discarded. Our assertion of the political relevance of "neocolonialism," and even of the more problematic "Third" and "Fourth Worlds," is intended not to endorse intellectual inertia but to point to a need to deploy all these concepts in a differential, contingent, and relational manner. It is not that one conceptual frame is "wrong" and the other "right," but rather that each frame only partly illuminates the issues. We can use them as part of a more mobile set of grids, a more flexible set of disciplinary and cross-cultural lenses adequate to the complex politics of contemporary location, while maintaining openings for agency and resistance.[81]

Postcolonial theory, in so far as it addresses complex, multilayered identities, has proliferated in terms having to do with cultural mixing: religious (syncretism); biological (hybridity); human-genetic (*mestizaje*); and linguistic (creolization). The word "syncretism" in postcolonial writing calls attention to the multiple identities generated by the geographical displacements characteristic of the post-independence era, and presupposes a theoretical framework, influenced by anti-essentialist poststructuralism, that refuses to police identity along purist lines. It is largely diasporic intellectuals, hybrids themselves (not coincidentally), who have elaborated this hybrid framework. And while the themes are old – "syncretism," "hybridity," *créolité*, and *mestizaje* had already been invoked decades ago by diverse Latin American modernisms – the historical moment is new.

The impulses behind the celebration of hybridity are themselves mixed. On one level, the celebration counters the colonialist fetishization of racial "purity." Colonialist discourse saw different races as different species, created at different times, and therefore forbidden to interbreed. The hostility to miscegenation was encapsulated in such pejorative terms as "half-caste," "mongrelization," and "mulattos" (seen as necessarily infertile). But while reacting against the colonialist mania for purity, contemporary hybridity theory also counterposes itself to the overly rigid lines of identity drawn by Third Worldist discourse. Although the barbed wire separating the medina from the European quarters of Algiers might have disappeared, postcolonial theory reminds us, the traces of French culture have not. French culture itself has been "Algerianized," while North Africans now in Europe occupy a new space of "beur" identity, one neither purely French nor simply North African.

The celebration of hybridity (through a switch in valence for stigmatized terms) coincides with the new historical moment of the post-independence displacements which generated dually or even multiply hyphenated identities (Franco-Algerian, Indo-Canadian, Palestinian-Lebanese-British, Indo-Ugandan-American, Egyptian-Lebanese-Brazilian). Post-independence identities, as the product of a conflictual merging, feature a more stressful hyphen, as it were, than those multiple identities deriving from a move between countries. Furthermore, diasporic identities are not homogenous. In some cases, qualitatively different displacements are piled on to other, earlier displacements. For Afro-diasporic communities, as Stuart Hall points out, the move to Europe comes in the wake of an already multilayered, traumatic history of displacement going back to the Middle Passage.[82]

In contemporary terms, postcolonial theory deals very effectively with the cultural contradictions generated by the global circulation of peoples and cultural goods in a mediated and interconnected world, resulting in a commodified, mass-mediated syncretism. One finds proleptic expression of this kind of syncretism in the Indian film *Shree 420* (Mr 420, 1955), where the Chaplinesque tramp figure (Raj Kapoor) sings *Mera joota hai Japani*: "My shoes are Japanese/My trousers are English/My red cap is Russian/But my heart is Indian." (The song is cited in *Mississippi Massala*, 1991.) Here the protagonist's syncretism is merely sartorial; his heart remains Indian. A number of more recent British films – *Sammy and Rosie Get Laid* (1987), *London Kills Me* (1991), *Young Soul Rebels* (1991), and *The Buddha of Suburbia* (1993) – bear witness to the tense postcolonial hybridity of former colonials growing up in what was once the "motherland." In the multicultural neighborhood of *Sammy and Rosie Get Laid*, the inhabitants have "lines out," as it were, to the formerly colonized parts of the globe. Many films focus on postcolonial diasporas in the First World: for example the Indian diaspora to Canada (*Massala*, 1991) or the US (*Unbidden Voices*, 1989; *Knowing Her Place*, 1990; *Mississippi Massala*), or the Iranian diaspora to New York in *The Mission* (1985). Indeed, one might speak of a genre of postcolonial hybrid films. A recent Hybrid State Films Festival featured films/videos about Ghanaians in England (*Testament*, 1988), Turks in Germany (*Farewell to False Paradise*, 1988), Indians in the US (*Lonely in America*, 1990), Iranians in the US (*The Suitors*, 1988), Algerians in France (*Le Thé au harem d'Archimède*, or Tea in the Harem, 1985), and Chinese in the US (*Full Moon over New York*, 1990).[83]

Occupying contradictory social and discursive spaces, then, hybridity is an unending, unfinalizable process which preceded colonialism and will continue after it. Hybridity is dynamic, mobile, less an achieved synthesis or prescribed formula than an unstable constellation of discourses. Tiana Thi Thanh Nga's *From Hollywood to Hanoi* (1993) renders this process through an autobiographical prism. Swept from South Vietnam to the US at the age of six, she narrates her development into a Vietnamese-American. As a teenager, she experiments with identities borrowed from female stars, "from Judy Garland to Jane Fonda and Tina Turner." As a minor actress in exploitation films, she soon exhausts the repertoire of orientalized roles available for Asian-American women. Upon arrival in Vietnam, she identifies with other "mixed" people, specifically the Vietnamese children of Black and White American soldiers. Shuttling back and forth between the US and Vietnam also means shuttling between different modes of performing identity: as American, as Vietnamese-American, as Vietnamese-American in South Vietnam, and as Vietnamese-American from South Vietnam in North Vietnam. Such hybrid identities are not reducible to a fixed recipe; rather, they form a changing repertory of cultural modalities. The hybrid diasporic subject is confronted with the "theatrical" challenge of moving, as it were, among the diverse performative modes of sharply contrasting cultural and ideological worlds.

The reversal of valence for what were once racist tropes ("syncretic," for example, recalls Christian prejudice against African religions) and the reversal of purist notions of identity should not obscure the problematic agency of "postcolonial hybridity." A celebration of syncretism and hybridity *per se*, if not articulated with questions of historical hegemonies, risks sanctifying the *fait accompli* of colonial violence. For oppressed people, even artistic syncretism is not a game but a sublimated form of historical pain, which is why Jimi Hendrix played the "Star Spangled Banner" in a dissonant mode, and why even a politically conservative performer like Ray Charles renders "America the Beautiful" as a moan and a cry. As a descriptive catch-all term, "hybridity" fails to discriminate between the diverse modalities of hybridity: colonial imposition, obligatory assimilation, political cooptation, cultural mimicry, and so forth. Elites have always made cooptive top-down raids on subaltern cultures, while the dominated have always "signified" and parodied as well as emulated elite practice. Hybridity, in other words, is power-laden and asymmetrical. Whereas historically assimilation by the "native" into a European culture was celebrated as part of the civilizing mission, assimilation in the opposite direction was derided as "going native," a reversion to savagery. Hybridity is also cooptable. In Latin America, national identity has often been officially articulated as hybrid and syncretic, through hypocritically integrationist ideologies that have glossed over subtle racial hegemonies.

As we suggested earlier, syncretism has always pervaded history and the arts. In architectural terms, the great mosque at Cordoba hybridizes the diverse styles that passed through Spain: Carthaginian, Greek, Roman, Byzantine, Arab-Moorish. Architectural syncretism can even be schizoid, as in the El Triunfo Church in Cuzco where the angels look like Spanish noblemen but the cherubs have indigenous faces. But while hybridity has existed from time immemorial, as civilizations conflict, combine, and synthesize, it reached a kind of violent paroxysm with European colonization of the Americas. Although mixing of populations predated the *conquista*, the colonizing process initiated by Columbus accelerated and actively shaped a new world of practices and ideologies of mixing, making the Americas the scene of unprecedented combinations of indigenous peoples, Africans, and Europeans, and later of immigratory diasporas from all over the world. These combinations have generated, especially in the Caribbean and in South America, a wide-ranging vocabulary of racial descriptive terms to account for all the permutations (*mestizo/a, mulato/a, creolo/a, moreno/a*). Mixing has not only been a reality but an ideology in which sex and race have played the major roles. Miscegenation (from the Latin to mix – *misce* – and race, stock, species – *genus*) has more negative connotations in English than *mestizaje* has in Spanish. Miscegenation calls attention to a taboo action of sexual mixing, while *mestizaje* endorses the long-term results of such mixing.

Throughout the Americas we find historical and literary figures, especially female figures (Pocahontas, Sacagawea, Malinche, Iracema, Guadalupe) who have become the foci of intense debates and symbolic struggles over the politics of *mestizaje*. In Mexico, the mythical figure of the "Virgin of Guadalupe" put a *mestizo* face on the Catholic religion, substituting for the Aztec goddess Tonantzin, and becoming paired in a Manichean fashion with the indigenous female slave/traitor/translator Malintzin (Malinche).[84] Gabriel Retes' *Nuevo Mundo* (New World, 1982) hints at the memory of Guadalupe in its story of Inquisition-like repression practiced against the native peoples of Mexico. In the film, forced conversion is accompanied by rape, torture, and murder, all presided over by priests. The natives, like the Jewish *conversos*, are obliged to feign allegiance to Catholicism. Their resistance takes visual, artistic form; they literally hide their own deities behind or inside of the Catholic saints. The film's climax involves the "miraculous" appearance of a *mestiza* virgin – transparently modeled on the Virgin of Guadalupe – fashioned by an indigenous painter pressured by the Church. The mass conversion of natives to Christianity, the film implies, was premised on mendacity and manipulation, while indigenous syncretism formed a tactic for cultural survival.

In the US, the Pocahontas story, meanwhile, is officially read as an exemplum of a noble savage woman's sacrificing her life to rescue her (White) love object from her barbarian tribe, a reading which excludes the narrative of rape, cultural destruction, and genocide. Yet some Native American "intepretative communities" read the Pocahontas narrative not as a romance but as a survivalist story, where Pocahontas' child is crucial to the story's meaning.[85] Pocahontas learns English ways in order to become an ambassador for her community and thus rescue it. The vexed question of the valence of racial-mixing stories, then, has implications for contemporary community identities. To read mixing as a simple choice on the indigene's part implicitly encodes a triumphalist Westernizing narrative, while reading mixing as a strategy for survival points to a history of colonization.

Syncretism is also linguistic. Thus New World English, which already syncretizes Germanic and Latinate sources, is further enriched by words and turns of phrase of African and indigenous origin. But linguistic syncretism also intersects with power. The point of departure for Ruiz's film *Het Dak Van de Walvis* (The Top of the Whale, 1981), for example, was the fact that certain tribes in Chile, due to their traumatic memory of genocide, spoke their own language only among themselves and never in front of a European. The resulting fable concerns a French anthropologist's visit to the last surviving members of a Patagonian tribe whose language has defied all attempts at interpretation. The film goes in and out of French, English, German, Spanish, Dutch, and the invented speech of the Patagonian Indians. At one point, the anthropologist discovers that the mysterious indigenous language in fact consists of one phrase; no matter what he shows them, they respond *yamas gutan*. When the anthropologist discovers later that the Indians change names each month and invent a new language every day, he returns to Europe in despair. Here the very refusal of dialog becomes a form of resistance. That the Indians do not let the anthropologist crack their code becomes a weapon of the weak against a non-dialogic hybridization.

The power-laden nature of syncretism applies even in such apparently innocuous realms as music and cuisine. Under New World slave regimes, African musical instruments (especially drums, which were associated with rebellions) were explicitly forbidden – a fact which seems rather remote now that African instruments have become standard equipment for many pop groups. Culinary syncretism, similarly, would at first glance seem a pure matter of gustatory pleasure, yet food too can be absorbed into political conflicts or evoke traumatic cultural memories. The Inquisition identified Sephardic Jewish *conversos* through the domestic presence of colanders used to drain the blood from meat, or through practices such as the non-mixing of milk and meat products. Thus while Jewish *kasher/taref* and Muslim *halal/haram* (permitted/forbidden) meat practices censured culinary mixing with other religions, these culinary-religious practices were themselves policed by outsiders.

Hybridization does not always exist on a conscious level. Recent research by the Southwest Jewish Archives points out that repressed Sephardic Jewish traditions remain alive even in predominantly Roman Catholic Mexican-American families in New Mexico and Texas, although the family members are not always conscious of the origins of the rituals. They do not understand why their grandmothers make unleavened bread called *pan semita* (Semitic bread), or why their rural grandparents slaughter a lamb in the spring and smear its blood on the doorway. The film *Last Marranos* (1990), meanwhile, chronicles the culture of contemporary Portuguese Jewish *conversos* who have been hiding their Jewishness for five centuries. They attend Mass and outwardly live as Catholics, yet behind closed doors light candles on Friday, bake matzah on Passover, and say "Adonai" instead of "Lord," creating as a result a syncretic Catholic-Jewish tradition, celebrating Christmas, for instance, as "Moses' birthday." In the absence of the founding texts, the ceremonies became an oral tradition, gradually dominated by women. The present-day attempts to "rejudaize" the *conversos* create tensions, ironically, because they are experienced by the older generation as a disruption of what have become their traditional, if hybrid, ways.[86]

The cultural terror of racialized slavery generated the Afro-diasporic offspring of Christianity and African religions: Santeria, Umbanda, Vodun, Xango, and so forth. For Africans in the New World, syncretism was a way of hiding their own religious practices under the cover of a Euro-Christian façade. Both indigenous and African religions in the Americas developed a culture of camouflage, of tricking the master by incorporating African *orixas* or indigenous deities into Christian practices. They transform historical repression into an affirmation of Afro culture in the diaspora. Dos Santos' *Amuleto de Ogum* (Ogum's Amulet, 1975) celebrates Umbanda, the syncretic Brazilian religion which combines Afro-Brazilian elements (the *orixas*, spirit possession) with Catholicism, Kabala, and the spiritism of Alain Kardec. *Amuleto* simply assumes Umbandista values without explaining or justifying them to the uninitiated. The audience is assumed to recognize the ceremony which "closes" the protagonist's body, to recognize his protection by Ogum: the warrior god of metal and the symbol, in Brazil, of the struggle for justice. At the same time, the film does not idealize Umbanda: one priest in the film works for popular liberation; the other is a greedy charlatan.

A film like *Amuleto* suggests the need for a kind of schema to plot out the different power relations within syncretism. In terms of *mestizaje*, for example, the spectrum would run from rape, at one extreme, to voluntary unions on the other, with marriage designed for assimilation or social mobility occupying the middle ground. Racial mixing could also be a survivalist strategy, as indigenous groups sometimes accepted Europeans as marriage partners so as to replenish the group in moments of demographic crisis. In religious terms, the spectrum moves from Inquisition-like practices and forced conversion at one extreme, to voluntary adherence at the other, with all sorts of intermediate forms occupying the middle ground: bottom-up Afro-Christian syncretism as a cover for actual faith in African spirits, top-down incorporation for purposes of proselytization (the priest or pastor who adds drums to accompany hymns, or who translates the Bible into indigenous languages). A strategic "bottom-up" syncretism, similarly, can take the form of selective appropriation of the dominant culture (whence the "subversive" antislavery readings of the Bible within African-American culture, or Handsome Lake's selective incorporation of Christian traditions), or of a dual life of parallel participations (whereby some native groups practiced both the dominant religion and their own tradition). The most egalitarian syncretisms have to do with what we would call "lateral syncretism," to be found, for example, in the mutually enriching collaborations between the diverse modalities of Afro-diasporic music. (We will return to the artistic manifestations of syncretism in chapter 8, "Esthetics of Resistance.")

POLYCENTRIC MULTICULTURALISM

If the discussion of postcolonial hybridity theory has been largely restricted to the academe, the debates about multiculturalist mixing have taken place in the wider public fora of newspapers, magazines, and radio and TV talk shows. And while postcolonial discourse usually focusses on situations outside the US, multi-culturalism is often seen as the name of a specifically American debate. In the North American context, multiculturalism has catalyzed an array of political responses, each with its favorite metaphors, many of them culinary: "melting pot," "ethnic stew," "tossed salad," "bouillabaisse," "stir-fry," "gumbo." For neoconservatives, multiculturalism is code for "left opposition" and "people of color," both ideal scapegoats now that the cold war has ended. Neoconservatives favor an imagery of purity and "standards," of medieval fortresses defended against barbarian siege. Militant nationalists, meanwhile, favoring originary metaphors of roots, of cultural wellsprings, regard multiculturalism ambivalently, both as cooptable by officialdom and as a strategic instrument for change and national regeneration. Liberals, finally, invoke the well-behaved "diversity" dear to college brochures, but reject the anti-Eurocentric drift of the more radical versions of multiculturalism. Positing the ideal of "color-blindness," liberals prefer metaphors evoking an innocuous pluralism: ceramic metaphors like "gorgeous mosaic," culinary metaphors like the "smorgasbord experience."

The concept of "multiculturalism," then, is polysemically open to various interpretations and subject to diverse political force-fields; it has become an empty signifier on to which diverse groups project their hopes and fears. In its more coopted version, it easily degenerates into a state or corporate-managed United-Colors-of-Benetton pluralism whereby established power promotes ethnic "flavors of the month" for commercial or ideological purposes. In institutional terms, Ada Gay Griffin posits a spectrum of models of multiculturalism, varying in their degree of participation by POCs (people of color): the IBM model (White executive staff plus a few token Blacks); the Spook model (a POC plots to empower other POCs); the Benetton model (POCs are visually conspicuous but decision-makers are White); the Abolitionist model (progressive Whites consult with POCs but retain power); the Nkrumah model (POCs transform a White institution into an organ responsive to their own concerns); and the Mugabe model (in a multiracial coalition, POCs enjoy decision-making power).[87] In other national contexts, multiculturalism radically alters its valence. In Canada, it designates official, largely cosmetic government programs – the object of satire in Srinivas Krishna's *Massala*, 1991 – designed to placate the *québecois*, Native Canadians, Blacks, and Asians. In Latin America, intellectuals worry about a new "multicultural" neocolonialism.

For us, the word "multiculturalism" has no essence; it points to a debate. While aware of its ambiguities, we would hope to prod it in the direction of a radical critique of power relations, turning it into a rallying cry for a more substantive and reciprocal intercommunalism. (If the term no longer serves this function, it should be dropped.) What is missing in much of the discussion of multiculturalism is a notion of ethnic relationality and community answerability. Neoconservatives accuse multiculturalists of pulling people apart, of Balkanizing the nation, of emphasizing what divides people rather than what brings them together, of summoning "ethnic" communities to form hermetically sealed enclaves, each with their own real or symbolic "militias." (TV images of strife in South Africa and former Yugoslavia, not to mention Los Angeles and New York, reinforce such fears.) That the inequitable distribution of power *itself* generates violence and divisiveness goes unacknowledged; that multiculturalism offers a more egalitarian vision of social relations is ignored. A radical multiculturalism, in our view, has to do less with artifacts, canons, and representations than with the communities "behind" the artifacts. In this sense a radical multiculturalism calls for a profound restructuring and reconceptualization of the power relations between cultural communities. Refusing a ghettoizing discourse, it links minoritarian communities, challenging the hierarchy that makes some communities "minor" and others "major" and "normative." Thus what neoconservatives in fact find threatening about the more radical forms of multiculturalism is the intellectual and political regrouping by which different "minorities" become a majority seeking to move beyond being "tolerated" to forming active intercommunal[88] coalitions.

Issues of multiculturalism, colonialism, and race must be discussed "in relation." Communities, societies, nations, and even entire continents exist not autonomously but rather in a densely woven web of relationality. Social communities and utterances "dialog" with one another; they are "aware of and mutually reflect one another" within the communality of the sphere of speech communication.[89] Racial and national diversity is therefore fundamental to *every* utterance, even to that utterance which on the surface ignores or excludes the groups with which it is in relation. This dialogical approach is in this sense profoundly antisegregationist. Although segregation can be temporarily imposed as a sociopolitical arrangement, it can never be absolute, especially on the level of culture. All utterances inescapably take place against the background of the possible responses of other social and ethnic points of view.

We would distinguish, therefore, between a cooptive liberal pluralism, tainted at birth by its historical roots in the systematic inequities of conquest, slavery, and exploitation,[90] and what we see as a more relational and radical *polycentric multiculturalism*. The notion of polycentrism, in our view, globalizes multiculturalism. It envisions a restructuring of intercommunal relations within and beyond the nation-state according to the internal imperatives of diverse communities.[91] Within a polycentric vision, the world has many dynamic cultural locations, many possible vantage points. The emphasis in "polycentrism," for us, is not on spatial or primary points of origin but on fields of power, energy, and struggle. The "poly," for us, does not refer to a finite list of centers of power but rather introduces a systematic principle of differentiation, relationality, and linkage. No single community or part of the world, whatever its economic or political power, should be epistemologically privileged.

Polycentric multiculturalism differs from liberal pluralism in the following ways. First, unlike a liberal-pluralist discourse of ethical universals – freedom, tolerance, charity – polycentric multiculturalism sees all cultural history in relation to social power. Polycentric multiculturalism is not about "touchy-feely" sensitivity toward other groups; it is about dispersing power, about empowering the disempowered, about transforming subordinating institutions and discourses. Polycentric multiculturalism demands changes not just in images but in power relations. Second, polycentric multiculturalism does not preach a pseudo-equality of viewpoints; its sympathies clearly go to the underrepresented, the marginalized, and the oppressed. Third, whereas pluralism is premised on an established hierarchical order of cultures and is grudgingly accretive – it benevolently "allows" other voices to add themselves to the mainstream – polycentric multiculturalism is celebratory. It thinks and imagines "from the margins," seeing minoritarian communities not as "interest groups" to be "added on" to a preexisting nucleus but rather as active, generative participants at the very core of a shared, conflictual history. Fourth, polycentric multiculturalism grants an "epistemological advantage" to those prodded by historical circumstance into what W. B. DuBois has called "double consciousness," to those obliged to negotiate both "margins" and "center" (or even with many margins and many centers), and thus somewhat better placed to "deconstruct" dominant or narrowly national discourses. Fifth, polycentric multiculturalism rejects a unified, fixed, and essentialist concept of identities (or communities) as consolidated sets of practices, meanings, and experiences. Rather, it sees identities as multiple, unstable, historically situated, the products of ongoing differentiation and polymorphous identifications.[92] Sixth, polycentric multiculturalism goes beyond narrow definitions of identity politics, opening the way for informed affiliation on the basis of shared social desires and identifications. Seventh, polycentric multiculturalism is reciprocal, dialogical; it sees all acts of verbal or cultural exchange as taking place not between discrete bounded individuals or cultures but rather between permeable, changing individuals and communities. Within an ongoing struggle of hegemony and resistance, each act of cultural interlocution leaves both interlocutors changed. (Henceforth, we will use the term "multiculturalism" in the more radical sense we have outlined here.)

NOTES

1   Raymond Williams, *Keywords: A Vocabulary of Culture and Society* (New York: Oxford University Press, 1976).
2   Jan Pieterse, "Unpacking the West: How European is Europe?," unpublished paper given us by the author, 1992.
3   On the African influence on modern dance, see Brenda Dixon, "The Afrocentric Paradigm," *Design for Arts in Education*, No. 92 (Jan./Feb. 1991), pp. 15–22.
4   Pieterse, "Unpacking the West," p. 16.
5   See C.M. Cipolla, *Before the Industrial Revolution: European Society and Economy 1000–1700* (New York: W.W. Norton, 1980), p. 222.
6   Pieterse, "Unpacking the West," citing J. Merson's *Road to Xanadu* (London: Weidenfeld and Nicolson, 1989).
7   See Joseph Needham, *The Grand Titration: Science and Society in East and West* (Toronto: University of Toronto Press, 1969).
8   See Alfredo Bosi, *Dialética da Colonização* (São Paulo: Companhia das Letras, 1992), pp. 11–19.
9   See H. Magdoff, *Imperialism: From the Colonial Age to the Present* (New York: Monthly Review Press, 1978), p. 108.
10 See Paul Johnson, "Colonialism's Back – and Not a Moment Too Soon," *New York Times Magazine* (April 18, 1993).
11 Ngũgĩ wa Thiong'o, *Decolonizing the Mind: The Politics of Language in African Literature* (London and Nairobi: James Currey/Heinemann Kenya, 1986).
12 See Heinz Dieterich, "Five Centuries of the New World Order," *Latin American Perspectives*, Vol. 19, No. 3 (Summer 1992).
13 See Jon Bennet, *The Hunger Machine* (Cambridge: Polity Press, 1987), p. 19.
14 Andre Gunder Frank, *Capitalism and Underdevelopment in Latin America* (Harmondsworth: Penguin, 1971), p. 33.
15 Eduardo Galeano, *The Open Veins of Latin America* (New York: Monthly Review Press, 1973), p. 12.
16 For a summary of the critiques of "world systems theory," see Jan Nederveen Pieterse, *Empire and Emancipation* (London: Pluto Press, 1990), pp. 29–45. See also Geoffrey Reeves, *Communications and the Third World* (London: Routledge, 1993). For a feminist critique, see Inderpal Grewal and Caren Kaplan, "Introduction: Transnational

Feminist Practices and Questions of Postmodernity," in Grewal and Kaplan, eds, *Scattered Hegemonies: Postmodernity and Transnational Feminist Practices* (Minneapolis: University of Minnesota Press, 1994).

17 See Ingrid Sarti, "Communication and Cultural Dependency: A Misconception," in Emile G. McAnany, Jorge Schnitman, and Noreene Janus, eds, *Communication and Social Structure* (New York: Praeger, 1981), pp. 317–34.

18 See Peter Hulme, *Colonial Encounters: Europe and the Native Caribbean 1492–1797* (London: Methuen, 1986), p. 2.

19 Quoted in Philip D. Curtin, ed., *Imperialism* (New York: Walker, 1971), pp. 194–5.

20 Albert Memmi, *Dominated Man* (Boston: Beacon Press, 1968), p. 186.

21 Middle Eastern people are called White on the US census forms, despite the fact they are multihued, and despite their not unfrequent victimization by Euro-American racism. For a related discussion, see Joseph Massad, "Palestinians and the Limits of Racialized Discourse," *Social Text*, No. 34, 1993.

22 Paul Gilroy, *There Ain't No Black in the Union Jack* (London: Hutchinson, 1987), p. 11.

23 Cedric J. Robinson, *Black Marxism: The Making of the Black Radical Tradition* (London: Zed, 1983), p. 27.

24 Frantz Fanon, "Racism and Culture," in *Présence Africaine*, Nos 8/9/10 (1956).

25 Whitney Young, "Exceptional Children: Text of a Keynote Speech," (1970), quoted in Judith H. Katz, *White Awareness* (Norman, Okla: University of Oklahoma Press, 1978).

26 Manning Marable expressed these views in a conference on the state of Black culture held at the Studio Museum in Harlem and at the Dia Foundation in Soho, New York, on the weekend of Dec. 6–8, 1991. Some of Marable's remarks are included in Gina Dent, ed., for a project by Michele Wallace, *Black Popular Culture* (Seattle, Wash.: Bay Press, 1992).

27 See Tzvetan Todorov, *On Human Diversity: Nationalism, Racism and Exoticism in French Thought*, trans. Catherine Porter (Cambridge, Mass.: Harvard University Press, 1993).

28 Quoted in Benita Parry, *Delusions and Discoveries: Studies on India in the British Imagination 1880–1930* (Berkeley: University of California Press, 1972).

29 See John Mohawk and Oren Lyons, eds, *Exiled in the Land of the Free* (Santa Fe, Calif.: Clear Light, 1992), p. 117.

30 See George Rawick, *From Sundown to Sunup: The Making of the Black Community*, quoted in David R. Roediger, *The Wages of Whiteness: Race and the Making of the American Working Class* (London: Verso, 1991), p. 95.

31 Roediger, *The Wages of Whiteness*, p. 106.

32 Ibid., p. 119.

33 Phyllis Rose, *Jazz Cleopatra: Josephine Baker in Her Time* (New York: Random House, 1989), p. 44.

34 See Toni Morrison, "The Pain of Being Black," *Time* (May 22, 1989), p. 120.

35 Ralph Ellison, *Shadow and Act* (New York: Vintage, 1972), p. 48.

36 Lillian Smith, *Killers of the Dream* (New York: W.W. Norton, 1949), cited in Jane Gaines, "Competing Glances: Who Is Reading Robert Mapplethorpe's *Black Book*?," in *New Formations*, No. 16 (Spring 1992).

37 The *Oxford English Dictionary*, discussing the meaning of the word "black" prior to the sixteenth century, lists the following associations: "Deeply stained with dirt; soiled, dirty ... Having dark or deadly purposes, malignant; pertaining to or involving death, deadly; baneful, disastrous, sinister ... Foul, iniquitous, atrocious, horrible, wicked." Spike Lee calls attention to such dictionary definitions in *X* (1992).

38 In film/television reports on the civil rights movement, racist Whites justify their

hostility to integration through the "argument" that "We're White, and they're Black," a meaningless truism unless one understands it to mean that moral "opposites" can never mingle without conflict.

39 See Etienne Balibar and Immanuel Wallerstein, *Race, Nation and Class: Ambiguous Identities* (London: Verso, 1991), pp. 37–67.

40 See Stuart Hall, "The Whites of Their Eyes: Racist Ideologies and the Media," in George Bridges and Rosalind Brundt, eds, *Silver Linings: Some Strategies for the Eighties* (London: Lawrence and Wishart, 1981), p. 36.

41 Philomena Essed, *Understanding Everyday Racism* (London: Sage, 1991), p. 37.

42 Quoted in David Spurr, *The Rhetoric of Empire: Colonial Discourse in Journalism, Travel Writing, and Imperial Administration* (Durham, NC: Duke, 1993), p. 105.

43 Originally in *Aberdeen Saturday Pioneer* (Dec. 20, 1891), but quoted in David E. Stannard, *American Holocaust: Columbus and the Conquest of the New World* (New York: Oxford University Press, 1992, p. 126).

44 General Schwarzkopf, during the Gulf war, similarly expressed concern over every one of "our boys," while portraying the Iraqis, the very people who were dying en masse, as people "who do not value life the way we do."

45 See Spurr, *The Rhetoric of Empire*, p. 24.

46 Broadcast on PBS, channel 13, on December 10, 1991.

47 Gary Peller, "Race against Integration," *Tikkun*, Vol VI, No. 1 (Jan./Feb. 1991), pp. 54–66.

48 See U.S. Mehta, "Liberal Strategies of Exclusion," *Politics and Society*, Vol. 18, No. 4 (1990), pp. 429–30.

49 See Todorov, *On Human Diversity*, p. 259.

50 Quoted in David Rieff, *Los Angeles: Capital of the Third World* (New York: Simon and Schuster, 1991), pp. 239–40.

51 See especially Aijaz Ahmad, "Jameson's Rhetoric of Otherness and the National Allegory," *Social Text*, No. 17 (Fall 1987), pp. 3–25, and Julianne Burton, "Marginal Cinemas," *Screen*, Vol. 26, Nos 3–4 (May–August 1985).

52 As Arjun Appadurai notes: "... for the people of Irian Jaya, Indonesianization may be more worrisome than American imperialism, as Japanization may be for Koreans, Indianization for Sri Lankans, Vietnamization for the Cambodians ... One man's imagined community is another man's political prison." See Arjun Appadurai, "Disjuncture and Difference in the Global Cultural Economy," *Public Culture*, Vol. 2, No. 2 (1990), pp. 1–24.

53 A related concept, Inderpal Grewal's "scattered hegemonies," is advanced by Grewal and Kaplan in their "Introduction: Transnational Feminist Practices and Questions of Postmodernity," which addresses the relationship between the "local" and the "global."

54 See Pierre Jalée, *The Third World in World Economy* (New York: Monthly Review Press, 1969), pp. ix–x.

55 Cited in ibid., pp. 3–8.

56 See Fernando Solanas and Octavio Getino, "Towards a Third Cinema," in Bill Nichols, ed., *Movies and Methods*, Vol. I (Berkeley: University of California Press, 1976.)

57 David Bordwell, Janet Staiger and Kristin Thompson, *The Classical Hollywood Cinema* (New York: Columbia University Press, 1985).

58 See Mark Schapiro, "Bollywood Babylon," *Image* (June 28, 1992).

59 Appadurai posits five dimensions of these global cultural flows:

1. ethnoscapes (the landscape of persons who constitute the shifting world in which people live);
2. technoscapes (the global configuration of technologies moving at high speeds

across previously impermeable borders);

3. financescapes (the global grid of currency speculation and capital transfer);
4. mediascapes (the distribution of the capabilities to produce and disseminate information and the large complex repertoire of images and narratives generated by these capabilities); and
5. ideoscapes (ideologies of states and counter-ideologies of movements, around which nation-states have organized their political cultures).

See Arjun Appadurai, "Disjunction and Difference in the Global Cultural Economy," *Public Culture*, Vol. 2, No. 2 (Spring 1990), pp. 1–24.

60 For a fuller definition see the "Special Rapporteur on the Problem of Discrimination against Indigenous Populations for the UN Sub-Commission on Prevention of Discrimination and Protection of Minorities," summarized and quoted in Saddruddin Aga Khan and Hassan bin Talal, *Indigenous Peoples: A Global Quest for Justice* (London: Zed, 1987). The term "Fourth World" has been used in many different ways. The discourse of global economy sometimes uses it to mean Third World countries without major resources, while Gordon Brotherston uses it to mean the Americas as the "fourth continent" after Asia, Europe, and Africa. See Brotherston, *Book of the Fourth World* (Cambridge: Cambridge University Press, 1992).

61 Jason W. Clay estimates that there are 5,000 such nations spread around the globe. See his "People, Not States, Make a Nation," *Mother Jones* (Nov./Dec. 1990).

62 *Cultural Survival Quarterly*, cited in Jerry Mander, *In the Absence of the Sacred: The Failure of Technology and the Survival of the Indian Nations* (San Francisco: Sierra Club, 1992), p. 6.

63 See John H. Bodley, *Victims of Progress* (Mountain View, Calif.: Mayfield, 1990), p. 5.

64 Quoted in Herman Merivale, *Lectures of Colonization and Colonies* (London: Green, Longman and Roberts, 1861), p. 541.

65 In 1907, Paul Rohrbach justified the German policy of appropriating the best Herero land:

> for people of the culture standard of the South African Natives, the loss of their free national barbarism and the development of a class of workers in the service of and dependent on the Whites is primarily a law of existence in the highest degree.

Quoted in John H. Wellington, *South West Africa and Its Human Issues* (Oxford: Oxford University Press, 1967), p. 196.

66 See Colin M. Turnbull, *The Mountain People* (New York: Simon and Schuster, 1972).

67 Quoted in Julian Burger's *The Gaia Atlas of First Peoples* (New York: Doubleday, 1990), p. 34. A high proportion of the plant-derived prescription drugs used worldwide were discovered following leads from indigenous medicine. The Hanunoo people of the Philippines, for example, distinguish 1,600 plant species in their forest, 400 more than scientists working in the same area.

68 See, for example, David MacDougall, "Beyond Observational Cinema," in Paul Hockings, ed., *Principles of Visual Anthropology* (The Hague: Mouton, 1975).

69 See Faye Ginsburg, "Aboriginal Media and the Australian Imaginary," *Public Culture*, Vol. 5, No. 3 (Spring 1993).

70 See Kate Madden, "Video and Cultural Identity: The Inuit Broadcasting Experience," in Felipe Korzenny and Stella Ting-Toomey, eds, *Mass-Media Effects across Cultures* (London: Sage, 1992).

71 Indigenous media have remained largely invisible to the First World public except for occasional festivals (for example the Native American film and video festivals held

regularly in San Francisco and New York City, or the Latin American Film Festival of Indigenous Peoples held in Mexico City and Rio de Janeiro).

72 Faye Ginsburg, "Indigenous Media: Faustian Contract or Global Village?," *Cultural Anthropology*, Vol. 6, No. 1 (1991), p. 94.

73 Ibid.

74 For a critical view of the Kayapo project, see Rachel Moore, "Marketing Alterity," *Visual Anthropology Review*, Vol. 8, No. 2 (Fall 1992), and James C. Faris, "Anthropological Transparency: Film, Representation and Politics," in Peter Ian Crawford and David Turton, eds, *Film as Ethnography* (Manchester: Manchester University Press, 1992). For Terence Turner's answer to Faris, see Turner's "Defiant Images: The Kayapo Appropriation of Video," Forman Lecture, RAI Festival of Film and Video in Manchester 1992, forthcoming in *Anthropology Today*.

75 See Terence Turner's account of his longstanding collaboration with the Kayapo in "Visual Media, Cultural Politics and Anthropological Practice," *Independent*, Vol. 14, No. 1 (Jan./Feb. 1991).

76 On the relationships between postmodernism and postcolonialism, see Kwame Anthony Appiah, "Is the Post- in Postmodernism the Post- in Postcolonial?," *Critical Inquiry*, No. 17 (Winter 1991).

If the rising institutional endorsement of "postcolonial" studies is on the one hand a success story for the PCs (politically correct), it is also a partial containment of the POCs (people of color) and the practitioners of ethnic studies, who feel displaced by the rise of postcolonial studies in US debates on racism.

77 As in the following:

> the literatures of African countries, Australia, Bangladesh, Canada, Caribbean countries, India, Malaysia, Malta, New Zealand, Pakistan, Singapore, South Pacific Island countries, and Sri Lanka are all post-colonial literatures. The literature of the USA should also be placed in this category ... What each of these literatures has in common beyond their special and distinctive regional characteristics is that they emerged in their present form out of the experience of colonization and asserted themselves by foregrounding the tension with the imperial power, and by emphasizing their differences from the assumptions of the imperial centre. It is this which makes them distinctively post-colonial.

See Bill Ashcroft, Gareth Griffiths and Helen Tiffin, *The Empire Writes Back: Theory and Practice in Post-Colonial Literatures* (London: Routledge, 1989), p. 2. We are not suggesting that this expanded use of the "postcolonial" is typical or paradigmatic.

78 Read for example, Zachary Lockman and Joel Beinin, eds, *Intifada: The Palestinian Uprising against Israeli Occupation* (Boston: South End Press, 1989), specifically Edward W. Said, "Intifada and Independence," pp. 5–22; also Edward W. Said, *After the Last Sky* (New York: Pantheon Books, 1986).

79 For discussions of the "post," see, for example, Robert Young, "Poststructuralism: The End of Theory," *Oxford Literary Review*, Vol. 5, Nos 1–2 (1982); R. Radhakrishnan, "The Postmodern Event and the End of Logocentrism," *Boundary 2*, Vol. 12, No. 1 (Fall 1983); Geoffrey Bennington, "Postal Politics and the Institution of the Nation," in Homi K. Bhabha, ed., *Nation and Narration* (London and New York: Routledge, 1990).

80 Although one can easily imagine the "postcolonial" traveling into Third World countries (more likely via the Indian diaspora within the Anglo-American academy than via India), significantly, the term has little currency in African, Middle Eastern, and Latin American intellectual circles, except occasionally in the restricted historical sense of the period immediately following the end of colonial rule.

81 For more on the "postcolonial," see Shohat, "Notes on the Postcolonial" and Anne

McClintock, "The Angel of Progress: Pitfalls of the Term 'Post-colonialism'," *Social Text*, Nos 31/32 (Spring 1992), pp. 84–98; Ruth Frankenberg and Lata Mani, "Crosscurrents, Crosstalk: Race, 'Postcoloniality' and the Politics of Location," in *Cultural Studies*, Vol. 7, No. 2, May 1993. See also *Public Culture*, No. 5 (Fall 1992).

82 Stuart Hall, "Cultural Identity and Cinematic Representation," *Framework*, No. 36 (1989), pp. 68–81.

83 The Hybrid State Film Series, curated by Coco Fusco in 1991, was a program of "parallel history," a year-long interdisciplinary project produced by Exit Art and directed by Jeanette Ingberman and Papo Colo.

84 For a discussion of Malinche and its implications for contemporary Chicana identity, see Norma Alarcon, "Traddutora, Traditora: A Paradigmatic Figure of Chicana Feminism," reprinted in Inderpal Grewal and Caren Kaplan, eds, *Scattered Hegemonies* (Minneapolis University of Minnesota Press, 1994); Gloria Anzaldua, "La Conciencia de la Mestiza: Towards a New Consciousness," in Gloria Anzaldua, ed., *Making Face, Making Soul, Haciendo Caras: Creative and Critical Perspectives by Women of Color* (San Francisco: Spinsters/Aunt Lute, 1987), pp. 377–89; Rachel Phillips, "Marina/Malinche: Masks and Shadows" in Beth Miller, ed., *Women in Hispanic Literature: Icons and Fallen Idols* (Berkeley: University of California Press, 1983), pp. 97–114; Jean Franco, "On the Impossibility of Antigone and the Inevitability of La Malinche: Rewriting the National Allegory," in Jean Franco, *Plotting Women: Gender and Representation in Mexico* (New York: Columbia University Press), pp. 129–46.

85 Rayna Green, "The Pocahontas Perplex: The Image of Indian Women in American Culture," in Ellen Carol Dubois and Vicki L. Ruiz, eds, *Unequal Sisters: A Multi-Cultural Reader in U.S. Women's History* (New York: Routledge, 1990); Beth Brant, "Grandmothers of a New World," *Woman of Power*, No. 16 (Spring 1990), pp. 4–47.

86 See Ella Shohat, "Staging the Quincentenary: The Middle East and the Americas," *Third Text*, No. 21 (Winter 1992–3).

87 See Ada Gay Griffin, "What's Mine Is Not Mine/What's Mine Is Ours/ What's Mine Is Yours/What's Yours Is Yours (Power Sharing in America)," *Felix*, Vol. 1, No. 2 (Spring 1992).

88 The phrase "intercommunalism," to the best of our knowledge, was first used by Huey Newton and the Black Panthers.

89 M.M. Bakhtin, "The Problem of Speech Genres," in *Speech Genres and Other Late Essays* (Austin: University of Texas, 1986), p. 91.

90 See Y.N. Kly, *The Anti-Social Contract* (Atlanta, Ga.: Clarity Press, 1989).

91 Samir Amin speaks of economic polycentrism in similar terms in his book *Delinking: Towards a Polycentric World* (London: Zed, 1985).

92 For a similar view, see Joan Scott, "Multiculturalism and the Politics of Identity," *October*, No. 61 (Summer 1992) and Stuart Hall, "Minimal Selves," in *Identity: The Real Me* (London: ICA, 1987).

2

FORMATIONS OF COLONIALIST DISCOURSE

"GREECE: WHERE IT ALL BEGAN"

A series of newspaper ads prepared by the Greek National Tourist Organization in 1991 featured alluring images of Aegean seascapes, classical monuments, and mythological icons, anchored by the captions "Greece: Where It All Began" and "Greece: Chosen by the Gods." Appealing to a presumably common myth of origins in order to promote a touristic pilgrimage to the sources of European civilization, the ads chart a pan-European imaginary, the "all" of the caption invoking a master-narrative of quasi-divine origin. Another ad in the same series

Plate 3 "Greece: where it all began"

features a painting of a beautiful White lad contemplating his aquatic mirror-image. The caption invites the viewer to reflect, like Narcissus, on "the crystalline purity of Greek waters." Yet this narrative of origins is itself specular and narcissistic: Europe looks in the mirror and is dazzled by its own beauty. Overwritten with the prestige of classical myth, the Greek waters invite the tourist into what is projected as a shared past. Ads for the equally crystalline waters of the Caribbean, by contrast, appeal not to historical origins but to "get-away-from-it-all" sensuality ("It's better in the Bahamas"), evincing little interest in the indigenous myths and history of the region. Both sets of ads reverberate with communal tensions about the meaning and interpretation of history. While the Greek ads are about remembering and reflecting, the Caribbean ads are about reawakening the dormant senses and, implicitly, about forgetting history. The former forges links to a European past, the latter obscures historical connections.

Another Greece-related ad, for an exhibit of classical sculpture, posits Greece as the site of the origin of democracy, and of the European self as Universal Humanity.[1] Titled "The Greek Miracle," the ad's text reads:

"We are all Greeks," the poet Shelley said. Born of democracy. Invention. Philosophy. Theatre. History. Sciences. And art, born from the democracy itself, makes us so. For out of 5th Century Greece, modern man was given life. Now the art of the Golden Age of Greece is here, to explore, embrace and revel in.... Art as evolution. As mankind. As free. As all ... And we, in awe, muse over the miracle of democracy. So yes, we are all Greeks.

Besides overlooking the slave-based nature of Greek "democracy," the ad posits history as "beginning" in Greece; a Eurocentric misnomer, since world history has no single point of origin, although some physical anthropologists speculate that the first human being was African and a woman.[2] Even during the classical period, history was played out around the globe, in China, in the Indus Valley, in Mesopotamia, in Africa, in what we now call the Americas, and indeed wherever there were human beings. Rather than the "Age" of Antiquity, as Samir Amin suggests, we should speak of the "Ages" of Antiquity. The Americas are dotted with antique ruins, with the pyramids and acropolises of Meso-America and "Turtle Island," but Eurocentric education rarely calls attention to them. Who tells us that Peruvian monumental architecture existed before Stonehenge? Or that when ancient Greece was falling under Roman hegemony, the Native American Adena culture had been flourishing for over 1,000 years?[3]

Meanwhile, some Afrocentric discourse posits Africa, and especially Egypt, as a site of origins.[4] The debate over origins is played out not only in the pages of books and in the halls of the academy, but also in the myriad forms of popular culture. In the rap music videos of KRSOne, for example, Egyptian pyramids furnish the backdrop for percussive rapped lectures on history. African-oriented culture also animates the street life of First World metropolises; identity is marketed, and nourished, through the sidewalk vending of papyrus, incense, jewelry, kente cloth, and books about African civilization. A whole genre of

T-shirt Afrocentrism explicitly links history, geography, and contemporary identity. One shirt popular around the time of Nelson Mandela's visit to the US in 1990 inscribes portraits of African and Afro-diasporic leaders on an Afrocentrically colored map of Africa, positing a line of noble descent – "Marcus Garvey, Malcolm X, Martin Luther King, Bob Marley, Nelson Mandela and Me" – framed by an admonition to an implicitly White addressee: "It's a Black Thing ... You Wouldn't Understand." The Afrocentric hip hop of X-Clan, meanwhile, portrays ancient Greece as the thief of Egyptian culture: "I am an African. I don't wear Greek/Must I be reminded of a legendary thief?" In X-Clan's music video "Heed the Word of a Brother" busts of Aristotle, Plato, and Socrates flash on the screen and then are irreverently dismissed.[5] The positing of an alternative Afrocentric version of history, while on one level reproducing the logic of a centered history, on another level inverts it; and, given the negative legacy of anti-African prejudice, reaffirms a genealogically productive past. Emphasized here is not so much the "origins" of civilization as the "beginnings" of political consciousness, with debates about Greece and Egypt becoming proxy battles for cultural prestige. Issues of origin become entangled with the political genealogy of diasporic identity.

The advent of colonialism inspired a retroactive rewriting of African history and its relation to classical Greek civilization. History was recast to conform to colonialist norms, in the name of an eternal "West" unique since its moment of conception. Whole continents were turned into eternal "slave continents." Martin Bernal describes the process in relation to Africa in his *Black Athena*:

> If it had been scientifically "proved" that Blacks were biologically incapable of civilization, how could one explain Ancient Egypt – which was inconveniently placed on the African continent? There were two, or rather, three solutions. The first was to deny that the Ancient Egyptians were black; the second was to deny that the Ancient Egyptians had created a civilization; the third was to make doubly sure by denying both. The last has been preferred by most 19th and 20th century historians.[6]

Bernal distinguishes between the "ancient model," which simply assumed classical Greek civilization's deep indebtedness to both African (Egyptian and Ethiopian) and Semitic (Hebraic and Phonecian) civilizations – and the "Aryan model" which developed in the wake of slavery and colonialism. The Aryan model had to perform ingenious acrobatics to "purify" classical Greece of all African and Asian "contaminations." It had to explain away, for example, the innumerable Greek homages to Afro-Asiatic cultures, Homer's description of the "blameless Ethiopians," and the frequent references to the *kalos kagathos* (handsome and good) Africans in classical literature.[7]

Eurocentric discourse has systematically degraded Africa as deficient according to Europe's own arbitrary criteria (the presence of monumental architecture, literate culture) and hierarchies (melody over percussion, brick over thatch, clothing over body decoration). Yet even by these dubious standards, precolonial

Africa was clearly a continent of rich and diverse culture – the scene of high material achievements (witness the ruins of Zimbabwe), widespread commercial exchange, complex religious beliefs and social systems, and diverse forms of writing (pictograms, ideograms, object scripts such as Alele and Ngombo). In the classical period, Aesop's (that is, the Ethiop's) fables had already fertilized the literary imagination of ancient Greece. Scholars have also established the complexity of Dogon astronomical knowledge: the *sigui* ritual, introduced by the mythical ancestor of the Dogons, Dyongu Seru (and filmed by Jean Rouch in the late 1960s), has been found to analogize and reflect the orbiting cycle of the star Sirius B.[8] And the Moorish Spaniard Leo Africanus, writing in the early sixteenth century, described the "magnificent and well-furnished court" of the King of Timbuktu, and "the great store of doctors, judges, priests, and other learned men . . . bountifully maintained at the King's cost and charges."[9]

There had been considerable contact between Africa and Europe over the centuries, and prior to 1492 the relative state of development of the two continents was roughly equal. Africa had a varied and productive economy, with strong metallurgical and textile industries. Africans developed ironworking and blast-furnace technology even before 600 BC, prefiguring techniques used in Europe only in the nineteenth century.[10] The textile exports of the eastern Congo during the early seventeenth century were as large as those of European textile-manufacturing centers such as Leiden.[11] Indeed, in the early years of the early Atlantic trade Europe had little to sell Africa that Africa did not already produce.[12] The "inferiority" of Africa and the African was thus an ideological invention. It demanded the "eradication within Western historical consciousness of the significance of Nubia for Egypt's formation, of Egypt in the development of Greek civilization, of Africa for imperial Rome, and more pointedly of Islam's influence on Europe's economic, political, and intellectual history."[13] The point is not that Africa should be complimented for "satisfying" competitive Euro-centric criteria for "civilization," nor that if Africa had accomplished less it would have somehow *deserved* colonization. Rather, it is to call attention to the constructedness of the supposedly unbridgeable gap between Europe and Africa.[14] (Hollywood cinema, as we shall see, sustained this artificial gap in such films as the *Tarzan* series, *Stanley and Livingstone* [1939], *Mogambo* [1953], and *Hatari* [1962], while African films, and video series such as Basil Davidson's eight-part *Africa: Anatomy of a Continent* [1984] and Ali Mazrui's nine-part *The Africans: A Triple Heritage* [1986], demystify the Eurocentric view of the Africa–Europe relationship.)

FROM *RECONQUISTA* TO *CONQUISTA*

The same double-edged process of combined mystification and defamation that has operated in relation to Africa has also operated in relation to the pre-Conquest Americas. Conventional historiography often paints a flattering picture of European life during the "Age of Discovery." Yet much of Europe in that period was the scene of fratricidal wars, Church-sponsored violence, and peasant rebellions, where life expectancy oscillated between the high teens and the low thirties.[15] The Americas meanwhile, though hardly the terrestrial paradise projected by European primitivist fantasy, were well populated, its people well nourished and relatively disease-free.[16] Although Europeans called the Americas the "New World," in fact some of its sites of occupation date back at least 30,000 years, to the point that many scholars now question the "priority" of the "Old World."[17] Europeans also called the land "empty," but contemporary estimates posit as many as 75 million to 100 million people living in the Americas in 1492. These peoples possessed a wide range of social systems, from egalitarian hunting and gathering groups to hierarchical kingdoms and oppressive empires. Despite the positive stereotype of the "ecological Indian," their actual practices were quite varied, although rarely as destructive as European practices. The indigenous peoples spoke hundreds of distinct languages, lived in both matrilineal (clan mother) and patrilineal formations, and were clearly able to live and govern themselves in very diverse environments. (The ethnocentric essentialism of Eurocentric history books which characterize these peoples variously as "fierce" and "warlike" or "gentle" becomes obvious when we transfer such qualifiers to European nationalities: the "fierce Italians"? the "gentle French"?) The attainments of indigenous peoples included ecologically minded agriculture, complex irrigation systems, intricate calendrical systems, trade networks extending for hundreds and even thousands of miles over land and sea (the communications system spreading out from Cuzco extended 25,000 miles), well-laid-out cities like Tenochtitlan and Cahokia, and such sophisticated social arrangements as the confederation of the Iroquois (Haudenosaunee) or the city-states of the Aztecs and Incas.[18] The zero as the basis of mathematics – as James Olmos tells his students in *Stand and Deliver* – was known to the Maya at least half a millennium before being discovered by Asian scholars; Europe received it later still via the Arabs.[19]

The notion of the indigenous peoples as "prehistoric" or "peoples without history" – in the double sense of lacking both textual historical records and meaningful development toward a goal – is another Eurocentric misnomer. First, there are *no* ahistorical peoples; and second, it is as accurate to say that Europeans became part of indigenous history as to say the reverse. Cortés' conquest of Mexico, for one historian, "was less a conquest than it was a revolt of dominated peoples," in the sense that Spanish firepower and cavalry would have been impotent without the Tlaxcaltec, Texcocoms, and others who joined the Spanish cause.[20] But for the demographic cataclysms provoked by massacre and the introduction of European diseases, Europeans might well have been absorbed or syncretized into native cultures, languages, and histories.

The *conquista* of the "New World" was ideologically buttressed by the prejudicial discourses articulated during the long *reconquista* of Iberia. The year 1492 was in this sense an absolutely crucial date, for in that year the conquest of the "New" World converged with the expulsion of 3 million Muslims and 300,000 Sephardi Jews from Spain. Columbus himself linked the two issues in a letter addressed to the Spanish throne: "Your Highnesses completed the war against the Moors ... after having chased all the Jews ... and sent me to the said regions of India in order to convert the people there to our Holy Faith."[21] Indeed, some scholars suggest that Columbus' voyages were partly financed by wealth confiscated from dispossessed Jews and Muslims.[22] The Crusades, which inaugurated "Europe" by reconquering the Mediterranean area, catalyzed Europeans' awareness of their own geocultural identity and established the principle that wars conducted in the interests of the Holy Church were axiomatically just. Feudal religiosity prepared the way for racialized conquest. The Crusades against Muslim "infidels" abroad coincided with anti-Semitic pogroms in Europe itself.[23] Jews were blamed for poisoning wells and spreading plagues, for killing Christian children to obtain their blood (the blood libel) and of countless other imaginary crimes, registered even in distinguished literary works like Chaucer's *Canterbury Tales*.

Although Christian Europe on the verge of the conquest of the New World was fearful of diverse "agents of Satan" – women, witches, heretics, and infidels[24]– Jews especially were the preferred scapegoats of the European ideological system.[25] Anti-Semitism, along with "anti-infidelism," provided a conceptual and disciplinary apparatus which, after being turned against Europe's internal "other" – the Jews – was then projected outward against Europe's external others – the indigenous peoples of Africa and the Americas.[26] Preexisting forms of ethnic and religious otherizing were transferred from Europe to its colonies, the presumed "godlessness" and "devil worship" of the indigenous people becoming a pretext for enslavement and dispossession. European Christian demonology thus set the tone for colonialist racism. In effect, a mammoth ideological apparatus was "recycled" in the Americas. Amerigo Vespucci's accounts of his own voyages, for example, drew on the stock of Jewish stereotypes to characterize the indigenous peoples of the Americas as savages, infidels, and sexual omnivores.[27] We discern, even, a partial congruency between the phantasmatic imagery projected on to both the internal Jewish "enemy" and the external "savage": "blood drinkers," "cannibals," "sorcerers," "devils."

Although life in Spain before the expulsion of Sephardi Jews and Muslims was characterized by a remarkable coexistence between three religious civilizations (Christian, Jewish, Muslim), the Inquisition in 1492, as an early exercise in European "self-purification," sought to punish and expel, or forcibly convert, Muslims and Jews. The same measures taken against the Jewish *conversos* were taken against the "converted" Muslims secretly practicing Islam (the *Moriscos*). The *reconquista*, which began with the fall of Toledo in the eleventh century and continued until the fall of Grenada in 1492, prepared the ground for subsequent *conquista* practices in the Americas. Discourses about Muslims and Jews crossed the Atlantic with the Spaniards, arming the conquistadors with a ready-made racist ideology. Centuries later, we find the same kind of "feedback" between internal and external racism in the link between colonialism and the Jewish Holocaust, seen by Aimé Césaire as a "crowning barbarism" which sums up the "daily barbarisms" of colonialism; tolerated and even applauded as long as they were applied only to non-European peoples.[28] (Ousmane Sembene's *Le Camp de Thioraye*, Camp at Thioraye, 1987, has a Senegalese soldier, interned at Dachau, reflect on the links between the two holocausts.) The road to Auschwitz, as David Stannard suggests, passed through Africa and the Americas.[29]

Many films have been made about the history of Christianity, but few films have shown the brutalities practiced by the Church in certain periods of its history. In 1562, for example, the Franciscan friar Diego de Landa used public torture to stamp out "heresy" among the Maya of the Yucatan. In just one of these episodes, 158 Mayans were killed, 30 committed suicide, many were crippled, and some 4,500 were tortured.[30] "The use of gunpowder against pagans," said Father Oviedo, "is the burning of incense to our Lord."[31] An exception to the general cinematic erasure of Church-sponsored violence is Arturo Ripstein's *El Santo Oficio* (The Holy Office, 1973), which deals with the efforts of the Holy See to spread the Inquisition into Mexico, and to enrich itself in the process. The film shows *conversos* forced to practice Judaism in secret. At one point they publicly pretend to bury a man in the Christian manner, then later rebury him secretly according to Judaic law. The finale shows them being burned at the stake, alongside "heretics," "witches," and indigenous "infidels," in a disciplinary staging of forced confession and punishment. Those who have refused to convert are burned alive, while the others are burned only after hanging, in an extravagant public spectacle whose transparent purpose is to intimidate all potential rebels. The perverse theatricality of the mass execution is turned by the film into a spectacle of denunciation.

Another film, the Argentinian Maria Luisa Bemberg's *Yo, Peor de Todas* (I, The Worst of All, 1990), speaks of Church repression as it affected Euro-Mexican women. Based on the life of the seventeenth-century scholar-philosopher-poet Sister (Sor) Juana Inés de la Cruz, the film shows Sor Juana becoming a nun in order to pursue her quest for knowledge. But the inquisitory surveillance closes in upon her, and even her erotically charged friendship with the Spanish Vice-Regent cannot guarantee her safety. Thus she is forced to declare herself "the worst of all" and accept Church-drawn boundaries of knowledge.[32]

THE COLUMBUS DEBATE

The so-called voyages of discovery inaugurated modernity, catalyzing a new epoch of European colonial expansion which culminated in its domination of the globe. For many revisionist historians, 1492 installed the mechanism of systematic advantage which favored Europe against its African and Asian rivals. Prior to 1492, according to J.M. Blaut, a movement toward modernization was taking place in various parts of Europe, Asia, and Africa. "Proto-capitalist" cities were developing, linked in a network of mercantile-maritime centers stretching from Western Europe to Eastern and Southern Africa and Asia. These centers were equal to Europe in demographic, technological, commercial, and intellectual terms. For instance, ambitious voyages were also being launched from non-European urban centers. Africans were sailing to Asia, Indians to Africa, Arabs to China. An Indian voyage went around the Cape of Good Hope and apparently 2,000 miles into the Atlantic circa 1420. After 1492, however, the massive injection of wealth from the New World, the use of forced indigenous-American and African labor, and the advantage of new markets in the Americas gave Europe the "edge" that turned it into a capitalist and colonialist giant.[33]

In this regard, the Columbus story is crucial to Eurocentrism, not only because Columbus was a seminal figure within the history of colonialism, but also because idealized versions of his story have served to initiate generation after generation into the colonial paradigm. For many children in North America and elsewhere, the tale of Columbus is totemic; it introduces them not only to the concepts of "discovery" and the "New World," but also to the idea of history itself. The vast majority of school textbooks, including very recent ones, as Bill Bigelow points out, describe and picture Columbus as handsome, studious, pious, commanding, audacious. Young pupils are induced to empathize with what are imagined to be his childhood dreams and hopes, so that their identification with him is virtually assured even before they encounter the New World others, who are described variously as friendly or fierce, but whose perspective is rigorously elided.[34] Only some voices and perspectives, it is implied, resonate in the world.

Cinematic recreations of the past reshape the imagination of the present, legitimating or interrogating hegemonic memories and assumptions. Mainstream films on Columbus prolong the pedagogy of pro-Columbus textbooks, thus indirectly influencing perceptions of colonial history. There is surprisingly little difference, in this regard, between the (British) David MacDonald film *Christopher Columbus* (1949) and the recent (1992) Salkind superproduction *Columbus: The Discovery*. Though half a century separates the two films, their idealizations of Columbus are virtually identical. Both films portray Columbus as a man of vision, an avatar of modernity and the Christian faith. Both laud his efforts to reach the New World despite the obstacles of superstition, ignorance, and envy. Both convey the view that Columbus was alone in thinking the world was round, when in fact he shared that knowledge with most educated Europeans and Arabs.[35] Both emphasize European antagonists, especially the aristocrat Bobadilla, and thus displace attention from the more fundamental antagonism between Europe and the indigenous peoples. In both films Columbus is charismatic, attractive, a loving father, a man whose fundamental motivations are not mercantile but religious (to convert the "heathen") and scientific (to prove his thesis about the shape of the globe.)

The 1949 film, featuring Fredric March as Columbus, is almost comically teleological, in that it has Columbus speak anachronistically of the "New World" at a time when the historical Columbus was unaware of that world's existence. Millions of benighted "heathens," the dialog informs us, are simply "waiting to be converted." Commentative music translates the film's Manicheism: the music associated with Columbus is choral and religious; that associated with the natives is ominous, provoking an acoustic sense of menace and encirclement. The music's orientalizing overtones replay Columbus' own transfer of cultural stereotypes from East Indies to West Indies. When Columbus arrives in the Caribbean, the mass of natives spontaneously applaud the conquest of their own land and seem to acquiesce in their own enslavement. They immediately abandon their own beliefs and culture, it is implied, and embrace the culture of Europe as irresistibly true. Their spontaneous genuflexions translate into veristic imaged representation of Columbus' own fantasy: that reading a document in Spanish (actually English) to uncomprehending natives signifies a legitimate transfer of ownership.

The historical Columbus' greed led him to demand, upon pain of hanging, that every Taino man, woman, and child over the age of fourteen deliver to him, every three months, a hawk's bell crammed with gold. The film's Columbus in contrast, is an outspoken critic of unfair trade: "We are here to convert the natives," he tells a greedy underling, "not to exploit them." Although the natives are supposedly played by indigenous people from the "Carib reserve" on the island of Dominica, they never achieve the status of characters, nor is their acting credited. They literally have no voice, no language, no dialog, and no apparent point of view beyond cheerful collaboration with European designs.[36] Exhibited in the Spanish court alongside the New World parrots, the Tainos show no discomfort in their role. Indeed, the parrots are granted more "voice" than the natives; they are allowed to squawk: "Long live the King! Long live the Queen! Long live the Admiral!"

Major elisions in *Christopher Columbus* include: the Inquisition; Columbus' involvement in the slave trade; the European massacres of natives, and indigenous rebellions against the Europeans. Although the film stages the well-known shipwreck of one of Columbus' ships, we are not told that the natives saved the shipwrecked sailors. (What does America owe the Native Americans, asks historian Francis Jennings, and answers: "America owes them its very existence.")[37] The selectively empathetic voice-over laments the toll of death and disease *among the colonists*, but ignores the demographic holocaust that engulfed the indigenous people. At the same time, the film sets up a clear class hierarchy among the European characters, conveyed through the gamut of accents from the elite British accent of the Old World courtiers, to Columbus' Anglified but recognizably American accent, to the Cockney accents of the superstitious sailors. Non-European races are clearly devalorized, while women are eclipsed by the emphasis on the strong masculine leader, and even the sailors are pictured as a mutiny-prone rabble: all choices which convey attitudes toward contemporary social relations.

The very title of the 1992 Salkind film – *Columbus: The Discovery* – betrays its makers' indifference to all those who have objected to the term "discovery." According to the producer, the film is an "adventure picture" combining "aspects of *Lawrence of Arabia* and *Robin Hood*," and featuring "no politics."[38] The generic choice of adventure film, the reference to an orientalist classic, and the tendentious use of the phrase "no politics" (actually meaning "no opposition politics") are in keeping with the film's general tone. That the Salkinds were the team behind the first *Superman* films (1978, 1981), *The Three Musketeers* (1974), and *Santa Claus – The Movie* (1985), and that the director (John Glen) is a veteran of several James Bond films, might have forewarned the spectator about the heroic paradigm into which Columbus was about to be placed. Since the film covers only Columbus' campaign to win the support of Queen Isabella, his first voyage, and his return in glory to Spain, it can ignore the death by massacre or disease that befell thousands of Caribbean Indians after his second voyage. From the beginning, it portrays Columbus as the personification of individual initiative overcoming bureaucratic inertia. A man of faith, he is shown as a critic of torture rather than the instigator of torture. Despite the historical Columbus' arcane views about so many subjects (mermaids, cannibals, devils), he is portrayed as the voice of modern rationality. That he is played by a handsome actor (George Corraface) further enforces spectatorial identification. Symphonic European music constantly supports the swelling ambition of Columbus' enterprise, while virtually every scene adds a humanizing touch. At one point, Columbus gives a young Jewish cabin boy a free ticket out of anti-Semitic Spain. The natives, meanwhile, are reduced to mute, admiring witnesses who regard White men as gods. They barely speak to one another, and seem to have no sense of community. The film portrays the native women as flirtatious toward the Europeans, while the *mise-en-scène* exploitively sets their nudity center-screen. No full picture of indigenous life, or of their reaction to the conquest, is developed.

Ridley Scott's film *1492: The Conquest of Paradise* (1992), meanwhile, is erratically revisionist but fundamentally protective of Columbus' good name. Here the scintillating beauty of the cinematography enfolds the violence of conquest into the ideology of the esthetic. The film references the present-day controversies surrounding Columbus, but in highly ambiguous ways. Covering more of Columbus' voyages than the other films (though the four voyages are reduced to three), it portrays him as occasionally brutal yet also as magnanimous. Once again, Columbus (Gerard Depardieu) is the central figure, subjectivized through voice-over, sycophantic close-ups, and empathetic music. Once again he is the voice of faith, science, and modernity. With sets built on location, the film shows the final siege of the Moors in Grenada and portrays Columbus, on the basis of no known historical evidence, as outraged by the Inquisition. Although he is seen as a dynamic entrepreneur, yet he is also a democrat, working and sweating alongside the commoners. Throughout we are sutured into his vantage point, while the music encodes a binarist perspective: choral music with ecclesiastical overtones cues sympathy for Columbus, while brooding dissonance subliminally instructs us to fear the natives, despite an otherwise positive portrayal. And indeed, on some levels the film does pay respect to indigenous culture. The Indians speak their own language, and complain that Columbus has never learned it. A native shaman takes care of the European sick, and in general the natives act with gentleness and dignity, though there is no hint that Columbus

Plate 4   The Discovery of Brazil

Plate 5   1492: The Conquest of Paradise

helped eradicate their complex civilizations. We see what looks like forced labor, but Columbus' crucial role in it is obscured; instead the film scapegoats an underling figure, a scheming Spanish nobleman who happens to look very much like an Indian, as the racist, and makes Columbus his antagonist. With the upgrading of the native image goes a parallel upgrading of Columbus. An enlightened version of the traditional history-book figure, he sympathizes with the Indians and treats them just as he treats Spanish noblemen. It is as if the film fused the personalities and ideologies of Columbus and the Spanish priest Bartolomé de las Casas, as if the "discoverer" had been retroactively endowed with the conscience of the radical priest.

The seven-hour PBS documentary *Columbus and the Age of Discovery* (1991), meanwhile, careens between occasional liberal-sympathetic images of indigenous people and a generally conservative glorification of Columbus' enterprise. The opening image of the ocean, followed by a caravelle, positions the spectator within the perspective of the voyagers from the very beginning. The orienting questions are: "Who was the man Columbus?" and "Should we celebrate Columbus' achievement as a great discovery ... or should we mourn a world forever lost?" The series thus confronts us with a dubious choice – celebrate Columbus or mourn a presumably vanished civilization – leaving no room for contemporary indigenous identities or for activism in the present. More importantly, the film is structured as a voyage/inquiry into Columbus' mind. There is no attempt to explore the cognition and understanding of the indigenous people. The series' subplot, meanwhile, revolves around the mobilization of the energies of the contemporary shipbuilders, navigators, cartographers, and historians who reenact Columbus' first voyage in replica vessels. Why would people today be so psychically and financially "invested," one wonders, in literally following in Columbus' tracks, if his voyage did not speak to them in quasi-mythic terms? Attitudes, one suspects, are being "replicated" along with the ships. (Entrepreneurs have often replicated the *Niña*, the *Pinta* and the *Santa Maria*; did they ever replicate a slave ship?)

For many Native Americans, to be asked to celebrate Columbus is the equivalent of asking Jews to celebrate Hitler.[39] Not only did Columbus inaugurate the transatlantic slave trade (in reverse) by taking six shackled Tainos back to Spain on his second voyage, his brief rule of "Hispianola" accounted for the deaths of some 50,000 people. Indeed, twenty-one years after his first landing, 8 million people had been killed by violence, disease, or despair.[40] Although Columbus' early diaries describe the natives as "the best people in the world and the most peacable" (16 December 1492), "gentle and ignorant of evil ... [not knowing] even how to kill one another" (12 November 1492), he proceeded to enslave and dispossess them. Columbus' split attitude toward the indigenous peoples made them simultaneously the best and the worst of humans, at once noble and savage. His radical dichotomizing of the Carib and the Arawak, the fierce cannibal and noble savage, marks a division within European perception of the indigene. "The old story of ferocious Caribs chasing timid Arawaks up the island chains from Venezuela, eating the men, possessing the women," as Peter Hulme and Neil Whitehead put it, "is endlessly repeated, even though fewer and fewer scholars accept it."[41] The good Indian/bad Indian binarism persists, we would add, even in revisionist, "pro-Indian" films like *The Emerald Forest* (1985), *Dances with Wolves* (1990) and *Black Robe* (1991). Although the three films pay homage to native culture, they still return to the colonial splitting of good/bad natives; the peace-loving "Invisible People" against the "Fierce People" in *The Emerald Forest*, the peaceful Sioux against the violent Pawnee in *Dances with Wolves*, the benevolent Hurons against the sadistic Iroquois in *Black Robe*.

Columbus' "America" was very much an intertextual invention shaped by Pliny's *Natural History*, Marco Polo's *Travels*, romances of chivalry, and Renaissance epic poems.[42] But despite Columbus' "literary" vision, New World literature did not begin with his arrival there. A "crass evolutionism" (Gordon Brotherston's words) celebrates the Semitic-Greek alphabet as the very pivot of human achievement, but portrays the indigenous peoples as pre-literate. Actually, however, there were many forms of phonetic and iconic script in the Americas: the knitted strings (*quipu*) and the *huacas* of the Inca, the dry painting of the Navajo (Dineh), the hieroglyphs of the Maya, the petroglyphs of the Pueblo peoples, the incised birchbark scrolls of the Midewiwin, the scrolls and wampum belts of the Algonquin, the screenfold books of Meso-America, the totem poles of the Pacific Coast.[43] (Indeed, Derrida appeals to such forms of *écriture* in his critique of Lévi-Strauss' phonocentrism in *De la Grammatologie*.) "American" literature also began with the songs, stories, dances, and dramatic productions of such peoples as the Chippewa, the Iroquois, the Inuit, the Mexicas, the Maya, and the Incas. The native tradition includes such works as the *Popol Vuh* (the Mayan encyclopedia of theogony, cosmogony, and astrology), the anonymous Incan verse drama *Ollantay*, the Maya Quiche tragedy *Rabinal Achi*, and the codex formed of mystical texts and prophecies attributed to the priest Chilam Balam.[44] This indigenous intertext still inspires contemporary literature. Leslie Marmon Silko's *Almanac of the Dead* (1991) revolves around an attempt to rescue a Mayan almanac hidden from the Spanish by native guardians. Miguel Angel Asturias' Nobel Prize-winning novel *Hombres de Maiz* (Men of Maize, 1949) draws on the *Popol Vuh* (a work which Asturias himself had translated); Octavio Paz redeploys the *Legend of the Suns* in *Piedra de Sol* (1957); Pablo Neruda invokes the messianic hope for the return of the Inca in *Alturas de Machu Picchu* (The Heights of Machu Picchu, 1950); and Mario de Andrade's *Macunaíma* (1928) draws on the dense *fabulae* of the Amazonian region.

Indeed, it is not unreasonable to speak of a clash of multiple intertexts, whereby European intruders, formed by readings from the scriptures, Herodotus, Marco Polo, King Arthur, chivalric romances, and fifteenth-century chronicles of African expeditions, encountered an indigenous culture that tried to account for the invaders through its own preexisting mythic systems, invoking the long-prophesied return of a divinity or hero (Quetzalcoatl in Mexico, Wiraqocha in the Andes), or the emergence of a great shaman (in the Tupi-Guarani cultural region).

67

While the Europeans tried to force the native peoples into a pre-set Biblical schema, the native peoples counterposed their own texts and beliefs to the Christian scriptures, as the Aztecs did to the Franciscans, the Tupi to the Capuchins, and the Algonquin to the Puritans.[45] The Europeans practiced a brutal *écriture*, literalizing what Derrida has called "the violence of the letter." Everywhere in the conquered world, they left signs, etching their power on indigenous faces through branding and changing toponymic names. At times, as Martin Lienhardt points out, the European "fetish of writing" turned *écriture* into a form of possession, "sanctified" by the religion of the book in whose name it was undertaken.[46] The imposition of European alphabetic systems was accompanied by the destruction of the traditional indigenous systems of notation, regarded as "inventions of the devil."[47] The same incendiarism that burned Jewish and Muslim texts also committed indigenous texts to the flames.

The story of the "voyages of discovery" to the "New World," like the fable of Europe's pure Greek origins, is a tale the West tells itself. Narrating a new beginning, it obscures not only the antecedent history in which the indigenous peoples had already explored, named, and mapped the entire hemisphere from Alaska to Tierra del Fuego,[48] but also the fact that Europe's new "beginning" was for the native peoples an ending, the destruction of their freedom and autonomy. Europe's morning of hope was for them a mourning for the loss of hope. Indigenous survivors of this holocaust wrote elegies to the pre-Columbian lost paradise, as in the sixteenth-century *Chilam Balam*:

> There was then no sickness;
> They had then no aching bones;
> They had then no high fever;
> They had then no smallpox;
> They had then no burning chest;
> ... at that time the course of humanity was orderly.
> The foreigners made it otherwise when they arrived here.[49]

'They made our flowers wilt," writes the Mayan prophet, "so that only their flowers could live."[50]

Today's critique of Columbus is sometimes considered anachronistic and unduly prosecutorial, a question of seeing Columbus through contemporary eyes, as if it were a question of a misplaced historical paradigm.[51] But this "critique of the critique" misses the point. First, the destruction of native peoples has not stopped; it is still going on all over the Americas. Second, in their own nonchalant reporting of European cruelties, many of the European documents from the Columbian period are self-indicting even within the European standards of the time. Third, the critique of Columbus does not so much involve the adoption of a *contemporary* perspective as of a *different* perspective: that of the native peoples and also of Columbus' critics *in his own time*. (History may be written by the winners, but the winners often quarrel.) Thus endorsing the anti-Columbus critique involves endorsing a whole series of opinions by contemporaneous clerics and legal scholars. It means endorsing the view of Spanish legal scholars such as Melchor Cano, who argued as early as 1546 that Spaniards had no right to take indigenous property, for "even if the inhabitants of [a] region hold things in common, foreigners cannot take possession of them without the consent of those who live there."[52] It means endorsing the view of Padré Antonio Vieira, who wrote from Brazil on April 4, 1654, to Portugal's King John IV, calling the domination of the indigenous peoples the "original and capital sin of the Portuguese State."[53] In 1511 in Santo Domingo, before an audience of royal officials of the province that included Columbus' son Diego, the Dominican friar Antonio de Montesinos excoriated the "tyrannical atrocities" imposed by the Spaniards on "innocent people."[54] In the same period Father Francisco de Vitoria, in his *Relectio de Indis*, rejected the concept of "discovery," and argued that conquest gave the Spanish no more right to American territory than the Indians would have had they conquered Spain.[55] At the same time, it would be wrong to idealize the various Christian dissenters from conquest, as Roland Jaffe's *The Mission* (1986) does, for example, when it overdraws the contrast between racist mercenary colonialists and compassionate antislavery Jesuits like Father Gabriel. Catholic critics did not renounce the Christian colonization of the native soul or the colonial enterprise in general; their denunciation was limited to genocidal practices and enslavement.

The contemporary debates in many ways echo those of the past. Even the debate about the word "discovery" is not new; in 1556, the Spanish regime officially decreed the substitution of the word *descubrimiento* (discovery) for the forbidden word *conquista* (conquest). The ritual sacrifices of the Aztecs, by the same token, were then and are still now ritually invoked (for example in *Newsweek*'s "Columbus Special Issue" of Fall/Winter 1991) to "justify" European conquest and to mask those "sacrificed" on the altar of European greed. The Aztec sacrifice rationale has certain difficulties, however, in that it falsely suggests that Europeans conquered *in order to* cleanse these regions of such practices, and fails to explain why Europeans also slaughtered other peoples *not* accused of such practices (the "friendly" Arawaks were destroyed along with the "fierce" Caribs). It also fails to explain why, if conquest constitutes a normal retribution for cruel practices, Europe itself would not be the legitimate object of such retribution for having practiced the Inquisition, torture at the rack, drawing and quartering, witch-burning, and countless other misdemeanors. And if the fact that indigenous groups occasionally feuded or fought is seen as justifying European conquest, would not the interminable squabbles of European nations justify the conquest of Europe by Native Americans?

In any case, the anticolonialist argument does not stand or fall on the moral qualities of native peoples – their humanity is sufficient argument against conquest. In Columbus' time, the Spanish priest Bartolomé de las Casas witnessed the massacres of the Indians by the conquistadors and denounced them in a book of 1520 addressed to King Charles V and entitled *The Devastation of the Indies: A Brief Account*. De las Casas described nothing less than a massive genocide, which reduced the native population in the first thirty years after

Cortés' landing from 25 million to 6 million souls. In forty years, he estimated, the internal actions of the Christians" had led to the unjust slaying of "more than twelve million men, women, and children."[56] De las Casas described Europeans taking "infants from their mothers' breasts ... [snatching] them by the arms and [throwing] them into the rivers, roaring with laughter and saying as the babies fell into the water, 'boil there, you offspring of the devil!'"[57] In a contemporary context, de las Casas' account resonates painfully with modern tales of Salvadoran soldiers tossing little children in the air to catch them on their bayonets.[58] The point of citing this catalog of horrors, in any case, is not moralistic but rather to emphasize the historical roots of contemporary debate.

De las Casas is the subject of at least one feature-length film: Mexican director Sergio Olhovich's *Bartolomé de las Casas* (1992). Structured as a series of flashbacks conveying the protagonist's evolving attitudes toward the New World and its inhabitants, the film emphasizes the priest's contradictions rather than his heroism. The film's esthetic is strikingly theatrical, characterized by chiaroscuro lighting of stylized interiors, tableaux effects, and an emphasis on close shots of tormented faces speaking in soliloquy – an intimist treatment for an epic subject. Armed conflicts between European and indigene, meanwhile, are not treated in a realistic manner but rather as a balletic combat of symbolic figures. Rather than idealizing de las Casas, Olhovich uses the Brechtian procedure of placing critiques of him in the mouths of his adversaries. "You claim you defend the Indians," says one critic, "but you yourself profit from them." Nor does the film obscure the fact that de las Casas at one point called for the importation of Africans as slaves, a suggestion he bitterly regretted later. When de las Casas tries to put into practice his democratic ideals along the coast of what is now Guatemala, the project turns out to be quixotic, an exercise in futility given the larger historical forces at play. But if the film does not idealize de las Casas, it does support his critique of the hypocrisy of a Church which offers "eternal life" in exchange for a lifetime of forced labor.

Bartolomé de las Casas stages the intense religious and juridicial debates which came in the wake of the *conquista*, the religious debate about Indian souls, the legal debate about Spanish claims on indigenous lands. The historical debate between de las Casas and Sepulveda is staged as a theatrical encounter between the King and his two counselors, one of whom, Sepulveda, offers theological rationalizations for material exploitation, while the other, de las Casas, criticizes conquest and enslavement in the name of Christian charity. When de las Casas argues that Spain should leave the New World to its original inhabitants, Sepulveda retorts that such a magnanimous gesture would only lead to a reversion to barbarism and idolatry. The film ends with the reading of de las Casas' final testament, calling for the Spanish to restore the stolen wealth to the Indians, for priests to learn indigenous languages, and for Spain to restore dignity to the "natural lords of these lands." A reflexive epilog has the camera dolly back to reveal director and crew as a cross of light covers the body of the dead de las Casas, symbolically identifying him with the crucified Christ.

REVISIONIST FILM AND THE QUINCENTENNIAL

The Columbus debate has been played out in the realms of official and popular culture. For the official celebrations of the quincentennial of 1992, millions of dollars were poured into international events, climaxing in the grand regatta, an international fleet of tall ships that sailed from Spain and arrived in New York Harbor for the Fourth of July. At the same time, widespread activism subverted the official celebration; Columbus, as Gary Wills put it, got "mugged" on the way to his own celebration. A group of Native Americans "landed" in Amsterdam, declared the land theirs, and set off for a European El Dorado rumored to be located somewhere near the Rhine. In the US, countless demonstrations, conferences, pedagogical projects, and media events created a counter-narrative. Even the dominant media paid attention to the protests. An anticolonial narrative was also performed via the "view-from-the-shore" projects, and through didactic films and videos whose titles clearly reveal their anticolonial thrust: *Surviving Columbus* (1990), *Columbus on Trial* (1992), *The Columbus Invasion: Colonialism and the Indian Resistance* (1992), *Columbus Didn't Discover Us* (1992), *Falsas Historias* (False Histories, 1992), *1492 Revisited* (1993), and *Outros Quinhentos* (Another Five Hundred Years, 1993).

Conventional literary and filmic narratives about "discovery," in contrast, from Columbus' *Diaries* through *Robinson Crusoe* to the quincentennial productions about Columbus, assume the point of view of the "discoverers." Most discovery narratives place the reader on a European ship, the land is sighted (usually through an anachronistic telescope), and the "Indians" are glimpsed on the beach or behind the trees. In his book *Fulcrums of Change*, Jan Carew projects a radically different perspective. He imagines the *Niña*, the *Pinta*, and the *Santa Maria* appearing against a steel-blue horizon, the Arawaks shouting the news about strange vessels "driven by shirts" and manned by bearded men armed with "gleaming sticks," performing indecipherable "rituals to a Sky God," and laying claim to all the lands in the name of some "chieftains" named Ferdinand and Isabella.[59]

Only recently have films begun to offer resistant commemorations of the conquest. An anti-quincentennial film *avant la lettre*, Glauber Rocha's *Terra em Transe* (Land in Anguish, 1967), an allegory about Brazilian politics, satirically reenacts the arrival of Pedro Cabral, the Brazilian Columbus, on the shores of Brazil in the year 1500. The right-wing figure of the film (named Porfírio Diaz after the Mexican dictator who slaughtered thousands of Indians), arrives from the sea carrying a huge cross, suggesting a myth of national origins. Bearing a black banner and a crucifix and dressed in an anachronistic modern-day suit, he is accompanied by a priest in an old Catholic habit, a sixteenth-century conquistador, and a symbolic feathered Indian. A huge cross is fixed in the sand as Diaz approaches it to kneel and perform a ritual evoking, for the Brazilian spectator, the famous "first Mass" celebrated in the newly "discovered" land, but in an anachronistic manner which stresses the metonymic and metaphoric

71

continuities between the *conquista* and contemporary oppression. Yoruba religious chants pervade the soundtrack, evoking the "transe" of the Portuguese title and suggesting, perhaps, an Afro-indigenous link.[60]

Land in Anguish anticipated a number of more recent revisionist films set in the early period of conquest films which relativize or even invert colonialist perspectives. The Mexican film *Cabeza de Vaca* (1989) tells the story of Alvar Nuñez Cabeza de Vaca, the shipwrecked Spaniard who traveled by foot from Florida to Texas. The film's source text, Alvar Nuñez's *Relación de los Naufragios* (Story of the Shipwrecked), is an early recounting of the Conquest as a story of failure. Inverting the usual roles, Nuñez portrays the Spaniards as vulnerable, as losing control, weeping, supplicating. And while a phantasmic cannibalism usually serves to justify European exploitation, here it is the Spanish who cannibalize one another and the natives who watch in horror.[61] Although the film portrays the Indians as menacing, even freakish, it does expose the underside of European religious proselytizing, and dares to suggest that the conquistadors, not the natives, might have been the real cannibals. The Venezuelan film *Jericó* (Jericho, 1990), meanwhile, largely adopts the indigenous perspective and shows extensive knowledge of the languages, histories, and cultural styles of the indigenous groups it portrays. While most Hollywood films have the "Indians" speak a laughable pidgin English, here the natives laugh at a European's garbled attempt to speak *their* language. The story describes the case of a European who "goes native." This was not in fact an infrequent occurrence during the first centuries of conquest: in Mexico, for example, Gonzalo Guerrero, a Spaniard kidnapped by Indians in the Yucatan, became a Cacique with tattooed face and pierced ears;[62] in North America, as Hector de Crevecoeur noted, thousands of Europeans became "white Indians" (to the point that some colonies passed laws against "Indianizing"), while "we have no examples of even one of these Aborigines having from choice become Europeans."[63] Some "white Indians" were attracted, by their own account, to the Indian sense of community, equality, the "ease of living [and] the absence of those cares and corroding solicitudes which so often prevail with us."[64]

Jericho concerns a Franciscan priest, Santiago, lone survivor of a sixteenth-century expedition led by the conquistador Gascuña in search of the mythic Mar del Sur. Although Santiago hopes spiritually to conquer the Indians, he is in fact spiritually conquered by them: as their captive, he comes to question his European attitudes toward religion, the body, the earth, and social life, and finally renounces his evangelical mission. In the end, he falls back into the hands of Spaniards, who regard his "going native" as a form of madness and heresy. What makes this revisionist captivity narrative so subversive is that it transforms the indigenous culture that official Europe regarded with fear and loathing into a seductive pole of attraction for Europeans. The real purpose of the Inquisition, Jorge Klor de Alva has suggested, was not to force the indigenes to become Europeans, but to keep Europeans from becoming indigenes.[65]

A number of revisionist films assert links between past and contemporary oppressions and resistances. The Cuban-Peruvian epic *Tupac Amaru* (1984) evokes indigenous resistance to Spanish-European domination in Peru, specifically the eighteenth-century Inca rebellion led by José Gabriel Condorcanqui Tupac Amaru, whose story is told in flashbacks from his trial by the Spanish.[66] A direct descendant of an Inca emperor (beheaded by the Spanish in 1572), whose name he borrowed, Tupac Amaru led a broad-based messianic rebellion against Spanish rule. In 1781 he entered the main plaza of Cuzco and announced that he was condemning the royal *corregidor*, Antonio Juan de Arriaga, to the gallows. A few days later he issued a decree liberating the slaves and abolishing taxes (*encomienda*) and forced labor (the *mita*). After a number of victories, he was betrayed and given over to the royalists, who had him drawn and quartered in the four directions of the Inca Empire, symbolically dismembering the indigenous reign that he was trying to install. The film begins and ends in the central square of Cuzco, in Inca cosmology the center (or "navel") of a universe that stretched anthropomorphically across a vast territory. By decapitating the Inca Emperor, the Spanish conquerers transformed the anthropomorphic figure of the Inca Empire (the *Inkarri* in Quechua) into a grimacing, contorted figure of pain, thus delegitimizing Cuzco as a center of power.[67] The film shows the Spanish punishment of Tupac Amaru and his family, watched by a distressed, benumbed indigenous crowd. (The historical torture and quartering of Tupac Amaru and his family lasted from ten in the morning to five in the afternoon of May 18, 1781.) We hear a pronouncement in Spanish: "The proceedings of this trial shall be destroyed. Not a trace shall remain of these unfortunate events nor a vestige of this accursed race." The camera swirls vertiginously, as if translating the despair of the crowd, after which the film segues into a black-and-white flash forward to a similar crowd – this time a modern-day political rally in 1975, held in the same square where Tupac Amaru was killed. The film thus contradicts the Spanish prophecy that "not a trace shall remain" and instead installs the terms of Inca prophecy, as a poem speaks of the head and body of the dismembered *Inkarri* coming back together in an apotheosis of liberation.

The Venezuelan film *Cubagua* (1987), an adaptation and update of the 1931 novel by Enrique Bernardo Nuñez, also moves between past and present, using tripled characters from the sixteenth century, the 1930s, and the present to show the continuities of exploitation. *Cubagua*'s male protagonist lives three different lives in three different periods: in 1520 as Lampugnano, an Italian helping the Spaniards extract pearls; in 1930 as an engineer helping North American oil companies; and in 1980 as an engineer working for a multinational company extracting minerals in the Amazon. His female counterpart, Nila, is a victim of the Spanish in the 1500s, a resistant chief's daughter in the 1930s, and an anti-imperialist journalist in the 1980s. Together, the characters help compose a portrait in transhistorical time of a country which has been colonized and neocolonized, but which has also displayed diverse forms of cultural and political resistance.[68]

The Brazilian film *Ajuricaba* (1977), similarly, stresses historical continuities

Plate 6 Global
discoveries: *Columbus
on Trial*

Plate 7 Cabral
"discovers" Brazil in
Land in Anguish

Plate 8 The
hallucinatory
conquistador in
O No Coronado!

Plate 9 The shadow of the conquest in *Surviving Columbus*

Plate 10 "Green Card" artwork by Inigo Manglano-Ovalle

Plate 11 Columbus on Trial

by shuttling between Indian resistance in the eighteenth century and resistance to multinational companies in the present. It tells the story of Ajuricaba, an eighteenth-century chief of the Manau tribe who fought against his people's enslavement and finally leaped to his death rather than be captured. Finally, Nelson Pereira Dos Santos' *Como Era Gostoso Meu Française* (How Tasty was My Frenchman, 1971) performs an "anthropophagic" critique of European colonialism, using the figure of cannibalism both to denounce the economic cannibalism of European colonialism and to suggest that contemporary Brazilians should emulate their Tupinamba forebears by devouring European technologies of domination in order to use them against Europe. Partly based on diaries written by Europeans such as Hans Staden and Jean de Lery, the film concerns a Frenchman captured by the Tupinamba and sentenced to death in response to massacres inflicted upon them by Europeans. Before he is ritually executed and eaten, however, he is given a wife (Sebiopepe, widow of one of the Tupinamba massacred by the Europeans), and is allowed to participate in the tribe's daily activities. In the last shot, the camera zooms into Sebiopepe's face as she casually chews her Frenchman without emotion, despite her previous close relationship with him. This image is followed by a quotation from a report on genocide committed by Europeans. Subverting the conventional identification with the European protagonist of the captivity narrative, the film maintains escape routes, maintaining an ironically neutral attitude toward the protagonist's being swallowed. The real scandal, the film implies, is genocide, not the ritual of devouring an "allegorical" representation of one's enemies.

In the US native Americans have also begun to make historical films from an indigenous point of view. George Burdeau's *Surviving Columbus* narrates the initial encounter between the conquistadors and the Zuni, giving pride of place to Zuni narratives within a communal atmosphere of domesticated storytelling. Seen from a Zuni perspective, the conquistadors become abstracted, depersonalized, Goya-esque figures of menace. Creek/Seminole filmmaker Bob Hicks' *Return of the Country* (1984) recalls the methods used in religious schools to oppress Native Americans – the separation of parents from children, enforced Eurocentric education, suppression of native languages and cultures. The film performs a millenarian overturning by reversing this oppressive situation: this time it is European language and culture that are outlawed (a White child is ordered to destroy his Bible), while the courts, the Congress, and the presidency are now in indigenous hands.

A number of didactic documentaries also tell the story of the conquest from the perspective of the conquered: Tainos, Mayas, Aztecs, Mohawks. *The Columbus Invasion: Colonialism and the Indian Resistance* combines sixteenth-century images with contemporary interviews with Native Americans. One native speaker cites a Maya prophecy that indigenous peoples, after 500 years of suffering, will unite, as the "eagle of the north meets the condor of the south." *Columbus Didn't Discover Us* cinematically "realizes" that prophecy by recording a panindigenous encounter held in the highlands of Ecuador in July 1990. *1492 Revisited* links past and present by featuring artwork from the *Counter Colon-ialismo* exhibition, along with interviews with Chicano and Native American artists and cultural critics. The British BBC documentary *Savagery and the American Indian* (1989), finally, plays on the trope of savage "wildness" by positing the Europeans, rather than the Native Americans, as wild and violent. At the same time it satirizes the folklore of ethnocentric prejudice – "They don't use the land, they have no religion" – by having it pronounced by the back-lit, bearded mouths of those the natives call the "hairy men."

Other films use avant-garde inflected tactics to critique the conquest. Lourdes Portillo's *Columbus on Trial* has the Chicano group Culture Clash perform a witty contemporary indictment of a Don Corleone-like Columbus, shown against the projected images of past colonial brutalities and contemporary racial conflicts. Acquitted by a coopted court, Columbus is finally killed by a Chicana. Cesary Jaworsky and John Petrizzelli's *Falsas Historias* has its grotesque conquistadors arrive in 1563 in a "New World" already polluted and dotted with shantytowns. Kidlat Tahimik's work-in-progress *Magellan's Slave* – its alternate title is *Memories of Overdevelopment* – is premised on the speculation that the first man actually to circumvent the globe was a Filipino slave whom Magellan picked up in Spain, and who completed Magellan's project after the Portuguese died. But the most outrageously avant-gardist of the antiquincentennial films is Craig Baldwin's *O No Coronado!* (1992), which is framed as a historical flashback within the mind of the conquistador Coronado as he falls off his horse – an apt metaphor for the carnivalesque dethroning that the film performs. Baldwin focusses on one of the more inept and deluded of the conquistadors, the one whose desperate search for the chimerical Seven Cities of Cibola led him into a fruitless, murderous journey across what is now the American southwest. To relate this calamitous epic, Baldwin deploys not only costumed dramatizations but also the detritus of the filmic archive: swashbucklers, pedagogical films, industrial documentaries. Found footage from diverse costume epics takes us back to the Old World origins of New World conquest in the Crusades and the *reconquista*. Educational footage of an atomic test site – found in the same region that Coronado exploited – is accompanied by a female voice-over pronouncing the prophecies of Native American seers: "Earthquakes shook the world ... fear was everywhere." Through the "prior textualizations" of tacky costume dramas and sci-fi films – Vincent Price (incarnating the Inquisition), the Lone Ranger, Charles Bronson – Coronado is portrayed as a Eurotrash exemplar of colonialism. The film ends with images of nuclear explosions, the apotheoses of instrumental reason, which Baldwin contrasts with a lone Indian using a reflecting mirror as a weapon – an evocation of their minimal means of resistance.

SLAVERY AND RESISTANCE

Prior to colonialism, slavery was traditionally based on the rationale of the "spoils of war," on the idea that the vanquished owed their very lives to the victor and therefore owed a lifetime of service. (This rationale is resurrected in Crusoe's enslavement of Friday in Defoe's novel.) Aristotle provided a rationale for slavery by arguing in the first book of the *Politics* that some individuals are "destined for slavery," but his criteria were explicitly *not* racial but ethical; the person destined for slavery is the person lacking in self-control. His stress was not on race but on class as a rationale for privilege. Colonialism subsequently "transferred" this class rationale from individuals to entire societies, seen as "slave nations" destined to be ruled. (In his attempt to justify enslavement of the native peoples of the Americas, Sepulveda explicitly racialized Aristotle's notion of the "natural slave.")

Slavery has existed in many forms, from before the dawn of recorded history through to the contemporary period; there is probably no group of people, Orlando Patterson writes, "whose ancestors were not at one time slaves or slaveholders."[69] But before colonialism, slavery in the Mediterranean and in Africa tended to amount to little more than domestic servitude. Absorbed into extended-family structures, the slave could accede to family rights, marry into the owner's family, and even inherit the owner's wealth.[70] According to John Thornton, slaves in Africa were the functional equivalents of the free tenants or hired workers of Europe. Giacinto Brugiotti da Vetralla described slaves in Central Africa as "slaves in name only" by virtue of their wide variety of employments as administrators, soldiers, and even royal advisors enjoying freedom of movement and elite lifestyles.[71] Our concern here is not to idealize African forms of slavery, nor to deny African elite complicity in the slave trade, but to point to a qualitative historical difference: only with colonialism and capitalism did slavery become modern, industrialized, tied to a mode of economic production and to a systematic ideology of racial superiority. Colonial-style slavery trafficked in racialized terror, displaying the logic of commodification in stark and hyperbolic form. The classic slave narrative of Olaudah Equiano (also known as Gustavus Vassa), an Igbo prince who was enslaved first in the African sense and then in the European-colonial sense, is eloquent in this regard. Equiano relates his horror when he falls from a relatively "benign" form of personal servitude into the mass horror of chattel slavery in North America; a system he describes as infinitely more horrendous and humiliating.[72]

O.E. Uya argues that since the fifteenth century the entire Black world has been under attack by colonialism, slavery, segregation, and the neocolonialism that "underdeveloped" Africa.[73] Eurocentric history downplays the central importance of slavery to European and Euro-American economies. (It also forgets that slavery was practiced against other groups such as Native Americans; it was not the exclusive "privilege" of Blacks.) Far from being a feudal holdover, the slave-based plantation system was an integral part of modernity; it involved heavy capital-ization, complex business organization, advanced industrial technology (milling, rum manufacture, transport).[74] Eurocentric history also downplays the extent of Black resistance to slavery. But Blacks resisted everywhere, and in diverse ways. There was an ideological connective, as Cedric Robinson puts it, between the African mutineers on the *Amistad* or the captors of the *Diane*; the maroon settlements in Pernambuco, Florida, Virginia, Jamaica, the Guianas and the Carolinas; the slave revolutionists of the Revolution in Haiti; the slave insurrectionists of the Caribbean ... [and] the black rebels of the regions of the Great Fish River, the Limpopo and the Zambesi in Southern Africa.[75]

Even the European "scramble for Africa" during the nineteenth century met constant resistance: the Matabele war, the Ashanti war, the Zulu revolt, the Mullah's revolt in Somaliland. Here, for Robinson, are the roots of Black radicalism as a specifically African response to oppression. Nor was this radicalism merely based on rejection of European norms; it was inscribed by African cosmologies, social structures, ideological constructions, and systems of justice.

A number of Cuban and Brazilian films – *La Ultima Cena* (The Last Supper, 1977), *El Otro Francisco* (The Other Francisco, 1975), *El Rancheador* (1974), *Maluala* (1979), *Sinha Moça* (1953) – have told stories of Black resistance to slavery. Carlos Diegues' *Ganga Zumba* (1963) and *Quilombo* (1984) memorialize the seventeenth-century fugitive slave republic Palmares, seen as the very prototype of a utopian democracy in the Americas. Palmares lasted almost a century in the face of repeated assaults from both the Dutch and the Portuguese. On the average, it withstood one Portuguese expedition every fifteen months.[76] At its height, the republic counted 20,000 inhabitants spread over numerous villages in the northeastern interior of Brazil, covering an area roughly a third the size of Portugal. Palmares bears witness to the capacity of Afro-Brazilians not only to revolt against slavery but also to imagine and mobilize an alternative life based on African norms. Economically self-sufficient, Palmares rejected the monoculture farming typical of colonial Brazil in favor of the diversified agriculture the freed Afro-Brazilians remembered from Africa, planting corn, beans, manioc, potatoes, and sugar cane on communally shared land. Palmarino kings were kings in the African sense of consensus ruler – not absolute monarchs but custodians of the common wealth. The Palmarino penal code was harsh, especially in the later period, but the people enjoyed basic civic and political equality. Along with the Black majority, Palmares welcomed Indians, *mestizos*, Jews, and renegade Whites, ultimately becoming a refuge for the persecuted of Brazilian society. Palmares has great contemporary resonance in Brazil, as Black nationalists invoke *quilombismo* and celebrate "Black Consciousness Day" on the anniversary of the death of the Palmarino leader Zumbi. Indeed, Black farmers still cultivate the land that their ancestors settled, and a *"quilombo* clause" could give land titles to 500,000 descendants of the free Black communities.[77]

Based on a historical novel by João Felicio dos Santos, *Ganga Zumba* focusses on a Black slave who discovers that he is the grandson of a King of Palmares. The film's portrait of slavery highlights forced labor, sadistic slave-drivers, and frequent whippings, rape, and murder, undercutting the idealized tableau of benign servitude painted by Lusophile historians like Gilberto Freyre. *Ganga Zumba* assumes a pro-Black perspective throughout, showing Blacks not as mere victims but as active agents. One scene shows a male slave and his lover entice a slave-driver in order to kill him – a scene unthinkable in any Hollywood film of the period. A Fanonian ode to insurrectional violence, the film applauds the slave's gesture as necessary and even laudatory.

In *Quilombo* (1983) Diegues returns to the same theme, taking advantage of a bigger budget as well as of recent historical research by Decio Freitas.[78] Sweeping over a historical period running from 1650 to 1695, the narrative moves through three distinct phases. In the first, a group of slaves, led by Ganga Zumba, flees a sugar plantation and makes its way to Palmares. In the second, Palmares, under Ganga Zumba, has become a prosperous independent community. In the third, another leader, Zumbi, is forced to lead the struggle against the colonists in an atmosphere dominated by internal tensions and external aggressions. The Palmarinos are ultimately massacred and Zumbi himself is killed, but the final intertitles inform us that outbreaks of resistance went on for another century. The overall movement of the film, then, is from spontaneous revolt through the building of a community, to the violent destruction of that community, with a final coda pointing to ongoing struggle.

Quilombo's gallery of characters includes Ganga Zumba, the African prince who leads the slaves out of bondage into the promised land of Palmares; Acotirene, a symbolic figure associated with African strength and spirituality; and Dandara, associated with the African spirit Iansã, whose performance of religious rituals saves Ganga Zumba. The character Samuel, meanwhile, represents the many Sephardi Jews and *conversos* who fled the Inquisition and took refuge in Brazil; his dialog brings to the flight of the slaves Biblical echoes of the exodus, the parting of the Red Sea, and the promised land. The film also valorizes Black culture by associating its characters with the *orixas* of Candomblé: Ganga Zumba is linked to the thunder god Xango, Zumbi to Ogum, the *orixa* of metal, agriculture, and war. At one point a venerable slave refuses the last rites in Latin and insists on singing in Yoruba. After his death, Ganga Zumba appears magically with Xango's ax in his hand. Thus the film foregrounds the symbolic value of African culture, while also insisting on the need for struggle. (The only problem with these homages to Yoruba religion is that Palmarino culture was in fact Bantu rather than Yoruba; the Yoruba were relative latecomers to Brazil.)[79] The film also betrays a kind of confusion of genres, shifting between utopian musical and realist history, with the result that it has neither the musical's charm (despite the excellence of Gilberto Gil's score) nor the grandeur of historical epic.

If diverse genres trip over one another in *Quilombo*, in Sergio Giral's *The Other Francisco* they are choreographed in a dialectical manner. Set in Cuba in a later period, and based on Cuba's first antislavery novel (Anselmo Suarez y Romero's *Francisco: El Ingenio o Las Delicias del Campo*, 1839), the film promotes interplay between diverse generic modes of presentation: a parodically melodramatic approach, "faithful" to the sentimental spirit of the novel; a staged

Plate 12 The machete that cuts cane can cut heads: Crispin in *The Other Francisco*

(anachronistically verité) documentary about the novel's context in the literary salons of the period; and a realistic reconstruction of the historical life of the enslaved. Taken together, the three modes emphasize exactly what is suppressed in the novel: the economic (free trade) motives behind the abolitionist movement, the catalyzing role of Black rebellion, and the artistic mediation of the story itself. In the novel, Francisco commits suicide when he learns that his true love Dorotea has surrendered to the lust of her White master. But the documentary-style segments suggest that a slave would never commit suicide over an ill-fated romance. And a voice-over narration informs us that pregnant slaves were forced to work in the fields through their ninth month, that infant mortality was near 100 per cent, and that many female slaves aborted their children to spare them a life of exploitation. The film's final section stages the slave uprisings missing from the novel. The slaves, Francisco among them, plan a rebellion. Their leader, Crispin – the polar antithesis of the docile Francisco of the novel – invokes revolutionary Haiti and, echoing Césaire, reminds them that "the same machete that cuts cane can cut heads." He calls for pan-African unity against divide-and-conquer attempts to separate Yoruba from Arara, Mina from Mandingo in Cuba. Here, the film transcends the implicit economism of the commentary in the earlier sections, as African religion takes on a central, energizing role. As Crispin, in traditional attire, ritualistically inspires the slaves to revolt, European symphonic music gives way to Afro-Cuban drums.

RENEGADE VOICES

Not all European writers have been uncritical or Eurocentric: many, in the tradition of de las Casas, have raised their voices against colonialist racism. In the sixteenth century the French philosopher Montaigne defended cultural relativism in "Des Cannibales," arguing that civilized Europeans were ultimately more barbarous than cannibals, since cannibals ate the flesh of the dead only to appropriate the strength of their enemies, while Europeans tortured and killed in the name of a religion of love:

> I think there is more barbarity in eating a live than a dead man, in tearing on the rack and torturing the body of a man still full of feeling, in roasting him piecemeal and giving him to be bitten and mangled by dogs and swine (as we have not only read, but seen within fresh memory, not between old enemies, but between neighbors and fellow citizens, and what is worse, under the cloak of piety and religion) than in roasting and eating him after he is dead.[80]

For Montaigne, Spanish genocide was motivated by greed: "so many cities razed to the ground, so many nations exterminated ... for a traffic in pearls and pepper!"[81] Montaigne also deployed an indigenous perspective to indict the barbarism of class in Europe itself. Reporting on the Tupinamba reaction to Europe, he wrote:

> They said that in the first place they thought it very strange that so many big men with beards, strong and armed ... should submit to obey a child, and that they did not rather choose one of their own number to command them. Secondly (they have a way of speaking of men as if they were halves of one another) that they had observed that there were men amongst us, full and gorged with all kinds of good things, and that their halves were begging at their doors, emaciated with hunger and poverty; and they thought it strange how these necessitous halves could suffer such injustice, and that they did not seize the others by the throat, or set fire to their houses.[82]

A few years later, Shakespeare devised the character of Caliban, whose name forms an anagram of "cannibal," for *The Tempest*, and had him curse the European Prospero for stealing his island: "for I am all the subjects that you have/ which first was mine own king." Aimé Césaire, in his 1969 version of the play, had to alter Shakespeare's text only slightly to turn it into an anticolonialist text. The hero of the Césaire version is the militant "Caliban X." "Call me X," says Caliban, "as one would say for a person ... whose name has been robbed." Césaire's Caliban denounces Prospero for teaching him to jabber his language well enough to follow orders but not enough to study science, and for projecting his libidinous fantasies on to him by accusing him of raping Miranda.[83]

Writing in 1719, a century after Shakespeare, Daniel Defoe created one of the West's archetypal colonial-adventurer heroes in *Robinson Crusoe*, a book which spawned hundreds of literary imitations, comic books, and films. Crusoe, we often forget, becomes wealthy through the slave trade and Brazilian sugar. Cast away on an island, his first thought on seeing human footprints, after years of solitude, is to "get a servant." As colonial explorer, he demiurgically moulds a whole civilization. He names "his" islander "Friday" in memory of the day he saved the native's life. (Friday, we recall, is the day God created Adam, strengthening the analogy between the "self-sufficient" Crusoe and God.) As Peter Hulme points out, Defoe centers two key episodes in Friday's education on aspects of Carib technology that were in fact borrowed by Europeans: the "barbecue" and the "canoe" (both indigenous words).[84] Crusoe's thinking thus exemplifies the double process of exaltation of the European self and devalorization of the non-European other that we have posited as typical of Eurocentric discourse.

Robinson Crusoe has generated an almost infinite chain of imitations and critiques. Derek Walcott's *Pantomime* has a master and slave rehearse a Crusoe–Friday mime, performing each other's roles within a power-laden play of specularity. Luis Buñuel's film adaptation of the Defoe novel casts satiric doubt (as does the novel) on Crusoe's religion – Friday is baffled by Christian theology – but leaves unquestioned certain aspects of colonialist discourse, such as the protagonist's paranoid projections of cannibals. More recent film adaptations, such as Jack Gold's *Man Friday* (1975), reveal a further tarnishing of Crusoe's heroic status, as a puritanical fable-cum-colonial-romance is turned into a

Plate 13 Colonial Pedagogy: Crusoe and Friday in *The Adventures of Robinson Crusoe*

counter-cultural, anticolonialist allegory. When the Crusoe (Peter O'Toole) of *Man Friday* explains the laws of ownership, Friday (Richard Roundtree) cannot understand why anyone would be so deranged as to believe in individual property. The film mocks Crusoe for his ledger-book mentality, his racism, his chauvinism, and his puritanical phobias (he spends years on a tropical island without removing his fur clothing). *Man Friday* also draws out the novel's homoerotic subtext. As has often been noted, Defoe's Crusoe seems less erotically energized by his wife, whom he marries and dispatches in a subordinate clause, than by Friday, whom he describes as "handsome" and "well-shaped." In *Man Friday* Crusoe alternates paternalistic mastery with erotic attraction. His fears of homosexual desire lead him to rampant paranoia and (literal) self-flagellation, to the bemusement of Friday, who does not share his erotic neuroses and inhibitions.

Man Friday performs a transvaluation of some of the conventional signs of the "other." While cannibalism is still a theme, it is now portrayed as a loving ingestion of one's dead relatives. Friday's fellow tribals are no longer the cardboard cannibals of the Defoe novel; they are individualized and exercise precise occupations, such as storyteller or craftsman. The film begins with an image of the transformation of the world from chaos to order, underlined by Crusoe's off-screen reading of the Biblical narrative of the creation. Next we see Crusoe's murderous encounter with Friday and the cannibals. But the film then reframes the narrative by switching to Friday's version of the same events. In a shift of perspectives, Friday reports Crusoe's fetishistic adoration of private property to his own tribespeople, who greet the very concept with gales of incredulous laughter, asking, "Do you mean to tell us this Crusoe fellow comes from a tribe of people who go around saying that 'this is mine' and 'this is yours'?" Yet despite the film's critique of Christian-Anglo puritanism, in the end it has Friday embody the ideal Christian, who patiently and lovingly tries to educate his errant master. While the revised title signals an apparent shift in focalization from master to slave, Friday's subjectivity ultimately serves a White counter-cultural utopia of festive and erotic community. Leaving Friday in a cultural and historical vacuum, the film does not dare to imagine his pre-Crusoe name, language, society; in sum we never learn who Friday is. The film critiques Eurocentrism, then, but remains Eurocentric in its incapacity to imagine Friday. While Césaire could reimagine Caliban from an anticolonial perspective in his version of *The Tempest*, *Man Friday* remains confined to an asymmetrical allegory in which one character is historically fleshed out, while the other is a counter-cultural token of innate Black wisdom and sensuality.

If *Robinson Crusoe* provides a paradigmatic image of colonialism, Jonathan Swift lampooned that institution in *Gulliver's Travels* (1726), which followed close on the publication of *Robinson Crusoe*. Although *Gulliver* came just thirteen years after a crucial date in the history of British colonialism – the "Asiento" which made slave traffic central to English economic expansion – the book's reception was generally apolitical, and *Gulliver's Travels* continues to be seen as an entertaining "classic" suitable for children. As Clement Hawes points out, this apolitical reading "forecloses the colonial dialectic on which the full satiric effect of the book depends," since the novel describes all the processes typical of colonization.[85] In the voyage to Laputa, Swift depicts a magnetically powered "flying island" that reigns over its dominions on the continent below and exacts tribute from them in a calculated reminiscence of colonial policy. It should be remembered that Swift was Irish – a citizen, that is, of the first of the British colonies, the prototype for all the others. One of his most bitter satires, "A Modest Proposal," ironically proposed the cannibalization of Irish children as a solution for the problem of starvation in poverty. But even if Swift had Ireland specifically in mind in *Gulliver*, his satiric barbs were also aimed at colonialism in general, as evidenced in the following indictment:

> A crew of pirates are driven by a storm they know not whither; at length a Boy discovers Land from the Topmast; they go on shore to rob and plunder; they see a harmless people, are entertained with kindness, they give the country a new name, they take formal possession of it for the king, they set up a rotten plank or a stone for a memorial, they murder two or three dozen of the natives, bring away a couple more by force for a sample, return home and get their Pardon ... And this execrable crew of butchers employed in so pious an expedition, is a modern colony sent to convert and civilize an idolatrous and barbarous people.[86]

Swift's imagery anticipates *Aguirre, der Zorn Gottes* (Aguirre, Wrath of God, 1972), Werner Herzog's film about the breakaway conquistador Lope de Aguirre (1518–61). Aguirre, having taken part in the Spanish suppression of indigenous rebellions in Peru, set out to find El Dorado, thought to be located at the headwaters of the Amazon. Although the film, which shows Europeans as victimized by the arrows and darts of faceless Indian snipers, offers no intimation of Inca grandeur and no profound critique of colonialism, it does at least focus on a conquistador manqué, who literally turns in circles. Herzog portrays Aguirre as a palpably deformed, quasi-Hitlerian icon of European megalomania and dementia, exposing the psychic roots of colonial conquest in sadism and paranoia. Obsessed with purity, Aguirre proposes founding the purest dynasty ever known by marrying his own daughter. The film also gives modest voice to colonialism's victims: the Indian Baltasar laments his lost way of life, and the Black slave Okello longs for freedom. When the only friendly Indian refuses to convert, the priest Carvajal, for whom "the Church must always side with the strong," kills him. The final moments of the film portray an extreme instance of colonial denial: as a raft laden with a delirious group of Spaniards is attacked by "Indians" from the shores, a dying soldier whispers: "This is not blood, this is not an arrow."

ANTINOMIES OF ENLIGHTENMENT AND PROGRESS

Time and again, the dispossession of indigenous peoples has been justified by the conceit of "the inevitable march of Western progress." It was in this "progressive" spirit that Andrew Jackson, in the wake of the Indian wars, censured the "sentimentality" (a present-day avatar of the same spirit might say "the cult of sensitivity") that would lament the fate of the indigenous peoples:

> To follow to the tomb the last of his race and to tread on the graves of extinct nations excite melancholy reflections. But true philantropy reconciles the mind to these vicissitudes as it does to the extinction of one generation to make room for another ... What good man would prefer a country covered with forests and ranged by a few thousand savages to our extensive Republic, studded with cities, towns, and prosperous farms [and] occupied by more than 12,000,000 happy people, and filled with all the blessings of liberty, civilization, and religion?[87]

Jackson's statement, part of his second annual message to Congress, orchestrates a number of Eurocentric leitmotifs: European material progress betokens European superiority (and provides retrospective justification for annihilation); settled peoples are superior to nomadic peoples (actually most Native American groups *were* settled); and the earth is to "have dominion" over rather than to collaborate with. The Native American peoples, according to this discourse, are "doomed by progress." The notion of the "disappearing Indian," sacrificed on the altar of the Western telos, indirectly soothes the European conscience by making genocide seem inevitable when in fact it was neither inevitable – cultural encounters need not involve genocide – nor complete, since millions of indigenous people, for example those who participated in the panindigenous rally documented in *Columbus Didn't Discover Us*, continue to survive and struggle in the Americas, living as vocal critics of the West's glorious claims of modernization and enlightenment.

At the same time, not all Europeans were anti-Indian; many became assimilated into native cultures. Even in Puritan New England, renegades like Thomas Morton, author of *New Canaan* (1636), danced with Indians around the maypole, trained them in the use of firearms, and found them "more full of humanity than the Christians."[88] For many philosophically inclined Europeans, indigenous people lived according to the egalitarian laws of Nature. In *History of America* (1777), William Robertson describes Indians as self-confident in their way of life and critical of that of Europeans:

> they regard themselves as the standard of excellence, as beings the best entitled, as well as the most perfectly qualified, to enjoy real happiness. Unaccustomed to any restraint upon their will or actions, they behold with amazement the inequality of rank, and the subordination which takes place in civilized life.[89]

Since the 1970s, Native American scholars and others have called attention to the influence of indigenous peoples on American democratic institutions. This was an influence the "founding fathers" themselves rarely denied; its erasure from history books reflects the same sort of retroactive rewriting of history we have seen with Africa and classical Greece. Revisionist scholars have emphasized salient features of Iroquois (Haudenosaunee) social and political life subsequently adopted by the founding fathers, such as the suspicion of authoritarian power ("that government governs best which governs least"), and the notion of checks and balances to prevent its concentration. Ben Franklin's idea of a "confederation," according to Donald Grinde Jr and Bruce Johansen, was borrowed from the confederation of the six Iroquois nations.[90] Indeed, the founding fathers' notions of liberty were strongly affected by Native American practices and beliefs. Arguing for public ownership of land, Tom Paine pointed to Native American society as lacking "those spectacles of human misery which poverty and want present to our eyes in all the towns and streets of Europe."[91] "I am convinced that those societies [like the Indians] which live without government," Thomas Jefferson told Edward Carrington on January 16, 1787, "enjoy in their general mass an infinitely greater degree of happiness than those who live under European governments."[92]

It was this appreciation of indigenous freedom that induced Jefferson to substitute the "pursuit of happiness" for "property" as the third leg of the natural rights tripod defended by followers of John Locke. It was no accident, Native American scholars point out, that the revolutionary "Sons of Liberty" disguised themselves as Mohawks, or that a statue of an Indian graces the Capitol building, or that the word "caucus" comes from the Algonquian language. In the 1950s, legal scholar Felix Cohen argued that the political ideals of American life emerged out of a "rich Indian democratic tradition" which was more radical than the constitution, since it included "universal suffrage for women as for men, the pattern of states that we call federalism [and] the habit of treating chiefs as servants of the people instead of their masters."[93] Indeed, speaking more generally, the idea of the egalitarian communal freedom of the native peoples, no matter how mediated or romanticized, has served as a kind of yeast or ferment which helped awaken Europe from the dogmatic sleep of authoritarianism. In the writings of Lévi-Strauss, Georges Bataille, Pierre Clastres, Eduardo Galeano, Kirkpatrick Sale, and Gerry Mander, it continues to play a role in provoking Western intellectuals to make deep anthropological critiques of the political and moral bases of Eurocentric civilization.

The cases of Franklin and Jefferson reflect the ambiguous inheritance of the Enlightenment, which was on the one hand profoundly liberating for certain strata within Europe and even outside it (for Haitian revolutionary Toussaint l'Ouverture, for example) and which on the other justified "progressive" subjugation of those who stood in Reason's way. Contemporaneous with Europe's rise to world power, the Enlightenment perpetuated, along with its progressive "overside," an imperialist, competitive, hierarchical underside. The "social contract" delineated by such philosophers as Locke, Rousseau, and Mill, which legitimized the establishment of the government of the US, was doubled by what Y.N. Kly calls the "antisocial contract" in which the idea of "equality among equals" came to entail an equal opportunity to disappropriate and exploit.[94] Indeed, few texts illustrate Walter Benjamin's aphorism that "there is no document of civilization which is not at the same time a document of barbarism" better than the American constitution. The principles enshrined there established two transcripts: one, public and written, for American men of European descent; and the other, largely unwritten, for non-European "minorities." The liberal theses of the "founding fathers," progressive as they were, were not meant to apply to "lesser peoples," just as Wilsonian "self-determination" in a later period was not meant to apply to non-European nations. Although in 1789 most of the sovereign territory of the US was unceded land occupied by Indians, the constitution made no provision for the cession, annexation, or accommodation of such peoples within the body of the Union.[95] Race was "submerged" in a double sense: the gendered Whiteness of the dominant group was submerged by going unnamed (an example of what Barthes calls "ex-nomination"), while the "Red" and the Black were submerged by euphemism or omission.

At the same time, the occasional expressed racism even of progressive European philosophers reveals the ethnocentric limits of the new "universal" knowledge. Indeed, many of the antinomies of Enlightenment thinking subsequently probed by Frankfurt School "critical theory," and later by Foucauldian archeology and Lyotardian postmodernism, were already evident in the eighteenth century.[96] For John Locke, Indians were to be classed with "children, idiots and illiterates" because of their inability to reason.[97] And David Hume, in a footnote to his 1748 essay "Of National Characters," claimed that "negroes were naturally inferior to the whites."[98] The empiricist philosopher did not submit "causality" between race and inferiority to his usual elaborate procedures of skepticism. Immanuel Kant was equally dubious of the intellectual capacities of Blacks, noting in his "Observations on the Feeling of the Beautiful and the Sublime" (1764) that Americans (that is, Native Americans) and Blacks "are lower in their mental capacities than all other races."[99] Among the French philosophes, Voltaire, while an opponent of slavery, also showed in his Traité de Metaphysique (1734) that he believed in Black inferiority.[100] And Rousseau, though he argued that inequalities were socially produced, also implied that some cultures were more evolved than others.[101] For many European philosophers, Black intelligence was perpetually on trial. Non-Europeans were called on to prove, for example by writing, what other races were granted as a birthright: their intelligence and humanity. The point is not that philosophers like Hume or Kant were *only* racists, or that they had nothing of value to say; but rather that racism, like sexism, came from the very heights of philosophical modernity.

Yet there were thinkers who took a different stance. Abbé Guillaume Reynal, author of Les Deux Indes (1776), invited the philosophically inclined to debate the proposal "Was the discovery of America a blessing or a curse to mankind?"; ultimately concluding that, given the "atrocious" traffic of slaves and the destruction of indigenous peoples, "only an infernal being" would answer the question in the affirmative.[102] The most passionately anticolonialist of the philosophes was Denis Diderot, who in his Supplément to Bougainville's voyage

88

warned Tahitians against Europeans armed "with crucifix in one hand and the dagger in the other," who would "force you to accept their customs and opinions."[103] In passages he contributed to Reynal's *Histoire des Deux Indes*, Diderot inverted the colonialist metonym of "beast and savage," advising the African Hottentots:

> Flee, unfortunate Hottentots! Flee! Hide in your forests. The ferocious beasts living in them are less frightening than the monsters of the empire under which you are about to fall ... Or if you have the courage, take your axes, take your bows, and rain your poisoned arrows on these foreigners.[104]

Like Montaigne, Diderot inverted the trope of barbarism, considering the colonizers the real barbarians. He even fantasized himself as a kind of anticolonialist guerilla *avant la lettre*, writing in 1781:

> Barbarous Europeans! The brillance of your enterprises does not impress me. Their success does not hide their injustice. In my imagination I have often embarked in those ships which bring you to distant countries, but once on land, and witness of your misdeeds, I separate myself from you and I join your enemies, taking arms against you, bathing my hands in your blood.[105]

Thus Diderot anticipated later radical renegades, for example the Sartre of the preface to Fanon's *The Wretched of the Earth* i.e. the European intellectual who identifies with the oppressed against European colonialism. (We will return to contemporary implications of renegadism in the final chapter.) He also denounced the hypocrisy of Europe's sentimental moralism in refusing sympathy to the peoples to whom it was materially indebted:

> Europe has been reverberating for a century with the most sublime moral maxims. The fraternity of all men is established in immortal writings ... Even imaginary sufferings provoke tears in the silence of our rooms and more especially at the theatre. It is only the fatal destiny of unfortunate blacks that fails to touch us. They are tyrannized, mutilated, burned, stabbed, and we hear about it coldly and without emotion. The torments of a people to whom we owe our delights never reaches our heart.[106]

If Hume used the term "nature" to deny Black humanity, Diderot deployed the same category to denounce slavery as a "crime against nature." But while Diderot called for African insurrection against the colonialists, Hegel, in *The Philosophy of History*, placed Africa outside the currents of history. Hegel, who knew nothing about Africa, argued that this continent forces us to abandon the very category of universality:

> Africa is no historical part of the World; it has no movement or development to exhibit. Historical movements in it – that is in its northern part – belong to the Asiatic or European world ... What we properly understand by

Africa, is the Unhistorical, Undeveloped Spirit, still involved in the conditions of mere nature.[107]

For Hegel, the only essential connection between Africans and Europeans was slavery, which he credited for "the increase in human feeling among the Negroes."[108] The indigenous cultures of Mexico and Peru, similarly, were for Hegel "spiritually impotent," and bound to "disappear to the extent that reason approaches."[109] China, by the same token, perpetuated a "natural vegetative existence,"[110] while in India Absolute Being was presented "in the ecstatic state of a dreaming condition."[111] It is the "necessary fate of Asiatic Empires," Hegel wrote, "to be subjected to Europeans."[112]

Although Marx turned Hegel on his head in some respects, in others he prolonged the Eurocentrism of Hegelian philosophy.[113] For Marx, the pre-capitalist societies of Asia and the Americas lived in a historically condemned temporality and would inevitably disappear before the productive march of progressive capitalism. As Native American critics point out, Marxist thought shares with capitalism the notion of productivity applied to human labor and the land.[114] Comtean positivism, meanwhile, saw the "order and progress" of human history as developing in predictable, universal stages. In *Time and the Other*, Johannes Fabian discerned a similar tendency within the science of classical anthropology – a desire to project the colonized as living "allochronically," in another time, associated with earlier periods of individual life (childhood) or of human history (primitivism). A "denial of coevalness" marked the state of the native culture as either "decadent" or "prehistoric." A frozen, inert, behind-the-times "tradition" was pitted against a vibrant "modernity," in a temporal displacement that masked the fact that what were in fact opposed were "not the same societies at different stages of development, but different societies facing each other at the same Time."[115]

Racism also left its mark on Enlightenment esthetics. The measurements and rankings characteristic of the new sciences were wedded to esthetic value judgments derived from an Apollonian reading of a de-Dionysianized Greece. Thus Aryanists like Carl Gustav Carus measured the divine in humanity through men's resemblance to Greek statues. The auratic religion of art, meanwhile, also worshipped at the shrine of Whiteness. bell hooks, Clyde Taylor, and Cornel West, among others, have denounced the "normative gaze" that has systematically devalorized non-European appearance and esthetics.[116] Where but among Caucasians, the British surgeon Charles White asked rhetorically, does one find "that nobly arched head, containing such a quantity of brain ... In what other quarter of the globe shall we find the blush that overspreads the soft features of the beautiful women of Europe?"[117] Although White's tumescent descriptions clearly hierarchize male brains over female beauty, they ultimately embrace White women for their genetic membership in the family of (White) man. In this spirit, countless colonial adventure novels, not to mention films like *Trader Horn* (1930) and *King Kong* (1933), show "natives" in naked adoration of the fetish of

White female beauty. It is only against the backdrop of this long history of glorification of Whiteness and the devalorization of Blackness that one can appreciate the emotional force of the counter-expression "Black is beautiful." (We will return to the issue of race, looks, and the cinema in chapter 8, "Esthetics of Resistance.")

In the nineteenth century, Eurocentric racism gained the aura associated with science as "objective" knowledge free from the taint of the subjective and contingent. (What passes for "objectivity," suggests Molefi Kete Asante, is really little more than a collective sense of European subjectivity.)[118] The same epoch saw the birth of biological racism; ancient prejudices were given a scientific stamp. Biological determinism argued that socioeconomic differences among races, classes, and sexes were the product of inherited genetic traits; the social was an epiphenomenon of biology. Decadence was attributed to race mixture; the *mestizo*, as Jan Pieterse points out, became "the personification of the dialectics of empire and emancipation, and was dreaded by racists as a monster, an infertile hybrid."[119] Certain contemporary methods of psychological and intellectual testing inherit determinist ideologies from this period, specifically the notion that "worth can be assigned to individuals and groups by *measuring* intelligence as a single quantity."[120] Common to all these currents is an arrogant monologism: there can only be one legitimate culture, one esthetic, one path to "mature" civilization, and all societies can be ranked according to their progression toward this single standard.

In the late nineteenth century, racist philosophy was reformulated as "Social Darwinism." Extrapolated from Darwin's theory of evolution by natural selection, this school of thought saw economic competition and even war as "tests" of racial virtue. Social determinists preached the "survival of the fittest," and "the fittest" always seemed to be European. "What a field of extermination," Robert Knox exulted in *The Races of Men*, "lies before the Saxon, Celtic, and Sarmatian races!"[121] For Karl Pearson, the "path of progress" was "strewn with the wreck of nations" and "the hecatombs of inferior races" become "the stepping stones on which mankind has arisen to the higher intellectual and deeper emotional life.[122] Social Darwinism offered a secular version of religious providence. The logic of natural extinction was coupled with an ideology of hierarchy, foreclosing any possibility of conversion or transformation. While the Inquisition's ideology of the *Limpieza de Sangre* (blood-cleansing) allowed for "purification" through conversion, nineteenth-century pure-blood theories provided no such escape-hatch. This was the ideology that led not only to colonial exterminations but also to the "Final Solution" which liquidated two-thirds of Europe's Jews.

Genetics overdetermined European culture in the nineteenth century, policing identity borders and protecting them from the anarchic fluidity of racial–sexual exchange. A mania for classification, measurement, and ranking – expressed in such pseudo-sciences as phrenology and craniometry – left no domain untouched. Every detail was mastered in the name of abstract hierarchies, and a capacity for abstraction was itself seen as a sign of superiority. (The "sociobiology" of texts

Plate 14 Colonial
classification: peoples of
the world

like Konrad Lorenz's *On Aggression* and Desmond Morris' *The Naked Ape* recycled Social Darwinism for the 1970s. Charles Murray and Richard Herrnstein perform a similar task for the 1980s and 1990s.) The British Channel 4 documentary *The Eye of the Empire* (1989) documents the nineteenth-century mania for classifying peoples by raiding the archives of imperial photographs, collected in books with titles like *Vol. IV: Medical Details, Male Series, North Anetaman Group of Tribes.* Human groups are placed within a "natural history" paradigm, subject to anthropometric studies and cranium measurements. Many of these photographs show the human object of study alongside a scientist wielding a tape measure. While Europeans are framed as artistic and familial "portraits," non-Europeans are framed as passive specimens of the "Peoples of the World."

European cinema, in its infancy, inherited the racist and colonialist discourse whose historical contours we have outlined here. Cinema, itself the product of "Western scientific discoveries," made palpable to audiences the master-narrative of the "progress of Western civilization," often through biographical narratives about explorers, inventors, and scientists. As the self-articulated product of scientific ingenuity, cinema saw itself as the avatar of a new kind of "inter-disciplinary" science which could make "other" worlds accessible. It could chart a map of the world like the cartographer; it could chronicle events like the historian; it could "dig" into the distant past like the archeologist; and it could anatomize the customs of "exotic" peoples like the anthropologist. In its role as pedagog, dominant cinema promised to initiate the Western spectator into unknown cultures, visualized as lived (à la Hegel) "outside" of history. Cinema thus became the epistemological mediator between the cultural space of the Western spectator and that of the cultures represented on the screen, linking separate spaces and figurally separate temporalities in a single moment of exposure.

NOTES

1   See *New York Times Magazine* (March 14, 1993).
2   See Donald Johanson and Maitland Edey, *Lucy: The Beginnings of Humankind* (New York: Simon and Schuster, 1981). Ethiopian commentators, being from the region where "Lucy" was "discovered," criticized the choice of a European name (a choice triggered by the Beatles song "Lucy in the Sky with Diamonds"). African-American filmmaker Alice Sharon Larkin points out that had she been making a documentary about "Lucy," she would have called her "what the Ethiopian children call her – 'Wonderful'" and would have had contemporary Ethiopian women talk about Lucy. See Alice Sharon Larkin, "Black Women Filmmakers Defining Ourselves: Feminism in Our Own Voice," in Deidre Pribram, ed., *Female Spectators* (London: Verso, 1988), p. 168.
3   See David E. Stannard, *American Holocaust: Columbus and the Conquest of the New World* (New York: Oxford University Press, 1992), p. 41.
4   Our own formulations try to avoid any "centering" or "originary" narrative in which geographical space becomes the source of world history and civilization. The "Afrocentric" view, though comprehensible as an attempt to combat an oppressive Eurocentrism, runs the risk of monologizing a very plural Africa by fetishizing the monumental culture of Egypt while neglecting other African cultures.
5   For more on the politics of hip hop, see Tricia Rose, "Never Trust a Big Butt and a Smile," *Camera Obscura*, No. 23 (May 1990); Jeffrey Louis Decker, "The State of Rap: Time and Place in Hip Hop Nationalism," *Social Text*, No. 34 (1993).
6   Martin Bernal, *Black Athena* (New Brunswick, NJ: Rutgers University Press, 1987), Vol. I, p. 241.
7   Frank Snowden documents contacts between the Africans of Kush and the Egyptians, Syrians, Greeks, and Romans from the third millennium BC in his *Before Color Prejudice: The Ancient View of Blacks* (Cambridge, Mass.: Harvard University Press, 1983).
8   Rouch filmed the ritual in 1967 in the film *La Caverne de Bongo* (1969). V.Y. Mudimbe sums up some of the debates about the Dogon in *The Invention of Africa* (Bloomington: Indiana University Press, 1988).
9   Leo Africanus, *History and Description of Africa* [c. 1518], quoted in David Killingray, *A Plague of Europeans* (Harmondsworth: Penguin, 1973), pp. 12–13.
10 See John Thornton, *Africa and Africans in the Making of the Atlantic World, 1400–1680* (Cambridge: Cambridge University Press, 1992), p. 46.
11 Ibid., pp. 43–71.
12 Ibid.

13   Cedric Robinson, *Black Marxism* (London: Zed, 1983), p. 4.
14   Patrick Buchanan was assuming this gap when he made his notorious comment that "Zulu immigrants to Virginia would be harder to assimilate than Englishmen." In a *New York Times* Op Ed piece (March 8, 1992), Stephen L. Carter pointed out that many Zulus in multilingual South Africa speak better English than the Europeans of whom Buchanan is so enamored. In a subsequent letter to the editor (dated March 9, 1992), Lorna Hahn observed that there are descendants of Zulus in present-day Virginia who not only actively participate in public life, but who "even became conservative Republicans." One must also interrogate the conservative fondness for invoking the Zulus for their rhetorical purposes, as in Saul Bellow's equally notorious observation about the lack of a "Zulu Proust." Is the word "Zulu" preferred because it has comic resonances for the Eurocentric ear, or because it phonetically includes the sound "zoo"?
15   See Ronald Wright, *Stolen Continents: The Americas through Indian Eyes since 1492* (Boston: Houghton-Mifflin, 1992), p. 12. Here is another historian's description:

> The frequent wars of this period organized violence on a large scale. On their way to and from battle, armies ravaged the countryside, bandits attacked travellers and held whole villages for ransom. Violence was a poison running through the bloodstream at all levels of society. People were killed casually, in quarrels, for cheating and gambling, for malicious gossip, in drinking bouts, and in urban riots.

See Milton Meltzer, *Columbus and the World around Him* (New York: Franklin Watts, 1990), p. 31.
16   See, for example, Alfred W. Crosby, *Ecological Imperialism: The Biological Expansion of Europe, 900–1900* (Cambridge: University of Cambridge Press, 1986).
17   See Gordon Brotherston, *Book of the Fourth World* (Cambridge: Cambridge University Press, 1992), p. 2. See also Sharon Begley, "The First Americas," *Newsweek* Columbus Special Issue (Fall/Winter 1991), p. 15.
18   To name just a few books from the vast bibliography dealing with indigenous life prior to Columbus, see Alvin M. Josephy Jr, *America in 1492* (New York: Alfred K. Knopf, 1992); Wright, *Stolen Continents*; Renny Golden, Michael McConnell, Peggy Mueller, Cinny Poppen, and Marily Turkovich, *Dangerous Memories: Invasion and Resistance since 1492* (Chicago: The Chicago Religious Task Force on Central America, 1991); and Rene Jara and Nicholas Spadaccini, eds, *Amerindian Images and the Legacy of Columbus* (Minneapolis: University of Minnesota Press, 1992).
19   See Brotherston, *Book of the Fourth World*, p. 3. Maurice Bazin points out that present-day Maya children, victims of a Eurocentric education, are not taught that their Olmec ancestors invented, three centuries before Christ, a numerical system fundamentally similar to the one used in the West. See Maurice Bazin, "Tales of Underdevelopment," *Race and Class*, Vol. XXVIII, No. 3 (1987).
20   In Eric R. Wolf, *Sons of the Shaking Earth* (Chicago: University of Chicago Press, 1959), pp. 154–5.
21   Quoted in Jean Comby, "1492: Le Choc des Cultures et l'Evangelization du Monde," *Dossiers de l'Episcopat Français*, No. 14 (October 1990), p. 16.
22   See Charles Duff, *The Truth about Columbus* (New York: Random House, 1936).
23   For an Arab-Muslim view of the Crusades, see Amin Malouf, *Les Croisades vues par les Arabes* (Paris: Gallimard, 1983).
24   See Jean Delumeau, *La Peur en Occident* (Paris: Fayard, 1978) and *Le Péché et la Peur* (Paris: Fayard, 1983).
25   See Joshua Trachtenberg, *The Devil and the Jews: The Medieval Conception of the Jew and Its Relation to Modern Anti-Semitism* (New York: Harper, 1943).

26   Jan Pieterse makes the more general point that many of the themes of European imperialism traced antecedents to the European and Mediterranean sphere. Thus the theme of civilization against barbarism was a carryover from Greek and Roman antiquity, the theme of Christianity against pagans was the keynote of European expansion culminating in the Crusades, and the Christian theme of "mission" was fused with "civilization" in the *mission civilisatrice*. See Jan Pieterse, *Empire and Emancipation* (London: Pluto Press, 1990), p. 240.

27   See Jan Carew, *Fulcrums of Change: Origins of Racism in the Americas and Other Essays* (Trenton, NJ: Africa World Press, 1988).

28   See Aimé Césaire, *Discourse on Colonialism* (New York: Monthly Review Press, 1972), pp. 14–15.

29   Stannard, *American Holocaust*, p. 246.

30   Here is a Spanish eyewitness account:

> When the Indians confessed to having so few idols ... the friars proceeded to string up many of the Indians, having tied their wrists together with cord, and thus hoisted them from the ground, telling them that they must confess all the idols they had, and where they were. The Indians continued saying they had no more ... and so the friars ordered great stones attached to their feet, and so they were left to hang for a space, and if they still did not admit to a greater quantity of idols they were flogged as they hung there, and had burning wax splashed on their bodies.

Quoted in Jara and Spadaccini, eds, *Amerindian Images and the Legacy of Columbus*, p. 31.

31   Quoted in Bernard McGrave, *Beyond Anthropology* (New York: Columbia University Press, 1989), p. 10.

32   For more on Hispanic nuns like Sor Juana, see Electa Arenal and Stacey Schlau, *Untold Sisters: Hispanic Nuns in Their Own Works* (Albuquerque: University of New Mexico Press, 1989).

33   J.M. Blaut, *The Colonizer's Model of the World: Geographical Diffusionism and Eurocentric History* (New York: Guilford Press, 1993), pp. 153–213.

34   Bill Bigelow, "Discovering Columbus, Re-reading the Past," in *Rethinking Columbus*, a special quincentenary issue of *Rethinking Schools* (1991).

35   The Muslim astronomer al-Battani measured the circumference of the earth (correct to three decimal places) 500 years before Columbus. See Ziaddin Sardar, "Lies, Damned Lies and Columbus," *Third Text*, No. 21 (Winter 1992–3). See also Hans Konig, *Columbus His Enterprise: Exploding the Myth* (New York: Monthly Review Press, 1976), pp. 29–30.

36   The production notes for *Christopher Columbus* speak of an intermediary between the Europeans and the "Caribs," a Cambridge graduate, Douglas Taylor, who "settled among them, married a beautiful young Carib girl ..." Taylor, we are told, became the "uncrowned King of the Carib reserve." Thus the venerable trope of the innate natural leadership qualities of White Europeans, reproduced in the various Tarzan films and in *King of the Cannibal Island* (1905) is recycled in the humble form of production notes.

37   See Francis Jennings, *The Invasion of America: Indians, Colonialism and the Cant of Conquest* (New York: W.W. Norton, 1975), p. 174.

38   See Bernard Weinraub, "It's Columbus against Columbus, with a Fortune in Profits at Stake," *New York Times* (May 21, 1992), p. C17.

39   Ward Churchill argues that the Third Reich was not so much a deviation from as a crystallization of the "dominant themes – racial supremacism, conquest and genocide – of the European culture Columbus so ably exemplifies." Churchill

explores in depth the Columbus/Hitler, or more accurately the Columbus/Himmler, parallel in "Deconstructing the Columbus Myth," *Anarchy* (Summer 1992).

40 See Chris Searle, "Unlearning Columbus," *Race and Class*, No. 33 (Jan.–March 1992), p. 69.

41 Peter Hulme and Neil L. Whitehead, eds, *Wild Majesty: Encounters with Caribs from Columbus to the Present Day* (Oxford: Clarendon, 1992), p. 3.

42 Emir Rodriguez Monegal and Thomas Colchie, eds, *The Borzoi Anthology of Latin American Literature*, Vol. I (New York: Alfred A. Knopf, 1977), p. 1.

43 On *écriture* in pre-Columbian America, see Brotherston, *Book of the Fourth World*.

44 See Eral E. Fitz, *Rediscovering the New World: Inter-American Literature in a Comparative Context* (Iowa City: University of Iowa Press, 1991).

45 "You say that our gods are not original/That's news to us/And it drives us crazy/It's a shock and a scandal." Taken from the Nahuatl text *Totecuyoane*, translated by Gordon Brotherston, in Brotherston, *Image of the New World: The American Continent Portrayed in Native Texts* (London: Thames and Hudson, 1979), pp. 63–9.

46 Martin Lienhardt, "Writing and Power in the Conquest of America," *Latin American Perspectives*, Vol. 74, No. 3 (Summer 1992), p. 81.

47 In the New World only some peoples, such as the Aztecs, had writing and thus the capacity to inscribe their perspective on the European invasion. Some of these accounts are gathered in the volume Miguel Leon-Portilla, ed., *The Broken Spears: The Aztec Account of the Conquest of Mexico* (Boston: Beacon Press, 1962).

48 On the indigenous mapping of the Americas, see Brotherston, *Book of the Fourth World*.

49 Quoted in Wright, *Stolen Continents*, p. 14.

50 Quoted in Leonardo Boff, *America Latina: Da Conquista à Nova Evangelização* (São Paulo: Attica, 1992), p. 9.

51 See for example Kenneth Auchinloss' introductory essay ("When Worlds Collide") to the Columbus Special Issue of *Newsweek* (Fall/Winter 1991).

52 Quoted in Anthony Pagden, *Spanish Imperialism and the Political Imagination* (New Haven, Conn.: Yale, 1990), p. 24.

53 Quoted in Boff, *America Latina*, p. 64.

54 Quoted in Bartolomé de las Casas, *History of the Indies*, trans. and ed. Andrée Collard (New York: Harper and Row, 1971), p. 184.

55 See Carlos Fuentes, *The Buried Mirror* (Boston: Houghton-Mifflin, 1992), p. 134.

56 Bartolomé de las Casas, *The Devastation of the Indies: A Brief Account* (New York: Seabury Press, 1974), p. 41.

57 Ibid., pp. 43–4.

58 See Doug Ireland, "Press Clips," *Village Voice* (March 23, 1993).

59 See Carew, *Fulcrums of Change*.

60 Rocha's use of African music, as if it existed in Brazil prior to the arrival of Europeans, is extremely suggestive, reminding us that "continental drift" theory suggests that Brazil and Africa were once part of a single land mass, and also anticipating Ivan Van Sertima's theory that Africans arrived in the New World "before Columbus." At the same time, Rocha deploys the music as part of an ironic reversal, since the Yoruba chants are repeatedly associated with the dictatorial figure of Porfírio Diaz. Although Europe posits African religion as irrational, hysterical, the film seems to suggest that in fact it is the European elite which is irrational, hysterical. Revelations about the "black magic" rituals according to which recently impeached President Fernando Collor, whose power in the Alegoas region goes back to the *capitanias* of the *conquista*, would stick pins into dolls representing his political opponents, confirm and literalize Rocha's prescience.

61 For a critical analysis of Alvar Nuñez's and other Spanish accounts of the conquest, see Beatriz Pastor, *Discurso Narrativo de la Conquista de America* (Havana: Casa de

las Americas, 1983). For information on Spanish cannibalism, see Stannard, *American Holocaust*, p. 216.

62 See Stephen Greenblatt, *Marvelous Possessions: The Wonder of the New World* (Chicago: University of Chicago Press, 1991), p. 141.

63 From Hector St John de Crevecoeur, *Letters from an American Farmer*, quoted in James Axtell, *The European and the Indian: Essays in the Ethnohistory of Colonial North America* (Oxford: Oxford University Press, 1982), p. 172.

64 See Axtell, *The European and the Indian*, p. 206.

65 Remarks made in a lecture given at New York University as part of the series "Rewriting 1492," organized by Robert Stam and held at New York University on October 9, 1992.

66 In Quechua *tupac* means the "real thing," while *amaru* refers to "serpent." "Tupac Amaru" is also the name of a rap group denounced by Dan Quayle.

67 We are indebted to Miriam Yataco and Euridice Arataia for their interpretations of the film in the light of Andean cosmology. For more on the *Inkarri*, see Brotherston, *Book of the Fourth World*.

68 We would like to thank Emperatriz Arreaza-Camero for providing us with a videotape of *Cubagua*. Her essay "*Cubagua*, or the Search for Venezuelan National Identity," provides a historically informed, in-depth study of the film. See *Iowa Journal of Cultural Studies* (1993).

69 See Orlando Patterson, *Slavery and Social Death: A Comparative Study* (Cambridge: Harvard University Press, 1982), p. vii.

70 See Basil Davidson, "Columbus: The Bones and Blood of Racism," *Race and Class*, No. 33 (Jan.–March 1992), p. 19.

71 See Thornton, *Africa and Africans in the Making of the Atlantic World, 1400–1680*, p. 87. There were cases, as with the Hausas, where enslaved Africans were literate and those who enslaved them were not.

72 "The Life of Olaudah Equiano" is included in Henry Louis Gates Jr, ed., *The Classic Slave Narratives* (New York: New American Library, 1987).

73 See O.E. Uya, "Conceptualizing Afro-American/African Realities," in J.E. Harris, ed., *Global Dimensions of the African Diaspora* (Washington, DC: Howard University Press, 1982). The idea that Europe underdeveloped Africa is elaborated in Walter Rodney, *How Europe Underdeveloped Africa* (London: Bogle-l'Ouverture, 1972), and in relation to Afro-America in Manning Marable, *How Capitalism Underdeveloped Black Africa* (Boston: South End Press, 1983).

74 Blaut, *The Colonizer's Model of the World*, p. 204.

75 Robinson, *Black Marxism* (London: Zed, 1983), p. 96.

76 R.K. Kent, "Palmares: An African State in Brazil," *Journal of African History*, Vol. VI, No. 2 (1965), pp. 167–9.

77 Musical groups from Bahia, specifically Olodum and Ile Aiye, have organized support for the present-day descendants of the *quilombos*, composing lyrics such as "*Quilombo*, here we are/my only debt is to the *quilombo*/my only debt is to Zumbi." See James Brooke, "Brazil Seeks to Return Ancestral Lands to Descendants of Runaway Slaves," *New York Times* (Sunday, Aug. 15, 1993), p. 3.

78 See Decio Freitas, *Palmares: A Guerra dos Escravos* (Rio de Janeiro: Graal, 1974).

79 We are indebted to Dan Dawson of the Caribbean Cultural Center for his comments on *Quilombo* as part of the "Rewriting 1492" series organized by Robert Stam and held at New York University on October 9, 1992.

80 Montaigne, "Of Cannibals" [1590], in *The Complete Essays of Montaigne*, trans. Donald Frame (Stanford, Calif.: Stanford University Press, 1957), pp. 155–6.

81 Montaigne, "Of Coaches" [1590], in *The Complete Essays of Montaigne*, pp. 131–2.

82 Montaigne, "Of Cannibals," in *The Complete Essays of Montaigne*, pp. 155–6. Lévi-Strauss claims Brazilian Indians asked him the same questions about class inequality.

83 See Aimé Césaire, *A Tempest*, trans. Richard Miller (New York: Ubu Repertory Theatre Publications, 1985).

84 See Hulme, *Colonial Encounters*, pp. 210–11.

85 See Clement Hawes, "Three Times around the Globe: Gulliver and Colonial Discourse," in *Cultural Critique*, No. 18 (Spring 1991).

86 Jonathan Swift, *Gulliver's Travels* (New York: Random House, 1958), p. 241.

87 President Andrew Jackson, in J.D. Richardson, ed., *A Compilation of the Messages and Papers of the Presidents, 1789–1897*, Vol. II, pp. 520–1.

88 The Thomas Morton story is well told by Richard Drinnon in *Facing West: The Metaphysics of Indian Hating and Empire-Building* (New York: Schocken, 1980).

89 William Robertson, *Works* (London, 1824), Vol. IX, pp. 94–5, quoted in Roy Harvey Pearce, *Savagism and Civilization* (Berkeley: University of California Press, 1988), p. 88.

90 See Donald A. Grinde Jr and Bruce E. Johansen, *Exemplar of Liberty: Native America and the Evolution of Democracy* (Los Angeles: American Indian Studies Center, University of California, 1991) and Bruce E. Johansen, *Forgotten Founders: How the American Indian Helped Shape Democracy* (Boston: Harvard Common Press, 1982). Both of these books carefully and quite cautiously document the Native American influence on American institutions, usually from the mouths of the founding fathers themselves.

91 Tom Paine, *Complete Writings*, ed. Foner, Vol. I, p. 610, quoted in Grinde and Johansen, *Exemplar of Liberty*, p 153.

92 Quoted in Johansen, *Forgotten Founders*, p. 98.

93 Felix Cohen, "Americanizing the White Man," originally published in *The American Scholar*, Vol. 21, No. 2 (1959) and quoted in Oren Lyons *et al.*, *Exiled in the Land of the Free* (Santa Fe, Calif.: Clear Light, 1992), p. 274.

94 See Y.N. Kly, *The Anti-Social Contract* (Atlanta, Ga.: Clarity Press, 1989).

95 Thus a civil polity very much concerned with contracts and legal documents knew how to avoid the issue when convenient. For more on this issue, see D.W. Meinig, "Strategies of Empire," in *Culturefront*, Vol. 2, No. 2 (Summer 1993).

96 See Pieterse, *Empire and Emancipation*, p. 56.

97 See P. Marshall and G. Williams, *The Great Map of Mankind: British Perceptions of the World in the Age of Enlightenment* (London: Dent, 1982), p. 192.

98 David Hume, "Of National Characters," *The Philosophical Works*, ed. Thomas Hill Greene and Thomas Hodge Grose, 4 Vols (Darmstadt: 1964), Vol. 3, p. 252, n. 1, quoted in Henry Louis Gates Jr., *Figures in Black* (New York: Oxford University Press, 1987), p. 18.

99 Immanuel Kant, "Observations on the Feeling of the Beautiful and the Sublime," quoted in Gates, *Figures in Black*, p. 19.

100 See M. Duchet, *Anthropologie et Histoire au Siècle des Lumières* (Paris: Maspero, 1971).

101 For further discussion see V.Y. Mudimbe, *The Invention of Africa: Gnosis, Philosophy, and the Order of Knowledge* (Bloomington: Indiana University Press, 1988), pp. 71–2.

102 Quoted in Kirkpatrick Sale, *The Conquest of Paradise: Christopher Colombus and the Columbian Legacy* (New York: Alfred A. Knopf, 1990), pp. 366–7.

103 Quoted in A. Moorhead, *The Fatal Impact: An Account of the Invasion of the South Pacific* (Harmondsworth: Penguin, 1987), p. 131.

104 Quoted in Yves Benot, *Diderot: de l'Athéisme à l'Anti-Colonialisme* (Paris: Maspero, 1970), p. 176. Benot has exhaustively perused Diderot's writings, including those absorbed into publications credited to others, such as *L'Histoire des Deux Indes*.

105 Quoted in Benot, *Diderot*, p. 172.

106 Ibid., p. 209.

107 G.W.F. Hegel, *The Philosophy of History*, trans. J. Sibree (New York: Dover, 1956), pp. 91–9.
108 Quoted in Paul Gilroy, *The Black Atlantic* (Cambridge, Mass.: Harvard University Press, 1993), p. 41.
109 Quoted in Boff, *America Latina*, p. 20.
110 Hegel, *The Philosophy of History*, p. 173.
111 Ibid., p. 139.
112 Ibid., pp. 142–3.
113 On orientalism in Marx see Edward Said, *Orientalism* (New York: Pantheon, 1979) and Ronald Inden, *Imagining India* (Oxford: Basil Blackwell, 1990).
114 For a Native American critique of the Eurocentric premises of Marxism, see Ward Churchill, ed., *Marxism and Native Americans* (Boston: South End Press, 1983).
115 Johannes Fabian, *Time and the Other: How Anthropology Makes Its Object* (New York: Columbia University Press, 1983), p. 155.
116 See Cornel West, *Prophesy Deliverance: An Afro-American Revolutionary Christianity* (Philadelphia: Westminster, 1982); Clyde Taylor, "Black Cinema in the Post-aesthetic Era," in Jim Pines and Paul Willemen, eds, *Questions of Third Cinema* (London: BFI, 1989); bell hooks, *Black Looks: Race and Representation* (Boston: South End Press, 1992).
117 Charles White, *Account of the Regular Gradation in Man*, quoted in Stephen Jay Gould, *The Mismeasure of Man* (New York: W.W. Norton, 1981), p. 42.
118 See Molefi Kete Asante, *Kemet, Afrocentricity and Knowledge* (Trenton, NJ: Africa World Press, 1990), p. 24.
119 See Pieterse, *Empire and Emancipation*, p. 360.
120 See Gould, *The Mismeasure of Man*, p. 20.
121 Robert Knox, *The Races of Men: A Fragment* (Philadelphia: Lea and Blanchard, 1850), p. 153.
122 Karl Pearson, quoted in Random House Historical Pamphlet, *Social Darwinism: Law of Nature or Justification of Repression?* (London: Random House, 1967), p. 53.

3

THE IMPERIAL IMAGINARY

The colonial domination of indigenous peoples, the scientific and esthetic disciplining of nature through classificatory schemas, the capitalist appropriation of resources, and the imperialist ordering of the globe under a panoptical regime, all formed part of a massive world historical movement that reached its apogee at the beginning of the twentieth century. Indeed, it is most significant for our discussion that the beginnings of cinema coincided with the giddy heights of the imperial project, with an epoch where Europe held sway over vast tracts of alien territory and hosts of subjugated peoples. (Of all the celebrated "coincidences" – of the twin beginnings of cinema and psychoanalysis, cinema and nationalism, cinema and consumerism – it is this coincidence with the heights of imperialism that has been least explored.) Film was born at a moment when a poem such as Rudyard Kipling's "White Man's Burden" could be published, as it was in 1899, to celebrate the US acquisition of Cuba and the Philippines. The first Lumière and Edison screenings in the 1890s closely followed the "scramble for Africa" which erupted in the late 1870s; the Battle of "Rorke's Drift" (1879) which opposed the British to the Zulus (memorialized in the film *Zulu*, 1964); the British occupation of Egypt in 1882; the Berlin Conference of 1884 which carved up Africa into European "spheres of influence"; the massacre of the Sioux at Wounded Knee in 1890; and countless other imperial misadventures.

The most prolific film-producing countries of the silent period – Britain, France, the US, Germany – also "happened" to be among the leading imperialist countries, in whose clear interest it was to laud the colonial enterprise. The cinema emerged exactly at the point when enthusiasm for the imperial project was spreading beyond the elites into the popular strata, partly thanks to popular fictions and exhibitions. For the working classes of Europe and Euro-America, photogenic wars in remote parts of the empire became diverting entertainments, serving to "neutralize the class struggle and transform class solidarity into national and racial solidarity."[1] The cinema adopted the popular fictions of colonialist writers like Kipling for India and Rider Haggard, Edgar Wallace and Edgar Rice Burroughs for Africa, and absorbed popular genres like the "conquest fiction" of the American southwest. The cinema entered a situation where European and American readers had already devoured Livingstone's *Missionary*

Travels (1857); Edgar Wallace's "Sanders of the River" stories in the early 1900s; Rider Haggard's *King Solomon's Mines* (1885); and Henry Morton Stanley's *How I Found Livingstone* (1872), *Through the Dark Continent* (1878), and *In Darkest Africa* (1890).

English boys especially were initiated into imperial ideals through such books as Robert Baden-Powell's *Scouting for Boys* (1908), which praised:

> the frontiersmen of all parts of our Empire. The "trappers" of North America, hunters of Central Africa, the British pioneers, explorers, and missionaries over Asia and all the wild parts of the world ... the constabulary of North-West Canada and of South Africa.[2]

The practical survivalist education of scouting, combined with the initiatory mechanisms of the colonial adventure story, were designed to turn boys, as Joseph Bristow puts it, into "aggrandized subjects," an imperial race who imagined the future of the world as resting on their shoulders.[3] While girls were domesticated as homemakers, without what Virginia Woolf called a "room of their own," boys could play, if only in their imaginations, in the space of empire. The fantasy of far-away regions offered "charismatic realms of adventure"[4] free from charged heterosexual engagements. Adventure films, and the "adventure" of going to the cinema, provided a vicarious experience of passionate fraternity, a playing field for the self-realization of European masculinity. Just as colonized space was available to empire, and colonial landscapes were available to imperial cinema, so was this psychic space available for the play of the virile spectatorial imagination as a kind of mental *Lebensraum*. Empire, as John McClure puts it in another context, provided romance with its raw materials, while romance provided empire with its "aura of nobility."[5]

THE SHAPING OF NATIONAL IDENTITY

Beliefs about the origins and evolution of nations often crystallize in the form of stories. For Hayden White, certain narrative "master tropes" shape our conception of history; historical discourse consists "of the provisions of a plot structure for a sequence of events so that their nature as a comprehensible process is revealed by their figuration as a story of a particular kind."[6] The nation of course is not a desiring person but a fictive unity imposed on an aggregate of individuals, yet national histories are presented as if they displayed the continuity of the subject-writ-large.[7] The cinema, as the world's storyteller *par excellence*, was ideally suited to relay the projected narratives of nations and empires. National self-consciousness, generally seen as a precondition for nationhood – that is, the shared belief of disparate individuals that they share common origins, status, location, and aspirations – became broadly linked to cinematic fictions. In the modern period, for Benedict Anderson, this collective consciousness was made possible by a common language and its expression in "print capitalism."[8] Prior to the cinema, the novel and the newspaper fostered imagined communities through their integrative relations to time and space. Newspapers – like TV news today – made people aware of the simultaneity and interconnectedness of events in different places, while novels provided a sense of the purposeful movement through time of fictional entities bound together in a narrative whole. As "bourgeois epic" (in the words of Georg Lukács), the novel inherited and transformed the vocation of the classical epic (for example *The Aeneid*) to produce and heighten national identity, both accompanying and crystallizing the rise of nations by imposing a unitary topos on heterogenous languages and diverse desires.

The fiction film also inherited the social role of the nineteenth-century realist novel in relation to national imaginaries. Like novels, films proceed temporally, their durational scope reaching from a story time ranging from the few minutes depicted by the first Lumière shorts to the many hours (and symbolic millennia) of films like *Intolerance* (1916) and *2001: A Space Odyssey* (1968). Films communicate Anderson's "calendrical time," a sense of time and its passage. Just as nationalist literary fictions inscribe on to a multitude of events the notion of a linear, comprehensible destiny, so films arrange events and actions in a temporal narrative that moves toward fulfillment, and thus shape thinking about historical time and national history. Narrative models in film are not simply reflective microcosms of historical processes, then, they are also experiential grids or templates through which history can be written and national identity figured. Like novels, films can convey what Mikhail Bakhtin calls "chronotopes," materializing time in space, mediating between the historical and the discursive, providing fictional environments where historically specific constellations of power are made visible. In both film and novel, "time thickens, takes on flesh," while "space becomes charged and responsive to the movements of time, plot and history."[9] There is nothing inherently sinister in this process, except to the extent that it is deployed asymmetrically, to the advantage of some national and racial imaginaries and to the detriment of others.

The national situation described by Anderson becomes complicated, we would argue, in the context of an imperial ideology that was doubly transnational. First, Europeans were encouraged to identify not only with single European nations but also with the racial solidarity implied by the imperial project as a whole. Thus English audiences could identify with the heroes of French Foreign Legion films, Euro-American audiences with the heroes of the British Raj, and so forth. Second, the European empires (what Queen Victoria called the "imperial family") were themselves conceived paternalistically as providing a "shelter" for diverse races and groups, thus downplaying the national singularities of the colonized themselves. Given the geographically discontinuous nature of empire, cinema helped cement both a national and an imperial sense of belonging among many disparate peoples. For the urban elite of the colonized lands, the pleasures of cinema-going became associated with the sense of a community on the margins of its particular European empire (especially since the first movie theaters in these countries were associated with Europeans and the Europeanized local bourgeoisies).[10] The cinema encouraged an assimilated elite to identify with "its" empire and thus against other colonized peoples.

If cinema partly inherited the function of the novel, it also transformed it. Whereas literature plays itself out within a virtual lexical space, the cinematic chronotope is literal, splayed out concretely across the screen and unfolding in the literal time of twenty-four frames per second. In this sense, the cinema can all the more efficiently mobilize desire in ways responsive to nationalized and imperialized notions of time, plot, and history. The cinema's institutional ritual of gathering a community – spectators who share a region, language, and culture – homologizes, in a sense, the symbolic gathering of the nation. Anderson's sense of the nation as "horizontal comradeship" evokes the movie audience as a provisional "nation" forged by spectatorship. While the novel is consumed in solitude, the film is enjoyed in a gregarious space, where the ephemeral communitas of spectatorship can take on a national or imperial thrust. Thus the cinema can play a more assertive role in fostering group identities. Finally, unlike the novel, the cinema is not premised on literacy. As a popular entertainment it is more accessible than literature. While there was no mass reading public for imperial literary fictions within the colonies, for example, there *was* a mass viewing public for imperial filmic fictions.

The dominant European/American form of cinema not only inherited and disseminated a hegemonic colonial discourse, it also created a powerful hegemony of its own through monopolistic control of film distribution and exhibition in much of Asia, Africa, and the Americas. Eurocolonial cinema thus mapped history not only for domestic audiences but also for the world. African spectators were prodded to identify with Cecil Rhodes and Stanley and Livingstone against Africans themselves, thus engendering a battle of national imaginaries within the fissured colonial spectator. For the European spectator, the cinematic experience mobilized a rewarding sense of national and imperial belonging, on the backs, as it were, of otherized peoples. For the colonized, the cinema (in tandem with other colonial institutions such as schools) produced a sense of deep ambivalence, mingling the identification provoked by cinematic narrative with intense resentment, for it was the colonized who were being otherized.

While the novel could play with words and narrative to engender an "aggrandized subject," the cinema entailed a new and powerful apparatus of the gaze. The cinematic "apparatus," that is to say the cinematic machine as including both the instrumental base of camera, projector, and screen and the spectator as the desiring subject on whom the cinematic institution depends for its imaginary realization, not only represents the "real" but also stimulates intense "subject effects." For Christian Metz, the cinematic apparatus fosters narcissism, in that the spectator identifies with him/herself as a "kind of transcendental subject."[11] By prosthetically extending human perception, the apparatus grants the spectator the illusory ubiquity of the "all-perceiving subject" enjoying an exhilarating sense of visual power. From the Diorama, the Panorama, and the Cosmorama up through NatureMax, the cinema has amplified and mobilized the virtual gaze of photography, bringing past into present, distant to near. It has offered the spectator a mediated relationship with imaged others from diverse cultures. We are not suggesting that imperialism was inscribed either in the apparatus or in the celluloid, only that the context of imperial power shaped the uses to which both apparatus and celluloid were put. In an imperial context the apparatus tended to be deployed in ways flattering to the imperial subject as superior and invulnerable observer, as what Mary Louise Pratt calls the "monarch-of-all-I-survey." The cinema's ability to "fly" spectators around the globe gave them a subject position as film's audio-visual masters. The "spatially-mobilized visuality"[12] of the I/eye of empire spiraled outward around the globe, creating a visceral, kinetic sense of imperial travel and conquest, transforming European spectators into armchair conquistadors, affirming their sense of power while turning the colonies into spectacle for the metropole's voyeuristic gaze.

CINEMA AS SCIENCE AND SPECTACLE

If the culture of empire authorized the pleasure of seizing ephemeral glimpses of its "margins" through travel and tourism, the nineteenth-century invention of the photographic and later the cinematographic camera made it possible to record such glimpses. Rather than remaining confined to its European home, the camera set out to "explore" new geographical, ethnographic, and archeological territories. It visited natural and human "wonders" (the Nile, the Taj Mahal) and unearthed buried civilizations (the excavations in Nubia), imbuing every sight with the wide-eyed freshness of the new machine. Yet the pioneers of the recorded image rarely questioned the constellation of power relations that allowed them to represent other lands and cultures. No one questioned how Egyptian land, history, and culture should be represented, for example, or asked what Egyptian people might have to say about the matter. Thus photographers making the grand oriental tour might record their own subjective visions, but in doing so they also drew clear boundaries between the subject looking and the object being looked at, between traveler and "traveled upon." Photographers such as George Bridges, Louis de Clercq, Maxime du Camp and filmmakers like Thomas Edison and the Lumière brothers did not simply document other territories; they also documented the cultural baggage they carried with them. Their subjective interpretations were deeply embedded in the discourses of their respective European empires.

The excitement generated by the camera's capacity to register the formal qualities of movement reverberated with the full-steam-ahead expansionism of imperialism itself. The camera was hired out to document the tentacular extensions of empire. Photographers and filmmakers were especially attracted to trains and ships, engines of empire that delivered raw materials from the interiors of Asia, Africa, and the Americas into the heart of Europe. Robert Howlett's photographs for the London *Times* of "The Bow of the Great Eastern" (1857) not only foreshadowed subsequent homages to the futurist esthetics of the machine, but also documented the construction of an unprecedentedly large ship as a matter of national pride and a confirmation of British supremacy at sea. The work of early photographers such as Felix Teynard, Maxime du Camp, Edouard-Denis Baldus, John Beasley Green, Louis de Clercq, and John Murray was supported, published, and exhibited by diverse imperial institutions. De Clercq, for example, was invited to accompany the historian Emmanuel-Guillaume Rey on a French government-sponsored expedition of 1859 to the Crusader castles of Syria and Asia Minor, a trip that generated the six volumes of *Voyage en Orient, Villes, Monuments, et Vues Pittoresques de Syrie*, along with the collection of historical artifacts now housed in the Oriental Antiquities Department of the Louvre. And Murray served in the East India Company army, where, like many Englishmen in India, he took up photography as a hobby. His work, first exhibited in London in 1857 during the "Indian Mutiny," was encouraged by the Governor-General of India, Lord Earl Canning, the same governor who suppressed the uprising and who, together with his wife Lady Charlotte Canning, was a major patron of photography in India.[13]

Travel photographers did not just document terrritories for military and governmental purposes, their photos also registered the advances of scientific activities, for example the archeological excavations of Greece and Egypt. Fascination with ancient monuments was mingled with admiration for the camera's capacity to provide a vivid sense of distant regions and remote times: a photo in Du Camp's album *Egypte, Nubie, Palestine et Syrie* (1852) – "Westernmost Colossus of the temple of Re, Abu Simbel, 1850" – shows the photographer's assistant atop the crown of Rameses II, illustrating both relative scale and a moment of mastery and possession. If bourgeois travelers cherished photographic moments of their own exploring – as in Du Camp's photo of Flaubert in Cairo in 1850 – the colonized had to bear the weight of a generic ethnographic gaze, as in the anonymous photograph "Women Grinding Paint, Calcutta, 1854." The camera also played a botanical and zoological role by documenting exotic fauna and flora. Louis Pierre Théophile Dubois de Nehant's "Another Impossible Task" (1854) shows the elephant "Miss Betsy," imported from India, in the Brussels Zoo, while Count de Motizon's photo (1852) captures Londoners admiring a hippopotamus captured on the banks of the White Nile. More than a servile scribe, the camera actively popularized imperial imagery, turning it into an exciting participatory activity for those in the motherland.

The social origins of the cinema were schizophrenic, traceable both to the "high" culture of science and literature and to the "low" culture of sideshows and nickelodeons. (At times the two cultures coalesced: the flying balloon in *Around the World in 80 Days*, designed to circle the world, is also the object of spectacle for enthusiastic Parisians.) The desire to expand the frontiers of science became inextricably linked to the desire to expand the frontiers of empire. The immediate origins of the cinema in Western science meant that filmic exhibition also entailed the exhibition of Western triumphs. The visible achievements of both cinema and science also graced the proliferating world fairs, which since the mid-nineteenth

Plates 15 and 16 Global ubiquity:
Around the World in 80 Days and
Simba: King of the Beasts

century had become the new "international" showplaces for the spectacular fruits of industrial and scientific progress.

The visualist inclinations of Western anthropological discourse[14] prepared the way for the cinematographic representation of other territories and cultures. The "ontologically" kinetic status of the moving image privileged the cinema not only over the written word but over still photography as well. It lent indexical credibility to anthropology, arming it with visual evidence not only of the existence of "others" but also of their actually existing otherness. Cinema in this sense prolonged the museological project of gathering three-dimensional archeological, ethnographic, botanical, and zoological objects in the metropolis. Unlike the more auratic and "inaccessible" elite arts and sciences, a popularizing cinema could plunge spectators into the midst of non-European worlds, letting them see and feel "strange" civilizations. It could transform the obscure *mappa mundi* into a familiar, knowable world.

Photography and the cinema often represented alien topographies and cultures as aberrant in relation to Europe. Operating on a continuum with zoology, anthropology, botany, entomology,[15] biology, and medicine, the camera, like the microscope, anatomized the "other." The new visual apparatuses demonstrated the power of science to display and even decipher otherized cultures; dissection and montage together constructed a presumably holistic portrait of the colonized. Technological inventions, in other words, mapped the globe as a disciplinary space of knowledge.[16] Topographies were documented for purposes of military and economic control, often on the literal backs of the "natives" who carried the cinematographers and their equipment. In the colonial context, the common trope of the "camera gun" (Marey's "fusil cinématographique") resonated with the aggressive use of the camera by the agents of the colonial powers.[17] "Primitive" peoples were turned into the objects of quasi-sadistic experimentation. This kind of aggression reached a paroxysm in the 1920s films of Martin and Osa Johnson,

where the filmmakers gleefully prodded Pygmies, whom they called "monkeys" and "niggers," to get sick on European cigars. In films such as *Trailing African Wild Animals* (1922) and *Simba* (1927), the Johnsons treated African peoples as a form of wildlife. The camera penetrated a foreign and familiar zone like a predator, seizing its "loot" of images as raw material to be reworked in the "motherland" and sold to sensation-hungry spectators and consumers, a process later fictionalized in *King Kong* (1933). There was no clue, in such films, as to how Europeans depended for their everyday survival in the field on the knowledge, intelligence, labor, and the "enforced subordination of people the white folk insisted on seeing as perpetual children."[18]

If cinema itself traced its parentage to popular sideshows and fairs, ethnographic cinema and Hollywoodean ethnography were the heirs of a tradition of exhibitions of "real" human objects, a tradition going back to Columbus' importation of "New World" natives to Europe for purposes of courtly entertainment. Exhibitions organized the world as a spectacle within an obsessively mimetic esthetic.[19] In the US, at a time roughly coincident with the beginnings of cinema, a series of fairs – the Chicago Columbian Exposition of 1893, the Omaha Trans-Mississippi Exposition in 1898, the Buffalo Pan-American Exposition in 1901, the St Louis "Louisiana Purchase" Exposition in 1904 – introduced millions of fairgoers to evolutionary ideas about race in an atmosphere of communal good cheer. The Chicago Columbian Exposition spatialized racial hierarchies in a quasi-didactic fashion by having the Teutonic exhibits placed closest to the "White City," with the "Mohammedan world" and the "savage races" at the opposite end. Racism and "entertainment," as Robert W. Rydell points out, became closely interwined.[20] The Omaha fair featured an exhibit on "the Vanquished Races," and in the Atlanta Exposition the Sioux were obliged to reenact their own defeat and humiliation at Wounded Knee. The Louisiana Purchase Exposition included a Filipino exhibit that made the Pacific Islands seem as much a part of "manifest destiny" as the conquest of the west. Such expositions gave utopian form to White supremacist ideology, legitimizing racial hierarchies abroad and muting class and gender divisions among Whites at home by stressing national agency in a global project of domination.[21]

Africans and Asians were exhibited as human figures with kinship to specific animal species, thus literalizing the colonialist zeugma yoking "native" and "animal," the very fact of exhibition in cages implying that the cages' occupants were less than human. Lapps, Nubians, and Ethiopians were displayed in Germany in anthropological-zoological exhibits.[22] The conjunction of "Darwinism, Barnumism [and] pure and simple racism" resulted in the exhibition of Ota Benga, a Pygmy from the Kasai region, alongside the animals in the Bronx Zoo.[23] A precursor to Epcott's global village, the 1894 Antwerp World's Fair featured a reconstructed Congolese village with sixteen "authentic" villagers. In many cases the people exhibited died or fell seriously ill. "Freak shows" too paraded before the West's bemused eye a variety of "exotic" pathologies. Saartjie Baartman, the "Hottentot Venus,"[24] was displayed on the entertainment circuit in England and France. Although her protrusive buttocks constituted the main attraction, the rumored peculiarities of her genitalia also drew crowds, with her racial/sexual "anomaly" constantly being associated with animality.[25] The zoologist and anatomist George Cuvier studied her intimately and presumably dispassionately, and compared her buttocks to those of "female mandrills, baboons ... which assume at certain epochs of their life a truly monstrous development."[26] After Baartman's death at the age of twenty-five, Cuvier received official permission for an even closer look at her private parts, and dissected her to produce a detailed description of her body inside out.[27] Her genitalia still rest on a shelf in the Musée de l'Homme in Paris alongside the genitalia of *"une négresse"* and *"une péruvienne"*[28] as monuments to a kind of imperial necrophilia. The final placement of the female parts in the patriarchally designated "Museum of Man" provides a crowning irony.

As the product of both science and mass culture, cinema combined traveling knowledge with traveling spectacles, conveying a view of the "world itself as an exhibition."[29] The study of a hypersexualized "other" in scientific discourse was paralleled by the cinema's scopophilic display of aliens as spectacle. Hollywood productions abounded in "exotic" images of moving native bodies, at times incorporating actual travelogs dug up from the archives, deployed in such films as the *Tarzan* series. Thus in a "double standard" erotics, the Production Code of the Motion Picture Producers and Directors of America, Inc, 1930–4, which censored Jane's two-piece outfit into one in later *Tarzan* films, left intact the naked African women in the background, evoking a *National Geographic*-style prurient delight in unilateral native nudity. The portrayal of dance rituals in such films as *The Dance of Fatima* (1903), *The Sheik* (1921), *Bird of Paradise* (1932), and *Sanders of the River* (1935) displayed alien flesh to hint at the masculinist pleasures of exploration. Hiding behind a respectable figleaf of "science" and "authenticity," ethnographic films focussed directly on the bouncing breasts of dancing women,[30] Hollywood films, under the surveillance of domestic moral majorities, relegated native nudity to the background, or restricted the imagery to minimal "native" garb. Formulaic scenes of dark frenzied bodies entranced by accelerating drum rhythms relayed a fetishized image of indigenous religions. Ceremonial possession (portrayed as a kind of mass hysteria) evoked the uncontrollable id of libidinous beings. Ethnographic science, then, provided a cover for the unleashing of pornographic impulses. The cinematic exposure of the dark body nourished spectatorial desire, while marking off imaginary boundaries between "self" and "other," thus mapping homologous spheres, both macrocosmic (the globe) and microcosmic (the sphere of carnal knowledge).

PROJECTING THE EMPIRE

The cinema combined narrative and spectacle to tell the story of colonialism from the colonizer's perspective. From the Lumière brothers' mocking portrayals of Muslim Arab religious and culinary habits in *Le Musulman Rigolo* (The Funny Muslim, 1902) and *Ali Bouffe à l'Huile* (Ali Eats with Oil, 1902), through the adventure tales of *Tarzan*, to the Westerner-in-the-pot cannibal imagery of the 1980s version of *King Solomon's Mines* and the scientific missions of *Indiana Jones* (1981, 1984, 1989), dominant cinema has spoken for the "winners" of history, in films which idealized the colonial enterprise as a philanthropic "civilizing mission" motivated by a desire to push back the frontiers of ignorance, disease, and tyranny. Programmatically negative portrayals helped rationalize the human costs of the imperial enterprise. Thus Africa was imaged as a land inhabited by cannibals in the Ernst Lubin comedy *Rastus in Zululand* (1910), Mexicans were reduced to "greasers" and "bandidos" in films like *Tony the Greaser* (1911) and *The Greaser's Revenge* (1914), and Native Americans were portrayed as savage marauders in *Fighting Blood* (1911) and *The Last of the Mohicans* (1920).

Each imperial filmmaking country had its own imperial genres set in "darkest Africa," the "mysterious East," and the "stormy Caribbean." It was in this imperializing spirit that Thomas Alva Edison staged battles against Filipino guerillas in the fields of New Jersey (with Blacks standing in for the Filipinos) and that J. Stuart Blackton staged the Spanish-American war using scale-model battleships in local bathtubs. Indeed, many of the early American one-reelers, such as *Cuban Ambush* (1898), *Roosevelt's Rough Riders* (1898), *Troop Ships for the Philippines* (1898), and *Landing of U.S. Troops near Santiago* (1902), glorified the imperialist binge in the Caribbean and the Philippines. Even filmmakers not conventionally associated with lauding imperialism betray a shared discourse of empire. Georges Méliès' filmography, for example, features a number of films related to expansionist voyages and orientalist fantasies: *Le Fakir – Mystère Indien* (1896), *Vente d'Esclaves au Harem* (1897), *Cléopatre* (1899), *La Vengeance de Bouddah* (1901), *Les Aventures de Robinson Crusoe* (1902), *Le Palais des Mille et une Nuits* (1905).[31] Similarly, in Méliès' *Le Voyage dans la Lune* (A Trip to the Moon, 1902; based on Verne's *From the Earth to the Moon*, 1865), the rocket's phallic penetration of the moon (the space frontier) recapitulates, on another level, the historical discourse of the other (imperial) "frontier." ("I would annex the planets if I could," Cecil Rhodes often said.) The film is structured like a colonial captivity narrative: spear-carrying skeleton creatures burst from the moon's simulacral jungle and capture the explorers, only to be defeated by the male explorers' gunlike umbrellas, which magically eliminate the savage creatures. Such a film, not in any obvious sense "about" colonialism, can thus be read as analogizing imperial expansion.

Many American films, for example *Beau Geste* (1939), filmed in Arizona but set in Morocco, praised the work of imperial confrères in the French Foreign Legion. Between 1911 and 1962, France itself made over 200 feature films set in North Africa, many of them memorializing the exploits of the Legion against native rebels.[32] But the British especially became masters of the imperial epic, as in the Korda trilogy *Sanders of the River* (1935), *Drums* (1938), and *The Four Feathers* (1939) and in the films produced by Michael Balcon: *Rhodes of Africa* (1936), *The Great Barrier* (1936), and *King Solomon's Mines* (1937). At a time when roughly one-fourth of the human race lived under British rule, many films preferred a nostalgic look back at the "pioneering" days of "exploration" to a frontal examination of the quotidian brutality of latter-day imperialism.[33]

Cedric Hardwicke as Livingstone conducting an African choir in "Onward Christian Soldiers" in *David Livingstone* (1936), Cecil Rhodes planning the Cape-to-Cairo railway before a map of Africa in *Rhodes of Africa*, Reginald Denny laying down imperial law to a native ruler in *Escape to Burma* (1955), Tarzan performing deeds of valor in the imperial service; such are the filmic epiphanies of empire. What Jeffrey Richards describes as the "square-jawed, pipe-smoking, solar-topeed English sahib," standing at the ramparts, scanning the horizon for signs of native restlessness, crystallized an ideal imperial figure for cinematic consumption. Actors such as Ronald Colman, C. Aubrey Smith, Clive Brook, David Niven, Basil Rathbone, George Sanders, and Ray Milland incarnated heroic virtue in what amounted to a form of celuloid ancestor worship. *Rhodes of Africa*, for example, paints a hagiographic portrait of the imperial patriarch, constructed as an exemplum of foresight and benevolence. Both Korda and Balcon stress the austere stoic virtues and natural authority of the British on foreign strands. In *Sanders*, a film based on the popular Edgar Wallace series, a colonial District Commissioner (Sanders) puts down an uprising in Nigeria and brings British law and order to the River Territories. The usual colonial splitting pits the good Black Chief Bosambo (Paul Robeson) against the evil King Mofalaba. Colonialism, as incarnated by the authoritative and likeable Sanders, is portrayed as natural, eternal, beneficent. Africans themselves, meanwhile, were enlisted to enact their own caricatures. The exploits of figures like Sanders, Tarzan, and Quartermain brought home to the domestic public an idealized version of what abstract imperial theories meant "on the ground."

The imperial thrust of many of these films requires no subtle deciphering; it is

Plates 17 and 18 The White man's burden: *Sanders of the River* and *Beau Geste*

right on the surface, often in the form of didactic forewords. *Sanders*, for example, is dedicated to the "sailors, soldiers and merchant adventurers ... who laid the foundations of the British Empire [and whose] work is carried on by the civil servants – the Keepers of the King's Peace." The preface to *Rhodes of Africa* suggests that Africans themselves endorsed Rhodes' enterprise; the Matabele, we are told, regarded Sanders as "a royal warrior, who tempered conquest with the gift of ruling." Elsewhere imperial ideology is explicitly expressed through dialog. Colonel Williams in *Wee Willie Winkie* (1937) tells Shirley Temple:

111

"Beyond that pass, thousands of savages are waiting to sweep down and ravage India. It's England's duty, it's my duty, to see that this doesn't happen." *Farewell Again* (1937) begins:

All over the world, wherever the Union Jack is flown, men, from castle and cottage, city and village, are on duty ... facing hardship, danger, death with only a brief glimpse of home. Each has his own joys and sorrows but a common purpose unites them – their country's service.

In such films, Britain's material interests in the imperialized world are masked by what Conrad's Marlowe would have called "redeeming ideas": the battle against savagery (*Wee Willie Winkie*), the struggle to abolish slavery (*Killers of Kilimanjaro*, 1959), the fight against fascism (*The Sun Never Sets*, 1940).

A positive image of empire was also encoded into law. The British in particular imposed censorship provisions throughout their empire. In Trinidad, the censorship code forbade "scenes intended to ridicule or criticise unfairly" British social life: "White men in a state of degradation amidst native surroundings, or using violence towards natives, especially Chinese, negroes and Indians," and "equivocal situations between men of one race and girls of another race."[34] In 1928 the Hong Kong censor told the American Consul-General that his duty was to uphold British prestige in "a small settlement of white men on the fringe of a huge empire of Asiatics." A United Artists agent in Hong Kong reported that banned subjects included "armed conflict between Chinese and whites" and portrayals of "white women in indecorous garb or positions or situations which would tend to discredit our womenfolk with the Chinese."[35] The British censorship codes applied to global audiences, pressuring American producers to respect them. In 1928, Jason Joy warned production personnel that the British would not permit "the portrayal of the white man and woman ... in a way that might degrade him or her in the eyes of the native, nor will they permit anything in films tending to incite the natives against the governing race."[36] At the same time, colonial powers tried to prevent the development of rival "native" cinemas. The growing power of Egyptian national cinema in the Arab world was perceived as troublesome by the French, leading them to form a special department "responsible for setting up a production centre in Morocco whose official mission was to oppose the influence of Egyptian cinema."[37]

Hollywood films also rendered service to empire by reconstructing colonial outposts in southern California. In Samuel Goldwyn's *The Real Glory* (1939), for example, soldiers of fortune and the American army quell a "terrorist" uprising in the Philippines. Despite the US' own historical origins in anti-British revolt, Hollywood films often demonstrated as much enthusiasm for European colonialism as did the European films. Hollywood made more films than the French did about the French Foreign Legion,[38] and American films like W.S. Van Dyke's *Trader Horn* (1931) and *Stanley and Livingstone* (1939) glorified British colonialism in Africa. George Stevens' *Gunga Din* (1939), similarly, showed three heroic British soldiers battling savage Punjabis in nineteenth-century India.

Furthermore, the fact that American stars such as Spencer Tracy in *Stanley and Livingstone* and Charlton Heston in *Khartoum* (1966) played British colonial heroes virtually ensured the sympathetic identification of the Euro-American public, thus playing out on a thespian level the historical lap-dissolve by which the British-dominated imperialism of the nineteenth century faded into the US-dominated imperialism of the twentieth. In Henry Hathaway's *Lives of a Bengal Lancer* (1934), starring Gary Cooper, a handful of British officers hold back a native rebellion. The older officers are played by British actors, the younger by Americans, suggesting a kind of imperial succession. As Richards points out, Shirley Temple, the top box-office attraction in Britain and the US from 1935 to 1938, played a central role in the imperial films.[39] *Wee Willie Winkie*, based on a Kipling story, featured her as an American girl in India who learns about England's mission from her British grandfather, the commanding officer of a frontier fort. While the grandfather – a figure of British colonialism – is overly rigid, the American granddaughter is flexible and adept at mediation and at one point actually intervenes in a war to reconcile a rebel Khan to the British Raj. Thus the English-American family becomes enlisted in a kind of imperial allegory. Temple's diplomatic "in-betweenness" reflects the historical in-betweenness of the US itself, as at once an anticolonial revolutionary power in relation to Europe, and a colonizing, hegemonic power in relation to Native American and African peoples. Upon arriving in India, Temple confuses the Indians (natives of India) with American "Indians" – committing Columbus' error, but in reverse. In a film released just two years later, *Susannah of the Mounties* (1939), she intervenes between the Royal Canadian Mounted Police and an "Indian" tribe, suggesting the substitutability of the two kinds of "Indian." (Shirley Temple Black's later nomination as Ambassador to Ghana provides a further twist on this trope of substitutability.) Moreover, three of the epics of British India, *Lives of a Bengal Lancer*, *Four Men and a Prayer* (1938), and *Gunga Din*, were remade as westerns, entitled respectively *Geronimo* (1940), *Fury at Furnace Creek* (1940), and *Soldiers Three* (1951). The imperial epic also provided the model for westerns like *Santa Fe Trail* (1940) and *They Died with Their Boots on* (1941), while *Charge of the Light Brigade* (1938) was the model for *Khartoum*. Thus a kind of imperial circularity recycled the formulae of European supremacy vis-à-vis globally dispersed others, with the White European always retaining his or her "positional superiority" (Edward Said's term).

The studios' predilection for spinning-globe logos also translated imperial ambition. The Lumières' location shootings of diverse "Third World" sites, such as India, Mexico, Egypt, and Palestine, inaugurated this imperial mobility. The globe logo became associated with several studios (Universal, RKO), and with the British Korda brothers' productions, many of whose films, such as *Drums*, *The Four Feathers*, and *The Jungle Book* (1942), concerned imperial themes. The globe image symbolically evokes divine powers, since the created world implies a Creator. Later, TV news updated this trope of "covering the world." In the 1950s, John Cameron Swayze used the globe-trotting motif in his *Camel News*

Caravan and contemporary news programs call attention to it through their spherical-line globes and illuminated maps. Recent TV coverage of international crises generated further elaborations of the trope. A Gulf war special, ABC's *A Line in the Sand*, had Peter Jennings walk on top of a colorful political map of the Middle East as a setting for a pedagogical tour of the region's history, in a "covering" at once temporal and spatial. The North American TV commentator literally steps on, sits on, and looks down on the map, bestriding the narrow world "like a colossus."[40]

In both cinema and TV, such overarching global points-of-view suture the spectator into the omniscient cosmic perspective of the European master-subject. Incorporating images of maps and globes, *Around the World in 80 Days*, (1956), for example, begins with its omniscient narrator hailing the "shrinking of the world" which occurred during the period that Verne was writing his book. (The prelude to the film includes the mandatory globus prop made to spin for the camera.) The idea of "shrinking" materializes the confident, scientific perspective of upper-class British men. "Nothing is impossible," says the David Niven character: "when science finally conquers the air it may be feasible to circle the globe in eighty hours." Thus he implicitly links the development of science to imperial control, an idea reinforced by the character's recurrent association with the strains of "Rule Britannia." In recent science-fiction films such as *Return of the Jedi* (1983), globality embraces spheres yet to be charted by NASA. The conquest of outer space cohabits with an underlying imperial narrative in which the visualization of another planet conforms to the representational paradigm of Third World "underdevelopment." A Manichean struggle pits the hero against the new land and its natives. The exotic, teddy-bear-like "Ewoks" – whose language, as in most colonial films, remains unintelligible – worship the high-tech Euro-American hero and defend him against repulsive, evil, irrational creatures. The hero's physical and moral triumph legitimates the enemy's destruction and the paternal transformation of the friendly "elements" into servile allies, authorizing his right to establish new outposts (and implicitly to hold on to old ones). Like early adventure films, spectacular sci-fi and star-war video-games visualize progress as a purposeful movement toward global ubiquity; if in the early films traveling the ocean entailed no boundaries, in the recent ones the sky is no longer the limit.

THE WESTERN AS PARADIGM

If the imperial adventure film conveyed the pleasures and benefits of empire, the western told the story of imperial-style adventures on the American frontier. Indeed, the link between the two imperial adventures, in the continental US and outside of it, has usually been obscured, the word "imperialism" usually being restricted in reference to the late nineteenth-century expansions beyond the continent into the Caribbean and the Pacific. As has often been noted, the high proportion of westerns in Hollywood's costume-film output – roughly one-fourth of all Hollywood features between 1926 through 1967 – is so striking as to betray a kind of national obsession.[41] Although relatively few films treat the American revolution, Washington, Jefferson, and Franklin, countless films treat the conquest of the west, Kit Carson, Billy the Kid, and General Custer. The central place of the "myth of the frontier" in the American imaginary has been eloquently discussed by Francis Jennings, Richard Slotkin, Richard Drinnon, Michael Rogin, John Cawelti, and others. Arguably the longest-lived of American myths, it traces its origins to the colonial period. The myth of the frontier has its ideological roots in some of the discourses addressed in the previous chapter: the competitive laws of Social Darwinism, the hierarchy of the races and sexes, the idea of progress. It gave exceptionalist national form to a more widespread historical process – the general thrust of European expansion into Asia, Africa, and the Americas. What Slotkin calls the "American-History-As-Indian-War" trope has consistently given a fantastical self-aggrandizing shape to "United Statesian" self-narration, with reverberations that echo through popular culture even today.

The western inherited a complex intertext embracing classical epic, chivalric romance, Indianist novel, conquest fiction, the paintings of George Catlin, and the drawings of Frederic Remington. It played a crucial pedagogical role in forming the historical sensibilities of generations of Americans. The western's macro-narrative was doubly "condensed," both temporally and spatially: of a "New World" history of almost four centuries, these films focus on the last 200 years, thus repressing situations of first contact when American land and culture were more obviously Indian, and when non-genocidal collaboration with the Indians was still possible. Films like *Drums along the Mohawk* (1939) and *Northwest Passage* (1940), set before 1800, are in this sense the exception; westerns usually place us at a historical moment when the penetration of the frontier is already well under way, when the characters' point of origin is no longer Europe but Euro-America, and when there is little likelihood that Native Americans will mount a successful resistance to European occupation. That westerns are not "easterns" is no accident, since "easterns," set on the eastern seaboard of an earlier generation's contact with Native Americans, might have stressed the "un-American" foreign-ness of White Europeans, bringing up some of the intriguing "what ifs?" of history.

Hollywood's Native America, as Ward Churchill puts it, "flourished with the arrival of whites," then "vanished somewhat mysteriously, along with the bison and the open prairie," in a story with no "before" and no "after."[42] As a result, there is no cinematic recognition of what Churchill calls "a white-free and autonomous past," no Iroquois, Sioux, or Cherokee (not to mention Aztec or Inca) counterpart to *Cleopatra* (1934, 1963), *The Robe* (1953), or *Ben Hur* (1926, 1959). Furthermore, even within an already condensed spatiotemporality, these westerns privilege a period of roughly fifty years, and return time and again to particular sites and events. Although historical Native Americans generally avoided direct confrontation with the White military – according to the National Parks Service, there were probably only six full-scale attacks on

Plate 19 Dominating vistas: John Wayne in *The Searchers*

US cavalry forts between 1850 and 1890 – the Indian raid on the fort, as the constructed bastion of settled civilization against nomadic savagery, nevertheless became a staple topos in American westerns.[43] Turned into aggressors, Native Americans became dispensable "pop-up targets for non-Indian guns."[44] The status of a hero, and indirectly of an actor, was defined by the number of Indians he could kill.[45]

Central to the western is the land. The reverent attitude toward the landscapes themselves – Monument Valley, Yellowstone, the Colorado River – occludes those to whom the land belonged and thus naturalizes expansionism. The land is regarded as both empty and virgin, and at the same time superinscribed with Biblical symbolism – "Promised Land," "New Canaan," "God's Earth." A binary division pits sinister wilderness against beautiful garden, with the former "inevitably" giving way before the latter: "The sturdy plant of the wilderness," Thomas Farnham writes, "droops under the enervating culture of the garden. The Indian is buried with his arrows and bow."[46] The dry, desert terrain furnishes an empty stage for the play of expansionist fantasies. Nor is it usually explained that the native populations portrayed as an intrinsic part of the landscape were for the most part driven there by the White expropriation of more fertile lands farther east.

A Manichean allegory also papers over two diametrically opposed views of the land and the soil: for most Native American cultures, land is not real estate for sale but is sacred both as historically consecrated and as the "mother" that gives (and needs) nurture.[47] In many indigenous languages, the concept of "selling land" is literally unspeakable, because there are no words to convey it; whence

116

Plate 20 The vision of the dominated: *Wiping the Tears of Seven Generations*

the absurdity of imagining that Europeans "bought" Manhattan for $24 and a few trinkets. For the European, on the other hand, the land was a soulless conglomeration of exploitable resources, and the Indians a wandering horde without a sense of property, law, or government. "Civilization," as one Secretary of War put it, "entails a love for exclusive property." Progress, said Senator Henry Dawes, depends on not holding land in common, since "selfishness is the basis of civilization."[48] For Europeans, land existed to be transformed and mono-grammed, as it were, by a human, societal presence. While for the Europeans land was a commodity that had to produce quickly or else be abandoned for greener pastures (or more golden mines), for the Native Americans land was a sacred trust irreparably damaged by conquest.

The very titles of westerns stress a mobile, and mobilizing, European claim on the land. A disproportionate number stress European-designed state borders – *Oklahoma Kid* (1939), *Colorado Territory* (1949), *The Texas Rangers* (1936), *California Conquest* (1952) – the irony of course being that a high proportion of American states (such as Alabama, Arizona), rivers (including the Ohio, Potomac), lakes (for example Huron, Ontario) and mountain ranges (the Adirondacks and Poconos, for instance) carry native names.[49] The titles themselves exhibit the Adamic/Promethean power to name: *El Dorado* (1967), *Northwest Passage* (1940), *The Last Frontier* (1956). A kind of occidentotropism ("Go West Young Man!") informs the films, conveying a thrusting, trailblazing purposiveness, a divinely sanctioned crepuscular teleology: *Red Sundown* (1956), *Union Pacific* (1939), *The Last Outpost* (1935, 1951), *Heaven's Gate* (1980). Other titles resonate more blatantly with westward-driving zeal – *Westbound* (1959), *Westward the Women* (1951), *The Way West* (1967). Such titles relay the "becoming" of the American nation, which reached its telos with the complete transmogrification of nature into culture, a point fully reached only in the age of cinema. The west was thus less a place than a movement, a going west, a moving horizon, a "vaguely realizing westward" in Robert Frost's phrase, a tropism in both senses of the word – a movement toward and a figure of speech.

The western projects a vision of wide-open possibility, a sense of vistas infinitely open in both space and time. Esthetically, this vision is expressed in wide-screen perspectives and soaring crane shots accompanying stampedes and cavalcades. The title of *How the West Was Won* (1936), a spectacular epic that follows an emigrant family from the Erie Canal in the 1830s to a settled home in the west fifty years and four generations later, sums up the theme of conquest and settlement. Western films inherit the vocation of frontier painting, exemplified by the Currier and Ives lithograph *Through to the Pacific*, where an allegorical landscape rich in symbols of material progress includes a train moving through an industrial town in the foreground toward "undeveloped" land stretching to the Pacific in the background. John Ford's *The Iron Horse* (1924), whose title itself is an anthropomorphic "Indianism," narrates a similar progression from a rustic past (before the railroad was built, when Indians attacked the wagon trains) to a dynamic adventure-filled present (during the construction of the railroad, when the Indians attack the workers), and an implied felicitous future (with the linking of the two railroads, symbolically the realization of the nation's manifest destiny, and the disappearance of Indians from the scene). A nation with continental ambitions crystallizes on the screen as diverse groups coalesce around a common project. The wild land is domesticated and envalued, with progress embodied in its metallic avatar, the locomotive, a vehicle often metonymically (Lumière's train station) and metaphorically associated with the cinema itself. A differential mode of emplotment encodes Enlightenment values of progress and development, assigning a comic "happy end," under the sign of providence, for the characters representing the West, and a tragic "doomed to extinction" emplotment for the West's "others." A narrative paradigm is enlisted to serve teleological notions of national progress and manifest destiny.

"Too bad," Duke Wayne says of Indian extinction in *Hondo* (1953); "it was a good way of life." The elimination of the Indian allows for elegiac nostalgia as a way to treat Indians only in the past tense and thus dismiss their claims in the present, while posthumously expressing thanatological tenderness for their memory. Here too the titles are revelatory of the idea that Indians live in historically condemned time: *The Vanishing Race* (1912), *The Last of the Mohicans* (1920, 1932, 1936, 1992), *The Last of the Redmen* (1947). An ambivalently repressive mechanism dispels the anxiety in the face of the Indian, whose very presence is a reminder of the initially precarious grounding of the American nation-state itself. For Native Americans, meanwhile, the memories were vivid and painful. In the filming of *The Indian Wars* (1914), traumatized Sioux were obliged to reenact their own historical defeat and humiliation at Wounded Knee:

The plan called for the battle to take place right over the Indian graves, which seemed to the Sioux a horrible desecration ... the Indians were resentful, remembering how the white soldiers had massacred their tribesmen and the women and children ... The greatest difficulty in getting these men together was to convince them that the purpose of this mobilization was merely to reproduce the wars and not to annihilate them, for when they saw the Hotchkiss guns, the rifles, revolvers and cases of ammunition, there was a feeling of unrest, as though the time had come when they were to be gathered in by the Great Spirit through the agency of the white men.[50]

In a temporal paradox, living Indians were induced to "play dead," as it were, in order to perform a narrative of manifest destiny in which their role, ultimately, was to disappear.

We are not suggesting that all westerns were made in a single mold, or that there were never sympathetic portrayals of Indians, or that westerns were free of ideological tensions and contradictions. Enormous differences, obviously, separate William S. Hart's *The Aryan* (1916) from "pro-Indian" westerns like *Broken Arrow* (1950) or *Devil's Doorway* (1970), and the general run of westerns from a going-native western like *Little Big Man* (1970), a satirical western such as *Buffalo Bill and the Indians, or Sitting Bull's History Lesson* (1976), or an implicitly anti-Vietnam-war western like *Soldier Blue* (1970), which appropriates the 1864 Sand Creek massacre of Cheyenne and Arapahos to allegorize the My Lai massacre in Vietnam. Even within specific subgenres there were notable differences. A captivity narrative, for example, could either portray White assimilation to Indian ways or convey a racist horror of sexual assault, to be avenged by "savage war." The western has also evolved historically, particularly since the 1960s when pro-Indian films began to promote identification, however condescendingly, with Indian cultural values. As Thomas Schatz points out, later westerns become reflective, projecting a less flattering vision of the expansionist project; the law-and-order heroes of the classic western give way to renegade antiheroes.[51] Post-1960s' "realistic" westerns depict the frontier as violent but unheroic, often presenting Native Americans with considerable sympathy.

Our point, then, is not to collapse differences among westerns, but rather to point to the genre's ideological premises and its general procedures for fostering identification. Generally speaking, the Hollywood western turned history on its head by making Native Americans appear intruders on their own land, and thus provided a paradigmatic perspective, as Tom Engelhardt points out, through which to view the whole of the non-White world.[52] Rarely do westerns show Native Americans as simply inhabiting the domestic space of their unthreatening daily lives, although it was *their* lives and habits that were brutally disrupted by western expansion. Native Americans are usually portrayed as mean-spirited enemies of the moving train of progress. The point-of-view in the western is premised on exteriority, within what Tom Engelhardt calls "an imagery of

119

encirclement." The besieged wagon train or fort forms the focus of attention and sympathy, and from this center familiar figures sally out against unknown attackers characterized by inexplicable customs and irrational hostility: "In essence, the viewer is forced behind the barrel of a repeating rifle and it is from that position, through its gun sights, that he [sic] receives a picture history of western colonialism and imperialism."[53] The point-of-view conventions consistently favor the Euro-American protagonists; they are centered in the frame, their desires drive the narrative; the camera pans, tracks, and cranes to accompany their regard. In films such as *Drums along the Mohawk*, the point-of-view can be said to follow a structure of concentric circles. The inner humanized circle – often including women and children – is threatened by a second circle of attackers, until a final outer circle – the cavalry – rescues the besieged first circle by annihilating the middle circle. The outer circle, as colonial *deus ex machina*, executes an environing providential order – cinematic shorthand for genocide. The possibility of sympathetic identifications with the Indians is simply ruled out by the point-of-view conventions; the spectator is unwittingly sutured into a colonialist perspective.

Dominant narratives about colonial encounters suggest that "we," while imperfect, are at least human, while the non-European "they" are irrational and subhuman. The "colonial proportion" decrees that many of "them" must die for each one of "us," a pattern repeated in films of Zulus fighting the British, Mexicans fighting the US cavalry, American soldiers against Japanese kamikaze bombers, and, most recently, American pilots against Iraqi conscripts. But while "they" die disproportionately, "we" must believe that "they" pose an apocalyptic threat. Richard Drinnon traces the process by which White hostility toward premodern "savages" has been recycled throughout American history. The process began with the "proto-victims," the Pequots massacred in 1637, when the Puritans made some 400 of them "as a fiery oven" in their village near the Mystic River and later finished off 300 more in the mud of Fairfield Swamp, in an early example of the "righteous massacres" that have so marked American history.[54] The founding arrogance of the Pequot massacre was subsequently expanded to the "Conquest of the West," after which it was extended to the Philippines during the "imperialist binge" at the end of the nineteenth century, where many of the commanding generals had fought in the Plains and Apache wars.[55] "The pigments of Indian-hating," writes Drinnon, "shaded off into coolie-hating, the Chinese exclusion act (1882) and the 'Yellow Peril' hysteria at the turn of the century."[56] During the Philippine-American war, soldiers writing home stressed the comparison. An officer who served in the Philippines wrote reporter Henry Loomis Nelson:

We exterminated the American Indians, and I guess most of us are proud of it, or, at least, believe the end justified the means; and we must have no scruples about exterminating this other race standing in the way of progress and enlightenment, if it is necessary.[57]

120

Another Asian war, the Vietnam war, also reverberated with echoes of the Indian wars. The same Custer story that provided John Ford with the plot for *Fort Apache* (1948) also provided Arthur Penn and Sidney Salkow with allegorical material with which to denounce the imperial folly of the Vietnam war. According to Frances Fitzgerald in *Fire in the Lake* (1973), the American elite saw the war as the:

> painless conquest of an inferior race [just as to] the American settlers the defeat of the Indians had seemed not just a nationalist victory, but an achievement made in the name of humanity – the triumph of light over darkness, of good over evil, of civilization over brutish nature.[58]

The very names of some of the military operations in Vietnam – "Rolling Thunder," "Sam Houston," "Hickory," and "Daniel Boone" – resonated with the memory, and the attitudes, of the American frontier history relayed in the western. Troops described Vietnam as "Indian country," while General Maxwell Taylor justified escalation as a case of moving the "Indians" away from the "fort" so that the "settlers" could "plant corn."[59] For Lyndon Johnson, Vietnam recalled the Alamo. Even the "domino theory," according to Drinnon, "was an updated, internationalized version of the older fear of pan-Indian movements that went back beyond the Pequots and the Narragansetts."[60] And more recently General Schwarzkopf compared Iraq to "Indian territory."

THE LATE IMPERIAL FILM

The colonial/imperial paradigm did not die with the formal end of colonialism, nor is the western paradigm limited to the wild west. Indeed, one could speak of a "submerged" imperial presence in many films – the South African diamond mines in the background of *Gentlemen Prefer Blondes* (1953), the French presence in Morocco in *The Man Who Knew too Much* (1954), the neocolonial backdrop of Disney films set in Latin America (*The Three Caballeros*, 1945, for example),[61] or the French domination, again in North Africa, in René Clair's *Les Belles des Nuits* (1952). Such attitudes seep even into innocuous television entertainments such as *Gilligan's Island*, seen by 2.5 million people per day as late as 1986, where the island, as Paul Sellors points out, is perceived as surrounded by barbarian tribes.[62] The same Rider Haggard novels that inspired filmmakers in the silent period were adopted again throughout the sound period, sometimes more than once. *King Solomon's Mines* was filmed again, often recycling the same footage, in 1937, 1950, 1959 (under the title *Watusi*), and 1985. The 1937 film features Paul Robeson as the Zulu Umbopa and has the witchdoctor Gogoul trap innocent Whites inside a volcano; as they are about to be butchered, an opportune solar eclipse confirms their pretense of being gods. The 1959 Kurt Neumann film *Watusi* reuses footage from the 1950 film, and has a missionary's daughter saved from "savages." The 1985 *King Solomon's Mines* borrows shamelessly from *Raiders of the Lost Ark* and recycles the most classic

121

colonialist imagery, such as hordes of spear-carriers and the venerable "Europeans-in-the-pot" cannibal motif. In a kind of desired Western history, the Made in Zimbabwe, the film in an amalgam of Manichean narratives, suggests that the real colonial foreigners in Africa were not the British or the French but the Turks and the Arabs, along with the German Nazis.[63]

It would be impossible, even pointless, to inventory all the films that relay a colonialist or imperialist perspective, but we can examine a symptomatic example. Andrew McLaglen's *The Wild Geese* (1978) extends the western conventions to post-independence Africa. Based on a novel by Daniel Carney, a White man from Rhodesia (now Zimbabwe) and a former member of the South African police, the film glorifies the White mercenaries who once propped up White-minority rule in places like South Africa and corrupt Black rule in places like Zaire. The film, which centers on the mercenaries' armed rescue of a deposed Central African President, features highly popular actors playing the mercenaries. Richard Burton plays a tough Bogart-like commander who hides a sensitive heart beneath his cynical surface. Richard Harris is a brilliant military technician who regretfully tears himself away from his young son to join the "mission." Roger Moore is a playboy-pilot and Hardy Kruger a South African policeman. The mercenaries form the central focus of our sympathy; they win us with their flawed humanity, their quirky eccentricities, and their boisterous Hawksian camaraderie. Killing Africans en masse, the film implies, somehow brings out the mercenaries' latent humanity.

In the racist hierarchies of *The Wild Geese*, White males stand at the apex, White women are essentially dispensable, and Africans are playthings for Western plans. The film adroitly camouflages its racism, however: a token Black is included in the mercenary force – massacres seem more palatable when the perpetrators are "integrated" – and the entire operation is in any case performed on behalf of a Black leader repeatedly characterized as "the best there is." (The "best there is," unfortunately, is portrayed as sick, helpless, dying, literally carried on the backs of the Whites.) Within this White rescue fantasy, the Black leader of the 1970s speaks oddly like the Sidney Poitier of the 1950s. Pleading for love and integration, he calls on Blacks to "forgive the White past" and on Whites "to forgive the Black present," thus canceling out centuries of slavery and colonialism in the misleading symmetry of an aphorism.

Despite its flimsy integrationist façade, itself rather anachronistic in the 1970s, *The Wild Geese* conforms to the generic conventions of the western as colonialist adventure film. Even mercenaries, recruited from the flotsam and jetsam of English society, the film suggests, are suited to exercise power over African life. Whether gamblers, drunkards, or opportunists, they remain human; they are "us." African life, meanwhile, comes cheap. The film consistently obeys the "colonial proportion" in the body count; scores, even hundreds of Blacks die for each White mercenary slain. At the same time, the film exploits our instinctive sympathy for any group performing a "mission." We are induced to glory in the "surgical precision" of a task well done, whatever its political motivation. The European right to determine Africa's destiny is simply assumed. *The Wild Geese* enlists the gamut of cinematic devices in the service of the mercenary cause. The camera places us behind the barrels of mercenary guns, from which vantage point we see Africans fall by the hundreds. History is neatly inverted, so that Africans, like Native Americans in the western, come to seem invaders in their own land. The cinematography, finally, celebrates the lyricism of warfare. Explosions are made beautiful and violent death graceful. Free-falling paratroopers float earthward in choreographed aerial shots: neocolonial war as *homo ludens*.

In the Reagan–Bush era, dominant cinema rediscovered the charms of the imperial/frontier narrative. *Red Dawn* (1984) returns to the encirclement imagery of the western, but this time it is the Cubans, the Soviets, and the (presumably Sandinista) Nicaraguans who take over the functional slot of the Indians. A literary eulogist of the Somoza regime in Nicaragua, Jack Coz, produced *The Last Plane Out* (1983), a defense of the dictator whom Roosevelt called "our son of a bitch." *Mountains of the Moon* (1989), meanwhile, recapitulates the Victorian explorer Richard Burton's search for the sources of the Nile, with weirdly colorful savages, presumably incapable of "discovering" the sources for themselves, as his witnesses. The Michael Caine vehicle *Ashanti* (1979) resurrects the venerable scenario of the British as the passionate enemies of slavery in Africa, seen also in films such as *Killers of Kilimanjaro* (1959) and *Drums of Africa* (1963). In *Doctor No* (1962), the British exercise benevolent rule over good-natured West Indians.

The 1980s and 1990s have witnessed a wave of elegiac narratives about the closing of the imperial period. The Raj nostalgia genre, exemplified by the TV series *The Jewel in the Crown* and by such films as *Staying On* (1980), *Passage to India* (1984), *Gandhi* (1982), *Heat and Dust* (1982), and *Kim* (1984), was denounced by Salman Rushdie as a transparent Thatcherite attempt to refurbish the image of empire, forming the "artistic counterpart of the rise of conservative ideologies in modern Britain."[64] Although Forster's novel *Passage to India* helped crystallized the beginnings of a change of attitude toward the British presence in India, David Lean's adaptation tones down the cautious anti-colonialism of the novel in the name of "balance." Richard Attenborough's *Gandhi*, as a spectacular epic about an ascetic, a *Triumph of the Will* for pacifists, pursues the "Great Man" view of history, subtly prettifying the British role. Some of the few critical colonial "nostalgia" films which, interestingly, have been made by French women (Claire Dénis' *Chocolat*, Marie-France Pisier's *Bal du Gouverneur*, and Brigitte Rouan's *Outremer*, all from 1990), shift their focus from male aggressivity to female domesticity, and to the glimmerings of a feminist/anticolonialist consciousness provoked by transgression of the taboo on inter-racial desire.

More often, colonialist imagery has been remarketed under the guise of humor and genre parody. Thus, in a moment of apparent imperial decline, Hollywood resuscitates the imperial romance, where the presumably parodic filmmaker celebrates the extinguished glories of "imperial conquest and dominion, of

Plate 21 The imperial family: *Indiana Jones and the Temple of Doom*

virtually magical mobility and power, and of exotic life at the outposts of empire."[65] The *Indiana Jones* series recycled Rider Haggard and Kipling for the Reagan–Bush era, charmingly resurrecting the colonial adventure genre. Even the films' adolescent qualities recall the pubescent energies of imperial adventure tales for boys. Set in the 1930s, the very heyday of the imperial film, the series, like comic books, is premised on an imperialized globe, in which archeology professors can "rescue" artifacts from the colonized world for the greater benefit of science and civilization. "Indy" operates with ease only in colonized countries, portrayed as ontologically corrupt, awaiting Western salvation. The series assumes an uncontested empire, with no trace of any viable anticolonial opposition. In the Egypt of 1936 of *Raiders*, there is no popular agitation against the British, just as in the Shanghai of 1935 there is no word of Mao's "Long March."[66] The India of *Indiana Jones and the Temple of Doom* (1984), similarly, betrays none of the civil disobedience against the British that led to the Government of India Act of 1935. In the world of Indiana Jones, Third World cultures are synopsized as theme park clichés drawn from the orientalist repertoire: India is all dreamy spirituality, as in the Hegelian account; Shanghai is all gongs and rickshaws. Third World landscapes becomes the stuff of dreamy adventure. In a classic splitting operation, the Third World is both demonized and infantilized: non-Western adult characters are evil (Mola Ram, Chattar Lal, Lao Che); children (Short Round and Little Maharajah) are eager, innocent, and pro-Western. In this imperial family order, the modernity embodied by the younger, pro-American children, will replace the hidebound tradition of the older, nationalist fathers. Indeed, the series shows most of the unwashed masses of the

Third World as passively waiting for Indy to save them from ambitious nationalists like Mola Ram, who constructs his own (religious) domino theory: "The British in India will be slaughtered. Then we will overrun the Moslems. Then the Hebrew God will fall. Then the Christian God will be cast down and forgotten." The blame-the-victim paradigm inherited from the western is globalized: the civilized West is threatened by the savage East, but the imperial family ultimately triumphs.

POSTMODERN WAR

That the imperial and Indian war conventions traced here, together with the Eurocentric tendencies of the media apparatus, have not reached an end became strikingly evident during the Persian Gulf war. The ground for the "popularity" of the war was prepared by a long intertextual chain: crusading anti-Islamic tales, captivity narratives, the imperial adventure novel, the "manifest destiny" western, and more recent militaristic films like *Star Wars* (1977), the *Rambo* series (1982, 1985, 1988) and *Top Gun* (1988). An orientalist and imperialist imaginary was reactivated for the ideological purposes of the warrior state.[67] The Gulf war was presented as a macro-entertainment, one with a beginning (Desert Shield), a middle (Desert Sword), and an end (Desert Storm), all undergirded by a fictive telos: the "New World Order." The futuristic overtones of the phrase meshed anachronistically with the medievalist connotations of "shield" and "sword," evocative of a religious substratum of Crusades against Muslim infidels. Network logos – "Countdown to War," "Deadline in the Desert," "America at the Brink" – communicated a throbbing sense of inevitability, of an inexorable slouching toward war; provoking, even, a kind of spectatorial *desire* for war. Talk of peace, following administration cues, was treated not as a hope but as a "nightmare scenario," a kind of "coitus interruptus" within an irresistible orgasmic march.[68]

Multigeneric, the Gulf war mini-series drew on the codes of the war film (soldiers silhouetted against the sky, thrilling martial music, *Top Gun* visuals); of the PBS educational show (military pedagogs with pointers, maps, and video blackboards); of sports programing (instant replay, expert-running commentary); and of the western (lines drawn in the sand, the implacable logic of the showdown). The Gulf war scenario had the elemental, childlike charm of the fable, the awesome pyrotechnics of apocalypse, and the didactic impulses of allegory. With this war, an already powerful media apparatus became "wedded" to another apparatus of the gaze – that of military simulation and surveillance. As a consequence, telespectators were encouraged to "enjoy" a quantum leap in prosthetic audio-visual power. Television news offered its spectator what Donna Haraway, in another context, calls the "conquering gaze from nowhere," a gaze that claims "the power to see and not be seen, to represent while escaping representation."[69] While TV coverage in general allows spectators to imagine themselves at the center of the globe's "hot spots," during the Gulf war the media coaxed spectators to spy, thanks to an almost pornographic kind of surveillance, on a whole geographical region, whose nooks and crannies lay open to the military's panoptic view.[70]

The fact that the military view literally *became* the spectator's view goes a long way toward explaining the massive public adherence in the US to the war. For quite apart from the pleasures of identification with a powerful military apparatus, the Gulf war coverage hyperbolized the normal pleasures of the televisual "apparatus" itself. While the semiotic theory of the cinematic apparatus requires "scanning" for television, since many of the factors that foster the realer-than-real subject effects in the cinema do not apply here, nevertheless TV does have its own pleasuring capacities and its own ways of encouraging spectatorial regression and narcissism. Indeed, TV affords pleasures even more multiform than those afforded by the cinema, for the televiewer identifies with an even wider array of viewpoints: notably those provided by film cameras, video-cameras, and their magnetic residue of images and sounds on tape, along with those provided by tapeless video-cameras directly transmitting images and sounds, all then relayed around the world through satellite transmission. TV thus confers perceptual powers in some ways superior to those of the relatively sluggish cinema, a medium that TV both includes and surpasses in its ability to "cover the world."[71] The smaller screen, while preventing immersion in a deep, enveloping space, encourages in other ways a kind of narcissistic voyeurism. Larger than the figures on the screen, we quite literally oversee the world from a sheltered position – all the human shapes parading before us in TV's insubstantial pageant are scaled down to Lilliputian insignificance, two-dimensional dolls, their height rarely exceeding a foot.

The Gulf war mobilized atavistic passions, as televisual spectatorship became deeply implicated in an attempt to corral multiethnic spectators into a jingoistic communalism. A "feel-good" war became an (ultimately ineffective) electoral ploy, as global and domestic politics became linked to the Nielsen ratings. Much as the encirclement imagery model in the western engages literal point of view – the looking through the sights of a rifle, or through the windows of a fort – Gulf war "spectators" were made to see through the point of view of American pilots, and even through that of "smart bombs." Media coverage endowed the spectatorial eye with what Paul Virilio calls the "symbolic function of a weapon."[72] The Gulf war telespectator, vicariously equipped with night-vision technology, infra-red vision, capable of zapping "enemy" tanks, planes, buildings, and heads of state, was prodded into feeling infinitely powerful. In a war where the same pilot's hand that released the missile simultaneously tripped the camera shutter, spectators were teleguided to see from the bomber's perspective, incorporated into the surveillance equipment, sutured into the sights of high-tech weaponry.

Gulf war media coverage paraded before the viewers innumerable candidates for what Metz calls "secondary identification," that is, identification with the human figures on the screen: the anchors, the correspondents, the generals, the

Plate 22 Peter Jennings "Striding the world like a Colossus"

experts, and the people interviewed on the street.[73] As "pivots" of identification, the anchors and correspondents played an especially crucial role. The latter-day descendants of the traveler and scientist heroes of the imperial adventure films, news anchors constitute authentic contemporary heroes. Their words have godlike efficacy; their mere designation of an event calls forth instant illustration in the form of animated miniatures, colorful maps, and live-action footage. As charismatic figures, comparable in power to the great stars of the cinema, the anchors facilitated a massive transfer of allegiance to the war, particularly in contexts where viewers lacked alternative sources of information and analysis.

During the Gulf war, the newscasters dropped their usual mask of neutrality and metamorphosed into partisan cheerleaders. The historical inertia of their reputation for "objectivity" functioned in favor of the war. The newscasters' pro-war stance took many forms: adjectival qualifications of the bombing as "beautiful" or "precise," facile references to soldier "heroes," the tendentious use of the word "patriotism" to refer only to pro-war actions and attitudes. Newscasters spoke of Iraq as the "enemy," as if they had personally joined the armed forces. Dan Rather "enlisted" by saluting the troops, Forest Sawyer by donning military fatigues, Howard Threlkel by frisking surrendering Iraqi prisoners. Throughout, the newscasters channeled empathy according to clear hierarchies of human value: at the apex stood Americans and Europeans, then came Israelis, then Arab allies, and lowest on the ladder were Arab enemies. Even the oil-suffocated cormorants in the Persian Gulf and the animals in the Kuwait

City Zoo garnered more sympathy than the Iraqi soldiers. The zealous citizens who sported "Nuke Iraq" T-shirts, or who patriotically roughed up people they took to be Arab-Americans (even those from countries allied to the US), intuitively understood the subliminal message sent out by the media: Third World life has no value a European (including an honorary European) need respect.

Although the Gulf war took place in the revised political context of the post-cold war period, many of the tropes, imagery, and narratives deployed were drawn from colonial/imperial discourse. Demonizing Saddam Hussein, the administration not only resuscitated the "just war" paradigm of World War II (thus making the war more amenable to Manichean dualisms of good versus evil than the "messy" Vietnam war), it also invoked the familiar paradigm of the "savage war" and of extermination as morality play. The premise of "savage war," according to Richard Slotkin, is the idea "that ineluctable political and social differences – rooted in some combination of "blood" and culture – make coexistence between primitive natives and Europeans impossible on any basis other than subjugation."[74] The psychological basis of public acceptance of massive force, in a situation of "savage war," is the expectation that a people (or leader) defined as savage will commit unimaginable atrocities, such as rape, massacre, or torture:

> once such a *threatened* or rumored atrocity has been avenged with an actual atrocity, the mechanisms of projection become more (rather than less) powerful. Although we hopefully assert that our vengeance has had a chastening effect on the enemy, our belief that the enemy is "savage" suggests that we may merely have given him an additional motive for vengeance.[75]

The melodramatic formula that cast Hussein as villain (a "Geronimo with Hitler's ambitions," as Slotkin puts it), Bush as hero, and Kuwait as the damsel in distress was a replay of countless colonial-western narratives. Basic to such narratives is the rescue of a White woman (and at times a dark one) from a dark rapist, and a happy conclusion entailing the restoration of a patriarchal-imperial world order and the punishment of the dark disobedient rapist, who must be humiliated in the name of the dishonored female. The Gulf war was fought in a gendered language, where the "rape of Kuwait" – the sexual violation of an innocent, passive, symbolically feminine persona – became the pretext for a manly penetration of Iraq. The metaphor of the rape of Kuwait, the circulating rumors about Iraqi rapes of Kuwaiti women, and the insinuation of possible rapes of American female soldiers by Iraqi captors became part of an imperial rescue fantasy eerily reminiscent of the medieval Crusades, when non-Christian enemies were also portrayed as licentious beasts.[76] At the same time, through a show of phallic vigor in the Gulf war, a senescent America imagined itself cured of the traumatic "impotence" it suffered in another war, in another Third World country – Vietnam.

Permeated by skull-and-crossbones-style male bonding, the Gulf war was machismo-driven from the start.[77] But in their mobilization of a national imaginary, the administration and the media were careful not to make jingoistic militarism the spectator's sole locus of identification. They also provided more warm, more stereotypically "feminine" and "progressive" points of identification. Along with the smart bombs came yellow ribbons, along with the martial fifes and drums came the strains of violins. For those disinclined to identify with military puissance *per se*, less masculinist entries for identification were available – with the "multicultural" army on the ground, with women taking military roles, with the advance for Blacks represented by the leadership of Colin Powell, with the homeside families concerned about their loved ones.

In the Gulf war as western, Iraqi conscripts played the role of the Indians. The western's imagery of encirclement entails not only a particular perspective of siege but also the inflation of the external threat. Thus the Iraqi army, a largely conscript force with mediocre weaponry, unable to conquer Iran much less the assembled might of the world's most powerful armies, was promoted to the "fourth army in the world." When diverse pragmatic rationales for the war (oil, jobs, the American way of life) failed to catch fire with the electorate, the administration tapped into two interrelated cultural strains – idealistic exceptionalism and puritanical vindictiveness. On the one hand, the administration sounded lofty goals of regional peace and the New World Order; on the other, it demonized Hussein as "a man of evil standing against human life itself." Here Bush stood well within the tradition of what Michael Rogin calls "political demonology" – the creation of monsters through the "inflation, stigmatization, and dehumanization of political foes."[78] The "moderate" and "pragmatic" Hussein of earlier political rhetoric, ally of American policy and the darling of American, British, and German corporations, was transformed into a reincarnation of Hitler with the rapidity with which enemies for "Hate Week" were fabricated in Orwell's *1984*. It was also within the logic of the Manichean allegory that Bush, invoking the venerable tradition of the righteous massacre, would ask for divine blessing for American armed forces in a National Day of Prayer, just as he thanked the pilots in the January 1992 bombings for "doing the Lord's work."[79] And since the Manichean allegory does not allow for two competing evils, or for lesser and greater evils, or for minor and major thugs, but only for good against evil, it also allows for only one legitimate outcome: the annihilation of evil in a ritual sacrifice or exorcism that "cleanses" the accumulated iniquity. "Allah creates," said one Gulf war ditty, "but we cremate."

While the media on the one hand forced a "dirty-handed" complicity with the war by positioning viewers among the soldiers – Ted Koppel placing us in the cockpit of a Saudi fighter, Diane Sawyer putting us inside a tank – they also symbolically cleansed those very same hands. The spectator was prompted to indulge infantile dreams of omnipotence, made to feel allied to immense destructive forces, but also to feel fundamentally pure and innocent. Any word or image implying that the American spectators or their tax dollars were somehow responsible for mass suffering would have destroyed the shaky edifice of non-culpability, an unflattering implication that might have hurt ratings. Despite its lethal violence (estimates of over 150,000 dead, with an equal number dying later due to disease and malnutrition), the Gulf war was fought in the name of American victimization, in the tradition of the many wars in which reiterated claims of self-defense have masked overwhelming, disproportionate power.

In "'Make My Day': Spectacle as Amnesia in Imperial Politics," Michael Rogin anatomizes the role of real and imaginary massacres in justifying military interventions. Citing Reagan's role-playing as Dirty Harry, Rogin recalls the context in which Clint Eastwood uses the phrase "make my day" in *Sudden Impact* (1983). In the scene, Eastwood is "daring a black man to murder a woman ... so that Dirty Harry can kill the black." In other words, "white men show how tough they are by resubordinating and sacrificing their race and gender others."[80] Running like a thread through North American history is the similar notion, recycled by countless westerns, that Indian "outrages" justified Euro-American massacres and appropriations. In 1622, in "A Declaration of the State of the Colonie and Affaires" in Virginia, Edward Waterhouse wrote with relief that "our hands which before were tied with gentleness and faire usage, are now set at liberty by the treacherous violence of the Savages [so that we may] invade the Country, and destroy them who sought to destroy us."[81] Waterhouse's declaration anticipates what one might call the "make my day" syndrome, a desire for an outrage to justify even greater violence. The Gulf war reiterated the trope of "regeneration through violence" (in Slotkin's words), the process whereby the fictive "we" of national unity is reforged through salutary massacres. That President Bush had been figuratively in bed with the dictator Hussein merely betrays the binaristic splitting off of one's own impulses on to a phantasmic other that is so typical of colonialist thinking.

Our point is not that some national essence induces the American public into war – obviously antiwar protest and antimilitarism are equally part of American history – nor to suggest that Hussein is an innocent Third World victim, but rather to map the ways point-of-view conventions and a powerful media apparatus can be mobilized to shape public opinion for militaristic purposes. But these televisual tactics would not have "worked" so effectively had spectators not already been thoroughly "primed" by innumerable westerns, adventure films, and imperial epics.

The Gulf war revealed not only the continued reign of the imperial imaginary, but also the limitations of certain variants of postmodernism. Jean Baudrillard's account of the implosive collapse of boundaries in a mass-mediated global society, for example, is exhilaratingly apt in its rendering of the "feel" of life in the simulacral world of the postmodern, but his conceptions are ultimately inadequate for a phenomenon such as the Gulf war. In an article in the *Guardian* a few days before the outbreak of the war, Baudrillard treated the impending conflict as an impossibility, a figment of mass-media simulation techniques without real-world referents.[82] And on March 29, 1991, shortly after the end of hostilities, playing with the Giraudoux title *La Guerre de Troie n'aura pas lieu* (The Trojan War Will Not Take Place, 1934), Baudrillard declared in *Libération* that "The Gulf War Has Not Taken Place."[83] On one level, there is no denying the descriptive canniness of Baudrillard's account. The representation of the most media-covered war in history did indeed seem to shift from classical realist representation to the brave new public-relations world of hyperreality. Not only was the war packaged as a spectatorial video-game, it also proliferated in simulacral strategies – computer simulations, fake bomb damage, fake missile silos, fake attacks, even fake heat to attract heat-seeking missiles. War on the electronic battlefield became a media experience *par excellence* even for its participants, demanding what Paul Virilio calls a *"dédoublement"* of observation – both an immediate perception and a media-inflected perception through video, radar, and computer simulation.[84]

But if the Gulf war revealed the descriptive aptness of the Baudrillardian account of postmodernism, it also signaled that paradigm's political vacuousness, its disempowering combination of extreme cognitive skepticism and political quietism. For what the Gulf war revealed were fundamental asymmetries in how the depthless surfaces of postmodernity are lived; asymmetries not only between the experience of television and the experience of war, but also between the experiences of the combatants and the spectators engaged on different sides of the war. Some groups watched the war from an antisceptic distance, while others lived it in the company of death, dismemberment, disease, and famine. Technology facilitated seeing and hearing on the one side, and obliterated it on the other. While Americans, as Jonathon Schell puts it, waged war in "three dimensions," the foe was trapped, "like the creatures in certain geometrical games, in two dimensions ... we kill and they die, as if a race of gods were making war against a race of human beings."[85]

If postmodernism has spread the telematic feel of First World media around the world, in sum, it has hardly deconstructed the relations of power that marginalize, devalue, and time and time again massacre otherized peoples and cultures.[86] Baudrillard's radically ahistorical account misses the fact that time is palimpsestic; we live in many times, not just in the "new" time of advertising and the media. In the case of the Gulf war, the most sophisticated technology was used in the service of ideas drawn from millennial sources, from Christian Crusades against Muslims to "savage wars" against Indians. With the Gulf war, the fact of mass death itself, the radical discontinuity between the living and the dead, reveals the limitations of a world seen only through the prism of the simulacrum.

NOTES

1   See Jan Pieterse's chapter on "Colonialism and Popular Culture" in his *White on Black: Images of Africa and Blacks in Western Popular Culture* (New Haven, Conn.: Yale University Press, 1992), p. 77.

2   Robert Baden-Powell, *Scouting for Boys*, quoted in Joseph Bristow, *Empire Boys: Adventures in a Man's World* (London: HarperCollins, 1991), p. 170.

3   Bristow, *Empire Boys*, p. 19.

4   Patrick Brantlinger, *Rule of Darkness: British Literature and Imperialism 1830–1914*

(Ithaca, NY: Cornell University Press, 1988), p. 11.

5   See John McClure, *Late Imperial Romance: Literature and Globalization from Conrad to Pynchon* (London: Verso, 1994).

6   Hayden White, *Tropics of Discourse* (Baltimore, Md.: Johns Hopkins University Press, 1978), p. 58.

7   Etienne Balibar writes: "The histories of nations are presented to us in the form of a narrative which attributes to these entities the continuity of a subject." See Etienne Balibar and Immanuel Wallerstein, *Race, Nation, Class: Ambiguous Identities* (London: Verso, 1991), p. 86.

8   Benedict Anderson, *Imagined Communities* (New York: Verso, 1983), pp. 41–6.

9   For more on the extrapolation of Bakhtin's notion of the chronotope, see Robert Stam, *Subversive Pleasures: Bakhtin, Cultural Criticism, and Film* (Baltimore, Md.: Johns Hopkins University Press, 1989); Kobena Mercer, "Diaspora Culture and the Dialogic Imagination," in Mbye Cham and Claire Andrade-Watkins, eds, *Blackframes* (Cambridge, Mass.: MIT, 1988); and Paul Willemen, "The Third Cinema Question: Notes and Reflections," in Jim Pines and Paul Willemen, eds, *Questions of Third Cinema* (London: BFI, 1989).

10 Movie theaters in the colonized world were at first built only in urban centers such as Cairo, Baghdad, Bombay. For early responses to the cinema in Baghdad, Ella Shohat has conducted a series of interviews with old Baghdadis from her own community, now dispersed in Israel/Palestine, England, and the US.

11 Christian Metz, "The Imaginary Signifier," in *The Imaginary Signifier: Psychoanalysis and the Cinema* (Bloomington: Indiana University Press, 1982), p. 51.

12 For more on the "mobilized gaze" of the cinema, see Anne Friedberg's discussion in *Window Shopping: Cinema and the Postmodern* (Berkeley: University of California Press, 1993).

13 The photographs discussed in this section can be found in Maria Hambourg, Pierre Apraxine, Malcolm Daniel, Jeff L. Rosenheim, and Virginia Heckert, *The Waking Dream: Photography's First Century*, Selections from the Gilman Paper Company Collection (New York: Metropolitan Museum of Art, 1993).

14 For critical studies of anthropological discourse see for example, Talal Asad, ed., *Anthropology and the Colonial Encounter* (Atlantic Highlands, NJ: Humanities Press, 1973); James Clifford and George Marcus, eds, *Writing Culture* (Berkeley: University of California Press, 1986); James Clifford, *The Predicament of Culture* (Cambridge, Mass.: Harvard University Press, 1988); Trinh T. Minh-ha, *Woman, Native, Other* (Bloomington: Indiana University Press, 1989); Edward Said, "Representing the Colonized: Anthropology's Interlocutors," *Critical Inquiry*, Vol. 15, No. 2, pp. 205–25.

15 Jean Rouch in his critique of ethnographic filmmaking suggested that anthropologists should not observe their subject as if it were an insect but rather as if it were a "stimulant for mutual understanding." See "Camera and Man" in Mick Eaton, ed., *Anthropology-Reality-Cinema*, (London: BFI, 1979), p. 62. Ousmane Sembene, ironically, accused Rouch himself of filming Africans "comme des insectes." See special issue on Rouch, *Cinemaction*, No. 17 (1982).

16 For more on the question of science and spectacle, see Ella Shohat, "Imaging Terra Incognita: The Disciplinary Gaze of Empire," *Public Culture*, Vol. 3, No. 2 (Spring 1990), pp. 41–70.

17 Etienne-Jules Marey, a French physiologist interested in animal locomotion and in wildlife photography, called his 1882 camera a "fusil cinématographique," because of its gunlike apparatus, which made twelve rapid exposures on a circular glass plate that revolved like a bullet cylinder. The same notion was later trained against the colonial powers themselves in the Third Cinema notion of the "camera gun" and "guerilla cinema."

18 Donna Haraway, *Primate Visions: Gender, Race, and Nature in the World of Modern Science* (New York: Routledge, 1989), p. 52.

19 Egyptians at an orientalist exposition were amazed to discover that the Egyptian pastries on sale were authentic. See Tim Mitchell, *Colonizing Egypt* (Berkeley: University of California Press, 1991), p. 10.

20 Robert W. Rydell, *All the World's a Fair* (Chicago: University of Chicago Press, 1984), p. 236.

21 Ibid.

22 See Pieterse, *White on Black*. On colonial safari as a kind of traveling mini-society see Donna Haraway, "Teddy Bear Patriarch: Taxidermy in the Garden of Eden, New York City, 1908–1936," *Social Text*, 11 (Winter 1984–5).

23 See Phillips Verner Bradford and Harvey Blume, *Ota Benga: The Pygmy in the Zoo* (New York: St Martins Press, 1992).

24 The African name of the "Hottentot Venus" remains unknown, since it was never referred to by those who "studied" her.

25 For further discussion on science and the racial/sexual body, see Sander Gilman, "Black Bodies, White Bodies: Toward an Iconography of Female Sexuality in Late Nineteenth-Century Art, Medicine, and Literature," *Critical Inquiry*, Vol. 12, No. 1 (Autumn 1985); and in conjunction with early cinema, see Fatimah Tobing Rony, "Those Who Squat and Those Who Sit: The Iconography of Race in the 1859 Films of Félix-Louis Regnault," *Camera Obscura* No. 28, 1992 (a special issue on "Imaging Technologies, Inscribing Science," ed. Paula A. Treichler and Lisa Cartwright).

26 "Flower and Murie on the Dissection of a Bushwoman," *Anthropological Review*, No. 5 (July 1867), p. 268.

27 Richard Altick, *The Shows of London* (Cambridge, Mass. and London: Harvard University Press, 1978), p. 272.

28 Stephen Jay Gould, *The Flamingo's Smile* (New York: W.W. Norton, 1985), p. 292. On a recent visit to the Musée de l'Homme, we found no traces of the Hottentot Venus; neither the official catalog, nor officials themselves, acknowledged her existence.

29 Mitchell, *Colonizing Egypt*, p. 13.

30 The lure of the breast found its way even to the cover of a book on ethnographic cinema, Karl Heider's *Ethnographic Film* (Austin: University of Texas Press, 1976), which features a cartoon of a "native" woman breast-feeding. Trinh T. Minh-ha's *Reassemblage* (1982), meanwhile, reflexively interrogates the focus on breasts in ethnographic cinema. The I-Max big-screen presentation *Secrets of the [Grand] Canyon* also reproduces the paradigm of Native American nudity/Euro-American dress.

31 Interestingly, Méliès' early fascination with spectacle dates back to his visits to the Egyptian Hall shows directed by Maskelyne and Cooke and devoted to fantastic spectacles.

32 For an analysis of the cinematic treatments of North Africa and the Arab world (especially in French films), see Pierre Boulanger, *Le Cinéma Colonial* (Paris: Seghers, 1975); Abdelghani Megherbi, *Les Algériens au Miroir du Cinema Colonial* (Algiers: Editions SNED, 1982; and also the section on "Arabian Nights and Colonial Dreams," in Richard Abel, *French Cinema: The First Wave 1915–1929* (Princeton, NJ: Princeton University Press, 1984).

33 For a survey of the British imperial films see Jeffrey Richards, *Visions of Yesterday* (London: Kegan and Paul, 1973).

34 From "Trinidad Government Principles of Censorship Applied to Cinematographic Films," internal circular in 1929, quoted in Ruth Vasey, "Foreign Parts: Hollywood's Global Distribution and the Representation of Ethnicity," *American Quarterly*, Vol. 44, No. 4 (December 1992).

35 Memo to United Artists, March 8, 1928, from the MPPDA (Motion Picture Producers and Directors of America, Inc) Archive, quoted in Vasey, "Foreign Parts."
36 A 1928 Resumé from the MPPDA Archive, cited by Vasey, "Foreign Parts."
37 Hala Salmane, Simon Hartog, and David Wilson, eds, *Algerian Cinema* (London: BFI, 1976). See also Ella Shohat, "Egypt: Cinema and Revolution," *Critical Arts*, Vol. 2, No. 4 (1983).
38 See Abel, *French Cinema*, p. 151.
39 See Jeffrey Richards, "Boys Own Empire," in John M. Mackenzie, ed., *Imperialism and Popular Culture* (Manchester: Manchester University Press, 1986.)
40 ABC's *A Line in the Sand* was broadcast on January 14, 1991, a day before the US "deadline" for Iraqi withdrawal from Kuwait.
41 The statistical figure is from Edward Buscombe, ed., *The BFI Companion to the Western* (New York: DaCapo, 1988), p. 35.
42 See Ward Churchill, *Fantasies of the Master Race: Literature, Cinema and the Colonization of American Indians*, ed. M. Annette Jaimes (Monroe, Maine: Common Courage Press, 1992), p. 232.
43 Cited in Ralph Friar and Natasha Friar, *The Only Good Indian: The Hollywood Gospel* (New York: Drama Book Specialists, 1972), p. 188.
44 See Churchill, *Fantasies of the Master Race*, p. 232.
45 "There's a hell of a part here for you," Raul Walsh would tell prospective actors, "you get to kill eight Indians." Raul Walsh interviewed by Richard Schikel in *Harper's* (October 1970).
46 Thomas Farnham, *Travels in the Great Western Prairies* [1843], in Thwaites, ed., *Early Western Travels*, Vol. XXVIII, pp. 123–4, quoted in Roy Harvey Pearce, *Savagism and Civilization* (Berkeley: University of California Press, 1988) p. 65.
47 In a pro-indigenous documentary entitled *To Protect Mother Earth* (1987), Native American women repeatedly lament what they call "the rape of Mother Earth."
48 Quoted in Noam Chomsky, *Year 501: The Conquest Continues* (Boston: South End Press, 1993), p. 232.
49 On Indian names, see Jack Weatherford, *Native Roots: How the Indians Enriched America* (New York: Ballantine, 1991). On Native American names in New York City, see Robert Steven Grumet, *Native American Place Names in New York City* (New York: Museum of the City of New York, 1981).
50 Passage from Henry Blackman Sell and Victor Weybright's *Buffalo Bill and the Wild West*, cited in Friar and Friar, *The Only Good Indian*, p. 74.
51 See Thomas Schatz, *Hollywood Genres* (New York: Random House, 1981).
52 Tom Engelhardt, "Ambush at Kamikaze Pass," in *Bulletin of Concerned Asian Scholars*, Vol. 3, No. 1 (Winter–Spring 1971).
53 Ibid.
54 See Richard Drinnon, *Facing West: The Metaphysics of Indian-Hating and Empire-Building* (New York: Schocken, 1980).
55 See Richard Slotkin, *Gunfighter Nation: The Myth of the Frontier in Twentieth-Century America* (New York: Atheneum, 1992), p. 110.
56 Drinnon, *Facing West*, p. 221.
57 Quoted in ibid., p. 314.
58 See Francis Fitzgerald, *Fire in the Lake: The Vietnamese and the Americans in Vietnam* (New York: Vintage, 1973), pp. 491–2.
59 See Slotkin, *Gunfighter Nation*, p. 3.
60 Drinnon, *Facing West*, p. 404.
61 On imperialism in Disney, see Ariel Dorfman and Armand Mattelart, *How to Read Donald Duck: Imperialist Ideology in the Disney Comic* (New York: International General, 1975); Julianne Burton, "Don (Juanito) Duck and the Imperial-Patriarchal

Unconscious: Disney Studios, the Good Neighbor Policy, and the Packaging of Latin America," in Andrew Parker, Mary Russo, Doris Sommer, and Patricia Yaeger, eds, *Nationalisms and Sexualities* (New York: Routledge, 1992); Eric Smoodin, *Animating Culture: Hollywood Cartoons from the Sound Era* (New Brunswick, NJ: Rutgers University Press, 1993).

62 Paul Sellors, "Selling Paranoia: *Gilligan's Island* and the Television Medium," unpublished paper.

63 The Arab League protested the film for this very reason. See *New York Times* (April 29, 1985), p .C13.

64 Salman Rushdie, "Outside the Whale," in *Imaginary Homelands* (London: Penguin, 1992).

65 The words are John McClure's, from *Late Imperial Romance* (London: Verso, 1994).

66 Our discussion here is indebted to Harel Calderon's unpublished paper, "I'm Goin' Home to Missouri, Where They Never Feed You Snakes before Ripping Your Heart out," written for a course in Third World cinema at New York University.

67 Ironically, General H. Norman Schwarzkopf himself speaks of this intertext in his recently published memoirs, where he complains of the pressure of the "hawks":

> These were guys who had seen John Wayne in *The Green Berets*, they'd seen *Rambo*, they'd seen *Patton*, and it was very easy for them to pound their desks and say: "By God, we've got to go in there . . . gotta punish that son of a bitch!" Of course, none of them was going to get shot at.

Quoted in *New York Times* (Sept. 20, 1992), p. 10.

68 The recurrent trope of the war being "on schedule" was as much narratological as military. January 15 was set as the date for war, as Serge Daney pointed out, much as a date is set for the opening of a Hollywood blockbuster. See Serge Daney, "Mais que fait la Police," *Libération* (Feb. 15, 1991), p. 16.

69 Donna Haraway, "Situated Knowledge: The Science Question in Feminism and the Privilege of Partial Perspective," included in Haraway, *Simians, Cyborgs and Women* (New York: Routledge, 1991), p. 188.

70 We focus here on the mechanisms of promoting identification; we do not suggest that these mechanisms were experienced in identical ways by, for example, Baghdadis or New Yorkers, Kuwaitis or Israelis, Christians or Muslims, leftists or rightists. Although the experience of war is mediated, there are differences within spectatorship. These spectatorial differences will be the subject of our last chapter.

71 See Robert Stam, "Television News and Its Spectator," in Ann Kaplan, ed., *Regarding Television* (Fredricksburg, Md.: AFI, 1983).

72 See Paul Virilio, *War and Cinema: The Logistics of Perception* (London: Verso, 1989).

73 For Metz on "secondary identification," see *The Imaginary Signifer.*

74 Slotkin, *Gunfighter Nation*, p. 12.

75 Ibid.

76 The media also painted Hussein in the colors of orientalist fantasies of sexual perversity and excess. Entertainment magazines and television shows luxuriated in voyeuristic projections about Hussein's putative sexual perversions, including still photos of his bunker bedroom, his harem, and stories about his presumed penchant for killing his lovers, especially those who could testify to his failures in bed. The cover of a *National Examiner* (March 12, 1991) carried the headline "Saddam Hussein's Bizarre Sex Life: A Recent CIA Report Reveals," with a photomontage of Hussein as a crossdresser in a mini skirt. Geraldo's talk show (March 4, 1991) featured a series of so-called experts' tititlating descriptions of torture, all delivered up to an insatiably repelled audience. Close-ups emphasized the responses of good

Americans shocked by this cruel dark-skinned leader, compared to Idi Amin, Qaddafi, Noriega, Hitler, and Stalin. Hussein was frequently nicknamed the "Butcher from Baghdad" and "The Thief from Baghdad." See Ella Shohat, "The Media's War," *Social Text*, No. 28, Vol. IX, (1991).

77   Pilots reportedly watched porn videos before ejaculating their bombs over Iraq, thus turning pent-up sexual energy into military aggression, and recapitulating the transmutation of sex into violence that Leslie Fiedler, in *Love and Death in the American Novel*, discerned as characteristic of the American novel.

78   Michael Rogin, *Ronald Reagan: The Movie* (Berkeley: University of California Press, 1987), p. xxi.

79   See William Alberts, "Prayer as an Instrument of War," Z (April 1991).

80   Michael Rogin, "'Make My Day': Spectacle as Amnesia in Imperial Politics," *Representations*, No. 29 (Winter 1990).

81   Quoted in Pearce, *Savagism and Civilization*, p. 11.

82   Jean Baudrillard, "The Reality Gulf," *Guardian* (Jan. 11, 1991).

83   Jean Baudrillard, "La Guerre du Golfe n'a pas eu lieu," *Libération* (March 29, 1991).

84   See Paul Virilio, "L'Acquisition d'Objectif," *Libération* (Jan. 30, 1991), p. 15.

85   See Jonathon Schell, "Modern Might, Ancient Arrogance," *Newsday* (Feb. 12, 1991), p. 86.

86   For more on the Gulf war, see Robert Stam, "Mobilizing Fictions: The Gulf War, the Media, and the Recruitment of the Spectator," *Public Culture*, Vol. 4, No. 2 (Spring 1992). This passage was written before the appearance of Christopher Norris' *Uncritical Theory: Postmodernism, Intellectuals, and the Gulf War* (Amherst: University of Massachussetts Press, 1992), which takes a parallel, although not identical, approach to the same topic. We are in full sympathy with Norris' critique of the "ideological complicity that exists between ... extreme anti-realist or irrationalist doctrine and the crisis of moral and political nerve among those whose voices should have been raised against the actions committed in their name" (p. 27).

4

TROPES OF EMPIRE

Within colonialist discourse, metaphors, tropes, and allegorical motifs played a constitutive role in "figuring" European superiority. For Hayden White, troping is "the soul of discourse," the mechanism without which discourse "cannot do its work or achieve its ends."[1] Although tropes can be repressive, a defense mechanism against literal meaning, they also constitute an arena of contestation; each is open to perpetuation, rejection, or subversion.[2] The idea of race, for example, can be seen as less a reality than a trope; a trope, as Henry Louis Gates Jr has pointed out, of difference. Apart from the association of "race" with metaphors of pedigree and horse-breeding, "race" also "tropes" through schematic exaggeration: people are not *literally* black, red, white, or yellow but display a wide spectrum of nuanced tones, which did not prevent Hollywood from painting actresses (for instance, Sarita Montiel in *Run of the Arrow*, 1957) with red makeup according to racial conventions. Even the notion of colors being clearly distinct is itself a trope; in fact, some "Black" people are lighter than some "White" people. A cognate trope is the notion of racial "blood," which has historically served to signify religious affiliation ("Jewish blood"), class belonging ("blue blood"), national appurtenance ("German blood"), and race ("black blood"). Still, the troped nature of "blood" did not prevent the US army, as late as World War II, from segregating "black" blood plasma from "white" blood plasma. Anxieties about other kinds of mixing, about the exchanges of other fluids, were projected on to blood itself. Despite their quasi-fictive nature, then, racial tropes exercise real effectivity in the world.

Tropological operations thus form a kind of figurative substratum within the discourse of empire. One key colonialist trope was "animalization." This was rooted in a religious and philosophical tradition which drew sharp boundaries between the animal and the human, and where all animal-like characteristics of the self were to be suppressed. Colonizing discourse, for Fanon, always resorts to the bestiary. Colonialist/racist discourse renders the colonized as wild beasts in their unrestrained libidinousness, their lack of proper dress, their mud huts resembling nests and lairs. A colonial zeugma yoked "savages and wild animals" as feral creatures ranging over "empty lands." President Andrew Jackson urged his troops to root out Indians from their "dens" and to kill their "women and

Plate 23 Erotic
animalization: Josephine
Baker in *Zou Zou*

whelps."[3] In Nazi propaganda, Jews were described, and visualized, as vermin. The racialization of the powerful myth of the "chain of being" led scientists to search for the "missing link" between the highest animal, usually thought to be the ape, and the lowest man, thought to be the Black.[4] Finally, the Social Darwinist metaphor of "the survival of the fittest" transferred a zoological notion to the realms of class, gender, and race. The animalizing trope surreptitiously haunts present-day media discourse, inflecting attitudes toward the poor and the homeless, many of them people of color, as "unfit" to survive and who therefore merit the pitiless life of "poor naked wretches."

Animalization forms part of the larger, more diffuse mechanism of naturalization: the reduction of the cultural to the biological, the tendency to associate the colonized with the vegetative and the instinctual rather than with the learned and the cultural. "Man becomes Man in opposition to Nature," as James Snead puts it, and "the Negro represents the Natural Man in all his wildness and indocility."[5] Colonized people are projected as body rather than mind, much as the colonized world was seen as raw material rather than as mental activity and manufacture. Colonialist tropes and topoi of colonialist discourse also display regional specificities. They associate Latin America, and especially Latin American women, with verbal epithets evoking tropical heat, violence, passion, and spice.

Plate 24 Exotic vegetalization: Carmen Miranda as fertility goddess in
The Gang's All Here

Thus Lupe Velez becomes "the Mexican Spitfire," Acquanetta the "Venezuelan Volcano," Olga San Juan the "Puerto Rican pepperpot," Marie Antoinette-Pons the "Cuban hurricane." Colonialist discourse is protean, multiple, adopting diverse and even contradictory rhetorics. It varies with region, with historical period, and with the ideological needs of the moment. It can condemn the Arab world for overdressing (the veil) and the indigenous world for underdressing (nudity). It can project Africa as hypermasculine, grossly corporeal, and incapable of abstraction, while projecting Asia as dreamy, feminine, and overly abstract. Africa can be a child and Asia a shriveled old man, but Europe always maintains a relational advantage. Both Asia and Africa are seen as constitutively deficient, while Europe always keeps its place at the apex of a value-laden hierarchy.

The trope of infantilization, meanwhile, projects the colonized as embodying an earlier stage of individual human or broad cultural development. Renan speaks of the "everlasting infancy of [the] non-perfectable races."[6] Scientific racists tried to "prove" that Black adults were anatomically and intellectually identical to White children.[7] The Black who comes into contact with Whites, claims a Belgian novel of 1868, "loses his barbarian character and only retains the childlike qualities of the inhabitants of the forest."[8] The racist habit of calling colonized men "boys," like the speech tic whereby some hautes bourgeoises lapse into baby

139

talk when they address Black people, is the linguistic marker of this attitude. "Who's the boy playing piano?", Bergman asks of Bogart in *Casablanca* (1942), referring to Dooley Wilson, an adult Black. The powerful girl-child Shirley Temple exercising leadership over the adult Bill Robinson in *The Littlest Rebel* (1935) offers the cinematic *mise-en-scène* of this trope. (Toni Morrison has her character Claudia, in *The Bluest Eye*, reserve a special hatred for Shirley Temple and a special love for Temple's friend, uncle, daddy – Bojangles.) For Native Americans, the trope of infantilization took statutory form; their presumed childlike nature made them "wards of the state." Brazilian "Indians" were not allowed to play themselves in films because of their legal status as children, and it was only in 1988 that the new Brazilian constitution recognized indigenous people as adult citizens.

The infantilization trope also posits the political immaturity of colonized or formerly colonized peoples, seen as Calibans suffering from what Octave Mannoni has called a "Prospero complex," that is, an inbred dependency on the leadership of White Europeans. The Black Congressional session in *The Birth of a Nation* (1915) where barefoot Black legislators chomp on chicken legs and swig whiskey projects an image of Black political immaturity. And the White request that Black civil rights activists be "patient," while less crudely racist, was covertly premised on this same idea of a lack of "maturity" for equality. The *in loco parentis* ideology of paternalistic gradualism assumed the necessity of White trusteeship. As diplomatic synonyms for "childlike," terms like "underdevelopment" project the infantilizing trope on a global scale. The Third World toddler, even when the product of a thousand years of civilization, is not yet in control of its body/psyche, and therefore needs the guiding hand of the more "adult" and "advanced" societies, gently pulling it into modern times.[9]

Working within many of these tropes are undergirding binarisms: order/chaos, activity/passivity, stasis/movement. Spatial tropes such as high/low devolve into symbolic hierarchies that simultaneously embrace class (the "lower class"), esthetics ("high" culture), the body (the "lower bodily stratum"), zoology ("lower" species), and the mind (the "higher and lower" faculties). Another spatial trope posits European life as central and non-European life as peripheral, when in fact the world is multicentered; life is lived centrally everywhere. Notions of depth and surface make European culture deep and profound, non-European culture shallow and "superficial," whether because excessively playful or because enmired in the brute struggle for subsistence. Finally, the trope of light/darkness, implicit in the Enlightenment ideal of rational clarity, envisions non-European worlds as less luminous, whence the notion of Africa as the "dark continent" and of Asians as "twilight people." Earlier religious Manicheisms of good and evil became transmuted into the philosophical binarism of rationality/light versus irrationality/darkness. Sight and vision are attributed to Europe, while the "other" is seen as living in "obscurity," blind to moral knowledge. Color, complexion, and even climatic hierarchies emerge, privileging light/day over darkness/night and light skin over dark skin. Somewhat contradictorily, it is not the clear-skied

Mediterranean but the cold cloudy North that forms the locus of rationality and morality, while the jungle and wilderness are projected as the tangled sites of violent impulse and anarchic lust. And all these binarisms are mapped on to others: sane/insane; pure/impure; reasonable/hysterical; healthy/unhealthy.

Metaphors, in sum, play a crucial if contradictory role in constructing Eurocentric hierarchies. Our focus here will be on a specific constellation of gendered tropes that link the colonized to eroticized geographies of "virgin land," to the projective imaginary of "dark continents," to exotically "veiled" territories, and to symbolic fantasies of rape and rescue.

ADAMS IN THE VIRGIN LAND

Europe's "civilizing mission" has often interwoven opposed yet linked narratives of Western penetration of inviting virginal landscapes[10] and of resisting libidinal nature. Samuel Eliot Morison, for example, in *Admiral of the Ocean Sea* (1942) recounts the European conquest of America in sexualized language: "Never again may mortal men hope to recapture the amazement, the wonder, the delight of those October days in 1492 when the New World gracefully yielded her virginity to the conquering Castilians."[11] Sir Walter Raleigh, similarly, described "a country that hath yet her mayden head, never sakt, turned, nor wrought."[12] And Crevecoeur reported in a letter: "Here nature opens her broad lap to receive the perpetual accession of new comers, and to supply them with food."[13] The early exaltation of the New World paradise gradually recoalesced around the idealized figure of the pioneer. The exaltation of the garden – the classical *locus ameonus* cherished by European writers – gave way to the exaltation of the cultivator. With this important addition, the garden metaphor evoked growth, increase, cultivation, and blissful agricultural labor,[14] and implied that the land, prior to Western penetration, was empty (just as the native was *tabula rasa*), uncultivated, undomesticated, without a legitimate (that is, settled European) owner.[15] Within this larger topos, subliminally gendered tropes such as "conquering the desolation" and "fecundating the wilderness" acquired heroic resonances of Western fertilization of barren lands. As Said suggests in relation to the orient, the metaphoric portrayal of the (non-European) land as coyly awaiting the touch of the colonizer implied that non-European continents could only benefit from colonial praxis.[16] The revivification of a wasted soil evoked a quasi-divine process of endowing life and meaning *ex nihilo*, a Promethean production of order from chaos, plenitude from lack. Indeed, the West's "Prospero complex" is premised on an East/South portrayed as a Caliban's isle, the site of superimposed lacks calling for Western/Northern transformation of primeval matter, in a phallocentric engendering of life from Adam's rib.[17]

The American hero, as R.W.B. Lewis points out, was celebrated as prelapsarian Adam, a New Man emancipated from history (that is, European history) before whom all the world and time lay available.[18] The American Adam (not an Eve but the solitary White man gazing westward) was a verbal demiurge blessed with the

141

divine prerogative of naming. He was also fundamentally innocent. Such a narrative clearly interweaves colonial and patriarchal discourses. In the Book of Genesis, the creation of the world involved the creation of Adam from earth (*adama* in Hebrew) in order to rule over nature. The power of creation is inextricably entwined with the power of naming – God lends Adam his naming authority as a mark of his rule, and Eve is "called Woman because she was taken out of man." Naming likewise played a crucial role in colonial history, as the "discoverer" gave names to places as a mark of possession ("America" as celebrating Amerigo Vespucci) or as indices of a European perspective ("Middle East," "Far East"). Colonialism stripped "peripheral" places and their inhabitants of their "unpronounceable" indigenous names and outfitted them with names marking them as colonial property. Often the names themselves were degrading, or the product of European misrecogitions. The Mexican province now called "Yucatan" (Mayan for "We don't know what you're talking about") got its name when the Spanish confused the local people's expression of bewilderment with a place name. The "Sioux," who refer to themselves as "Dakota" ("allies"), were named through a French condensation of the Ojibwa word *nadowe-ls-lw* ("snake," "enemy"). The "Navajos" (thieves), so called by the Spanish, are currently petitioning to be officially recognized by their original name "Dineh" ("the people").

The notion of an American Adam obscured the fact that there were already people in the New World when the settlers arrived – cautious estimates suggest a population of roughly 75 million[19] – and that the settlers had scarcely jettisoned their deeply ingrained Old World cultural baggage. Here "virginity," reflected incidentally in the naming of the "Virgin Island," must be seen in diacritical relation to the metaphor of the European "motherland." A "virgin" land is presumably available for defloration and fecundation; ownerless, it becomes the property of its "discoverers" and cultivators. The "purity" that the term implies masks the dispossession of an already cultivated land and its resources. (In Mexico, giant pyramids such as La Venta were found under what looked like "virgin" forest; remnants of ancient crop fields are turning up in what were thought to be untouched biospheres.[20]) It was to the settlers' advantage to project an already fecund land, in indigenous terminology a "mother" – in Kuna *abia ayala* ("adult," "fecund" land) – as metaphorically virgin, "untouched," and therefore awaiting a master.[21] The "virgin" trope still informs contemporary discourse. The Amazonian rainforest, interlinked with human cultures for millennia, including agricultural chiefdoms that lasted for 2,000 years in a vast rural economy sustaining millions of people, is still referred to by journalists, including ecologically minded journalists, as "virgin" forest, in what amounts to a romantic variation on the trope.[22] And modern scientists refer to epidemics introduced into a community without immunities as "virgin soil epidemics."[23]

Gendered colonial metaphors are visibly rendered in Jan Van der Straet's pictorial representation of the discovery of America, which shows Vespucci, bearing European emblems of power and meaning (cross, armor, compass),[24] and behind him the vessels that will bring the treasures of the New World paradise back to Europe. Before him is a welcoming naked woman, the Indian America, and in the background are visual hints of cannibalism. If the indigenous woman is portrayed as a harmonious extension of nature, Vespucci is made to represent scientific mastery.[25] Here the conqueror, as Michel de Certeau puts it, "will write the body of the other and inscribe upon it his own history."[26]

Interlinked with the coy virgin metaphor is the opposite pole of libidinous wild femininity. This "no man's land" or wilderness may be characterized as resistant, harsh, and violent, a country of savage landscapes to be tamed; "shrew" peoples (Native Americans, Africans, Arabs) to be domesticated; and desert to be made to bloom. The split discourse of virginal and libidinal nature, homologous to the madonna/whore dichotomy, operates even in the same text. Ultimately, this serves the trope of rescue resuscitated during recent neocolonial wars (Grenada, Panama, Kuwait). Whereas "virginity" underlines the land's availablity, thus calling "logically" for a fecundating penetration, libidinousness subliminally invokes the need for a policing operation. Colonialist discourse oscillates between these two master tropes, alternately positing the colonized as blissfully ignorant, pure, and welcoming on the one hand, and on the other as uncontrollably wild, hysterical, and chaotic, requiring the disciplinary tutelage of the law.

The King Vidor film *Bird of Paradise* (1932), the story of a romance between an American sailor and a South Seas "native," exemplifies this politically charged paradox. The South Seas native woman (Dolores del Rio) metaphorizes her land; she betokens the "natural" paradise untouched by "civilization." But the very same ecologically harmonious landscape which yields a cornucopia of food abruptly metamorphoses, during the course of the film, into a threatening volcanic universe, a disordered hysterical body, as pastoral nature is inundated by the lava which swallows and sucks into itself the very beauty to which it had given birth. In the traditional equation between nature and woman, the South Seas heroine mirrors these opposites of Edenic pacificity and infernal danger. We first see her rescuing the trapped American hero from a shark; a crucial shot shows her swimming underwater with knife in mouth. Later she initiates an amphibious erotic ballet both under water and on land, leading to the narrative's inevitable punishment both of female initiation and of miscegenation. The woman gives up her life in the superstitious belief that it will save her lover; she is sacrificed by her possessed people. (Hollywood later banned all interracial affairs except in the context of the Pacific Ocean, since the "union of a member of the Polynesians and allied races of the Island groups with a member of the white race is not ordinarily considered a miscegenetic relationship.")[27] For her volcano-worshipping tribe, only human sacrifice can placate the angry Lava God, a treatment of religion which recalls the colonialist view of primitive religions as consisting of idolatrous worship of personified nature deities. If the initial images associate the del Rio character with peaceful water, the final shots superimpose her image over flames – an infernal punishment for the sexually hungry subaltern as well as for the pre-scientific natives.

143

Bird of Paradise advances an orientalist conflation of exoticism and eroticism; a theme picked up later in such films as *Sayonara* (1957) and *The World of Suzie Wong* (1960). The European is enchanted and seduced, but always returns home after having enjoyed the foreign woman/country without ever questioning his own cultural values. He "goes native" but ultimately recovers from his "traveling disorder" to become the delegate of the virtues of science, technology, and modernity. Nor is the sexualization of the colonial relation confined to narratives of colonial encounter. Nineteenth-century European representations of ancient civilizations, stimulated by archeological discoveries, also deployed gendered tropes to project the imperial present on to past encounters between West and East. And the nineteenth-century Romantic depiction of the ancient orient of Babylonia and Egypt, reproduced in films such as D.W. Griffith's *Intolerance* (1916) and Cecil B. de Mille's *Cleopatra* (1934), projected the "East" as feminine. In *Intolerance* Babylon signifies sexual excess, building on the description of the city in the Book of Revelation as "the Mother of Harlots and of the Abominations of the Earth." De Mille's *Cleopatra* articulates this view by having the sexually manipulative Cleopatra addressed as "Egypt" and by presenting the orient as the scene of carnal delights. The monumental architecture, domestic detail, and quasi-pornographic feasts in these films reflect an infatuation with the ancient East's material abundance that was shared by colonial travel

Plate 25 The iconography of a feminized Egypt: *Cleopatra (1934)*

literature, which also obsessively detailed oriental sensual excesses. The subjection of Cleopatra and Egypt is not without contemporary colonial overtones: the Roman court seems to consist of aristocratic Englishmen, who make sarcastic jibes at the idea that Rome could ever be ruled by the presumably Black Cleaopatra. And this despite the fact that Hollywood esthetic conventions turn the historically dark Cleopatra into a European-looking White woman, just as Christ has gradually been de-Semiticized in Western iconography.

In this sense, cinema enacted a historiographical and anthropological role, writing (in light) the cultures of "others." The silent films' penchant for graphological signifiers such as hieroglyphs (in the diverse versions of *Cleopatra*), Hebrew script (*Intolerance*), or the pages of an open book (as in "The Book of Intolerance," along with the didactic "notes" accompanying the intertitles), point to Hollywood's role as archivist and historian. By associating itself with writing, and particularly with "original" writing, early cinema lent a grand historical and artistic aura to a medium still associated with circus-like entertainments. Linking a new, apprentice art to ancient times and "exotic" places, it laid claim to quasi-archeological powers, resuscitating forgotten civilizations both on screen and architecturally in the various pseudo-Egyptian movie palaces. Made in a period when colonized peoples were asserting a counter-identity vis-à-vis their colonizers, these films suppress contemporary conflicts in favor of a romantic, nostalgic search for the lost Eastern origins of the West. Only this contextual feature explains a structuring absence in Hollywood's representations of Egypt, Babylonia, and the (Biblical) Holy Land: the absence of portrayals of the contemporary colonized *Arab* orient and its nationalist struggles. The films define the orient as ancient and mysterious, epitomized by an iconography of papyruses, Sphinxes and mummies, whose existence and revival depends on the revivifying "look" and "reading" of the Westerner. The putative rescue of the past, in other words, suppresses the present and thus legitimates by default the availability of oriental space for Western geopolitical maneuvers. The filmic mummified zone of ancient civilizations, in sum, forms part of the representation of the historical role of the West in the imperial age.

MAPPING *TERRA INCOGNITA*

In the manner of Western historiography, Eurocentric cinema narrates penetration into the Third World through the figure of the "discoverer." In most Western films about the colonies such as *A Bird of Paradise*, *Wee Willie Winkie* (1937), *Black Narcissus* (1947), *The King and I* (1956), and *Lawrence of Arabia* (1962), the status of hero falls to the voyager (often a scientist) who masters a new land and its treasures, the value of which the "primitive" residents had been unaware. It is this construction of the consciousness of "value" as a pretext for (capitalist) ownership that legitimizes the colonizer's act of appropriation. In *Lawrence of Arabia* and the *Indiana Jones* series of the 1980s, the camera relays the hero's dynamic movement across a passive, static space, gradually stripping the land of its "enigma" as the spectator wins visual access to oriental treasures through the eyes of the explorer-protagonist. In *Lawrence of Arabia*, a romantic "genius" inspires and leads the passive Arab masses, an interpretation of history that Arab historians have vigorously challenged.[28] The unveiling of the mysteries of an unknown space becomes a rite of passage allegorizing the Westerner's achievement of virile heroic stature.

The sexual relation has provided one of the most common tropes for scientific and philosophical knowing: knowledge becomes involved with metaphors of eroticized scrutiny, penetration, and consummation.[29] There is a vast traditional discourse positing nature as feminine – as for example in Francis Bacon's idea that in so far as we learn the laws of nature through science, we become her (sic) master, as we are now, in ignorance, "her thralls."[30] In the colonial context, this discourse has clear geopolitical implications. The desire to dominate a new land forms part of the philosophy of the period of early colonial history, in which epistemology in part modeled itself on geography. Bacon analogizes expanding scientific knowledge and European geographical expansion:

> [A]s the immense regions of the West Indies had never been discovered, if the use of the compass had not first been known, it is no wonder that the discovery and advancement of arts hath made no greater progress, when the art of inventing and discovering of the sciences remains hitherto unknown."[31]

And Bacon finds it "disgraceful," that "while the regions of the material globe ... have been in our times laid widely open and revealed, the intellectual globe should remain shut up within the narrow limits of old discoveries."[32] Traveling into the watery infinity of the ocean, the Faustian overreacher voyaging beyond the Pillars of Hercules aims to discover a *terra incognita* on the other side of the ocean. Systematizing the paths, as Hans Blumenberg points out, guarantees that the accidents of things coming to light ultimately lead to a universal acquaintance with the world.[33] The logic of explorers from Robinson Crusoe to Indiana Jones, in this sense, is based on the hope that "nature" conceals in its "womb" still more mysteries, outside the familiar paths of the power of imagination. This context illuminates cinema's symptomatically frequent image of the Western hero discovering the "unknown" in caves in non-European lands, a motif found both in the Kipling-based *The Jungle Book* (1942) and in the Forster-based *Passage to India* (1984), as well as in *Raiders of the Lost Ark* (1981) and *Indiana Jones and the Temple of Doom* (1984).

The aura of scientificity inscribed by images of maps and globes also helped legitimize colonial narratives about treasure islands. It was during the Renaissance, after all, that Europe's ability to map graphically intimated the continent's potential dominion over all the globe. The growing science of geography inspired numerous narratives about the mapping of new regions. European cartographic inscription, with the drawn compass serving as the imprimatur of scientific authority, determined the status and significance of places. The full tale of transforming the unknown into known is conveyed through titles and captions, as well as through drawings of places and characters. Artistic conventions of the time personify the world's continents as female, while individualizing them in stereotyped ways, with luxurious Asia sumptuously dressed, Africa either stylishly Moorish or barely clothed, and America as the naked savage.[34] A 1586 map of America labeled "Terra Septemtrionalis Incognita" cartographically "writes" the history of the "discovery" of 1492. There is a sailing ship, and at the bottom Columbus and his men encounter nude, largely female "natives." Below, we read a caption in Latin: "America annos Dm 1492 a Christophoro Colombo nomine Regis Castello primum detecta." ("Columbus who in the year 1492 was the first to have found America in the name of the King of Spain.") The left-to-right sequence takes us from the "discovery" on the left to the realization of the map on the right. Cartography, in other words, is contextualized as the byproduct of scientific discoveries and of heroic discoverers. The narrative of mastery is finally metaphorized through the denuded "native" body occupying the space behind Columbus.

Geography was microcosmically reflected in travel narratives and exploration fictions revolving around the drawing or deciphering of a map (often the instrument for the telos of rescue) and the map's authentication through contact with the "new-found" land. Cinema has often used map imagery to plot the topographies touched by its adventurer heroes, implicitly celebrating its own technological superiority both to the novel's mere verbality and to the static nature of drawings and still photography. Numerous films set in Africa begin their narrative of "making sense" of an obscure continent through a map. The ethnographic film *The Sudan* (Museum of Natural History, 1953) begins with a map of Africa, entitled "Africa, the Dark Continent," accompanied by a male voice-over asserting: "If anything could have slain the fable of the Dark Continent, it would have been the motion picture. The camera's eye sees nothing but reality." In films as recent as *Raiders of the Lost Ark* and *Indiana Jones and the Temple of Doom*, not to mention the PBS documentary *Columbus and the Age of Discovery* (1992), animated arrows moving over maps signify the progress of the Westerner. Cinema thus represents itself as the contemporary heir of a more ancient visual medium: cartography.

Films often superimpose maps over shots of landscapes, subliminally asserting a "claim," a kind of optical "deed," to the land. *Around the World in 80 Days* (1956) feminizes national maps by imaging "native" women on the backs of maps of specific countries (the protagonist's balloon, "La Coquette," is also a "she"). *King Solomon's Mines* (1937, 1950, 1985) similarly genderizes the relation between the explorer and "his" topography.[35] In the second shot of Menahem Golan's 1985 adaptation, a small sculpture of a nude woman engraved with Canaanite signs is glossed by an archeologist as a map leading to the twin mountains called the Breasts of Sheba, whose caves hide King Solomon's diamond mines. The camera voyeuristically tilts down on the female body/map, scrutinizing it from the excited perspective of the archeologist and the antique dealer in whose store he found it. The road to the utopia of capital entails simultaneously deciphering the map and mastering the female body; the legendary twin peaks and the cave metaphorize the desired goal of plunder. The land itself is sexualized to resemble the female anatomy. The spectator is initiated into these enigmatic sites via the eroticized vantage point of the hero and his female companion, the archeology professor's daughter. The climactic deciphering of the map's coded language and the uncovering of the land's hidden resources run parallel to the fertile narrative of the constitution of the couple.

EXCAVATING THE DARK CONTINENT

Hollywood's ethnography has been premised on the cinema's capacity to initiate the Western spectator into an unknown culture. This premise operates even when films set in "exotic" lands and ancient times have no Western characters, for example the Babylon section of *Intolerance*, *The Thief of Baghdad* (1924), and *Kismet* (1944), where oriental heroes and heroines are played by White stars. Orientalist films invite the spectator on a temporal/spatial tour of a celluloid-preserved culture, implicitly celebrating cinema's capacity to promote panoramic spectacle and temporal voyeurism. Evoking André Bazin's view of cinema as possessing a "mummy complex,"[36] the cinematic capturing of the unknown has created a locus for popular anthropologizing and archeologizing. Often the spectator, identified with the gaze of the West (whether embodied by a Western male/female character or by a Western actor/actress masquerading as an oriental), comes to master, in a remarkably telescoped period of time, the codes of a foreign culture shown as simple, unself-conscious, and susceptible to facile apprehension. The films thus reproduce the colonialist mechanism by which the orient, rendered as devoid of any active historical or narrative role, becomes, as Edward Said suggests, the object of study and spectacle.[37] Any possibility of representing dialogic interaction is excluded from the outset.

The portrayal of a "Third World" region as underdeveloped is often reinforced by a topographical reductionism that figures the orient as desert and, metaphorically, as dreariness. The desert, a frequent verbal and visual motif in orientalist films, forms the timeless backdrop against which history is played out. While the Arab in *Lawrence of Arabia*, *Exodus* (1960), and *Raiders of the Lost Ark* is associated with underdevelopment, the Westerner is associated with productive, creative pioneering, with the masculine redemption of the wilderness. A culturally overdetermined geographical-symbolic polarity, on a double East/West and South/North axis, informs colonialist films. As if in a reversion to deterministic climate theories such as those of Madame de Staël or Hippolyte Taine, Eurocentric cinema has shaped an "East" or "South" visual ecology of irrational primitivism and dangerous instincts. The barren land and the blazing sands metaphorize the exposed "hot" uncensored passions of the orient; in short, the world of the out-of-control id.

The orient is also sexualized through the recurrent figure of the veiled woman, whose mysterious inaccessibility, mirroring that of the orient itself, requires Western unveiling to be understood. Ironically, veiled women in orientalist paintings, photographs, and films expose more flesh than they conceal.[38] This process of exposing, even literally denuding, the dark female, comes to allegorize the availability of Eastern land for Western penetrating knowledge and possession. Freud's metaphor of "the dark continent," similarly, functions on the boundaries of the epistemological and the sexual within colonial discourse. Freud wraps female sexuality in metaphors of darkness and obscurity drawn from the realms of archeology and exploration – the metaphor of the "dark continent," for example, was derived from a book by the Victorian "explorer" Stanley.[39] Seeing himself as explorer and discoverer of new worlds, Freud in *Studies on Hysteria* compared the psychoanalyst to the archeologist; the act of "clearing away the pathogenic psychical material layer by layer" is analogous "with the technique of excavating a buried city."[40] The analogy, made in the context of a discussion of a woman patient (Elisabeth Von R.), calls attention to the therapist's role in locating obscure trains of thought. As Freud puts it in his first-person account: "I would penetrate into deeper layers of her memories at these points, carrying out an investigation under hypnosis or by the use of some similar technique."[41]

Freud's "dark continent" and his psychoanalytic discourse of "penetrating deeply" into the "neurosis of women," thanks to a science which can give a "deeper and more coherent" insight into femininity,[42] carry significant political overtones. Penetration, as Toril Moi suggests, is very much on Freud's mind as he approaches femininity,[43] including, one might add, "the dark continent" of female sexuality. He sometimes deploys the language of violence: "we force our way," he writes, "into the internal strata, overcoming resistances at all times."[44] (Symptomatically, Freud never elaborates on the lived reality of rape in his writings.) The unveiling of the unconscious requires an obscure object in order to sustain the very desire to explore, penetrate, and master. David Macey's suggestion that psychoanalysis posits femininity as being in excess of its rationalist discourse, and then complains that it cannot explain it,[45] also applies to the positioning of the Third World "other" in colonial discourse. Returning to the figure of ancient Eastern civilizations, Freud employs myths such as those of the Sphinx and of Oedipus to draw parallels between the "development of civilization" and that of the psyche. (Although Freud never speculated at length on Egyptian mythology, over half of his private collection of antiquities reportedly consisted of ancient Egyptian sculptures and artifacts.)[46] The psychoanalyst who heals by unearthing the suppressed past (most of Freud's studies of hysteria were conducted in relation to women) resembles the archeologist, who recovers the hidden past or strata of civilization (usually "found" in Third World lands). Freud's epistemology, like that of classical archeology, assumes the (White) male as the bearer of knowledge who penetrates woman and text, while she, as a remote region, allows herself to be explored until truth is uncovered. Freudian science, as Ludmilla Jordanova puts it in her study of scientific imagery, "is a masculine viewer, ... anticipating full knowledge of nature, which is presented as the naked female body."[47]

As figures of threatening darkness, both "woman" and "native" must be controled through the systematic unearthing of the hidden. Just as psychoanalysis observed the details of hysteria, anthropology documented possession rituals. The notion of a "disordered body" demarcates the sexualized and racialized object of the scientific gaze and the institutionalized power-laden modes of study. This apparatus has left no imaginative space for what Fanon has termed "creative madness,"[48] a possibility evoked in Jean Rouch's critical ethnographic film *Les Maîtres Fous* (1955), which documents the possession rituals of the West African Hauka cult. Here the trance ritual testifies to a collective exorcism of alien domination. Corporeal disorder allegorizes a broader political disorder. The parodic mimicry of the colonizer by the possessed colonized links the symptoms of colonialism to the original trauma of colonial encounters. Fanon, in explicit criticism of Freud's Eurocentric psychoanalytic work, explains mental "disorder" as a symptom of political disorder and of power relations.[49] The disorders of the female and colonized body, in this sense, can be considered as reaction formations, or even as an exorcism and transcendence of patriarchal and colonial pathologies. Indeed, psychoanalytic praxis itself must be historicized, taking into account the power European psychoanalysts exercised over the mentally confined colonized, who were disciplined to confess to the (colonizer) psychoanalyst, for example, not in Arabic but in French.[50]

Freud's analogy between the development of the psyche and that of civilization must also be understood in relation to the culture of empire. (We are not suggesting that it is *reducible* to that culture.) The nineteenth-century medical and biological sciences were at pains to prove that certain features of the brain and sexual organs were the mark of lower primitive civilizations, thus lending scientific prestige to the contemporaneous political infantalization of White women and native peoples. The psychoanalytic postulation of id/superego, to some extent, parallels the primitive/civilized dichotomy in colonial discourse. (This binarist discourse has its variant in sociology, particularly in T.E. Parson's 1950s school of modernization which divides societies into primitive and less developed, and modern and more complex.) Questions of temporality in the analogy between the layers of civilization and those of the psyche are, in other words, historically charged. The relegation to a primal-time frame provides an apologia for the literal (geographical) and metaphoric (institutional) domination of space. Penetration into the enigmas of the various "interiors" is embedded in the imperial discoveries and expansions of the nineteenth century, and implicitly in the scientific discoveries which expand upon the alien's "aberrations".

Thus the term "dark continent" implicitly celebrates both geographical and psychic discoveries, in a manner reminiscent of Bacon's analogy between geographical and philosophical explorations. The role of Africa in anticolonial writing further illuminates the metaphors of light/darkness and the tropes of discovery. For Aimé Césaire and Fanon, as for Marcus Garvey and Malcolm X, Africa is not "dark" but rather the source of "enlightenment," particularly for its diaspora. The (re)discovery of Africa by Afro-diasporic intellectuals ever since the Negritude movement reverses notions of European discovery and colonial mimicry:

> If we want to turn Africa into a new Europe, and America into a new Europe, then let us leave the destiny of our countries to the Europeans ... But if we want humanity to advance further, if we want to bring it up to a different level than that which Europe has shown it, then *we must make discoveries*.[51] (emphasis added)

The (re)discovery of Africa returns the anticolonial intellectual to the site of the collective trauma of the first encounters with the "discoverers." Fanon's repeated references to history lessons about "our ancestors, the Gauls" critiques colonial pedagogy for perpetuating the neurotic disorder of the colonized.[52] Thus the discovery of one's ancestry can form part of a therapeutic recovery. Analyzing the rupture provoked by colonialism bespeaks a revolt against a present colonial dispossession.

MUMMIES AND EGYPTOLOGY

The interweaving of archeology and psychoanalysis touches on a nineteenth-century motif in which the voyage into the origins of the orient becomes a voyage into the interior colonies of the "self." As Said points out in *Orientalism*, for Lamartine, "Un voyage en Orient [était] comme un grand acte de ma vie intérieure".[53] Cinema's implicitly archeological role in deciphering buried civilizations at times becomes explicit in stories of archeological rescue missions. (The disciplinary origins of archeology as the search for the "roots of civilization," as we have seen, are both temporally and ideologically linked to imperial expansion.) Numerous films, from the *Mummy* series (particularly from the 1930s through the 1940s) to the *Indiana Jones* series, reproduce the colonialist topos by which Western "knowledge" of ancient civilizations "rescues" the past from oblivion. *Raiders of the Lost Ark*, for example, legitimizes the sequestering of the Egyptian heritage within metropolitan museums – an ideology also implicit in *Intolerance*, *Cleopatra*, and the *Mummy* series. (These films are often programed in museums featuring Egyptological exhibitions.)

Symptomatically, *Raiders of the Lost Ark* assumes a disjuncture between contemporary and ancient Egypt which only the Western scientist can bridge, since he alone can grasp the full significance of the ancient archeological objects. Set in the mid-1930s, when most of the world was still under colonial rule, the film naturalizes the colonial presence in Egypt, eliding a history of Arab nationalist revolts against foreign domination and reducing the Egyptian people to ignorant non-entities who happen to be sitting on a land full of historical treasures, much as the Arabs happen to "sit" on oil. The American archeologist of *Raiders* is searching, in a sense, for the Eastern roots of Western civilization. He liberates the ancient Hebrew ark from illegal Egyptian possession while also

Plates 26 and 27 The Mummy (1932) and *Raiders of the Lost Ark*:
Western knowledge rescues the Egyptian past from oblivion

rescuing it from immoral Nazi control, subliminally reinforcing American and Jewish solidarity against the Nazis and their Arab assistants.[54] *Raiders of the Lost Ark* develops parallel linked plots in which the female protagonist, Marion, and the ark become twin objects of the hero's search for harmony. The necklace which leads to the ark is first associated with Marion, who herself becomes the object of competing nationalist male desires. Like the ark, she is abducted by the Nazis and their Arab assistants, followed by Dr Jones' simultaneous rescue of both Marion and the ark. The premise of cinema's voyages into unknown regions – whether mental or geographical – is that the Westerner both already *knows* the orient (in the epistemological and Biblical senses) and at the same time rescues it from its own obscurantism. Marked by temporal and spatial ruptures, the archeological master-narrative implies a notion of historical "strata" within a politicized "geology." The deep stratum, in the literal and figurative sense, is unearthed by the Westerners, while the recent, "superficial" level is associated with the Arabs.

Much of the historical archive of what we now call the "Third" and "Fourth" Worlds was "discovered," seized, commodified, moved to Western institutions, and "reconceptualized to fit into the economic, cultural, political and ideological needs of people from distant societies."[55] Pharaonic and Babylonian monuments ended up in European and American museums, while pre-Columbian Mayan and Aztec texts – the Florentine Codex, for example – are named after their present-day European locations. A number of films, notably the Marker/Resnais *Les Statues Meurent Aussi* (Statues Also Die, 1953), have spotlighted this cultural massacre. And an African film, Ugbona's *The Mask* (1980), has Major Obi, Agent 009, sent on a mission to London to recover African artifacts from the British Museum. (Ishmael Reed, in *Mumbo Jumbo*, 1972, portrays Western museums as penal institutions, "centers of detention" for the Third World's sacred artifacts.)

The museological fetishizing of cultures is also criticized in the Egyptian film *Al Mumia* (The Mummy, 1969), distributed in the US as *The Night of Counting the Years*. Based on the case of the discovery of Pharaonic tombs in the Valley of the Kings in 1881, a year before the British colonization of Egypt, the film opens with a French Egyptologist, Gaston Maspero, telling his colleagues about the black-market trade in antiquities from the reigns of pharaohs such as Ahmose, Thutmose III, and Rameses II. The government's archeological commission, under Maspero, delegates an expedition headed by a young Egyptian archeologist to investigate the location of the tombs in Thebes in order to end the thievery. In Thebes, meanwhile, the Upper Egyptian Horobbat tribe has been surviving by extracting artifacts from the Pharaonic tombs. Its chief has just died, and his sons must be initiated by his brother into the secret of the mountain. Still in mourning for their father's death, the sons are repelled by the dissection of a mummy aimed at retrieving a gold necklace depicting the sacred "Eye of Horus." They must choose between two grave options: the vulture-like looting of ancient tombs, with the desecration of mummies, or the betrayal of their father's secret to the outside world, with a consequent loss of income vital for feeding hungry Horobbat mouths. Revealing the secret out of respect for "the dead," whom the Horobbat elders view as nothing but leathery cadavers, would entail that their family and tribe famish. The village elders assassinate the older brother when he refuses to sell an artifact on the black market. The younger brother, Wannis, is torn between his guilt that he owes his life to ancient Egyptian corpses ("How many bodies did my father violate in order to feed us?", he asks his mother) and the condemnation of his people to destruction. As he wanders through the ruins of Thebes and Karnak – for him, not simply mementos of an older civilization, but living reminders of his childhood playground memories – long-take swirling camera movements render his ethical and even epistemological vertigo, the conflict between his responsibilities to his Egyptian heritage and his immediate responsibility for present-day lives. After being reassured that the "effendi archeologists" are trying to understand Egypt's past rather than plunder it, he reveals the secret knowledge to Maspero's assistant. Before the village can prevent it, the expedition empties the graves and carries out the mummies, destined for the museum.

The Mummy is set in the late nineteenth century, at the height of imperial Egyptology. By the time Britain occupied Egypt, in 1882, the country had been bereft of many of its archeological treasures, which are still on exhibit in London, Paris, and New York as stony testimonials to the progress of Western science. The heroic, almost sanctimonious language of the mission's archeological reports on the 1881 discovery describes their rescue of the ancient East's powerful kings from Arab clans in a way that associates the Westerner with emperors and royal dynasties. The positing of a rupture between past and present-day Egypt conveniently empowers the Western claim over Egypt's past,[56] thus naturalizing the presence of the Rosetta Stone, for example, in the British Museum. Shadi Abdel Salam's film implicitly challenges this archeological master-narrative by foregrounding the voices of those on the margins of Egyptological texts. If the film opens with an archeological project and ends with its successful accomplishment, it also undermines that mission by focussing on the concrete dilemmas of living Egyptians in relation to their past. A non-diegetic musical motif based on Upper Egypt's popular music ("Al Arian"), along with a slow rhythm evocative of the regional atmosphere, further conveys the cultural force of the Egyptians' environment.[57] Significantly, the film does not end with the safe placement of the artifacts in a museum, but rather with the slow departure of the boat carrying the Egyptologists and the mummies, seen from the perspective of the devastated tribe. The film ends, then, with the emptiness left in the wake of the European intrusion. The women of the Horabbat tribe are said to have mourned when the mummies were taken, yet Shadi Adbel Salam, in long-shot and through depsychologized editing, presents a unified, communal silent gaze in which the only voice of protest is the whistling wind. Far from conveying the triumphant conclusion of the archeological narrative, that silent gaze unveils the cataclysmic rupture in Egyptian lives, thus subverting the self-celebratory Egyptological definition of dispossession.[58]

Archeological reports often inadvertently relay metaphors that suggest the mercantile underpinnings of their own profession. In his account of the 1881 discovery, the archeologist Howard Carter, who worked on the unearthing of Tut-ankh-Amen's tomb, writes, "Incredible as it may seem the secret was kept for six years, and the family, with a banking account of forty or more dead pharaohs to draw upon, grew rich."[59] Abdel Salam's *The Mummy*, in contrast, emphasizes the ambivalent relationships between the Egyptian people and their ancient heritage. The tribe lives on theft, yet its deprived circumstances imply a critique of the imperial class system. The archeological redemption, in other words, must be seen in its historical and cultural context as taking away the only power the tribe possessed while bringing nothing in return. It would be simplistic, however, to view *The Mummy* as merely a condemnation of Egyptology. The film illuminates class relations within the colonial dynamic which obliges the tribe to deal with the "small" black-market dealers, for the "effendis" from Cairo will not even pay the tribe and have them arrested. Imperial circumstances force the small village to regard the ancient artifacts as a means of survival, a system in which their secret becomes their only power. From their perspective, the effendis are strangers, cut off from national reality. Unlike Western representations of Egypt, *The Mummy* does not stress the grandeur of the ancient kingdom of Egypt at the expense of contemporary Arab lives; rather, it exposes the palimpsestic complexity of Egyptian identity.

As an allegory of Egyptian identity, *The Mummy* offers a meditation on the destiny of a national culture. As Abdel Salam says: "We have a national culture but it lies buried at the bottom of the memory of the people who are not always aware of its great values."[60] Speaking in an improbably literary Arabic (rather than an existing dialect), the villagers embody both the Arab cultural heritage and continuity with the ancient past – emphasized, for example, through the ancient-Egyptian-style eye makeup of the actress Nadia Lutfi. In a symbolic, syncretic

Plate 28 The Mummy (1969): amplifying the voices on the margins
of the Egyptological texts

155

continuity of Pharaonic and Arab Egypt, the film associates the ancient "Eye of Horus" – first shown in close-up, as if looking at the brothers (and directly at the spectator) – with the Arab gesture of *hamsa*, the hand extended against the evil eye, seen on the boat on which the older brother is murdered. Shots of a gigantic monumental fist similarly accompany a dialog between Wannis and a migrant worker about "a hand holding a fate no one can read" and "what fate can you read in a stone hand?," suggesting the hazardous nature of reading fate in the hands of the monuments. The contemporary popular Middle Eastern culture of reading fate in the hand, in sum, is implicitly contrasted with the immortal grandeur but also the lifelessness of mere monuments.[61]

The imagistic dialog between Arab Egypt and the pre-Arab past is further rendered through montage, for example when a shot of the agonized Wannis gazing up at a gigantic monument is juxtaposed with a high-angle shot of him as if from the monument's point-of-view. The presentation of Egypt's national identity as an amalgam of histories and cultures evokes formulations (by the writers Taha Hussein and Tawfiq al-Hakim, for instance) of Egyptian identity as a synthesis of Pharaonic past, Arabic language, and Islamic religion. The film's opening intertitle (drawn from *The Book of the Dead*), promising that he who departs shall also return, and the final intertitle imploring the dead to "wake up," must also be seen within the context in which the film was produced.[62] During the period after the 1967 war and Egypt's defeat by Israel, the Nasser regime lost much of its allure, provoking a general despair and a felt need for critical reassessment. The ancient inscription of resurrection, in this sense, is also allegorically a call for a national rebirth of the Egypt of the late 1960s.

RAPE AND THE RESCUE FANTASY

The topos of rescue in colonial discourse forms a crucial site in the battle over representation. Not only has the Western imaginary metaphorically rendered the colonized land as female to be saved from her environ/mental disorder, it has also given prominence to more literal narratives of rescue, specifically of Western and non-Western women – from polygamous Arabs, libidinous Blacks, and macho Latinos. Many films – *The Birth of a Nation* (1915), *The Last of the Mohicans* (1920), *Drums along the Mohawk* (1939), *The Searchers* (1956) – have perpetuated the rape and rescue trope, by which virginal White women, and at times dark women, are rescued from dark men. The figure of the dark rapist, like that of the African cannibal, catalyzes the narrative role of the Western liberator as integral to the colonial rescue fantasy. In the case of the orient, it also carries theological overtones of the inferiority of the polygamous Islamic world to the Christian world as encapsulated by the celibate priest or the monogamous couple.

In the chromatic sexual hierarchies of colonialist narratives, White men and women occupy the center of the narrative, with the White woman as the desired object of both male protagonists and male antagonists. Third World women – when not merely erotic tokens of their virgin lands – are marginalized, appearing

156

largely as sexually hungry subalterns. In one scene in *The Sheik* (1921), Arab women – some of them Black – quite literally fight over their Arab man. While the White woman has to be lured, made captive, virtually raped to awaken her repressed desire, the Arab/Black/Latin woman is driven by raging libido. A split discourse, then, posits the colonized land and its inhabitants both as virginal and as obscenely desiring, thus calling for a Victorian repression of sexuality, particularly female sexuality.[63]

The positing of female sexual enslavement by polygamous dark men becomes especially ironic when we recall the historical subjection of enslaved African-American women to the polygamous behavior of White male slaveowners.[64] In her 1860 narrative, *Inside Views of Southern Domestic Life*, Louisa Picquet portrayed the sexual exploitation of Black women as being at the core of White southern hyprocisy. Whites opposed the "heathenism of the Turkish harem," she observed, but were harems any

> worse than what is constantly practiced, with scarce a word of unfavorable comment, in our Christian land? Our chivalrous southern gentlemen beget thousands of slaves; and hundreds of children of our free white citizens are sold in the southern slave markets every year.[65]

Images of Black/Arab women in "heat" versus "frigid" White women mythically elide the history of subordination of Third World women by First World men. The hot/frigid dichotomy implies three interdependent axioms within the sexual politics of colonialist discourse: first, the sexual interaction of Black/Arab men and White women can *only* involve rape (since White women cannot possibly desire Black or Arab men); second, the sexual interaction of White men and Black or Arab women *cannot* involve rape (since Black or Arab women are in perpetual heat and desire the White master); and third, the interaction of Black or Arab men and Black/Arab women *also* cannot involve rape, since both are in perpetual heat. It was this racist *combinatoire* that generated the (largely unspoken) rationale for the castration and lynching of African-American men, thought to be a threat to White women, and the immunity of White men to punishment for the rape of African-American women. The denial of any erotic intercourse between Europeans and non-Europeans had the further advantage of maintaining the myth of the West's ethnic "purity."

The national and racial hierarchies of the cinema allegorize extra-discursive social intercourse. In the period of the Good Neighbor policy, Hollywood tried to enlist Latin America for hemispheric unity against the Axis powers. As European film markets were reducing their film consumption due to the war, Hollywood, in hopes of South American markets, flooded the screens with films on "Latin American" themes. Interestingly, the trope of "good neighbor" very rarely entailed the neighborly intimacies of interracial or inter-national marriage. Marginalized within the narrative, and often limited to roles as entertainers, the Latin American characters in *The Gang's All Here* (1943), *Too Many Girls* (1940), and *Weekend in Havana* (1941) tend at the films' finales to be exactly at the point from which they began, in contrast with the teleologically evolving North American protagonists. The musical numbers in these films provide the spectacle of exotic difference and function narratively to unite the North American couples vis-à-vis the South Americans.

The generic division of labor typical of films such as *The Gang's All Here* has the North American protagonists Alice Faye and James Ellison perform the "serious" or romantic numbers such as "A Journey to a Star," while the Latin American characters, most extravagantly exemplified by Carmen Miranda, perform "excessive" numbers involving swaying hips, exaggerated facial expressions, kitsch sexy costumes, and "think-big" style props. Miranda's figure in the number "The Lady with the Tutti-Frutti Hat" is dwarfed by gigantesque vegetative imagery. The final idealized image of her as a virtual fertility goddess reverberates textually with the opening of the number where very material goods from the South are unloaded in the US; the North here celebrates the South as the fecund feminine principle that gives birth to the goods the North consumes. The bananas in Miranda's song not only enact the agricultural reductionism of Latin America's monocultural products but also form phallic symbols, here raised by "voluptuous" Latinas over circular, quasi-vaginal forms. (But the Latina, as the lyrics suggest, will take her hat off "only for Johnny Smith," much as the "oriental" woman in films such as *The Road to Morocco*, 1942, would only remove her veil for the Anglo-American man.) Josephine Baker too often wore skirts of jiggling bananas, comparable to "perky, good-natured phalluses."[66]

Gender and colonial discourses intersect in Hollywood's exploitation of Asia, Africa, and Latin America as the pretexts for eroticized images, especially from 1934 through the mid-1950s when the restrictive Production Code forbade "scenes of passion" and required the upholding of the sanctity of marriage at all times. Miscegenation, nudity, sexually suggestive dances or costumes, and "excessive and lustful kissing" were prohibited, while adultery, illicit sex, seduction, or rape could only be suggested indirectly, and then only if absolutely essential to the plot and severely punished at the end. The Western obsession with the harem, for example, was not only crucial for Hollywood's visualization of the orient, it also authorized a proliferation of sexual images projected onto an otherized elsewhere, much as the orient, Africa, and Latin America played a similar role for Victorian culture.

Exoticizing and eroticizing the Third World allowed the imperial imaginary to play out its own fantasies of sexual domination. Even silent era films featured eroticized dances, improbable mélanges of Spanish and Indian choreographies, plus a touch of Middle Eastern belly-dancing (*The Dance of Fatima*, 1903; *The Sheik*, 1921; and *Son of the Sheik*, 1926). These mélanges recall the frequent superimposition within orientalist paintings of visual traces of civilizations as diverse as Arab, Persian, Chinese, and Indian[67] – a painterly version of the musical's "mark of the plural." An oriental setting (most of the films about Asia, Africa, and Latin America were studio-shot) provided Hollywood filmmakers with license to expose flesh without risking censorship; they could display the bare skin of Valentino, Douglas Fairbanks, and Johnny Weissmuller beside scores of women, from Myrna Loy, Maureen O'Sullivan, and Marlene Dietrich dancing with her legs painted gold to Dolores Grey moving her hips, with the "realistic" alibi of depicting less "civilized" cultures. In the desert and the jungle, the traditional slow-paced courtship leading to marriage could also be speeded up through racy fantasies of sexual "freedom" and domination, and specifically with fantasies of polygamy and even the rape of presumably repressed White women. The display of rape in a "natural" despotic environment continues to the present; for example, in the several attempted rapes of Brooke Shields in *Sahara* (1983). For a puritanical society and a film industry still hemmed in by moralistic codes, colonized lands provide a scene for violent eroticism.

As an early instance of erotic violence, *The Birth of a Nation* obsessively links sexual and racial phobias in what seems a guilt-ridden denegation of White man's history of raping Black women. The animalistic "Black" Gus attempts to rape the virginal White Flora, much as the "mulatto" Lynch tries to force Elsie into marriage, and the "mulatta" Lydia accuses an innocent White man of sexual abuse while sexually manipulating the naive politician Stoneman. The threat of African-American political assertion is metaphorized by Black sexual potency. Meanwhile, the only non-threatening Black figure, the "loyal" mammy, is portrayed as completely desexualized. It is Blacks' putative hypersexuality that foils and provokes (White) masculinist patriotism; the attempted rape of Flora catalyzes the grand act of White "liberation." The film's opening intertitle blames the African presence in America for having planted "the first seed of disunion," and the portrayal of idealized harmony between north and south (and masters and slaves) before abolition scapegoats libidinous Blacks for destroying the nation. The rescue of Flora, of Elsie, and of the besieged northerners and southerners (once again united "in common defence of their Aryan birthright") operates as a didactic allegory whose ground is the Klansmen's vision of the right "order of things." The closure of a regionally "mixed" marriage confirms national unity and establishes a sexual order in which the virginal desired White woman is available only to the White man. Finally, the superimposition of the Christ figure over the celebrating family provides a religious benediction for the "birth" of the new nation. This abstract, metaphysical birth masks a more concrete birth no less relevant to the conception of the American nation: that of the children born of raped Black women. Naming the mulatto "Lynch," similarly, crudely blames the victims of White-on-Black violence. As a final twist, Griffith shows the White man as manifesting a latent desire to rape innocent White women via a blackface surrogate, as if burnt cork were camouflaging the identity of the real perpetrator.

Even when not involving rape, erotic interaction in films prior to the 1960s was severely limited by apartheid-style racial codes. The same Hollywood that could project "mixed love" stories between Anglo-Americans and Latins, Asians, or Arabs – preferably incarnated by Euro-American performers (Valentino in *The Sheik*; Dorothy Lamour in *The Road to Morocco*; Maureen O'Hara in *They Met in Argentina*, 1941; or Yul Brynner in *The King and I*, 1956)[68] – was more

159

inhibited in relation to potential African and Native American sexual partners. In such films as *Call Her Savage* (1932), *Imitation of Life* (1934, 1959), *Pinky* (1949), *Far Horizons* (1955), *The Oklahoman* (1957), and *High Noon* (1952), a fear of blood-tainting bars the "half breed" (Native American, African-American, or Mexican) female protagonists from mixed marriages, even though the roles are usually played by White actresses. In these films the female protagonists withdraw by making the sacrifice of returning to their tribe, people, or country; in others (*Broken Arrow*, 1950; *Across the Wide Missouri*, 1951) they are sacrificed for their Pocahontas-style attempts to form a bridge between the races. Even a "utopian" genre like the musical, formulaically devoted to the constitution of the couple, could not support a protagonist of color; only the melodrama provided the generic space for a (usually doomed) interracial romance. Contemporary TV "dating game" shows, interestingly, adhere to a revised version of ethnic segregation: Whites date Whites, Blacks date Blacks, Latinos date Latinas, Asians date Asians, and so forth.

The Production Code of the Motion Picture Producers and Directors of America, Inc, 1930–4 explicitly states: "Miscegenation (sex relations between the white and black races) is forbidden."[69] This delegitimizing of the romantic union between White and Black is linked to a broader exclusion of Africans, Asians, and Native Americans from participation in social institutions. Translating the obsession with "pure blood" into legal language, southern miscegenation laws, as African-American feminists such as Anna Julia Cooper and Ida B. Wells pointed out as early as the end of the nineteenth century, were designed to maintain White male supremacy and to prevent the possible transfer of property to Blacks in the post-abolition era. "Race" as a biological category, as Hazel Carby formulates it, was subordinated to race as a political category.[70] This exclusionary ideology explains the Production Code's blanket censorship of sexual violence and brutality, thus foreclosing any portrayal of racial and sexual violence toward African-Americans and implicitly wiping the memory of rape, castration, and lynching from the American record.[71] The Production Code, in other words, forestalled the possibility of a denunciatory counter-narrative from the perspective of people of color, for whom sexual violence by Whites has often been a core historical experience. By contrast, a film by an Afro-Cuban director, Sergio Giral's *El Otro Francisco* (The Other Francisco, 1975) could foreground White sexual violence against Black women during slavery as a system of control of the Black family. Haile Gerima's *Bush Mama* (1975), similarly, focalizes the contemporary rape of a Black woman by a White L.A.P.D., and proceeds entirely from the woman's perspective.

Anticolonialist intellectuals have also resorted to narratives of rape and rescue. Both Césaire and Fanon, inverting the colonial paradigm, have compared colonialism itself to rape and ravage. Fanon has condensed the horrors of colonialism through incendiary images of brutality toward colonized women, made to carry the burden of representing the corpus of the nation: "Arrested, tortured, raped, shot down, [the Algerian woman] testifies to the violence of the occupier and to his inhumanity.[72] Césaire similarly excoriates the "adventurers who slashed and violated and spat on Africa to make the stripping of her easier."[73] Nationalist intellectuals thus interrupted the colonialists' exemplary tales of sexual violence and heroic sacrifice by appealing to the actual history of sexual violence and dispossession wrought against "Third World" women themselves. The "Third Worldist" construction of the "national," in other words, shifted and subverted the colonial perspective; since colonialist discourse relied on gendered language to articulate its mission of progress, anticolonial critique called up the elided history of the rape of Third World women. Yet by positing the nation as a haven for "our" women, anti-colonialism also clung to a masculinist fantasy of rescue.

THE IMAGINARY OF THE HAREM

Like voyeuristic anthropology and moralistic travel literature, dominant cinema projected a puritanical obsession with sexuality. Western male heroic desire finds an outlet in *Harum Scarum* (1965), which features a carnival-like orient reminiscent of Las Vegas (itself situated in the desert sands of Nevada) and offering harem-like nightclubs. The film opens with Elvis Presley – attired in "oriental" headwrap and vest – arriving on horseback in the desert. Upon arrival he leaps off his horse to free a woman from two malicious Arabs who have tied her to a stake. The triumphant rescuer later sings:

> I'm gonna go where desert sun is; where the fun is; go where the harem girls dance; go where there's love and romance – out on the burning sands, in some caravan. I'll find adventure where I can. To say the least, go East, young man. You'll feel like the Sheik, so rich and grand, with dancing girls at your command. When paradise starts calling, into some tent I'm crawling. I'll make love the way I plan. Go East – and drink and feast – go East, young man.

In orientalist discourse, material abundance, the product of imperial enterprises, functions as part of the generic utopia of the musical, constituting itself as a projected (masculinist) fulfillment of what is desired and absent within the sociopolitical status quo. The harem images offer an "open sesame" to an alluring and tantalizingly forbidden world, seen as infinitely desirable to the instinctual primitive presumably inhabiting all men. In *Kismet* (1955), for example, the harem master's panopticon-like device allows him to watch his many women without their knowledge. Authorizing a voyeuristic entrance into an inaccessible private space, the harem dream reflects a masculinist utopia of sexual omnipotence.[74] (These fantasies are recycled in contemporary erotic literature – *Turkish Delights, The Lustful Turk* – which emphasizes interracial sadomasochism and "sexual practices, beyond the Western imagination.")

The topos of the harem in contemporary popular culture draws, of course, on a long history of orientalist fantasies. In actuality, Western voyagers had little

Plates 29 and 30
Incarnations of the Sheik:
from Rudolph Valentino to
Elvis Presley

access to harems; indeed, the Arabic etymology of the word "harem" (*harim*) refers to something "forbidden" and "sacred." Yet Western texts delineate harem life with self-confident precision, rather like European orientalist studio paintings (for instance, Ingres' *Turkish Bath*, 1862) painted without visiting the orient. The *in loco* paintings by artists who did travel to the East, such as Delacroix, generally served to authenticate an *a priori* phallocentric vision. The harem was described through paradigms furnished by European translations of *A Thousand and One Nights* (*Alf Laila wa Laila*), tales often translated quite loosely to satisfy the European taste for a passionately violent orient,[75] best encapsulated in the figure of Salome, whose Semitic origins were highlighted by the nineteenth-century orientalist ethnographic vogue (the work of Hugo von Habermann and Otto Friedrich, for instance).

Whereas Eurocentric discourse has defined the harem as simply a male-dominated space, a sign of "oriental despotism," other accounts have emphasized the harem as a privileged site of female interaction and even of Sapphic fantasy. In Hanan Al-Shaykh's novel *Women of Sand and Myrhh* (*Misk al-Ghazal*), for example, the wives of patriarchal men themselves have lesbian relations within a supportive female community. Historical accounts by Middle Eastern women testify to a system that allowed women access to other women, providing a shelter for the exchange of ideas and information safe from the eyes and ears of men.[76] (Contemporary Middle Eastern vestiges of this tradition are found in regular all-female gatherings in which women, as in the harems, carnivalize male power through jokes, stories, singing and dancing.) Largely an upper-class phenomenon, the historical harem, as Leila Ahmed points out, was in fact most striking in its domesticity. Memoirs written by harem women depict a complex familial life and a strong network of female communality across class lines. Despite their subordination, harem women often owned and ran their property, and at times exercised political power. The harem, although fundamentally patriarchal in nature, was clearly a site of contradictions.[77] Yet it has been subjected to an ahistorical discourse which leaves unquestioned the West's own sexual oppressions; exercised, for instance, in the Victorian system of domestic "solitary confinement" for upper-middle-class women.[78]

European women formed an enthusiastic readership for the nineteenth-century orientalist poetry of Beckford, Byron, and Moore, anticipating their later spectatorial enthusiasm for such orientalist films as *The Sheik* and *The Thief of Baghdad* (1924). As travelers, however, their discourse on the harems oscillates between orientalist narratives and more dialogical testimonies. Western women at times participated in the Western colonial gaze, with writings which dwell voyeuristically on oriental clothes, postures, and gestures, exoticizing the female "other."[79] If male narrators were intrigued by the harem as the scene of lesbian sexuality, female travelers, who had more access to female spaces, undermined and re-oriented the pornographic imagination of the harem. Interestingly, the detailed description of Turkish female bodies in Lady Mary Wortley Montagu's letters, particularly those drawn from her visit to the *hammam* (baths), points to a subliminal erotic fascination with the female "other," a fascination that masquerades, at times, as a male gaze:

> I perceiv'd that the Ladys with the finest skins and most delicate shapes had the greatest share of my admiration, tho their faces were sometimes less beautiful than those of their companions. To tell you the truth, I had the

wickedness enough to wish secretly that Mr. Gervase could have been there invisible. I fancy it would have very much improv'd his art to see so many fine Women naked in different postures.[80]

Female travelers were also compelled to compare their own oppression with that of Middle Eastern women. Wortley Montagu often measures the freedom of English vis-à-vis Turkish women, suggesting the paradoxes of harems and veils:

> Tis very easy to see that they have more liberty than we have, no woman of what rank soever being permitted to go in the streets without two muslins, one that covers her face all but her eyes and another that hides the whole dress ... You may guess how effectually this disguises them, that there is no distinguishing the great lady from her slave, and 'tis impossible for the most jealous husband to know his wife when he meets her, and no man dare either touch or follow a woman in the streets ... The perpetual masquerade gives them entire liberty of following their inclinations without danger of discovery.[81]

In fact, Wortley Montagu implicitly suggests the Turkish women's awareness not only of their own oppression but also of that suffered by European women. Recounting the day she was undressed in the *hammam* by the lady of the house, who was struck at the sight of her stays, she quotes the lady's remark that "the Husbands in England were much worse than in the East; for they ty'd up their wives in boxes, of the shape of their bodies."[82]

The popular image-making of the orient internalized the codes of male-oriented travel narratives. Strong continuities link Hollywood's ethnography with Hollywood's pornography, which often latently inscribes harems and despots even in texts not set in the orient. What might be called "harem structures," in fact, permeate Western mass-mediated culture. Busby Berkeley's production numbers, for example, project a harem-like structure reminiscent of Hollywood's mythical orient; like the oriental harem, they house a multitude of women serving, as Lucy Fischer suggests, as signifiers of male power over infinitely substitutable females.[83] The *mise-en-scène* of both harem scenes and musical numbers is structured around the scopic privilege of the master in an exclusionary space inaccessible to other men. Berkeley's panopticon-like camera links visual pleasure to the aerial surveillance of orchestrated female movement. The camera's omnipresent mobile gaze, its airborne prowling along confined female torsos, embodies the overarching look of the absent/present master – that is, of the director/producer and, vicariously, of the spectator. Berkeley's production numbers tend to exclude any visible male presence, but position the spectatorial gaze as that of a lone despot entertained by a bevy of enticing females. Rendered virtually identical, the women in these numbers evoke the analogy between the musical show and the harem not only as a textual construct but also as a studio practice, whose casting practices are conceived as a beauty contest (a "judgment of Paris"). Speaking of his casting methods, Berkeley recounted a day in which he interviewed 723 women in order to select only three: "My sixteeen regular girls were sitting on the side waiting; so after I picked the three girls I put them next to my special sixteen and they matched just like pearls."[84] (The harem decorative-pearl trope is of course a staple of male-oriented TV commercials.)

All-female spaces have been represented very differently in alternative feminist cinema. Documentaries such as Atteyat El-Abnoudi's *Ahlam Mumkina* (Permissible Dreams, Egypt, 1983) and Claire Hunt and Kim Longinotto's *Hidden Faces* (Britain, 1990) examine female agency within Egyptian society. Both films feature sequences where Egyptian women speak together about their lives in the village, recounting in ironic terms their dreams and struggles with patriarchy. Through its critical look at the Egyptian feminist Nawal el Saadawi, *Hidden Faces* explores the complex class, regional, and religious frictions among women working together to create alternative institutions. Elizabeth Fernea's *The Veiled Revolution* (1982) shows Egyptian women redefining not only the meaning of the veil but also the nature of their own sexuality. And Moroccan filmmaker Farida Ben Lyazid's feature *Bab Ilsma Maftouh* (A Door to the Sky, 1989) offers a positive gloss on the notion of an all-female space, counterposing Islamic feminism to orientalist fantasies. The film tells the story of a Moroccan woman, Nadia, who returns from Paris to her family home in Fez. That she arrives in Morocco dressed in punk clothing and hairstyle makes us expect an ironic tale about a Westernized Arab feeling out of place in her homeland. But instead, Nadia rediscovers Morocco and Islam and comes to appreciate the communitarian world of her female relatives. She is instructed in the faith by an older woman, Kirana, who has a flexible approach to Islam: "Everyone understands through his own mind and his own era." As Nadia awakens spiritually, she gradually abandons the idea of the West as a site for her liberation, and sees Arab/Muslim society as a possible space for fulfillment. Within the Islamic tradition of women using their wealth for social charity, she turns the family's spacious home into a shelter for battered women. At the same time, the film is not uncritical of the patriarchal abuses of Islam, for example the laws which count women as "half persons" and which systematically favor the male in terms of marriage and divorce. The film's esthetic, meanwhile, favors the rhythms of contemplation and spirituality, in slow camera movements that caress the contoured Arabic architecture of courtyards and fountains and soothing inner spaces. Dedicated to a historical Muslim woman, Fatima Fihra, the tenth-century founder of one of the world's first universities, *A Door to the Sky* envisions an esthetic that affirms Islamic culture, while inscribing it with a feminist consciousness, offering an alternative both to the Western imaginary and to an Islamic fundamentalist representation of Muslim women. Whereas contemporary documentaries show all-female gatherings as a space for resistance to sexual patriarchy and religious fundamentalism, *A Door to the Sky* uses all-female spaces to point to a liberatory project based on unearthing women's history within Islam, a history that includes female spirituality, prophecy, poetry, and intellectual creativity as well as revolt, material power, and social and political leadership.[85]

THE DESERT ODYSSEY

Although the imperial narrative is ultimately masculinist, the ambiguous role of European female characters, as in the case of the harem, complicates the analysis. Here the intersection of colonial and gender discourses generates a shifting, contradictory subject positioning. Whether as traveler, settler, nurse, or scientist, a Western female character can simultaneously constitute "center" and "periphery," identity and alterity. In the imperial narratives, furthermore, a Western woman can be subordinated to Western man and yet exercise domination over non-Western men and women. This textual relationality homologizes the historical positioning of colonial women who have sometimes played an ambiguous role in relation to colonized people (both men and women).[86] In many films, colonial women become the instrument of the White male vision, and are granted a gaze more powerful than that of non-Western women and men. This ephemeral superiority granted European women in a colonial context is exemplified in *The Sheik*. Based on Edith Hull's novel, the George Melford film first introduces the spectator to the Arab world in the form of the "barbarous ritual" of the marriage market, depicted as a casino lottery where Arab men select women to serve as "chattel slaves." At the same time, the Western woman character, usually the object of the male gaze in Hollywood films, is endowed in the East with an active (colonial) gaze; she temporarily becomes the sole delegate, as it were, of Western civilization. The "norms of the text" (Boris Uspensky's phrase) are represented by the Western male, but in his absence the White woman becomes the center of civilizing consciousness.[87]

Michael Powell's and Emeric Pressburger's *Black Narcissus* (1947), a film about the "civilizing mission" of British nuns in India, rings curious variations on these themes. While the narrative is largely focalized through the nuns, the textual norms are ultimately embodied by the British man. His initial "prophecy" that the wild mountains of India will elude Christian proselytization is confirmed by the finale, when physical catastrophe and mental chaos undermine the religious order and symbolically punish the nuns. Yet while the British man dominates the intra-European encounters, the nuns are privileged filters and centers of consciousness in relation to the "natives" (both men and women). We find a variation on the same theme in *Out of Africa* (1985), supposedly a "feminist" film about female self-exploration, yet one that scapegoats the female protagonist as the carrier of colonialist ideology and makes her lover (Robert Redford's character) the bearer of the liberal "norms of the text."

In sum, the colonialist discourse on gender has Western women occupy a relatively powerful position on the surface of the text, but only as the bearers of a gaze more colonial than sexual. Contemporary media occasionally pick up on this colonial topos, as when Ralph Lauren "Safari" ads, shot largely in African locations, appeal to the upper-class woman's freedom to travel and "realize herself." Evocative images of a White woman traveler in a jungle environment – face veiled by gauze hanging from a colonial helmet, dressed in a white trouser suit and carrying a suitcase, waiting for an old-style airplane, or surrounded by dark bodies – are juxtaposed with diary entries: "A world of romance without boundaries." In these friction-producing moments, the national identity of the White female "character" is relatively privileged over the sexual identity of dark male figures. A similar ambivalence operates in relation to Third World male characters, whose punishment for interracial desire is accompanied by spectatorial gratification for a male sexual gaze as intermittently relayed by a darker man. These contradictions between racial and sexual hierarchies become accentuated in the recent liberal nostalgia-for-empire films featuring venturesome female protagonists, and thus presumably appealing to a feminist audience, while still reproducing colonialist narrative and cinematic conventions. The desexualization of the "good" African or Indian (servant) man in *Gorillas in the Mist* (1989), *A Passage to India* (1984), and *Out of Africa*, not unlike the desexualization of the female domestic servant in *The Birth of a Nation* and *Gone with the Wind* (1939), becomes linked to the White woman's temporary occupation of the (White) "pater" position toward the "natives."

Exoticist films also authorize subliminally transsexual tropes, as the orient provides an outlet for a carnivalesque play with national and gender identity. Isabelle Adjani is disguised as an Arab male rebel in *Ishtar* (1987), and Brooke Shields as an American male racer in the Sahara desert in *Sahara*, while Rudulph Valentino (*The Sheik* and *Son of the Sheik*), Douglas Fairbanks (*The Thief of Baghdad*), Elvis Presley (*Harum Scarum*), Peter O'Toole (*Lawrence of Arabia*), Warren Beatty and Dustin Hoffman (*Ishtar*) all masquerade in Arab disguise. This masquerading manifests a latent desire to transcend fixed national and gender identities. In *The Sheik*, the Agnes Ayres character, assisted by Arab women, wears an "Arab" female dress to penetrate the oriental "marriage market," assuming the "inferior" position of the Arab woman in order, paradoxically, to empower herself with a gaze on oriental despotism. The gender-switching in more recent films such as *Sahara* and *Ishtar* allows for harmless deviations from

Plates 31 and 32 Homoeroticism and transvestitism in the orient:
Lawrence of Arabia and *Sahara*

"feminine" body language. In counter-narratives such as *The Battle of Algiers* (1966), as we shall see, gender and national disguises carry a very different signification: rebel Algerian women disguise themselves in Western "modern" dress, dying their hair blonde and acting coquettishly with French soldiers. Here it is the Third World that masquerades as the West, not as an act of self-effacing mimicry but as a way of sabotaging the colonial regime.

Since Western male clothing, as a result of "the Great Masculine Renunciation,"[88] has been limited to austere, colorless costumes, the fantastic orient allows the imagination to go exuberantly "native." It was the widely disseminated popular images in newspapers and newsreels of T.E. Lawrence in flowing Arab costume that in part inspired films such as *The Sheik* and *Son of the Sheik*, whose bisexual appeal can be located in their closet construction of Western man as "feminine."[89] Yet the coded "feminine" look is played out in the safe space of the oriental oasis. David Lean's Lawrence, while conforming to the classic norms of heroic manliness, is also bathed in a homoerotic light. When accepted by the Arab tribe he is dressed all in white, and at one point is set on a horse, moving delicately, captured like a bride. Unsheathing his sword, the O'Toole character shifts the gendered signification of what is usually a phallic symbol by using it as a mirror to look at his own newly acquired "feminine" oriental image. More generally, the relationship between Lawrence and the Omar Sharif character gradually modulates from initial male rivalry to an implied erotic complicity, in which Sharif is associated with female imagery, best encapsulated in the scene where he is seen empathizing with the tormented Lawrence in misty eyed close-up. The subtext of interracial homoerotism in *Lawrence of Arabia* forms part of a long tradition that runs from *Robinson Crusoe* and *Huckleberry Finn* to *Around the World in 80 Days* (in the figures of Phileas Fogg and his dark servant Passepartout).[90] The archly colonialist *Trader Horn* (1930) develops a strong homoerotic subtext in the relation between the White adventurer protagonist and his Black servant, whom he verbally abuses throughout the film but whom he carries and caresses when the servant is wounded. The film's emotional paroxysm comes in a lachrymose homage after the death of the Black "boy," now transfigured in a nostalgia-drenched superimposition of the lost love object. Most texts about empire, from the Western genre to recent nostalgia-for-empire films such as *Mountains of the Moon* (1989), prefer intra-European homoeroticism, however; male explorers, deprived of women and "forced" into physical intimacy, weave bonds of affection and desire in the course of travails in unknown, hostile lands. Homoeroticism, then, can permeate even heterosexist narratives of empire.

Within this same symptomatic dialectic we may also find White heterosexual desires displaced on to African, Arab, and Latino men, who play the id to the Western masculinist superego. In *The Sheik*, for example, Valentino, as long as the spectator knows him only as an Arab, acts as the id. Revelation of his status as the son of Europeans, however, transforms him into a superego figure who risks his life to rescue the English woman from "real" Arab rapists.[91] And the English woman overcomes her sexual repression only in the desert, after the Sheik repeatedly provokes her. Valentino, the "Latin lover," is here projected into an "exotic" space where he can act out sexual fantasies unthinkable in a contemporaneous American or European setting. The desert in this sense functions narratively as the site of moral liminality. Orientalist films often begin in the city – where European civilization has already tamed the East – but withhold the most dramatic conflicts for the desert; where defenseless White women can easily become the captives of romantic sheiks or evil Arabs. The positioning of a "rapeable" White woman by a lustful male in an isolated desert locale gives displaced expression to a masculinist fantasy of despotic control over the Western woman "close to home," suspending any intervening protective code of morality. Puritanical Hollywood thus censures (White) female adventurousness, and the male tyranny of harems and rapes – but only, paradoxically, as a way of gratifying Western interracial sexual desires.

The male rescue fantasy and the chastening of female rebellion also undergird the narrative of a more recent reworking of *The Sheik* and *Son of the Sheik*, Golan's *Sahara*. In *Sahara*, Dale (Brooke Shields), feisty race-car driver and only daughter of a 1920s car manufacturer, is presented as recklessly overassertive for penetrating the male domain of the oriental desert and competing in a "men only" race. She disguises herself as a man, adopts a male profession, and emulates male technological mastery. Captured by tribesmen, she becomes a prized commodity fought over within and between tribes. The camera's fetishization of her body, however, ironically betrays the Western predilection for rendering star bodies as commodities. Scenes of Shields wrestling with her captors not only suture the Western spectator into a national rescue operation but also invite him/her to participate in orgiastic voyeurism. The desire for the Western woman, and the fear of losing control over her, are manifested in her punishment through Arab rape. At the finale, however, Shields, courageous winner of the race, decides "on her own" to return to the noble (White) "sheik" who has risked his life to rescue her. She could have won independence, yet she "voluntarily" chooses the ancient ways of gender hierarchy.

Indeed, it is sometimes implied that women, while offended by Arab-Muslim rapists, actually *prefer* masterful men like Valentino.[92] Following the opening of *The Sheik*, columnists asked Valentino: "Do women like masterful men?" To which the star replied: "All women like a little cave-man stuff. No matter whether they are feminists, suffragettes or so-called new women, they like to have a masterful man who makes them do things he asserts."[93] The author of the novel, Edith Hull, expressed similar opinions: "There can be only one head in a house. Despite modern desire for equality of sexes I still believe that physically and morally it is better that the head should be the man."[94] Edith Hull's novel and Monic Katterjohn's adaptation gratify a projected Western female desire for an "exotic" lover, for a romantic, sensual, passionate (but non-lethal) play with the *Liebestod*,[95] a release of the id for the (segregated) middle-class occidental woman. In this sense the phantasm of the orient can be incorporated by Western women as part of a broader colonial discourse on the "exotic", while simultaneously constituting an imaginary outlet for suppressed sexual desires.

When literalized through the rescue of a woman from a lascivious Arab, the rescue fantasy not only allegorizes the rescue of the orient from its own instinctual destructiveness but also addresses a didactic *Bildungsroman* to women at home, perpetuating by contrast the myth of the sexual egalitarianism of the West. The exoticist films of the 1920s, like those of today, delegitimized Third World national identities *and* gave voice to an anti-feminist backlash, responding to the threat to institutionalized patriarchal power presented by the women's suffrage movements and the nascent feminist struggle. In this sense the narrative of Western female travelers in the Third World can be read as a didactic allegory insinuating the dangerous nature of the "uncivilized man" and by implication lauding the freedom presumably enjoyed by Western women. In *The Sheik* and *Sahara*, the Western woman at first rebels against the "civilized tradition" of marriage, calling it "captivity," only later to become the literal captive of libidinous dark men. (Third World women, in these narratives, display no desire to rebel or to explore the world.) Transgressing male space (penetrating the marriage market by masquerading as an Arab woman in *The Sheik*, masquerading as a male racecar driver in *Sahara*), the White female protagonists' hubris, their failure to appreciate the Western males who protect them against desert Arabs, leads to a "fall" and the "pedagogical" chastening of attempted rape. The "homecoming" of this desert odyssey, then, is the disciplinary punishment of female fantasies of liberation and the spectator's renewed appreciation of the existing sexual, racial, and national-imperial order.

NOTES

1 Hayden White, *Tropics of Discourse* (Baltimore, Md.: Johns Hopkins University Press, 1978), p. 2.
2 For the view of tropes as repressive, see Harold Bloom, *A Map of Misreading* (New York: Oxford University Press, 1975), p. 91.
3 Quoted in David E. Stannard, *American Holocaust: Columbus and the Conquest of the New World* (New York: Oxford University Press, 1992).
4 See George L. Mosse, *Toward the Final Solution: A History of European Racism* (London: Dent, 1978).
5 James Snead, "Repitition as a Figure of Black Culture," in Russell Ferguson, Martha Gever, Trin T. Minh Ha, and Cornel West, eds., *Out There: Marginalization and Contemporary Cultures* (Cambridge, Mass.: MIT Press, 1990).
6 Ernst Renan, *The Future of Science* (Boston: Roberts Roberts, 1891), p. 153.
7 See Stephen Jay Gould, *The Mismeasure of Man* (New York: W.W. Norton, 1981), p. 40.
8 Cited in Jan Pieterse, *White on Black: Images of Africa and Blacks in Western Popular Culture* (New Haven, Conn.: Yale University Press, 1992), p. 89.
9 Within postwar cosmology, Carl Pletsch has suggested, the First World nations were seen as the most developed because shaped according to scientific, rational knowledge; the Second World nations were viewed as developed, but held back by socialist ideology; and the Third World was seen as "developing." See Carl Pletsch,

"The Three Worlds, or the Division of Social Scientific Labor, circa 1950–1970," *Comparative Studies in Society and History*, Vol. XXIII, No. 4 (1981), pp. 565–90.

10   See Edward Said's notion of the "feminization" of the orient in *Orientalism* (New York: Vintage, 1978); Francis Barker, Peter Hulme, Margaret Iversen, and Diana Loxley, eds, *Europe and Its Others*, Vols 1 and 2 (Colchester: University of Essex, 1985), especially Peter Hulme, "Polytropic Man: Tropes of Sexuality and Mobility in Early Colonial Discourse" (in Vol. 2) and Jose Rabasa, "Allegories of the Atlas" (in Vol. 2).

11   Samuel Eliot Morison, *Admiral of the Ocean Sea* (Boston: Little, Brown, 1942), Vol. I, p. 308.

12   Sir Walter Raleigh, "Discovery of Guiana." Cited in Susan Griffin, *Woman and Nature: The Roaring Inside Her* (New York: Harper and Row, 1978), p. 47. See also Louis Montrose, "The Work of Gender in the Discourse of Discovery," *Representations*, No. 33 (Winter 1991).

13   St John de Crevecoeur, *Letters from an American Farmer*, 1782. Cited in Henry Nash Smith, *Virgin Land: The American West as Symbol and Myth* (Cambridge, Mass.: Harvard University Press, 1950), p. 121.

14   See Smith, *Virgin Land*. For nineteenth-century North American expansionist ideology, see Richard Slotkin, *The Fatal Environment: The Myth of the Frontier in the Age of Industrialization, 1800–1890* (Middletown, Conn.: Wesleyan University Press, 1985).

15   Jerry Mander points out that when a Russian nuclear satellite fell out of orbit to earth in 1978, it was said to have broken in hundreds of bits along an "unpopulated icy wasteland" which was in fact inhabited by twenty-six communities of Dene and Inuit, who had been living there for 20,000 years. See Jerry Mander, *In the Absence of the Sacred* (San Francisco: Sierra Club Books, 1992), p. 99.

16   The cinema, in the American western or in the Israeli pioneer film, often relayed this discourse. For a discussion of the gendered representation of Palestine in Israeli cinema, see Ella Shohat, *Israeli Cinema: East/West and the Politics of Representation* (Austin: University of Texas Press, 1989).

17   On women and the American frontiers see Annette Kolodny, *The Lay of the Land: Metaphors as Experience and History in American Life and Letters* (Chapel Hill: University of North Carolina Press, 1975); and *The Land before Her: Fantasy and Experience of the American Frontiers, 1630–1860* (Chapel Hill: University of North Carolina Press, 1984).

18   R.W.B. Lewis, *The American Adam: Innocence, Tragedy, and Tradition in the Nineteenth Century* (Chicago: University of Chicago Press, 1959). Hans Blumenberg, interestingly, points out in relation to Francis Bacon that the restitution of paradise, as the goal of history, was supposed to promise magical facility. The knowledge of nature for him is connected to his definition of the paradisiac condition as mastery by means of the word. See Blumenberg, *The Legitimacy of the Modern Age*, trans. Robert Wallace (Cambridge, Mass.: MIT Press, 1983).

19   For population estimates, see Russel Thornton, *American Indian Holocaust and Survival: A Population History since 1492* (Norman: University of Oklahoma, 1987), pp. 22–5.

20   See Carol Kaesuk Yoon, "Rain Forests Seen as Shaped by Humans," *New York Times* (July 27, 1993), p. C1.

21   See Leonardo Boff, *America Latina: Da Conquista à Nova Evangelização* (São Paulo: Attica, 1992), p. 16.

22   See "Complex Farming Found in Amazon," *New York Times* (April 3, 1990), p. C12.

23   Alfred W. Crosby, "Virgin Soil Epidemics as a Factor in the Aboriginal Depopulation in America," *William and Mary Quarterly*, Third Series, No. 33 (1976), pp. 289–99.

24 Jan Van der Straet's representation of America has been cited by several scholars; Michel de Certeau, "Avant Propos," in his *L'Ecriture de l'Histoire* (Paris: Gallimard, 1975); Olivier Richon, "Representation, the Despot and the Harem: Some Questions around an Academic Orientalist Painting by Lecomte-du-Nouy (1885)," in Barker *et al.*, eds, *Europe and Its Others*, Vol. 1.

25 The gendered colonial encounter draws on a preexisting genderized discourse which opposes "man and nature." See Griffin, *Woman and Nature*; Carol MacCormack and Marilyn Strathern, eds, *Nature, Culture and Gender* (Cambridge: Cambridge University Press, 1980).

26 De Certeau, "Avant Propos."

27 Olga Martin, *Hollywood's Movie Commandments: Handbook for Motion Picture Writers and Reviewers* (New York: Scribners, 1937).

28 See for example Suleiman Mousa, *T.E. Lawrence: An Arab View*, trans. Albert Butros (New York: Oxford University Press, 1966).

29 For more on the sexualization of science, see Ludmilla Jordanova, *Sexual Visions: Images of Gender in Science and Medicine between the Eighteenth and Twentieth Centuries* (Madison: University of Wisconsin Press, 1988)

30 See Francis Bacon, *Advancement of Learning and Novum Organum* (New York: Colonial Press, 1899).

31 Ibid., p. 135.

32 Francis Bacon, "Novum Organum" in *The Works of Francis Bacon*, ed. James Spedding, Robert Ellis, and Douglas Heath (London: Longmans and Co., 1870), p. 82.

33 Here is the full Blumenberg quote:

> So much had remained concealed from the human spirit throughout many centuries and was discovered neither by philosophy nor by the faculty of reason but rather by accident and favorable opportunity, because it was all too different and distant from what was familiar, so that no preconception (*praenotio aliqua*) could lead one to it.
>
> (Blumenberg, *The Legitimacy of the Modern Age*, p. 389)

34 John Higham, "Indian Princess and Roman Goddess: The First Female Symbols of America," *Proceedings of the American Antiquarian Society*, No. 100 (1990), p. 48.

35 For an analysis of Haggard's *King Solomon's Mines* and the sexualization of maps, see Anne McClintock, "Maidens, Maps, and Mines: The Reinvention of Patriarchy in Colonial South Africa," *South Atlantic Quarterly*, Vol. 87, No. 1 (Winter 1988).

36 Bazin's Malraux-inspired statement in the opening of "The Ontology of the Photographic Image" attempts to offer a partial psychoanalysis of the cinema, suggesting that "at the origin of painting and sculpture there lies a mummy complex." (*What Is Cinema*, trans. Hugh Gray [Berkeley: University of California Press, 1967], p. 9.) The ritual of cinema, in this sense, is not unlike the Egyptian religious rituals which provided "a defense against the passage of time," thus satisfying "a basic psychological need in man, for death is but the victory of time." Bazin offers an existentialist interpretation of the mummy, which, at the same time, undermines Egyptian religion itself; since the ancient Egyptians above all axiomatically *assumed* the reality of life after death – toward which the mummy was no more than a means.

37 Said, *Orientalism*. One can posit at least seven subgenres of the Hollywood orientalist film: (1) stories concerning contemporary Westerners in the orient (*The Sheik*, 1921; *The Road to Morroco*, 1942; *Casablanca*, 1942; *The Man Who Knew Too Much*, 1956; *Raiders of the Lost Ark*, 1981; *Sahara*, 1983; *Ishtar*, 1987); (2) films concerning "orientals" in the First World (*Black Sunday*, 1977; *Back to the Future*, 1985); (3) films based on ancient history, such as the diverse versions of *Cleopatra*; (4) films based on contemporary history (*Exodus*, 1960; *Lawrence of Arabia*, 1962); (5) films

based on the Bible (*Judith of Bethulia*, 1913; *Samson and Delilah*, 1949; *The Ten Commandments*, 1956); (6) films based on *The Arabian Nights* (*The Thief of Baghdad*, 1924; *Oriental Dream*, 1944; *Kismet*, 1955); (7) films in which ancient Egypt and its mythologized enigmas serve as pretext for contemporary horror-mystery and romance (the *Mummy* series). See Ella Shohat, "Gender in Hollywood's Orient," *Merip*, No. 162 (January–February, 1990), pp. 40–3.

38   Mallek Alloula examines this issue in French postcards of Algeria. See *The Colonial Harem*, trans. Myrna Godzich and Wlad Godzich (Minneapolis: University of Minnesota Press, 1986).

39   Freud associates Africa and femininity in *The Interpretation of Dreams* when he speaks of Haggard's *She* as "a strange book, but full of hidden meaning . . . the eternal feminine . . . *She* describes an adventurous road that had scarcely even been trodden before, leading into an undiscovered region." *The Standard Edition of the Complete Psychological Works of Sigmund Freud*, ed. James Strachey (London: Hogarth Press and Institute of Psycho-Analysis), pp. 453–4.

40   Joseph Breuer and Sigmund Freud, *Studies on Hysteria*, trans. James Strachey in collaboration with Anna Freud (New York: Basic Books, 1957), p. 139.

41   Ibid., p. 193.

42   Sigmund Freud, "On Transformations of Instinct as Exemplified in Anal Eroticism," in *The Standard Edition of the Complete Psychological Works of Sigmund Freud*, 2nd edn., Vol. XVII, London: Hogarth Press, 1953–1974, pp. 129, 135.

43   Toril Moi, "Representation of Patriarchy: Sexuality and Epistemology in Freud's Dora," in Charles Brenheimer and Claire Kahane, eds., *In Dora's Case: Freud, Hysteria, Feminism* (London: Virago, 1985), p. 198.

44   Breuer and Freud, *Studies on Hysteria*, p. 292.

45   David Macey, *Lacan in Contexts* (London and New York: Verso, 1988), pp. 178–80.

46   Stephen Salisbury, "In Dr. Freud's Collection, Objects of Desire," *New York Times*, September 3, 1989.

47   Jordanova, *Sexual Visions*, p. 87.

48   Frantz Fanon, *The Wretched of the Earth*, trans. Constance Farrington (New York: Grove Press, 1964), p. 95.

49   Frantz Fanon, *Black Skin, White Masks*, trans. Charles Markmann (New York: Grove Press, 1967), p. 56. Fanon states: "The discoveries of Freud are of no use to us here" (p. 104). His critique, particularly of the concept of the family as the "source" of major psychoanalytical inquiry, is suggested through his repeated question about the possibility of applying the "family" model to the colonized. If the "family" is a miniature of the nation, he asks, then where would the colonized "fit"? For more on Fanon's reservations about psychoanalysis, see Patrick Taylor, *The Narrative of Liberation* (Ithaca, NY: Cornell University Press, 1989). On Fanon, Freud, and the "dark continent," see Ella Shohat, "Imaging Terra Incognita," *Public Culture*, Vol. 3, No. 2 (Spring 1991).

50   The notion of archeology is not separable from culture. If Freud elided patriarchal culture as part of his discussion of the (female) disorder, Fanon was involved in sociotherapy, which perceived pathology in historical terms. Fanon engages in an "archeology" of culture in order to understand madness in context. This is evident in the article coauthored with his colleague François Sanchez, "The Attitude of the Maghreb Muslim toward Madness." Any cure, Fanon argues, must take "native" history and tradition into account. See *Revue Pratique de Psychologie de la Vie Social et d'Hygiene Mentale*, No. 1 (1956).

51   Fanon, *The Wretched of the Earth*, p. 315.

52   Our reading of Fanon might seem to contradict certain emphases in his work. Fanon suggests, in a semi-materialist fashion, that "the discovery of the existence of a Negro

civilization in the fifteenth century confers no patent of humanity on me. Like it or not, the past can in no way guide me in the present moment" (*Black Skin, White Masks*, p. 225). Yet this point does not ultimately contradict the liberatory "structure of feelings" that the symbolic return to Africa offers colonized Blacks, and which Fanon himself discusses.

53 See Said, *Orientalism*, p. 177.

54 Linking Jews to the history, politics and culture of the West must be seen as continuous with Zionist discourse which has elided the, largely, Third World Arab history and culture of Middle Eastern Sephardic Jews. For a full discussion of the ethnic/racial problematics generated by Zionist discourse, see Ella Shohat, "Sephardim in Israel: Zionism from the Standpoint of Its Jewish Victims," *Social Text*, Nos 19/20 (Fall 1988). This debate was continued in part in *Critical Inquiry*, Vol. 15, No. 3 (Spring 1989) in the section "An Exchange on Edward Said and Difference"; see especially, Edward Said, "Response," pp. 634–46.

55 See Sally Price, *Primitive Art in Civilized Places* (Chicago: University of Chicago Press, 1989), p. 5.

56 Howard Carter and A.C. Mace's narrative of their predecessor's 1881 discovery, for example, links the Egyptologists' rescue of mummies to the ancient Egyptian priests' protection of their kings:

> There, huddled together in a shallow, ill-cut grave, lay the most powerful monarchs of the ancient east, kings whose names were familiar to the whole world, whom no one in his wildest moments had ever dreamed of seeing. There they had remained, where the priests in secrecy had hurriedly brought them that dark night three thousand years ago; and on their coffins and mummies, neatly docketed, were the records of their journeyings from one hiding place to another. Some had been wrapped, and two or three in the course of their many wanderings had been moved to other coffins. In forty-eight hours – we don't do things quite so hastily nowadays – the tomb was cleared; the kings were embarked upon the museum barge.

See Shirley Glubok, ed. *Discovering Tut-ankh-Amen's Tomb*, abridged and adapted from Howard Carter and A.C. Mace, *The Tomb of Tut-ankh-Amen*, (New York: Macmillan, 1968), p. 15.

57 In an interview following the screening of *The Mummy* on Egyptian television, Shadi Abdel Salam was criticized for relying on a Western musician when Egypt has its own musicians. Abdel Salam insisted that the Italian musician was chosen for his technical knowledge, and that his role was basically to arrange preexisting popular Egyptian music. Hassan Aawara, "*Al Mumia*," *Al Anba*, October 30, 1983 (in Arabic).

58 In addition to Edward Said's major critical writings on orientalist discourse on Egypt, see also Timothy Mitchell, *Colonising Egypt* (Cambridge: Cambridge University Press, 1988).

59 Glubok (ed.), *Discovering Tut-ankh-Amen's Tomb*, p. 15.

60 Guy Hennebelle, "Chadi Abdel Salam Prix Georges Sadoul 1970: "'La Momie' est une Réflexion sur le Destin d'une Culture Nationale," *Les Lettres Françaises*, No. 1366, December 30, 1977, p. 17.

61 This meditation on the mightiest pharoahs – "What Became of Them?" – recalls Shelley's "Ozymandias."

62 See *The Book of the Dead*, ed. E.A. Wallis Budge (London: Arkana, 1989).

63 The mystery in the *Mummy* films which often involves a kind of *Liebestod* or haunting heterosexual attraction – for example *The Mummy* (1932), *The Mummy's Curse* (1944), *The Mummy's Hand* (1940) – in this sense allegorizes the mysteries of sexuality itself.

64 In her autobiography, Harriet Jacobs focusses on the sexual oppression she suffered as a slave woman. Her daily struggle against racial/sexual abuse involved her master, determined to turn her into his concubine, his jealous wife, who added her own harassments, and a future Congressman, who, after fathering her children, did not keep his promise to set them free. *Incidents in the Life of a Slave Girl Written by Herself*, Fagan Yellin, ed. (Cambridge, Mass.: Harvard University Press, 1987).

65 Louise Picquet, *Louisa Picquet, the Octoroon: or, Inside Views of Southern Domestic Life* (New York: the author, 1860), pp. 50–2, cited in Manning Marable, *How Capitalism Underdeveloped Black America* (Boston: South End Press, 1983), p. 75.

66 Phyllis Rose, *Jazz Cleopatra* (New York: Random House, 1989), p. 97.

67 For example, Ferdinand-Victor-Eugene Delacroix, as Lawrence Michalak points out, borrowed Indian clothing from a set designer for his models, threw in some "Assyrian" motifs from travel books and Persian miniatures, and invented the rest of the Maghreb from his imagination. "Popular French Perspectives on the Maghreb: Orientalist Painting of the Late 19th and Early 20th Centuries," in *Connaissances du Maghreb: Sciences Sociales et Colonisation*, Jean-Claude Vatin, ed. (Paris: Editions du Centre National de la Recherche Scientifique, 1984).

68 For an analysis of interracial romance in *The King and I*, see Caren Kaplan, "Getting to Know You: Travel, Gender, and the Politics of Postcolonial Representations in *Anna and the King of Siam* and *The King and I*," in Ann Kaplan and Michael Sprinker, eds, *Crosscurrents: Late Imperial Culture* (London: Verso, 1994).

69 Citations from the Production Code of the Motion Picture Producers and Directors of America, Inc 1930–4 are taken from Garth Jowett, *Film: The Democratic Art* (Boston: Little, Brown, 1976).

70 Hazel V. Carby, "Lynching, Empire, and Sexuality," *Critical Inquiry*, Vol. 12, No. 1 (Autumn 1985).

71 On rape and racial violence see, for example, Jacquelyn Dowd Hall, "'The Mind that Burns in Each Body': Women, Rape, and Racial Violence," in Ann Snitow, Christine Stansell, and Sharon Thompson, eds., *Powers of Desire* (New York: Monthly Review Press, 1983).

72 Frantz Fanon, *A Dying Colonialism*, trans. Haakon Chevalier (New York: Grove Press, 1967), p. 66.

73 Aimé Césaire, "Introduction" to Victor Schoelcher, *Esclavage et Colonisation* (Paris: Presses Universitaires de France, 1948), p. 7.

74 Fellini's *8½*, meanwhile, mocks the protagonists's King Solomon-style harem as amplifying the protagonist's actual lived polygamy.

75 For the orientalist ideology undergirding the translations of *A Thousand and One Nights* to European languages, see Rana Kabbani, *Europe's Myths of Orient* (Bloomington: Indiana University Press, 1986).

76 See, for example, Huda Shaarawi, *Harem Years: The Memoirs of an Egyptian Feminist (1879–1924)*, trans. Margot Badran (New York: Feminist Press at City University of New York, 1987); Fatima Mernissi, *Dreams of Trespass: Tales of a Harem Girlhood* (Reading, Mass.: Addison-Wesley, 1994). See also Mervat Hatem, "The Politics of Sexuality and Gender in Segregated Partiarchal Systems," *Feminist Studies*, Vol. 12, No. 2 (Summer 1986).

77 For a critique of Eurocentric representation of the harem see Leila Ahmed, "Western Ethnocentrism and Perceptions of the Harem," *Feminist Studies*, Vol. 8, No. 3 (Fall 1982). See also Emily Apter, "Female Trouble in the Colonial Harem," *Differences*, Vol. 4, No. 1 (1992); Inderpal Grewal, *Home and Harem: Imperialism, Nationalism and the Culture of Travel* (Durham, NC: Duke University Press, forthcoming 1995).

78 The artistic representation of the solitary confinement of upper-middle-class Western women within the household is fascinatingly researched and analyzed by Bram

Dijkstra, *Idols of Perversity* (New York: Oxford University Press, 1986).

79 For a critique of Western feminism and colonial discourse see, for example, Chandra Talpade Mohanty, "Under Western Eyes: Feminist Scholarship and Colonial Discourses," *Boundary*, Vol. 2, No. 12 (Spring/Fall 1984); Gayatri Chakravorty Spivak, *In Other Worlds: Essays in Cultural Politics*, Chapter 3: "Entering the Third World" (New York and London: Metheun, 1987); Marnia Lazreg, "Feminism and Difference: The Perils of Writing as a Woman on Women in Algeria," *Feminist Studies*, Vol. 14, No. 3 (Fall 1988).

80 Robert Halsband, ed., *The Complete Letters of Lady Mary Wortley Montagu*, Vol. I (Oxford: Oxford University Press, 1965), p. 314.

81 Robert Halsband, ed., *The Selected Letters of Lady Mary Wortley Montagu* (New York: St. Martin's Press, 1970), pp. 96–7.

82 Halsband, ed., *The Complete Letters of Lady Mary Wortley Montagu*, Vol. I, pp. 314–15.

83 For an analysis of the "mechanical reproduction" of women in Busby Berkeley's films, see Lucy Fischer, "The Image of Woman as Image: The Optical Politics of *Dames*," in Patricia Erens, ed., *Sexual Strategems: The World of Women in Film* (New York: Horizon Press, 1979).

84 Quoted in Fischer, "The Image of Woman as Image," p. 44.

85 See Fatima Mernissi, *The Forgotton Queens of Islam*, trans. Mary Jo Lakeland (Minneapolis: University of Minnesota Press, 1993).

86 See, for example, Cynthia Enloe, *Bananas, Beaches, and Bases: Making Feminist Sense of International Politics* (Berkeley: University of California Press, 1989), pp. 19–41. See also Nupur Chaudhuri and Margaret Strobel, eds, *Western Women and Imperialism: Complicity and Resistance* (Bloomington: Indiana University Press, 1992); Vron Ware, *Beyond the Pale: White Women, Racism and History* (London: Verso, 1992); Margaret Strobel, *European Women in British Africa and Asia* (Bloomington: Indiana University Press, 1990).

87 The White-woman's-burden ideology in films like *The King and I* (1956) and *Out of Africa* (1985) contrasts with the view advanced in such films as Ousmane Sembene's *La Noire de ...* (Black Girl, 1966), where the relationship between the Senegalese maid and her French woman employer is clearly oppressive, or with the relationship portrayed in Mira Hamermesh's documentary on South Africa, *Maids and Madams* (1985).

88 See J.C. Flugel, *The Psychology of Clothes* (London: Hogarth Press, 1930). For an extended discussion of Flugel's writing on fashion see Kaja Silverman, "The Fragments of a Fashionable Discourse," in *Studies in Entertainment: Critical Approaches to Mass Culture*, ed. Tania Modleski (Bloomington: Indiana University Press, 1986); also see Kaja Silverman, *The Acoustic Mirror: The Female Voice in Psychoanalysis and Cinema* (Bloomington: Indiana University Press, 1988), pp. 24–7.

89 The American journalist Lowell Thomas was instrumental in the popularization of the T.E. Lawrence myth in the West; his show, which consisted of lecture and footage he shot from the Middle East front, was, after a short time, moved to Madison Square Garden. See John E. Mack, *A Prince of Our Disorder: The Life of T.E. Lawrence* (Boston: Little, Brown, 1976), p. 276.

90 Leslie Fiedler argues that homoerotic friendship between White men and Black or indigenous men is at the core of the classic American novel. See Fiedler, *Love and Death in the American Novel* (New York: Criterion Books, 1960).

91 Interestingly, Leslie Fiedler's *The Inadvertent Epic* comments on another White woman novelist, Margaret Mitchel, whose *Gone With the Wind* is structured according to scenarios of interethnic rapes.

92   For an analysis of Valentino and White female spectatorship, see Miriam Hansen, "Pleasure, Ambivalence, Identification: Valentino and Female Spectatorship," *Cinema Journal*, Vol. 25, No. 4 (Summer 1986).

93   *Movie Weekly*, November 19, 1921.

94   Ibid.

95   Denis de Rougement traces the *Liebestod* motif in part to Arabic poetry. See de Rougement, *Love in the Western World*, trans. Montgomery Belgion (New York: Harper and Row, 1974).

5

STEREOTYPE, REALISM AND THE STRUGGLE OVER REPRESENTATION

Much of the work on ethnic/racial and colonial representation in the media has been "corrective," devoted to demonstrating that certain films, in some respect or other, "got something wrong" on historical, biographical, or other grounds of accuracy. While these "stereotypes and distortions" analyses pose legitimate questions about social plausibility and mimetic accuracy, about negative and positive images, they are often premised on an exclusive allegiance to an esthetic of verisimilitude.[1] An obsession with "realism" casts the question as simply one of "errors" and "distortions," as if the "truth" of a community were unproblematic, transparent, and easily accessible, and "lies" about that community easily unmasked. Debates about ethnic representation often break down on precisely this question of "realism," at times leading to an impasse in which diverse spectators or critics passionately defend their version of the "real."

THE QUESTION OF REALISM

These debates about realism and accuracy are not trivial, not just a symptom of the "veristic idiocy," as a certain poststructuralism would have it. Spectators (and critics) are invested in realism because they are invested in the idea of truth, and reserve the right to confront a film with their own personal and cultural knowledge. No deconstructionist fervor should induce us to surrender the right to find certain films sociologically false or ideologically pernicious, to see *Birth of a Nation* (1915), for example, as an "objectively" racist film. That films are only representations does not prevent them from having real effects in the world; racist films can mobilize for the Ku Klux Klan, or prepare the ground for retrograde social policy. Recognizing the inevitability and the inescapability of representation does not mean, as Stuart Hall has put it, that "nothing is at stake."

The desire to reserve a right to judgment on questions of realism comes into play especially in cases where there are real-life prototypes for characters and situations, and where the film, whatever its conventional disclaimers, implicitly makes, and is received as making, historical-realist claims. (Isaac Julien's *Looking for Langston*, 1989, dodges the problem through a generic "end run" by labeling itself as a "meditation" on Langston Hughes.) The veterans of the 1960s

Plate 33 History whitewashed in *Mississippi Burning*

civil rights struggle are surely in a position to critique *Mississippi Burning* (1988) for turning the movement's historical enemy – the racist FBI which harassed and sabotaged the movement – into the film's heroes, while turning the historical heroes – the thousands of African-Americans who marched and braved beatings and imprisonment and sometimes death – into the supporting cast, passive victim-observers waiting for official White rescue.[2] This struggle over meaning matters because *Mississippi Burning* might induce audiences unfamiliar with the facts into a fundamental misreading of American history, idealizing the FBI and regarding African-Americans as mute witnesses of history rather than its makers.[3] Thus although there is no absolute truth, no truth apart from representation and dissemination, there are still contingent, qualified, perspectival truths in which communities are invested.

Poststructuralist theory reminds us that we live and dwell within language and representation, and have no direct access to the "real." But the constructed, coded nature of artistic discourse hardly precludes all reference to a common social life. Filmic fictions inevitably bring into play real-life assumptions not only about space and time but also about social and cultural relationships. Films which represent marginalized cultures in a realistic mode, even when they do not claim to represent specific historical incidents, still implicitly make factual claims. Thus critics are right to draw attention to the complacent ignorance of Hollywood portrayals of Native Americans, to the cultural flattening which erases the geographical and cultural differences between Great Plains tribes and those from other regions, which have Indians of the northeast wearing Plains Indians clothing and living in Hopi dwellings, all collapsed into a single stereotypical figure, the "instant Indian" with "wig, war bonnet, breechclout, moccasins, phony bead-work."[4]

Many oppressed groups have used "progressive realism" to unmask and combat hegemonic representations, countering the objectifying discourses of patriarchy and colonialism with a vision of themselves and their reality "from within." But this laudable intention is not always unproblematic. "Reality" is not self-evidently given and "truth" is not immediately "seizable" by the camera. We must distinguish, furthermore, between realism as a goal – Brecht's "laying bare the causal network" – and realism as a style or constellation of strategies aimed at producing an illusionistic "reality effect." Realism as a goal is quite compatable with a style which is reflexive and deconstructive, as is eloquently demonstrated by many of the alternative films discussed in this book.

In his work, Mikhail Bakhtin reformulates the notion of artistic representation in such a way as to avoid both a naive faith in "truth" and "reality" and the equally naive notion that the ubiquity of language and representation signifies the end of struggle and the "end of history." Human consciousness and artistic practice, Bakhtin argues, do not come into contact with the "real" directly but rather through the medium of the surrounding ideological world. Literature, and by extension cinema, do not so much refer to or call up the world as represent its languages and discourses. Rather than directly reflecting the real, or even refracting the real, artistic discourse constitutes a refraction of a refraction; that is, a mediated version of an already textualized and "discursivized" socioideo-logical world. This formulation transcends a naive referential verism without falling into a "hermeneutic nihilism" whereby all texts become nothing more than a meaningless play of signification. Bakhtin rejects naive formulations of realism, in other words, without abandoning the notion that artistic representations are at the same time thoroughly and irrevocably social, precisely because the discourses that art represents are *themselves* social and historical. Indeed, for Bakhtin art is incontrovertibly social, not because it represents the real but because it constitutes a historically situated "utterance" – a complex of signs addressed by one socially constituted subject or subjects to other socially constituted subjects, all of whom are deeply immersed in historical circumstance and social contingency.

The issue, then, is less one of fidelity to a preexisting truth or reality than one of a specific orchestration of ideological discourses and communitarian per-spectives. While on one level film is mimesis, representation, it is also utterance, an act of contextualized interlocution between socially situated producers and receivers. It is not enough to say that art is constructed. We have to ask: Constructed for whom? And in conjunction with which ideologies and dis-courses? In this sense, art is a representation not so much in a mimetic as a political sense, as a delegation of voice.[5] Within this perspective, it makes more sense to say of The Gods Must Be Crazy (1984) not that it is untrue to "reality," but that it relays the colonialist discourse of official White South Africa. The racist discourse of the film posits a Manichean binarism contrasting happy and noble but impotent Bantustan "Bushmen," living in splendid isolation, with dangerous but incompetent mulatto-led revolutionaries. Yet the film camouflages its racism by a superficial critique of White technological civilization. A discursive approach to *First Blood (Rambo)* (1983), similarly, would not argue that it "distorts" reality, but rather that it "really" represents a rightist and racist discourse designed to flatter and nourish the masculinist fantasies of omnipotence characteristic of an empire in crisis. By the same token, representations can be convincingly verisimilar, yet Eurocentric, or conversely, fantastically "inaccurate," yet anti-Eurocentric. The analysis of a film like *My Beautiful Laundrette* (1985), sociologically flawed from a mimetic perspective – given its focus on wealthy Asians rather than more typically working-class Asians in London – alters considerably when regarded as a constellation of discursive strategies, as a provocative symbolic inversion of conventional expectations of a miserabilist account of Asian victimization.

That something vital is at stake in these debates becomes obvious in those instances when entire communities passionately protest the representations that are made of them in the name of their own experiential sense of truth. Hollywood stereotypes have not gone unremarked by the communities they portrayed. Native Americans, very early on, vocally protested misrepresentations of their culture and history.[6] A 1911 issue of *Moving Picture World* (August 3) reports a Native American delegation to President Taft protesting erroneous representations and even asking for a Congressional investigation. In the same vein, the National Association for the Advancement of Colored People (NAACP) protested *Birth of a Nation*, Chicanos protested the *bandido* films, Mexicans protested *Viva Villa!* (1934), Brazilians protested *Rio's Road to Hell* (1931), Cubans protested *Cuban Love Song* (1931), and Latin Americans generally protested the caricaturing of their culture. The Mexican government threatened to block distribution of Hollywood films in Mexico if the US film industry did not stop exporting films caricaturing Mexico, Mexican Americans, and the Mexican revolution. More recently, Turks protested *Midnight Express* (1978), Puerto Ricans protested *Fort Apache the Bronx* (1981), Africans protested *Out of Africa* (1985) and Asian-Americans protested *The Year of the Dragon* (1985). Native Americans so vigorously protested the TV series *Mystic Warrior*, based on Ruth Beebe Hill's Ayn Rand-inflected pseudo-Indian saga *Hanta Yo* (1979), that the film version could not be made in the US. One American Indian Movement pamphlet distributed during protests offered ironic guidelines on "How to Make an Indian Movie":

How to make an Indian Movie. Buy 40 Indians. Totally humiliate and degrade an entire Indian nation. Make sure all Indians are savage, cruel and ignorant ... Import a Greek to be an Indian princess. Introduce a white man to become an "Indian" hero. Make the white man compassionate, brave and understanding ... Pocket the profits in Hollywood.

181

Critical spectators can thus exert pressure on distribution and exhibition, and even affect subsequent productions. While such pressure does not guarantee sympathetic representations, it does at least mean that aggressively hurtful portrayals will not go unchallenged.

Although total realism is a theoretical impossibility, then, spectators themselves come equipped with a "sense of the real" rooted in their own experience, on the basis of which they can accept, question, or even subvert a film's representations. In this sense, the cultural preparation of a particular audience can generate counter-pressure to a racist or prejudicial discourse. Latin American audiences laughed Hollywood's know-nothing portrayals of them off the screen, finding it impossible to take such misinformed images seriously. The Spanish-language version of *Dracula*, for example, made concurrently with the 1931 Bela Lugosi film, mingled Cuban, Argentine, Chilean, Mexican, and peninsular Spanish in a linguistic hodge-podge that struck Latin American audiences as ludicrous. At the same time, spectators may look beyond caricatural representations to see the oppressed performing self. African-Americans were not likely to take Step'n Fetchit as a typical, synecdochic sample of Black behavior or attitudes; Black audiences knew he was acting, and understood the circumstances that led him to play subservient roles. In the same vein, in a kind of double consciousness, spectators may enjoy what they know to be misrepresentations; Baghdadi spectators could enjoy *The Thief of Baghdad* (1940), for example, because they took it as an escapist fantasy, as a Western embroidery of an already fantastic tale from *A Thousand and One Nights*, with no relation to the "real" historical Baghdad.

THE BURDEN OF REPRESENTATION

The hair-trigger sensitivity about racial stereotypes derives partly from what has been labeled the "burden of representation." The connotations of "representation" are at once religious, esthetic, political, and semiotic. On a religious level, the Judeo-Islamic censure of "graven images" and the preference for abstract representations such as the arabesque cast theological suspicion on directly figurative representation and thus on the very ontology of the mimetic arts.[7] Representation also has an esthetic dimension, in that art too is a form of representation, in Platonic or Aristotelian terms, a mimesis. Representation is theatrical too, and in many languages "to represent" means "to enact" or play a role. The narrative and mimetic arts, to the extent that they represent ethos (character) and ethnos (peoples) are considered representative not only of the human figure but also of anthropomorphic vision. On another level, representation is also political, in that political rule is not usually direct but representative. Marx said of the peasantry that "they do not represent themselves; they must be represented." The contemporary definition of democracy in the West, unlike the classical Athenian concept of democracy, or that of various Native American communities, rests on the notion of "representative government," as in the

182

rallying cry of "No taxation without representation." Many of the political debates around race and gender in the US have revolved around the question of self-representation, seen in the pressure for more "minority" representation in political and academic institutions. What all these instances share is the semiotic principle that something is "standing for" something else, or that some person or group is speaking on behalf of some other persons or groups. On the symbolic battlegrounds of the mass media, the struggle over representation in the simulacral realm homologizes that of the political sphere, where questions of imitation and representation easily slide into issues of delegation and voice. The heated debate around which celebrity photographs, whether of Italian-Americans or of African-Americans, will adorn the wall of Sal's Pizzeria in Spike Lee's *Do the Right Thing* (1989) vividly exemplifies this kind of struggle within representation.

Since what Memmi calls the "mark of the plural" projects colonized people as "all the same," any negative behavior by any member of the oppressed community is instantly generalized as typical, as pointing to a perpetual backsliding toward some presumed negative essence. Representations thus become allegorical; within hegemonic discourse every subaltern performer/role is seen as synecdochically summing up a vast but putatively homogenous community. Representations of dominant groups, on the other hand, are seen not as allegorical but as "naturally" diverse, examples of the ungeneralizable variety of life itself.[8] Socially empowered groups need not be unduly concerned about "distortions and stereotypes," since even occasionally negative images form part of a wide spectrum of representations. A corrupt White politician is not seen as an "embarrassment to the race;" financial scandals are not seen as a negative reflection on White power. Yet each negative image of an underrepresented group becomes, within the hermeneutics of domination, sorely overcharged with allegorical meaning as part of what Michael Rogin calls the "surplus symbolic value" of oppressed people; the way Blacks, for example, can be made to stand for something beside themselves.[9]

This sensitivity operates on a continuum with other representations and with everyday life, where the "burden" can indeed become almost unbearable. It is this continuum that is ignored when analysts place stereotypes of so-called ethnic Americans, for example, on the same level as those of Native Americans or African-Americans. While all negative stereotypes are hurtful, they do not all exercise the same power in the world. The facile catch-all invocation of "stereotypes" elides a crucial distinction: stereotypes of some communities merely make the target group uncomfortable, but the community has the social power to combat and resist them; stereotypes of other communities participate in a continuum of prejudicial social policy and actual violence against dis-empowered people, placing the very body of the accused in jeopardy. Stereotypes of Polish-Americans and Italian-Americans, however regrettable, have not been shaped within the racial and imperial foundation of the US, and are not used to justify daily violence or structural oppression against these communities. The media's tendency to present all Black males as potential delinquents, in contrast, has a searing impact on the actual lives of Black people. In the Stuart case in Boston, the police, at the instigation of the actual (White) murderer, interrogated and searched as many Black men as they could in a Black neighborhood, a measure unthinkable in White neighborhoods, which are rarely seen as representational sites of crime. In the same way, the 1988 Bush campaign's "allegorical" deployment of the "Black buck" figure of Willie Horton to trigger the sexual and racial phobias of White voters, dramatically sharpened the burden of representation carried by millions of Black men, and indirectly by Black women.

The sensitivity around stereotypes and distortions largely arises, then, from the powerlessness of historically marginalized groups to control their own representation. A full understanding of media representation therefore requires a comprehensive analysis of the institutions that generate and distribute mass-mediated texts as well as of the audience that receives them. Whose stories are told? By whom? How are they manufactured, disseminated, received? What are the structural mechanisms of the film and media industry? Who controls production, distribution, exhibition? In the US, in 1942, the NAACP made a compact with the Hollywood studios to integrate Blacks into the ranks of studio technicians, yet very few have become directors, scriptwriters, or cinematographers. Minority directors of *all* racial groups constitute less than 3 per cent of the membership of the almost 4,000-member Directors' Guild of America.[10] An agreement between several film unions and the US Justice Department in 1970 required that minorities be integrated into the industry's general labor pools, but the agreement's good intentions were undercut by growing unemployment throughout the industry and by a seniority system that favored older (therefore White male) members. The most recent report on Hollywood employment practices released by the NAACP reveals that Blacks are underrepresented in "each and every aspect" of the entertainment industry. The 1991 study, entitled "Out of Focus – Out of Synch," claims that Blacks are unable to make final decisions in the motion picture process. Despite the success of people like Oprah Winfrey, Bill Cosby, and Arsenio Hall, only a handful of African-Americans hold executive positions within film studios and television networks. Although Blacks purchase a disproportionate share of domestic movie tickets, nepotism, cronyism, and racial discrimination combine to bar Blacks and Black-owned businesses from the industry.[11] Spike Lee speaks of a "glass ceiling" restricting how much money will be spent on Black-made films, based on the assumption that Blacks cannot be trusted with large sums of money.[12] And Blacks are not the only disadvantaged group in this respect. While producers assume that Italian-American directors should direct films about Italian Americans, for example, they choose Anglos to direct films about Latinos.[13]

Furthermore, in that the Hollywood system favors big-budget blockbusters, it is not only classist but also Eurocentric, in effect if not in explicit intention; to be a player in this game one needs to have economic power. Third World filmmakers are asked, in practice, to worship an unreachable standard of cinematic "civility." Moreover, many Third World countries themselves reinforce hegemony by discriminating against their own cultural productions. (Brazilian TV, for example, systematically favors American films.) In the news and information fields, similarly, it is First World institutions (CNN, AP, and the rest) that provide the filter for the world's news. Distribution advantages too tend to lie with the First World countries. Hollywood films often arrive in the Third World "preadvertised," in that much of the media hype revolving around big-budget productions reaches the Third World through journalistic articles and TV even before these films are released locally. American popular music also buttresses the dissemination of Hollywood films, with movies such as *Saturday Night Fever* (1977), *Purple Rain* (1984), *Truth or Dare* (1991), and *The Bodyguard* (1992) all arriving preadvertised by airtime, given that their music has been played on multinational-dominated radio and TV. Even the Oscar ceremonies constitute a powerful form of advertising; the audience is global, yet the product promoted is almost always American, the "rest of the world" usually being corraled into the restricted category of "foreign film."

The "Third World," then, is doubly weakened by cinematic neocolonialism. Brazilian filmmaker/poet Arnaldo Jabor has denounced this situation in an incendiary poem entitled "Jack Valenti's Brazilian Agenda":

> Jack Valenti,
> with Republican grin, star-spangled tie,
> diamond smile and the pale semblance of the perfect
> executive
> hints of Dick Tracy, George Wallace, Westmoreland, Liberace,
> Billy Graham, and so many other robots of infinite guffaw,
> at exactly this moment
> with his portfolio of indestructible designs
> and the audacity that our Foreign Debt has lately given
> international executives,
> Jack Valenti will descend from his astral airplane
> into the land of promised and overdue payments

Jabor inventories the psychic deformations caused by Hollywood:

> ... under Valenti's non-Brazilian shoes
> the red carpets of hospitality will roll
> and no one will see the cinematic crimes in the air
> nor the remains of our poor dead minds,
> no one will see the wounds
> since there will be no corpse
> no coroner to discover the bruises in our soul
> purple wounds, pink wounds, rainbow wounds
> stardust in our eyes, the tatooed people we have become

> of Hollywood's thousand and one adventures
> invisible victims of a thousand dazzling fairy wounds
> Eastmancolor burns
> seven-colored napalm
> kodak-yellow of our hunger

For Jabor, even dominant narrative conventions form part of an imperial mindset:

> ... In a few hours,
> Valenti will take from his portfolio of indestructible designs
> the most sacred values of the imperial Occident:
> logic, symmetry, continuity,
> beginning, middle, end,
> the happy end, the "individual" and
> the sinister American vision of goodness.[14]

Jabor's poem assumes a situation in which Hollywood films, with easy access to Third World distribution circuits, display tantalizingly opulent production values virtually impossible for the Third World to emulate and often inappropriate to its concerns. The astronomical budget of one First World blockbuster may be the equivalent of decades of production for a Third World country. As such films bludgeon audiences with their maximum-impact Dolby Sound thrill-a-minute style, they create what one might call a "Spielberg effect" of seduction and intimidation for Third World filmmakers and spectators. At the same time, economic neocolonialism and technological dependency raise filmmaking costs in the Third World itself, where imported film, cameras, and accessories often cost two or three times as much as in the "First World." Even well-established Third World filmmakers are likely to find their work blocked by First World-dominated channels of distribution, and when US distributors buy their films it is often at derisory prices. Major Arab filmmakers – the Egyptian Youssef Chahine, for example – have rarely enjoyed commercial openings in the US. Even radical directors remain dependent on multinational companies for their equipment and film stock. And the film stocks themselves may be said to discriminate against darker-complected people: they are sensitive to particular skin tones and must be "stopped down" or specially lit for others. In *A Diary of a Young Soul Rebel*, Isaac Julien attributes the difficulty in lighting dark and light skin in the same frame to the fact that film technology favors lighter skin tones.[15] The celluloid itself is racially inscribed.

The Eurocentrism of audiences can also inflect cinematic production. Here the dominant audience, whose ideological assumptions must be respected if a film is to be successful, or even made at all, exerts a kind of indirect hegemony. "Universal" becomes a codeword for palatable to the Western spectator as the "spoiled child" of the apparatus. A number of big-budget anti-apartheid films – *Cry Freedom* (1987), *A World Apart* (1988), and *A Dry White Season* (1989) – betray traces of "representational adjustments" as the values of a radical liberation

186

struggle are watered down for a predominantly liberal American audience. In these films, Rob Nixon argues, the challenge of bridging cultural difference becomes "overlaid with problems of profound ideological incompatibility." As a result, the story of Steve Biko in *Cry Freedom* gives way to a story of the "friendship that rocked the world." The radical discourse of the Black Consciousness movement is replaced with a "palatable liberal discourse of moral decency and human rights." Nixon contrasts the experience of *Cry Freedom* with the more radical *Mapantsula* (1989), a film that, simply to be made, had to disguise itself as an "apolitical gangster movie." In *Mapantsula*, moralistic concerns do not shoulder aside strategic institutional questions. The film's refusal to observe the "mass market conventions of translating a radical South African narrative into a white-mediated, liberal idiom" resulted in its failure to draw a major distributor.[16]

The production processes of individual films, their means of production and relations of production, bring up questions concerning the filmmaking apparatus and the participation of "minorities" within that apparatus. It seems noteworthy, for example, that in multiethnic but White-dominated societies such as South Africa, Brazil, and the US, Blacks have tended to participate in the filmmaking process mainly as performers rather than as producers, directors, and scriptwriters. In South Africa, Whites finance, script, direct, and produce films with all-Black casts. In the US in the 1920s, all-White filmmaking crews shot all-Black musicals like *Hearts in Dixie* (1929) and *Hallelujah* (1929). Blacks appeared in these films, just as women still frequently do in Hollywood, as images in spectacles whose social thrust is primarily shaped by others: "Black souls as White man's artifact" (Fanon). And since commercial films are designed to make profits, we must also ask to whom these profits go. J. Uys, the director of *The Gods Must Be Crazy*, paid his star actor N!Xau only 2,000 Rand for *Gods I* and 5,000 Rand for *Gods II*.[17] Similarly, it was not blacks who profited from the American blaxploitation films of the early 1970s; these films were financed, produced, and packaged by the same Whites who received the lion's share of the profits. The thousands of Black Brazilians who played at an out-of-season carnival, with virtually no pay, for the benefit of Marcel Camus' French cameras, never saw any of the millions of dollars that *Black Orpheus* (1959) made around the world.[18]

To a certain extent, a film inevitably mirrors its own processes of production as well as larger social processes. At times, minoritarian filmmakers directing films about police harassment have themselves been harassed by police. During the making of Haile Gerima's *Bush Mama* (1975), a film partly about police repression in the inner cities, the crew members themselves became police targets; Black men with cameras, the police assumed, like Black men with guns, could be up to no good.[19] In other cases, we find a contradiction between a film's overt politics and its politics of production. The presumably anticolonial film *Gandhi* (1982), dedicated to the patron saint of non-violent struggle, deployed a differential pay scale that favored European technicians and performers. In

Hearts of Darkness (1989), the documentary about the production of *Apocalypse Now* (1979), Francis Ford Coppola speaks of the low cost of Filipino labor. In this sense he inherits the same privileges accorded the corporate manager who relocates to the Third World to take advantage of local cheap labor.

Victor Masayesva's *Imagining Indians* (1992) explores the commodification inflicted on Native American culture when it is filtered through a Eurocentric industry, even when those doing the filtering are "sympathetic to the Indian." More precisely, the film examines the problematic negotiations between the Hopi and the producers of *Dark Wind*, a film shot on Hopi land (not yet released at the time of writing). Combining interviews with native extras on Hollywood films, excerpts from the films discussed, sequences showing sacred sites, and a staged story of a native woman's encounter with a condescending White dentist, the film shows the tribal elders raising objections to the project but ultimately going along with it, in a process that recalls the treaty negotiations between indigenous nations and the US government. At times, native resistance has been more aggressive. When Werner Herzog tried to film *Fitzcarraldo* (1982) with Aguaruna Indians, the newly formed Aguaruna Council objected, refusing to be represented in the way Herzog planned, and even surrounded Herzog's camp and forced the crew to move downriver.[20]

The importance of the participation of colonized or formerly colonized people in the process of production becomes obvious when we compare Gillo Pontecorvo's *La Battaglia di Algeria* (Battle of Algiers, 1966) to his later *Burn* (1970). In the former film, a relatively low-budget ($800,000) Italian-Algerian co-production, Algerian non-professional actors represent themselves in a staged reconstruction of the Algerian war of independence. The Algerians were intimately involved in every aspect of the production, with actors often playing their own historical roles at the very sites where the events took place. They collaborated closely with screenwriter Franco Solanas, who rewrote the scenario numerous times in response to their critiques and observations. As a result, the Algerians exist as socially complex people, and as agents of national struggle. Pontecorvo's multimillion dollar *Burn*, on the other hand, involved no such collaboration. An Italo-French co-production, the film casts Marlon Brando as a British colonial agent against Evaristo Marques, a non-professional actor of peasant background. By pitting one of the First World's most charismatic actors against a completely inexperienced Third World non-professional chosen only for his physiognomy, Pontecorvo, while on one level subverting the star system, on another disastrously tips the scales of spectatorial fascination in favor of the colonizer, in a film whose didactic intention, ironically, was to support anticolonial struggle. The lack of Caribbean participation in the film's production leads to a one-dimensional portrayal of the colonized, seen as shadowy figures devoid of cultural definition.

THE RACIAL POLITICS OF CASTING

Film and theater casting, as an immediate form of representation, constitutes a kind of delegation of voice with political overtones. Here too Europeans and Euro-Americans have played the dominant role, relegating non-Europeans to supporting roles and the status of extras. Within Hollywood cinema, Euro-Americans have historically enjoyed the unilateral prerogative of acting in "blackface," "redface," "brownface," and "yellowface," while the reverse has rarely been the case. From the nineteenth-century vaudeville stage through such figures as Al Jolson in *Hi Lo Broadway* (1933), Fred Astaire in *Swing Time* (1936), Mickey Rooney and Judy Garland in *Babes in Arms* (1939), and Bing Crosby in *Dixie* (1943), the tradition of blackface recital furnished one of the most popular of American pop-cultural forms. Even Black minstrel performers like Bert Williams, as the film *Ethnic Notions* (1987) points out, were obliged to carry the mark of caricature on their own bodies; burnt cork literalized, as it were, the trope of Blackness.

Political considerations in racial casting were quite overt in the silent period. In *The Birth of a Nation* subservient Negroes were played by actual Blacks, while aggressive, threatening Blacks were played largely by Whites in blackface. But after protests by the NAACP, Hollywood cautiously began to cast black actors in small roles. Nevertheless, even in the sound period, White actresses were called on to play the "tragic mulattas" of such films as *Pinky* (1949), *Imitation of Life* (1959), and even of the Cassavetes underground film *Shadows* (1959). Meanwhile, real-life "mulattas" were cast for Black female roles – for example Lena Horne in *Cabin in the Sky* (1943) – although they could easily have "passed" for White roles. In other words, it is not the literal color of the actor that mattered in casting. Given the "blood" definition of "Black" versus "White" in Euro-American racist discourse, one drop of "Black blood" was sufficient to disqualify an actress like Horne from representing White women.

African-Americans were not the only "people of color" to be played by Euro-Americans; the same law of unilateral privilege functioned in relation to other groups. Rock Hudson, Joey Bishop, Boris Karloff, Tom Mix, Elvis Presley, Anne Bancroft, Cyd Charisse, Loretta Young, Mary Pickford, Dame Judith Anderson and Douglas Fairbanks Jr are among the many Euro-American actors who have represented Native American roles, while Paul Muni, Charlton Heston, Marlon Brando, and Natalie Wood are among those who have played Latino characters. As late as *Windwalker* (1973), the most important Indian roles were not played by Native Americans. Dominant cinema is fond of turning "dark" or Third World peoples into substitutable others, interchangeable units who can "stand in" for one another. Thus the Mexican Dolores del Rio played a South Seas Samoan in *Bird of Paradise* (1932), while the Indian Sabu played a wide range of Arab-oriental roles. Lupe Velez, actually Mexican, portrayed Chinese, "Eskimos" (Inuit), Japanese, Malayans, and American-Indian women, while Omar Sharif, an Egyptian, played Che Guevara.[21] This asymmetry in representational power has generated intense resentment among minoritarian communities, for whom the casting of a non-member of the "minority" group is a triple insult, implying (a) you are unworthy of self-represention; (b) no one from your community is capable of representing you; and (c) we, the producers of the film, care little about your offended sensibilities, for we have the power and there is nothing you can do about it.

These practices have implications even on the brute material level of literal self-representation, that is, the need for work. The racist idea that a film, to be economically viable, must use a "universal" (i.e. white) star, reveals the intrication of economics and racism. That people of color have historically been limited to racially designated roles, while Whites are ideologically seen as "beyond" ethnicity, has had disastrous consequences for "minority" artists. In Hollywood, this situation is only now changing, with star actors like Larry Fishburne, Wesley Snipes, and Denzel Washington winning roles originally earmarked for White actors. At the same time, even "affirmative action" casting can serve racist purposes, as when the role of the White judge in the novel *Bonfire of the Vanities* (1990) was given to Morgan Freeman in the Brian de Palma film, but only as a defense mechanism to ward off accusations of racism.

Nor does chromatically literal self-representation guarantee non-Eurocentric representation. The system can simply "use" the performer to enact the dominant set of codes; even, at times, over the performer's objection. Josephine Baker's star status did not enable her to alter the ending of *Princess Tam Tam* (1935) to have her North African (Berber) character marry the French aristocrat instead of the North African servant, or to marry the working-class Frenchman played by Jean Gabin in *Zou Zou* (1934). Instead, Zou Zou ends up alone, performing as a caged bird pining for the Caribbean. Despite her protests, Baker's roles were circumscribed by the codes that forbade her screen access to White men as legitimate marriage partners. Their excessive performance styles allowed actresses like Josephine Baker and Carmen Miranda to undercut and parody stereotypical roles, but could not gain them substantive power. Even the expressive performance of the politically aware Paul Robeson was enlisted, despite the actor's protests, in the encomium to European colonialism in Africa that is *Sanders of the River* (1935). In recent years Hollywood has made gestures toward "correct" casting; African-American, Native American, and Latino/a performers have been allowed to "represent" their communities. But this "realistic" casting is hardly sufficient if narrative structure and cinematic strategies remain Eurocentric. An epidermically correct face does not guarantee community self-representation, any more than Clarence Thomas's black skin guarantees his representation of African-American legal interests.

A number of film and theater directors have sought alternative approaches to literally self-representative casting. Orson Welles staged all-Black versions of Shakespeare plays, most notably his "Voodoo Macbeth" in Harlem in 1936. Peter Brook, similarly, cast a rainbow of multicultural performers in his filmic adaptation of the Hindu epic *The Mahabaratha* (1990). Glauber Rocha deliberately confused linguistic and thespian self-representations in his *Der Leone Have Sept Cabecas* (1970), whose very title subverts the linguistic positioning of the spectator by mingling five of the languages of Africa's colonizers. Rocha's Brechtian fable animates emblematic figures representing the diverse colonizing nations, suggesting imperial homologies among them by having an Italian-accented speaker play the role of the American, a Frenchman play the German and so forth.

Such antiliteral strategies provoke an irreverent question: what is wrong with non-originary casting? Doesn't acting always involve a ludic play with identity? Should we applaud Blacks playing Hamlet but not Laurence Olivier playing Othello? And have not Euro-American and European performers often ethnically substituted for one another (for example, Greta Garbo and Cyd Charisse as Russians in *Ninotchka*, 1939, and *Silk Stockings*, 1957)? Casting, we would argue, has to be seen in contingent terms, in relation to the role, the political and esthetic intention, and to the historical moment. We cannot equate a gigantic charade whereby a whole foreign country is represented by players not from that country and is imagined as speaking a language not its own (a frequent Hollywood practice), with cases where non-literal casting forms part of an alternative esthetic. The casting of Blacks to play Hamlet, for example, militates against a traditional discrimination that denied Blacks any role, literally and metaphor-ically, in both the performing arts and in politics, while the casting of Laurence Olivier as Othello prolongs a venerable history of deliberately bypassing Black talent. We see the possibilities of epidermically incorrect casting in *Seeing Double* (1989), a San Francisco Mime Troupe play about the Israeli-Palestinian conflict, where an ethnically diverse cast takes on shifting roles in such a way as to posit analogical links between communities. An African-American actor plays both a Palestinian-American and a Jewish-American, for example, thus hinting at a common history of exclusion binding Blacks, Jews, and Arabs.

THE LINGUISTICS OF DOMINATION

The same issues of self-representation arise in relation to language. As potent symbols of collective identity, languages are the foci of deep loyalties existing at the razor's edge of national and cultural difference. Although languages as abstract entities do not exist in hierarchies of value, languages as lived operate within hierarchies of power. Inscribed within the play of power, language becomes caught up in the cultural hierarchies typical of Eurocentrism. English, especially, has often served as the linguistic vehicle for the projection of Anglo-American power, technology, and finance. Hollywood films, for their part, betray a linguistic hubris bred of empire. Hollywood proposed to tell not only its own stories but also those of other nations, and not only to Americans but also to the other nations themselves, and always in English. In Cecil B. de Mille epics, both the ancient Egyptians and the Israelites, not to mention God, speak English. By ventriloquizing the world, Hollywood indirectly diminished the possibilities of linguistic self-representation for other nations. Hollywood both profited from and itself promoted the world-wide dissemination of the English language, thus contributing indirectly to the subtle erosion of the linguistic autonomy of other cultures.

Since for the colonizer to be human was to speak the colonizing language, colonized people were encouraged to abandon their languages. Ngũgĩ wa Thiong'o tells of Kenyan children being punished for speaking their own languages, made to carry plaques saying "I am stupid,"[22] a situation portrayed in the Senegalese film *Le Symbole* (1994). But the colonized are denied speech in a double sense, first in the idiomatic sense of not being allowed to speak, and second in the more radical sense of not being recognized as capable of speech.[23] It is this historical sense of tying tongues that has provoked protest against countless films, where linguistic discrimination and colonialist "tact" go hand in hand with condescending characterization and distorted social portraiture. The "Indians" of classic Hollywood westerns, denuded of their own idiom, mouth pidgin English, a mark of their inability to master the "civilized" language. In many First World films set in the Third World, the "word of the other" is elided, distorted, or caricatured. In films set in North Africa, for example, Arabic is an indecipherable murmur, while the "real" language of communication is the French of Jean Gabin in *Pépé le Moko* (1936) or the English of Bogart and Bergman in *Casablanca* (1942). In Lean's *Lawrence of Arabia* (1962), which is pretentiously, even ostentatiously sympathetic to the Arabs, we hear almost no Arabic at all but rather English spoken in a motley of accents, almost all of them (Omar Sharif's being the exception) having little to do with Arabic. And, more recently, Bertolucci's *The Sheltering Sky* (1991), set in North Africa, privileges the English of its protagonists and does not bother to translate Arabic dialog. Given this film history, the relative advance of *Dances with Wolves* (1990), and *Black Robe* (1991), trigger hopes for a sea-change in linguistic representation.

Many Third World filmmakers have reacted against the hegemonic deployment of European languages in dominant cinema. Although English, for example, has become the literary *lingua franca* for postcolonials like Ben Okri, Derek Walcott, Bharati Mukherjee, Salman Rushdie, and Vikram Seth, and in this sense is no longer the possession of its original "owners," it has also been met with the anti-neocolonial demand of return to one's linguistic sources. Ngũgĩ wa Thiong'o's challenge to African writers – that they write in African rather than European languages – has to some extent been taken up by African filmmakers, for whom the use of African languages (with subtitles) is standard procedure. Ousmane Sembene, for example, has filmed in diverse African languages, notably Diola and Wolof. Sembene has also foregrounded the issue of language and power within the colonial situation. His *Xala* (1974), for example, links issues of linguistic and social representation. The protagonist, El Hadji, a polygamous Senegalese businessman, embodies the neocolonized attitudes of the African elite so vehemently denounced by Fanon. Sembene structures the film around the opposition of Wolof and French. While the elite don African dress and make nationalist speeches in Wolof, they speak French among themselves and reveal European suits beneath their African garb. Many of the characterizations revolve around the question of language. El Hadji's first wife, Adja, representing the precolonial African woman, speaks Wolof and wears traditional clothes. The second wife, Oumi, mimics European fashions, affects French, and wears wigs, sunglasses, and low-cut dresses. Finally, El Hadji's daughter, Rama, representing the progressive hybrid of Africa and Europe, knows French but insists on speaking Wolof to her francophile father, who prefers she seal her lips. Instead, she performs what Gloria Anzaldúa calls "linguistic code-switching" in the face of censorious forces, "transforming silence with (an)other alphabet."[24] Thus conflicts involving language-shifts are made to carry a strong charge of social and cultural tension.

As a social battleground, language forms the site where political struggles are engaged both collectively and intimately. People do not enter simply into language as a master code; they participate in it as socially constituted subjects whose linguistic exchange is shaped by power relations. In the case of colonialism, linguistic reciprocity is simply out of the question. In Sembene's *La Noire de* ... (Black Girl, 1966), the female protagonist Diouana stands at the convergence of multiple structures of inequality – as Black, as maid, as woman – and her oppression is conveyed specifically through language. Diouana overhears her French employer say of her: "She understands French . . . by instinct . . . like an animal." The colonialist here transforms a defining human character-istic – the capacity for language – into a sign of animality, even though Diouana knows French while her employers, after years in Senegal, know nothing of her language and culture. It is this regime of linguistic non-reciprocity which distinguishes colonial bilingualism from ordinary linguistic dualism. For the colonizer, the refusal of the colonized's language is linked to the denial of political self-determination, while for the colonized mastery of the colonizer's tongue testifies both to a capacity for survival and a daily drowning out of one's voice. Colonial bilingualism entails the inhabiting of conflicting psychic and cultural realms.

The neocolonial situation, in which the Hollywood language becomes the model of "real" cinema, has as its linguistic corollary the view of European languages as inherently more "cinematic" than others. The English phrase "I love you," some Brazilian critics argued without irony in the 1920s, was intrinsically more beautiful than the Portuguese *eu te amo*. The particular focus on amorous language reflects not only the lure of Hollywood's romantic model of cinema projecting glamor and popular stars, but also an intuitive sense of the erotics of linguistic neocolonialism – that is, the sense that the imperializing language exercises a kind of phallic power and attraction. Carlos Diegues' *Bye Bye Brazil* (1980), titled in English even in Brazil, looks at English, as it were, "through" Brazilian Portuguese. The name of the film's traveling entertainment troupe – Caravana Rolidei – phonetically transcribes the Brazilian pronunciation of the English "holiday," in a spirit of creative distortion. This refusal to "get it straight" reveals a typical colonial ambivalence, melding sincere affection and resentful parody. The Chico Buarque theme song features expressions like "bye bye," "night and day," and "OK" as indices of the Americanization (and in this case the multinationalization) of a world where Portuguese-speaking Amazonian tribal chiefs wear designer jeans and backwoods rock groups sound like the Bee Gees, embodying a palimpsestic America. In sum, the issue of linguistic self-representation does not simply entail a return to "authentic" languages but rather the orchestration of languages for emancipatory purposes.[25]

WRITING HOLLYWOOD AND RACE

Important work has already been done on the ethnic/racial representation of oppressed communities within Hollywood cinema. Critics such as Vine Deloria, Ralph and Natasha Friar, Ward Churchill, Annette Jaimes, and many others have discussed the binaristic splitting that has turned Native Americans into blood-thirsty beasts or noble savages. Native American critics have denounced the "redface" convention, the practice of having non-Native Americans – White (Rock Hudson), Latino (Ricardo Montalban), or Japanese (Sessue Hayakawa) – play Native American roles. They have also pointed to the innumerable representational blunders of Hollywood films, which have had Indians perform grotesque dog-eating rituals (*The Battle at Elderbush Gulch*, 1913), and wrist-cutting ceremonies (*Broken Arrow*, 1950), and have misascribed specific ceremonies to the wrong tribes (the Sioux Sun-Dance presented as the *okipa* ceremony of the Mandans). Churchill points out that even "sympathetic" films like *A Man Called Horse* (1970), hailed as an authentic, positive portrayal, depicts a people "whose language is Lakota, whose hairstyles range from Assiniboi through Nez Perce to Comache, whose tipi design is Crow, and whose Sun Dance ceremony ... [is] typically Mandan."[26] The film has the Anglo captive teach the Indians the finer points of the bow, a weapon which had been in use by Native Americans for countless generations, thus demonstrating "the presumed inherent superiority of Eurocentric minds."[27]

How can one account for Hollywood films that show some sensitivity to issues of self-representation? A popular film like *Dances with Wolves* demonstrates the need for a nuanced multivalent analysis. The film did break ground by casting Native Americans to play themselves, yet it was less politically audacious in placing its story in the distant past, cordoned off from the contemporary struggles of living native people. However, a thoroughgoing analysis must see the film as contradictory, affirming at the same time that it (1) constitutes a relatively progressive step for Hollywood in its adoption of a pro-indigenous perspective, and (2) in respecting the linguistic integrity of the Native Americans; yet that (3) this progressive step is in part undermined by the traditional split portrayal of bad Pawnees/good Sioux; that (4) it is further compromised by its elegiac emphasis on the remote past and (5) by the foregrounding of a Euro-American protagonist and his (6) idyll with a non-Indian lover; yet that (7) this Euro-American

focalization, given the mass audience's identificatory propensities, also guaran-
teed the film's wide impact; and (8) that this impact indirectly helped open doors
for Native American filmmakers, without (9) introducing major institutional
changes within the industry, but also (10) altering the ways in which such films
are likely to be made in the future, while (11) still forming part, ultimately, of a
capitalist/modernist project that has fostered the destruction of Native American
peoples.[28] A textually subtle, contextualized analysis, then, must take into
account all these apparently contradictory points at the same time, without lapsing
into a Manichean good film/bad film binaristic schema, the "politically correct"
equivalent of "bad object" criticism.[29]

A number of scholars, notably Donald Bogle, Daniel Leab, James Snead, Jim
Pines, Jacquie Jones, Pearl Bowser, Clyde Taylor, and Thomas Cripps, have
explored how preexisting stereotypes – for example the jiving sharpster and
shuffling stage sambo – were transferred from antecedent media to film. In *Toms,
Coons, Mulattoes, Mammies and Bucks*, Bogle surveys representations of Blacks
in Hollywood cinema, especially foregrounding the unequal struggle between
Black performers and the stereotypical roles offered them by Hollywood. Bogle's
very title announces the five major stereotypes:

1. the servile "Tom" (going back to Uncle Tom in *Uncle Tom's Cabin*);
2. the "Coon" (Step'n Fetchit is the archetypal example), a type itself
   subdivided into the "pickanniny" (the harmless eye-popping clown figure)
   and the Uncle Remus (naive, congenial folk philosopher);
3. the "Tragic Mulatto," usually a woman, victim of a dual racial inheritance,
   who tries to "pass for White" in such films as *Pinky* and *Imitation of Life*;
   or else the demonized mulatto man, devious and ambitious, like Silas Lynch
   in *Birth of a Nation*;
4. the "Mammy," the fat, cantankerous but ultimately sympathetic female
   servant who provides the glue that keeps households together (the Aunt
   Jemima "handkerchief head" is one variant), such as Hattie McDaniel in
   Gone with the Wind; and
5. the "Buck," the brutal, hypersexualized Black man, a figure of menace
   inherited from the stage, whose most famous filmic incarnation is perhaps
   Gus in *Birth of a Nation*, and which George Bush resuscitated for electoral
   purposes in the figure of Willie Horton.

Bogle's book goes beyond stereotypes to focus on the ways African-American
performers have "signified" and subverted the roles forced on them. For Bogle,
the history of Black performance is one of battling against confining types and
categories, a battle homologous to the quotidian struggle of three-dimensional
Blacks against the imprisoning conventions of an apartheid-style system. It is
interesting to compare Bogle's largely implicit theory of performance in film with
James C. Scott's anthropology of performance and resistance in everyday life. If
we see performance as completely determined from above, Scott argues, we
"miss the agency of the actor in appropriating the performance for his own

195

ends."[30] Thus subaltern performance encodes, often in sanitized, ambiguous ways, what Scott calls the "hidden transcripts" of a subordinated group. A kind of "euphemization" occurs when hidden transcripts are expressed within power-laden situations by actors who prefer to avoid the sanctions that a direct statement might bring. At their best, Black performances undercut stereotypes by individualizing the type or slyly standing above it. The "flamboyant bossiness" of McDaniel's "Mammy" in *Gone with the Wind*, her way of looking Scarlett right in the eye, within this perspective, indirectly translates hostility toward a racist system. Bogle emphasizes the resilient imagination of Black performers obliged to play against script and studio intentions, their capacity to turn demeaning roles into resistant performance. Thus "each major black actor of the day managed to reveal some unique quality of voice or personality that audiences immediately responded to. Who could forget Bojangles' urbanity? Or Rochester's cement-mixer voice? Or Louise Beavers' jollity? Or Hattie McDaniel's haughtiness?"[31] Performance itself intimated liberatory possibilities.

Historically, Hollywood has tried to "teach" Black performers how to conform to its own stereotypes. Beavers' voice had no trace of dialect or southern patois; she had to school herself in the southern drawl considered compulsory for Black performers. Robert Townsend's *Hollywood Shuffle* (1987) satirizes these racial conventions by having White directors oblige Black actors to conform to White stereotypes about Blackness. The White directors give lessons in street jive, gestures and mannerisms, all of which the Black actor-protagonist finds distasteful. The protagonist's own dream, presented in a fantasy sequence, is to play prestigious hero roles such as Superman and Rambo or tragic roles like King Lear. The desire for dignified and socially prestigious dramatic roles reflects a desire to be taken seriously, not always to be the butt of the joke, to win access to the generic prestige historically associated with tragedy and epic, even if Townsend's film relays this desire, paradoxically, in parodic form.

Apart from studies on Native Americans and African-Americans, important work has also been done on the stereotypes of other ethnic groups. In *The Latin Image in American Film*, Allen Woll points to the substratum of male violence common to Latino male stereotypes – the bandido, the greaser, the revolutionary, the bullfighter. Latina women, meanwhile, call up the heat and passionate salsa evoked by the titles of the films of Lupe Velez: *Hot Pepper* (1933), *Strictly Dynamite* (1934), and *Mexican Spitfire* (1940). Arthur G. Pettit, in *Images of the Mexican American in Fiction and Film*, traces the intertext of such imagery to the Anglo "conquest fiction" of writers like Ned Buntline and Zane Grey. Already in conquest fiction, Pettit argues, the Mexican is defined negatively, in terms of "qualities diametrically opposed to an Anglo prototype." Anglo conquest authors transferred to the *mestizo* Mexicans the prejudices previously directed toward the Native American and the Black. They excoriate miscegenation and repeatedly sound the theme of the inevitable decline and degeneracy of Mexicans due to race mixing: "the Spaniards and their 'polluted' descendants have comitted racial and national self-genocide by mixing voluntarily with inferior dark-skinned races."[32]

In conquest novels, Mexicans are not called Mexicans but "greasers," "yallers," "mongrels," and "niggers". Hollywood inherited these stereotypes – the bandido, the greaser, the "half-breed" whore – along with the positively connoted elite figures of the Castillian gentleman and the high-caste Castillian woman. Morality, in such works, is color-coordinated; the darker the color, the worse the character.[33]

A number of didactic documentaries address the issue of stereotypes. *The Media Show: North American Indians* (1991) critically dissects the portrayal of "Indians" in Hollywood films (including *Dances with Wolves*). Phil Lucas and Robert Hagopian's *Images of Indians* (1979) examines Hollywood films as purveyors of Native American stereotypes. This documentary is divided into five half-hour segments: "The Great Movie Massacre" examines the warrior image of the Indian; "Heathen Injuns and the Hollywood Gospel" addresses the misrepresentation of indigenous religion; "How Hollywood Wins the West" focusses on the one-sided representations of history; "The Movie Reel Indians" speaks of industry attitudes toward Native Americans; and "Warpaint and Wigs" speaks of the constructedness and artificiality of the Hollywood Indian. *Black History: Lost, Stolen, and Strayed* (1967), narrated by Bill Cosby, criticizes the historical misrepresentations and stereotypical portrayals of Blacks. Marlon Riggs' *Ethnic Notions* stresses the pain caused by stereotypes incarnated in racist cartoons, toys, and films, and alternates citations of racist materials with interviews with African-American performers and scholars. Gloria Ribe's *From Here, from This Side* (1988) deploys Hollywood films and archival material to communicate a vision of cultural domination from the Mexican side. The Edward Said-narrated *In the Shadow of the West* (1984) critiques orientalist imagery in part through conversations with Palestinians, Lebanese, and Arab intellectuals living in the US. Renee Tajima and Christine Choy's *Who Killed Vincent Chin?* (1988), a film about the murder by White autoworkers of a Chinese-American whom they took to be Japanese, uses media materials in its portrayal of anti-Asian discrimination. Valerie Soe's *All Orientals Look the Same* (1986) undercuts the orientalizing "mark of the plural" by having very diverse Asian-American faces dissolve into one another. Christine Choy's and Renee Tajima's *Yellow Tale Blues* (1990) juxtaposes media imagery with the actual situations of Asian-Americans. Shu Lea Cheang's *Color Schemes* (1989) spoofs American melting-pot ideals through the metaphor of "color wash" to explore the ambiguities of racial assimilation. Twelve performers evoke four ethnic "wash cycles": soak, wash, rinse, extract. Deborah Gee's *Slaying the Dragon* (1987), finally, uses film clips (for example, from *The World of Suzie Wong*, 1960) and interviews to show how Asian women have been stereotyped as docile and exotic.

Riggs' *Color Adjustment* (1991) chronicles the history of Black representation on TV, moving from the caricatural days of *Amos and Andy* through Black sitcoms like *Good Times* and through *Roots* up to the ultimate Black American family: the Huxtables of *The Cosby Show*. Throughout, *Color Adjustment* speaks less about "authentic" representation than about the fundamental paradigm lurking behind most of the shows – the idealized suburban nuclear family. In one of the quoted programs, *All in the Family*, Edith Bunker praises Black progress: "They used to all be servants, and maids, and waiters, and now they're lawyers and doctors. They've come a long way on television!" But this simulacral meliorism, *Color Adjustment* suggests, is deeply inadequate. Even if TV were peopled exclusively by African-American doctors and lawyers, the concrete situation of African-Americans would not thereby be substantially improved. *Color Adjustment* underlines this contrast between media image and social reality by suggestively juxtaposing sitcom episodes with documentary street footage, sometimes by way of contrast (*The Brady Bunch* versus police attacks on civil rights marches), sometimes by way of comparison (scenes of anti-bussing demonstrators hurling racial epithets juxtaposed with Archie Bunker's racial inanities). *Fade to Black* (1989), finally, aggressively orchestrates very diverse materials: a capsule history of Blacks in films, Althusser-influenced theoretical interventions, clips from feature films (*Vertigo*, 1958; *Taxi Driver*, 1976), rap music and a hard-hitting voice-over commentary. The voice-overs by two Black men contrast White verbal denials of racism with everyday "proxemic" expressions of fear and hostility: the White motorist who clicks the car door lock upon seeing a Black man, the White matron who clutches her purse upon seeing a Black man approach.

THE LIMITS OF THE STEREOTYPE

We would like both to argue for the importance of the study of stereotyping in popular culture and to raise some methodological questions about the underlying premises of character- or stereotype-centered approaches. (We are not implying that the work of the writers just mentioned is reducible to "stereotype analyis.") To begin, the stereotype-centered approach, the analysis of repeated, ultimately pernicious constellations of character traits, has made an indispensable contribution by:

1. revealing oppressive patterns of prejudice in what might at first glance have seemed random and inchoate phenomena;
2. highlighting the psychic devastation inflicted by systematically negative portrayals on those groups assaulted by them, whether through internalization of the stereotypes themselves or through the negative effects of their dissemination; and
3. signaling the social functionality of stereotypes, demonstrating that they are not an error of perception but rather a form of social control, intended as what Alice Walker calls "prisons of image."[34]

The call for "positive images," in the same way, corresponds to a profound logic which only those accustomed to having their narcissism stroked can fail to understand. Given a dominant cinema that trades in heroes and heroines, "minority" communities rightly ask for their fair share of the representational pie as a simple matter of representational parity.

198

At the same time, the stereotype approach entails a number of theoretical-political pitfalls. First, the exclusive preoccupation with images, whether positive or negative, can lead to a kind of *essentialism*, as less subtle critics reduce a complex variety of portrayals to a limited set of reified formulae. Such criticism is procrustean; the critic forces diverse fictive characters into preestablished categories. Behind every Black child performer the critic discerns a "pickaninny"; behind every sexually attractive Black actor a "buck"; behind every corpulent or nurturing Black female a "mammy." Such reductionist simplifications run the risk of reproducing the very racial essentialism they were designed to combat.

This essentialism generates in its wake a certain *ahistoricism*; the analysis tends to be static, not allowing for mutations, metamorphoses, changes of valence, altered function; it ignores the historical instability of the stereotype and even of language. Some of the basic terminology invoked by Bogle was not always anti-Black. The word "coon," for example, originally referred to rural Whites, becoming a racial slur only around 1848. At the time of the American revolution, the term "buck" evoked a "dashing, virile young man"; and became associated with Blacks only after 1835.[35] Stereotype analysis also fails to register the ways that imagery might be shaped, for example, by structural changes in the economy. How does one reconcile the "lazy Mexican" from the "greaser films" with the media's present-day "illegal alien" overly eager to work long hours at half pay? On the other hand, images may change, while their function remains the same, or vice versa. Riggs' *Ethnic Notions* explains that the role of the Uncle Tom was not to represent Blacks but rather to reassure Whites with a comforting image of Black docility, just as the role of the Black buck, ever since Reconstruction, has been to frighten Whites in order to subordinate them to elite manipulation, a device invented by southern Dixiecrats but subsequently adopted by the Republican Party. The positive images of TV sitcoms with Black casts, such as *Different Strokes* and *The Jeffersons*, Herman Gray argues, idealize "racial harmony, affluence, and individual mobility" and thus "deflect attention from the persistance of racism, inequality, and differential power."[36] The Huxtables' success, as Jhally and Lewis put it, "implies the failure of the majority of black people."[37] Contemporary stereotypes, moreover, are inseparable from the long history of colonialist discourse. The "sambo" type is on one level merely a circumscribed characterological instantiation of the infantilizing trope. The "tragic mulatto", in the same vein, is a cautionary figure premised on the trope of purity, the loathing of mixing characteristic of a certain racist discourse. Similarly, many of the scandalously racist statements discussed in the media are less eccentric views than throwbacks to colonialist discourses. Seen in historical perspective, TV commentator Andy Rooney's widely censured remark that Blacks had "watered down their genes" is not a maverick "opinion" but rather a return to the nostrums of "racial degeneracy" theories.

A recent *Tom Brokaw Report* (April 1993) on the subject of immigration illustrates the need to historicize the discussion of stereotyping and media racism. In the report, we accompany the efforts of the border police to catch "illegal aliens" coming from Mexico. In the greenish light of surveillance cameras, we see the "aliens" making their way over fences, across highways, through cracks. The portrayal suggests a kind of ineradicable vermin who proliferate like mice and are just as difficult to stomp out. One of "them" appears briefly, not to explain their perspective but only to warn that nothing will stop them, that arrest and expulsion are not major obstacles. There is no historicization, nothing about the brutality of the border police, and no explanation that this entire area was once part of Mexico, that "illegal" Mexicans were there before "legal" Anglos, and that many Chicanos and Mexicans regard themselves as part of a transborder nation. We then move to New York, where a Black Dominican medic reports on the high levels of crime in the neighborhood he serves; he calls for more "selective" immigration. After hearing about the "bad" ethnics (predictably Black and Latino), we meet the "good ethnics": this time Russian Jews who work hard, do not complain, and are deeply appreciative of America's gifts. The same signs shift valence according to an ethnic hierarchy. Both Dominicans and Russians are shown dancing, for example, but only with the Russians does the voice-over "anchor" the dancing as a sign of "*joie de vivre*." Then we meet another "model minority," a Korean businessman who "teaches discipline" to young Blacks, who praise the Korean for improving their neighborhood. The Koreans, we are told, work long hours, respect their elders, and get ahead, but their success causes resentment. (Given the LA rebellions, we suspect that the "resenters" might be Blacks and Latinos.) Three White male "experts" address us: one, a liberal, argues for tolerance; the other two argue for greater restrictions. The few Black voices in the program speak up not for their community but rather for other communities (the Koreans) or for stricter immigration policy; no one speaks up for the Blacks. Not a word about racism, about widely divergent histories and relations to colonialism, slavery, or capitalism.

A moment's reflection reveals why this scenario seems so familiar. We are hearing echoes of the nineteenth-century racial hierarchy theories developed by such thinkers as Hegel, Gobineau, and Renan, now embedded in "culture of poverty" ideology. For Gobineau, Blacks are on the lowest rung, incapable of development, while the "Yellow" race is superior to the Black, but still passive and susceptible to despotism. The White race, characterized by intelligence, orderliness, and a taste for liberty, occupies the top position. For Renan too, Blacks (along with indigenous peoples) are at the bottom, with Asians as an "intermediate race" and White Europeans positioned at the top. In the Brokaw program, the qualities posited have changed (the Asians are no longer passive but rather hardworking; European Jews, once the object of anti-Semitic hostility, have been promoted), yet the basic hierarchizing mechanism remains intact. White superiority is not so much asserted as assumed – Whites are the objective ones, the experts, the uncontroversial ones, those who cause no problems, those who judge, those "at home" in the world, whose prerogative it is to create laws in the face of alien disorder.

The focus on "good" and "bad" characters in image analysis confronts racist discourse on that discourse's favored ground. It easily slides into *moralism*, and thus into fruitless debates about the relative virtues of fictive characters (seen not as constructs but as if they were real flesh-and-blood people) and the correctness of their fictional actions. This kind of anthropocentric moralism, deeply rooted in Manichean schemas of good and evil, leads to the treatment of complex political issues as if they were matters of individual ethics, in a manner reminiscent of the morality plays staged by the right, in which virtuous American heroes do battle against demonized Third World villains. Thus Bush/Reagan regime portrayals of its enemies drew on the "Manichean allegories" (in the words of Abdul Jan Mohamed) of colonialism: the Sandinistas were portrayed as latter-day bandidos, the *mestizo* Noriega was made to incarnate Anglo phobias about Latino men (violent, drug-dealing, voodoo-practicing), and Saddam Hussein triggered the intertextual memory of Muslim fanatics and Arab assassins.

The media discussion of racism often reflects this same personalistic bias. Mass-media debates often revolve around sensational accusations of *personal* racism; the accusation and the defense are framed in individual terms. Accused of racism for exploiting the image of Willie Horton, Bush advertised his personal animosity toward bigotry and his tenderness for his little brown grandchildren, exemplifying an ideological penchant for personalizing and moralizing essentially political issues. The usual sequence in media accusations of racism, similarly, is that the racist statement is made, offense is expressed, punishment is called for: all of which provokes a series of counter-statements – that the person in question is not racist, that some of the person's best friends belong to the race in question, and so forth. The process has the apparently positive result of placing certain statements beyond the pale of civil speech; blatant racism is stigmatized and punished. But the more subtle, deeper forms of discursively and institutionally structured racism remain unrecognized. The discussion has revolved around the putative racism of a single individual; the problem is assumed to be personal, ethical. The result is a lost opportunity for antiracist pedagogy: racism is reduced to an individual, attitudinal problem, distracting attention from racism as a systematic self-reproducing discursive apparatus that itself shapes racist attitudes. Stereotypic analysis is likewise covertly premised on *individualism* in that the individual character, rather than larger social categories (race, class, gender, nation, sexual orientation), remains the point of reference. Individual morality receives more attention than the larger configurations of power. This apolitical approach to stereotypes allows pro-business "content analysts" to lament without irony the TV's "stereotyping" of American businessmen, forgetting that television as an institution, at least, is permeated by the corporate ethos, that its commercials and even its shows are commercials *for* business.

The focus on individual character also misses the ways in which social institutions and cultural practices, as opposed to individuals, can be misrepresented without a single character being stereotyped. The flawed mimesis of many Hollywood films dealing with the Third World, with their innumerable ethnographic, linguistic, and even topographical blunders, has less to do with stereotypes *per se* than with the tendentious ignorance of colonialist discourse. The social institutions and cultural practices of a people can be denigrated without individual stereotypes entering into the question. The media often reproduce Eurocentric views of African spirit religions, for example, by regarding them as superstitious cults rather than as legitimate belief-systems, prejudices enshrined in the patronizing vocabulary ("animism," "ancestor worship," "magic") used to discuss the religions.[38] Within Eurocentric thinking, superimposed Western hierarchies work to the detriment of African religions:

1. oral rather than written, they are seen as lacking the cultural imprimatur of the religions "of the Book" (when in fact the text simply takes distinct, oral-semiotic form, as in Yoruba praise songs);
2. they are regarded as polytheistic rather than monotheistic (a debatable hierarchy and in any case a misrepresentation of most African religions);
3. they are viewed as superstitious rather than scientific (an inheritance from the positivist view of religion as evolving from myth to theology to science), when in fact all religions involve a leap of faith;
4. they are considered disturbingly corporeal and ludic (danced) rather than abstractly and austerely theological;
5. they are thought insufficiently sublimated (for example, involving actual animal sacrifice rather than symbolic or historically commemorative sacrifice); and
6. they are seen as wildly gregarious, drowning the personality in the collective transpersonal fusions of trance, rather than respecting the unitary, bounded individual consciousness. The Christian ideal of the *visio intellectualis*, which Christian theology inherited from the neo-Platonists, flees in horror from the plural trances and visions of the "transe" religions of Africa and of many indigenous peoples.[39] In a less Eurocentric perspective, all these "deficiencies" might become advantages: the lack of a written text precludes fundamentalist dogmatism; the multiplicity of spirits allows for historical change; bodily possession betokens an absence of puritanical asceticism; the dance and music are an aesthetic resource.

Diasporic syncretic religions of African origin are almost invariably caricatured in dominant media. The affiliation of such "voodoo" films as *Voodoo Man* (1944), *Voodoo Woman* (1957), and *Voodoo Island* (1957) with the horror genre already betrays a viscerally phobic attitude to African religion. But in recent films positivist phobias about "magical" practices, coupled with monotheist diabolization of "godless" rituals, still surface. *The Believers* (1986) presents Santeria as a cult dominated by ritual child-murderers, in a manner reminiscent of the "unspeakable rites" invoked by colonialist literature. Any number of films eroticize African religion in a way that betrays ambivalent attraction and repulsion. *Angel Heart* (1987) has Lisa Bonet, as Epiphany Proudfoot the voodoo priestess, thrash around with Mickey Rourke in a sanguinary love scene. Another Mickey Rourke vehicle, *Wild Orchid* (1989), exploits the religious atmosphere of the Afro-Brazilian religion Candomblé as what Tomas Lopez-Pumarejo calls an "Afro-dysiac." And the Michael Caine comedy *Blame it on Rio* (1984) stages Umbanda as a frenetic orgy in which the priestess (*mãe de santo*) doles out amorous advice in English to tourists.[40] The electronic media also participate in these defamatory portrayals. Local "Eyewitness News" reports, in New York at least, present Santeria as a problem for law enforcement, or as an issue of "cruelty to animals." Habitual chicken-eaters, forgetful of the scandalous conditions of commercial poultry production, become horrified at the ritual slaughter of small numbers of chickens, while officials openly call for an "end to Santeria," a call unthinkable in the case of "respectable" religions.[41] In sum, Eurocentric procedures can treat complex cultural phenomena as deviant without recourse to a character stereotype.

A moralistic and individualistic approach also ignores the contradictory nature of stereotypes. Black figures, in Toni Morrison's words, come to signify polar opposites: "On the one hand, they signify benevolence, harmless and servile guardianship and endless love," and on the other "insanity, illicit sexuality, chaos."[42] A moralistic approach also sidesteps the issue of the relative nature of "morality," eliding the question: positive for whom? It ignores the fact that oppressed people might not only have a *different* vision of morality, but even an *opposite* vision of a hypocritical moralism which not only covers over institutional injustice but which is also oppressive in itself. Even the Decalogue becomes less sacrosanct in bitter situations of social oppression. Within slavery, for example, might it not be admirable and therefore "good" to lie to, manipulate, and even murder a slave-driver? The "positive image" approach assumes a bourgeois morality intimately linked to status quo politics. What is seen as "positive" by the dominant group, for instance the acts of those "Indians" in westerns who spy for the Whites, might be seen as treason by the dominated group. The taboo in Hollywood was not so much on "positive images" but rather on images of racial anger, revolt, and empowerment.

The privileging of character over narrative and social structure places the burden on oppressed people to be "good" rather than on the privileged to remove the knife from the back. The counterpart of the "good Black" on the other side of the racial divide is the pathologically vicious racist: Richard Widmark in *No Way Out* (1950) or Bobby Darin in *Pressure Point* (1962). Such films let "ordinary racists" off the hook, unable to recognize themselves in the raving maniacs on the screen. And in order to be equal, the oppressed are asked to be better, whence all the stoic "ebony saints" (Bogle's words) of Hollywood, from Louise Beavers in *Imitation of Life* (1934 version), through Sidney Poitier in *The Defiant Ones* (1961), to Whoopi Goldberg in *Clara's Heart* (1988). Furthermore, the saintly Black forms a Manichean pair with the demon Black, in a moralistic schema reminiscent of that structuring *Cabin in the Sky*. Saints inherit the Christian tradition of sacrifice and tend to be desexualized, deprived of normal human attributes, along the lines of the "Black eunuch," cast in decorative or subservient poses.[43] The privileging of positive images also elides the patent differences, the social and moral heteroglossia (Bakhtin's term signifying "many-languagedness"), characteristic of any social group. A cinema of contrivedly positive images betrays a lack of confidence in the group portrayed, which usually itself has no illusions concerning its own perfection. A cinema in which all the Black characters resembled Sidney Poitier might be as much a cause for alarm as one in which they all resembled Step'n Fetchit. It is often assumed, furthermore, that control over representation leads automatically to the production of "positive images." But African-made films like *Laafi* (1991) and *Finzan* (1990) do not offer positive images of African society; rather, they offer critical African perspectives on African society. The demand that Third World or minoritarian filmmakers produce only "positive images," in this sense, can be a sign of anxiety. Hollywood, after all, has never worried about sending films around the world which depict the US as a violent land. Rather than deal with the contradictions of a community, "positive image" cinema prefers a mask of perfection.

Image analysis, furthermore, often ignores the issue of function. Tonto's "positive" image, in the *Lone Ranger* series, is less important than his structural subordination to the White hero and to expansionist ideology. Similarly, a certain cynical integrationism simply inserts new heroes and heroines, this time drawn from the ranks of the oppressed, into the old functional roles that were themselves oppressive, much as colonialism invited a few assimilated "natives" to join the club of the "elite." *Shaft* (1971) simply inserts Black heroes into the actantial slot formerly filled by White ones to flatter the fantasies of a certain sector (largely male) of the Black audience. Even the South African film industry under apartheid could entertain with Black Rambos and Superspades.[44] Other films, such as *In the Heat of the Night* (1967), *Pressure Point*, the *Beverly Hills Cop* series with Eddie Murphy (1984, 1987), and, more complexly, *Deep Cover* (1992), place Black characters in highly ambiguous roles as law-enforcers. The television series *Roots*, finally, used positive images as part of a cooptive version of Afro-American history. The series' subtitle – "The Saga of an American Family" – signals an emphasis on the European-style nuclear family (retrospectively projected on to Kunta's life in Africa) in a film which casts Blacks as just another immigrant group making its way toward freedom and prosperity in democratic America. As Riggs' *Color Adjustment* points out, *Roots* paved the way for *The Cosby Show* by placing an upscale Black family in the preexisting "slot" of the idealized white family sitcom, with Cliff Huxtable as benevolent *paterfamilias*; a liberal move in some respects but one still tied to a conservative valorization of family. John Downing, in contrast, finds *The Cosby Show* more ideologically ambiguous, on the one hand offering an easy pride in African-American culture, and on the other celebrating the virtues of middle class existence in order to obscure structural injustice and racial discrimination.[45]

PERSPECTIVE, ADDRESS, FOCALIZATION

A "positive image" approach also ignores the question of perspective and the social positioning both of the filmmakers and the audience. We cannot equate the stereotyping performed "from above" with stereotyping "from below," where the stereotype is used as it were "in quotes," recognized as a stereotype and used to new ends. The theater group Culture Clash, for example, invokes stereotypes about Chicanos, but always within a sympathetic Chicano perspective. The notion of positive images disallows this kind of "insider satire," the affectionate self-mockery by which an ethnic group makes fun of itself. Spike Lee's *School Daze* (1988) also applies stereotypes for its own purposes, subverting the segregationist connotations of the all-Black musical in order to explore intraracial tensions within the African-American community. *School Daze* comically stages the ideological and class tensions between White-identified and Black-identified African-Americans. Instead of resorting to the usual community-delegate status of African-Americans, the film liberates narrative space to play out the contradictions of a heterogenous community, demonstrating the confidence of a director who, whatever his notorious blindspots (especially in terms of gender and sexuality), is ready to give voice to a polyphony of conflicting voices. Indeed, questions of address are as crucial as questions of representation. Who is speaking through a film? Who is imagined as listening? Who is actually listening? Who is looking? And what social desires are mobilized by the film?

A "positive image" approach also elides issues of point-of-view and what Gerard Genette calls "focalization." Genette's reformulation of the classic literary question of "point-of-view" reaches beyond character perspective to the structuring of information within the story world through the cognitive-perceptual grid of its "inhabitants."[46] The concept is illuminating when applied to liberal films which furnish the "other" with a "positive" image, appealing dialog, and sporadic point-of-view shots, yet in which European or Euro-American characters remain radiating "centers of consciousness" and "filters" for information, the vehicles for dominant racial/ethnic discourses. Many liberal Hollywood films about the Third World or about minoritarian cultures in the First World deploy a European or Euro-American character as a mediating "bridge" to other cultures portrayed more or less sympathetically. The First World journalists in *Under Fire* (1983), *Salvador* (1986), *Missing* (1982), *The Year of Living Dangerously* (1983), and *Circles of Deceit* (1982) inherit the "in-between" role traditionally assigned to the colonial traveler and later to the anthropologist: the role of the one who "reports back." The mediating character initiates the spectator into otherized communities; Third World and minoritarian people, it is implied, are incapable of speaking for themselves. Unworthy of stardom either in the movies or in political life, they need a go-between in the struggle for emancipation.

The character whose point-of-view predominates need not be the "carrier" of the "norms of the text." Oswaldo Censoni's *João Negrinho* (1954), for example, is entirely structured around the perspective of its focal character, an elderly

Brazilian ex-slave. But while the film seems to present all its events from João's point of view, apparently to elicit total sympathy with him, what it in fact elicits sympathy for is a paternalistic vision of "good" Blacks leaving their destiny in the hands of well-intentioned White abolitionists. One finds a related ambiguity in liberal films that privilege European mediators over their Third World object of sympathy – the Palestinians in *Hanna K.* (1983), the Indians in *Passage to India* (1984), the African-Americans in *Mississippi Burning*, the Nicaraguans in *Under Fire*, the Indians in *City of Joy* (1990). A recent episode of the TV show *Travel* (April 26, 1992), similarly, glorifies an elderly British woman who helps children in Peru. The *mise-en-scène* foregrounds her as she leads the group singing of "My Bonnie Lies over the Ocean." Throughout she is focalized as a kind of haloed White savior of the oppressed, within an ideology that posits individual altruism as the sole legitimate force for social change. The Third World characters have a subsidiary function in such films and reports, even though their plight is the thematic focus. Media liberalism, in sum, does not allow subaltern communities to play prominent self-determining roles, a refusal homologous to liberal distaste for non-mediated self-assertion in the political realm. In *City of Joy*, what is portrayed as the unrelieved misery of Calcutta – "an inexhaustible object of Christian charity" in the words of Chidananda das Gupta – becomes the scene of Patrick Swayze's *bildungsroman*.[47] The "other" becomes a trampolin for personal sacrifice and redemption.

To make its didactic thrust palatable to a Western audience, *Hanna K.*, like other recent Middle East thrillers such as *Circles of Deceit* and *The Little Drummer Girl* (1984), has its First World protagonist (Jill Clayburgh) explain Third World oppression. Particularly in the courtroom sequences, Hanna not only speaks for the Palestinian Selim but is positioned by the *mise-en-scène* as physically (and ideologically) closer to the spectator. Dialog and *mise-en-scène* construct her narrative dominance, aligning the spectator with her apolitical humanism. At the same time, the narrative structure allows the spectator to know only as much as she knows, an equation of knowledge between spectator and protagonist that makes possible the film's pedagogical strategy. In the *Bildungsroman* chronicling Hanna's journey from ignorance to awareness of political and sexual inequalities, the spectator's consciousness gradually becomes inseparable from hers.[48] In films like this, all the ideological points-of-view are integrated into the authoritative liberal perspective of the narrator-focalizer, who, godlike, oversees and evaluates all the positions.

Some liberal films practice a slightly more critical twist on this *bildungsroman* technique. The Dutch film *Max Havelaar* (1978), directed by Fons Rademakers, adapts a popular Dutch novel by Eduard Douwes Dekker (pen name Multatuli), an exposé of colonialism by a civil servant who experienced it first hand. Although the film simplifies the novel's complex system of multiple narrations, it does retain two central elements: the story of Havelaar, a well-intentioned colonial administrator, and the story of the novelist's search for a publisher. After some success as a minor government official on the island of Celebes in

Indonesia, Havelaar is given an Assistant Residency in Lebak, a remote outpost on Java. There he sails into what turns out to be a nest of vipers: his predecessor, we learn, has been poisoned and the murder has been covered up by a falsified medical report. Havelaar confronts the native Regent, a man of duplicitous charm whose enigmatic smile masks despotic greed and who treats the people of Lebak as virtual slaves. Hoping to persuade the Regent to mend his ways, Havelaar offers him money from his own pocket to pay the natives for their work. The Regent smiles benignly, accepts the money, and goes on exploiting. Enraged, and naively assuming that the colonial administration shares his revulsion at the Regent's misdeeds, Havelaar brings his campaign to the Dutch bureaucracy, where he discovers that Dutch colonial officials are accomplices in the Regent's crimes. The corruption stretches all the way from his colonial outpost to the Dutch King. Shorn of both his position and his illusions, Havelaar returns to Holland. His heroic reformism is portrayed as a kind of quixotic madness. About to dive into shark-infested waters, he speaks grandly of his "mission." "Yes," someone replies, "but do the sharks know about that?" Humanitarian do-gooders, the film implies, are apt to be devoured by colonialist sharks. While Havelaar irritates the sharks, he is also unable to join the colonized fishes. His predicament is that of the "colonialist who refuses" (in Memmi's words); social contradiction permeates his every word and gesture. The film's innovation, however, lies in having a bridge character mediate not so much between audience and subject as between the contradictions of colonialism itself.

Thunderheart (1991), a fictionalized version of the struggle of the Oglala-

Plate 34 Compromise focalization: Val Kilmer in *Thunderheart*

Sioux against FBI repression in the 1970s, meanwhile, is focalized through a hybrid character whose sense of identity is radically transformed during the course of the film. The FBI agent (Val Kilmer), on the reservation to investigate a murder, at first denies the Native American side of his identity – he has a Sioux grandfather – then evolves into a fighter on behalf of Native Americans. Parallel to his discovery of the identity of the murderers goes a discovery of his own suppressed identity. The spectator accustomed to liberal point-of-view conventions is surprised to find that the "norms of the text" evolve dramatically during the course of the film. Whereas Hanna in *Hanna K.* merely learns more about the world, without fundamentally altering her structure of thought, the FBI agent in *Thunderheart* presumably undergoes a fundamental change in orientation. Affected by what he learns on the reservation, illuminated by visions, he switches cultural/political allegiance, bringing the spectator with him.[49]

CINEMATIC AND CULTURAL MEDIATIONS

A privileging of social portrayal, plot and character often leads to a slighting of the specifically cinematic dimensions of the films; often the analyses might as easily have been of novels or plays. A throughgoing analysis has to pay attention to "mediations": narrative structure, genre conventions, cinematic style. Eurocentric discourse in film may be relayed not by characters or plot but by lighting, framing, *mise-en-scène*, music. Some basic issues of mediation have to do with the *rapports de force*, the balance of power as it were, between foreground and background. In the visual arts, space has traditionally been deployed to express the dynamics of authority and prestige. In pre-perspectival medieval painting, for example, size was correlated with social status: nobles were large, peasants small. The cinema translates such correlations of social power into registers of foreground and background, on screen and off screen, speech and silence. To speak of the "image" of a social group, we have to ask precise questions about images. How much space do they occupy in the shot? Are they seen in close-ups or only in distant long shots? How often do they appear compared with the Euro-American characters and for how long? Are they active, desiring characters or decorative props? Do the eyeline matches identify us with one gaze rather than another? Whose looks are reciprocated, whose ignored? How do character positionings communicate social distance or differences in status? Who is front and center? How do body language, posture, and facial expression communicate social hierarchies, arrogance, servility, resentment, pride? Which community is sentimentalized? Is there an esthetic segregation whereby one group is haloed and the other villainized? Are subtle hierarchies conveyed by temporality and subjectivization? What homologies inform artistic and ethnic/political representation?

A critical analysis must also be alive to the contradictions between different registers. For Ed Guerrero, Spike Lee's *Jungle Fever* (1991) rhetorically condemns interracial love, yet "spreads the fever" by making it cinematically

208

appealing in terms of lighting and *mise-en-scène*.[50] Ethic/ethnic perspectives are transmitted not only through character and plot but also through sound and music. As a multitrack audio-visual medium, the cinema manipulates not only point-of-view but also what Michel Chion calls "point-of-hearing" (*point-d'écoute*).[51] In colonial adventure films, the environment and the "natives" are heard as if through the ears of the colonizers. When we as spectators accompany the settlers' gaze over landscapes from which emerge the sounds of native drums, the drum sounds are usually presented as libidinous or threatening. In many Hollywood films, African polyrhythms become aural signifiers of encircling savagery, acoustic shorthand for the racial paranoia implicit in the phrase "the natives are restless." What is seen within Native American, African, or Arab cultures as spiritual and musical expression becomes in the western or adventure film a stenographic index of danger, a motive for fear and loathing. In *Drums along the Mohawk* (1939), the "bad" Indian drums are foiled by the "good" martial Euro-American drums which evoke the beneficent law and order of White Christian patriarchy. Colonialist films associate the colonized with hysterical screams, non-articulate cries, the yelping of animal-like creatures; the sounds themselves place beast and native on the same level, not just neighbors but species-equals.

Music, both diegetic and non-diegetic, is crucial for spectatorial identification. Lubricating the spectatorial psyche and oiling the wheels of narrative continuity, music "conducts" our emotional responses, regulates our sympathies, extracts our tears, excites our glands, relaxes our pulses, and triggers our fears, in conjunction with the image and in the service of the larger purposes of the film. In whose favor do these processes operate? What is the emotional tonality of the music, and with what character or group does it lead us to identify? Is the music that of the people portrayed? In films set in Africa, such as *Out of Africa* (1985) and *Ashanti* (1979), the choice of European symphonic music tells us that their emotional "heart" is in the West. In *The Wild Geese* (1978), classicizing music consistently lends dignity to the White mercenary side. The Roy Budd score waxes martial and heroic when we are meant to identify with the Whites' aggressivity, and sentimental when we are meant to sympathize with their more tender side. The Borodin air commonly called "This Is My Beloved," associated in the film with the mercenary played by Richard Harris, musically "blesses" his demise with a tragic eulogy.

Alternative films deploy sound and music quite differently. A number of African and Afro-diasporic films, such as *Faces of Women* (1985), *Barravento* (1962), and *Pagador de Promessas* (The Given Word, 1962), deploy drum ouvertures in ways that affirm African cultural values. The French film *Noir et Blanc en Couleur* (Black and White in Color, 1976) employs music satirically by having the African colonized carry their colonial masters on their backs, but satirize them through the songs they sing: "My master is so fat, how can I carry him? . . . Yes, and mine has stinky feet . . ." Films by African and Afro-diasporic directors like Sembene, Cisse, and Faye not only use African music but celebrate it. Julie Dash's *Daughters of the Dust* (1990) deploys an African "talking drum" to drive home, if only subliminally, the Afrocentric thrust of a film dedicated to the diasporic culture of the Gullah people.

Another key mediation has to do with genre. A film like Preston Sturges' *Sullivan's Travels* (1942) raises the question of what one might call the "generic coefficient" of racism. In ·this summa of cinematic genres, Blacks play very distinct roles, each correlated with a specific generic discourse. In the slapstick land-yacht sequences, the Black waiter conforms to the prototype of the happy-go-lucky servant/buffoon; he is sadistically "painted" with whiteface pancake batter, and excluded from the charmed circle of White sociality. In the documentary-inflected sequences showing masses of unemployed, meanwhile, Blacks are present but voiceless, very much in the left-communist tradition of class reductionism; they appear as anonymous victims of economic hard times, with no racial specificity to their oppression. The most remarkable sequence, a homage to the "all-Black musical" tradition, has a Black preacher and his congregation welcome the largely White prison-inmates to the screening of an animated cartoon. Here, in the tradition of films like *Hallelujah* (1929), the Black community is portrayed as the vibrant scene of expressive religiosity. But the film complicates conventional representation: first, by desegregating the genre; second, by having Blacks exercise charity toward Whites, characterized by the preacher as "neighbors less fortunate than ourselves." The preacher exhorts the congregation not to act "high-toned," for "we is all equal in the sight of God." When congregation and prisoners sing "Let My People Go," the music, the images, and the editing forge a triadic link between three oppressed groups: Blacks, the prisoners, and the Biblical Israelites in the times of the Pharaoh, here assimilated to the cruel warden. The Sturges who directs the "Black musical" sequence radically complicates the Sturges who directs the slapstick sequence; racial attitudes are generically mediated.

The critique-of-stereotypes approach is implicitly premised on the desirability of "rounded" three-dimensional characters within a realist-dramatic esthetic. Given the cinema's history of one-dimensional portrayals, the hope for more complex and "realistic" representations is completely understandable, but should not preclude more experimental, anti-illusionistic alternatives. Realistic "positive" portrayals are not the only way to fight racism or to advance a liberatory perspective. Within a Brechtian esthetic, for example, (non-racial) stereotypes can serve to generalize meaning and demystify established power, at the same time that the characters are never purely positive or negative but rather are the sites of contradiction. Parody of the kind theorized by Bakhtin, similarly, favors decidedly negative, even grotesque images to convey a deep critique of societal structures. At times, critics have mistakenly applied the criteria appropriate to one genre or esthetic to another. A search for positive images in shows like *In Living Color*, for example, would be misguided, for that show belongs to a carnivalesque genre favoring anarchic bad taste and calculated exaggeration, as in the parody of *West Side Story* where the Black woman sings to her Jewish orthodox lover: "Menahem, Menahem, I just met a man named Menahem." (The show is of course open to other forms of critique.) Satirical or parodic films may be less concerned with constructing positive images than with challenging the stereotypical expectations an audience may bring to them. The performance piece in which Coco Fusco/Guillermo Gomez Peña exhibit themselves as "authentic aborigines" to mock the Western penchant for exhibiting non-Europeans in zoos, museums, and freak shows, prods the art world audience into awareness of its own complicity. The question, in such cases, lies not in the valence of the image but rather in the drift of the satire.

What one might call the generic defense against accusations of racism – "It's only a comedy!," "Whites are equally lampooned!," "All the characters are caricatures!," "But it's a parody!" – is highly ambiguous, since it all depends on the modalities and the objects of the lampoon, parody, and so forth. The classic Euro-Israeli film on Asian and African Jews, *Sallah Shabbati* (1964), for example, portrays a Sephardi protagonist, but from a decidedly unSephardi perspective. As a naif, Sallah on one level exemplifies the perennial tradition of the uninitiated outsider figure deployed as an instrument of social and cultural critique or distanciation. But in contrast with other naif figures such as Candide, Schweik, or Said Abi al Nakhs al Mutasha'il (in Emil Habibi's *Pesoptimist*), who are used as narrative devices to strip bare the received wisdom and introduce a fresh perspective, Sallah's naiveté functions less to attack Euro-Israeli stereotypes about Sephardi Jews than to mock Sallah himself and what he supposedly represents – the "oriental," or "black," qualities of Sephardim. In other words, unlike Jaroslav Hašek, who exploits the constructed naiveté of his character to attack European militarism rather than using it as a satire of Schweik's backwardness, the director, Kishon, molds Sallah in conformity with socially derived stereotypes in a mockery of the Sephardi "minority" (in fact the majority) itself. The grotesque character of Sallah was not designed, and was not received by Euro-Israeli critics, as a satire of an individual but rather as a summation of the Sephardi "essence." And within the Manichean splitting of affectivity typical of colonialist discourse, we find the positive – Sephardim are warm, sincere, direct, shrewd – and negative poles – they are lazy, irrational, unpredictable, primitive, illiterate, sexist. Accordingly, Sallah (and the film) speaks in the first-person plural "we," while the Ashkenazi characters address him in the second-person plural, "you all." Kishon's anti-Establishment satire places on the same level the members of the Establishment and those outside it and distant from real power. Social satire is not, then, an immediate guarantor of multiculturalism. It can be retrograde, perpetuating racist views, rather than deploying satire as a community-based critique of Eurocentric representations.[52]

The analysis-of-stereotypes approach, in its eagerness to apply an *a priori* grid, often ignores issues of cultural specificity. The stereotypes of North American Blacks, for example, are only partly congruent with those of other multiracial New World societies like Brazil. Both countries offer the figure of the noble, devoted slave: in the US the Uncle Tom, in Brazil the *Pai João* (Father John). Both also offer the female counterpart, the devoted woman slave or servant: in the US the "mammy," in Brazil the *mãe preta* (Black mother), both products of a

211

plantation slavery where the children of the master were nursed at the Black mammy's breast. With other stereotypes, however, the cross-cultural analogies become more complicated. Certain characters in Brazilian films (Tonio in *Bahia de Todos os Santos*, 1960; Jorge in *Compasso de Espera*, Making Time, 1973) at first glance recall the tragic mulatto figure common in North American cinema and literature, yet the context is radically different. First, the Brazilian racial spectrum is not binary (Black or White) but nuances its shades across a wide variety of racial descriptive terms. Although color varies widely in both countries, the social construction of race and color is distinct, despite the fact that the current "Latinization" of American culture hints at a kind of convergence. Second, Brazil, while in many ways oppressive to Blacks, has never been a rigidly segregated society; thus no figure exactly corresponds to the North American "tragic mulatto," schizophrenically torn between two radically separate social worlds. The "passing" notion so crucial to American films such as *Pinky* and *Imitation of Life* had little resonance in Brazil, where it is often said that all Brazilians have a "foot in the kitchen"; in other words, that they all have a Black ancestor somewhere in the family. This point is comically demonstrated in the film *Tenda dos Milagres* (Tent of Miracles, 1977), when Pedro Arcanjo reveals his racist adversary Nilo Argilo, the rabid critic of "mongrelization," to be himself part Black. The mulatto figure can be seen as dangerous only in an apartheid system and not in a system dominated by an official, albeit hypocritical, integrationist ideology like Brazil's. In Brazil, the figure of the mulatto became surrounded with a different set of prejudicial connotations, such as that of the mulatto as "uppity" or pretentious. On the other hand, this constellation of associations is not entirely foreign to the US; Griffith's *Birth of a Nation*, for example, repeatedly pinpoints mixed-race mulattos as ambitious and dangerous to the system.

The Brazilian film *Macunaíma* (1969), by Joaquim Pedro de Andrade, illustrates some of the pitfalls both of a misdirected search for "positive images" and of a culturally misinformed reading. An adaptation and updating of the modernist novel of the same name by Mario de Andrade (1928), *Macunaíma* transforms the ultimate negative stereotype – cannibalism – into a positive artistic resource. Fusing the discourse of fellow modernist Oswald de Andrade's anthropophagical movement with the theme of cannibalism that runs through the novel, the director turns cannibalism into the springboard for a critique of both repressive military rule and the predatory capitalist model of Brazil's shortlived "economic miracle." The cannibalist theme is treated in all its variations: people so hungry they eat themselves; an ogre who offers Macunaíma a piece of his leg; the urban guerilla who devours him sexually; the cannibal-giant-capitalist Pietro Pietra with his anthropophagous soup; the capitalist's wife who wants to eat him alive; and finally the man-eating siren who lures him to his death. We see the rich devouring the poor, and the poor devouring each other. The left, meanwhile, while being devoured by the right, purifies itself by eating itself, a practice which the director calls the "cannibalism of the weak."[53]

Given *Macunaíma*'s raucously Rabelaisian esthetic, it would be misguided to look for "positive images," or even for conventional realism. Virtually all the film's characters are two-dimensional grotesques rather than rounded three-dimensional characters, and the grotesquerie is democratically distributed among all the races, while the most archly grotesque characters are the Italian-Brazilian industrialist cannibal and his ghoulish spouse. The case of *Macunaíma* provides an object lesson in the cultural differentiation of spectatorship. In Brazil, a number of factors militate against a reading of the film as racist. First, Brazilians of all races tend to see Macunaíma as representing a spoof on their "national personality" rather than on some racial "other," seeing both the Black and White Macunaímas as a national rather than as a racial archetype. Second, Brazilians would likely be aware of the novel's status as a national classic (never accused of being racist) by a Brazilian of mixed race. Third, Brazilians are less prone to allegorize their own films racially. Since the whole issue of racial portrayal is somewhat less "touchy" in Brazil – an ambiguous fact in itself – the films are not made to bear such a strong "burden of representation." Fourth, North American viewers are less likely to be aware of the associations surrounding the figure of Grande Otelo for Brazilians, who will probably see his role in the film as just one more role in a variegated career, not as emblematic of Blackness. (At the same time, the tendency in the 1940s and 1950s to cast Grande Otelo in comically desexualized roles did reflect a flight from portrayals of mature Black characters.) Fifth, the misunderstanding also derives from a difference between filmic and literary cinematic representation, between verbal suggestiveness and iconic specificity. In the novel, Macunaíma is transformed into a *principe lindo* (a comely prince); there is no racial specification. The film, in contrast, must choose actors to play roles, and actors come with racial characteristics. Thus the fable-like evocativeness of "comely prince" gives way to the physical presence of the Euro-Brazilian actor Paulo José, chosen more for his thespian talents than for his Whiteness, but leading in other contexts to racialized misreadings. The director might be accused, then, not so much of racism as of insensitivity; first, for appearing to posit a link between Blackness/ugliness (a link with very painful historical/intertextual resonances), and second, for failing to imagine the ways that his film might be read in non-Brazilian contexts. At the same time the metaphor of the multiracial Brazilian "family," common to both novel and film, should not be seen as entirely innocent; first because the national ideology of mixed race glossed over racial hierarchies, and second because that metaphor has historically relegated Black Brazilians to the status of "poor cousins" or "adopted children." But such a critique should begin only *after* the film has been understood within Brazilian cultural norms, and not as the application of an *a priori* schema.

THE ORCHESTRATION OF DISCOURSES

One methodological alternative to the mimetic "stereotypes-and-distortions" approach, we would argue, is to speak less of "images" than of "voices" and "discourses." The very term "image studies" symptomatically elides the oral and the "voiced." A predilection for aural and musical metaphors – voices, intonation, accent, polyphony – reflects a shift in attention, as George Yudice suggests, from the predominantly visual logical space of modernity (perspective, empirical evidence, domination of the gaze) to a "postmodern" space of the vocal (oral ethnography, a people's history, slave narratives), as a way of restoring voice to the voiceless.[54] The concept of voice suggests a metaphor of seepage across boundaries that, like sound in the cinema, remodels spatiality itself, while the visual organization of space, with its limits and boundaries and border police, forms a metaphor of exclusions and hierarchical arrangements. It is not our purpose merely to reverse existing hierarchies – to replace the demogoguery of the visual with a new demogoguery of the auditory – but to suggest that voice (and sound) and image be considered together, dialectically and diacritically. A more nuanced discussion of race and ethnicity in the cinema would emphasize less a one-to-one mimetic adequacy to sociological or historical truth than the interplay of voices, discourses, perspectives, including those operative within the image itself. The task of the critic would be to call attention to the cultural voices at play, not only those heard in aural "close-up" but also those distorted or drowned out by the text. The analytic work would be analogous to that of a "mixer" in a sound studio, whose responsibility it is to perform a series of compensatory operations, to heighten the treble, deepen the bass, amplify the instrumentation, to "bring out" the voices that remain latent or displaced.

Formulating the issue as one of voices and discourses helps us get past the "lure" of the visual, to look beyond the epidermic surface of the text. The question, quite literally, is less of the color of the face in the image than of the actual or figurative social voice or discourse speaking "through" the image.[55] Less important than a film's "accuracy" is that it relays the voices and the perspectives – we emphasize the plural – of the community or communities in question. While the word "image" evokes the issue of mimetic realism, "voice" evokes a realism of delegation and interlocution, a situated utterance of "speaking from" and "speaking to." If an identification with a community voice/discourse occurs, the question of "positive" images falls back into its rightful place as a subordinate issue. We might look at Spike Lee's films, for example, not in terms of mimetic "accuracy" – such as the lament that *Do the Right Thing* portrays an inner city untouched by drugs – but rather in terms of voices/discourses. We can regret the absence of a feminist voice in the film, but we can also note its repeated stagings of wars of community rhetorics. The symbolic battle of the boomboxes featuring African-American and Latino music, for example, evokes larger tensions between cultural and musical voices. And the final quotations from Martin Luther King and Malcolm X leave it to the spectator to synthesize two complementary modalities of resistance, one saying: "Freedom, as you promised," the other saying: "Freedom, by any means necessary!"

It might be objected that an analysis of textual "voices" would ultimately run into the same theoretical problems as an analysis centered on "images." Why should it be any easier to determine an "authentic voice" than to determine an "authentic image?" The point, we would argue, is to abandon the language of "authenticity" with its implicit standard of appeal to verisimilitude as a kind of "gold standard," in favor of a language of "discourses" with its implicit reference to community affiliation and to intertextuality. Reformulating the question as one of "voices" and "discourses" disputes the hegemony of the visual and of the image-track by calling attention to its complication with sound, voice, dialog, language. A voice, we might add, is not exactly congruent with a discourse, for while discourse is institutional, transpersonal, unauthored, voice is personalized, having authorial accent and intonation, and constitutes a specific interplay of discourses (whether individual or communal). The notion of voice is open to plurality; a voice is never merely a voice; it also relays a discourse, since even an individual voice is itself a discursive sum, a polyphony of voices. What Bakhtin calls "heteroglossia," after all, is just another name for the socially generated contradictions that constitute the subject, like the media, as the site of conflicting discourses and competing voices. A discursive approach also avoids the moralistic and essentialist traps embedded in a "negative-stereotypes" and "positive-images" analysis. Characters are not seen as unitary essences, as actor-character amalgams too easily fantasized as flesh-and-blood entities existing somewhere "behind" the diegesis, but rather as fictive-discursive constructs. Thus the whole issue is placed on a socioideological rather than on an individual-moralistic plane. Finally, the privileging of the discursive allows us to compare a film's discourses not with an inaccessible "real" but with other socially circulated cognate discourses forming part of a continuum – journalism, novels, network news, television shows, political speeches, scholarly essays, and popular songs.[56]

A discursive analysis would also alert us to the dangers of the "pseudo-polyphonic" discourse that marginalizes and disempowers certain voices, then pretends to dialog with a puppet-like entity already maneuvered into crucial compromises. The film or TV commercial in which every eighth face is Black, for example, has more to do with the demographics of market research and the bad conscience of liberalism than with substantive polyphony, since the Black voice, in such instances, is usually shorn of its soul, deprived of its color and intonation. Polyphony does not consist in the mere appearance of a representative of a given group but rather in the fostering of a textual setting where that group's voice can be heard with its full force and resonance. The question is not of pluralism but of multivocality, an approach that would strive to cultivate and even heighten cultural difference while abolishing socially-generated inequalities.

NOTES

1 Steve Neale points out that stereotypes are judged simultaneously in relation to an empirical "real" (accuracy) and an ideological "ideal" (positive image). See Neale, "The Same Old Story: Stereotypes and Difference," *Screen Education*, Nos 32–3 (Autumn/Winter 1979–80).

2 For more on FBI harassment of civil rights activists, see Kenneth O'Reilly, *"Racial Matters": The FBI's Secret File on Black America, 1960–1972* (New York: Free Press, 1989).

3 Pam Sporn, a New York City educator, had her high-school students go to the south and video-interview civil rights veterans about their memories of the civil rights struggle and their reactions to *Mississippi Burning*.

4 See Gretchen Bataille and Charles Silet, "The Entertaining Anachronism: Indians in American Film," in Randall M. Miller, ed., *The Kaleidoscopic Lens: How Hollywood Views Ethnic Groups* (Englewood, NJ: Jerome S. Ozer, 1980).

5 Kobena Mercer and Isaac Julien, in a similar spirit, distinguish between "representation as a practice of depicting" and "representation as a practice of delegation." See Kobena Mercer and Isaac Julien, "Introduction: De Margin and De Centre," *Screen*, Vol. 29, No. 4 (1988), pp. 2–10.

6 An article in *Moving Picture World* (July 10, 1911), entitled "Indians Grieve over Picture Shows," reports on protests by Native Americans from southern California concerning Hollywood's portrayal of them as warriors when in fact they were peaceful farmers.

7 Religious tensions sometimes inflect cinematic representation. A German film company plan in 1925 to produce *The Prophet*, with Muhammad as the main character, shocked the Islamic University Al Azhar, since Islam prohibits representation of the Prophet. Protests prevented the film from being made. Moustapha Aaqad's *The Message* (Kuwait, Morocco, Libya, 1976), in contrast, tells the story within Islamic norms, respecting the prohibition of graven images of the Prophet, representation of God and holy figures. The film traces the life of the Prophet from his first revelations in AD 610 to his death in 632, in a style which rivals Hollywood Biblical epics. Yet the Prophet is never seen on the screen; when other characters speak to him they address the camera. The script was approved by scholars from the Al Azhar University in Cairo.

8 Judith Williamson makes a similar point in her essay in *Screen*, Vol. 29, No. 4 (1988), pp. 106–12.

9 See Michael Rogin, "Blackface, White Noise: The Jewish Jazz Singer Finds his Voice," *Critical Inquiry*, Vol. 18, No. 3 (1992), pp. 417–44.

10 Michael Dempsey and Udayan Gupta, "Hollywood's Color Problem," *American Film* (April 1982).

11 See *New York Times* (Sept. 24, 1991).

12 See interview with Spike Lee, "Our Film Is Only a Starting Point," *Cineaste*, Vol. XIX, No. 4 (March 1993).

13 See Gary M. Stern, "Why the Dearth of Latino Directors?," *Cineaste*, Vol. XIX, Nos 2–3 (1992).

14 Translation by Robert Stam and Randal Johnson. A full English version of the poem can be found in Randal Johnson and Robert Stam, *Brazilian Cinema* (Rutherford, NJ: Fairleigh Dickinson University Press, 1982; republished Austin: University of Texas Press, 1987; rev. edn, New York: Columbia University Press, 1995).

15 See Isaac Julien and Colin MacCabe, *A Diary of a Young Soul Rebel* (Bloomington: Indiana University Press, 1991).

16 See Rob Nixon, "Cry White Season: Apartheid, Liberalism, and the American Screen," *South Atlantic Quarterly*, No. 90, Vol. 3 (Summer 1991).

17 Reported in *Vrye Weekblod* (Nov. 17, 1989), cited in Keyan Tomaselli, "Myths, Racism and Opportunism: Film and TV Representations of the San," in Peter Ian Crawford and David Turton, eds, *Film as Ethnography* (Manchester: University of Manchester Press, 1992), p. 213.

18 The White Brazilian musicians who worked on *Black Orpheus* were also exploited. The French producer Sacha Gordine refused songs already written for the source play in order to be able to copyright the songs in French, with a contract that gave him 50 per cent of the profits on highly popular songs, while the composer and lyricist (Tom Jobim and Vinicius de Moraes) got only 10 per cent. See Rui Castro, *Chega de Saudade* (São Paulo: Companhia das Letras, 1992).

19 See Clyde Taylor, "Decolonizing the Image," in Peter Steven, ed., *Jump Cut: Hollywood, Politics and Counter Cinema* (Toronto: Between the Lines, 1985), p. 168.

20 See Jean Franco, "High-Tech Primitivism: the Representation of Tribal Societies in Feature Films," in John King, Ana Lopez, and Manuel Alvarado, eds, *Mediating Two Worlds* (London: BFI, 1993).

21 Clear social hierarchies also inform the practice of substitutional casting. The evolution of casting in Israeli cinema, for example, reflects changing strategies of representation. The heroic-nationalist films of the 1950s and 1960s, which focussed on the Israeli-Arab conflict, typically featured heroic Euro-Israeli Sabras, played by European Jews (Ashkenazis), fighting villainous Arabs, while Sephardi Arab-Jewish actors and characters were limited to the "degraded" roles of Muslim Arabs. In most recent political films, in contrast, Israeli-Palestinian actors and non-professionals play the Palestinian roles. Such casting allows for a modicum of "self-representation." And at times the Palestinian actors have actually forced radicalization of certain scenes. In some films Palestinian actors have even been cast as Israeli military officers (for example, Makram Houri in *The Smile of the Lamb* (1986) and in the Palestinian-Belgium film *Wedding in Galilee*, 1987). For more on the ideology of casting in Israeli cinema, see Ella Shohat, *Israeli Cinema: East/West and the Politics of Representation* (Austin: University of Texas Press, 1989).

22 See Ngũgĩ wa Thiong'o, *Moving the Center: The Struggle for Cultural Freedoms* (London: James Currey, 1993), p. 33.

23 See David Spurr, *The Rhetoric of Empire* (Durham, NC: Duke University Press, 1993), p. 104.

24 Gloria Anzaldúa, ed., *Making Face, Making Soul: Hacienda Caras* (San Francisco: Aunt Lute, 1990), pp. xxii, 177.

25 For more on language and power, see Ella Shohat and Robert Stam, "Cinema after Babel: Language, Difference, Power," *Screen*, Vol. 26, Nos 3–4 (May–August 1985).

26 See Ward Churchill, *Fantasies of the Master Race: Literature, Cinema and the Colonization of American Indians* (Monroe, Maine: Common Courage Press, 1992), p. 237.

27 Ibid., p. 238.

28 For a thorough discussion of *Dances with Wolves* from a Native American point of view, see Edward Castillo's essay in *Film Quarterly*, Vol. 44, No. 4 (Summer 1991).

29 See Christian Metz, "The Imaginary Signifier," in *The Imaginary Signifier: Psychoanalysis and the Cinema* (Bloomington: Indiana University Press, 1982).

30 James C. Scott, *Domination and the Arts of Resistance: Hidden Transcripts* (New Haven, Conn.: Yale University Press, 1990), p. 34.

31 Donald Bogle, *Toms, Coons, Mulattoes, Mammies and Bucks* (New York: Continuum, 1989), p. 36.

32 See Arthur G. Pettit, *Images of the Mexican American in Fiction and Film* (College Station: Texas A and M University Press, 1980), p. 24.

33 Critics have also performed extended analyses of specific films from within this perspective. Charles Ramirez Berg analyzes *Bordertown* (1935), the first Hollywood sound film to deal with Mexican-American assimilation and the film which laid down the pattern for the Chicano social problem film. Among the narrative and ideological features Berg isolates are:

1. stereotypical inversion (that is, upgrading of Chicanos coupled with the denigration of the Anglos, portrayed as oversexed blondes (Marie), materialistic socialites (Dale), and inflexible authority figures (the judge)));
2. undiminished stereotyping of other marginalized groups (for example Chinese-Americans);
3. the assimilationist idealization of the Chicana mama as the "font of genuine ethnic values";
4. the absent father (Anglo families are complete and ideal; Chicano families are fragmented and disfunctional); and
5. the absent non-material Chicana (implying the inferiority of Chicanas to Anglo women).

See Charles Ramirez Berg, "*Bordertown*, the Assimilation Narrative and the Chicano Social Problem Film," in Chon Noriega, ed., *Chicanos and Film* (New York: Garland, 1991).

34 Quoted in *Prisoners of Image: Ethnic and Gender Stereotypes*, (New York: Alternative Museum, 1989).

35 See David R. Roediger, *The Wages of Whiteness: Race and the Making of the American Working Class* (London: Verso, 1991), pp. 88–9.

36 Herman Gray, "Television and the New Black Man: Black Male Images in Prime-Time Situation Comedy," *Media, Culture and Society*, No. 8 (1986), p. 239.

37 See Sut Jhally and Justin Lewis, *Enlightened Racism: The Cosby Show, Audiences and the Myth of the American Dream* (Boulder, Colo.: Westview Press, 1992), p. 137.

38 For a critique of Eurocentric language concerning African religions, see John S. Mbiti, *African Religions and Philosophy* (Oxford: Heinemann, 1969).

39 See also Alfredo Bosi's brilliant analysis of the confrontation between Catholicism and the Tupi-Guarani religion in his *Dialetica da Colonização* (São Paulo: Companhia das Letras, 1992).

40 For positive portrayals of African religions, we must look to African (*A Deusa Negra*, 1979), Brazilian (*A Força de Xango*: The Force of Xango, 1977) and Cuban (*Patakin*, 1980) features, and to documentaries such as Angela Fontanez's *The Orixa Tradition*, Lil Fenn's *Honoring the Ancestors*, Maya Deren's *The Divine Horsemen*, and Gloria Rolando's *Oggun* (1991).

41 The 1993 Supreme Court decision allowing the animal sacrifices associated with Santeria was in this sense a landmark affirmation of religious rights.

42 Toni Morrison, ed., *Race-ing Justice, En-gendering Power: Essays on Anita Hill, Clarence Thomas, and the Construction of Social Reality* (New York: Pantheon, 1992), p. xv.

43 See Jan Pieterse, *White on Black: Images of Africa and Blacks in Western Popular Culture* (New Haven, Conn.: Yale University Press, 1992), p. 207.

44 Ibid., p. 106.

45 On *The Cosby Show*, see John D.H. Downing, "*The Cosby Show* and American Racial Discourse," in Geneva Smitherman-Donaldson and Teun A. van Dijk, eds, *Discourse and Discrimination* (Detroit: Wayne State University Press, 1988); Gray, "Television and the New Black Man," in Todd Gitlin, ed., *Watching Television* (New York: Pantheon, 1987), pp. 223–42; Mark Crispin Miller, "Deride and Conquer," in Gitlin, ed., *Watching Television*; and Mike Budd and Clay Steinman, "White Racism and the

Cosby Show," *Jump Cut*, No. 37 (July 1992).

46 See Gerard Genette, *Narrative Discourse: An Essay in Method*, trans. Jane E. Lewin (Ithaca, NY: Cornell University Press, 1980).

47 See Chidananda das Gupta, "The Politics of Portrayal," *Cinemaya*, Nos 17–18 (Autumn–Winter 1992–3).

48 For more on liberalism in *Hanna K.*, see Richard Porton and Ella Shohat, "The Trouble with Hanna," *Film Quarterly*, Vol. 38, No. 2 (Winter 1984–5).

49 Antonio Prieto-Stanbaugh points out a kind of homology between the protagonist, who sympathizes with the Sioux but ultimately leaves the reservation, and the filmmaker Michael Apted and screenwriter John Fusco, who sympathized with the Sioux and, in the case of Fusco, even lived on the reservation, but who ultimately returned to fame and fortune in the White world (unpublished student paper for a course at New York University).

50 See Ed Guerrero, "Fever in the Racial Jungle," in Jim Collins, Hilary Radner, and Ava Preacher Collins, eds, *Film Theory Goes to the Movies* (London: Routledge, 1993).

51 Michel Chion, *Le Son au Cinéma* (Paris: Cahiers, 1985).

52 For more on the fissures between the ethnic-racial and the national in Israeli cultural practices, see Shohat, *Israeli Cinema*.

53 See Johnson and Stam, *Brazilian Cinema*, pp. 82–3.

54 See George Yudice, "Bakhtin and the Subject of Postmodernism," unpublished paper.

55 Two of Clyde Taylor's defining traits of New Black Cinema – the link to the Afro-American oral tradition, and the strong articulation of Black musicality – are aural in nature, and both are indispensable in Black Cinema's search for what Taylor himself calls "its voice." See Clyde Taylor, "Les Grands Axes et les Sources Africaines du Nouveau Cinema Noir," *CinemAction*, No. 46 (1988).

56 James Naremore's analysis of *Cabin in the Sky* deploys this kind of discursive analyis with great precision and subtlety. Naremore sees the film as situated uneasily among "four conflicting discourses about blackness and entertainment in America": a vestigial "folkloric" discourse about rural Blacks; NAACP critique of Hollywood imagery; the collaboration between mass entertainment and government; and the "posh Africanism of high-toned Broadway musicals." See James Naremore, *The Films of Vincent Minnelli* (Cambridge: Cambridge University Press, 1993).

6

ETHNICITIES-IN-RELATION

SUBMERGED ETHNICITIES

Although issues of race and ethnicity are culturally omnipresent, we have been arguing, they have often been filmically submerged. This textual repression exists on a continuum with the repression of race in other areas. The American constitution, for example, by speaking as if all Americans were equal and free, "submerged" the presence of enslaved Blacks and dispossessed Native Americans, much as today the buried labor of Third World people (migrant labor, "illegal aliens," groundskeepers, nannies) is camouflaged, literally "undocumented." At the same time, the constitution "veiled" White patriarchal domination in falsely universalist language, normalizing the power of White male institutions and identities.[1] This tension between presence and absence points to a possible reconceptualization of race and ethnicity in the media. Rather than restricting our attention to the texts' explicit racial discourse, we will see even the "non-ethnic" text as a field for excavation and reconstruction. And instead of the traditional "image" analysis applied to an unproblematized notion of "minorities," we will explore the ethnic and racial undertones and overtones "haunting" the text. The challenge, then, is to render visible, or at least audible, the repressed multiculturalism even of dominant texts.

A polycentric multicultural approach, we have been arguing, sees issues of race and national representation within a complex and multivalent relationality. In this chapter, we would like to explore the methodological and textual implications of ethnic/racial relationality, both "within" and "between" cultures, for mainstream narrative cinema. Ethnic image studies have often pitted isolated minorities against a fixed and hegemonic Euro-American power structure, usually within the framework of a single national formation. They have not registered the structural analogies underlying dominant representations of marginalized groups, or the interplay of social and sexual displacements, projections, allegories and dialogisms among the diverse communities. While the cultural influence of "minorities" on the dominant culture is obvious – for example, the striking Africanization/ Latinization of North American music/dance – it is easy to overlook the interethnic and international contradictions, syncretisms, and hybridities among the diverse "margins." Nor has image studies globalized its analysis to see representations within the broader transnational context of other multicultural societies, notably those of the Americas.

Since race is a constitutive rather than a secondary feature of American national identity, we should not be surprised to find racial undertones and overtones haunting Hollywood films, just as the repressed stories, the sublimated agonies, and the buried labor of people of color "haunt" everyday social life. For example, an inferential ethnic presence informs Hollywood films set outside of the US. Since all Americans, except for Native Americans, trace their origins to other nations or continents, Hollywood's geographical and historiographical constructs have a visceral impact for "America's" communities. And since immigration is at the core of the official master-narrative, the sympathetic portrayal of certain lands of origin and the caricaturing of others has indirectly legitimated links to Europe while undermining links to Asia, Africa, and Latin America. In this sense, Hollywood has imagined a monocultural history for a multicultural America (and for a multicultural world). Making numerous films about ancient Greece (*Helen of Troy*, 1955; *Ulysses*, 1955; *Alexander the Great*, 1956), imperial Rome (*Quo Vadis*, 1951; *Ben Hur*, 1925, 1959; *Julius Caesar*, 1953), the Crusades (*The Crusades*, 1935), and the Vikings (*The Vikings*, 1958), and about an interminable procession of occidental heroes and heroines (Joan of Arc, Robin Hood, Henry the Eighth, Captains Kidd and Hook, Marie Antoinette, and Napoleon), it has rarely produced films about their counterparts in Asia, Africa, and Latin America.

Many epidermically "White" films bear the traces of an erased multicultural presence. John Ford's *Grapes of Wrath* (1940), like the John Steinbeck novel on which it is based, focusses on the plight of Okies expelled from their land, yet fails to remind us that the Okies had themselves deprived Native Americans of the same land a half-century before, and that these same Native Americans had themselves been displaced from lands further to the East. Yet the film carries tell-tale traces of the erased culture, in the form of place names ("Cherokee County") and in a single shot of a picturesque reservation along Highway 66. A film like *Dead Poet's Society* (1989), similarly, treats an elite, lily-white 1950s milieu, yet encodes the boys' revolt against private-school repression as culturally Black (in the form of the boys' tapped-out polyrhythms) or Black at one remove (in the form of their "White negro" emulations of Beat poetry), and Native American (the boys' ritual activities in the sacred liminal space of the cave). Indeed, the boys' warpaint and drums anticipate the contemporary men's movement, in which White men put on Indian headdresses and carry spears on weekend retreats, in a primitivist attempt to release the "barbaric yawp" of the dark Iron Man repressed at the bottom of the White male psyche.[2]

When one rereads Hollywood classics as it were "from the margins," reconstructing the cultural voices drowned out or reduced to a whisper, one begins to hear other voices. One hears African-American voices, for example, even in an all-White film like *Rear Window* (1954): the voice of Nat King Cole echoed in the group singing of "Mona Lisa," the faint jazzistic overtones in the

Franz Waxman score, the telephone voice of Detective Doyle's Black-sounding maid. Hitchcock's *Vertigo* (1958), similarly, both foregrounds and represses Latino voices. There, the White male and female protagonists are both possessed by a traumatic past (Scottie's vertigo, "Madeleines' fixation" on Carlotta). Might this trauma relate on some level to San Francisco's suppressed Spanish-Mexican history, referenced through verbal and visual allusions (such as the city's Spanish name and architecture, including sites such as Mission Dolores), and more specifically through the haunting iconographic presence of the (Hispanic) Carlotta Valdez?[3] The archeological layers of Carlotta's psyche can also be read as hidden strata of the national identity. Her dispossession from wealth and maternity, her final despairing suicide, might be seen as allegorizing US/Mexican relations; her framed muteness, in the museum, conveys her Hispanic voiceless-ness.[4] A metaphor for her city, Carlotta can be recognized only via the "White" gaze – Madeleine/Judy's and Scottie's – as well as through Hitchcock's inscription of her (Hispanic) city on the screen, inadvertently defining her story as part of the haunting unconscious of American history. In the same film, the voyage to the Sequoia forest indirectly evokes an even deeper submerged stratum – that is, pre-Columbian indigenous history. The dates inscribed on the concentric lines of the sequoia trunk convey a Christian narrative (Christ, Columbus) but the tree itself calls up other lives from an even more ancient past.

A multifocal analysis discerns submerged ethnic voices even in the absence of delegate characters. *Raiders of the Lost Ark* (1981), for example, not only posits the availability of Third World space for the play of First World interests and curiosity, it also reveals a hidden Jewish substratum, even in the absence of Jewish characters. By liberating the ancient Hebrew ark from illegal Egyptian posses-sion, the American hero also rescues it from Nazi sequestration, allegorically reinforcing American and Jewish solidarity against Nazis and their Arab collaborators. The geopolitical alignments here are as clear as in the (perhaps inadvertent) allegory of de Mille's *The Ten Commandments* (1956), where a WASPish Charlton Heston incarnates the Hebrew Moses struggling against menacing Egyptians, thus allegorizing, in a 1950s context, the contemporary conflict of Israel and the US versus Egyptians and other Arabs. That *Raiders* ends with the US army guarding the "top secret" ark – with the ark's active complicity – further buttresses this sense of geopolitical alliances. Just as the ancient Egyptians dispossessed the Hebrews of their ark, so do the Nazis in the film's putative present (the 1930s). But in a kind of time-tunnel, Harrison Ford can be seen as fighting the Nazis in the name of a Jewish shrine, although the word "Jewish" is never pronounced. In this fantasy of liberation from a history of victimization, Biblical myths of wonders wrought against ancient Egyptians are now redeployed against the Nazis – miracles conspicuously absent during the Holocaust. The Hebrew ark itself miraculously dissolves the Nazis, saving Indiana Jones from the Germans, who, unlike the Americans, ignore the divine injunction against looking at the Holy of Holies. The Jewish religious prohibition against looking at God's image, and the censure of "graven images," triumphs over the Christian predilection for religious visualization. Instantiating the typical paradox of cinematic voyeurism, the film punishes the hubris of the "Christian" who dares to gaze at divine beauty, while also generating spectacular visual pleasure for the viewer.

DIALECTICS OF PRESENCE/ABSENCE

Because racial multiplicity exists at the very kernel of the American historical experience, relationality, we argue, should be central for the critical and historiographic accounts of American cinema. From *The Jazz Singer* (1927) and *Swing Time* (1936), through *The Gang's All Here* (1943) and *Porgy and Bess* (1959), to *Funny Girl* (1968) and *New York, New York* (1977), the musical genre in particular has articulated ethnic heterogeneity, whether explicitly or, more often, implicitly, through music and dance. Many musicals thematize the struggle between the high culture of opera and legitimate theatre and the "low" culture of vaudeville and popular music, a struggle that is also racial. Here we will explore a number of interlinked issues concerning relational ethnicity and film studies methodology, and especially the cinematic, narrative, generic, and cultural mediations of ethnicity/race. For Richard Dyer, for example, the Hollywood musical performs an artistic "change of signs" whereby the negatives of social existence are turned into the positives of artistic transmutation.[5] The musical serves up a utopian world of abundance, energy, intensity, transparency and community, in the place of the everyday social inadequacies of scarcity, exhaustion, dreariness, manipulation, and solitude. This utopia gives us the kinetic sensation, as Jane Feuer puts it, of what it would "feel like to be free."[6]

It is the musical's evocation of social harmony that makes the genre appropriate for discussing ethnicities-in-relation. Yet the genre's staging of this harmony also makes Dyer's "community" problematic, since the "imagined community" of the classic musical is usually limited to the dominant White group, eliding even a "managed" interracial collective harmony. Whether set in the midwest – (*Meet Me in St. Louis*, 1944; *Oklahoma!*, 1955), New York (*Dames*, 1934; *Shall We Dance*, 1937), or Hollywood (*Show Girl in Hollywood*, 1930; *Singin' in the Rain*, 1952) – the musical orchestrates a monolithically White communal harmony that represses awareness of America's multicultural formation. Highlighting the exclusionary nature of the musical's communality illuminates the dialectics of presence/absence of marginalized communities even in exclusively White-cast films which almost despite themselves reveal the suppressed "others" through music and dance. The musical's sparse allusions to marginalized cultures usually occur in the fantasy space of the song-and-dance numbers; as in *A Star Is Born* (1954) and *It's Always Fair Weather* (1955), where Asiatics, Scots, and Latinos are evoked in bricolage-style dance sequences. The subaltern presence, then, is largely inferential; it inflects the representation without any literal representations of "ethnic/racial" themes or even characters.

African-American performance has influenced all American arts, yet this influence has often gone acknowledged, or, worse, has been appropriated without credit. The exclusion of Afro/Latin American performers from the musical seems especially anomolous in musicals that exploit African-American and Afro-Latin music. The tradition of blackface "minstrel" recital exemplified by Al Jolson in *Hi Lo Broadway* (1933), Fred Astaire in *Swing Time*, Mickey Rooney and Judy Garland in *Babes in Arms* (1939), and Bing Crosby in *Dixie* (1943) provides an iconic paradigm of the simultaneous presence and absence of marginalized communities. Premised on the myth of the benevolent plantation, minstrelsy clearly constitutes an ambivalent mockery of Blackness.[7] The presence of "Blackness" as mask (a pathological reversal of the Fanonian formula of *Black Skin White Masks*), and the veiled presence of African-American music and dance in numerous films paradoxically marks Afro-American *absence* from the screen.[8] Historically, the minstrel shows evolved largely in the north and were performed without any substantive familiarity with southern culture, with slavery, or even, for that matter, with African-Americans themselves.[9] Indeed, blackface became a popular craze at the very moment that genuinely Black performers and celebrations such as Black coronation festivals were being driven underground.[10] But African-American traces remain in such shows, apparent in body movements or gestures appropriated from Blacks – for example in the "Louisiana Hayride" number in *The Band Wagon* (1953), or in the "Remember my Forgotten Man" number in *Gold Diggers of 1933*, or in "Fascinating Rhythm" in *Girl Crazy* (1943), or in the "Broadway Rhythm" number in *Singin' in the Rain* where the performers shake their hands, gospel-like, in the air.

In musicals, then, the African-American voice was suppressed both historically and musically, since Black musical idioms became more associated on the screen with "White" stars, authorizing a Euro-American signature on what were basically African-American cultural products. In a power-inflected form of ambivalence, the same dominant society that "loves" ornamental snippets of Black culture excludes the Black performers who might best incarnate it. These politics of racial representation were not "unconscious," they were the object of explicit debate and negotiation within the Hollywood production system, rent by the competing influences of southern (and northern) racists, liberals, Black public advocacy groups, censors, nervous producers, and so forth. Thomas Cripps describes the processes by which Blackness was edited out of Hollywood films: the way an all-Black family became White during the scripting process of *Till the End of Time* (1946); or the way the African-American music that inspired George Gershwin was gradually cut out of the biopic *Rhapsody in Blue* (1945), leaving Paul Whiteman to "make a lady out of jazz"; or the way Frank Yerby's critique of plantation mythology became a formula romance in *The Foxes of Harrow* (1947); or the way *Lydia Bailey* (1952) turned from a story about Toussaint l'Ouverture and the Haitian revolution into a White-focalized romance.[11]

Set in a Hollywood studio in the 1940s, Julie Dash's *Illusions* (1982) calls attention to these exclusionary practices by foregrounding a Black singer who lends her singing voice to a White Hollywood star. Like *Singin' in the Rain*,

224

Illusions reflexively focusses on the cinematic technique of postsynchronization or dubbing. But while the former film exposes the intraethnic appropriation whereby silent movie queen Lina Lamont (Jean Hagen) appropriates the silky dubbed voice of Kathy Selden (Debbie Reynolds), *Illusions* reveals the racial dimension of this same procedure. The film features two "submerged" Blacks: Mignon Dupree (Lonette McKee), invisible as an African-American studio executive "passing for White," and Esther Jeeter (Rosanne Katon), the invisible singer hired to dub the singing parts for White film star Leila Grant. Jeeter performs the vocals for a screen role denied her by Hollywood's institutional racism. Black talent and energy are sublimated into a haloed White image. But by reconnecting the Black voice with the Black image, the film makes the Black presence "visible" and therefore "audible," while depicting the operation of the erasure and revealing the film's indebtedness to Black performance. But if Gene Kelly can expose the injustice and bring harmony in the world of *Singin' in the Rain*, Lonette McKee has no such power in *Illusions*, in a studio significantly named the "National Studio."

Illusions references the historical fading in of the African-American image into Euro-American entertainment, suggesting that while Black sounds were often welcome (for example on the radio) Black images remained taboo, as if their iconic presence would be incendiary after such a long disappearing act. As Du Bois reports, the Fisk Jubilee Singers once performed from a Brooklyn organ loft,

Plate 35 Illusions: the racial dialectics of presence/absence

"lest pious congregationalists see their black faces before they heard their heavenly voices."[12] A similar dialectic of presence and absence has operated toward other groups, as in the evocations of Latina, African, and Japanese women in the song "Les Girls" in *Les Girls* (1957), of Chinese in the Shanghai Lil number in *Footlight Parade* (1933) of Native Americans in "Crazy Horse" in *The Girl Most Likely* (1957), and of Latins in *Pal Joey* (1957). The Sinatra song "Small Hotel" shifts midstream into Latin rhythms, subliminally authorizing the Euro-American characters to move their bodies in a more openly sensual way. The same sensuality effect occurs with the cha-cha dancing in the number "Too Bad We Can't Go back to Moscow" and in the African-American melody of "Red Blues" in *Silk Stockings* (1957). That film, within what Rick Altman designates as the musical's "dual-focus narrative,"[13] stages a kind of cold-war romantic imperialism, painting the West as an eroticized pleasure palace in contrast to the austere Soviet lifestyle. Yet what signifies the vibrancy of Anglo-American culture are Latin and African-American rhythms, while the sources of these signifiers, Afro/Latin-American people themselves, remain invisible. North American hegemony represents itself to a competing ideological discourse (Soviet communism) in an ethnically "exotic" spirit. While the Soviets are associated with dull Old World "high art," the North Americans are associated with an effervescent popular culture defined in Latinized/Africanized terms, precisely that which constitutes the "non-American" within the hegemonically imagined American nation.[14]

In some films, African-American culture becomes a kind of structuring absence. Paul Whiteman's *King of Jazz* (1930), for example, celebrates "jazz," here synonymous with popular music in general, but largely ignores African-Americans. The few references to Blacks are patronizing ones: Whiteman's safari to "darkest Africa"; lyrics about "darkies" and the "Mississippi Mud"; a version of "Old Black Joe"; and a single shot of the maestro holding a "pickaninny." Jazz is said to emerge from the "voodoo drum," but the drumming we hear is completely unAfrican; a monorhythmic beat simply accelerates and gets louder rather than being elaborated and complicated. A caricatural finale represents the peoples who contributed to jazz by superimposing a series of musical ensembles, representing various *European* ethnicities, over a symbolic melting pot. Stereotypically accoutered mini-pageants represent the Italians, the Swedes, the French, but there is no African or African-American ensemble. The blended images and sounds metaphorize the "melting pot," vocalizing Euro-American history while silencing the African dimension even where it is most obvious.

In the same vein, the Disney cartoon *Saludos Amigos* (1941) features Afro-Brazilian music and even African instruments (the cuica, the berimbau) in its animated portrait of the Africanized city of Salvador, Bahia, but rigorously avoids suggesting that Black people actually live there. *Birth of the Blues* (1941) does include Black performers, but privileges Bing Crosby as the leader of the Basin Street Hot-Shots as they struggle for a hearing in New Orleans, with jazz trombonist Jack Teagarden in tow. (The film was loosely based on the formation of Nick LaRocca's Original Dixieland Jazz Band, reportedly the first Euro-American group to play Afro-American music.) *High Society* (1956) has Louis Armstrong appear as himself, but makes Bing Crosby the official spokesperson and legitimator of jazz for the East Coast elite. In the song "Now You Has Jazz," it is Crosby who educates the White spectators as to "how jazz music is made" while introducing the Black band and jazz instruments; Afro-American cultural production is mediated through the Euro-American musical authority of Crosby as filter for the "peripheral" culture. Films like this clearly reproduce the colonialist discourse by which Europe serves as global impresario or stage manager, while non-European cultures remain the raw material for the enter-tainment industry. (An exception to such patterns was Orson Welles' planned "Jazz Story," a proposed section of *It's All True* featuring Duke Ellington and Louis Armstrong, which was to show White musicians trying to steal musical ideas from Black musicians while being unable to imitate them. *It's All True* is discussed later in this chapter.)

By speaking for marginalized communities, Hollywood indirectly blocked their self-representation. Musicals generally cast "minority" performers only in isolated sequences, usually without granting them the status even of secondary characters. Often the "ethnic" characters lack even the most basic marker of identity: a name. In *The Band Wagon*, it is Astaire's singing and dancing in the "Shine on Your Shoes" number that awakens the otherwise dormant dancing talent of the African-American shoeshine, used as a merry kinetic object, in an objectifying device reminiscent of Busby Berkeley's depersonalizing rhetoric of gender. LeRoy Daniels as the shoeshine "boy" (kneeling) shines Astaire's shoes and brushes his clothes. Astaire sits in a raised chair, a kind of throne, as the Black man caters to his whims. In both literal and metaphoric senses, Astaire sings while Daniels remains "voiceless"; Astaire leads, Daniels follows. Just as images of White women beautifying themselves in *Dames* are made to yield up their quantum of spectacle, so the shoeshine in *The Band Wagon* forms part of the esthetic dynamics of the production number. In *High Society*, similarly, Crosby's singing "inspires" Louis Armstrong's "echoes" on the trumpet, thus symbolically reversing the historical relation between African-American and Euro-American music.[15] The racial division of prestige in *High Society*, moreover, credits Bing Crosby as a classical musician who plays jazz while the jazzmen are portrayed as ignorant of "classical music." What all these appropriations have in common is a desire for an otherness whose presence is made possible, paradoxically, only through erasure. Black entertainment becomes a kind of errant fetish; just as an African mask could be torn from its social habitus and placed in a museum, so Black-style popular culture could be separated off from the Black communities and performers that gave it birth.

The racial dialectics of presence/absence become particularly complicated when we take White "ethnicities" into account. Since immigrants, especially European-Jewish immigrants, played a major and contradictory role in Hollywood, the study of American cinema is perforce also the study of those

Plate 36 The kinetics of servitude: Fred Astaire and Leroy Daniels in *The Band Wagon*

immigrants' projected "American dream," their oneiric extrapolation of the image that hegemonic America would desire for itself.[16] Their ways of expressing, repressing, and sublimating America's ethnic multiplicity provide a barometer for evolving racial attitudes and discourses. Despite the disproportionate role of Jewish immigrants in the film industry, until the late 1960s Hollywood films did not foreground Jewishness, which generally remained only a euphemistic "closet" presence. Even 1950s and 1960s films shot or set in New York (*On the Town*, 1949; *It's Always Fair Weather*), downplay the ethnic and racial diversity of the metropolis. The post-Holocaust "problem film" *Gentleman's Agreement* (1947), where Gregory Peck plays a journalist who pretends to be a Jew, also betrays acute anxiety in the face of a fully articulated Jewishness.[17] Worried about anti-Semitism, the immigrants repressed their own images from the public sphere, as if afraid that any self-declared appearance as Jews might threaten a precariously achieved security.

A relational approach to representation would take into account both a racial dimension – the Whiteness of European-Jewish immigrants – and an ethnic/religious dimension – their Jewishness. In *The Jazz Singer* the cantor's son runs away from home and from the emotive music of Kol Niderei to become a jazz singer in the face of his father's disapproval. The older immigrant generation gesticulates melodramatically, while the eager-to-assimilate younger generation

228

incarnated by Jolson uses such gestures largely in blackface. This expressive mask was an index not only of a conditioned Jewish self-censorship in the name of "Americanness," but also of the production of Black absence.[18] Jackie Rabinowitz/Jack Robins' identity crisis is articulated in blackface, beyond the usual stage entertainment framing. His mirror reflects not his literal self but the image of the Jewish community, echoing, as the intertitles suggest, the "call of his race." The reconcilation between two differentially empowered White worlds is summed up at the finale, as Jolson belts out "Mammy" to his weeping Yiddeshe-Mamma. His wrestling with the anomalies of identity in the "New World" is played out along the shady specular boundaries between European-Jewish and African-Black identities; Blackness becomes a sign of the dilemmas of White/Jewish ethnicity vis-à-vis Anglo culture.

Jewish entertainers took the preexisting racist tradition of blackface from vaudeville, but endowed it with a communitarian intonation. For Irving Howe, American Jews allegorized their historical sorrow through Black expressivity; blackface became iconic of exclusion.[19] As the Jolson character is told in *The Jazz Singer*: "There are a lot of jazz singers but you have tears in your eyes." Blackface, according to Howe, "became a mask for Jewish expressiveness, with one woe speaking through the voice of another," enabling Jewish performers to reach a spontaneous assertiveness in the performance of their ethnic selves.[20] Thanks to the black mask, Jews could repossess, as it were, an emotional heritage of shtetl expressivity, while at the same time conveniently displacing it on to a group seen as inferior in status. As a site of contradictions, the Jewish minstrel figure combined an intuition of historical affinities with rank opportunism, including the classic opportunism of affirming one's "Americanness" by denigrating Blacks. The "two-woes" parallelism suggested by Howe is asymetrical, however, since the Jewish-American minstrel was not simply the vehicle of a Jewish woe, but also an appropriation of the exoticized signs of Blackness as constructed in the Jim Crow era.

There were of course clear affinities linking Blacks and Jews as groups historically oppressed by Eurocentrism. In the collective consciousness of both traditions, narratives of slavery and diaspora have played a major role. The yearly Passover celebration of the Exodus tale of the Israelites' escape from Egyptian enslavement took on contemporary echoes of anti-Semitic persecution. Meanwhile, Bible-based Black spirituals translated the same experience into African-American idiom: "When Israel was in Egypt land ... Let my people go." The Jewish themes of exile, the Promised Land, and return became part of a "signifying" Black language testifying to the Afro-diasporic experience, rendered for example in *The Harder They Come* (1973), and in Rastafarianism and reggae with its lyrical lietmotifs of "Babylon," "Jerusalem," and the "Lion of Judah." The Afro-diasporic revoicing of Hebraic texts, however, emphasized historical analogies of oppression and, unlike the Jewish-American appropriation of a folklorized Blackness, did not take place in a caricatural show-business context. African Americans, unlike Jews, had little power over their own self-representation or over that of others; Black marginalization was both more extreme and more constitutive of the "center." While for Blacks America was the site of relentless oppression, for Jews it was a place of hope. Jews *chose* to immigrate to the US, and their assimilation was eased by the facility with which they could "pass" for the socially normative ethnicity. African-Americans, like Asians and Native Americans, could not conveniently mask their features. And although European Jewish immigrants were obliged more or less to conform to the institutionalized decorum of American life, in Hollywood they still wielded the power to prevent anti-Semitic imagery. The norm of the "melting pot" was therefore experienced differently by the two communities. Jewish characters could easily achieve assimilated status, as in *The Jazz Singer*, and assimilated Jewish actors such as John Garfield and Kirk Douglas could become stars. But African-Americans, undisguisably "different," were forced to perform the roles assigned them within the segregated space of all-Black films.

EROTIC ALLEGORIES

Films made in multiracial societies reveal a clear tendency toward "allegory," in Fredric Jameson's sense of texts which metaphorize the public sphere even when narrating apparently private stories, and where "the personal and the political, the private and the historical, become inextricably linked."[21] The ethnic hierarchies of the cinema allegorize, in other words, extra-discursive social intercourse. While interracial romance was taboo in most classic Hollywood films, a number of them, such as *The Jazz Singer* and *The Jolson Story* (1946), show White interethnic romances in such a way as to project allegories (even quasi-didactic allegories) of ethnic tensions and reconciliation, in which youthful mixed couples microcosmically unite, or attempt to unite, their conflicting communities. Thus ethnic and class conflicts are "resolved" through "acceptance" and implied harmony. Al Jolson in *The Jazz Singer* is torn between the world of the cantor, synecdochic of his Ashkenazi Jewish heritage, and that of a Broadway jazz singer, symbolizing the contemporary America embodied by his Anglo-American girlfriend. The film's closure celebrates the New World utopia of the "melting pot": a Jewish cantor becomes a jazz singer without discarding his heritage. The melded Jewish/Black music provides the soundtrack for the constitution of a "mixed" Jewish-gentile couple. Such mixed marriages typically take place among "White" ethnicities, however, and presume assimilation on the part of the "ethnic" character.

In the musical's exclusionary version of ethnic utopia, embodied in such films as *Follow the Fleet* (1936), *Annie Oakley* (1935) and *Oklahoma!*, the representatives of marginalized groups, when they do appear, are not allowed to violate the principles of purity and social order. The overwhelming majority of the love stories in musical comedies avoid any hint of miscegenation by focalizing a glamorous heterosexual White couple, best epitomized by Ginger Rogers and Fred Astaire. In *Swing Time* the narrative role of Rogers' Latin lover (George

Metaxa) is to catalyze her relationship with Astaire, the Anglo who woos Rogers away from the libidinal Latin – a variation on the romantic plot of *Top Hat* (1935), which again features a volatile Latin lover character (Erik Rhodes). While the Anglo-American entertainers occupy center stage, the Latin and Black entertainers barely appear outside the musical numbers. The occasional mixed couples appear only in periods of acute economic lust on the part of North American corporations. In *Flying down to Rio* (1933), for example, where Dolores del Rio discards her Brazilian lover for a North American,[22] the film's mythical discourse of love, as Brian Henderson points out, masks a crude promotion of the new airline route of New York–Rio de Janeiro and the merged imperial interests of Panamerican and RCA.[23]

In the period of the Good Neighbor policy, Hollywood attempted to enlist Latin America in the anti-Axis cause. As European film markets declined due to World War II, Hollywood, in hopes of Latin American markets and pan-American political unity, flooded the screens with Latin American heroes, stars, locales, and, especially, music and dance. (Swing, in this period, gave way to rhumba.) But Latin Americans (and Afro-Americans) were almost invariably marginalized by the narrative and cinematic codes, and were usually limited to roles as entertainers within the musical numbers. The musical's disjunctive structure made possible an ethnic division of labor, counterpointing a relatively "realistic" mode of narrative for the White characters against implausibly ludic musical numbers for the Latinos, the delicious artifice of the latter providing narrative license for "exotic" display.

The musical thus allotted its narrative "spaces" in ethnic and national terms, homologizing segregationist attitudes in the larger society. The musical numbers not only furnished the spectacle of difference but also functioned narratively to unite the North American couple vis-à-vis the "Latins." In *Guys and Dolls* (1955), for example, the erotic metamorphosis of the Salvation Army worker during her visit to Havana is ignited by the sweeping music and dance that trigger her romance with Marlon Brando. In this sense, the musical heightened the presence of marginalized communities not otherwise allowed into the space of the "real" (assumed to be "White" and Euro-American) without ever granting them a substantive equality. (Retrospective clips from the Johnny Carson *Tonight Show* reveal a latter-day echo of this division of labor: while welcome as performers on stage, Blacks are not often invited into the inner sanctum of Carson's symbolic "home".) Marginalized and ossified within the narrative, the Latin characters in *The Gang's All Here*, *Too Many Girls* (1940), *Pan-Americana* (1945) and *Weekend in Havana* (1941) tend at the finale of each film to be left at the same point from which they began, unlike the North American protagonists who go on to new phases in their lives. Set outside any properly narrative development, the Latin performers are set outside of history; their presence is "tolerable" only on the decorative level of music and dance. Character interaction allegorizes the larger North/South relation, translating an ambivalent attraction and repulsion toward cultural difference.

231

GOOD NEIGHBORS AND BORDER CROSSERS

Hollywood filmmaking, even in a period when the threat of fascism generated a "Popular Front" liberal stance, generally remained cautious, if not outright reactionary, on issues of race. One of the major attempts radically to revise the racial conventions and ideologies in this same period was Orson Welles' largely finished but never released *It's All True*. In 1942, as a representative of the Good Neighbor policy, Welles went to Brazil to make a "pan-American documentary." He filmed two sequences, one highlighting the Black contribution to the Rio de Janeiro carnival, the other celebrating four real-life *mestizo* fishermen or *jangadeiros* (raftsmen) who traveled over a 1,000 miles by raft to present their social grievances to Brazil's President Vargas. The production methods and esthetic of *It's All True*, part of which is now viewable thanks to the efforts of Richard Wilson, Bill Krohn, Catherine Benamou, and Myron Meisel and their partial reconstruction of *It's All True* (1993), stand in striking contrast to the conventional Hollywood approach both to race and to Latin America. Rather than displaying North American stars against "exotic" backdrops, the usual practice in Hollywood films set in Latin America, *It's All True* was designed to promote local talent, much of it Black: well-known carnival orchestras like Chiquinho, Fon-Fon, and Dédé; Brazilian composers and instrumentalists such as Pixinguinha, the composer of "Carinhoso." The key performer was to be the brilliant Black actor Sebastião Prata (also known as "Grande Otelo," the future lead in *Macunaíma*, 1969), whose role would be to "personalize" the carnival sequence.[24]

The conventional paradigm for the representation of Latin America was premised on a notion of the continent's political incapacity and cultural nullity. (Even Hollywood's attempts to ingratiate itself with Latin American audiences through "positive" portrayals, in such films as *Down Argentine Way*, 1940, foundered on the shoals of studio ignorance and condescension.) Welles consciously marked off his difference from the usual Hollywood procedures by attempting to paint a more knowing portrait of Brazil than that offered by such films as *Flying Down to Rio* and *That Night in Rio* (1941). The mere desire to move beyond stereotype, however, is hardly sufficient; cultural and historical knowledge is essential. It was in this sense that *It's All True* constituted a radical departure from Hollywood modes of production and representation. Welles commissioned research by a number of well-known Brazilian writers (Alex Viany, Clovis de Gusmao, Edgar Morel, Ernani Fornari, Luiz Edmondo, Rui Costa, Ayres de Andrade Jr), and this research tells us a good deal about Welles, about North/South relations, and about what a completed *It's All True* might have looked like. First, it reflected Brazilian views rather than the opinions of Hollywood "experts." Second, the range of the subjects covered – slavery, sugar and coffee plantation economies, social conditions, popular culture, and political institutions – was astonishingly broad. Third, the material was undogmatic; the emphasis was on polyphonic debate and lively differences of opinion. Fourth, the orientation was toward Brazilian popular culture and more particularly its liberatory movements: the Black fugitive-slave republic of Palmares, the antislavery revolts, the millennial movement led by Antonio Conselheiro. Welles saw the *jangadeiro* episode, for example, as part of an ongoing tradition of popular Brazilian resistance to oppression, since past *jangadeiros* had been instrumental in the struggle against slavery, and in the present they were still articulating popular demands. (Jacaré, the leader of the *jangadeiros*, was a labor activist with a price on his head, and the Brazilian elite was not pleased that Welles devoted such loving attention to a "rabble rouser.") The image of *mestizo* raftsmen struggling for justice on the high seas recalls what Paul Gilroy calls the "chronotope of the ship" as a conduit of pan-African communication within the

Plate 37 Grande Otelo
in *It's All True*

Plate 38 The chronotope
of the *jangada*

history of the Black Atlantic, with the same *jangadas* that were once used to spirit slaves to freedom now being used to press social demands.

The research Welles commissioned would have alerted him, if he had not already been aware of it, to the indispensable Black role in carnival. But Welles in 1942 was already well attuned to the power and complexity of what Robert Farris Thompson calls "black Atlantic civilization." More than a tolerant liberal, Welles was a passionate opponent of racism and anti-Semitism. In a period of extreme racism, of segregation in the south and discrimination in the north, Welles was an active participant in antilynching and anti-Mexican discrimination campaigns, and used his radio programs and newspaper columns to excoriate racism as the American version of Nazism. Welles was attracted to Black themes and Black performers, as exemplified by his early interest in John Brown in "Marching Song," by the "Voodoo" *Macbeth* he staged with an all-Black cast in Harlem in 1936, by his 1940 theatrical adaptation of Richard Wright's *Native Son*, and by his involvement in the Duke Ellington/Louis Armstrong "Jazz Story" project originally slated to form part of *It's All True*. It was only when Welles realized that samba was the Brazilian counterpart to jazz and that both were expressions of African diaspora culture in the New World, that he abandoned the New Orleans setting of "Jazz Story" in favor of another Africanized New World carnival city, Rio de Janeiro, and that he replaced the Afro-American music called jazz with the Afro-Brazilian music called samba. Songs such as "Didn't He Ramble" gave way to Brazilian tunes like "Bahia" and "Praca Onze," and Duke Ellington and Louis Armstrong made way for Pixinguinha and Grande Otelo.

Before World War II, even the most significant Black musical stars tended to be relegated to the "ghetto" of unprestigious two-reelers. Such films as *Birth of the Blues* and *Syncopation* (1943) were among the few timidly favorable treatments of jazz, but these films were usually White-focalized. Welles' approach in *It's All True* sharply challenged the racial and esthetic conventions of Hollywood filmmaking. Nor was he merely chameleonizing to the more relaxed racial mores of Brazil, for he went further than the equivalent Brazilian productions of the period in foregrounding Black life, culture, and performance. Edgar Morel, hired by Welles to research the raftsmen story, describes Welles as a "vehement anti-racist" and attributes much of the hostility toward him to the fact that he enjoyed the company of Blacks and that he treated carnival as a "Black" story. As a result, the film was hounded by a racism which came both from the Euro-Brazilian elite – not eager to expose the "secret" of Brazil's Blackness – and from higher-ups in the RKO production hierarchy and the Rockefeller Committee of the Coordinator of Inter-American Affairs. A memorandum from the Rockefeller Committee to RKO recommends that *It's All True* "avoid any reference to miscegenation," and suggests that the studio should "omit sequences of the film in which mulattos or mestizos appear conspicuously."[25]

There were also complaints from RKO executives, and from some members of the production crew, that Welles was overemphasizing the Black element and showing too much "ordinary social intercourse" between Blacks and Whites in carnival, a feature that might offend some North American viewers. A July 1942 letter from William Gordon, of the film's production team, to an RKO executive complains about Welles "indiscriminate intermingling of blacks and whites."[26] Citing Goldwyn's deletion of two close shots of Black members of Gene Krupa's orchestra in *Ball of Fire* (1941), Gordon argues for the deletion of all such shots. An RKO memorandum from studio head Koerner to Gordon, meanwhile, notes that "the heroes on the raft are referred to as Indians," a perspective that "will be impossible to sell to audience, especially south of the Mason-Dixon line." The democratic, antiracist spirit animating Welles' project was antithetical to such colonizing attitudes. Welles wanted to show Brazilian heroes, not North American stars against Brazilian backdrops. That *It's All True* could laud a Black *sambista* from the *favelas* and a quartet of *mestizo* fisherman as authentic popular heroes speaks volumes about the distance that separated the film from the ambient racism of the time.[27]

STAGING AMERICAN SYNCRETISM

Welles' work in the early 1940s, that of a multiculturalist *avant la lettre*, was in certain ways prophetic of the heightened ethnic consciousness of the late 1960s. This consciousness brought with it a resurgent embrace of America's cultural diversity, whether through *Roots*-like recuperation of the past, through narratives set in the "old country" (as in the European shtetl of *Fiddler on the Roof*, 1971) or through films that foregrounded the multiethnicity of contemporary America (*Nashville*, 1975; *Hair*, 1979; *Fame*, 1980; and *Dirty Dancing*, 1987). As early as 1961, *West Side Story* had stylized ethnic conflicts, conveying the ironic motto "everything is alright in America/if you are white in America." (The satire here is largely restricted to the musical numbers.) Still, utopian longing for ethnic and social harmony permeates the finale of this recycled Shakespearean tragedy, where the lovers, "somewhere, someday," hope to "find a new way of living."

In the wake of Rock 'n' Roll and the swelling White consumption of Black musical culture, early 1960s films such as *Bye Bye Birdie* (1963) have Euro-American performers emulate Afro-American-style singing and dancing, in contrast to the segregated filmic zone of earlier "Black" musicals such as *Cabin in the Sky* (1943). *Bye Bye Birdie* alludes to Elvis Presley, but suppresses the Afro-American sources of Rock 'n' Roll. Recent nostalgia musicals like *Dirty Dancing* and *Hairspray* (1988), by contrast, enthusiastically foreground the Black and Latino influence on "White" popular culture, projecting communal utopias in which Euro-American characters are viscerally "possessed" or "entranced" by the very Afro-American or Latin cultures repressed in antecedent cinema. Yet *Dirty Dancing*, and even the independent production *Hairspray*, retain the old hierarchies in focalization, narratively privileging the Euro-American (in these cases the marginalized White working-class or Jewish middle-class) perspective, even though it is Afro-Latin music/dance that energizes the film.

Films such as *Dirty Dancing*, *Breakin'* (1984), *Salsa* (1988), and even

Forbidden Dance (1991) celebrate the pluralistic integration of "ethnic" music and dance into "mainstream" American culture. In *La Bamba* (1987), the class ascendency of the Chicano character lends allegorical spice to the American dream. In *Dirty Dancing* the Jewish characters emulate the mainstream Anglo culture, whereas the working-class White male protagonist is powerfully drawn to Latin/Black rhythms and dancers. The film ends with integration through Eros: the excluded, even forbidden, "dirty" music and dance formerly played only in ghettoized surroundings, as well as their lower-class performers, are accepted in an atmosphere of communal harmony. Sensuously swaying the hips becomes a collectively desired fantasy of the Jewish middle class. The final image of the dancing couple surrounded by the White "ethnic" community applauding and mimicking their movements encapsulates the film's liberal integrationist vision.

American popular culture bears constant witness to the "dialog" less between different marginalized communities than between Euro-American culture and its diverse "others." In film, this dialog has often taken the form of hero-and-sidekick (the Lone Ranger and Tonto, ethnicized latter-day avatars of Don Quixote and Sancho Panza), or of hero and valet (Jack Benny and Rochester), or of hero and entertainer (Rick and Sam in *Casablanca*, 1942). In *The Defiant Ones* (1958) Tony Curtis and Sidney Poitier carry a chain-heavy allegory of racial interdependency. The 1970s and 1980s offer more upbeat versions of the biracial "buddy film": Richard Pryor and Gene Wilder in *Stir Crazy* (1980) and *See No Evil* (1989); Eddie Murphy and Nick Nolte in *48 Hours* (1982); Billy Crystal and Gregory Hines in *Running Scared* (1986); and Mel Gibson and Danny Glover in *Lethal Weapon* I, II and III (1987, 1989, 1991). Films like *Driving Miss Daisy* (1991), *Grand Canyon* (1992), *Passion Fish* (1992), and *White Men Can't Jump* (1992) similarly place Black–White dialog at the center of their concerns. The appeal, including the box-office appeal, of such films suggests that they touch something deep within the national unconscious, a historically conditioned longing for interracial harmony. Leslie Fiedler in *Love and Death in the American Novel* traces the literary origins of these epiphanies of racial harmony back to Crusoe and Friday, Natty Bumppo and Chingachgook, Ishmael and Queequeeg, Huck and Jim – relationships that for Fiedler have homoerotic overtones. And indeed images of ethnic utopia percolate all through American popular culture, from the perennial Thanksgiving celebrations through the latest multiethnic music videos. One finds echoes of this utopian trope in contemporary TV talk shows (Arsenio, Oprah), MTV (Janet Jackson's "Rhythm Nation," Lionel Ritchie's "All Night Long"), soft-drink commercials, TV sports, public service announcements, and in the amiable multiethnic camaraderie of Eyewitness News. The challenge, however, is to translate the utopian energies behind these consolatory representations of ethnic harmony into the necessary mobilization for structural change that alone can make racial equality a quotidian reality.

In a multiracial society, the self is inevitably syncretic, especially when a preexisting cultural polyphony is amplified by the media. This syncretism is first of all linguistic: in cities like New York the language itself is hybrid, consisting of Yiddishized English, Anglicized Spanish, and so forth. When Rupert Pupkin, in Scorsese's *King of Comedy* (1983), calls his female sidekick, Masha, "el schmucko supremo," he gives voice to the hybridized language of the city. This process of cultural syncretism began even before the American revolution, as diverse African nations (such as Fulani, Hausa, Ibo) and Native American nations (Iroquois, Cherokee, Huron) culturally commingled with one another, and as Euro-Americans appropriated not only the vocabulary but also the military tactics and political thinking of Native American peoples, along with the musical and religious styles (and the labor) of African-Americans. Cultural syncretism takes place both at the margins and between the margins and a changing mainstream, resulting in a conflictual yet creative intermingling of cultures. Indigenous, Afro-American and local-immigrant, diasporic and exile experiences play against one another in a "non-finalized" polyphony.

It is no accident that any number of American films stage the processes of ethnic syncretism: White men learning Native American ways in films like *Hombre* (1967) and *A Man Called Horse* (1970); Richard Pryor showing Gene Wilder how to "walk Black" in *Silver Streak* (1976); Eugene Martoni learning to play the blues at the feet of Willie Brown in *Crossroads* (1985); Appalachian Whites, Italians, and Black Americans collaborating musically (and politically) in *Matewan* (1987); young (White) boy David learning Jamaican patois from Clara in *Clara's Heart* (1988); Chinese immigrants learning street slang from Chicanos in *Born in East L.A.* (1987); Woody Allen armed with Wonder Bread and crucifix and ready for conversion in *Hannah and Her Sisters* (1985); Charlie Parker in a yarmulka jazzing up a Hassidic wedding in *Bird* (1988); Whoopie Goldberg teaching White nuns Motown dance routines in *Sister Act* (1992). Indeed, any binary grid which pits Anglo Whiteness against Black/Red/Yellow others inevitably misses the complex contradictory gradations of syncretized culture. One merit of Spike Lee's *Do the Right Thing* (1989) is that it foregrounds not only the tensions but also the begrudging affinities between Italian-Americans and African-Americans. The film implicitly calls attention to how some members of recent immigrant communities have used Blacks as a kind of "welcome mat," as a way of affirming, through anti-Black hostility, their own insecure sense of American identity. (In *Jungle Fever*, 1991, some Italian-Americans almost come to blows over insinuations of "black blood.") At the same time, the film highlights more subtle interactions between the two communities by having the Italians act just a little "Black" and the Blacks act just a little "Italian." We learn from the published screenplay that Lee even thought of having Giancarlo Esposito, who is himself half Black and half Italian, play a character called "Spaghetti Chitlins." (The metaphor drawn from cuisine is highly apposite, since American cuisine is now multicultural, having been soul-foodized, taco-ized, felafelized, and sushi-ized.) A polyphonic historical process has in effect generated the rich peculiarities and syncretisms of North American popular culture. American music and dance, to take another example, now thoroughly meld European and African traditions: there is no contemporary White popular music that does not trace some of its roots to Africa. Virtually all of the participants, Black and White, in the music video "We Are the World," for example, sing in a melismatic, improvisational gospel style that has everything to do with the spirit of Black musicality.

Recent films have facilitated a syncretic space of racial transformation. Woody Allen's *Zelig* (1983) features a bizarre chameleon-man with an uncanny talent for taking on the accent and ethnicity of his interlocutors. Born White and Jewish, he subsequently becomes Native American, African-American, Irish, Italian, Mexican, and Chinese. (His Brazilian counterpart Macunaíma is born Indian and Black but subsequently transforms himself into a White Portuguese prince and a French divorcé.) Films like *Black Like Me* (1964), *Watermelon Man* (1970), *Soul Man* (1986), *True Identity* (1987), and *Made in America* (1993) all play on this trope. Sandra Bernhard, in the opening sequence of *Without You I Am Nothing* (1989), sings "My Skin is Black" and is lit, and dressed, so as to appear Black. As Masha in Scorsese's *King of Comedy*, the same actress speaks of wishing she were Black, much as Woody Allen, in *Annie Hall* (1977), suggests that smoking grass makes White college students think they've become Billie Holliday. But the trope is hardly limited to film. Lou Reed sang "I Wanna Be Black" on the album "Street Hassle" (1979), just as the all-White rap group Young Black Teenagers speak of being "Proud To Be Black," arguing that "Blackness is a state of mind." Standup comics, similarly, constantly cross racial boundaries through a kind of racial ventriloquism. Whoopi Goldberg impersonates (presumably White) "valley girls," while Billy Crystal impersonates (presumably Black) jazz musicians. These racial metamorphoses reach their apotheosis in Michael Jackson's "Black or White" music video, where morphing scrambles a succession of multiethnic faces into an infinity of hybridized combinations.

As a chameleon-man who literally *becomes* his ethnic neighbors, Zelig especially illustrates the opportunistic appropriations typical of a mobile, heteroglot culture. Each of Zelig's metamorphoses is informed by a deep social and cultural logic; each carries its specific weight of historical association. Zelig's recurrent switch to Blackness, for example, is deeply rooted in the experience of a European anti-Semitism which insistently associated Jewishness and Blackness. The KKK, we are told, views Zelig as a "triple threat" precisely because of his multiple otherness as Black, Jew, and Native American. Not only does Zelig the Jew chameleonize to other oppressed communities, he also chameleonizes to his fellow swimmers in the European immigrants' melting pot. The film can thus be seen as illustrating, in this reading, the process by which diverse ethnicities meet, clash, and interact in the streets of a city like New York. *Zelig* renders syncretism visible by offering us a figure who is at once Woody Allen, and therefore White and Jewish, *and* Black, Indian, Chinese, and Irish. The dialogical encounter is not a complete merging, but a "hybridization" and "assimilation" of the other's word. These metamorphoses render palpable the constant process of synchresis that occurs when ethnicities brush against and rub off on one another in a crowded ambivalent space of cultural interaction.[28]

At times interracial dialogism inflects a film's textual strategies. Think for example of Robert Altman's *Nashville* (1975) and its alternating montage between the soporific intoning of Haven Hamilton's country-style bicentennial song "Two Hundred Years" in one recording studio, and the rousing chant of a Black hand-clapping gospel song (improbably led by an out-of-tune Lily Tomlin) in the studio next door. Altman suggestively juxtaposes two musical styles, each redolent of what Bakhtin would call the "accents" and "intonations" of a "socio-ideological world." Rather than polyphony, we are given a contrastive diaphony or counterpoint: in one studio, the bland music of jingoistic complacency – "we must be doing something right to last 200 years" – presided over by an authoritarian singer who would expel longhaired dissidents from the room; in the other, a soulful participatory music forged during the same 200 years, but informed by the perspective of a historical memory that includes slavery and segregation. The gospel scene is observed, furthermore, by an effusive BBC journalist, played by Geraldine Chaplin, who makes inane ethnocentric comments about darkest Africa and missionaries converting natives. The revolution celebrated by the bicentennial, Altman reminds us, was fought against this journalist's ancestors, the British, who had in common with White North Americans an oppressive relation to Black people.[29]

Emilio de Antonio's satirical documentary about Richard Nixon, *Milhouse: A White Comedy* (1971), offers an even more incisive instance of ethnic/racial counterpoint. De Antonio counterposes the voice of Nixon extolling "law and order" against a Black voice describing what transpired in Miami's Black community during the Republican convention in that city. The ensuing images decode Nixon's grand phrases about "order" to reveal their subsurface significa-tion: the intention to crush any outbreaks of Black rebellion. The next montage plays off Nixon's innocuous "I See a Day" speech against Martin Luther King's stirring "I Have a Dream" oration – whose rhetoric and syntax the Nixon speech clearly pilfers – showing transparent sympathy for the emotional force and political commitment of the latter while mocking the petit-bourgeois mediocrity of the former. Nixon's voice, promulgating the myth of "equal opportunity," gradually gives way to the resonant authority of King's denouncing, in the powerful accents of the southern Black preacher, the barriers to equality while articulating a distant-yet-imaginable promised land of racial harmony. The two voices are counterposed at a dialogical angle, generating a social message far transcending the content of the two individual discourses.

If ethnic and racial relations have often been repressed or submerged in mainstream representation, some recent parody films call up a veritable "return of the repressed." Though scarcely radical, these films do partly subvert racial hierarchies by exposing the silences of the American master-narrative. John Waters' *Hairspray*, for example, stages a synergistic coalition of marginalized figures. The overweight White working-class female protagonist and her "mother," played by the male actor Divine, together with the Afro-American community, defeat the racists, suggesting the utopia of a non-supremacist America. At the finale the protagonist and her Black-style "bug" dance win over the "all-American girl" and her racist fans. One scene satirizes White paranoia by having African-Americans play with the racist expectations of a White matron "stranded" in a Black ghetto. By focalizing the scene through the neighborhood's Black residents, Waters sutures the spectator into an antiracist viewpoint. Similarly, John Sayles, in *The Brother from Another Planet* (1984), represents two terrified white midwesterners from the perspective of the patrons of a Harlem bar. The finale of *Hairspray* celebrates the triumph of various "margins," culminating in the policeman's participation in the collective dance.

Mel Brooks' *Blazing Saddles* (1974), meanwhile, orchestrates a "trialog" between Jews, Blacks, and Native Americans, subjecting the western genre to a corrosively comic revision. Much of the film's humor plays off the stereotypical expectations audiences bring to film. Here the Whites sing "Ole Man River" and the Blacks sing "I Get No Kick from Champagne," and the Black sheriff (Cleavon Little) has a Gucci saddle. Instead of the western's usual segregationist discourse of Anglo-American heroes foiling evil "Indians" and Mexicans, Brooks' parody western calls up elided histories and suppressed voices. It opens with a historical episode usually omitted from the Hollywood master-narrative: the forced labor of Blacks and Chinese on the railroad, their mistreatment by racist and greedy cowboys (with Slim Pickens in a satirically recast version of his traditional western roles), and the confiscation of Native American land under the paternalistic alibi of "their own protection." Furthermore the "gunslinger" Gene Wilder, who in another ethnically revisionist film, *The Frisco Kid* (1979), plays the schlemeil Rabbi in the west, here joins the Black sheriff (Cleavon Little) to rescue the town from judicial injustice and cowboy vandalism, ultimately winning the marginalized some share of land and equality. The film also provocatively revises generic and historiographical conventions through the carnivalesque inversion that transforms an exploited Black laborer into a sheriff. One scene visualizes the Cleavon Little character's story about his family's travel to the west: obliged to follow the end of the trail, even when Indians are about to attack, the Blacks are denied entry to the White folks' circle. The "Indians," meanwhile – Brooks plays the Chief in redface – are not demonic but sympathetic, and they let the Blacks go. Speaking Yiddish, the Indian Chief addresses the Blacks as "schvarzes" and prevents his Indian companion from killing them. Here Brooks aligns Native Americans, Jews, and African-Americans as groups all marginalized, in different ways, by the Eurocentric master-narrative. When the Black family continues to travel, the Chief notes that "they are darker than us": on one level a self-mocking allusion to Jewish racism toward Blacks, on another an acknowledgment of the different colors not as binary opposites but as nuances on a spectrum, and a hint at the affinities among all three groups as having been objectified and oppressed on a pseudo-biological basis.

Brooks' Yiddish-speaking Indian follows in the tradition of Jewish entertainers such as Fanny Brice, who used to sing "I'm an Indian," and in the tradition of "Indianist" poetry written by Jewish immigrants as a way of displacing their own sense of marginality on to Native Americans, forging a link between Europe's external and internal "other." A Lenny Bruce monolog even voiced the bitter irony of the Native American by having one complain: "Oh Christ! The white people are moving in – you let one white family in, and the whole neighborhood will be white." Bruce thus lampooned the urban ethnic phobias directed against stigmatized groups, but by placing the comment in the mouth of a Native American he also called attention to the European expropriation of Native American land. The concept of the "Indian," in other words, is employed as a mode of indirect enunciation, a political metaphor constucting one's own ethnic subjectivity through (an)other. These stagings of mass-mediated syncretism, while groping toward a dialogical inter-change, hardly exhaust the possibilities of oppositional syncretism – possibilities to which we will return in a later chapter.

THE MUTUAL ILLUMINATION OF CULTURES

Within dialogism, entire genres, languages, and even cultures are susceptible to what Bakhtin calls "mutual illumination." This illumination takes place both "within" and "between" cultures and thus provides a model for dialogical cross-cultural study. One consequence of Eurocentrism, for example, is that North Americans tend to look to Europe for self-definition and self-understanding, rather than to the other multiracial societies of our hemisphere. Yet the question of ethnic representation in North American cinema might be profitably studied within the relational context of the cinematic representations offered by the other racially plural societies of the Americas, with their shared history of colonialism, slavery, and immigration.

Throughout the Americas, we find variations on the same racial theme: the shifting relationalities among the fundamental triad of indigenous "Reds," African "Blacks," and European "Whites," augmented by various immigrant strains. The proportions may vary, but the fact of racial heterogeneity obtains almost everywhere, including in the US. But while Latin Americans have known their continent to be *mestizo*, many Euro-Americans have resisted the recognition that North American culture is also *mestizo*, mixed, hybrid. While the syncretic nature of other societies is "visible," the syncretic nature of North American society often remains hidden. Where the Latin American and Caribbean discussion of national identity – for thinkers such as Justo Sierra, José Vasconcelos, Carlos Fuentes, and Octavio Paz in Mexico, for Edouard Glissant and Aimé Césaire in the Caribbean, and for Mario de Andrade, Paulo Prado, and Gilberto Freyre in Brazil – has generally been premised on racial multiplicity, the dominant North American vision of national identity has generally been premised on an unstated yet none the less normative "Whiteness."

While the North American national character has been explained as a function of the puritanical religious character of the country's founders (by Perry Miller), or of the impact of the frontier experience on the national personality (by Frederick Jackson Turner and R.W.B. Lewis), or of the shaping power of egalitarian political institutions (De Toqueville's analysis), theorists of national identity have tended to downplay its specifically racial dimension. Latin American intellectuals, by contrast, have tended, at least since the beginning of the nineteenth century, to conceive national identity in racially plural terms. The Brazilian poet Olavo Bilac, writing in the 1920s, saw Brazilian art as the "loving flower of three sad races."[30] Anthropologist Gilberto Freyre in the 1930s viewed Brazil's racial diversity as the key to its creativity and originality. We are not suggesting that Latin America theorists have been less racist – indeed, some excoriated racial mixing as a source of "degeneracy," while others developed official integrationist ideologies to mask class and social stratification. Yet Latin Americans have surely been more insistent on the primordial role of racial determinants in forming "national character." What Freyre was fond of calling a "New World in the Tropics" was for him made possible by the cultural fusion of three genetically equal races (the Portuguese, the Indian, and the African), each of which, he believed, had made an invaluable contribution, even if he tended to romanticize slavery and "folklorize" the Black and indigenous contributions. Brazilian filmmaker Joaquim Pedro de Andrade's planned adaptation of Freyre's *Casa Grande e Senzala* (The Big House and the Slave Quarter), never finished because of the director's untimely death, would have dramatically staged (and critically updated) Freyre's theories.[31] The script reveals that the film would have orchestrated a kind of polyphonic encounter of Brazil's various source cultures, offering diverse racial perspectives – indigenous, Afro-Brazilian, Portuguese – on the national experience. There was to be a place for indigenous resistance (warfare and anthropophagy), for Black resistance (the film refers to the *quilombos* or fugitive slave republics), and even for Sephardic Jews fleeing the Inquisition.

A cross-cultural "mutually illuminating" dialogical approach stresses not only the analogies within specific national film traditions – for instance, the analogies between the representation of African-Americans and Native Americans within Hollywood cinema – but also the analogies and disanalogies between the representations of both groups in Hollywood cinema and their representation in the other multiethnic film cultures of the Americas. Such a comparative approach juxtaposes whole constellations of representational practices. It is revelatory, for example, to compare Brazil's cinematic treatment of indigenous peoples to that of the US, and the relation of that treatment to the representation of Blacks. While Blacks were a frequent (if much abused) presence in North American silent cinema, they form a kind of structuring absence within Brazilian silent cinema – the exceptions being adaptations of *Uncle Tom's Cabin* (1910), of Azevedo's *Mulato* (1917), and of *A Escrava Isaura* (The Slave Isaura, 1929). On the other hand, the film histories of both countries feature scores of silent films devoted to the "Native American" or the "Native Brazilian." Both cinemas offer numerous adaptations of nineteenth-century "Indianist" novels, of José de Alencar's *Iracema* in Brazil, for example, or of James Fenimore Cooper's *The Last of the Mohicans* in the US. (In Brazil, there were four filmic adaptations of *O Guarani* and three of *Iracema* in the silent period alone.) In a broader sense, the tradition of "Indianist" works continues up to the present in both countries, as is evidenced by TV series like *O Guarani* in Brazil and films like *The Last of the Mohicans* (1992) in the US.

Brazilian cinema, however, lacks the western's depiction of Native Americans as dangerous war-whooping savages; there is no "imagery of encirclement" pitting threatened Whites against screaming hordes. Instead, the early Brazilian films recapitulate the values of the romantic "Indianist" movement, portraying the indigenous populace as healthy, pure, and heroic, as *bravos guerreiros*, nostalgic exemplars of a vanished golden age. The myths purveyed in these works, moreover, are myths of racial syncretism and fusion. They constitute what Doris Sommer calls "foundational fictions," in which "star-crossed lovers . . . represent particular regions, races, parties, or economic interests which should naturally come together."[32] Like the Indianist novelists, the filmmakers saw Brazil as a fusion of the indigenous peoples with the European element into a new entity called "the Brazilian," a fusion embodied in the marriage of the Indian Iracema and the Frenchman Martins in *Iracema*, or in the love of the indigenous Peri and the European Ceci in the same novelist's *O Guarani*. *O Guarani* concludes with the symbolic merging of two rivers, a metaphor for the melding of the indigenous peoples with those of Europe. By contrast, North American novelistic and filmic treatments of the Native American more frequently emphasize the doomed nature of love between European and Native American. Where Brazilian culture celebrates miscegenation, if ambiguously, in North America the idea of miscegenation has tended to generate fear and paranoia.

But this difference in the representation of racial relations does not make Brazilian cinema ultimately more "progressive" toward the indigenous peoples of Brazil. First, Brazilian cinema's celebration of the Indian as "brave warrior," the spiritual source and symbol of Brazil's nationhood, the mark of its difference from Europe, involved an element of bad faith toward Indians: the exaltation of the "disappearing" Indian is dedicated to the very group victimized by literal and cultural genocide. Second, the positive image of the Indian in these novels (and the films based on them) was premised on an asymmetrical compact between two imaginary aristocracies – European and indigenous – who were in fact locked in brutal conflict. Third, the ambiguous "compliment" to the Indians was a means of avoiding the vexed question of Blacks and slavery. The proud history of Black rebellion in Brazil was ignored; the brave Indian, it was subtly insinuated, resisted slavery, while Blacks did not. The White literary and filmmaking elite in Brazil preferred to treat the safely distant and mythically connoted Indian, symbol of the national difference from the detested Portuguese, over the more problematically present Black, victim of a slavery abolished just a decade before the cinema's inauguration in Brazil.

A relational methodology would also go beyond a bipolar comparative approach between single nations to a more broadly conceived diasporic or transnational approach. A truly multicultural media studies would perform a conceptual "remapping" of the field within a global space. Here we will suggest only a few utopian possibilities. A pan-American remapping of the cinema, for example, would chart the intersections and tangencies of the diverse New World cinemas, counterpointing whole constellations of representational practices within a relational context. In the wake of illuminating comparative studies of slavery, for example, one might study the "cinemas of slavery." If one excepts the TV series *Roots* and Herbert Biberman's film *Slaves* (1974), and occasional documentaries like *Cimmarrones* (1979), mainstream American media have rarely thematized the issue of Black resistance to slavery. Latin American films, on the other hand, as we saw in the case of *Ganga Zumba* (1963) and *Quilombo* (1984), have often touched on this theme. The Brazilian film *Sinha Moça* (1953), a costume drama set around the time of abolition, shows the institution of slavery as morally repugnant and even provides glimpses of Black anger and rebellion – mass flight, arson, insurrection. Sampaio's *A Marcha* (The March, 1977) features the soccer star Pelé as a Black freedman who liberates slaves on the eve of emancipation. One could then extend the discussion by including other Latin American films about Black resistance such as Giral's *El Otro Francisco* (The Other Francisco, 1974), *Maluala* (1979), and *Placido* (1986); and Alea's *La Ultima Cena* (The Last Supper, 1976). An "Atlanticist" approach to the cinema would embrace African-American directors like Spike Lee, Charles Burnett, Bill Duke, Charles Lane, Marlon Riggs, Bill Greaves, Camille Billops, Ayoka Chenzira, Zeinabu Davis, and Julie Dash; Caribbean Black directors such as Sergio Giral, Felix LeRoy, Sarah Maldoror, and Euzhan Palsey; Brazilian directors including Zozimo Balbul and Antonio Pitanga; Black British directors like Isaac Julien, Maureen Blackwood, and John Akomfra; and African directors such as Ousmane Sembene, Souleyman Cisse, Ola Balogun, Med Hondo, Idrissa Ouedraogo, Haile Gerima, and Safi Faye. (Film programmers rather than academics seem to be in the vanguard of this kind of remapping.) While a neo-African diasporic esthetic is clearly discernible in the music of the Americas – seen in the polymorphous interfecundations of samba, reggae, salsa, soca, calypso, and hip hop – subsurface commonalities of sensibility might also be discerned in diasporic cinema, especially since diasporic music so often forms an integral esthetic and structural ingredient in the films.

Speaking more generally, we would argue for a relational pedagogical strategy that would shuttle constantly between dominant and alternative media, so as to enable a contrapuntal reading of a shared, conflictual history.[33] A media teacher or programmer might show a paternalistic film about Africa like *Out of Africa* (1985) or *Mister Johnson* (1990), but counterpoint it with an anticolonialist film by an African such as *Emitai* (1971) or *Le Camp de Thioraye* (The Camp at Thioraye, 1987). Teach Vidor's orientalist *Bird of Paradise* (1932), with its exoticized pseudo-South Seas woman, next to *Nice Coloured Girls* (1987), which registers an Aboriginal feminist perspective on English discourse of interracial erotica. Place an all-White 1940s musical like *Girl Crazy* alongside *Illusions*, which pinpoints precisely the racial subtexts and elisions of such films. Show *Fame*, where the minority characters abandon their ethnicity in favor of art and social mobility, but juxtapose it with Leon Ichaso's *Crossover Dreams* (1985), where the success myth is debunked and shown as hollow. Teach *Imitation of Life* alongside Muriel Jackson's *The Maids* (1985) as a reflection on domestic labor since slavery. Juxtapose the Hollywood film *Glory* (1989), with its White-oriented focalization, with *The Massachusetts 54th Colored Infantry* (1991), Jacqueline Shearer's Black-focalized documentary on the same topic. Show *Gone with the Wind*, but compare it to Giral's *The Other Francisco*, a deconstruction of another sentimental abolitionist novel. In this way, cinema studies or history teachers become cultural activists, orchestrating illuminating clashes of perspectives and esthetics, intellectual montages not of shots but of films and discourses. Through film, diverse cultural experiences become concurrent and relatable. The point of such an exercise in contrapuntal dialogisms, in any case, is to suggest that entire civilizations are susceptible to "mutual illumination," that in an age where cultural circulation, if in many respects asymmetrical, is still global and multivoiced, whole continents are implicated in one another, not only economically but also culturally.

NOTES

1   Toni Morrison, Hazel Carby, bell hooks, Coco Fusco, Caren Kaplan, Ruth Frankenberg, Edward Ball, George Yudice, and Richard Dyer are among the many critics and theorists who have problematized the notion of "Whiteness."

2   One could easily perform parallel analyses of European cinema in terms of a submerged colonial presence. Witness for example the coded references to the war in Algeria in the films of the French New Wave: a brief radio mention of Algeria in *Cléo de 5 à 7* (1962), whose protagonist is frightened by African masks, the presumably North African cellmate of Jean-Pierre Leaud in *400 Coups* (1959), the unspecified war for which the protagonist embarks in *Adieu Phillipine* (1962), the fragmented references to Algeria in *Muriel* (1956). (Only Jean Rouch and Chris Marker brought the War center stage in such films as *Chronique d'un Eté*, 1961, and *Le Joli Mai*, 1962.)

3   David Rieff, in *Los Angeles: The Capital of the Third World* (New York: Simon and Schuster, 1991), refers to the Mexican presence in California as "a kind of subtext to the otherwise oblivious triumphalism of . . . California" (p. 66).

4   As a Hispanic, Carlotta Valdez resembles the high-caste "Castillian" heroines of conquest fiction. For a feminist analysis of *Vertigo* which also takes sociological factors into account, see Virginia Wright Waxman, "The Critic as Consumer: Film Study and the University, *Vertigo*, and the Film Canon," *Film Quarterly*, Vol. 39, No. 3 (1986), pp. 32–41.

5   Richard Dyer, "Entertainment and Utopia," in Bill Nichols, ed., *Movies and Methods*, Vol. 2 (Berkeley: University of California Press, 1985).

6   Jane Feuer, *The Hollywood Musical* (Bloomington: Indiana University Press, 1982), p. 84.

7   See Jan Pieterse, *White on Black: Images of Africa and Blacks in Western Popular Culture* (New Haven, Conn.: Yale University Press, 1992), p. 134, citing A. Saxton, "Blackface Minstrelsy and Jacksonian Ideology," *American Quarterly* (1983).

8   Henry Louis Gates Jr notes the iconographic links between Blackness, the harlequin, and the minstrel figure, whereby the "inherent nobility of Harlequin the Black Clown [became] transformed by degrees into the ignoble black minstrel figure." See Gates,

Figures in Black (New York: Oxford University Press, 1987), pp. 51–3.

9 For more on the origins of the minstrel show, see Joseph Boskin, *Sambo* (New York: Oxford University Press, 1986).

10 See David R. Roediger, *The Wages of Whiteness* (London: Verso, 1991), p. 104.

11 See Thomas Cripps, *Making Movies Black* (New York: Oxford University Press, 1993).

12 W.E.B. Du Bois, *The Autobiography of W.E.B. Du Bois* (New York: International Publishers, 1968), p. 122. (Quoted in Gilroy, *The Black Atlantic* [Cambridge, Mass.: Harvard University Press, 1993], p. 116.)

13 Rick Altman, *The American Film Musical* (Bloomington: Indiana University Press, 1989), pp. 16–58.

14 This opportunistic foregrounding of Black cultural achievement exists on a continuum with the State Department's diplomatic exploitation of Black jazz musicians such as Louis Armstrong and Dizzy Gillespie for world tours during the early decades of the cold war.

15 *Bells Are Ringing* (1960) is in this sense an anomaly, for unlike many contemporaneous musicals it violates the usual hierarchies by having its Latino character not only teach Judy Holliday the cha-cha, thus connecting the rhythms to a specific ethnos, but also shows a bicultural conversancy with European classical music.

16 For more on the important Jewish presence in Hollywood, see Robert Sklar, *Movie Made America: A Cultural History of American Movies* (New York: Random House, 1975); and Neal Gabler, *An Empire of Their Own: How the Jews Invented Hollywood* (New York: Doubleday, 1988).

17 The reasons for Jewish producers' suppression of Jewish presence on the screen, despite their relative power in the industry, are discussed by Patricia Erens, *The Jew in American Cinema* (Bloomington: Indiana University Press, 1984); and Lester Friedman, *Hollywood Image of the Jew* (New York: Frederick Ungar Publishing, 1982).

18 The later bio-pic *The Jolson Story* does foreground the Black influence on his singing, especially recounting Jolson's fascination with Blues musicians in New Orleans.

19 See Irving Howe, *The World of Our Fathers* (New York: Vintage, 1978).

20 Ibid., p. 563.

21 Fredric Jameson, "Third World Literature in the Era of Multinational Capitalism" *Social Text*, No. 15 (Fall 1986).

22 In another exceptional mixed-ethnic marriage, in *They Met in Argentina* (1941), the "Latina" Maureen O'Hara is wooed away by James Ellison from her Latin boyfriend Alberto Vila.

23 See Brian Henderson's "A Musical Comedy of Empire," *Film Quarterly*, Vol. 35, No. 2 (Winter 1981–2).

24 Already well known in Brazil as a theatrical and nightclub performer as well as an actor in the so-called carnivalesque films or *chanchadas*, Otelo subsequently played in well over 100 films ranging from Burle's *Moleque Tião* (1943), a film based on his own life, to *Macunaíma* (1969) through Herzog's *Fitzcarraldo* (1982), and indeed has figured prominently in all the crucial phases of Brazilian cinema since the 1930s. Welles repeatedly characterized Grande Otelo as one of the world's preeminent comic actors and a "multi-talented performer," and described him as a Black blend of Mickey Rooney and Charlie Chaplin.

25 Quoted by Servulo Siqueira, in "Tudo é Verdade," *Folha de São Paulo* (Dec. 2, 1984).

26 These documents and memoranda are to be found in the Welles collection at Lilly Library, Indiana University.

27 For more on Welles and *It's All True*, see Robert Stam, "Orson Welles, Brazil, and

the Power of Blackness," in a special issue on Welles from *Persistance of Vision*, No. 7 (1989). See also the essays by Catherine Benamou and Susan Ryan in the same issue. Catherine Benamou is writing a dissertation on the subject of *It's All True* in the Cinema Studies Department at New York University.

28   For more on syncretism in *Zelig*, see Stam/Shohat, "*Zelig* and Contemporary Theory: Meditation on the Chameleon Text," *Enclitic*, Vol. IX, Nos 1–2 (1987).

29   Elsewhere this kind of racial exchange is more positive in nature, evoking a complex play of identifications between ethnicities. Take, for example, the brief sequence in Haskel Wexler's *Medium Cool* (1969) where Eileen, a poor southern White woman migrated to Chicago, is watching a television report concerning the assassination of Martin Luther King. The words and images of King's "I Have a Dream" speech trigger flashback memories of her own southern Baptist upbringing, thus evoking Black/White commonalities rooted in historical experience, to wit the fact that historically Blacks were not only forced to "learn" Christianity, they also "taught" preaching to admiring Whites, with the result that the Black rhetorical style ended up by inflecting the White style of preaching. See Albert J. Raboteau, *Slave Religion* (New York: Oxford University Press, 1978).

30   The Olavo Bilac phrase is found in his *Poesias* (Rio de Janeiro: Alvez, 1964). The fundamental reference for Gilberto Freyre is *Casa Grande e Senzala*, published in English as *The Masters and the Slaves*, trans. Samuel Putnam (New York: Alfred A. Knopf, 1956).

31   We are grateful to Lula Buarque de Hollanda, who worked as a research coordinator on the project, for giving us a copy of the script of the proposed film.

32   See Doris Sommer, "Irresistible Romance: The Foundational Fictions of Latin America," in Homi K. Bhabha, ed., *Nation and Narration* (London: Routledge, 1990).

33   Edward Said, in *Culture and Imperialism*, also argues for a "contrapuntal" hermeneutics, although he arrives at the concept via different route. Our analysis emerges from our extrapolation and reaccentuation of Bakhtinian conceptual categories such as "dialogism," "mutual illumination," "excess seeing," "polyphony," and "mutual relativization." These concepts were explored with regard to comparative reading strategies in Robert Stam, *Subversive Pleasures* (Baltimore: Johns Hopkins University Press, 1989).

7

THE THIRD WORLDIST FILM

At a time when the *grands récits* of the West have been told and retold ad infinitum, when a certain postmodernism (Lyotard's) speaks of an "end" to metanarratives and when Fukayama talks of an "end of history," we must ask: precisely whose narrative and whose history is being declared at an "end"?[1] Dominant Europe may clearly have begun to deplete its strategic repertoire of stories, but Third World people, First World "minorities," women and gays and lesbians, have only begun to tell, and deconstruct, theirs. For the Third World, this cinematic counter-telling basically began with the postwar collapse of the European empires and the emergence of independent Third World nation-states.[2] In the late 1960s and early 1970s, in the wake of the Vietnamese victory over the French, the Cuban revolution, and Algerian independence, Third Worldist film ideology was crystallized in a wave of militant manifesto essays – Glauber Rocha's "Esthetic of Hunger" (1965), Fernando Solanas and Otavio Getino's "Towards a Third Cinema" (1969), and Julio Garcia Espinosa's "For an Imperfect Cinema" (1969) – and in declarations and manifestoes from Third World film festivals calling for a tricontinental revolution in politics and an esthetic and narrative revolution in film form.[3] Within the spirit of a politicized auteurism, Rocha called for a "hungry" cinema of "sad, ugly films," Solanas-Getino for militant guerilla documentaries, and Espinosa for an "imperfect" cinema energized by the "low" forms of popular culture.

Although on one level the "new cinemas" of the Third World came in the wake of the European "new" movements – neorealism, *nouvelle vague* – their politics were far to the left of their European counterparts. The manifestoes of the 1960s and 1970s valorized an alternative, independent, anti-imperialist cinema more concerned with provocation and militancy than with auteurist expression or consumer satisfaction. The manifestoes contrasted the new cinema not only with Hollywood but also with their own countries' commercial traditions, now viewed as "bourgeois," "alienated," and "colonized." Just as the French *nouvelle vague* filmmakers raged against *le cinéma de papa*, so Brazil's Cinema Novo directors, for reasons as much Oedipal as political, rejected the entertainment-oriented *chanchadas* and the European-style costume epics of film studios like Vera Cruz, much as the young Egyptian filmmakers rejected the "Hollywood on the Nile" tradition. And the "new cinema" directors from India, for example Satyajit Ray, rejected both Hollywood and the commercial tradition of the Bombay musical, preferring the model of the European art film. In retrospect, the "New Waves" seem to have been overly binaristic in their rejection of antecedent commercial film traditions; the tendency in subsequent years has been to emphasize indigenous precursors and films (for example, Kamal Selim, *Al Azima*, or The Determination, 1939, in Egypt; and Dhiren Ganguly, *Bilat Ferat*, or England Returned 1921, in India) and at times to recover, if only through parody, consecrated popular traditions. (Buñuel's critical resurrections of popular genres such as the melodrama and the *comedia ranchera*, in his Mexican films of the 1950s, opened a path later followed by directors like Arnaldo Jabor and Raul Ruiz.) And even though Hollywood was seen as a political antagonist, the antipathy to Hollywood was never total. To take only two examples, Glauber Rocha's first film review was of the westerns of John Sturges; Carlos Diegues was fond of King Vidor and John Ford.

After the "euphoric" period of Third World cinema, the early manifestoes were critiqued, positions were modified and updated, while cinematic praxis evolved in myriad directions. In this chapter and the next we will examine a range of alternative media practices, largely produced by Third Worldist and minoritarian filmmakers. What follows is not intended as a "survey"; rather, our focus is on specific films which exemplify noteworthy strategies with special clarity or flair. The resistant practices of such films and videos are neither homogeneous nor static; they vary over time, from region to region, and in genre, going from epic costume drama to personal small-budget documentary. Their esthetic strategies range from "progressive realist" to Brechtian deconstructivist to avant-gardist, tropicalist, and resistant postmodern. Rather than exalting a single "correct" strategy or esthetic, an approach alien to our polycentric perspective, we call for multiple strategies and modalities; it is the repertory of these approaches, in all their diversity and even contradictions, that we would like to examine.

REWRITING COLONIAL HISTORY

Colonialism, for Fanon, is "not satisfied merely with holding a people in its grip ... By a kind of perverted logic, it turns to the past of the people, and distorts, disfigures and destroys it."[4] In the face of Eurocentric historicizing, Third World and minoritarian filmmakers have rewritten their own histories, taken control over their own images, spoken in their own voices. It is not that their films substitute a pristine "truth" for European "lies," but that they propose counter-truths and counter-narratives informed by an anticolonialist perspective, reclaiming and reaccentuating the events of the past in a vast project of remapping and renaming.

This rewriting has operated within a double time-frame: the reinscription of the past inevitably also rewrites the present. While revisionist historical films such as *Jericó* (Jericho, 1990) and *Quilombo* (1984), as we saw earlier, challenged Eurocentric accounts of the early years of European conquest, other films have

249

rewritten more recent events. Med Hondo's *Sarrouina* (Queen Sarrouina, 1987) tells of an African woman at the end of the nineteenth century who outwitted the French and saved her people from colonialism. Filipino filmmaker Eddie Romero's *Ganito Kami Noon, Papano Kayo Ngayon* (This is the Way We Were Then: How Are You Now?, 1976) treats the nationalist coming-to-consciousness of a Filipino just before the war against Spain. Jorge Sanjines' *El Coraje del Pueblo* (The Courage of the People, 1971) dramatically restages a 1967 massacre of Bolivian tin miners, and is enacted by the miners themselves.

A number of films were made simultaneous with anticolonial struggles, from National Liberation Front (FLN) films in Algeria, through Fidelista films during the anti-Battista campaign, to FRELIMO films in Mozambique, and the work of the Radio Venceremos Film and Video Collective and the El Salvador Film Institute in El Salvador. Other films were made with the luxury of historical hindsight, after the consolidation of independence. In the wake of the revolution of 1948, the Chinese film industry celebrated the victory against the Kuomintang in films like *Red Banner on Green Rock* (1951) and *Victory of the Chinese People* (1950). Sembene's *Emitai* (1971), meanwhile, reached back into the relatively recent past of Senegalese resistance to French colonialism during World War II, and specifically the refusal of Diola women to supply French soldiers with rice. The same director's *The Camp at Thioraye* (1987) treats the similar rebellion of Senegalese soldiers who refuse to accept unequal pay in the French army, a refusal for which they are unceremoniously massacred. Niazi Mustafa's *Shitan Alayil* (Satans of the Night, 1958) chronicles British colonial oppression in Egypt. Mohamed Lakhdar-Hamina's *Assifat al-Aouraz* (Wind from the Aures, 1965) tells a fictional story about Algerian popular struggle against the French. The same director's *Waqai Sinin al-Jamr* (Chronicle of the Years of Embers, 1975) offers an epic account of the century of struggle that culminated in the Algerian revolution. Omar Khleifi's *Al-Fajr* (The Dawn, 1966) and *Fallaga* (The Fellaheen, 1970) deal with the Tunisian liberation struggle; Sarah Maldoror's *Sambizanga* (1972) with the liberation struggle in Mozambique, Ahmed Rachedi's compilation film *L'Aube des Damnés* (Dawn of the Damned, 1965) with anticolonial struggles throughout Africa.

In Egypt in the wake of the 1952 revolution, films such as Hussein Didky's *Yaskut al Istiamar* (Down with Imperialism, 1953), Henri Barakat's *Fi Baitouna Ragoul* (A Man in Our House, 1961), and Ibrahim Hilmy's *Kilo Tissa wa Tissaine* (Kilometer 99, 1955) celebrated popular participation in anticolonial history. Other films hailed Arab support for the Palestinians: Niazi Mustafa's *Samara Sinai* (The Dark Girl of the Sinai, 1958), Kamal el-Cheikh's *Ardh al Salam* (Land of Peace, 1955). Films such as Niazi Mustafa's *Sajine Abou Zabaal* (Abou Zabaal, Prisoner, 1956), Izzedine Zulficar's *Port Said* (1957), and Hassan al Imam's *Hub min Nar* (Fiery Love, 1957) depicted the Suez war of 1956. Nasser's commitment to anticolonial struggle was also reflected in the sympathetic portrayal of the Algerian struggle for independence in Youssef Chahine's *Jamila al Jazairiyya* (Jamila the Algerian, 1958), a film whose portrayal of French torture and Algerian solidarity thematically anticipates Pontecorvo's *The Battle of Algiers* (1966).

Many of the Third World films conduct a struggle on two fronts, at once esthetic and political, synthesizing revisionist historiography with formal innovation. Humberto Solas' *Lucia* (1968) rejects the conventional single fiction in favor of a complex tripartite structure, with each episode set in a different historical period (colonial 1895, bourgeois revolutionary 1933, postrevolutionary 196...), each revolving around a woman named Lucia (creole aristocrat, middle-class urban, rural-worker class), each in a distinct genre (Viscontian tragic melodrama, Bertolucci-style New Wavish political and existential drama, Brechtian farce) and each with its own visual style (dark, hazy, brightly lit). The result is to show how inseparable historical interpretation is from stylistic mediation. Med Hondo's *Soleil O* (1970) mixes documentary and fiction, dream and dance in a poetic exorcism of colonialism. The same director's *West Indies* (1979) sets a cinematic opera on a slave ship, calling attention to both oppression and resistance during five centuries of colonial domination and revolt. Solas too uses operatic techniques to tell a story about Chilean miners in his *Cantata de Chile* (1975). Paul Leduc's *Reed: Insurgent Mexico* (1973) tells the story of the Mexican revolution in a reflexive, deconstructive manner. Any number of films mingle documentary and fiction, in a politicized variation on a stylistic trademark of the *nouvelle vague*. Manuel Octavio Gomez's *La Primera Carga del Machete* (First Charge of the Machete, 1969), for example, reconstructs a 1868 battle against the Spanish in Cuba as if it were a contemporary documentary, using high-contrast film, hand-held camera, direct-to-camera interviews, ambient light, and so forth.

One of the many Third Worldist films portraying independence struggles was Pontecorvo's *The Battle of Algiers*, which, although directed by an Italian (in collaboration with the Algerians), is thoroughly imbued with the spirit of Fanonian Third Worldism. An early European commercial feature treating anticolonial wars of liberation, the film reenacts the Algerian war for independence from France, a war that raged from 1954 to 1962, costing France 20,000 lives and Algeria a million and a half lives. *The Battle of Algiers* offers a marked contrast to the French and American films set in North Africa where the Arabs form a passive backdrop to the heroic exploits of European heroes and heroines. Whether French (*Pépé le Moko*, 1936) or American (*Morocco*, 1930; *Casablanca*, 1942), the films exploit North Africa mainly as an exotic setting for Western love dramas, a decor dotted with palm trees and lazily traversed by camels. They illustrate perfectly Fanon's description of the imperial vision, in which "the settler makes history; his life is an epoch, an Odyssey," while against him "torpid creatures, wasted by fevers, obsessed by ancestral customs, form an almost inorganic background for the innovating dynamism of colonial mercantilism."[5] A crucial innovation of *The Battle of Algiers* was to invert the Eurocentric focalizations typical of the western and the imperial adventure film. Instead, Pontecorvo deploys identificatory mechanisms on behalf of the colonized, presenting the Algerian struggle as an inspirational exemplum for other colonized peoples. Sequence after sequence provides audio-visual glosses on Fanonian ideas, beginning with the film's dualistic conceptualization of a socially riven urban space. The repeated pans linking the native medina and the French city contrast the settler's brightly lit town, in Fanon's words a "well-fed town, an easygoing town; its belly ... full of good things," with the native town as a "place of ill fame, peopled by men of evil repute."[6] The dividing line between these two worlds, for the film as for Fanon, is formed by barbed wire and barracks and police stations, where "it is the policeman and the soldier who are the official, instituted go-betweens, the spokesman of the settler and his rule of oppression." The contrasting treatments provoke sympathy for the Algerians. While the French are in uniform, the Algerians wear everyday civilian dress. For the Algerians, the casbah is home; for the French it is a frontier outpost. The iconography of barbed wire and checkpoints, the cinematic topos of fascist occupations within Europe, elicits our sympathy for a struggle against a foreign, European, occupant in *The Battle of Algiers*.

In most European features set in North Africa, Arabic exists only as a background murmur, an incomprehensible babble. In *The Battle of Algiers*, in contrast, the Algerian characters, although bilingual, generally speak in Arabic (with subtitles for European audiences); they are granted linguistic and cultural dignity. Instead of being shadowy background figures, picturesquely backward at best and hostile and menacing at worst, they are foregrounded. Neither exotic enigmas nor imitation Frenchmen, they exist as people with agency. While never caricaturing the French, the film exposes the crushing logic of colonialism and fosters our complicity with the Algerians. It is through their eyes, for example, that we witness a condemned rebel's walk to his execution. It is from within the casbah that we see and hear the French troops and helicopters. Counter to the western paradigm, this time it is the colonized who are encircled and menaced and with whom we are made to empathize. By embedding the story of the temporary defeat of the FLN insurgents within the larger story of their final triumph, the very structure of *The Battle of Algiers* creates the impression of inevitable victory by the colonized over the colonizers. Their trilling cries rising as if from nowhere, and the streams of people feeding into swelling demonstrations of solidarity, stress the futility of the French attempt to defeat a whole people bent on independence.

Although *The Battle of Algiers* superficially centers on the character Ali-la-Pointe, the film in fact has a collective protagonist: the Algerian people. Ali is offered as a typical figure, a characteristic product of colonialism who hustles to survive until he is transformed by participation in a political cause. Just one of many leaders, he forms part of an organization, the FLN, which in turn is supported by the mass of Algerians. *The Battle of Algiers* subscribes to a left popular esthetic in which historical struggle is not narrated through idealized star actors and heroic characters but through the mass movement of peoples. Indeed, the film develops a constant dialectic between individual and community; certain personalities step briefly into the foreground only to recede again into the mass.

Hardly the classic heavies of anti-Nazi films, the French are simply profession-als following orders. Colonel Mathieu is not deranged or maniacal; he is charming, articulate, and honorable, straightforward about the reality of torture and "rational" in its defense. He ultimately represents the rationality of a system, the inherent logic of colonialism. Both sides are shown as capable of generosity as well as cruelty. Both are humanly (but never tragically) flawed. Throughout, Pontecorvo resists the temptation of melodrama to stress the crucial issue: colonialism. But the refusal of melodrama does not signify a refusal to take sides: in fact the film endorses the FLN's violent revolt as a legitimate and necessary response to oppression, and posits the violence of the colonizer as the systematic, rationalized expression of a retrograde system.

One sequence, in which three Algerian women masquerade as Europeans in order to pass the French checkpoints and plant bombs in the European sector, is particularly subversive in controverting traditional patterns of identification. Many critics were impressed with the filmmakers' honesty in showing FLN terrorist acts against civilians, and lauded this sequence for its "objectivity." But that the film shows such acts is ultimately less important than *how* it shows them; the signified of the diegesis (terrorist actions) is less important than the mode of address and the positioning of the spectator. The film makes us *want* the women to complete their task, if not out of conscious political sympathy then through the specific mechanisms of cinematic identification: scale (close-up shots individual-ize the women); off-screen sound (we hear the sexist comments of the French soldiers as if from the women's aural perspective); and especially point-of-view editing. By the time the women plant the bombs, spectatorial identification is so complete that the audience is not shocked even by a series of close shots of one of the bombers' potential victims. The eyeline matches between close shots of the Algerian woman and of her intended French victims both engender and disturb identification with the French; for although the patrons of the café she attacks are humanized by close-ups, the film has already prepared the spectator to feel "at home" within the bomber's perspective, to sense the reasons for such a mission. Historical contextualization and formal mechanisms have shortcircuited the reflex rejection of terrorism.

Other devices also solicit spectatorial complicity. The narrative placement of this sequence within the film presents the women's action as the fulfillment of the earlier FLN promise to respond to the French bombing of the casbah. Everything conspires to portray the bombing as an expression of the rage of an entire people rather than the will of a fanatical minority, a considered political task reluctantly undertaken rather than an erratic outburst. Pontecorvo thus hijacks the apparatus of "objectivity" and the formulaic techniques of mass-media reportage (hand-held cameras, frequent zooms, long lenses) to express political views that would be anathema to the dominant media. The technically degraded image, as opposed to the high-grade image of the conventional feature film, becomes the sign and guarantor of "authenticity." For the First World mass media, "terrorism" means only anti-establishment violence, never state terrorism or government-sanctioned aerial bombardments. But *The Battle of Algiers* presents anticolonialist violence as a response to colonialist terror: in Fanon's words, "the violence of the colonial regime and the counterviolence of the native balance each other and respond to each other in an extraordinary reciprocal homogeneity."[7] If the media has usually presented colonial repression as a retaliatory response to "leftist subversion," *The Battle of Algiers* inverts this sequence, revealing the political dimension of syntagmatic organization.

The *mise-en-scène*, meanwhile, creates other anticolonialist variants, for example on the classic cinematic and painterly topos of women dressing in front of a mirror. In Western iconography, mirrors are often the instruments of vanitas, or of loss of identity. Here they are a revolutionary tool. The lighting highlights the women's faces as they remove their veils, cut and dye their hair, and apply makeup so as to look more European. They look at themselves as they put on an enemy identity, ready to perform their national task but with no apparent vindictiveness toward their future victims. Whereas in other sequences Algerian women use the veil to mask acts of violence, here they use European dress for the same purpose. Hassiba, first seen in traditional Arab dress, her face covered by a veil, might in a Western context be received initially as a sign of the exotic, yet soon she becomes an agent in a national transformation where masquerading as the colonizer plays a crucial role. As the sequence progresses, we become increasingly close to the three women; though we become close to them, paradoxically, as they perform as Europeans. At the same time, we are made aware of the absurdity of a system in which people warrant respect only if they look and act like Europeans. The film thus demystifies the French colonialist myth of "assimilation," the idea that a select coterie of well-behaved Algerians could be "integrated" into French society in a gesture of progress and emancipation. Algerians can assimilate, the film suggests, but only at the price of shedding everything characteristically Algerian about them – their hair, their clothes, their religion, their language.

The French soldiers treat the Algerians with discriminatory scorn and suspicion, but greet the Europeans with amiable "bonjours." And the soldiers' sexism leads them to misperceive the three women as French and flirtatious when in fact they are Algerian and revolutionary. *The Battle of Algiers* thus underlines the racial and sexual taboos of desire within colonial segregation. As Algerians, the women are the objects of a military as well as a sexual gaze; they are publicly desirable for the soldiers, however, only when they masquerade as French. They use their knowledge of European codes to trick the Europeans, putting their own "looks" and the soldiers' "looking" (and failure to see) to revolutionary purpose. (Masquerade also serves the Algerian male fighters who dress as Algerian women to better hide their weapons.) Within the psychodynamics of oppression the slave, the colonial, the woman know the mind of the oppressor, while the converse is not true. In *The Battle of Algiers*, they deploy this cognitive asymmetry to their own advantage, consciously manipulating ethnic, national, and gender stereotypes in the service of their struggle.

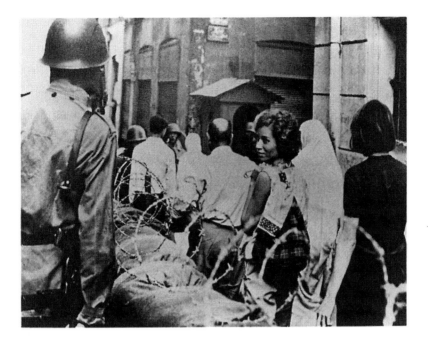

Plate 39 Masquerade as stratagem: passing the checkpoint in *The Battle of Algiers*

At the same time, it would be a mistake to idealize the sexual politics of *The Battle of Algiers*. The women in the film largely carry out the orders of the male revolutionaries. They certainly appear heroic, but only in so far as they perform their service for the "nation." The film does not ultimately address the two-fronted nature of their struggle within a nationalist but still patriarchal revolution.[8] In privileging the nationalist struggle, *The Battle of Algiers* elides the gender, class, and religious tensions that fissured the revolutionary process, failing to realize that, as Anne McClintock puts it, "nationalisms are from the outset constituted in gender power" and that "women who are not empowered to organize during the struggle will not be empowered to organize after the struggle."[9] The final shots of the dancing Algerian woman waving the Algerian flag and taunting the French troops, superimposed on the title "July 2, 1962: the Algerian Nation is born" has a woman "carry" the allegory of the "birth" of the Algerian nation. But the film does not bring up the contradictions that plagued the revolution both before and after victory. The nationalist representation of courage and unity relies on the image of the revolutionary woman, precisely because her figure might otherwise evoke a weak link, the fact of a fissured revolution in which unity vis-à-vis the colonizer does not preclude contradictions among the colonized.[10]

255

THE ESTHETIC OF HUNGER

A salient feature of the Third World cinema of the 1960s and 1970s was an attempt, at once theoretical and practical, to formulate an esthetic and a production method appropriate to the economic situation of Third World nations. *The Battle of Algiers* cost $800,000, a relatively low budget for a First World feature, but Third World filmmakers have often been obliged to work with budgets far below even this relatively modest level.[11] In the early 1960s, Brazil's Cinema Novo directors defended what Glauber Rocha, in a famous manifesto, called an "esthetic of hunger." Rejecting the relative luxury of antecedent Brazilian commercial cinema, these directors constructed filmic "allegories of underdevelopment," turning scarcity itself, as Ismail Xavier has put it, "into a signifier,"[12] much as the Judaic allegorical tradition turned slavery and exile into badges of honor. In a symbiosis of theme and method, the lack of technical resources was metaphorically transmogrified into an expressive force; misery, in Gilles Deleuze's words, was "raised to a strange positivity."[13]

Cinema Novo undermined the bureaucratic hierarchies of conventional production, seeking a language adequate to the precarious conditions of a "Third World" country and capable of conveying a constructive and dis-alienating vision of social experience. For Rocha, "our originality is our hunger." But even before Rocha coined the expression "esthetic of hunger," Nelson Pereira dos Santos embodied that esthetic in *Vidas Secas* (Barren Lives, 1963), a film about poverty in Brazil's arid northeast. *Barren Lives* subjectivizes a group, the peasantry, that since Neolithic times has represented the majority population of the planet, yet is almost never represented in cinema which favors the First World middle class as both subject and interlocutor.

The difficult circumstances in which Third World filmmakers work are largely unrecognizable to their First World colleagues. Apart from low budgets, import duties on materials, and "under the line" production costs many times higher than in the US or Europe, they also confront limited, less affluent markets than those of the First World. Furthermore, they must compete with the glossy, high-budget foreign films unceremoniously "dumped" in their countries. These differences in production inevitably inflect both the ideology and the esthetics of the films. "Hunger" characterizes not only the subject and esthetic of *Barren Lives*, but also its production methods. The total production cost of the film was $25,000, while another film on a similar topic, *Grapes of Wrath*, made twenty-three years earlier, cost thirty times as much. *Barren Lives* could not afford a highly paid star for its central role, and thus poverty loses some of the glamor associated with an actor like Henry Fonda. Indeed, the distance between John Ford's 1940 adaptation of the Steinbeck novel and dos Santos' adaptation of *Barren Lives* is the distance that separates southern California from the arid Brazilian backlands and Hollywood studio production from 1960s Third World filmmaking.

Both *Grapes of Wrath* and *Barren Lives* are naturalist novels (published only a year apart) treating the same subject: drought and migration. Just as the droughts of the dustbowl drive the Joads from Oklahoma west to California, the *secas* of the northeast drive Fabiano and his family to the cities of the south of Brazil. In both works the trajectory of a single family comes to encapsulate the destiny of thousands of oppressed migrants. In the one case the oppressors are real-estate companies and agrobusiness; in the other, landowners and their accomplices. There are contrasts as well as similarities between the social portrayals of the two novels. The Okies of *The Grapes of Wrath* may be an oppressed group within the US, but in global terms they are relatively affluent. The Joads have a broken-down truck and some basic necessities; Fabiano and family have only their blistered feet and a single trunk of possessions. The Okies may be only precariously literate, but they are presented as loquacious homespun philosophers who discourse eloquently on the resilient survival skills of the people. The illiterate peasants of *Barren Lives*, in contrast, have a tenuous grasp even on spoken language, communicating only in gestures, grunts, and monosyllables. The Okies, consequently, are better equipped for resistance. While Tom Joad is armed with literacy and class-consciousness, Fabiano has inchoate resentment and an inarticulate impulse to revolt.

Barren Lives cinematizes the novel's third-person "indirect free style" – that is, a mode of discourse that begins in the third person ("he thought") and then quietly modulates into a more or less direct, but still third-person, presentation of a character's thoughts and feelings. The discourse of the Ramos novel, like that of Flaubert's *Madame Bovary*, is highly subjectivized; the verbal material is articulated through the points of view of the characters, within a hierarchy of power that passes from Fabiano to his wife Vitoria down to the two boys and even the dog. Ramos empathetically projects himself into the minds and bodies of characters very different from himself; his prose brings us right into the physical being of his peasant subjects. (In a *tour de force*, he provides even the dog Baleia with visions of a canine afterlife.) In the film, interior monolog in the indirect free style disappears in favor of direct dialog. Fabiano's internal wrestlings with language are dropped; we are given only the fact of his inarticulateness. But the film does retain a kind of democratic distribution of subjectivity, the focus passing from Fabiano to Vitoria, to the two boys, and to the dog, and through diverse cinematic registers. Classically, and most obviously, the film uses point-of-view editing to structure identification. One sequence alternates shots of Baleia watching and panting with shots of rodents scurrying through the brush. The film also subjectivizes through camera movement: low-angled hand-held traveling shots evoke a boy's experience of traversing the *sertão*; a vertiginous camera swirl suggests the younger boy's dizzy fall. Other subjectivizing procedures include exposure (a blanched, overexposed shot of the sun blinds and dizzies both character and spectator); camera angle (the camera inclines with the movement of the boy's head); and focus (Baleia's vision goes out of focus as Fabiano stalks him, as if the dog were bewildered by his master's behavior).

Like *Grapes of Wrath*, *Barren Lives* elaborates the analogy, characteristic of naturalist fiction and rooted in nineteenth-century biologism and Social Darwinism,

Plate 40 Esthetic of hunger: *Barren Lives*

between human beings and animals. The twist in both the novel and film versions of *Barren Lives* is that the metaphor emerges not in the descriptive passages but in the words of the characters themselves, in a manner that diverges sharply from naturalist conventions. Fabiano and Vitoria complain constantly of being forced to live like animals. Sleeping in a feather bed takes on overweening importance to them because it represents the ideal of no longer living like animals. They are very much aware of their inability to communicate through language, yet when Vitoria kills her parrot for food, she justifies her action by saying "It didn't even talk." Thus Ramos (and dos Santos) avoids the biologistic reductionism typical of naturalist novels, where the characters become the passive playthings of a grim determinism. Instead, it is social structures that "animalize" people, who consciously resist animalization.

Barren Lives is a highly sensitive "reading" of a classic novel, but it also makes a specifically cinematic contribution. Ramos' literary style, especially adept at rendering physical sensation and concrete experience, is transmuted into cinematic *écriture*. The cinematography is dry and harsh, like the landscape. Indeed, the film's director of photography, Luiz Carlos Barreto, has been credited with "inventing" a light appropriate to Brazilian cinema: unable to afford the expensive 20,000 watt lights used in Hollywood and Europe to fill in shadowy areas in high-contrast daylight locations, he turned necessity into cinematic virtue, for example by sacrificing full exposure in favor of silhouetted human figures against sundrenched backdrops, light flaring into the camera lens, back-lit vultures

258

perched on skeletal trees. Elsewhere, ambient light spills through the open windows and large doors of provincial houses. Bypassing the expensive tubular track used in Hollywood, a shaky hand-held camera renders the tentative, precarious mobility of the family's odyssey through the *sertão*. At the same time, in the wake of Figueroa's work with Buñuel in *Los Olvidados* (1950), the filmmakers avoid the estheticization of poverty.

The film's ingenious soundtrack, meanwhile, provides an instance of the "structural use of sound" (Noel Burch's phrase). The non-diegetic sounds of the creaking wheels of an ox cart accompanying the film's credits are subsequently "diegetized," when we see an ox cart simultaneously with the sound. At another point, the creaking of the cart modulates, in a kind of aural "pun," into the (diegetic) sound of a scraping violin. Over the course of the film, the sound of the ox cart becomes a kind of auditory synecdoche for the northeast, both by its denotation (the ox cart evoking the region's technical backwardness) and by its connotation, the very unpleasantness of the sound constituting a structure of aggression. Indeed, the opening shot of *Barren Lives* already intimates a certain aggressivity toward the spectator. A laconic camera records the snail-like progress of four human figures and a dog across an inhospitable landscape. Their slow approach suggests the cultural distance between the peasant characters and the middle-class urban spectator. At the same time, the shot's unconventional prolongation (it lasts four minutes) warns the spectator not to expect the fast pacing and high density of incident that characterize "entertainment" films. The mimetic incorporation of the lived tempo of peasant life forms part of the film's meaning; the spectator's experience will be symbolically "dry," like that of the characters.

First World cinema, on the rare occasions that it talks about peasants, usually sentimentalizes them as passive victims or as exempla of pastoral purity. *Barren Lives*, rather than sensationalizing its subject through pathos and drama, portrays only the most quotidian of events in a world where very little "happens." Rather than rude transcendental poets, strumming guitars and mouthing the rustic wisdom of simple folk, the characters are moving in their very inarticulateness, their unequal struggle with language. Rather than making them exemplary victims of a quasi-metaphysical injustice, the film portrays the characters as simply oppressed by a social situation. They are neither more nor less noble than other people. Rather than relieving the visual and temporal austerity with a lush musical score, the film offers only harsh sounds (the squawking of the parrot, the grating creak of the cart). Rather than allowing picturesque scenery to compensate for the aridity of the subject, the film presents images as harsh, overexposed, and inhospitable as the *sertão* itself. One watches only at the price of certain discomfort; the relentlessly blinding light leaves the spectator, like the protagonists, without an oasis. Eschewing even the melodramatic plot and emotive scores of many neorealist films, *Barren Lives* elicits no pastoral nostalgia for a simpler time and place and entertains no mystical attitude toward the land.

In the ideological and material conditions of the early 1960s, *Barren Lives* represented one possible model: austere budgets, improvisational technique, a style grafting Bressonian minimalism and avant-gardist aggression on to a neorealist base. Popular audiences, however, were not necessarily eager to look at their own poverty on the screen. The film, and the "esthetic of hunger," left unanswered the question of spectatorial pleasure, a question to which we shall return.

THIRD CINEMA AND MILITANT DOCUMENTARIES

While Pontecorvo was restaging the Algerian war of independence, and dos Santos was registering the misery of the *sertão*, other Third World filmmakers were forging a militant anticolonialist cinema in documentary form. The late 1960s were heady days for revolutionary cinema. World-wide decolonization seemed to suggest revolution everywhere in the Third World, while First World revolutionary movements promised an overthrow of the imperial system from within "the belly of the beast." At the same time, dominant film form and Hollywood hegemony were being challenged virtually everywhere. The avant-garde militant documentary was a characteristic product of this period in both First and Third Worlds. And if there are two avant-gardes, the formal and the theoretical-political,[14] then the Argentinian film *La Hora de los Hornos* (Hour of the Furnaces, 1968), by Fernando Solanas and Octavio Getino, surely marks one of the high points of their convergence. "The struggle to seize power from the enemy," Solanas and Getino write in "Towards a Third Cinema," is the "meeting ground of the political and artistic vanguards engaged in a common task which is enriching to both."[15] Fusing political radicalism with artistic innovation, *Hour of the Furnaces* revives the historical sense of the term "avant-garde" as connoting political as well as cultural militancy, teasing to the surface the military metaphor submerged in the term – the image of an advanced contingent reconnoitering unexplored and dangerous territory. The film resuscitates the venerable analogy of camera and gun, charging it with a precise revolutionary signification. (Art becomes, as Walter Benjamin said of the Dadaists, "an instrument of Ballistics.") At the same time, *Hour*'s experimental language is indissolubly wedded to its political project; it is the articulation of one with the other that generates the film's meaning and secures it relevance.

It is in this exemplary two-fronted struggle, rather than in the historical specificity of its politics, that *Hour* retains some partial vitality as a model. Subsequent events, if they have not completely discredited the film's political analyses, have thoroughly relativized them. Virtually everywhere around the globe, the late 1960s were the "hour of the furnaces," and *Hour of the Furnaces*, as a quintessential product of the period, forged the incandescent expression of their glow. At the time, tricontinental revolution, under the symbolic egis of Frantz Fanon, Che Guevara, and Ho Chi Minh, was deemed imminent, lying in wait just around the next bend of the dialectic. But under the combined onslaught of external threats and internal repression, revolutionary flames dwindled into embers, as much of the Third World settled into the diminished expectations of an era of neoliberalism and IMF austerity programs. In Argentina, Perón – the last hope simultaneously of the revolutionaries and of the elite – returned from exile only to die shortly thereafter. His political heirs veered rightward, until a putsch installed a regime that killed thousands of its opponents (a campaign of oppression registered in such films as *La Historia Oficial* (The Official Story, 1986), *Las Madres de la Plaza de Mayo* (The Mothers of Playa de Mayo, 1987), and *La Amiga* (The Woman Friend, 1989) followed by a return to the drastically modified (neoliberal) Peronism of Menem). Rather than being surprised by revolution, Argentina, and *Hour* with it, was ambushed by an historical equivocation.

Hour is structured as a tripartite political essay. The first section, "Neocolonialism and Violence," reveals Argentina as an amalgam of European influences: "British Gold, Italian Hands, French Books." A series of "Notes" ("The Daily Violence," "The Oligarchy," "Dependency") explores various forms of neocolonial oppression. The second section, "An Act for Liberation," subdivides into a "Chronicle of Peronism," covering Perón's rule from 1945 through his deposition in 1955, and "Chronicle of Resistance," detailing the opposition struggle during Perón's exile. The third section, "Violence and Liberation," consists of an open-ended series of interviews, documents, and testimonials.

While reawakening the military metaphor dormant in the term "avant-garde," *Hour* also literalizes the trope of the "underground." Filmed clandestinely in cooperation with militant cadres, it was made in the interstices of the system and against the system. Situating itself on the periphery of the periphery, the film brashly disputes the hegemony both of the dominant model of "First Cinema," and of auterism ("Second Cinema"), proposing instead a "Third Cinema," independent in production, militant in politics, and experimental in language. As a poetic celebration of the Argentine nation, it is "epic" in the classical as well as the Brechtian sense, weaving disparate material (newsreels, eyewitness reports, TV commercials, photographs) into a rich historical tapestry. A cinematic summa, its strategies ranging from straightforward didacticism to operatic stylization, the film borrows freely from avant-garde and mainstream, fiction and documentary, cinema verité and advertising. It inherits and extends the work of Eisenstein, Vertov, Ivens, Rocha, Birri, Resnais, Buñuel and Godard.

Hour's most striking feature is its openness. But whereas "openness" in art usually evokes plurisignification and a calculated multiplicity of equally legitimate readings, *Hour* is stridently unequivocal, even propagandistic. Its ambiguities derive more from the vicissitudes of history than from the intentions of its authors. The film's openness lies elsewhere, and first of all in its process of production. Coming from Argentina's traditional Europeanized left, Solanas and Getino set out to make a socially minded short documentary about the country's working class. Through the filmmaking experience, however, they evolved toward a left Peronist position. The production process, in other words, inflected their own ideological trajectory in ways that they themselves could not fully have predicted. (One need not endorse the specific nature of this inflection to appreciate the fact that it is there.) Once aware of the tenuous nature of their initial "certainties," the filmmakers opened their project to the criticisms and suggestions of the Argentinian working class. Under the pressure of their critique, the film underwent a series of mutations. Rather than perform the *mise-en-scène* of preconceived opinions, the film's making entailed inquiry and search. The reformist short became a revolutionary manifesto.

Second, *Hour* is open in its very structure as a text. At key points the film raises questions – "Why did Perón fall without a struggle? Should he have armed the people?" – and proposes that the audience debate them, interrupting the projection to allow for discussion. Elsewhere, the authors appeal for supplementary material, soliciting collaboration in the film's writing. The "end" of the film refuses closure by inviting the audience to respond to and extend the text: "Now it is up to you to draw conclusions, to continue the film. You have the floor." The challenge was concretely taken up by Argentine audiences, at least until dictatorship ended the experiment.

While some film theorists claim that the cinema allows only for deferred communication, *Hour*, by opening itself up to person-to-person debate, "stretches" this claim to its very limits. A provocative amalgam of cinema, theater, and political rally, it welds the space of representation to the space of the spectator, thus making possible "real" and immediate, if unequal, dialog. The passive cinematic experience, that *rendezvous manqué* between exhibitionist and voyeur, is transformed into a "theatrical" encounter between human beings present in the flesh. The two-dimensional space of the screen gives way to the three-dimensional space of theater and politics. The film mobilizes activity rather than self-indulgent fantasy. Rather than vibrating to the sensibility of an auteur, the spectators are encouraged to "author" their own collective narrative. Rather than placing a hero on the screen, the film suggests that audience members are history's real protagonists. Rather than a place of regression, the cinema becomes a political stage on which to act.

Because of its activist stance, *Hour* was dangerous to make, to distribute, and, on occasion, to see. When a repressive regime makes filmgoing a clandestine activity punishable by prison or torture, the mere act of viewing comes to entail political engagement. With *Hour*, cinephilia, at times a surrogate for political action, became in Argentina a life-endangering activity, placing the spectator in a boobytrapped space of political commitment. Instead of the mere firecracker under the seats of the Dadaists, the spectator was faced with the distant but real possibility of gunfire in the cinema. All the celebrated "attacks on the voyeurism of the spectator" pale next to this threatened initiation into political brutality. Brecht contrasted the kind of artistic innovation easily absorbed by the apparatus with the kind that threatens its very existence. *Hour* attempts to ward off cooptation by a stance of radical interventionism and by various textual strategies. Rather than hermetically sealing itself off from life, the text makes itself permeable to history and practice, calling for co-conspirators and not consumers.

262

The three major sections begin with overtures (orchestrated quotations, slogans, and rallying cries) which suggest that the spectators have come not to enjoy a show but to participate in an action taking place in what the authors call "liberated space" and "decolonized territory." The spoken and written commentary addressed directly to the spectator fosters a discursive relationship, the "I-you" of "discourse" rather than the "he-she-it" voyeurism of "story." The film's dedication to Che Guevara, the partisan language, the final exhortation to action, all obey the Brechtian injunction to force the audience to "take sides." At times, the call for commitment reaches discomforting extremes for the spectator hoping for the usual warm bath of escapism. Quoting Fanon's remark that "all spectators are cowards or traitors" (neither option flatters), *Hour* at times calls for readiness for martyrdom – "To choose one's death is to choose one's life." Here the seeker of entertainment might justifiably feel that the demands for commitment have escalated unacceptably.

Hour also shortcircuits spectatorial passivity by making intense intellectual demands. Taken together, its written titles and spoken commentary form a more or less continuous essay, one reminiscent in rhetorical power of the authors it cites – Fanon, Césaire, Sartre. At once broadly discursive and vividly imagistic, this essay-text, the film's "brain," organizes the images and provides their principle of coherence; images take on meaning in relation to text rather than the other way around. The staccato intercutting of black frames and incendiary titles generates a dynamic *ciné-écriture*; the film writes itself. Vertovian titles explode pyrotechnically, rushing toward and retreating from the spectator, their graphic presentation often mimicking their signification. The word "liberation" proliferates and multiplies, in a graphic, kinetic reminiscence of Che's call for "two, three, many Vietnams." Or, in a rude challenge to the "primacy of the visual," the screen goes blank while a disembodied "acousmatic" voice addresses us from the darkness.

The voice-over commentary participates mightily in the film's work of demystification. Just as for Benjamin the caption of a photograph could tear it away from fashionable clichés and grant it "revolutionary use-value," so here the commentary shatters the official picture of the world. An idealizing painting that celebrates Argentina's political independence is undercut by the off-screen verbal account of the financial deals that betrayed the country's economic independence. Formal sovereignty is exposed as the façade masking material subjugation. Similarly, shots of the bustling port of Buenos Aires are accompanied by an analysis of a systematic impoverishment: "What characterizes Latin American countries is, first of all, their dependence – economic dependence, political dependence, cultural dependence." The spectator is taught to distrust images, to pierce the veil of appearances, to dispel the mists of ideology through an act of revolutionary decoding.

Much of *Hour*'s persuasive power derives from its ability to visualize ideas, to give abstract concepts clear accessible form. The sociological abstraction "oligarchy," for example, is concretized by shots of the "fifty families" that monopolize much of Argentina's wealth. The "oligarchy" comes into focus in the faces of recognizable, accountable individuals. "Class society" becomes the image ("quoted" from Fernando Birri's film *Tire Dié*, 1960) of desperate child beggars running alongside trains in the hope of a few pennies tossed by blasé middle-class passengers. "Systematic violence" is rendered by images of the state's apparatuses of repression – prisons, armored trucks, bombers. The title "No Social Order Commits Suicide" segues to four quick-cut shots of the military. Césaire's depiction of the colonized – "Disposessed, Marginalized, Condemned" – gives way to shots of workers, literally "up against the wall," undergoing police interrogation. Thus *Hour* engraves its ideas on the spectator's mind. The images do not explode harmlessly, dissipating their energy; fusing with ideas, they detonate in the minds of the audience.

Parody and satire also form part of the strategic arsenal of *Hour of the Furnaces*. One sequence, a sight-seeing excursion through Buenos Aires, has the irreverence of Buñuel's sardonic tour of Rome in *L'Age d'Or* (1930). The images are the usual ones in travelog films – government buildings, monuments, busy thoroughfares – but the voice-over is dipped in acid. Rather than exalt the city's cosmopolitan charm, the commentary anatomizes its class structure: the highly placed comprador bourgeoisie, the middle-class ("eternal in-betweens, protected and used by the oligarchy") and the fuss-budgety petit bourgeois, "eternal crybabies, for whom change is necessary, but impossible." Symbolic monuments of national pride are treated as petrified emblems of colonial servility. As the camera zooms out from an equestrian statue of one of Argentina's founding fathers (Carlos de Alvear), an ironic off-screen voice remarks: "Here monuments are erected to the man who said: 'these provinces want to belong to Great Britain, to accept its laws, obey its government, live under its powerful influence.'"

Satiric vignettes pinpoint the retrograde nostalgia of the Argentine ruling class. Their cemetery, "la Recoleta," bears baroque testimonial to an atrophied way of life, where they try to "freeze time" and "crystallize history." Just as Vertov uses split screen to symbolically destroy the Bolshoi Theater in *Man with the Movie Camera* (1928), Solanas and Getino "annihilate" the cemetery's neoclassical statues. In a completely artificial time and space, the statues are made to "dialog" in shot/reaction to the music of an Argentine opera whose words ("I shall bring down the rebel flag in blood") remind us of the aristocracy's historical capacity for savage repression. Still another vignette pictures the annual cattle show in Buenos Aires, interweaving shots of the crowned heads of the prize bulls with the faces of the aristocracy. The bulls – inert, sluggish, well-pedigreed – present a suggestive analog to the oligarchs that breed them. Metonymic contiguity coincides with metaphoric transfer as the auctioneer's descriptions of the bulls ("admire the expression, the bone structure") are yoked, in a stunning cinematic zeugma, to the looks of bovine self-satisfaction on the faces of their owners.

On occasion, Solanas and Getino enlist the unwitting cooperation of their satiric targets by letting ruling-class figures indict themselves through their own discourse. As newsreel-style footage shows an Argentinian writer, surrounded by jewelry-laden dowagers, at an official reception, a parodic off-screen voice sets the tone: "And now let's go to the Pepsi Cola Salon, where Manuel Mujica Lainez, member of the Argentine Academy of Letters, is presenting his latest book *Royal Chronicles*." Then we hear Lainez boast (in non-synchronous sound) of his international prizes, his European formation, his "deep sympathy for the Elizabethan spirit." No professional actor could better incarnate the intellectual bankruptcy and fossilized attitudes of the elite, with its yearning for Europe, its hand-me-down culture, and its snide ingratitude toward the people who made its privileges possible.

Solanas and Getino also radicalize and reelaborate the avant-garde heritage. One sequence fuses Eisenstein with Warhol by intercutting scenes inside a slaughterhouse with pop-culture advertising icons, investing Eisenstein's celebrated non-diegetic metaphor in *Strike* (1924) with specifically Argentine resonances. In Argentina, where livestock is a basic industry, many workers can barely afford the meat that they themselves produce. Yet advertising encourages these same workers to consume the products of multinational companies. The livestock metaphor, anticipated in the earlier prize-bull sequence, is taken up again by a shot of the exterior of a slaughterhouse, coinciding with an account of police repression against striking workers. The juxtaposition of advertising images and slaughterhouse scenes evokes advertising itself as slaughter, its numbing effect imaged by the mallet striking the ox unconscious. The vapid accompanying music by the Swingle Singers (Bach grotesquely metamorphosed into Ray Conniff) counterpoints the brutality of the images, while underlining the ads' shallow plastic cheeriness.

In *Hour*, minimalism – an esthetic quite appropriate to the exigencies of Third World film production – reflects practical necessity as well as artistic strategy. Time and again, unpromising footage is transmogrified into art, as the alchemy of montage transforms the base metals of titles, blank frames, and percussive sounds into the gold and silver of rhythmic virtuosity. Static two-dimensional images (photos, posters, ads, engravings) are dynamized by editing and camera movement. Still photos and moving images sweep by at such velocity that we lose track of where movement stops and stasis begins. The most strikingly minimalist gesture is the holding of a close-up of Che Guevara's face in death for a full five minutes. The effect of this inspirational death mask is paradoxical. Through the "having-been-there" of photography, Che returns our glance from beyond the grave. His face seems mesmerizingly present; his expression one of defiant undefeat. At the same time, the photo gradually assumes the look of a cracked revolutionary icon. The long contemplation of this image demystifies and unmasks: we become conscious of the frame, the technical imperfections, the filmic material itself.

Elsewhere, an iconoclastic sequence entitled "Models" invokes Fanon's final exhortation in *The Wretched of the Earth*: "Let us not pay tribute to Europe by creating states, institutions and societies in its mould. Humanity expects more

Plate 41 Revolutionary icon:
Che Guevara in death

from us than this caricatural and generally obscene imitation." As the commentary derides Europe's "racist humanism," the image track parades the most highly prized artifacts of European high culture: the Parthenon, *Déjeuner sur l'Herbe*, Roman frescoes, portraits of Byron and Voltaire. In an attack on the ideological hierarchies of the spectator, hallowed art works are lap-dissolved into meaningless metonymy. As in the postcard sequence from that other *locus classicus* of anti-high-art semioclasm, Godard's *Les Carabiniers* (1963), the most cherished monuments of Western culture are equated with the commercialized fetishes of consumer society. Classical portraiture, abstract painting, and Crest toothpaste are leveled as merely diverse brands of imperial export.

This demolition job on Western culture is not without its ambiguities, however, for Solanas and Getino, like Fanon before them, are imbued with the very culture they so vehemently denigrate. *Hour* betrays a cultivated familiarity with Flemish painting, Italian opera, French cinema; it alludes to the entire spectrum of highbrow and popular culture. This attack is also an exorcism, fruit of an ambivalent love–hate relationship with European culture. The same lap-dissolves that obliterate classical art also highlight its beauty. And as our Godard comparison suggests, the film's scorn for "culture" finds ample precedent within Europes's own antitraditionalist modernism, which asked, in Mayakovsky's

266

words, that the classics be "cast from the steamboat of modernity." (The dismissal of earlier art as a waste of time recalls the *antepassatismo* of the futurists, and Marinetti's call to "spit each day on the altar of art.") But if *Hour* draws on a certain avant-garde, it eludes its model's vacuity by politicizing what might have been purely formalist exercises. The ironic pageant of high-art images in the "Models" sequence, for example, is accompanied by a discourse on the colonization of Third World culture. Another sequence, combining shots of bourgeois Argentinians lounging poolside with vapid cocktail dialog about pop art, highlights the elite's Eurocentric fondness for a politically innocuous avant-garde, a taste that is as much the product of fashion and commodity fetishism as styles in shirts and jeans.

Our embrace of this critique of an apolitical avant-garde does not entail a total endorsement of the film's global politics. *Hour* shares with what one might call the heroic-masochistic avant-garde a vision of a kind of apocalyptic self-sacrifice in the name of future generations. Artistic avant-gardes, as Renato Poggioli and Massimo Bontempelli have suggested, often cultivate the image, and symbolically suffer the fate, of military ones; they serve as advanced cadres "slaughtered" (if only by the critics) to prepare the way for the regular army or the new society. The vision of self-immolation on the altar of the future ("Pitié pour nous qui combattons toujours aux frontières/De l'illimité et de l'avenir") merges in the film with a quasi-religious subtext that draws on the language and imagery of martyrdom, death, and resurrection: subliminal Dantesque structuring takes us from the *inferno* of neocolonial oppression through the *purgatorio* of revolutionary violence to the *paradiso* of national liberation. In this sense, the film confuses political with moral and religious categories. Its subsurface millenarianism may partly explain the film's power, but in some ways undermines its political thrust. This religious substratum becomes linked to a binaristic approach to relations between First World and Third World, and a folding of cultural categories into those of political economy. The film conveys a puristic notion of cultural identity, as if there really were an originary Argentinian identity free of European and North American cultural influences. First and Third Worlds are portrayed as hermetically separated realms, their commerce consisting solely in the "penetrations" of imperialism. The critique of English as a colonialist language forgets that Spanish is equally colonial. The music of African-American artists and the hippie "peace and love" movements are seen as equal in "corrupting" power to the CIA and the Pentagon. The film's rhetoric of authenticity masks the colonial-settler origins of the Argentine national formation. A more complex view would see both First and Third Worlds as mixed sites, as culturally and politically multiple, as indigenous, African and European: all the loci of both hegemony and resistance.

Armed with the luxury of retrospective lucidity, we can also better discern the deficiencies of the Fanonian and Guevarist ideas informing the film. *Hour* shares Fanon's faith in the therapeutic value of violence. But while violence can in certain circumstances be an effective political language, a key to resistance or to

267

the taking of power, it is quite another thing to value it as therapy for the oppressed in every situation. *Hour* universalizes a theory associated with only one specific point in Fanon's ideological trajectory (the point of maximum disenchantment with the European left) and with a precise historical situation (French colonialism in Algeria). And by making Guevara its model revolutionary, the film ignores weaknesses in his ultra-voluntarist strategy, which often turned out to be ineffective or even suicidal. Guerilla strategists have often underestimated the repressive power of the governments in place and overestimated the objective and subjective readiness of the "people" for revolution.[16] The ideal of the heroic warrior who personally exposes himself to combat, furthermore, permeates the film's masculinist nationalism, reflected even in the film's language ("El Hombre").

As a left-Peronist film, *Hour* also partakes of the historical ambiguities of that movement. The film rightly identifies Perón as a Third World nationalist *avant la lettre* rather than the "fascist dictator" of Eurocentric mythology. Indeed, while the film does score Peronism's failures (its refusal to attack the oligarchy, its failure to arm the people, its constant oscillation between "popular democracy" and the "dictatorship of bureaucracy") the film ultimately sees Perón as the "objectively revolutionary" embodiment of the proletarian movement, the figure through whom the Argentine working class became gropingly aware of its collective destiny. By breaking the neocolonial stranglehold on Argentina's economy, Peronism was preparing the way for authentic socialist revolution. This is a vision that fails to place Peronism in the context of Latin American populism, with its tendency to flirt with the right with one hand and caress the left with the other. As a tactical alliance, Peronism constituted a labyrinthine tangle of contradictions, a fragile mosaic which shattered, not surprisingly, with its leader's demise.

Two of Peronism's major contradictions are to a certain extent inscribed in the film. Wholeheartedly anti-imperialist, Peronism was only half-heartedly anti-monopolist, since the industrial bourgeoisie allied with it was more frightened of the working class than it was of imperialism. And although *Hour* calls for socialist revolution, it also reflects the political ambiguity both in Peronism and in the concept of "Third Cinema:" the "Third," while obviously referring to the "Third World," also echoes Perón's call for a "third way" or intermediate path between socialism and capitalism. The film's radical feel derives less from its undergirding politics than from its orchestration of the revolutionary intertext, its aural and visual evocation of global revolution. The strategically placed allusions to Fanon, Che Guevara, Ho Chi Minh, and Stokely Carmichael create a kind of "*effet de radicalité*" rather like the "*effet de réel*" cited by Barthes in connection with the strategic details of classic realist fiction. The second, related contradiction within Peronism has to do with its constant swing between democracy and authoritarianism. In populism, personal charisma and plebean style often mask a deep scorn for the masses. Egalitarian manners create the simulacrum of equality between the elite and the people. At once manipulative and participatory, strong-armed and

268

egalitarian, *Hour* shares this ambiguity. It speaks the language of popular expression ("Your ideas are as important as ours") but also resorts to hyperbolic language and sledgehammer rhetoric.

History has not shown the filmmakers as totally failed prophets, however. The film's indictment of neocolonial dependency remains relevant, as does its critique of the Argentine Communist Party, which supported the junta because it repressed only the non-Stalinist left. The film also points up the capacity for violence of an elite that has "more than once bathed the country in blood," a capacity subsequently manifested in the violent, anti-Semitic repressiveness of the junta. Whatever its political ambiguities, *Hour* stands as a landmark in one phase of revolutionary cinema. By allying itself with a concrete political movement, it practices a cinematic politics of "dirty hands." If its politics are at times populist, its filmic strategies are not: it assumes that ordinary spectators are ready for linguistic experimentation, capable of grasping the exact meaning of an image or of a sound montage. It respects its audience by proposing a cinema that is simultaneously a tool for consciousness-raising, an instrument for analysis, and a catalyst for action. *Hour* in this sense is a treasury of transformalist strategies, an advanced seminar in the politics of art and the art of politics. By avoiding the twin traps of an empty iconoclasm on the one hand and a "correct" but formally nostalgic militancy on the other, it strives toward the realization of a scandalously utopian and only apparently paradoxical idea: that of a majoritarian avant-garde.

Another militant documentary from the same period, *La Batalla de Chile* (The Battle of Chile, 1973–6), by Patricio Guzman and the Equipe Tercer Año collective, provides an illuminating comparison with *Hour*. Shot during the period of the Allende government in Chile, but completed in exile later, the film was collectively authored in the heat of militancy, at considerable danger to the filmmakers themselves. But while *Hour* develops a quasi-religious cult of self-sacrifice, *The Battle of Chile* recognizes the possibility of death soberly and without mystification. While Solanas and Getino were left-Peronist, Guzman and his collaborators were part of the non-sectarian Marxist left, the intellectual wing of the mass movement that in 1970 had generated a manifesto that called for a "revolutionary cinema" to be "born of the conjunction of the artist and the people, united in a single aim: liberation." This is not the place to register the circumstances in which *The Battle of Chile* was made; they are already well registered elsewhere.[17] Rather, we want to compare the film's strategies to those of *Hour*.

Like *Hour*, *The Battle of Chile* is a film of epic length (four and a half hours) divided into three parts: "Insurrection of the Bourgeoisie"; "The Coup d'Etat"; and "Popular Power." The differences begin with genre: if *Hour* is agitprop, *The Battle of Chile* is an analytic documentary. (In fact, its makers were critical of *Hour*'s heavy-handedness.) The filmmakers eschewed a number of classic documentary modes, such as strict chronology, thematic compilation footage, a day-in-the-life approach, and so on. Instead, they synthesized these methods in a dialectical style that combined their advantages. The plan was to emphasize nodal points in the struggle between the left (led by Allende) and the right (the military, the fascist "Patria y Libertad," the right wing of the Christian Democratic Party): how would the left try to take power and restructure Chilean society, and what would the right do to stop them? The film focusses on key battlegrounds – the parliament, the economy, the universities, the media. Within this topical approach, the filmmakers combine political analysis (made before, during, and after the filming) and on-the-spot filmmaking performed in the heat of the political and ideological battle. For spectators accustomed to militant left filmmaking, the surprises and reversals derive from Chile's anomolous status as the first country to move toward socialism through elections. Left-wing opposition to a capitalist state usually implies a derisive rejection of "bourgeois legality," but here it was the socialist government that defended legality (the constitution, legislative procedure, elections) and the right that found that legality no longer served its purposes. Whereas police forces in leftist films are generally portrayed as an occupying army, here they are the guarantors of the Allende administration and of democratic government. And whereas leftist films are generally sympathetic to striking workers, here the strikers are elite accomplices of the bosses trying to undermine socialism.

The major difference in strategy between *Hour* and *The Battle of Chile* has to do with the positioning of the spectator. Where *Hour* strives constantly for rhetorical effect, *The Battle of Chile* eschews rhetoric in favor of recording history in the making. It makes no effort to proselytize, yet is none the less moving, perhaps precisely because of this refusal. Seeing the film long after the events it records, in the knowledge that many of the activists it shows were killed, imprisoned, or exiled after General Pinochet overthrew the Allende government, makes the film a poignant experience. The ordinary Chileans on the screen, rather than the authors "behind" the film, are eloquent, living refutations of the cliché phrase "inarticulate masses." Lucid about politics, their passion is ultimately to change the quality of their own collective life. Where most films lead us to identify with individual characters, here the identification is with a community of aspiration. *Battle of Chile* generates the excitement we normally associate with a fiction film, but its drama is built into the events themselves, events seized by very agile and aware filmmakers who used their understanding of the political dynamics of events to tell them where to film, where to place the camera and microphone.

While *Hour* and *The Battle of Chile* are both self-referential, *The Battle of Chile* achieves its reflexivity by showing signs of the production process (the sound boom, calls for "cut," and so on) rather than through intertextual ironies. The two films also deploy sound and music in very different ways: whereas *Hour* uses non-diegetic music (classical music, pop, opera, tango) for didactic and ironic ends, *The Battle of Chile* features only diegetic music (percussion played at marches, martial music for military parades). While *Hour*'s montagist strategies betray the influence not only of Eisenstein and the avant-garde but also of TV commercials, the editing of *The Battle of Chile* is self-effacing. It favors

270

single-shot sequences in a kind of politicized Bazinianism that respects not only the spatiotemporal integrity of the materials, but also the integrity of the people who speak, including those with whom the filmmakers do not agree. Yet the overall structure conveys a subtle class-inflection, conveyed not in the "cheap shots" of contrastive parallel editing but rather in the film's undergirding social architectonics. Class differences inform everything we see: members of the elite address the filmmakers as "Sir," common people say *compañero*; the elite drive cars, the common people go to demonstrations on foot or in trucks; elite women wear layers of makeup, working-class women adorn themselves simply; the elite overestimates its electoral chances (not surprising since the dominant anti-Allende media consistently flatter the revanchist fantasies of the right), while the left is more lucid. The intermittent off-screen narration admittedly lacks the febrile brilliance of *Hour*; but its purpose here is not to display brilliance but to provide essential information. One remarkable sequence was filmed by an Argentinian during an attempted coup. He films a soldier firing directly at him: the soldier kills him, the camera blurs as it falls to the ground. Since the shot is directed at the camera, in cinematic terms at ourselves as spectators, the sequence has a remarkable impact, analogous in some ways to the direct-to-camera/ spectator effects of certain Hitchcock films, yet here it conveys what the commentary itself calls "the very face of fascism."

ALLEGORIES OF IMPOTENCE

For Fredric Jameson, all Third World texts are "necessarily allegorical," in that even those invested with an apparently private or libidinal dynamic "project a political dimension in the form of national allegory: the story of the private individual destiny is always an allegory of the embattled situation of the public third-world culture and society."[18] We do not endorse Jameson's somewhat hasty totalization of *all* Third World texts – it is impossible to posit any single artistic strategy as uniquely appropriate to the cultural productions of an entity as heterogenous as the "Third World," and allegory is in any case relevant to cultural productions elsewhere, including those of the First World. Nevertheless, the concept of allegory, here conceived in a broad sense as any kind of oblique or synecdochic utterance soliciting hermeneutic completion or deciphering, does strike us as a productive category for dealing with many Third Worldist films.[19]

Allegory is not an entirely new phenomenon in the cinemas of what was later called the Third World. The Brazilian film *Paz e Amor* (Peace and Love, 1910) spoofs a fantasy King, Olin I, a barely disguised anagram of Brazil's President Nilo Peçanha. During the 1930s and 1940s in India, the female star "fearless Nadia" rescued oppressed peoples from foreign tyrants, in ways which were read at the time as anti-British allegories.[20] But in the more recent history of Third World cinema we find at least two major strands of allegory: first, the teleological Marxist-inflected nationalist allegories of the early period, where history is revealed as the progressive unfolding of an immanent historical design; second,

271

the modernist self-deconstructing allegories of the later period, where the focus shifts from the "figural" signification of the onward march of history to the fragmentary nature of the discourse itself, and where allegory is deployed as a privileged instance of language-consciousness in the context of the felt loss of larger historical purpose. A third variant, indifferently teleological or modernist, might be found in those films where allegory serves as a form of protective camouflage against censorious regimes, where the film uses the past to speak of the present, as in de Andrade's *Os Inconfidentes* (The Conspirators, 1971), or subversively adapts a classic, as in dos Santos' adaptation of Machado de Assis' *O Alenista* (The Psychiatrist, 1970). The allegorical tendency available to all art becomes exaggerated in the case of repressive regimes, perhaps, especially where intellectual filmmakers, profoundly shaped by nationalist discourse, feel obliged to speak for and about the nation as a whole.

Here we will focus on three films, set in Brazil, Senegal, and Israel/Palestine respectively, in which literal or figurative impotence serves to allegorize the social, political, and economic predicaments of Third World nations. We may begin with a frankly allegorical Brazilian film: Glauber Rocha's *Terra em Transe* (Land in Anguish, 1967), a film which fuses a baroque, avant-garde esthetic (inflected by Shakespeare, Eisenstein, Welles, Brecht, and Resnais) with a corrosive critique of the left-populist politics that failed to prevent Brazil's military coup against the left-leaning government of João Goulart in 1964. The film's title, referring not to a character but to a *terra* (land) in *transe* (a reference to the spirit possession of Afro-Brazilian religion), virtually trumpets allegorical intentions. The film further points to its own allegorical nature by setting its action not in the country recognizable as Brazil – its obvious setting – but in the mythical land of El Dorado, a name evoking European projective fantasies about golden cities in Latin America.

Organized around the flashback memories of its dying protagonist, *Land in Anguish* traces the zigzagging political allegiances of an artist/intellectual named Paulo Martins. After supporting the right-wing leader Porfírio Diaz, Paulo moves leftward to support the populist Vieira. Fearful of electoral defeat, the right wing stages a coup d'état, transparently modeled on the 1964 coup in Brazil. Brought back to the starting point of the film, we see the by now radicalized Paulo hand Vieira a gun, a symbol of the popular resistance that Vieira lacks the courage to invoke and support. Cross-cutting alternates Paulo's final agony with the coronation of the dictator Diaz, and a long-held final shot shows a silhouetted Paulo with uplifted rifle.

Shocking its progressive audience by breaking with the Manichean schemas of leftist political art, *Land in Anguish* was initially denounced as "fascist" by the same militants who later came to appreciate the acuity of its analysis. Lumping together the conspiratorial right and the incompetent left as two faces of elite power, *Land in Anguish* portrays left populism as a pseudo-democratic masquerade, a "tragic carnival." The film animates synthetic characters representing vast historical forces, characters *à clef* who solicit allegorical decipherment on the spectator's part. Porfírio Diaz, named after the Mexican dictator who waged savage campaigns against the Indian populations of the northern Mexican states, embodies the Latin American version of Iberian despotism. His political career parallels that of the Brazilian politician Carlos Lacerda, who evolved from youthful leftism to hysterical anticommunism, and who directly collaborated with the US to bring about the 1964 coup. Vieira, the liberal politician, combines the traits of a number of Brazilian populist leaders (Getulio Vargas, João Goulart, Janio Quadros, Miguel Arraes, Leonel Brizola). The character Sara represents the Communist Party, whose policy it then was to support populists like Vieira. The company called EXPLINT (Company of International Exploitation) finally represents the multinational corporations involved in the coup.

Paulo Martins, himself a contradictory, at times even reprehensible figure, provides a critical portrait of a whole generation of leftist intellectuals. In this neobaroque allegory of disenchantment, conveyed in a volcanic effluvium of words, sounds, and images, Paulo represents the poet abroad in the world of class struggle and coups d'état. His habitual mode of speech, simultaneously frenetic and solemn, is poetic: he speaks in *Hamlet*-like soliloquies, appearing in close-up with a non-synchronous voice expressing his inner speech, in a manner reminiscent of the Orson Welles adaptations of Shakespearean tragedies. Furthermore, he shares significant traits with Hamlet – an overheated imagination, a perverse virtuosity of language, a rigorous skepticism coexisting with an exasperated idealism, and a view of himself as the legitimate heir to power. Like Hamlet, he is the more or less lucid critic of an ambient corruption in which he himself participates.

The baroque esthetics of *Land in Anguish* are linked to those of one of the least realistic of artistic genres – opera. Rocha, a passionate devotee of the "cinema-opera" of Welles and Eisenstein, has operatic music, especially that of Verdi and his Brazilian epigone Carlos Gomes, pervade the soundtrack. Paulo's death itself recalls the protracted agonies of opera, where characters die eloquently, interminably, and in full voice. The technique too is operatic, allegorical; the coup d'état, for example, is figured not as a modern-day exercise of force but rather as a baroque palace intrigue, a usurpation, a coronation. In his famous essay on epic theater, Brecht expressed a desire to make opera contemporary and democratic. For him, it procured a certain realism, then annihilated it by having everyone sing. In the terms of Brecht's comparison between epic and dramatic theater, *Land in Anguish* invariably falls into the epic category. Rather than incarnating a process, it tells its story with narrative distance. Rather than involving the audience emotionally, it transforms it into a critical observer of the contradictions of character. We identify with Paulo yet at the same time see him critically. He is, as Walter Benjamin said of the protagonist of Brecht's *A Man's a Man*, "an empty stage on which the contradictions of our society are acted out."

The critical undercutting of Paulo's status as hero only partly explains the shortcircuiting of identification, which also derives from the film's core esthetic strategy – its refusal of the conventions of dramatic realism. *Land in Anguish* underlines its antirealist intentions through that ultimate implausibility – the posthumous narrator. The narrative is constantly derailed, deconstructed, reel-aborated, while spatio-temporal discontinuity is exacerbated by dizzying camera movements, jump cuts, and an autonomous, discontinuous soundtrack. The film stages a conflictual dialog of styles and rhetorics, so that the meaning partly emerges from the creative tension among diverse modalities of filmic *écriture*. Rocha devours cinematic styles with anthropophagic gusto: set alongside the Wellesian influence are the styles of direct cinema (direct-to-camera interviews, ambient light) and Eisensteinian montage (*faux raccords*, socially emblematic personages). Rather than merely cite the filmic intertext, Rocha transforms it. One moment evokes the famous sequence from *Battleship Potemkin* (1925) where the goateed Doctor Smirnov, responding to the sailors' complaints about the food, uses his lorgnette to examine maggot-covered meat, then pronounces it "perfectly healthy and ready to be eaten." Rocha has his Senator, who has just lavished Panglossian praise on El Dorado's perfect society, use his glasses in identical fashion to examine the corpse of a murdered representative of the people. The analogy is clear: in both cases the corrupt representatives of established power look at but refuse to see the most glaring evidence of social ills.

Land in Anguish operates a double demystification – one political, the other esthetic; it deconstructs two styles of representation. On the one hand it deconstructs populism as a political style of representation by performing the *mise-en-scène* of its contradictions. For Rocha, populism offers only the simulacrum of participation; it incites the people to speak, but represses them when their voice becomes too strident. It invites the people into the palace, then murders them if they become too militant. The film questions the romantic idealization of the "people" by having its protagonist designate an inarticulate popular representative and ask: "Can you imagine this man in a position of power?" On another level, the film rejects an esthetic style of representation, which might also be labeled "populist." A populist art speaks to the people in simple and transparent language, for fear of not "communicating." It practices the sugar-coated-pill theory of art; it is sweet in order to be useful. To get its message across, it offers the public its habitual dosage of cinematic gratifications – intrigue, suspense, romance, spectacle. It treats them as if they needed only a simplistic, redundant, prettifying art, just as the populist Vieira speaks of "the people" but does nothing to advance their political maturation. *Land in Anguish* attacks Hollywoodean film language, as Arnaldo Jabor points out, not through the masochistic "drying up" of language or the "destruction of discourse" in the fashion of the European avant-garde, but rather through the "famished, voracious excess of the critical baroque."[21]

The audacity of *Land in Anguish* consists in its superimposition of a twin critique, one on the level of political economy and geopolitics (the alliance of multinational corporations and the Brazilian elite against workers, peasants, and left intellectuals) and the other a cultural-anthropological critique involving music, architecture, gestures, symbols, and decors, that transforms these historical agents into grotesque exempla of historical forces.[22] The film establishes a resonance between the protagonist's poetic delirium and the general atmosphere of doubt and hysteria that marks the political process. Drawing on both baroque theater and the allegorical pageantry of Brazilian carnival, *Land in Anguish* shows Brazil as an unstable cultural amalgam – Afro-indigenous *mestizo* – subject to an overarching European domination. It gives proleptic expression to what later came to be called the "crisis of totalizations": that is, the spreading skepticism about historical master-narratives such as Marxism with its faith in a history ordered by the progressive laws of dialectical materialism. It also shows that the underlying faith of first-phase Cinema Novo films such as *Barren Lives* was being corroded. While the earlier films spoke in confident and prophetic tones, the later films are marked by disillusionment and a feeling of impotence.

If impotence is figurative in *Land of Anguish*, it is quite literal in Ousmane Sembene's *Xala* (1974). The film revolves around a fable of impotence, in which the protagonist's *xala*, a divinely sanctioned curse of impotence, comes to symbolize the neocolonial servitude of the Black elite in countries like Senegal. (The novel and film of *Xala* were of course key references in Jameson's landmark essay.) The protagonist, El Hadji, is a polygamous Senegalese businessman who becomes afflicted with *xala* on the occasion of taking his third wife. In search of a cure, he visits various medicine men, who fail to cure him. At the same time, he suffers reverses in business, is accused of embezzlement and ejected from the Chamber of Commerce. In the end, he discovers that the *xala* resulted from a curse sent by a Dakar beggar whose land El Hadji had expropriated. The protagonist finally recovers by submitting to the beggar's demand that he strip and be spat upon; the film ends with a freeze-frame of his spittle-covered body.

In the world of *Xala*, the patriarchal structures of colonialism have given way to indigenous African class and gender oppression, precluding the utopia of liberation promised by nationalist discourse. Impotence thus betokens post-independence patriarchy as failed revolution. Here, the traditional ritual of marriage provides a structuring device for a political story. Indeed, with its intimate setting, the film demonstrates the inseparability of the private and the political. News of the protagonist's wedding-night impotence quickly spreads through the community, provoking the most diverse speculations about its origins. As Françoise Pfaff points out, each of the protagonist's wives plays an allegorical role, representing the Senegalese people at different stages and in different relations to colonization and to tradition: the dignified, patient traditional wife Awa, the trendy Westernized Oumi, and the object of sexual consumerism N'gone.[23]

Laura Mulvey sees *Xala* as a reflection on the various discourses on the fetish as "something in which someone invests a meaning and a value beyond its actual meaning or value." Fetishism is itself allegorical, she points out, in that it calls "attention to a nodal point of vulnerability, whether within the psychic structure of an individual or the cultural structure of a social group."[24] As a symptom, the fetish requires, like allegory, an act of decipherment. For Mulvey, Marx turned the

275

Plate 42 Marriage and commodity fetishism in Sembene's *Xala*

discourse of fetishism, a discourse rooted in Eurocentric prejudice against African religions, back against Europe itself, and Freud used it to define the furthest limits of the psyche's primitive credulity, thus turning the issue away from its anthropological roots toward broader questions of signification. The Sembene film articulates the psychosexual with the socioeconomic, turning the protagonist's impotence into a symptom of something else: the neocolonial dependency of the Black African elite.

Since Third World films raise questions of identity and power, their representations of sexuality are particularly charged. In the Palestinian film *Urs bilGalil* (Wedding in Galilee, 1987), the allegorical strategies hinge again on the ritual of marriage and the wedding-night: events by their very nature overdetermined with meaning due to their implicit uniting of families, histories, and genealogies, a feature here exacerbated by the political conflict between Israelis and Palestinians. The story revolves around the desire of the Mukhtar of a Palestinian village in Galilee to marry off his son in a memorable ceremony. But the Israeli military have imposed a curfew, forcing him to ask the governor's permission to continue the celebrations till nightfall. The governor approves on condition that he and his staff be invited to attend. As in *Xala*, the private/public distinction breaks down: marriage and wedding become the pretext for a kind of social x-ray. The marriage ritual crystallizes the community (which collectively prepares and

276

dresses the bride and the groom), bringing to the surface all its latent tensions: between Israel and Palestine, between the patriarch and his bridegroom son, between diverse political forces within the community. Here the groom is not only impotent, he is unwilling and even hostile, for he resents his father's authoritarian gesture of arranging the marriage under the auspices of Israeli authority. Israeli military infiltration of the wedding makes sexual penetration impossible, leading to the brides's self-defloration.

Produced before the Intifada on the West Bank and in Gaza, *Wedding* is the first major Palestinian fiction film to be made by a "1948 Palestinian," that is by an Israeli Palestinian, in this case one (Michel Khleifi) who left Nazareth in 1970 for Belgium. The film interweaves a number of intra-Palestinian discourses. The camera oscillates among diverse perspectives, contrasting the attitudes of the young radicals born under Israeli occupation with those of the older, "patient" generation. The Palestinian community is shown to be riven by ideological, sexual, familial, and generational tensions. As with his earlier documentary *Al Dhikrayat al Khasibah* (Fertile Memories, 1980), Khleifi interweaves the longer history of Palestinian dispossession with the narratives of the historically evolving roles of women under the occupation. But unlike many pro-Palestinian Arab directors, he refuses to separate "internal" problems from "external" challenges.[25] One may object to the film's masculinist preference for female versus male nudity, yet women characters do exercise a strong presence in the story, indeed a presence in inverse proportion to their officially acknowledged place in the village depicted. It is the women who nurture the collective memory. On their shoulders rests the burden of the insistent, daily struggle for familial and national preservation. Their roles provide glimpses of liberation while also registering the impasses of patriarchal society. Their steadfast, quiet resistance is presented as more mature than the heroic posturings of the male militants. Indeed, Khleifi's attention to women and children, and to the sporadic, quasi-Oedipal attempts at revolt on the part of young men, was in some ways anticipatory of more recent alterations in power relations within the Palestinian community on the West Bank and Gaza, where children and women became a major force in the uprising.[26]

Although *Wedding* alludes to the differences, gaps, and tensions within the Palestinian community, it also reflects a common struggle against occupation, along with a common history and cultural identity rooted in the land and its past. Images of Palestinian lives on the screen thus challenge the denial of Palestinian existence, whether through the physical elimination of Palestinian villages and fields, or through the verbal-ideological obfuscation implicit in terms like "natives" and "nomads." In this sense, the camera's painstaking, affectionate scrutiny of rural ceremonies and rituals, and the film's evocation of the people's love of the land and its fruits, makes less an anthropological than a simple political point: "We are here, and we exist." The fluid movement from character to character and the blending of diverse discourses and languages (daily slang, proverbs, popular rhymes, sloganistic speeches, hallucinatory poetic monologs) suggests the nation's textured complexity.

While the Zionist "Prospero complex" associates vegetation and fruitfulness with the pioneers who "made the desert bloom," *Wedding* connects earth, crops, trees, vegetation, and abundance of food with the Palestinians. At the same time, it links violence to the land with the Israelis, who plant mines in the fields to sabotage the Palestinian people's agriculture and, symbolically, their "fruitfulness." Meanwhile, the documentation of the details of Palestinian-Arab culture (the bride's henna ceremony, the *hamsa* image on the wall, the villagers' singing and dancing) reinforces a sense of permanence, a stubborn refusal to disappear. And just as Jewish weddings ritualistically evoke the memory of Zion, so Palestinian weddings, especially in the context of occupation, become catalysts for national desire, celebrations of collective memories and hopes.

If *Wedding* vividly accentuates Palestinian lives in a way radically opposed to the Western media's image of "terrorists," it also mingles customs, times, and places in order to sustain the idea of a Palestinian nation. The wedding ceremony, for example, mingles Muslim and Christian Palestinian customs. This presentation of Palestinian identity as predominantly national rather than religious (on the part of a filmmaker of minority Christian descent) is significant in a Euro-Israeli context, where Christian Palestinians are subtly perceived as "better," and where official discourse devalues Palestinian nationalism by speaking of the "non-Jewish minorities." Although subordination to martial law was abolished for Israel's Palestinians in 1966 (only to be installed a year later in the newly occupied territories), *Wedding* portrays a Palestinian village under military control in Galilee, within Israel, in the present. This conflation implies that Palestinian land within the boundaries of pre-1967 Israel can be seen as occupied as well; even if Israeli-Palestinians can legally take part in the Israeli political process, they are excluded in a "Jewish state" whose very definition equates nation and religion. Even if they carry Israeli passports, their national identity remains inseparable from that of the Palestinians on the West Bank and in Gaza. Shot in various villages in Galilee and in the West Bank, the film also condenses varied topographies and architectural styles, in order, once again, to underline a single national identity. Despite the attempts to undermine Palestinian unity, *Wedding* valorizes the linked destinies and dreams of 1948 and 1967 Palestinians and those of the diaspora.

The film's narrative structure also reinforces national legitimization. By focussing on a Palestinian ritual circumscribed by Israeli power, the film subverts the Western and Israeli media trope of Arabs besieging Israel and Palestinians disrupting Israeli routines. A tale with Palestinians at the center and Israelis as "visitors" inverts a narrative that favors the land's "original," that is Jewish, inhabitants over its present-day Arab "guests." In Palestinian eyes, Israel represents just one more invasive foreign power arriving in the wake of the Turks and the British. This point is articulated in the monologs of the old man who rambles, in the present tense, about the Turks. *Wedding in Galilee*, like *Fertile Memories*, suggests that Palestinian memory is not only alive but also fertile, capable of giving birth to new beginnings.

Some of the film's sequences are explicitly allegorical. For example, Palestinians and Israelis together coax a mare out of a field that the Israelis have mined, evoking a vision of a dialogical future; instead of mines and rifles, gentleness and dialog. The pastoral epilog showing the Mukhtar's child running in the fields underlines a desire for harmony in a bloodstained land, as if closing the circle opened at the beginning of the film, where the voices of Palestinian children at play dissolve into the roar of Israeli jets. Coming after the soldiers' evacuation of the village, this epilog implies a wish for a liberated future. Palestinian and Israeli national cultures pervade each other's memories and tales, but from a Palestinian standpoint a dialogical future will be made possible only by an end to the occupation. As the groom's sister puts it provocatively to an Israeli soldier: "You will have to take off your uniform if you want to dance."

THIRD WORLDIST REFLEXIVITY

Many Third Worldist films are preoccupied with the relation between intellectuals and the marginalized masses to whom they offer what Benjamin called "mediated solidarity." Seeing themselves as part of a general national trajectory, Third Worldist filmmakers have reflexively addressed their own position vis-à-vis the people they aspire to represent. At the same time, these filmmakers are haunted by the specter of cultural colonialism, of being too servile toward the dominant model. They express their creative personalities, but as part of a larger collective project: the consolidation of a national cinema. Working consciously with issues long elaborated in filmic and extra-filmic texts, the filmmaker almost necessarily becomes reflexive, dialoging with the received body of belief and method, directly or indirectly discussing cinema itself within the films. Each work becomes a methodological sample of possible strategies, at once "about" a subject and "about" itself.

Here Third Worldist cinema is in step, of course, with international cinema, with its ever-greater tendency to reflexivity, whether modernist (early Godard), Brechtian (late Godard), or postmodernist (Atom Egoyan). But there are also national specificities at work, rooted in the marginal and syncretic nature of Third World cultural experiences. Historically multicultural, often fluent in a number of languages, defined as at the margins yet thoroughly co-implicated with the "center," Third World artists tend to be language- and culture-conscious, inhabiting a peculiar realm of irony where words and images are seldom taken at face value. Whatever the root cause of the phenomenon, techniques of metacinema and reflexivity have been virtually ubiquitous in Third Worldist cinema in recent decades, appearing in a variety of genres – documentaries, fictive documentaries, linear-Marxist and postmodern deconstructionist narratives.[27] (We mean reflexivity here in a broad sense to refer to films that in some way foreground the filmmaker, the film's production, its textual procedures, its intertext or its reception.) We find reflexivity in the Cuban films *Hasta Cierto*

Punto (Up to a Certain Point, 1984) and *Adorables Mentiras* (Adorable Lies, 1991); in the Mexican film *Mi Querido Tom Mix* (My Dear Tom Mix, 1991); in the Egyptian films *Hadutha Misriyya* (An Egyptian Story, 1982) and *Al Qahira* (Cairo, 1991); in the Indian film *Bhumika* (The Role, 1977); and in the Brazilian films *Cinema Inocente* (Innocent Cinema, 1979) and *A Dama de Cine-Shanghai* (The Lady of Cinema Shanghai, 1987). Here we will examine a number of films that are reflexive in the most obvious and literal sense: they focus on the filmmaking process itself, always in ways that stress the particularities of filmmaking in the Third World.

While disadvantaged in relation to their First World counterparts, Third World filmmakers are often members of the elites of their own countries. Mrinal Sen's *Aakaler Sandhane* (In Search of Famine, 1980) explores the contradictions inherent in this situation. This Indian film centers on a film crew, led by its director (Dhritiman Chatterjee), which goes to a remote village to shoot a film entitled *Aaakaler Sandhane*, a fictive study of the real Bengal famine of 1943. Sen highlights the social abyss separating the urban middle-class filmmakers from the impoverished rural world they attempt to portray. The title itself is ironic: only artists enjoy the luxury of "searching" for famine. Despite the leftist anthems they sing en route to the village, the crew remains incorrigibly bourgeois – tourists on a whirlwind tour of misery. Their pampered intervention has disastrous consequences: their consumerism triggers drastic changes in the local economy, raising the cost of essential goods. ("They're not only filming a famine," a

Plate 43 In Search of Famine: the contradictions of filming misery

280

wizened peasant remarks, "they're creating one.") The actors and actresses, meanwhile, have internalized the ideals of Hollywood glamor and the star system, so that one actress complains that her peasant role obliges her to wear unfashionable clothes. With their conversation sprinkled with trendy English expressions, the filmmakers are deeply imbued with colonialist culture, and themselves exercise a kind of internal colonialism over the people who are their subjects. One moment especially captures their privileged condescension: looking at old photographs, the filmmakers guess by their grain and hue at the year of the famine they represent. A human tragedy becomes the pretext for a parlor game.

But the filmmakers are not the only objects of critique. The 1943 famine itself is revealed as a sociohistorical rather than "natural" phenomenon, a byproduct of the war economy thrust on India by the British. The local elite, its wealth and privileges acquired by dubious means, plays a complicit role. The film also mocks cultural colonialism by displaying an advertisement for *The Guns of Navarone* (1961), "Starring the greatest beauty in the world, Anthony Quinn, in the lead." Sen also critiques patriarchal attitudes. When Devika, the starlet, is discovered to be unsuitable for her role, a search is begun for a replacement; the well-to-do fathers who volunteer their daughters are shocked to learn that the role is that of a village woman who turns to prostitution for survival. No one condemns a male actor for playing a drunk or a pimp, someone remarks, but everyone condemns an actress for playing a prostitute. The film ends with what by now has become a reflexive topos: the filmmakers decide not to make the film, but the audience knows the film has in fact been made, and that it is called *In Search of Famine*.

Eduardo Coutinho's metadocumentary *Cabra Marcado para Morrer*, 1984 (literally "Man Marked for Death" but translated into English as "Twenty Years After"), in some respects offers a counter-example to *In Search of Famine* in that it demonstrates the political efficacy of Third World filmmaking, deploying reflexivity to offer a capsule history of Brazil, and of Brazilian cinema, since the early 1960s. Coutinho's initial project, conceived in the optimistic years before the 1964 coup d'état, was to reconstruct dramatically the real-life political assassination, in 1962, of peasant leader João Pedro Teixeira. João Pedro's actual comrades in work and struggle were to perform at the actual site of the events, and among the "actors" would be the deceased leader's widow Elizabete. The coup interrupted the filming, however; the filmmakers and peasant participants were dispersed and the material already shot had to be hidden from the newly installed junta. Almost two decades later, encouraged by the liberalization of the 1980s, Coutinho sought out the hidden footage and the original "performers," now spread around the country by years of hardship and oppression. In the final film, the participants in the original film watch themselves on the screen, their faces and lives bearing witness to the scars left by dictatorship.

Elizabete, João Pedro's widow, is a key figure in *Twenty Years After*. She has carried on her husband's militancy, leading demonstrations and even traveling to Brasilia to denounce his murder. Coutinho discovers her in another state, under another name, cut off from former friends and from much of her family – all

281

necessary, she explains, "in order not to be exterminated." After bitter repression, she reencounters her family, reassumes her true name, and reaffirms her political convictions. In her capacity for disappearing, surviving, and then reappearing, as Roberto Schwarz points out, she resembles the filmmaker himself.[28] The emotion generated by the film, as Schwarz indicates, arises from the encounter of a committed filmmaker with an authentic popular heroine who, despite everything, manages to trace the path of her political trajectory, just as the filmmaker manages to complete his project. In a renewed confluence of political cinema and popular struggle, the cineaste offers efficacious solidarity with the peasant leader. The dispersion and disintegration of the family and the erasure of identity under repression point to the generation's suffering. But the descent into hell is doubled by a reverse journey that leads, if not to paradise, at least to an altered historical conjuncture. Tracing a two-decade process, the cinema literally intervenes in the life of the oppressed. The story of the film begun, brutally interrupted, and now completed is mingled with the story of the people with whom the filmmaker dialogs. Thanks to the film, Elizabete Teixeira emerges from the underground and recomposes her identity, just as political cinema continues, but in a different mode.

The filmmakers' 1960s meeting with the widow is paralleled by quotations of the highly didactic cinema of the period – a mélange of *Salt of the Earth* (1954) style realism with the populist idealism promoted by the leftist Popular Centers of Culture. The 1980s meeting, on the other hand, takes place in the era of network television and of revisionist "voice-of-the-other" documentaries. The filmic language is now more dialogical, less inclined to pontificate and more inclined to listen. The film itself manifests this evolution by adroitly interweaving traditional documentary procedures, especially off-screen commentary, with the more contemporary techniques of TV reportage usually practiced by Coutinho, now a TV professional linked to the well-known series *Globo Reporter*. We see his crew working within the frame, making us acutely aware that a film is being made before our eyes. *Twenty Years After* thus offers a telescoped representation not only of the history of Brazil but also of Brazilian cinema, in a synthesis at once political, social, anthropological, and filmic.

Iskandariya Leh? (Alexandria Why ...?, 1979), Youssef Chahine's semi-autobiographical film about an aspiring filmmaker haunted by Hollywood dreams, meanwhile, offers an Egyptian perspective on the imperializing film culture of the US. Chahine's protagonist begins as a Victoria College student who adores Shakespeare's plays and Hollywood movies. The film is set in the 1940s, a critical period for the protagonist and for Egypt: Allied troops were then stationed in the country and Axis forces threatened to invade Alexandria. Although *Alexandria Why ...?* focusses on the would-be filmmaker, its subplots offer a multiperspectival study of Egyptian society, describing how different classes, ethnicities, and religions – working-class communists, aristocratic Muslim homosexuals, middle-class Egyptian Jews, petit-bourgeois Catholics – react to Eyptian-Arab nationalism. The subplots stress the diversity of Egyptian experience, but the unanimity of the reaction to European colonialism. One story, for example, reaffirms the "Arabness" of Egypt's Arab Jews, through a romance subplot involving a communist of Muslim working-class background and a Jewish-Egyptian woman, daughter of a middle-class anti-Zionist communist.[29] Thus Chahine undoes the simplistic equation of all Jews with Zionism, and with Europeanness, undermining the Eurocentric binarism of Arab versus Jew and evoking instead a complex history of nationalist struggle which includes Egyptian Jews (even sometimes as leaders, as in the case of Ya'aqub Sanua).

Alexandria Why ...? weaves diverse materials – newsreels, clips from Hollywood films, staged reconstructions, Chahine's own youthful amateur films – into an ironic collage. The opening credit sequence mingles black and white 1940s travelog footage of Alexandria beaches with newsreel footage of Europe at war, implementing a "peripheral" Egyptian perspective on Europe. In the following sequence we watch a series of newsreels and Hollywood musicals along with the spectators in Alexandria. The musicals are subtitled in Arabic (Egypt was a translation center for the Middle East), while the newsreels have an Arabic voice-over, suggesting a "return to sender" message from the "periphery." An anthology of musical clips featuring Hollywood stars and songs such as "I'll Build a Stairway to Paradise" are inserted into a reception context redolent of First World/Third World economic and military relations as well as of the worldwide hegemonization of the American dream. The "Three Cheers for the Red, White and Blue" number, for example, at once charming and intimidating in its climactic image of cannons firing at the camera, celebrates American power and renders explicit the nationalist subtext of First World "entertainment."

The movie-going scenes suggest a kind of obsession, a repetitive ritual of filmgoing. Meanwhile, the Egyptian musical scenes, directed by the protagonist, clearly mock Americanizing fantasies. These numbers affect a kitschy, "underdeveloped" mimicry of Hollywood production values. As Egyptian performers emulate the formulae of the Hollywood-Latino musical, they also point to Hollywood's role in disseminating imagery of the Third World. One Egyptian actor, sporting poncho and sombrero, plays a mariachi-style guitar, much as an earlier sequence featured the Argentinian song "Perfidia." It is Hollywood and its distribution network, we are reminded, that popularized Latin American performers like Carmen Miranda, and dances like the tango, rhumba, and the cha-cha among the middle classes of the Middle East and the Third World generally. But Chahine satirizes Westernizing mass-mediated culture not on originary grounds but rather on cultural and ideological ones. The grandiose stairs of the Egyptian musical performance parody the lavish stairway-to-paradise number featured earlier. The clumsy mimicry of the Hollywoodeanized dancing contrasts with an earlier nightclub sequence in which Egyptian women perform Arabic songs while a drunken British soldier in the audience tries to sing in English; the soundtrack amplifies the women's singing, symbolically letting Arabic overtake English.

Alexandria Why ...? interweaves documentary and staged theatrical fiction in innovative ways. Impossibly fluid movement matches, for example, take us from

Plate 44 Egypt as Europe's battlefield: *Alexandria Why...?*

newsreel material to staged footage to theatrical play. World War II actuality footage is manipulated to incorporate the film's characters; whether the material is diegetic or non-diegetic is deliberately blurred. The theatrical sketch, meanwhile, reduces the European powers to a stereotypical cultural emblem; Hitler's moustache, Churchill's cigar, a French chef, an Italian pizza. In a reversal of tradition, the colonized now caricature the colonizer. Indeed, Egyptians cast themselves as their European colonizers, but finally remove the Hitler mask in a reflexive gesture that reveals their Egyptianness. As representatives of Allied and Axis powers chase each other chaotically across a sandy stage (as well as across the generically contradictory space of documentary and fiction), all mumbling their own idioms, the Egyptian characters watch, spectators of an alien imperialist war in their own land. They hold a sign in Arabic: "From here no one passes" (an evocation of Egyptian anticolonialist slogans), but the rapidly transmuting European colonizers, both Allies and Axis, blithely ignore the sign. The irrationality usually projected by Western orientalism on to Arabs here boomerangs against the Europeans.

The final sequences mock the power that replaced European colonial power in Egypt after World War II – the US – deriding the chimera of Americanization that enthralls both the protagonist and, allegorically, middle-class Egyptians generally. On arriving in the musical's national homeland, he is greeted by the Statue of Liberty transformed into a toothless, loudly laughing woman. By 1979, when *Alexandria Why...?* was made, the view of the US as a liberating force had given way to bitter disillusionment. The Statue of Liberty is shown via 1940s studio-style back-projection, but whereas Hollywood often exploited scenic matte shots to show exotic locales, the Egyptian film deploys the same technique to mock the industrialized fantasies of American mass-culture. The tacky papier-maché quality of Chahine's Statue of Liberty metaphorizes the factitious nature of Third World idealizations of North American freedom, particularly in the context of the postwar Middle East, where the US has come to represent both an alluring model and a new imperialism supplanting European colonialisms.[30]

BEYOND THE NATIONAL

Any serious discussion of Third World cinema must engage the complex question of the "national." As the products of national industries, produced in national languages, portraying national situations and recycling national intertexts (literatures, folklores), all films are of course national, just as *all* films, whether Hindu mythologicals, Mexican melodramas, or Third Worldist epics, project national imaginaries. But if First World filmmakers seem to float "above" petty nationalist concerns, it is because they take for granted the projection of a national power that facilitates the making and the dissemination of their films. Third World filmmakers, on the other hand, cannot assume a substratum of national power. Rather, relative powerlessness generates a constant struggle to create an elusive "authenticity" to be constructed anew with every generation.

Third Worldist filmmakers see themselves as part of a national project, but the concept of the national is contradictory, the site of competing discourses. Quite apart from the historical and ideological ambiguities of nationalism – the slippage between the original meaning of "nation" as racial group and its later meaning as politically organized entity, and the oscillation between nationalism's progressive and regressive poles – nationalism changes its valence in different historical and geographical contexts. A proactive European nationalism – such as Nazi Germany's *lebensraum* ambitions against its neighbors – cannot be equated with reactive nationalisms like those of Latin America, where nationalism is directed not against neighbors but rather against the hegemonic power to the north. Nor can an atomizing nationalism (such as that currently fracturing the former Yugloslavia) be equated with the agglutinative nationalism of diasporic movements, which call both for local integrity and for larger interwoven collectivities. At the same time, we reject the binaristic dichotomy of a "good" Third World nationalism, and a "bad" First World nationalism. Third World nationalisms can mimic the worst features of their First World antagonists; what began as liberatory can become oppressive, and what was already oppressive (for instance in relation to gender and sexuality) can become more so.

Some of the early Third Worldist discussions of nationalism took it as axiomatic that the issue was simply one of expelling the foreign to recover the national, as if the nation were a kind of "heart of the artichoke," to be found by peeling away the outer leaves, or as if, to change the metaphor, the nation were the ideal sculpted form lurking within the unworked stone. Roberto Schwarz calls this view the "national by subtraction"; that is, the assumption that the simple elimination of foreign influences will automatically allow the national culture to emerge in its native glory.[31] In many Third World countries, the project of eliminating the foreign and recuperating the national was shared by both left and right, except that each gave the words "national" and "foreign" a different political inflection. For right-wing "national-security" ideologists, it was an "alien" Marxism that had to be excised, while for the left it was imperialism and the multinational corporations.

We need not linger here on the deficiencies of the right-wing analysis, but the ambiguities of the left-wing position deserve exploration. First, the topos of a unitary nation camouflages the possible contradictions among different sectors of Third World society. The nation-states of the Americas, of Africa and Asia, as we saw earlier, often "cover" the existence of indigenous nations within them. Second, the exaltation of "the national" provides no criteria for distinguishing what is worth retaining in the "national tradition." A sentimental defense of patriarchal social institutions simply because they are "ours" can hardly be seen as emancipatory. Indeed, many Third World films criticize exactly such institutions: *Xala* criticizes polygamy, *Finzan* (1989) and *Fire Eyes* (1993) critique female genital mutilation, while films like *Allah Tanto* (1992) focus on the political repression exercised even by a pan-Africanist hero like Sekou Toure, and *Guelwaar* (1992) satirizes religious divisions within the Third World nation. Third, all nations are heterogenous, at once urban and rural, male and female, religious and secular, native and immigrant, and so forth. The view of the nation as unitary muffles the "polyphony" of social and ethnic voices within heteroglot cultures. Third World feminists especially have highlighted the ways in which the subject of the Third World nationalist revolution has been covertly posited as heterosexual and masculine. Fourth, the precise nature of the national "essence" to be recovered is elusive and chimerical. Some locate it in the precolonial past, or in the country's rural interior (the African village, for example), or in a prior stage of development (the pre-industrial), or in a non-European ethnicity (for instance, the indigenous or African strata in the nation-states of the Americas). But often even the most prized national symbols are indelibly marked by the foreign. Cultural practices seen as prototypically Brazilian, for example, come from elsewhere; palm trees from India, soccer from Britain, the samba from Africa. Recently, scholars have emphasized the ways in which national identity is mediated, textualized, constructed, "imagined," just as the traditions valorized by nationalism are "invented."[32] Any definition of nationality, then, must see it as partly discursive in nature, must take class, gender, and sexuality into account, must allow for racial difference and cultural heterogeneity, and must be dynamic, seeing "the nation" as an evolving, imaginary construct rather than an originary essence.

Third Worldists often fashioned their idea of the nation-state according to the European model, in this sense remaining complicit with a Eurocentric Enlightenment narrrative. And the nation-states they built often failed to deliver on their promises. In terms of race, class, gender, and sexuality in particular, many of them remained, on the whole, ethnocentric, patriarchal, bourgeois, and homophobic. At the same time, reducing Third World nationalism to a mere echo of European nationalism ignores the international realpolitik that obliged the colonized to adopt a discourse and a practice of the nation-state precisely in order to end colonialism. The formation of Third World nation-states often involved a double process of on the one hand joining diverse ethnicities and regions that had been separate under colonialism, and on the other partitioning regions in a way that forced regional redefinition (Iraq/Kuwait) and a cross-shuffling of populations (Pakistan/India). Furthermore, political geographies and state borders do not always coincide with what Said calls "imaginary geographies," whence the existence of "internal emigrés," nostalgics, rebels – that is, groups of people who share the same passport but whose relations to the nation-state are conflicted and ambivalent. In the postcolonial context of the constant flux of peoples, affiliation with the nation-state becomes highly partial and contingent.[33]

The decline of Third Worldist euphoria brought with it a rethinking of political and cultural and esthetic possibilities, as the rhetoric of revolution began to be greeted with a certain skepticism. Meanwhile, the socialist-inflected national liberation struggles of the the 1960s and early 1970s were harassed economically and militarily, violently discouraged from becoming revolutionary models for post-independence societies. A combination of IMF pressure, cooptation, and "low-intensity warfare" obliged even socialist regimes to collaborate with transnational capitalism. Some regimes grew repressive toward those who wanted to go beyond a purely nationalist revolution to restructure class, gender, region, and ethnic relations. As a result of external pressures and internal self-questioning, the cinema too gave expression to these mutations, as the anti-colonial thrust of earlier films gradually gave way to more diversified themes. This is not to say that artists and intellectuals became less politicized, only that cultural and political critiques took new and different forms.

Largely produced by men, Third Worldist films were not generally concerned with a feminist critique of nationalist discourse. They often favored the generic (and gendered) space of heroic confrontations, whether set in the streets, the casbah, the mountains, or the jungle. The minimal presence of women corre-sponded to the public place assigned women both in the anticolonialist revolutions and within Third Worldist discourse, leaving women's "private" struggles unacknowledged. Women occasionally carried the bombs, as in *The Battle of Algiers*, but only in the name of a "Nation." More often women were made to carry the "burden" of national allegory (the Algerian woman dancing with the flag in *The Battle of Algiers*; the Argentinian prostitute whose image is underscored by the national anthem in *Hour of the Furnaces*; the *mestiza* journalist in *Cubagua*, 1987, as embodiment of the Venezuelan nation) or scapegoated as personifications of imperialism (the allegorical "whore of Babylon" figure in Rocha's films). Gender contradictions have been subordinated to anticolonial struggle: women have been expected to "wait their turn." Purely nationalist discourse cannot apprehend the layered, dissonant identities of diasporic or postcolonial subjects. The minoritarian/Third World films of the 1980s and 1990s, by contrast, do not so much reject the "nation" as interrogate its repressions and limits. While often embedded in the autobiographical, they are not always narrated in the first person, nor are they "merely" personal; rather, the boundaries between the personal and communal, like the generic boundaries between documentary and fiction, are constantly blurred. The diary form, the voice-over, the personal written text, now bear witness to a collective memory of colonial violence. While early Third Worldist films documented alternative histories through archival footage, interviews, testimonials, and historical reconstructions, generally limiting their attention to the public sphere, the films of the 1980s and 1990s use the camera less as revolutionary weapon than as monitor of the gendered and sexualized realms of the personal and the domestic, seen as integral but repressed aspects of collective history The "post-Third Worldist" films of the 1980s and 1990s display a certain skepticism toward metanarratives of liberation, but do not necessarily abandon the notion that emancipation is worth fighting for. Rather than fleeing from contradiction, they install doubt and crisis at the very core of the films. Rather than a grand anticolonial metanarrative, they favor heteroglossic proliferations of difference within polygeneric narratives, seen not as embodiments of a single truth but rather as energizing political and esthetic forms of communitarian self-construction. These new forms are the subject of our next chapter.

NOTES

1 Lyotard, despite his skepticism about "metanarratives," endorsed the Persian Gulf war in a collective manifesto published in *Libération*, thus indirectly endorsing Bush's metanarrative of a "New World Order."

2 There were of course implicitly anticolonial films, prior to this period, in such countries as India, Egypt, and Mexico. Many Latin American films celebrated creole nationalist heroes such as Tiradentes in Brazil and Martin Fierro in Argentina. But such films were not articulated in relation to anticolonialist movements *per se*.

3 The various festivals – in Havana, Cuba (dedicated to New Latin American cinema), in Carthage, Tunisia (for Arab and African cinemas), in Ouagadougou, Burkina Faso (for African and Afro-diasporic cinemas) – gave further expression to these movements.

4 Frantz Fanon, *The Wretched of the Earth* (New York: Grove Press, 1964), p. 210.

5 Ibid., p. 51.

6 Ibid., pp. 38–9.

7 Ibid., p. 88.

8 Pontecorvo recently (1991) returned to Algiers to make *Gillo Pontecorvo Returns to Algiers*, a film about the evolution of Algeria during the twenty-five years that had elapsed since *The Battle of Algiers* was filmed, and focussing on topics such as Islamic fundamentalism, the subordinate status of women, the veil, and so forth.

9 Anne McClintock, "No Longer in a Future Heaven: Women and Nationalism in South Africa," *Transition*, 51 (1991), p. 120.

10   For a fuller discussion of *The Battle of Algiers*, see Robert Stam, *The Battle of Algiers: Three Women Three Bombs* (New York: Macmillan Films Study Extract, 1975); and Joan Mellen, *Filmguide to The Battle of Algiers* (Bloomington: Indiana University Press, 1975).

11   For production information about *The Battle of Algiers*, see Mellen, *Filmguide to The Battle of Algiers*. Mellen points out that Pontecorvo had thought of engaging Warren Beatty to play Colonel Mathieu, a choice that would have been more expensive and would have undercut the scrupulous historicity of the film.

12   See Ismail Xavier, "Allegories of Underdevelopment," New York University Ph.D. dissertation, 1982 (Ann Arbor: University of Michigan Microfilms, 1984).

13   See Gilles Deleuze, *Cinema Two: Time-Image*, trans. Hugh Tomlinson and Robert Galeta (Minneapolis: University of Minnesota Press, 1989), p. 222.

14   See Peter Wollen, "The Two Avant-Gardes," reprinted in Peter Wollen, *Readings and Writings: Semiotic Counter Strategies* (London: Verso, 1982).

15   See Fernando Solanas and Octavio Getino, "Towards a Third Cinema," in Michael Chanan, ed., *Twenty Five Years of the New Latin American Cinema* (London: BFI, 1983).

16   Gérard Chaliand, in *Mythes Révolutionnaires du Tiers Monde* (Paris: Editions du Seuil, 1976) criticizes the machismo which led Latin American guerillas to expose themselves to combat even when their presence was not required, thus resulting in the death of most of the guerilla leaders. Chaliand contrasts this attitude with the more prudent procedures of the Vietnamese, who during fifteen years of war did not lose even one of the fifty members of the Central Committee of the South Vietnamese National Liberation Front.

17   For more on *The Battle of Chile*, see Julianne Burton, "Politics and the Documentary in People's Chile," in Julianne Burton, ed., *Cinema and Social Change in Latin America: Conversations with Filmmakers* (Austin: University of Texas Press, 1986), and Ana M. Lopez, "*The Battle of Chile*: Documentary, Political Process, and Representation," in Julianne Burton, ed., *The Social Documentary in Latin America* (Pittsburgh, Penn.: Pittsburgh University Press, 1990).

18   See Fredric Jameson, "Third World Literature in the Era of Multinational Capitalism," *Social Text*, No. 15 (Fall 1986). And for a critique of the Jameson essay, see Aijaz Ahmad, "Jameson's Rhetoric of Otherness and the 'National Allegory'," *Social Text*, No. 15 (Fall 1986).

19   One unfortunate aspect of Jameson's essay is that it does not recognize the extent to which theories of national allegory had already been developed within the Third World itself. In Brazil, for example, the idea of national allegory, although it does not always go by that name, has been a constant at least since the 1920s modernistas. For more on cinema and national allegory, see Ismail Xavier's 1982 dissertation: "Allegories of Underdevelopment," revised and published in Brazil as *Alegorias do Subdesenvolvimento* (São Paulo: Brasiliense, 1993). See also Robert Stam and Ismail Xavier, "Transformations of National Allegory: Brazilian Cinema from Dictatorship to Redemocratization," in Robert Sklar and Charles Musser, eds, *Resisting Images* (Philadelphia: Temple University Press, 1990). We would like to thank Ismail for allowing us to use the "shared territory" of that essay. For national allegories in the context of Israel/Palestine, see Ella Shohat, "Master Narrative/Counter Readings: The Politics of Israeli Cinema," in Sklar and Musser, eds, *Resisting Images*; and Shohat, "Anomalies of the National: Representing Israel/Palestine," *Wide Angle*, Vol. 11, No. 3 (1989).

20   Behroze Gandhy and Rosie Thomas make this point in their essay "Three Indian Film Stars," in Christine Gledhill, ed., *Stardom: Industry of Desire* (London: Routledge, 1991).

21   See Arnaldo Jabor, "Sim, Gosto Se Discute," *Rio Capital* (April/May 1993).

22 See "Do Golpe Militar a Abertura: A Resposta do Cinema de Autor," in Ismail Xavier, Jean-Claude Bernardet, and Miguel Pereira, *O Desafio do Cinema* (Rio: Zahar, 1985).

23 See Françoise Pfaff, "Three Faces of Africa: Women in *Xala*," *Jump Cut*, No. 27 (1977).

24 Laura Mulvey, "*Xala*, Ousmane Sembene 1976: The Carapace that Failed," in *Third Text*, Nos 16/17 (Autumn/Winter 1991).

25 Palestinian film production, from the establishment of "Unity Cinema" in 1967 through "Palestinian Cinema Group" in 1973 to "The Palestinian Cinema Organization," under the auspices of the PLO, has always been intended as an instrument for the promotion of the Palestinian national cause and the registering of revolutionary events related to the Palestinian resistance. Virtually all production, therefore, has been devoted to news and documentary films – a situation common in societies struggling for political definition (and reminiscent, ironically, of Zionist film production in the pre-state era). The few fiction films sympathetic to the Palestinian cause – for example, *The Dupes* (Al-Mukhdu'un, 1972), by the Egyptian filmmaker Tewfiq Salleh, and *Kafr Qassem* (1973), by the Lebanese Borhane Aalawiyye – were made by non-Palestinian Arabs. Aalawiyye's film is a recreation of a 1956 massacre of Palestinian villagers by the Israeli army, shortly before the end of the joint Anglo-Franco-Israeli attack on Egypt in 1956. But whereas this film demonizes the Israelis – for example by having a Palestinian observe in the streets of Tel Aviv the sale of a presumably popular toy: a guillotine cutting off the head of an Arab in a keffiya – *Wedding in Galilee* does not reduce the oppression of the Palestinian people to a Manichean schema of good Palestinians versus evil Israelis.

26 See Nahla Abdo, "Women of the Intifada: Gender, Class and National Liberation," *Race and Class*, Vol. 32, No. 4 (April/June 1991).

27 For more on reflexivity, see Robert Stam, *Reflexivity in Film and Literature* (New York: Columbia University Press, 1985, reprinted 1992).

28 See Roberto Schwarz, "O Fio da Meada," in Schwarz, *Que Horas São* (São Paulo: Companhia das Letras, 1987).

29 Chahine portrays Egyptian Jews, positively, as connected to the Socialists fighting for an equal and just Egyptian society, forced to evacuate Egypt fearing the Nazis' arrival, and thus immigrating to Palestine/Israel. Here the film structures point-of-view so that the Egyptian Jew views the clashes between Euro-Israelis and Palestinians together with Arabs from the Arab point of view; realizing that the rights of one people are obtained at the expense of another people, he returns to Egypt. The film thus distinguishes between Arab (Sephardi) Jews and European (Ashkenazi) Jews, a distinction reinforced at the end of the film through the protagonist's arrival in the US and his encounter with Ashkenazi Hassidim, implicitly suggesting the distance between his Jewish-Egyptian friends (with whom he shares a similar culture) and European Jews. Such a representation, however, is rather rare in Arab fiction and the film was banned by several Arab countries, even though it was approved by Palestinian organizations. Sephardi filmmakers have insisted on Arab-Jewish identity, as in the documentaries *Anahnu Yehudin Arism be Israel* (We Are Arab Jews in Israel, 1978) by the Moroccan–Israeli Yigal Nidam, and *I Miss the Sun* (1983) by the Egyptian-American Mary Halawane.

30 The critique of the US must be seen in a context when Sadat's opening to Israel triggered hostile reaction in Egypt and the Arab world.

31 See Roberto Schwarz, "Nacional por Subtração," in his *Que Horas São*.

32 See Benedict Anderson, *Imagined Communities: Reflections on the Origins and Spread of Nationalism* (London: Verso, 1983); and E.J. Hobsbawm and Terence Ranger, eds, *The Invention of Tradition* (Cambridge: Cambridge University Press, 1983).

33 Diasporic communities, Michael Hanchard suggests, express allegiance less to spatially fixed nation-states than to an attitude toward time. The African diaspora forms an "imagined community" whose "social movements can be thought of as speed mobilized in an historical moment in order to shorten the duration – the time – of oppression." Diverse "velocities of existence" operate within a single time, "exploding the myth of unified, stable national-statist collective identities." Michael Hanchard, "A Notion of Afro-Diasporic Time," paper presented at a workshop on "The World the Diaspora Makes," University of Michigan, June 5–7, 1991, and kindly sent to us by the author.

8

ESTHETICS OF RESISTANCE

Oppositional cinemas in both the First and Third Worlds have explored a wide spectrum of alternative esthetics. This spectrum includes films and videos that bypass the formal conventions of dramatic realism in favor of such modes and strategies as the carnivalesque, the anthropophagic, the magical realist, the reflexive modernist, and the resistant postmodernist. These alternative esthetics are often rooted in non-realist, often non-Western or para-Western cultural traditions featuring other historical rhythms, other narrative structures, other views of the body, sexuality, spirituality, and the collective life. Post-Third Worldist, they interrogate nationalist discourse through the grids of class, gender, sexual, and diasporic identities. Many incorporate paramodern traditions into clearly modernizing or postmodernizing esthetics, and thus problematize facile dichotomies such as traditional/modern, realist/modernist, modernist/postmodernist.

In our view, the projection of Third World cultural practices as untouched by avant-gardist modernism or mass-mediated postmodernism is often subliminally imbricated with a view of the Third World as "underdeveloped," or "developing," as if it lived in another time-zone apart from the global system of the late capitalist world. Like the sociology of "modernization" and the economics of "development," the esthetics of modernism (and of postmodernism) often covertly assume a telos toward which Third World cultural practices are presumed to be evolving. Even such an acute cultural theorist as Fredric Jameson, in his writings on Third World literature and cinema, tends to underestimate the radical revisioning of esthetics performed by Third World and diasporic artists. Although he is (thankfully) inconsistent on this point, Jameson in his unguarded moments at times seems to conflate the terms of political economy (where he projects the Third World into a less developed, less modern frame), and those of esthetic and cultural periodization (where he projects it into a "premodernist" or "pre-postmodernist" past). A residual economism or "stagism," normally anathema to a thinker like Jameson, here leads to the equation of late capitalist/postmodernist and precapitalist/premodernist, as when he speaks of the "belated emergence of a kind of modernism in the modernizing Third World, at a moment when the so-called advanced countries are themselves sinking into full postmodernity."[1] Elsewhere, he recalls with a certain ironic distance the old First World leftist fantasy invested in "the hope, then called Third Worldism, that precapitalist societies who came to modernization only in relatively recent times, would somehow be able to overleap everything crippling for the industrial west in its experience of capitalism."[2]

Thus the Third World, the object of idealization in an earlier phase, becomes the object of disenchantment in a later phase. In Jameson's prose the Third World always seems to lag behind, not only economically but also culturally, condemned to a perpetual game of catch-up in which it can only repeat on another register the history of the "advanced" world. When the First World reaches the stage of late capitalism and postmodernism, the Third World hobbles along toward modernism and the beginnings of capitalism. Jameson thus ignores the world systems theory that sees First and Third Worlds as living the same historical moment although the Third World lives that moment under the mode of oppression. A seventeenth-century slave-based plantation, for instance, was also an industrial system, involving heavy capitalization and advanced technology, and was therefore an integral part of global modernity. A different cultural theory would posit the neologistic cultures of Latin America, for example, as the products of uneven development and of multifaceted transactions with other cultures, and as the privileged scenes of copy and pastiche, as themselves the proleptic site of postmodernist practices. For us, "postmodern" is not an honorific, nor are Third World postmodernisms necessarily identical to those of the First World. A more adequate formulation would see time as scrambled and palimpsestic in all the Worlds, with the premodern, the modern, the postmodern and the paramodern coexisting globally, although the "dominant" might vary from region to region. Thus the Pennsylvania Dutch and Silicon Valley technocrats both live in "postmodern" America, while the "Stone Age" Yanomami and the hyper-sophisticated Euro-Brazilians of São Paulo both live in Brazil, yet the Yanomami use video while the sophisticates adhere to "primitive" Afro-Brazilian religions.

Part of the burden of this chapter is to call attention to the esthetic innovations of Third World modernist and paramodernist movements. The valorization of "sleaze, punk, trash, and garbage" that Jameson posits as characteristic of First World postmodernism, for example, was already present in the palpably grubby "dirty screens" of the Brazilian "esthetics of garbage" movement of the late 1960s. Quite apart from the confluence of Brechtian modernism and Marxist modernization in the "New Cinemas" of Cuba (Alea), Brazil (Guerra), Senegal (Sembene), and India (Sen), there have been many modernist and avant-garde films in the Third World, going all the way back to films like *São Paulo: Sinfonia de uma Cidade* (São Paulo: Symphony of a City, 1928) and *Limite* (1930), both from Brazil, and forward through the Senegalese director Djibril Diop Mambete's *Touki-Bouki* (1973), the Mauritanian Med Hondo's *Soleil O* (1970) and *West Indies* (1975), and the Tunisian Ferid Boughedir's *La Mort Trouble* (Murky Death, 1970), to the underground movements of Argentina and Brazil, through Kidlat Tahimik's anticolonialist experiments in the Philippines (which Jameson, to his credit, does reference).

293

Plate 45 The archaic
postmodern: *Touki-Bouki*

One cannot assume, then, that "avant-garde" always means "White" and "European," or that Third World art, as Jameson sometimes seems to imply, is always realist or premodernist.[3] The esthetic exchange, furthermore, was always two-way. The debt of the European avant-gardes to the arts of Africa, the Pacific region, and the Americas has been extensively documented. The British sculptor Henry Moore, to take just one example, modeled his recumbent statues on the Chac Mool stone figures of ancient Mexico. Although it may be true that it was the "impact of surrealism," as Roy Armes suggests, "that liberated the Caribbean and African poets of Negritude from the constraints of a borrowed language,"[4] it was also, we would argue, African and Asian and American indigenous art that liberated the European modernists by provoking them to question their own culture-bound esthetic of realism. Even the equation of "reflexivity" with European modernism is questionable. The Meso-American *teoamoxtli* or cosmic books feature *mise-en-abyme* images of deerskin drawn upon the deerskins of which they are made, just as the *Popol Vuh* "creates itself in analogy with the world-making it describes or narrates."[5] In Africa, meanwhile, scholars such as Karin Barber of the University of Ife (Nigeria) have discerned common elements in deconstruction and Yoruba *oriki* praise poetry, specifically indeterminacy, intertextuality, and constant variability.[6] And for Henry Louis Gates Jr (in *The Signifying Monkey*), the Yoruba trickster figure Eshu-Elegbara emblematizes the deconstructive "signifying" of African-derived art forms. "Third World" esthetic practices, in sum, cannot be corraled into the narrow, segregated categories suggested for them by Euro-diffusionist notions of art history.

THE ARCHAIC SOURCES OF
ALTERNATIVE ESTHETICS

The beginnings of cinema did not only coincide with the heights of imperialism; they also coincided with the agonizing paroxysms of the veristic project as expressed in the realist novel, in the naturalist play (with real meat hanging in stage butcher shops), and in obsessively mimetic exhibitions. Despite its superficial modernity and technological razzle-dazzle, dominant cinema inherited the mimetic aspirations that Impressionism had relinquished in painting, that Jarry as well as the symbolists had attacked in the theater, and that Joyce and Woolf had undermined in the novel. And while the "progressive realism" (in the words of Roman Jakobson) exemplified by some of the films analyzed earlier offers an invaluable artistic and political strategy for combatting the "regressive realism" of the colonialist master-narrative, a realist or, better, illusionist style is just one of many possible strategies; one marked, furthermore, by a certain provinciality. Vast regions of the world, and long periods of artistic history, have shown little allegiance to or even interest in realism. Kapila Malik Vatsayan speaks of a very different esthetic that held sway in much of the world:

> A common esthetic theory governed all the arts, both performing and plastic, in South and South East Asia. Roughly speaking, the common trends may be identified as the negation of the principle of realistic imitation in art, the establishment of a hierarchy of realities where the principle of suggestion through abstraction is followed and the manifestation in the arts of the belief that time is cyclic rather than linear ... This tradition of the arts appears to have been persuasive from Afghanistan and India to Japan and Indonesia over two thousand years of history.[7]

In India, a 2,000-year tradition of theater circles back to classical Sanskrit drama, which tells the myths of Hindu culture through an esthetic based less on coherent character and linear plot than on subtle modulations of mood and feeling (*rasa*). Chinese painting, in the same vein, has often ignored both perspective and realism. Much African art, similarly, has cultivated what Robert Farris Thompson calls "mid-point mimesis," that is to say, a style that avoids both illusionistic realism and hyperabstraction.[8] Non-realist traditions also exist within the West, of course, and in any case there is nothing intrinsically "bad" about occidental realism. But as the product of a specific culture and historical moment, it is only one band on a wider esthetic spectrum.

Just as the European avant-garde became "advanced" by drawing on the "archaic" and "primitive," so non-European artists, in an esthetic version of "revolutionary nostalgia," have drawn on the most traditional elements of their cultures, elements less "premodern" (a term that embeds modernity as telos) than "paramodern." In the arts, the distinction archaic/modernist is often not pertinent, in that both share a refusal of the conventions of mimetic realism. It is thus less a question of juxtaposing the archaic and the modern than of deploying the archaic in order, paradoxically, to modernize, in a dissonant temporality which combines a past imaginary communitas with an equally imaginary future utopia. In their attempts to forge a liberatory language, for example, alternative film traditions draw on paramodern phenomena such as popular religion and ritual magic. In some recent African films, such as *Yeelen* (1987), *Jitt* (1992), and *Kasarmu Ce* (This Land is Ours, 1991), magical spirits become an esthetic resource, a means for breaking away, often in farcical ways, from the linear, cause-and-effect conventions of Aristotelian narrative poetics, a way of defying the "gravity," in both senses of that word, of chronological time and literal space.

In Nigeria, filmmaker Ola Balogun explains, it is less appropriate to speak of "performing arts" than of "ritual or folk performances ... ceremonies of a social or religious nature into which dramatic elements are incorporated."[9] The values of African religious culture of which Balogun speaks have come to inform not only Nigerian cinema but also a good deal of Afro-diasporic cinema, for example Brazilian films like Rocha's *Barravento* (1962), Cavalcanti's *A Força de Xango* (The Force of Xango, 1977), dos Santos' *Amuleto de Ogum* (Ogum's Amulet, 1975); Cuban films like *Patakin* (1980) and *Ogum* (1990), and African-American films like Julie Dash's *Daughters of the Dust* (1990), Thomas Allen Harris' *Heaven, Earth & Hell* (1993), Zeinabu Davis' *Cycles* (1989) and Ayoka Chenzira's *Zajota and the Boogie Spirit* (1989) – all of which inscribe African (usually Yoruba) religious symbolism and practice. Indeed, the preference for Yoruba religious symbolism is itself significant, since the performing arts – music, dance, costume, narrative, poetry – are integral to Yoruba transe religion itself, unlike religions where the performing arts are grafted on to a theological/ textual core.

Haile Gerima's *Sankofa* (1993) synthesizes the modern and the traditional through an Afro-magical *egungun* esthetic: an esthetic that invokes the spirits of the ancestors as embodiments of a deep sense of personal and collective history.[10] Named after an Akan word for "recuperating what's lost," the film begins with a drummed invocation exhorting the ancestral spirits to "rise up, step out, and tell your story." An urgent whispered voice-over exhorts: "Spirit of the dead, rise up and possess your bird of passage, come out, you stolen Africans, spirits of the dead, you raped, castrated, lobotomized." This device of a collective call by a presiding spirit, turned into a structural refrain, authorizes a transgenerational mingling of the present (a bewigged Black fashion model posing against the backdrop of the Mina slave fort) and past (the fort's former historical atrocities). In a kind of psychic and historical time-machine, the fashion model becomes possessed by Shola, a nineteenth-century house slave, and is made to experience the cruelties, the rapes and the brandings of slavery, and to acknowledge her kinship with her own enslaved ancestors. (The woman, in this didactic allegory, is made to bear the burden of contemporary alienation.) Gerima repeatedly pans over friezes of Black faces, evoking an ocular chorus, bypassing an individualizing point-of-view structure to evoke a community of the gaze. Rather than being passive victims, Blacks exercise leadership even under the constraints of slavery.

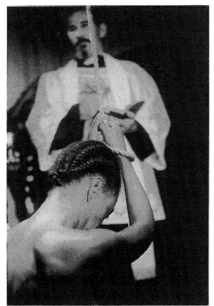

Plates 46 and 47 Afro-diasporic memory: *Sankofa* and *Daughters of the Dust*

The narrative forms a multifocal, communitarian *bildungsroman*: the fashion model confronts the sources of her own alienation and the "headman" who beats slaves becomes a double agent working for liberation. Nor is this a monolithic community, since it includes field slaves and house slaves, and even foremen who whip other slaves. The cultural facets of African life (communal childcare, herbal remedies, the primordial role of music and stories) are constantly stressed. Orality exists both as a diegetic presence – characters literally tell stories/histories of Africa, of the Middle Passage – and as a metacinematic device structuring the entire film as a collective narration, where disembodied voices exhort, prophesy, exorcize, criticize, all in a "polyrhythmic" style where avant-garde inflected moments of esthetic contemplation alternate with dramatic moments of decisive action.

An "archaic" orality takes the form both of oral stories and of oral *methods* of storytelling. For Bakhtin, the "autographed literature" of personal authorship is a mere drop in the ocean of anonymous oral folk literature. And indeed, written literature has often revitalized itself through spoken literature. African writers like Chinua Achebe, Wole Soyinka, and Ousmane Sembene draw on the taproot of the oral – proverbs, trickster tales, religious mythologies.[11] Italo Calvino, meanwhile, has his storyteller describe the Amazonian cosmos of myth and legend as the "primeval magma," the ultimate source of the world's narrative oxygen and energy.[12] Mario de Andrade drew on this same "magma" to create *Macunaíma*

297

(1928), a novel whose freedom of invention derives in part from the totemic and animistic matrix of Amazonian myths, creating a world where characters metamorphose into animals and turn into stars after death, as they do in Amerindian legends. Both the film and the novel exploit the antimimetic logic of folktales, which never pretend to realism, tending rather to spatial and temporal indeterminacy. The interbreeding of folktales from disparate traditions forms part of a productive *combinatoire* by which the collective language of the tribe is transformed into literary/filmic parole.

Ignoring the oral-formulaic origins of some of Europe's own founding narratives, such as *The Iliad* and *Beowulf*, Eurocentric thinking tends to equate the "non-literate" with the "*ill*iterate." It values literacy over orality, and assigns the prerogative of interpreting history to the literate European. But one can appreciate literacy as a useful tool and still question the equation of the written with the lofty, the serious, the scientific, and the historical, and of the oral with the backward, the frivolous, and the irrational.[13] The orality/literacy hierarchy has been questioned, in diverse ways, by thinkers such as Derrida (with his critique of phonocentrism), Hayden White (with his "leveling" of history and myth) and Bakhtin (with his dehierarchizing notion of "speech genres"), and has been radically challenged by the mixed-mode "oral writing" of feminists of color such as Gloria Anzaldúa, Audre Lorde, bell hooks, and Cherrie Moraga. Many films present "bottom-up" history conveyed through popular memory, legitimizing oral history by "inscribing" it on the screen. History, these films suggest, can also take the oral form of stories, myths, and songs passed on from generation to generation. The fecundating power of oral tradition is especially apparent in African and Afro-diasporic cinema. Souleymane Cisse's *Yeelen* (1987), for example, stages one of the oral epics, a kind of quest or initiation story, of the Bambara people. But even in films not based on oral narratives, such as Idrissa Ouedraogo's *Yaaba* (1989), we find a cinema of the utterance, a cinema marked by the pauses, the repetitions, and the rhythms of speech.

In Africa, the reinscription of the oral has often served a practical purpose: Sembene, for example, turned from novelist to filmmaker in order to reach non-literate audiences. He wanted to become the "mouth and ears" of society, the one who "reflects and synthesizes the problems, the struggles, and the hopes of his people."[14] Here the cinema inherits the social function (but not the conservative ideology) of the *griot*, the oral archivist of the tribe, the praise singer who tells of births, deaths, victories, and defeats. (The communal oral expression of the *griot* paradigm might be contrasted with the more individualist "camera pen" of the French New Wave.) As Cheryl Chisholm puts it, the *griot*:

> keeps the past alive in the minds and hearts of the group and, in the shaping of the recitation, the consensus of the group about its own identity evolves through time. The *griot* comments on the past in the light of the present and vice versa, communicating not in the disengaged, third person voice that has been the hallmark of conventional Western history, but in a manner fully

engaged with the ongoing drama of the group.[15]

Although *griots per se* are increasingly marginal to contemporary African life (indeed, Momar Thiam's *Sa Dagga*, 1982, charts the arc of their decline), their style of oral narration, deployed as a formal resource, informs a number of African and Afro-diasporic films.[16] In *Jom* (1981) a *griot*-narrator articulates the themes of the film, often direct to camera.

Manthia Diawara delineates some of the mediations operating between the oral traditions themselves and their filmic reelaboration; more important than the explicit traces of oral literature in film (presence of the *griot*, heroes and heroines borrowed from the oral tradition), he argues, are the deep structural transformations the cinema effects in the narrative points of view. Rather than merely being "faithful" to the oral tradition, in other words, films can transform that tradition. *Wend Kunni* (1982), for example, "incorporates an oral rendering of the tale which it also subverts." Diawara enumerates the film's diverse myth-kernels in terms of Proppian-Greimasian "functions," emphasizing the subversion of these myths for feminist and revolutionary purposes. If the *griot*'s narrative implies a restoration of the traditional order, the film points to the hope of a new order. In the oral tradition, a woman who defies the elders' advice to remarry is a witch; in *Wend Kunni* the "witch" is a harmless soul with a sick son and a missing husband. The film thus practices the "subversive deployment of orality." The story is "deterritorialized," its meaning transformed.[17]

But oral-inflected narratives are hardly limited to African films, nor are *griots* the only models of orality. Trinh T. Minh-ha speaks of "spinning and weaving [as] a euphonious heritage of wo/mankind handed on from generations of weavers within the clapping of the shuttle and the creaking of the block – which the Dogon call the 'creaking of the Word.'"[18] Felix de Rooy's *Almacita de Desolato* (1986) weaves legends from Curaçao, Aruba, and Bonnaire to narrate a symbolic battle between creative and destructive forces in a turn-of-the-century Afro-community in Curaçao. In both Gerima's *Ashes and Embers* (1982) and Dash's *Daughters of the Dust*, the voiced tales of elderly women relate repressed histories of resistance passed down across the generations, while Charles Burnett's *To Sleep with Anger* (1990) draws on the oral tradition of the trickster figure.[19] Native American films also draw on the taproot of orality. Victor Masayesva's *Itam Hakim, Hopiit* (We, Someone, the Hopi People, 1982) features one of the last male members of the storytelling Bow clan telling both his personal story and the story of Hopi emergence and the Pueblo revolt of 1680. In both George Burdeau and Larry Walsh's *Surviving Columbus* (1990) and Pat Ferrero's *Hopi: Songs of the Fourth World* (1983), elders tell the tribal history, thus throwing up an oral and mythic challenge to the Eurocentric version of the conquest, blurring the boundaries between documentary history (with its rationalist-scientist assumptions) and poetic myth-telling. Meanwhile, *Coyote Goes Underground* (1989) enacts oral legends (in claymation) about the trickster figure Coyote, while *Ancient Spirit, Living Word – the Oral Tradition* (1983) and *Live and Remember* (1986) stress oral tradition as a link to the past and a key to the future.

Despite their postmodern aura, the high-tech *griots* of rap music also root their art in orality. Largely the creation of Black and Latino working-class teenagers, rap music ultimately derives from African call-and-response patterns and their interanimation of performer and listener. The multiple strands woven into rap include disco, preaching, street funk, radio disk jockeys, be-bop singers, Cab Calloway, tap dancers, standup comics, the Last Poets, Gil Scott Heron, Muhammed Ali, doo-wop groups, ring games, skip-rope rhymes, prison and army songs, signifying and "the dozens," all the way back to the *griots* of Nigeria and Gambia.[20] Rap's free-wheeling raid on the intertext, furthermore, bypasses the bourgeois proprieties of copyright. Found bits from other songs, political speeches and advertisements are "sampled" and placed in ironic mutually relativizing relationships. Rap music videos recycle the voices and images of Black martyrs and ancestors such as Malcolm X and Martin Luther King in a "versioning" which sets up a direct line to African culture heroes, to the African-American intertext, and, as "Black Folks' CNN" (Chuck D's term), to the community.[21]

The question of orality illustrates the pitfalls of imposing a linear narrative of cultural "progress," in the manner of "development" theory, which sees people in traditional societies as mired in an inert preliterate past, incapable of change and agency. In the arts, the esthetic reinvoicing of tradition can serve purposes of *collective* agency in the present. The very name of the Palestinian theater group Al Hakawati (The Storyteller) evokes the tradition of the Arab storyteller, but the group's performances incorporate that figure in a generic spectrum that includes classical Arabic poetry, popular proverbs, and historical narration, all presented in a postmodern mélange that ironizes the developmentalist claims of the Zionist project. For Teshome Gabriel, Third World cinema (we would say a certain "trend" within Third World cinema) privileges formal strategies specific to oral cultures – repeated face-to-face narrations, a favoring of collective engagement over consumerist entertainment, participation over passivity.[22] In this vein, some recent African films create a kind of village or extended family esthetic to foster a collective space within a modernist or postmodernist paradigm. Jean-Pierre Bekolo's *Quartier Mozart* (1992), which portrays a Cameroonian neighborhood (the "Mozart Quarter" of the title), never sutures us via point-of-view editing into the individual desires of single characters of either gender; sexuality, as in carnival, becomes a quasi-public affair. In the film's "magical" format, a sorceress (Maman Thekla) helps a schoolgirl, "Queen of the Hood," enter the body of a man ("My Guy") in order to explore gendered boundaries. The sorceress takes the shape of "Panka," familiar from Cameroonian folklore, who can make a man's penis disappear with a handshake. While the magical devices of *Quartier Mozart* are on one level "archaic" – in that they translocate traditional folktale motifs into a contemporary setting – the style is allusively postmodern (referring especially to Spike Lee and his witty direct-address techniques), media-conscious (the neighborhood girls adore Denzel Washington), and music-video slick.

A film like *Quartier Mozart* makes one suspect that the resources of the cinema have barely begun to be tapped. One imagines a cinema which would rethink film from the standpoint of transpersonal desire, which would "socialize," as it were, the formulaic procedures of conventional scriptwriting based on individual motivations and conflicts, proposing instead: **ethnic** exposition, **social** antagonist, **racial** *anagnorisis* (self-recognition), *community* catharsis. *Daughters of the Dust*, for example, subverts the monadic unity of a psychologizing point of view to emphasize a community of aspiration, in the spirit of the African anti-Cartesianism of "I am, because we are; and since we are, therefore I am,"[23] or of the Vietnamese language where there is no pronoun "I" as such but only "your servant."[24] For Toni Cade Bambara, *Daughters of the Dust* eschews the Hollywood protocol of hero-dominated narrative in favor of a "non-linear, multi-layered unfolding." The emphasis is on a "shared space (wide-angled and deep-focus in which no one becomes backdrop to anyone else's drama) rather than dominated space (foregrounded hero in sharp focus, others Othered in background blur.)"[25] The events of *Daughters*, while technically set in 1902 at Ibo Landing in the Sea Islands of South Carolina, actually take place in in-between time, a time pregnant both with painful memory and with the long-term possibilities of freedom. Present time resonates with the echoes of the past; as children fall atop one another in a game, for example, we hear groaning reminiscent of the Middle Passage where Africans were piled together in the slave ships.[26] In *Daughters*, props, dresses, hairstyles, hand gestures become as important as characters because they embody historical traces, cultural metonyms.

Other films offer a provocative symbiosis of orality and music, pointing to the possibility of a transformed esthetic where music is not subordinate to the image and the diegesis but rather would form a kind of primordial matrix from which the film itself would emerge. Music might then play the role in film that it has often played in village or community life, where it is an energizing presence at once artistic, spiritual, and practical, whose function is communitarian rather than individualist-consumerist. Or music can relay a historical and social gestus (according to Brecht). Both *Frida* (1984) and *The Ballad of Gregorio Cortez* (1983) convey historical events and social attitudes through the Mexican border folk ballads called *corridos*. The blind balladeer's songs in Rocha's *Deus e Diabo na Terra do Sol* (Black God White Devil, 1964), meanwhile, based on the *cordel* tradition of the Brazilian northeast, lend an "epic" quality in both the folk-epic and the Brechtian sense, cuing changes of tone, substituting for dialog, "triggering" camera movement, drawing morals.[27] For Rocha, this "archaic" tradition itself contains "modernist" elements – telegraphic style, the refusal of mimesis. Eschewing the conventional use of music as mood-setter, *Terra em Transe* (Land in Anguish, 1967) similarly exploits the social connotations of specific musical traditions to evoke the characters' cultural-political allegiances: the right-wing dictator is associated with opera (Verdi and his Brazilian epigone, Carlos Gomez); the populist politician with samba; and the Rocha-like intellectual protagonist with Villa-Lobos, a composer who, like the director himself, produces erudite elaborations of popular leitmotifs.

CARNIVALESQUE SUBVERSIONS

Another "archaic" source of alternative esthetics is "carnival," a counter-hegemonic tradition with a history that runs (to speak only of Europe) from Greek Dionysian festivals (and classical Greece, we recall, was itself an amalgam of African, Semitic, and Greek elements) and the Roman Saturnalia, through the grotesque realism of the medieval "carnivalesque" (Rabelasian blasphemies, for example) and baroque theater, to Jarry, Surrealism, and on to the counter-cultural art of recent decades. But although European real-life carnivals have generally degenerated into the ossified repetition of perennial rituals, it would be Eurocentric to speak of the "end of carnival." Nearly all cultures have carnival-like traditions. Among the Navajos (Dineh), there are special rituals for overturning good order and respectable esthetics. The concept of *rasquachismo* (from Nahuatl), similarly, evokes deliberate bad taste and the breaking of taboos.[28] For the Hopi, ritual clowns are those who violate conventional expectations in a spirit of gay relativity.[29] In Latin America and the Caribbean carnival remains a living, vibrant tradition, where a profoundly *mestizo* culture builds on indigenous and African traditional festivities to forge an immensely creative cultural phenomenon. What was remote and merely metaphoric for European modernism – magic, carnival, anthropophagy – was familiar and quasi-literal for Latin Americans. It was partly his contact with such festivals, and with Haitian Vodun, that led the Cuban writer Alejo Carpentier to formulate the contrast of the *real maravilloso americano* and the quotidian magic of Latin American life with Europe's labored attempts to resuscitate the marvelous.[30] It would be wrong, furthermore, to see such carnivals as archaic; they are dynamically evolving phenomena, incorporating even the contemporary mass media. Indeed, more and more North American and European cities are developing mini-carnivals linked to the presence of Latin American, Caribbean, and African immigrant communities.

As theorized by Bakhtin, carnival embraces an anticlassical esthetic that rejects formal harmony and unity in favor of the asymmetrical, the heterogenous, the oxymoronic, the miscegenated. Carnival's "grotesque realism" turns conventional esthetics on its head in order to locate a new kind of popular, convulsive, rebellious beauty, one that dares to reveal the grotesquerie of the powerful and the latent beauty of the "vulgar." In the carnival esthetic, everything is pregnant with its opposite, within an alternative logic of permanent contradiction and non-exclusive opposites that transgresses the monologic true-or-false thinking typical of a certain kind of positivist rationalism.

Carnival favors an esthetic of mistakes, what Rabelais called a *gramatica jocosa* ("laughing grammar") in which artistic language is liberated from the stifling norms of correctness and decorum. Against the static, classic, finished beauty of antique sculpture, carnival counterposes the mutable, transgressive "grotesque body," rejecting what might be called the "fascism of beauty": the construction of an ideal type or language of beauty in relation to which other types are seen as inferior "dialectal" variations. The carnival esthetic exalts even "base" products of the body, all that has been banned from respectable representation because official decorum remains chained to a Manichean notion of the body's fundamental uncleanliness. Carnivalesque art is thus "anticanonical"; it deconstructs not only the canon, but also the generating matrix that creates canons and grammaticality. And if carnival is antigrammaticality, the dominant model of cinema, with its neat sequencing of beginning, middle, and end, would seem to constitute grammaticality. Waxing speculative, we might see the problem-solving mode of the classic narrative, in which highly motivated characters work toward clear and realizable goals, as instantiating an anticarnivalesque, individualist, and competitive *Weltenschauung*. Dominant cinema esthetics relay time as a linear succession of events related through cause and effect, rather than conveying an associative time linked to rituals and festivals. In an ethos where "time is money," dominant cinema commercializes time in carefully measured sequences. And the blockbuster "entertainment" esthetic, in this same perspective, can be seen as "productivist" in that every moment has to count, produce its specific quantum of effect and spectacle.

The concept of "laughing grammar" reminds one of how Black musicians have historically turned "lowly" materials (washboards, tubs, oil drums) into vibrant musicality, or how jazz artists have stretched the "normal" capacities of European instruments by playing the trumpet "higher" than it was supposed to go, by "hitting two keys, mis-hitting keys (like Monk did), flubbing notes to fight the equipment."[31] In such cases, the violation of esthetic etiquette and decorum goes hand in hand with an implicit critique of conventional social and political hierarchies. Arthur Jaffa speaks of the cinematic possibilities of "Black visual intonation," whereby "irregular, nontempered (nonmetronomic) camera rates and frame replication ... prompt filmic movement to function in a manner that approximates black vocal intonation," forging the filmic equivalent of the tendency in Black music to "treat notes as indeterminate, inherently unstable sonic frequencies rather than ... fixed phenomena."[32] What would be the equivalent in film, one wonders, of the role of repetition and variation typical of African-based musics? What would be the cinematic correlative of melisma? Of a blue note? Of a suspended beat? Of call-and-response antiphony? Of a polyrhythmic style where the organizing pulse is precisely the beat which is not heard but which the audience feels?

The possibilities of an "aesthetic of mistakes" are suggestively evoked in William Greaves' *SymbioPsychoTaxiPlasm – Take One* (1967). In this reflexive film, the filmmaker-in-the-film becomes the catalyst whose very refusal to direct instigates a revolt (devoutly desired by the director) on the part of actors and crew. During the filming of "Over the Cliff" in Central Park – consisting of endless reshooting of the same scene of marital breakup – as a decoy, the director provokes the crew and cast to film themselves arguing about the director's manipulative refusal to direct. With Miles Davis' *In a Silent Way* on the soundtrack, the film is built, like jazz itself, on signifying "mistakes": the film runs out, the camera jams, the actors become restless and irritable. The film analogizes jazz's relation to the European mainstream by performing a filmic critique of dominant cinema conventions and subtly evoking, in a *tour de force* of improvisation, multiple resistances and insurgent energies against diverse authoritarianisms and oppressions.

Although the carnivalesque principle at its most radical goes far beyond merely inverting existing power relations, we need not scoff at "mere" inversion. Oppressed people might have difficulty in imagining the precise contours of an alternative society, James Scott argues, but they have no trouble at all imagining a reversal of the existing distribution of status and rewards within a "counter-factual social order."[33] The millennial theme of a world upside down, where the last shall be first and the first last, for Scott, "can be found in nearly every major cultural tradition in which inequities of power, wealth, and status have been pronounced."[34] Thus the Saturnalia of ancient Rome, carnival in the Caribbean, and the Feast of Krishna in India all translate popular insurgency through images of millennarian reversals. These reversals pop up in surprising places, for example in *Rufus Jones for President* (1933), a short film in which a six-year-old Sammy Davis Jr becomes President of the US. While framed as a pure fantasy, the film provides an outlet for dreams of Black power. It recalls not only Black-led and African-influenced entertainments such as "Negro Election Day," "Jubilee," and the various Black coronation and emancipation festivals but also the carnival topos of the *puer rex* (boy king).[35]

Historically, carnivals have been politically ambiguous affairs, sometimes constituting symbolic rebellions by the disenfranchised; at other times fostering the festive scapegoating of the weak by the strong (or by the slightly less weak). Carnivals, and carnivalesque artistic practices, are not *essentially* progressive or regressive; it depends on who is carnivalizing whom, in what historical situation, for what purposes, and in what manner. Actual carnivals form shifting configurations of symbolic practices, complex crisscrossings of ideological manipulation and utopian desire, their political valence changing with each context. Official power has at times used carnival to channel energies that might otherwise have fueled popular revolt, but just as often carnival has provoked elite anxiety and been the object of official repression. C.L. Barber documents this repressive process in Elizabethan England, Peter Stallybrass and Allon White in the England of later periods, while Mike Davis speaks in *City of Quartz* of the destruction of carnivalesque public spaces in Los Angeles, replaced by a "Skinnerian orchestration" which produces a "veritable commercial symphony of swarming, consuming monads moving from one cashpoint to another."[36] Brazilian historians have spoken of the repression of carnival in Brazil, where the hostility toward it has often been linked to anti-Black racism and an animus against Afro-Brazilian religious expression. Nelson Pereira dos Santos' *Tenda dos Milagres* (Tent of Miracles, 1977) addresses the link between racism and the repression of carnival in turn-of-the-century Bahia, while the Sankofa production *Territories* (1985) addresses the inability of the official British media to comprehend the yearly Caribbean carnivals held in Notting Hill, or to critique the police repression of such activities.

The appeal of the contemporary mass media, in our view, derives partly from their capacity to relay, in however compromised a manner, the distant cultural memory (or the vague future hope) of an egalitarian carnival-like *communitas*. Indeed, popular culture reverberates constantly with the textual echoes of carnival. Thus Eddie Grant's music video "Dance Party" draws on the carnival trope of "dancing in the streets," as Pepsi commercials also do, while Lionel Ritchie's "All Night Long" conveys the literal accents of Caribbean carnival in a music video whose music, lyrics, and visuals celebrate a choreographed takeover of public space, a multiracial utopia in which even policemen foresake authoritarianism to twirl their batons and breakdance.

Carnival has taken very diverse forms in the cinema. There are films that literally thematize carnival (*Orfeu Negro*, 1959), films that anarchize institutional hierarchies (*Born in Flames*, 1983), films that foreground the "lower bodily stratum" (Richard Pryor's "Concert" films), films that favor grotesque realism and antigrammaticality (the "esthetic of garbage" films from Brazil), films that celebrate social and racial inversions (Alea's *The Last Supper*, 1976). Brazilian cinema especially has always been deeply impregnated by the cultural values associated with carnival. The *chanchadas* or *filmes carnavalescos* (carnivalesque films), the musical comedies popular from the 1930s through the 1950s, were not only released at carnival time but were intended to promote the annual repertory of carnival songs. Their parodic strategies are premised on North American hegemony; they assume that the audience has already been inundated by North American cultural products. In political terms, as João Luiz Vieira points out, they are almost always ambivalent, mingling national pride with idealization of the foreign, internalized as "ideal ego." The *rapports de force* between idealization and critique vary from film to film. In some films, Brazilian cinema itself becomes the object of attack, scapegoat for the incapacity of an underdeveloped country to copy the American cinema's powerful technological efficiency. In others, parody becomes a means to subvert canonized codes.[37]

One reflexive-modernist *chanchada*, for Vieira, especially encapsulates these ambiguities. *Carnaval Atlantida* (1952) proposes a model of cinema based on sublime debauchery and carnivalesque irony. The subject of *Carnaval Atlantida* is filmmaking itself, and, more specifically, the inappropriateness of the Hollywood model for Brazil. The film follows a Euro-Brazilian film director, Cecilio B. de Milho (Cecil B. de Corn), who abandons his plan for an epic production of the story of Helen of Troy in the implicit recognition that the conditions of Brazilian cinema are not propitious for a film on such a grand scale. The genre's Hollywood-dictated standards, with ostentatious sets and the proverbial cast of thousands, are simply not feasible in a Third World country. (The Brazilian parodies of American films, as Vieira points out, tend to focus on superproductions such as *King Kong* and *Jaws*, providing a pretext for the directors to mock both the American films and the Brazilian inability to imitate their glossy and high-tech production values.) Against the overreaching de Milho, other characters argue for a more popular, less lofty adaptation, recommending that the director discard the proposed epic in favor of a carnival film. In one sequence, de Milho explains his conception of *Helen of Troy*, demonstrating both the Brazilian internalization of Hollywood standards and a possible alternative to them. His elitist, grandiose vision is contrasted with the point-of-view of two Afro-Brazilian studio janitors and aspiring scriptwriters (Colé and Grande Otelo), through whose eyes we move from de Milho's "scene" to the scene as they imagine it: the Black singer Blecaute (Blackout) appears dressed in Greek costume singing "Dona Cegonha," a carnival samba written for that year's celebration, accompanied by Grande Otelo tripping over his toga. European themes, then, had to be parodically relocated within the context of Brazilian carnival. "*Helen of Troy* won't work," de Milho is told, "the people want to dance and move." The Hollywood/Greek model is dropped in favor of Afro-Brazilianized popular culture.

The 1970s and 1980s witnessed a "recarnivalization" of Brazilian cinema, not only as a key trope orienting the filmmakers' conception of their own production, but also as a means of renewing contact with the popular audience. The stories of Diegues' *Xica da Silva* (1976) and Walter Lima Jr's *Chico Rei* (1982), for example, were first presented as samba-school pageants for Rio's carnival. Indeed, Diegues conceived both *Xica da Silva* and *Quilombo* (1984) as *samba-enredos* (samba-narratives), that is, as formally analogous to the collections of songs, dances, costumes, and lyrics which form part of the annual samba-school pageants. Fernando Cony Campos' *Ladrões de Cinema* (Cinema Thieves, 1977) stages the same analogy by having his marginalized *favelado* protagonists (dressed up, significantly, as "Indians") steal filmmaking equipment from American tourists visiting Rio's carnival. The *favelados* conceive the film they plan to make – concerning an abortive Brazilian revolt against Portuguese colonialism – as a kind of samba school narration.

Carnival, then, is not only a living social practice but also a general, perennial fund of popular forms and festive rituals; it promotes participatory spectacle, a "pageant without footlights" erasing the boundaries between spectator and performer. As a kind of dress-rehearsal for utopia, carnival suspends hierarchical distinctions, barriers, norms, and prohibitions, installing instead a qualitatively different kind of communication based on "free and familiar contact." Carnival sees social and political life as a perpetual "crowning and uncrowning" and the permanence of change as a source of hope. What is suspended in carnival is first of all "hierarchical structure and ... everything resulting from socio-hierarchical inequality or any other form of inequality among people."[38]

MODERNIST ANTHROPOPHAGY

Inverting the colonialist trope of the cannibal, recent critical discourse has been rich in cannibalistic imagery turned toward Europe itself. In *Columbus and Other Cannibals* Jack Forbes, for example, defines imperialism and exploitation as forms of cannibalism; bell hooks speaks of the consumption of "ethnic" fashions as "eating the other"; and Dean MacCannell detects cannibalistic undertones in the everyday idiom of corporate executives: "cut-throat competition," "picking brains," corporate "headhunting."[39] The First World cinema of recent decades, meanwhile, has also been rife with cannibals, from New Wave art films like Godard's *Weekend* (1967) and Pasolini's *Porcile* (1968), to critical ethnographic films such as *Cannibal Tours* (1988), to more pop productions which include *Eating Raoul* (1982), *Parents* (1988), *Silence of the Lambs* (1991), *Alive!* (1991), *Delicatessen* (1992) and *The Resurrected* (1993) – reflecting, perhaps, a loss of moral self-confidence on the part of the West.[40] The exiled Chilean filmmaker Raul Ruiz also associates cannibalism with the West in *Le Territoire* (The Territory, 1981). Mircea Eliade's epigraph on the film describes cannibalism as an impressive "invention of the human spirit," a matter "as complex, as harmonious and as worthy of respect as a Gothic cathedral." In Ruiz's parable, a group of Americans end up in a small medieval town in southern France, and later lose their way in the snow and are gradually converted to cannibalism. Western society, Ruiz suggests, is not as far from "savagery" as it likes to think.

What is less well known is that the Brazilian modernists of the 1920s made the trope of cannibalism the basis of an insurgent esthetic, calling for a creative synthesis of European avant-gardism and Brazilian "cannibalism," and invoking an "anthropophagic" devouring of the techniques and information of the superdeveloped countries the better to struggle against domination. Just as the aboriginal Tupinamba Indians devoured their enemies to appropriate their force, the modernists argued, Brazilian artists and intellectuals should digest imported cultural products and exploit them as raw material for a new synthesis, thus turning the imposed culture back, transformed, against the colonizer. The modernists also called for the "de-Vespucciazation" of the Americas (the reference is to Amerigo Vespucci) and the "de-Cabralization" of Brazil (referring to Pedro Cabral, Brazil's Portuguese "discoverer"). The *Revista de Antropofagia* (Cannibalist Review) laments that Brazilians continue to be "slaves" to a "rotting European culture" and to a "colonial mentality."[41] At the same time, the notion of "anthropophagy" assumes the inevitability of cultural interchange between "center" and "periphery," and the consequent impossibility of any nostalgic return to an originary purity. Since there can be no unproblematic recovery of national origins undefiled by alien influences, the artist in the dominated culture should not ignore the foreign presence but must swallow it, carnivalize it, recycle it for national ends, always from a position of cultural self-confidence. The "cannibalist" and "carnivalist" metaphors have in common the appeal to "oral" rituals

307

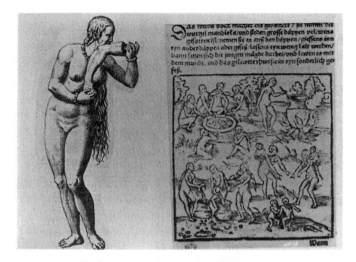

Plates 48 and 49
Anthropophagic
critique and culinary
cinema:
*How Tasty Was My
Frenchman* and
King Solomon's Mines
(1985)

of resistance, their evocation of a transcendence of self through the physical or spiritual commingling of self and other, and their call for the "cordial mastication" and critical recycling of foreign culture.

In two manifestos – "Manifesto of Brazilwood Poetry" (1924) and "Anthropophagic Manifesto" (1928) – Brazilian poet/dramatist Oswald de Andrade pointed the way to an artistic practice at once nationalist, modern, multicultural, and pleasurable. In the earlier text, de Andrade called for an "export-quality" poetry that would not borrow imported European models but would find its roots in everyday life and popular culture. Where colonialist discourse had posited the Carib as a ferocious cannibal, as a diacritical index of Europe's moral superiority,

Oswald called for a revolution infinitely "greater than the French revolution": the "Carib revolution," without which "Europe wouldn't even have its meager declaration of the rights of man."[42] Although the cannibalist metaphor was also circulated among European avant-gardists, cannibalism in Europe, as Augusto de Campos points out, never constituted a cultural movement, never defined an ideology, and never enjoyed the profound resonances within the culture that it did in Brazil. The nihilism of Dada had little to do with what de Campos calls the "generous ideological utopia" of Brazilian anthropophagy.[43] Only in Brazil did anthropophagy become a key trope in a longstanding cultural movement, ranging from the first "Cannibalistic Review" in the 1920s, with its various "dentitions," through Oswald de Andrade's speculations in the 1950s on anthropophagy as the philosophy of the technicized primitive, to the pop-recyclings of the metaphor in the Tropicalist movement of the late 1960s.

As exploited by the Brazilian modernists, the cannibalist metaphor had a negative and a positive pole. The negative pole deployed cannibalism to reveal the exploitative Social Darwinism of class society. But the positive pole was ultimately more suggestive: radicalizing the Enlightenment valorization of indigenous Amerindian freedom, it highlighted aboriginal matriarchy and communalism as a utopian model. "The Indian," de Andrade wrote, "had no police, no repression, no nervous disorders, no shame at being nude, no class struggle, no slavery."[44] Synthesizing insights from Montaigne, Nietzsche, Marx, and Freud, along with what he knew of Native Brazilian societies, he portrayed indigenous culture as offering a more adequate social model than the European one, a model based on the full enjoyment of leisure. Playing on the Portuguese word *negocio* – "business," but literally "neg-ocio," or the negation of leisure – de Andrade offered a proto-Marcusean encomium to *sacer-docio* or "sacred leisure."[45] For the Indians, having once been enslaved by Europeans, work in the European sense connoted misery and subordination, and in any case productivism was for them not the alpha and omega of existence. Here again we find a literalization of the metaphors of the European avant-garde. The Dadaists too had called for "progressive unemployment" and Breton's Surrealist "rules" had forbidden regular work. Brazilian artist-intellectuals, however, had the advantage of being able to point to existing indigenous societies quite free both from work, in the occidental sense of salaried labor, and from coercive power. And these societies lived not in poverty but in material abundance.[46] The two poles of the cannibalist metaphor were of course complementary in that the cannibalism-as-critique motif contemplates the melancholy distance separating contemporary society from the imagined ideal communitas of the Amerindian. "At the heart of every utopia," de Andrade wrote, "there is not only a dream but also a protest."[47]

This revalorization of a ludic life must be seen against the backdrop of modernity's productivist and pleasure-denying work ethic and its historical aversion to "subsistence cultures" – a term that itself translates hostility by evoking a desperate struggle for a meager living rather than a proud self-sufficiency within abundance.[48] It is as if any relatively pleasurable life based on

309

communally held land could provoke irritation on the part of "progressive," hardworking puritans. (The film *Savagery and the American Indian* stages precisely this puritanical hostility toward what the puritans saw as the "unserious," "unproductive" ways of Native Americans.) For some thinkers, the capital offense of non-European tribal peoples was not that they lived differently but that they lived enjoyably.[49] Renata Salecl, in an argument that recalls George Bernard Shaw's definition of puritanism as "that terrible fear that someone, somewhere is having a good time," suggests that this ludophobia arises when an inhibition of one's own pleasure assumes the symptomatic form of attacks on the pleasures of others.[50]

The Brazilian anthropophagy movement mingled homages to indigenous culture with esthetic modernism. Indeed, it not only called itself modernism (*modernismo*) but saw itself as allied to and conceptually parallel to European avant-garde movements like Futurism, Dada, and Surrealism. Much later, the movement came to inflect Brazilian cinema through the cultural movement called Tropicalism, which emerged in Brazil in the late 1960s. Like Brazilian modernism (and unlike European modernism), Tropicalism fused political nationalism with esthetic internationalism. As recycled for the 1960s, "anthropophagy" implied a transcendence of Cinema Novo's Manichean opposition between "authentic Brazilian cinema" and "Hollywood alienation." As expressed in the theater, music, and cinema, Tropicalism aggressively juxtaposed the folkloric and the industrial, the native and the foreign. Its favored technique was an aggressive collage of discourses, an anthropophagic devouring of varied cultural stimuli in all their heterogeneity. Tropicalist filmmakers framed a resistant strategy premised on a low-cost "esthetic of garbage." Where the earlier metaphor of an "esthetics of hunger" had evoked famished victims redeeming themselves through violence, the garbage metaphor proposed an aggressive sense of marginality, of surviving within scarcity, of being condemned to recycle the materials of dominant culture. A garbage style was seen as appropriate to a Third World country picking through the leavings of an international system dominated by First World capitalism.

In this spirit, Rogerio Sganzerla's *Bandido da Luz Vermelha* (Red Light Bandit, 1968) orchestrates an improbable collage of preexisting materials and clichés into an ironic conflation of genres. In his story of the rise and fall of a famous outlaw mythologized by the mass media, Sganzerla shows an anthropophagic openness to intertextual influences, including those of Hollywood and the mass media. Rejecting the purism of Cinema Novo, he turns Hollywood against Hollywood through tactics of discursive collage in a style that would later be called "postmodern." Calling the film a "film-summa, a western, a musical documentary, detective story, chanchada, and science fiction," Sganzerla turns it into a compilation of pastiches, a kind of cinematic writing in quotation marks. *Red Light Bandit* posits a homology, as Ismail Xavier points out, between a red-light district in a Third World country as a "realm of garbage" and the text itself as a collection of film and mass-media refuse. The garbage principle works in the film both "horizontally," through the contiguity of heterogenous and mutually relativizing discourses, and "vertically," through the superimposition, at the same syntagmatic points, of multiple elements, for example through the overlaying of voice-over narration with richly incompatible different types of music playing simultaneously. Thus *Red Light Bandit* modifies and transforms Cinema Novo's favorite esthetic procedure – the erudite elaboration of popular culture – promiscuously mingling the languages of city and country, metropole and periphery, condensing modes of discourse usually thought to be separate and antithetical.

If cannibalism is metaphoric in *Red Light Bandit*, it is quite literal in another Tropicalist-inflected film, *Macunaíma*, which, as we have seen, turns the theme into a springboard for a critique of repressive military rule and of the predatory capitalist model of the shortlived Brazilian "economic miracle." *Macunaíma* synthesizes intellectual reflection and popular appeal, and thus answers the question of pleasure not always addressed by the more austere or militant Third Worldist films. It manages this synthesis by fusing the erudite anthropophagy of the novel on which it is based with a comic-episodic narration reminiscent of Buster Keaton and the Marx Brothers. The film assured its own commercial success by renewing contact with that most popular Brazilian film genre, the *chanchada*, by featuring key *chanchada* stars like Grande Otelo and Zeze Macedo along with songs popular from the *chanchada* period. Of the two poles of the cannibalist metaphor, *Macunaíma* clearly emphasizes the negative pole, exploiting the anthropophagic motif in order to expose Brazil's predatory class structure. As Joaquim Pedro de Andrade puts it in his preface to the film:

> Cannibalism is an exemplary mode of consumerism adopted by underdeveloped peoples ... The traditionally dominant, conservative classes continue their control of the power structure – and we rediscover cannibalism ... The present work relationships, as well as the relationships between people, are still basically cannibalistic. Those who can, "eat" others through their consumption of products, or even more directly in sexual relationships. Cannibalism has merely institutionalized and cleverly disguised itself.[51]

Macunaíma's tangential relationship with Tropicalism is evident not only in its anthropophagic theme but also in its camp and gaudy colors, its emphasis on the lack of national character (the subtitle of the novel is "The Hero without any Character"), and its mélange of high-art tradition and mass-mediated culture. The film extends the allegorical social critiques of Cinema Novo, but performs them with an oblique humor and cunning that caught even the censors off guard.

Artur Omar's *Triste Tropico* (1974) also touches on the issue of anthropophagy. Best defined as a fictive anthropological documentary, the film's title, transparently alluding to Lévi-Strauss' ethnographic memoir about Brazil, triggers an evocative chain of cultural associations. While Lévi-Strauss went from Europe to Brazil only to discover the ethnocentric prejudices of Europe, the protagonist of

Triste Tropico goes to Europe – and here his trajectory parallels that of innumerable Brazilian intellectuals – only to discover Brazil. Thus the film inserts itself into the ongoing discussion of Brazil's problematic cultural relationship to Europe, a discussion undergoing frequent changes of etiquette: "Indianism," "nationalism," "modernism," "Tropicalism." *Triste Tropico* is not a Tropicalist film, however; it is a distanced reflection on the whole notion of the "Tropics" as Europe's other, as something exotic.

Triste Tropico constantly alters its relation to the spectator. The opening shots – traffic in São Paulo, old family album photographs – lead us to expect a fairly conventional documentary. The off-screen narrator, speaking in the stilted delivery to which canonical documentaries have accustomed us, tells us about a certain Arthur Alvaro de Noronha, known as Dr Arthur, who returned from studies in Paris to practice medicine in Brazil. Home-movie footage shows a man with his family; we infer that the man is Dr Arthur. In Paris, we are told, the doctor became friendly with André Breton, Paul Eluard, and Max Ernst. This is our first clue that a truly surreal biography awaits us. As the film continues, two things happen. First, the narration becomes progressively more improbable and hallucinatory. The doctor becomes involved with Indians, compiles an almanac of herbal panaceas, becomes an indigenous Messiah, and finally degenerates into sodomy (an exclamatory intertitle underlines the horror!) and cannibalism, thus recapitulating the trajectory of a certain body of colonialist literature. Second, the descent of the story into this parodic Brazilian *Heart of Darkness* coincides with our own descent into a tangled jungle of cinematic confusion. The images gradually detach themselves from the narration, becoming less and less illustrative and more and more disjunctively chaotic. We begin to suspect that we have been the dupes of an immense joke, as if Borges had slyly rewritten Conrad, and that the illustrious Dr Arthur is merely the figment of the imagination of the director, whose name, we may remember, is also Arthur.

The central procedure of *Triste Tropico* is to superimpose an impeccably linear (albeit absurd) narration on extremely discontinuous sounds and images. While the off-screen narration is coherent (within the limits of its implausibility), all the other tracks – image, music, noise, titles – form a serial chaos, an organized delirium of wildly heterogenous materials: amateur movies, European travel footage, shots of Rio's carnival, staged scenes, archival material, clips from other films, engravings, book covers, almanac illustrations. The music constitutes an anthology of Brazilian, American, Argentinian, and Cuban materials, inserted briefly and discontinuously, as if someone were rapidly turning a radio dial. Within this audio-visual bricolage we encounter certain structured oppositions: some specifically cinematic (black/white versus color; old footage versus new) and some broadly cultural (coast and interior; "raw" Brazil and "cooked" Europe; Apollonian order and Dionysian frenzy; *la pensée sauvage* and *la pensée civilisée*), but presented in such a way as to offer what would now be called a postmodern take on structuralism.

Plate 50 Border Brujo

SYNCRETISM AS ARTISTIC STRATEGY

Brazilian "anthropophagy," in melding European avant-gardism with indigenous cultural motifs, can be seen as just one of many ways in which syncretism has served as a perennial resource for the arts. While the Brazilian modernists spoke of the "technical Indian" who absorbs European technique into indigenous culture, Native (North) American artists perform their own kind of anthropophagy. Everything brought in from Europe, says Jimmie Durham,

> was transformed with great energy ... We took glass beads, horses, wool blankets, wheat flour for fry bread ... and immediately made them identifiably "Indian" things. We are able to do that because of our cultural integrity and because our societies are dynamic and able to take in new ideas.[52]

This anthropophagic approach might take as its own motto Salman Rushdie's words about his *Satanic Verses* as celebrating "hybridity, impurity, intermingling, the transformation that comes of new and unexpected combinations of human

313

beings, ideas, politics, movies, songs [and which] rejoices in mongrelization and fears the absolutism of the Pure."[53] The culinary metaphors typical of multicultural discourse often imply a fondness for this kind of mélange. Significantly, Indian filmmakers speak of blending the *massalas* – literally, Hindi for "spices," but metaphorically, "creating something new out of old ingredients" – as a key to their recipe for making films.[54] Indeed, the word *massala* forms part of the titles of two Indian diasporic films, one Indo-Canadian (*Massala*, 1991) and the other Indo-American (*Mississipi Massala*, 1991). In the former film, the god Krishna, portrayed as a gross hedonist, appears to a nostalgic Indian grandmother thanks to an interactive VCR. While mocking the official multiculturalism of Canada, the filmic style itself serves up a kind of *massala*, where the language of the Hindu "mythological" mingles with the language of MTV and the mass media. In the diasporic-British film *Pot Boiler* (1993), meanwhile, the tensions of a marriage between an Indian woman and a Caribbean man are both expressed and resolved through cuisine, as foods and spices interpenetrate in the hybrid space of a wedding party, while the superimposed names of spices "float" in the air of the kitchen.

Music especially has been syncretic. The mutually enriching collaborations between the diverse currents of Afro-diasporic music – yielding such hybrids as "samba-reggae," "samba-rap," "jazz-tango," "rap-reggae" and "roforenge" (a blend of rock, forro, and merengue) in the Americas – offer examples of "lateral syncretism," or syncretism on a "sideways" basis of rough equality. Diasporic musical cultures mingle with one another, while simultaneously also playing off the dominant media-disseminated tradition of First World, especially American, popular music, itself energized by Afro-diasporic traditions. An endlessly creative multidirectional flow of musical ideas thus moves back and forth around the "Black Atlantic" (Gilroy's phrase); for example, between cool jazz and samba in bossa nova, between soul music and ska in reggae. Afro-diasporic music displays an anthropophagic capacity to absorb influences, including Western influences, while still being driven by a culturally African bass note. In the Americas, musicians such as Stevie Wonder, Taj Mahal, Ruben Blades, Gilberto Gil, and Caetano Veloso not only practice syncretic forms of music but also thematize syncretism within their lyrics.[55] The new fluidities of cultural exchange enabled by cable and satellite TV, meanwhile, generate such phenomena as "Hindi rap." In the Middle East and North Africa, musicians and groups like Ziad Al-Rahabani and Marcel Khalife (Lebanon), Sabreen (West Bank, Palestine), Natural Alternative, Boustan, and Yair Dalal (Israel), and Cheb Khaled (Algeria) practice innovative combinations of diverse Arabic musical forms along with jazz, rock, samba, and reggae. Cheb Khaled's "Khaled," for example, features a mélange of folk, rai, funk, reggae, and flamenco, while his "Didi" video mixes images of Sufi dancing, Moorish art, and hip hop dancing.

Such richly syncretic musical forms evoke the question: what would this kind of syncretism mean in the cinema? Indian cinema, for example, can be seen as syncretic in its cinematic language. The popular Hindi films of the 1950s, as Ravi

Vasudevan points out, mingled plots drawn both from Hindu mythology and from Hollywood, with esthetic styles ranging from a relatively realist mode to anti-illusionistic tableaux effects rooted in folk painting, and were condemned by critics for what in fact was their esthetic strength – their mixing of cultural and cinematic modes.[56] Countries like India offer countless examples of a multi-faceted and constantly changing artistic syncretism. Salman Rushdie's homage to syncretism thus builds on a long tradition within Indian thought and history. (It is no accident that the syncretic protagonist of *Satanic Verses*, Gibreel Farishta, is a representative of what Sumita Chakravarty calls that "supremely hybrid form, the commercial Hindi film.")[57] The sixteenth-century Moghul Akhbar the Great tried to install a new religion – *din-ai-ilahi* (religion of God) – which would borrow the best elements from Hinduism and Islam. The vertical strata of the columns of his "Fatehpur Sikkri" palace near Agra, paying homage to diverse religious and linguistic cultures, demonstrate a kind of programmatic multi-culturalism *avant la lettre*. Indian cinema has also practiced an esthetic politics of the impure. Here we see a striking discontinuity between the esthetic and the political realms. Two films produced in the wake of the partition of India and Pakistan, *Anarkaii* (1953) and *Mughal-e-Azam* (The Grand Moghul, 1960), which glorify Moghul culture specifically and Indo-Islamic culture generally, were adored by the same Hindu audience that was attacking Muslims in the streets.[58] Many Muslim actors and actresses – Dilip Kumar, Meena Kumari, Nargis – continued to be wildly popular even at the height of Hindu–Muslim tensions.

Indian cinema is rich in narrative homages to syncretism and to an inter-communal tolerance that is now very much endangered. The character Biswamb-har Roy, in Satyajit Ray's *Jalsaghar* (The Music Hall, 1958), is as much Muslim as Hindu, to the point that it is difficult to say where the one ends and the other begins. Shayam Benegal's *Junoon* (1978), similarly, stresses the tolerance reigning between different religious communities within India at the time of the 1857 "sepoy Mutiny." As the narrative moves from a Christian to a Hindu to a Muslim family, religious differences and affinities are woven into the fabric of everyday life. In the Hindu home, Hindi mantras are recited, while in the Muslim home the family members answer the call of the muezzin. We are struck, as Hema Ramachandran points out, by the ways that the film shows Muslim life, with its poetry and music and *gawali* performances, as "irrevocably intertwined with the larger history of the [Indian] nation."[59] And here we encounter the limits of syncretism, for all this cultural intertwining has not managed to prevent tension and even violence between the Muslim and Hindu communities. Cultural and political borders are not necessarily congruent.

As a meld of European Jewish, Sephardi-Mizrahi and Palestinian cultures, Israel/Palestine too is rich in conflictual syncretisms. Named after a popular oriental-Sephardic pastry, the "Bourekas" genre in Israeli cinema is a product of conflicts between European and Mizrahi (Oriental) Jews featured within the framework of melodrama or comedy. The mainstream critics (largely Ashkenazi-European) who denounced the films as "vulgar," "cheap," "Levantine," and even "anti-cinema" were blind to the playful, carnivalesque and even self-reflexive aspects of Bourekas films such as *Rak Hayom* (Today Only, 1976), *Hamesh Meot Elef Shahor* (Half a Million Black, 1977), *Gonev mi Ganav Patur* (He Who Steals from a Thief Is Not Guilty, 1977) and *Badranit baHatzot* (Midnight Entertainer, 1978). The link between the Bourekas and Egyptian, Lebanese, Indian, Turkish, and Iranian cinema derives from Jewish displacement from these same film-producing countries; filmmaker George Ovadia, for instance, had worked in the Iraqi and Iranian film industries. This link is kept alive by the frequent screenings of such films in movie theaters and on Jordanian, Lebanese, Egyptian, and Israeli TV (particularly the Friday night screenings of Egyptian films, popular with the Bourekas audience), as well as through video rentals and cable television. Thus in a country set in the Middle East, but whose hegemonic imaginary inclines toward the West, the Bourekas genre has provided the meeting site for diverse oriental-Arab Jewish cultures, from India to Morocco. Just as the popular music of Sephardi singers such as Zohar Argov, Ofra Haza, and Zehava Ben melds various Middle Eastern music traditions, the Bourekas cinema syncretizes a wide range of Middle Eastern cinematic cultures, testifying to an emergent identity forged in the face of imposed westernization.

Syncretism has been an absolutely crucial thematic and esthetic resource in Caribbean and Latin American cinema. The theme predates the cinema, of course, and the region is rich in neologistic evocations of cultural mixture: *mestizaje, diversalité, creolité, Antillanité, raza cosmica*. The *mestizo* pan-American art of Mexican painters Rivera, Siqueiros, and Orozco could creatively juxtapose, as occurred in Rivera's Detroit murals, the metallic imagery of Fordist industry, and the stony grandeur of Aztec or Mayan sculpture. Mexican filmmakers like Emilio Fernandez (El Indio), working with Gabriel Figueroa, carried on this tradition through a syncretistic mélange of Hollywood esthetics and Mexican muralism. Paul Leduc picks up the same tradition at a later point, first in his *Frida*, where he creates a cinematic analog to the style of Frida Kahlo's paintings, and later in his *Barroco* (1988), a free adaptation of Alejo Carpentier's *Concierto Barroco* (1974), where the themes of *mestizaje*, artistic syncretism, and colonialism all come into play. Like Carpentier's novel, Leduc's film has us make the same journey as Columbus and the conquistadors, but in reverse, with Mexico as the starting point. The novel's two central characters, the Mexican *mestizo* Amo and the Afro-Caribbean Filomenio, suggest the racially synthetic character of Latin American culture from the outset. With scenes set in Mexico, Cuba, Spain, and Italy, the film offers us a tour of the syncretic cultures of the Americas (indigenous fertility rituals, Afro carnivals, Christian Holy Week processions) along with a compendium of musical styles (mariachi, salsa, bolero, flamenco, Yoruba ceremonial music, Catholic liturgical chants), in a baroque concert of musical tensions and affinities. Thus *Barroco* roots its images and sounds in a culture at once indigenous, African, Moorish-Spanish, Sephardi-Jewish, and European Christian.

Mexico is not alone in such syncretic productions. Venezuelan director Diego

Risguez's *Orinoko, Nuevo Mundo* (Orinoco, New World, 1986) combines the visions and fantasies of European visitors (Spanish conquistadors, English pirates) to the Amazon, juxtaposed with a quasi-ethnographic account of the Yanomami tribes of the Orinoco River. The same director's *Amerika, Terra Incognita* (1988) stages the processes of *mestizaje* as taking place within Europe, between an imprisoned native Prince and a Spanish damsel. *Ava and Gabriel* (1990), by the Caribbean filmmaker Felix de Rooy, also practices syncretism in the arts. The story revolves around a Black painter in Dutch-dominated Curaçào in 1948 who wants to paint a Black Madonna. Syncretism in *Ava and Gabriel* is not only painterly but also linguistic, in that the dialog is spoken in a number of languages (Dutch, English, French, and Papiamento, the last of which itself mixes Dutch, Spanish, and African languages). The video *Border Brujo* (The Shaman, 1990), for its part, features "border artist" Guillermo Gomez-Peña as the shape-shifting incarnation of a multicultural critique of US hegemony. Finally, Raul Ruiz, although he does not thematize syncretism in such literal terms, can be seen as a syncretic diasporic artist, in that he takes all of the world's myths and forms and fictions as his province in a dazzling *combinatoire* with multicultural overtones but without a multicultural agenda. In films like *Three Crowns of the Sailor* (1982), Ruiz practices an esthetic of digression, multiplying stories but always returning to a central theme or situation. Far from an austere esthetic of hunger, Ruiz practices a gluttonous absorption and proliferation of styles. As Zuzana Pick points out, *Three Crowns of the Sailor* mingles European sailor stories with mariner legends of the southern Chilean coast (for example, that of the giant sea monster Caleuche) in a film whose ship drops anchor, as it were, in Tampico, Dakar, Singapore, and Tangiers.[60] Within Ruiz's narratological syncretism, the entire world becomes a story or image bank on which to draw.

Brazilian cinema has been especially rich in filmic syncretism, deploying it both as theme and as formal strategy. The opening sequence of *Macunaíma*, for example, shows a family whose names are indigenous, whose epidermic traits are African and European and *mestizo*, whose clothes are Portuguese and African, whose hut is indigenous and backwoods, and whose manner of giving birth is indigenous. The plot of another Brazilian film *Pagador de Promessas* (The Given Word, 1962) revolves around the conflicting values of Catholicism and Candomblé, evoked through the manipulation of cultural symbols, setting in motion a cultural battle, for example, between *berimbau* (an African instrument consisting of a long bow, gourd and string) and church bell, thus synecdochically encapsulating a larger religious and political struggle. *Tent of Miracles* counterposes opera and samba to metaphorize the larger conflict between Bahia's White elite and its subjugated *mestizos*, between ruling-class science and Afro-inflected popular culture. Brazilian cinema often does more than merely reflect a preexisting syncretism; it actively syncretizes, counterpointing cultural forces in non-literal ways. Rocha's *Land in Anguish* uses Candomblé to evoke the *transe* of the title, while inverting its conventional associations to suggest that the truly superstitious, those "in trance," are not the impoverished Black practitioners of

317

Afro-religions but rather the mystical powermongers of the White political elite. Syncretic textual strategies, in sum, are not merely additive; rather they counterpoint cultural elements in a space of clash and interchange.

THE POETICS OF DISEMBODIMENT

A number of recent diasporic film/video works treat issues of postcolonial identity within a post-Third Worldist esthetic and ideology. The Sankofa production *Passion for Remembrance* (1986) thematizes post-Third Worldist discourses and fractured diasporic identity, in this case Black British identity, by staging a "polylog" between the 1960s Black radical as the (somewhat puritanical) voice of nationalist militancy, and the "new," more playful voices of gays and lesbians, all within a derealized reflexive esthetic. Films such as that of the Algerian-French novelist Assia Djebar's *Nouba Nisa al Djebel Shnua* (The Nouba of the Women of Mount Chenoua, 1978), Mona Hatoum's *Measures of Distance* (1988), and Elia Suleiman's *Homage by Assassination* (1990) break away from earlier macro-narratives of national liberation, reinvisioning the "nation" as a heteroglossic multiplicity of trajectories. While anticolonialist, these experimental films call attention to the diversity of experiences within and across nations. Colonialism, by simultaneously aggregating communities fissured by glaring cultural differences and separating communities marked by equally glaring commonalities, turned many Third World nation-states into artificial and contradictory entities. Films produced in the First World, in particular, raise questions about dislocated identities in a situation marked by the mobility of goods, ideas, and peoples in a "multinationalized" global economy.

While most Third Worldist films assumed the fundamental coherence of national identity, with the expulsion of the colonial intruder fully completing the process of national becoming, diasporic films call attention to the fault lines of gender, class, ethnicity, religion, partition, migration, and exile. Many of the films explore the identitary complexities of exile – from one's own geography, from one's own history, from one's own body – within innovative narrative strategies. Fragmented cinematic forms come to homologize cultural disembodiment. Caren Kaplan's observations about a reconceived "minor" literature as deromanticizing solitude and rewriting "the connections between different parts of the self in order to make a world of possibilities out of the experience of displacement,"[61] are exquisitely appropriate to two autobiographical films by Palestinians in exile: Elia Suleiman's *Homage by Assassination* and Mona Hatoum's *Measures of Distance*. *Homage by Assassination* chronicles Suleiman's claustrophobic reality in New York during the Persian Gulf war, foregrounding multiple failures of communication: a radio announcer's aborted efforts to reach the filmmaker by phone; the filmmaker's failed attempts to talk to his family in Nazareth (in Israel/Palestine); his impotent look at old family photographs; despairing answering-machine jokes about the Palestinian situation. The glorious dream of nationhood and return is here reframed as a Palestinian flag on a TV monitor, the land as a map on a wall, and the return (*Aawda*) as the "return" key on a computer keyboard. At one point Suleiman receives a fax from a friend, who narrates her family history as an Arab Jew, her feelings during the bombing of Iraq and the Scud attacks on Israel, and the story of her displacement from Iraq, through Israel/Palestine, and then on to the US.[62] The communications media become the imperfect means by which dislocated people retain their national imaginary, while also struggling for a place in new countries (the US, Britain) whose foreign policies have concretely impacted on their lives. *Homage by Assassination* invokes the diverse spatialities and temporalities marking the exile experience. A shot of two clocks, in New York and in Nazareth, points to the double spatiotemporality lived by the diasporic subject, a temporal doubleness underlined by an intertitle saying that the filmmaker's mother, due to the Scud attacks, is adjusting her gas mask at that very moment. The friend's letter similarly stresses the fractured space-time of being in the US while identifying with relatives in both Iraq and Israel.

In *Measures of Distance*, the Palestinian artist Mona Hatoum explores the renewal of friendship between her mother and herself during a brief family reunion in Lebanon in the early 1980s. The video relates the fragmented memories of diverse generations: the mother's tales of the "used-to-be" of Palestine, Hatoum's own childhood in Lebanon, the civil war in Lebanon, and the current dispersal of the filmmaker and her sisters in the West. (The cinema, from *The Sheik*, 1921, to *Out of Africa*, 1985, has generally preferred showing Western women in the East rather than Eastern women in the West.) As images of the mother's hand-written Arabic letters to the daughter are superimposed over dissolves of the daughter's color slides of her mother in the shower, we hear an audio-tape of their conversations in Arabic, along with excerpts of their letters as translated and read by the filmmaker in English.

The voice-over and script of *Measures of Distance* narrate a paradoxical state of geographical distance and emotional closeness. The textual, visual, and linguistic play between Arabic and English underlines the family's serial dislocations, from Palestine to Lebanon to Britain, where Mona Hatoum has been living since 1975, gradually unfolding the dispersion of Palestinians over diverse geographies. The foregrounded letters, photographs, and audio-tapes call attention to the precarious means by which people in exile maintain cultural identity. In the mother's voice-over, the repeated phrase "My dear Mona" evokes the diverse "measures of distance" evoked by the video's title. Meanwhile, background dialog in Arabic, recalling their conversations about sexuality and Palestine, recorded in the past but played in the present, parallels shower photos of the mother, also taken in the past but looked at in the present. The multiplication of temporalities continues in Hatoum's reading of a letter in English: to the moments of the letter's sending and its arrival is added the moment of Hatoum's voice-over translation for the English-speaking viewer. Each layer of time evokes a distance at once temporal and spatial, historical and geographical; each dialog is situated, produced, and received in precise historical circumstances.

The linguistic play also marks the distance between mother and daughter, while their separation instantiates the fragmented existence of a nation. When relentless bombing prevents the mother from mailing her letter, the screen fades to black, suggesting an abrupt end to communication. Yet the letter eventually arrives via messenger, while the voice-over narrates the exile's difficulties of maintaining contact with one's culture. The negotiation of time and place is here absolutely crucial. The videomaker's voice-over reading her mother's letters in the present interferes with the dialog recorded in the past in Lebanon. The background conversations in Arabic give a sense of present-tense immediacy, while the more dominant English voice-over speaks of the same conversation in the past tense. The Arabic-speaking viewer labors to focus on the Arabic conversation and read the Arabic script, while also listening to the English. If the non-Arabic-speaking spectator misses some of the film's textual registers, the Arabic-speaking

Plates 51 and 52 The scripted body of exile: *Homage by Assassination* and *Measures of Distance*

320

spectator is overwhelmed by competing images and sounds. This strategic refusal to translate Arabic is echoed in Suleiman's *Homage by Assassination*, where the director (in person) types out Arab proverbs on a computer screen, without providing any translation. These diasporic media artists thus cunningly provoke in the non-Arabic-speaking spectator the same alienation experienced by a displaced person, invoking, through inversion, the asymmetry in cultural exchange between exiles and their "host" communities. At the same time, they catalyze a sense of community for the minoritarian-speech community, a strategy especially suggestive in the case of diasporic filmmakers, who often wind up in the First World precisely because colonial/imperial power has turned them into displaced persons.

Measures of Distance also probes issues of sexuality and the female body in a kind of self-ethnography, its nostalgic rhetoric concerning less the "public sphere" of national struggle than the "private sphere" of sexuality, pregnancy, and children. The women's conversations about sexuality leave the father feeling displaced by what he dismisses as "women's nonsense." The daughter's photographs of her nude mother make him profoundly uncomfortable, as if the daughter, as the mother writes, had "trespassed on his possession." To videotape such intimate conversations is not a common practice in Middle Eastern documentary cinema, or, for that matter, in any cinema. (Western audiences often ask how Hatoum won her mother's consent to use the nude photographs and how she broached the subject of sexuality.) Paradoxically, the exile's distance from the Middle East authorizes the exposure of intimacy. Displacement and separation make possible a transformative return to the inner sanctum of the home; mother and daughter are together again in the space of the text.

In Western popular culture, the Arab female body, whether in the form of French cards of veiled bare-breasted women or of the Hollywood images of harems and belly-dancers, has functioned as a sign of the exotic. But rather than adopting a nationalist patriarchal strategy that "covers up" the colonized female body, censuring female nudity, Hatoum deploys the diffusely sensuous, almost pointillist images of her mother's nakedness to tell a more complex story with nationalist overtones. She uses diverse strategies to veil the images from voyeuristic scrutiny: already hazy images are concealed by text (fragments of the mother's correspondence, in Arabic script) and are difficult to decipher. The superimposed words in Arabic script serve to "envelop" and "bar" the mother's body, metaphorizing her inaccessibility and visually undercutting the intimacy verbally expressed in other registers. The nature of existence in exile is thus conjured up by superimposed fragmentations: fragments of letters, of dialog, and of the mother's *corps morcellé* (rendered as hands, breasts, belly). The blurred and fragmented images evoke the dispersed collectivity of the national family itself.[63] Rather than evoking a longed-for ancestral home, *Measures of Distance*, like *Homage by Assassination*, affirms the process of recreating identity in the liminal zone of exile.[64] Video layering makes it possible for Mona Hatoum to capture the fluid, multiple identities of the diasporic subject.

PARADIGMS OF LOOKS

Exile can also take the form of estrangement from one's own body. Dominant media have long disseminated the hegemonic esthetic inherited from colonialist discourse, an esthetic which exiled people of color from their own bodies. Until the late 1960s, the overwhelming majority of Anglo-American fashion journals, films, TV shows, and commercials promoted a canonical notion of beauty within which White women (and secondarily White men) were the only legitimate objects of desire. In so doing, the media extended the longstanding philosophical valorization of Whiteness explored in earlier chapters. European homages to the ideal of White beauty implicitly devalorize the appearance of people of color. For Gobineau, the "white race originally possessed the monopoly of beauty, intelligence and strength."[65] For Buffon, "[Nature] in her most perfect exertions made men white."[66] Fredrich Bluembach called White Europeans "Caucasians" because he believed that the Caucasus mountains were the original home of the most beautiful human species.[67]

The hegemony of this Eurocentric gaze, spread not only by First World media but even at times by Third World media, explains why *morena* women in Puerto Rico, like Arab-Jewish (Sephardi) women in Israel, dye their hair blonde, why Brazilian TV commercials are more suggestive of Scandinavia than of a Black-majority country, why "Miss Universe" contests can elect blonde "queens" even in North African countries, and why Asian women perform cosmetic surgery in order to appear more Western. (We are not questioning the aspect of agency involved in such transformations, but highlighting the patterns informing such practices.) The mythical norms of Eurocentric esthetics come to inhabit the intimacy of self-consciousness, leaving severe psychic wounds. A patriarchal system contrived to generate neurotic self-dissatisfaction in *all* women (whence anorexia, bulimia, and other pathologies of appearance) becomes especially oppressive for women of color by excluding them from the realms of legitimate images of desire. At the same time, recently there have been reverse currents linked to the central role of African-Americans in mass-mediated culture: Whites who thicken their lips and sport dreadlocks, fades, or cornrows. From a multicultural feminist perspective, these cross-cultural transformations can be exempla of "internal exile," "appropriation," or renegadism, but on another they evoke the possibility of an open, non-essentialist approach to looks and identity.

The supposedly oxymoronic naming of the "Hottentot Venus," as we saw earlier, was aggressive and Eurocentric. A collage by Renee Green turns this same "oxymoron" against its originators. The piece juxtaposes a photograph of a White man looking through a camera; a fragment of a nineteenth-century drawing of the torso of a White woman in a hoop skirt; a fragment of another torso, this time of the nude "Hottentot"; and finally, an image of the Grand Tetons (the Big Breasts). A text accompanying the collage calls attention to the undercurrents of desire within the scientific enterprise:

The subinterpreter was married to a charming person, not only a Hottentot in figure, but in that respect a Venus among Hottentots. I was perfectly aghast at her development. I profess to be a scientific man, and was exceeding anxious to obtain accurate measurements of her shape.

The collage evokes a hierarchy of power. The man looking evokes Cuvier, the scientist who measured the Hottentot Venus. By fragmenting the African woman's buttocks, Green exaggerates what for the White scientists was already exaggerated. Juxtaposing this image with a fragmented depiction of a White woman whose fashionably hooped skirt also shapes artificially outsized buttocks, she implies that both the African and the European woman have been constructed for masculinist pleasures: one as the acme of coy virginal beauty, adorned with flowers and delicately held fan; the other, naked, imagined as an exemplum of gross corporality supposedly to be looked at without pleasure, only for the sake of the austere discipline of science. Both drawings easily slide into the image of nature, of the Grand Tetons. The letter A appears next to the White woman, B to the Black, and AB to the Grand Tetons (Big Breasts), and a punning C ("see") to the White man with camera. The strategic use of European representations of an African woman to underline social ironies about sexuality, gender, and race exploits a boomerang technique; a descendant of Africans literally reframes the prejudicial images of an earlier African woman as a kind of posthumous indictment.

The racialized body has been subjected not only to the indignities of the auction block, to rape, branding, lynching, whipping, stun-gunning, and other kinds of physical abuse but also to the cultural erasure entailed in esthetic stigmatization.

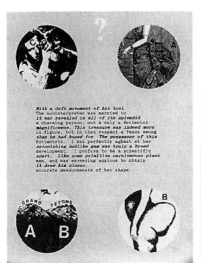 

Plates 53 and 54 Returning the Colonial Gaze: Renee Green's "Hottentot Venus" and Coco Fusco/Gomez Peña's "Two Undiscovered Amerindians"

323

Many Third World and minoritarian feminist film and video projects suggest strategies for coping with the psychic violence inflicted by Eurocentric esthetics, foregrounding the racialized body as the site of both brutal oppression and creative resistance. Black creativity turned the body, as a singular form of "cultural capital," into what Stuart Hall calls a "canvas of representation."[68] A number of recent independent films and videos – notably Ayoka Chenzira's *Hairpiece: A Film for Nappy-Headed People* (1985), Camille Billops's *Older Women and Love* (1987), Ngozi A. Onwurah's *Coffee Coloured Children* (1988), Shu Lea Cheang's *Color Schemes* (1989), Pam Tom's *Two Lies* (1989), Maureen Blackwood's *Perfect Image?* (1990), Helen Lee's *Sally's Beauty Spot* (1990), and Kathe Sandler's *A Question of Color* (1993) – meditate on the racialized female body to narrate issues of identity. These semi-autobiographical texts link fragmented diasporic identities to larger issues of representation, recovering complex experiences in the face of Eurocentric mass culture. *Perfect Image?*, for example, satirizes the mass-mediated ideal of a "perfect image" by focussing on the representation and self-representation of two Black British actresses, one light-skinned and the other dark, lampooning the system that generates self-dissatisfaction in very diverse women, all of whom see themselves as "too" something – too dark, too light, too fat, too tall. Their constant shifting of personae evokes a diversity of women, and thus prevents any essentialist stereotyping along color lines in the Afro-diasporic community.

Pathological syndromes of self-rejection – Black skins/White masks – form the psychic fallout of racial hegemony. Given the construction of dark bodies as ugly and bestial, resistance takes the form of affirming Black beauty. The Black Power movement of the 1960s, for example, transformed kinky hair into proud, Afro hair. Sandler's *A Question of Color* traces tensions around color-consciousness and internalized racism in the African-American community, a process summed up in the popular dictum: "If you're white, you're all right/if you're yellow, you're mellow/if you're brown, stick around/but if you're black, stay back." (Such tensions formed the subject of Duke Ellington's musical composition "Black, Brown and Beige.") Hegemonic norms of skin color, hair texture, and facial features are expressed through such euphemisms as "good hair" (that is, straight hair) and "nice features" (meaning European-style features), and in inferentially prejudicial locutions such as "dark *but* beautiful" or in admonitions not to "look like a Ubangi." The film registers the impact of the "Black is Beautiful" movement, while regarding the present moment as the contradictory site of the resurgent Afrocentrism of some rap music together with lingering traces of old norms. One interview features a Nigerian cosmetic surgeon who de-Africanizes the appearance of Black women, while the film reflects on the valorization of light-skinned Black women in rap video and MTV. Sandler also probes intimate relations to expose the social pathologies rooted in color hierarchies; the darker-skinned feel devalorized and desexualized, while the lighter-skinned, to the extent that their own community assumes they feel superior to it, are obliged to "prove" their Blackness. Filtering down from positions of dominance, chromatic hierarchies sow tensions among siblings and friends, all caught by Sandler's exceptionally sensitive direction.

In all these films, internalized models of White beauty become the object of a corrosive critique. Not coincidentally, many of the films pay extraordinary attention to hair as the scene both of humiliation ("bad hair") and of creative self-fashioning as a "popular art form" articulating "esthetic solutions," in Kobena Mercer's words, to the "problems created by ideologies of race and racism."[69] Spike Lee, even before the "conking" scene in his 1992 *Malcolm X*, had addressed the subject of hair in *School Daze* (1988). Rather than satirizing the feminine beautifying process in general, Lee's musical focusses on "White" (European) versus Black (African) models of Beauty. One stylized production number, set in a beauty salon, foregrounds the politics of hair within the Afro-American community. While the White-aspiring "Wannabees" reject the African look – "Don't you wish you had hair like this/then the boys would give you a kiss ... caint cha, don't cha hair stand on high/caint cha comb it and don't you try" – the politically conscious "Jigaboos" mock them: "Don't you know my hair is so strong/it can break the teeth out the comb ... I don't mind being BLACK/go on with your mixed-up head/I ain't gonna never be 'fraid."[70] The dancers hold, respectively, Vivien Leigh and Hattie McDaniel style fans, reflexively alluding to Hollywood representations of race relations, and implicitly to their impact on the Afro-American self-image. The number lends an esthetic corollary to Malcolm X's dictum that the White man's worst crime was to make the Black man hate himself.

Ayoka Chenzira's ten-minute animated short *Hairpiece: A Film for Nappy-Headed People* similarly addresses hair and its vicissitudes in order to narrate African-Americans' history of exile from the body as well as the utopia of empowerment through Afro-consciousness. In a dominant society where beautiful hair is that which "blows in the wind," *Hairpiece* suggests an isomorphism between vital, rebellious hair and the vital, rebellious people who "wear" the hair. Music by Aretha Franklin, James Brown, and Michael Jackson accompanies a collage of Black faces (from Sammy Davis to Angela Davis). Motown tunes underscore a quick-paced visual inventory of relaxers, gels, and curlers – devices painfully familiar to Black people, and particularly to Black women. The film's voice-over and "happy ending" might seem to imply an essentialist affirmation of "natural African beauty," but as Kobena Mercer points out in another context, "natural hair" is not itself African; it is a syncretic construct.[71] Afro-diasporic hairstyles, from the "Afro" of the 1960s and 1970s to cornrows, dreadlocks, and fades, are not emulations of "real" African styles but rather neologistic projections of diasporic identity. The styles displayed at the film's finale, far from being examples of "politically correct" hair, rather assert a cornucopia of diasporic looks, an empowering expression of a variegated collective body. Satirizing the Black internalization of White esthetic models, the film provokes a comic catharsis for spectators who have experienced the terror and pity of self-colonization.[72]

Ngozi A. Onwurah's lyrical semi-autobiographical film *Coffee Coloured Children*, meanwhile, speaks of the Black body as hemmed in by racism. The daughter of a White mother and an absent Nigerian father, the film's narrator recalls the pain of growing up in an all-White English neighborhood. The opening sequence intimates the kind of racist harassment the family suffered; a racist youth defiles their front door with excrement, while the mother, in voice-over, worries about protecting her children from feeling somehow responsible for the violence directed at them. The narrative conveys the traumatic self-hatred provoked by imposed paradigms. In one scene, the daughter dons a blonde wig and white makeup in front of a mirror, trying to emulate a desired Whiteness. If *The Battle of Algiers* made the mirror a revolutionary tool, here it becomes the speculum for a traumatized identity, that of a Black skin literally masked with whiteness. The simple act of looking in a mirror is revealed to be multiply specular, as one looks even at oneself through the eyes of many others: those of one's family, one's peers, one's racial others, as well as through the panoptic eyes of the mass media and of consumerist culture. The scars inflicted on the victims of this esthetic hegemony are poignantly suggested in a bath sequence where the children frantically try to scrub off a Blackness lived as pain.[73] The narrator's voice-over relating the cleansing ritual is superimposed on a close shot of rapid scrubbing, blurred so as to suggest bleeding, an apt image for colonialism's legacy inscribed on the body of children, a testament to the internalized stigmata of a devastating esthetic regime.

While Third World and First World minoritarian women have experienced diverse histories and sexual oppressions, they have also shared a common status as colonial exotics, portrayed as wiggling bodies graced with Tutti Frutti hats, as lascivious dark eyes peering from behind veils, as feathered dark bodies slipping into trance to accelerating rhythms. Escaping these paradigms, Tracey Moffatt's *Nice Coloured Girls* interweaves tales about contemporary urban Australian Aboriginal women and their "captains" (sugar daddies) with tales of Aboriginal women and White men over 200 years before. Moffatt interrogates the hackneyed conventions of the "Aboriginal film," proposing instead the formal experimentalism of *Nice Coloured Girls* itself.[74] And in sharp contrast to the colonial construction of the Aboriginal female body seen as a metaphorical extension of an exoticized land, *Nice Colored Girls* places dynamic, irreverent, resourceful Aboriginal women at the center of the narrative, offering a multitemporal perspective on their "nasty" actions – mild forms of prostitution and conning White Australian men into spending money. By shuttling between present-day Australia and past texts, voices, and images, the film contextualizes their behavior in relation to the asymmetrical exchanges typical of colonial encounters. Two temporally and spatially distinct but conceptually interlinked frames – one associated with images of the sea (or its painterly representation) and set in the past, the other set in a pub in contemporary Australia – contextualize the encounter. In one early pub sequence, an Aboriginal man and woman step behind a frosted glass door to smoke a joint. As their film-noirish silhouettes undulate to the diegetic pub music, a British-accented male voice-over reads excerpts from a historical journal describing an Aboriginal woman's breasts, teeth, and face. The evocation of an earlier historical meeting conditions the viewer's comprehension of latter-day encounters.

Rather than searching for an "authentic" Aboriginal culture, *Nice Coloured Girls* constructs a "genealogy" of criminality. While from the vantage point of Eurocentric decorum the Aboriginal women are amoral schemers, the historical context of settler colonialism and its sexualized relations to both land and women switches the ethical and emotional valence. In the pub, the women demonstrate their resilient capacity to survive and to outwit marginalization. Whereas images of the past are set inside a ship, or in daylight on the shore, images from the present are set in the night time city, pointing to the historical "neonization," as it were, of Aboriginal space. The film can thus be seen as a "revenge" narrative in which Aboriginal women trick Euro-Australian men into fantasizing a "fair" exchange of sex and goods, then take their money and run.

Racial and sexual relations from past (the encounter between Europeans and Aborigines in 1788) and present (1987) are interwoven through overlapping images, music, texts, and voice-over. The opening sequence superimposes a text by an early English "explorer" over a dark urban skyscraper, accompanied by the sounds of rowing and of labored rhythmic breathing. While the male voice-over narrates extracts from journals of the "settlement" of Australia in 1788, subtitles convey the thoughts of present-day Aboriginal women. Whereas the voice-over is in the first person, the subtitles relay a collective voice. The images reinforce the subtitled version, relaying the women's perspective on their trapped "captains," deconstructing the journals not by correcting the historical record but rather through a discursive critique of their racist and masculinist thrust.

The title of *Nice Coloured Girls* is itself ironic, foreshadowing the film's subversion of the "positive" image of "nice" colored girls as the objects of colonial exoticization, and the valorization of the "negative" image of "nasti-ness." The historical encounters are reconstructed in a minimalist antirealist style, a symbolic evocation rather than a "realistic" depiction. By foregrounding the artifice of its production through stylized sets, excessive performance style, and ironic subtitles, the film undermines any expectation of sociologically "authentic" or ethically "positive" representations. Image, sound, and text mutually amplify and contextualize one another, militating against any authoritative history. The constant changes of discursive register – verité-style hand-held camera, voice-over ethnographic texts, subtitled oral narratives, American soul music of obscure diegetic status – undermine any univocal mode of historical narration.

Nice Coloured Girls challenges a whole series of discursive, generic, and disciplinary traditions. Looking at official Anglo-Australian discourse through the deconstructive eyes of the Aboriginal women, this densely layered text mocks the prurient "ethnographic" fascination with Aboriginal sexuality. Rather than reversing the dichotomy of sexualized Third World women and virginal European women by proposing an equally virginal image of Aboriginal women, the film rejects the binaristic mode altogether by showing "nastiness" as a creative response to a specific economic and historical conjuncture.

MEDIA JUJITSU

The Brazilian "anthropophagic" movement, as we saw earlier, called for an art which would devour European techniques the better to struggle against European domination. And if we substitute "dominant" and "alternative," or "mass" and "popular," for "Europe" and "Brazilian," we begin to glimpse the global contemporary relevance of its critique. By appropriating an existing discourse for its own ends, anthropophagy *assumes* the force of the dominant discourse only to deploy that force, through a kind of artistic jujitsu, *against* domination. Such an "excorporation" steals elements of the dominant culture and redeploys them in the interests of oppositional praxis. Indeed, from Rocha's "esthetic of hunger" to the Tropicalist "esthetics of garbage," from Claire Johnston's feminist "counter-cinema" to Henry Louis Gates Jr's "signifying-monkey" esthetic and Paul Leduc's "salamander" (as opposed to dinosaur) esthetic, from Jean Rouch's *ciné-transe* and Teshome Gabriel's "nomadic esthetics" to Kobena Mercer's "diaspora esthetics," from Deleuze/Guattari's "minor" esthetic to Espinosa's *ciné imperfecto* and Ishmael Reed's neo-hoodoo esthetic, many alternative esthetics have in common the twin anthropophagic notions of revalorizing what had been seen as negative and of turning tactical weakness into strategic strength. (Even "magic realism" inverts the view of magic as irrational superstition.)

Don Featherstone's *Babakiueria* (1988) illustrates what we mean by "media jujitsu" by ironically reversing Euro-Australian discourses and policies toward Aborigines. The film begins with the Aboriginal "discovery" of a White-inhabited Australia. Since the first White "natives" they see are enjoying a picnic barbecue, the invading Aborigines, in a parodic example of colonial misrecognition, name the continent "Babakiueria." Framed as Aboriginal TV reportage, *Babakiueria* has an Aboriginal woman reporter initiate the spectator into the "strange culture" of Whites. Mingling the discourses of anthropology and social welfare, she introduces us to a "typical White family," residing in a "typical White house" in a "typical White ghetto" and practicing "typical White rituals": a father who works and a mother who stays home, children who study their culture (in a class on the A-bomb) and an ethos of "strong family ties" (they call their grandmother three times a year). We are introduced to their religious practice of "making donations to prayer tokens" while they "watch trained horses run in a circle." We are told of the White "predilection for violence" (evidenced in documentary clips of soccer brawls) and for pollution and garbage. Seen through an Aboriginal grid, Euro-Australian customs are estranged and colonial practices (the denial of self-representation, forced adoptations, and relocation programs) formerly applied to Aborigines are now applied to Whites. The "Minister of White Affairs" insists that all the citizens of Babakiueria join in the bicentennial celebrations of the "discovery." White political opposition is dismissed as the work of outside agitators and is brutally repressed by the police. The report's final claim that White violence is abating coincides with a tossed brick coming through the window. In *Babakiueria*, Euro-Australian representations of Aborigines boomerang against their perpetrators.

We also find a martial-art esthetic in Philippine director Kidlat Tahimik's *Mababangong Bangungot* (Perfumed Nightmare, 1977). Like Artur Omar's *Triste Tropico*, the film conducts an ironic odyssey in the form of a reflexive pseudo-documentary memoir which mocks the positing of the First World as the ideal ego of the neocolonized world, all in an improvisational style reminiscent of the "esthetic of garbage." The film tells the story of a young Filipino taxi-driver, head of his local "Werner von Braun" fan club and honorary Grand Marshal of the club's Miss Universe contest. Apart from being the film's (dubiously reliable) narrator, Tahimik himself appears as the main character, who exhibits at the outset all the pathological symptoms of neocolonial dependency: he systematically prefers the foreign to the local – steel to bamboo, rockets to jeepneys, English to Tagalog. Even his inner voice has become confounded with that of Voice of America broadcasts. The protagonist's secret dream is to fly beyond the "nets" of provincial "backwardness" into the soaring flight of modernity as incarnated in the tumescent missiles of Werner von Braun. Taken to Paris by an American bubble-gum magnate, the protagonist glimpses the squalid underside of European modernity in the form of razed housing and urban blight. After having his protagonist uncritically embrace American patriotism, Tahimik casts doubt on such ideals. From being an admirer of the rationalist West, the character begins to dabble with the Filipino mysticism incarnated by his friend Kaya, a striking visionary figure with a contorted face and a giant butterfly tattoo on his chest. Kaya expresses skepticism about the "ghost of progress," recommending instead the "quiet strength of bamboo." In the end, the film plays off Filipino mysticism against rationalist modernity, and artisanal, low-budget improvisational poetic cinema against industrialized, big-budget prosaic commercial cinema, without leaving any doubt about the film's corrosive attitude toward Europe's "superiority." At the same time, as Fredric Jameson suggests, the film proposes jeepney-style bricolage as an alternative model of esthetic production, one outside assembly-line alienation, with a "kind of Brechtian delight with the bad new things that anybody can hammer together for their pleasure ... another jeepney, an omnibus and omnipurpose object that ferries its way back and forth between First and Third Worlds with dignified hilarity."[75]

Contemporary video and computer technologies facilitate media jujitsu. Instead of an "esthetic of hunger," video-makers can deploy a kind of cybernetic minimalism, achieving maximum beauty and effect for minimum expense. Video switchers allow the screen to be split, divided horizontally or vertically with wipes and inserts. Keys, chroma-keys, mattes and fader bars, along with computer graphics, multiply audio-visual possibilities for fracture, rupture, polyphony. An electronic "quilting" can weave together sounds and images in ways that break with linear character-centered narrative. In such texts, multiple images can be "hung" on the screen like so many paintings in a gallery, obliging spectators to choose which image to contemplate, without losing themselves in any single image. All the conventional decorum of dominant narrative cinema – eyeline matches, position matches, the 30° rule, cutaway shots – is superseded by proliferating polysemy. The

Plates 55, 56, 57
Media jujitsu:
Babakiueria (top),
Slaying the Dragon
(right), and
*Introduction to the
End of an Argument*
(left)

spatial co-presence of multiple images within the rectangle of the screen establishes syntagamic possibilities denied to single-image cinema. The centered perspective inherited from Renaissance humanism is relativized, the multiplicity of perspectives rendering identification with any one perspective difficult. Spectators have to decide what the juxtaposed images have in common, or how they conflict; they have to make real the syntheses latent in the audio-visual material. The capacity for palimpsestic overlays of images and sounds facilitated by electronics and cybernetics opens the doors to a renovated, multichannel, polyphonic esthetic. Meaning can be generated not through the drive and thrust of individual desire as encapsulated by a linear narrative, but rather through the interweaving of mutually relativizing layers of sound, image, and language.

A number of texts perform media jujitsu by coercing Hollywood films and commercial TV into comic self-indictment, deploying the power of the dominant media against their own Eurocentric premises. The ludicrous catalog of media Arabs (assassins, terrorists, fanatics), drawn from cartoons, newscasts, fiction films, and even game shows, in Elia Suleiman and Jayce Salloum's *Muqaddima Li Nihayat Jidal* (An Introduction to the End of an Argument, 1990) hilariously deconstructs mass-media orientalism. Set against more critical materials, the sheer repetition of the caricatural images makes the stereotypes fall of their own weight. The performances of Spiderwoman Theater, a group of three Native American (Cuna/Rappahanock) sisters, as documented in *Sun, Moon and Feather* (1989), carnivalize Hollywood stereotypes by having two of the sisters mimic and sing along with Nelson Eddy and Jeanette MacDonald performing "Indian Love Call" in such a way as to break open the Eurocentric frame and "re-Indianize" Hollywood caricatures. Carlos Anzaldua's tape *It's a Dictatorship, Eat!* (1983) weaves clips from commercials, news, and fiction films, along with mock-reportage scenes, into a critique of the symbiotic complicities between Reaganite policies and an acquiescent media. Sherry Millner and Ernest Larsen's *The Desert Bush* (1991) combines pop culture images and artifacts – *Lawrence of Arabia*, war movies, toys, George Bush speeches, *Thousand and One Nights*-style intertitles – to critique the media's Persian Gulf war. In *From Hollywood to Hanoi* (1993), Tiana Thi Thanh Nga performs jujitsu by absorbing clips of her own orientalized performances in commercial films (as B-movie karate queen, as oriental sexpot) into her own guerilla filmmaking portrayal of her odyssey from reflex anticommunist – as a child she was told that Ho Chi Minh would devour her if she did not eat her vegetables – into diasporic struggler for reconciliation between Vietnam and the US.

It might be objected that jujitsu tactics place one in a perpetually reactive or parasitic posture of merely deconstructing or reversing the dominant. We would argue, however, that these films are not merely defensive. Rather, they express an alternative sensibility and shape an innovative esthetic. By defamiliarizing and reaccentuating preexisting materials, they rechannel energies in new directions, generating a space of negotiation outside of the binaries of domination and subordination, in ways that convey specific cultural and even autobiographical inflections. We are not suggesting, in any case, that jujitsu should ever be the only alternative strategy. We would argue for multiple strategies, for infiltrating the dominant, transforming the dominant, kidnapping the dominant, creating alternatives to the dominant, even ignoring the dominant. In a context of marginalization, however, jujitsu becomes crucial. Since anti-Eurocentric discourse has historically been placed in a defensive position, it is virtually obliged to turn the hegemonic discourse against itself. All systems of domination, we assume, are "leaky"; the point is to turn such leaks into a flood. Instead of waiting passively for the culture industry to deliver its blockbusters, therefore, instead of waiting for the next Madonna music video with its possibly recuperable subversions, instead of letting the industry do our politics for us, teachers and critics might create and support popular culture along a wider spectrum which would include the kinds of films and videos discussed here: critical First World mass-media texts, Third World films and video, rap music video, the politicized avant-garde, didactic documentaries, the camcorder militancy of media activists, the self-mocking minimalism of public access cable such as "Paper Tiger" or "Deep Dish."[76]

In their respect for difference and plurality, and in their self-consciousness about their own status as simulacra, and as texts that engage with a contemporary, mass-mediated sensibility without losing their sense of activism, the best of the jujitsu films constitute examples of what Hal Foster has called "resistance postmodernism." Jorge Furtado's *Isle of Flowers* (1990) brings Brazil's "garbage esthetic" into a self-consciously postmodern esthetic. Described by its author as a "letter to a Martian who knows nothing of the earth and its social systems," Furtado's fifteen-minute short uses Monty Python-style animation, archival footage, and parodic/reflexive documentary techniques to indict the distribution of wealth and food around the world. The "isle of flowers" of the title is a Brazilian garbage dump where the famished poor are allowed ten minutes to scrounge for food. But this denunciatory material is woven into an ironic treatise about pigs, tomatoes, racism, and the Holocaust (archival footage shows Jews being thrown, garbage-like, into death camp piles). Furtado invokes the old carnival motif of pigs and sausage, but with a political twist; here the pigs eat better than people. We are given a social examination of garbage; the truth of a society is in its detritus. Rather than having the margins invade the center, as in carnival, here the center creates the margins, or, better, there are no margins; the urban bourgeois family is linked to the rural poor via the sausage and the tomato within a web of global relationality. The title of another Brazilian "garbage" film, Eduardo Coutinho's documentary *Boca de Lixo* (The Scavengers, 1993), is triply allusive: literally translated as "mouth of garbage," the title also evokes "red-light district" and "garbage cinema." The film centers on poor Brazilians who live and survive thanks to a garbage dump outside of Rio. But rather than take a miserabilist approach, Countinho shows us people who are inventive, ironic, and critical (they tell the director what not to film and what interpretative mistakes to avoid). Instead of the suspect pleasures of a condescending "sympathy," the middle-class spectator is confronted by vibrant people who dare to dream and to talk back.

332

But one need not look so far for examples of resistant postmodernism. Popular music, which now almost invariably comes accompanied by visuals, offers countless examples. Unlike classical music, which requires a distanced and contemplative attitude, popular music encourages movement and tries to abolish the separation between performer and spectator within a kinetic, energizing, percussive style. In the 1980s, Robert Mugge's *Black Wax* featured Gil Scott Heron satirizing Ronald Reagan in such media-conscious songs as "B-Movie." The rap videos of Ziggy Marley, the Jungle Brothers, Public Enemy, Queen Latifa, KRSOne, and Arrested Development, similarly, show awareness of the media-saturated nature of the contemporary imaginary, yet do not fall into cynical nihilism. Marley's "Bold Our Story" offers a crash-course in Afro-literacy (complete with a reading list). Queen Latifah's "Ladies First" dishes out Afro-feminism, while Public Enemy's rap video "Burn, Hollywood, Burn" satirizes the stereotypical images proffered by Hollywood. "Can't Truss It" invokes the historical continuities, in a postmodern age supposedly indifferent to history, between the racialized terror of slavery and contemporary police brutality. Such work, as Manthia Diawara points out, has helped create a vibrant Black public sphere, disdainful of integration yet attracting, paradoxically, a host of White admirers and imitators.[77] And in Brazil pop musician intellectuals like Chico Buarque de Holanda, with his samba allegories, Gilberto Gil, with his musical essays on the politics of syncretism (such as "From Bob Dylan to Bob Marley"), and Caetano Veloso, in songs like "Something is Out of Order in the New World Order," provide a model of pleasurable, danceable political/artistic praxis.[78] For decades at the cutting edge of political and esthetic innovation (and of reflexion on the cultural moment and on their own practice), these artists are actively engaged in the political issues of their time. "Popular" in both the box-office sense and the Bakhtinian carnivalesque sense, they are community-based intellectuals. Brazilian musical groups like Olodum and Ile Aiye, meanwhile, not only make their own music videos but also create community schools for practical and anti-Eurocentric education, while constructing "carnival factories" to provide jobs. Their audio-visual-musical texts demonstrate art's capacity to give pleasurable form to social desire, to open new grooves, to mobilize a sense of possibility, to shake the body-politic, to appeal to deeply rooted but socially frustrated aspirations for new forms of work and festivity and community, crystallizing desire in a popular and mass-mediated form.

NOTES

1 Fredric Jameson, *The Geopolitical Aesthetic: Cinema and Space in the World System* (Bloomington and London: Indiana University Press and BFI, 1992), p. 1.
2 Ibid., p. 186.
3 We have in mind both Jameson's "Third World allegory" essay ("Third World Literature in the Era of Multinational Capitalism," *Social Text*, No. 15, Fall 1986) and his *Geopolitical Aesthetic*.

4   See Roy Armes, *Third World Filmmaking and the West* (Berkeley: University of California Press, 1987), p. 27.

5   See Gordon Brotherston, *Book of the Fourth World* (Cambridge: Cambridge University Press), p. 48.

6   See Karin Barber, "Yoruba Oriki and Deconstructive Criticism," *Research in African Literature*, Vol. 15, No. 4 (Winter 1984).

7   Quoted in Armes, *Third World Filmmaking and the West*, p. 135.

8   See Robert Farris Thompson, *African Art in Motion: Icon and Act* (Berkeley: University of California Press, 1973).

9   Ola Balogun, "Traditional Arts and Cultural Development in Africa," *Cultures*, No. 2 (1975), p. 159.

10 *Egungun*, as practiced in Brazil, calls up representations of male ancestors. For a documentary presentation of *Egungun*, see the Carlos Brasbladt film entitled, simply, *Egungun* (1985).

11 Comparing Sembene's *Mandabi* (1968) to two trickster tales – "Amanse" (in Ashanti) and "Leukthi Hare" (in Wolof) – Mbye Cham sees a common thematic thread of "greed and corruption within a social framework where only scoundrels live well." See Mbye Cham, "Art and Society in Oral Narrative and Film," in I. Okpewho, *The Oral Performance in Africa* (Ibadan: Spectrum, 1990).

12 Italo Calvino, *If on a Winter's Night a Traveller*, p. 94, quoted in Gerald Martin, ed., *Journeys through the Labyrinth* (London: Verso, 1989), p. 306.

13 Hollywood cinema, interestingly, often conveys a bookish view of history, not only by basing so many films on written sources but also through formulaic ouvertures featuring book covers or turning pages.

14 Quoted in Françoise Pfaff, *The Cinema of Ousmane Sembene* (Westport, Conn.: Greenwood, 1984), p. 29.

15 Cheryl Chisholm, "Voice of the Griot: African-American Film and Video," in Barbara Abrash and Catherine Egan, eds, *Mediating History* (New York: New York University Press, 1992), p. 22.

16 For more on the relations between oral narrative and contemporary media, see Victor Bachy, ed., *Tradition Orale et Nouveaux Medias* (Brussels: OCIC, 1989).

17 See Manthia Diawara, "Oral Literature and African Film: Narratology in *Wend Kunni*," in Paul Willemen and Jim Pines, eds, *Questions of Third Cinema* (London: BFI, 1989).

18 Trinh T. Minh-ha, "Grandma's Story," in Brian Wallis, ed., *Blasted Allegories* (New York: New Museum of Contemporary Art/Cambridge, Mass.: MIT Press, 1987).

19 African-American "orature," for Clyde Taylor, implies a "taste for semantic ambiguity, a fascination with bold, extravagant metaphor, a 'cool' sensibility, a funky explicitness, and frequently, a prophetic mode of utterance." See Clyde Taylor, "Decolonizing the Image," in Peter Stevens, ed., *Jump Cut: Hollywood, Politics and Counter-Cinema* (Toronto: Between the Lines, 1986).

20 See David Toop, *The Rap Attack: African Jive to New York Hip Hop* (London: Pluto Press, 1984).

21 See Dick Hebdige, *Cut'n Mix: Culture, Identity and Caribbean Music* (London: Methuen, 1987). The basic text on rap is Tricia Rose, *Black Noise* (Wesleyan: Wesleyan, 1993).

22 See Teshome Gabriel, "Towards a Critical Theory of Third World Films," in Willemen and Pines, eds, *Questions of Third Cinema*, p. 40. Paul Willemen, in the same volume, argues that Gabriel's schema, while suggestive, in some ways constitutes a "premature globalization."

23 See John S. Mbiti, *African Religions and Philosophy* (Oxford: Heinemann, 1969), pp. 108–9.

24 Patricia Williams calls attention to this relational use of Vietnamese pronouns in her *The Alchemy of Race and Rights* (Cambridge, Mass.: Harvard University Press, 1991), p. 62.

25 See Toni Cade Bambara and bell hooks, *Daughters of the Dust: The Making of an African American Woman's Film* (New York: New Press, 1992).

26 Manthia Diawara also analyzes this sequence. See his introduction to *Black American Cinema: Aesthetics and Spectatorship* (New York: Routledge, 1993).

27 See Graham Bruce, "Alma Brasileira: Music in the Films of Glauber Rocha," in Randal Johnson and Robert Stam, eds, *Brazilian Cinema* (Rutherford, NJ: Fairleigh Dickinson Press, 1982; republished Austin: University of Texas Press, 1987).

28 Lucy Lippard, *Mixed Blessings: New Art in a Multicultural Age* (New York: Pantheon, 1990), p. 201.

29 Ibid., p. 202.

30 See Alejo Carpentier, "De lo Real Maravilloso Americano," *Ciné Cubano*, No. 102 (1982), pp. 12–14.

31 Arthur Jaffa, "69," in Gina Dent, ed., *Black Popular Culture* (Seattle, Wash.: Bay Press, 1992), p. 266.

32 Ibid., pp. 249–54.

33 James C. Scott, *Domination and the Arts of Resistance* (New Haven, Conn.: Yale University Press, 1990), p. 80.

34 Ibid.

35 On these Black-led entertainments in antebellum America, see David R. Roediger, *The Wages of Whiteness: Race and the Making of the American Working Class* (London: Verso, 1991).

36 Mike Davis, *City of Quartz* (New York: Vintage, 1992), p. 257.

37 See João Luiz Vieira, "Hegemony and Resistance: Parody and Carnival in Brazilian Cinema" (Ph.D. Dissertation, New York University 1984). See also João Luiz Vieira and Robert Stam, "Parody and Marginality," in Manuel Alvarado and John O. Thompson, eds, *The Media Reader* (London: BFI, 1989).

38 See M.M. Bakhtin, *Problems of Dostoevsky's Poetics*, trans. Caryl Emerson (Minneapolis: University of Minnesota Press, 1984), pp. 122–3.

39 See Jack Forbes, *Columbus and Other Cannibals* (New York: Autonomedia, 1992); bel hooks, *Black Looks: Race and Representation* (Boston: South End Press, 1992); and Dean MacCannell, *Empty Meeting Grounds* (London: Routledge, 1992).

40 Diane Scheinman, a student of cinema studies at New York University, is currently writing a dissertation on this subject, entitled "Consuming Passions: Cannibalism and Cinema."

41 For more on modernist "anthropophagy," see Robert Stam, "Of Cannibals and Carnivals," in Stam, *Subversive Pleasures; Bakhtin, Cultural Criticism and Film* (Baltimore, Md.: Johns Hopkins University Press, 1989).

42 For an English version of the "Cannibalist Manifesto," see Leslie Bary's introduction to and translation of the poem in *Latin American Literary Review*, Vol. XIX, No. 38 (July–Dec. 1991).

43 Alfred Jarry in his "Anthropophagie,"(1902) spoke of that "branche trop negligée de l'anthropophagie" and in "L'Almanach du Pere Ubu" addressed himself to "amateur cannibals." The Dadaists entitled one of their organs *Cannibale* and in 1920 Francis Picabia issued the "Manifeste Cannibale Dada."

44 Oswald de Andrade's various manifestoes are collected in *Do Pau-Brasil e Antropofagia as Utopias* (From Brazil-wood to Anthropophagy and to the Utopias) (Rio de Janeiro: Civilização Brasileira, 1972). Translations by Robert Stam.

45 Oswald de Andrade's vision is confirmed by Pierre Clastres' anthropological research into the same Brazilian indigenous groups of which de Andrade spoke. Clastres

describes these groups as tropical "affluent societies" (not in the contemporary sense but in the sense of having surplus food) and as societies without social hierarchy or political coercion. See Pierre Clastres, *Society against the State* (New York: Zone Books, 1987).

46 See Clastres, *Society against the State* for a critique of the ethnocentrism of a classic anthropology accustomed to conceiving political power in terms of hierarchized and authoritarian relations of command and obedience and therefore incapable of theorizing Tupinamba culture and society.

47 Quoted in Augusto de Campos, *Poesia, Antipoesia, Antropofagia* (São Paulo: Cortez e Moraes, 1978).

48 On European hostility to "subsistence societies," see Jerry Mander, *In the Absence of the Sacred: The Failure of Technology and the Survival of the Indian Nations* (San Francisco: Sierra Club Books, 1991); and Marshall Sahlins, *Stone Age Economics* (Chicago: Aldine, 1972).

49 See MacCannell, *Empty Meeting Grounds*.

50 See Renata Salecl, "Society Doesn't Exist," *American Journal of Semiotics*, Vol. 7 Nos 1/2 (1991), pp. 45–52.

51 Joaquim Pedro de Andrade, "Cannibalism and Self-Cannibalism," in Johnson and Stam, eds, *Brazilian Cinema.*

52 Quoted in Lippard, *Mixed Blessings*, p. 183.

53 See Salman Rushdie, "In Good Faith: A Pen against the Sword," *Newsweek* (Feb. 12, 1990), p. 52.

54 See Rosie Thomas, "Indian Cinema: Pleasures and Popularity," *Screen*, Vol. 26, Nos 3–4 (May–August 1985).

55 Paul Simon is a relative latecomer to this mode of music; his "Spirit of the Saints" offers not "strong syncretism," but rather a kind of mismatch between individualist lyrics and the collective energies of the *batucadas* of Olodum. At the same time, those who accuse Paul Simon of "stealing" would presumably not argue the converse, for example that John Coltrane "stole" the music of "My Favorite Things." The issue is not of ethnic copyright but of the concrete successes or failures of specific collaborations.

56 See Ravi Vasudevan, "Shifting Codes, Dissolving Identities," *Journal of Arts and Ideas* (New Delhi), Nos 23–4 (Jan. 1993).

57 See Sumita Chakravarty, *National Identity in Indian Popular Cinema, 1947–1987* (Austin: University of Texas Press, 1993).

58 See Vijay Singh, "Les Films Indiens, Héritiers de Deux Traditions," *Le Monde Diplomatique* (July 1993).

59 We are indebted to the insights of Hema Ramchandran in her unpublished paper entitled simply *Junoon*.

60 See Zuzana M. Pick, *The New Latin American Cinema: A Continental Project* (Austin: University of Texas, 1993), p. 180.

61 Caren Kaplan, "Deterritorializations: The Rewriting of Home and Exile in Western Feminist Discourse," *Cultural Critique*, No. 6 (Spring 1987), p. 198.

62 The friend in question is Ella Shohat.

63 Or as the letters put it: "This bloody war takes my daughters to the four corners of the world." This reference to the dispersion of the family, as metonym and metaphor for the displacement of a people, is particularly ironic given that Zionist discourse itself has often imaged its own national character through the notion of "the ingathering of exiles from the four corners of the globe."

64 *Measures of Distance* in this sense goes against the tendency criticized by Hamid Naficy which turns nostalgia into a ritualized denial of history. See Naficy, "The Poetics and Practice of Iranian Nostalgia in Exile," *Diaspora*, No. 3 (1992).

65 Quoted in Brian V. Street, *The Savage in Literature* (London: Routledge and Kegan Paul, 1975), p. 99.

66 Georges-Louis Leclerc de Buffon, *The History of Man and Quadrupeds*, trans. William Smellie (London: T. Cadell and W. Davies, 1812), p. 422. Quoted in Tzvetan Todorov, *On Human Diversity*, trans. Catherine Porter (Cambridge, Mass.: Harvard University Press), p. 105.

67 George Mosse, *Toward the Final Solution: A History of European Racism* (London: Dent, 1978), p. 44.

68 Stuart Hall, "What is this 'Black' in Black Popular Culture," in Dent, ed., *Black Popular Culture*, p. 27.

69 Kobena Mercer, "Black Hair/Style Politics," *New Formations*, No. 3 (Winter 1987).

70 The lyrics are cited in Spike Lee (with Lisa Jones), *Uplift the Race: The Construction of School Daze* (New York: Simon and Schuster, 1988).

71 Mercer, "Black Hair/Style Politics."

72 Not surprisingly, the film has been screened in museums and churches, and even for social workers and hairstylists, as a provocative contemplation of the intersection of fashion, politics, and identity.

73 The association is especially ironic given the colonial legacy of slavery and servitude, in which Black men (janitors) and women (maids) were obliged to clean up the "mess" created by White Europeans.

74 *Nice Coloured Girls'* juxtaposition of ethnographic diaries/writings and Aboriginal images is hardly coincidental, since the first photographic and cinematographic representations of Aborigines reflected the culture-bound ethnography of White settlers (Walter Baldwin Spencer's 1901 footage of the Arrente tribe performing a kangaroo dance and rain ceremony marks the historical beginning of ethnographic filmmaking about the Aboriginies.) See Karl C. Heider, *Ethnographic Film* (Austin: University of Texas Press, 1976), p. 191.

75 Jameson, *The Geopolitical Aesthetic*, p. 211. Filipina critic Felicidad C. Lim argues that Jameson ignores the actual conditions obtaining in the Saroo jeepney factory, a privately owned monopoly aided by the Marcos regime and the site of alienated labor rather than a "utopic cooperative." Lim, unpublished paper, 1993.

76 We would like here to call attention to the Media Alternatives Project (MAP), established in 1990 to introduce multicultural perspectives into American history teaching thorugh the use of independent film/video. See B. Abrash and C. Egan, eds, *Mediating History: The Map Guide to Independent Video* (New York: New York University Press, 1992).

77 Manthia Diawara, "Black Studies, Cultural Studies: Performative Acts," *Afterimage*, Vol. 20, No. 3, October 1992).

78 For more on Brazilian popular music, see Charles Perrone, *Masters of Contemporary Brazilian Song: MPB 1965–1985* (Austin: University of Texas, 1989) and Robert Stam, *Subversive Pleasures*.

9

THE POLITICS OF MULTICULTURALISM IN THE POSTMODERN AGE

The decline of revolutionary utopian hopes over recent decades has led to a remapping of political and cultural possibilities. Since the 1980s one finds, even on the left, a self-reflexive and ironic distance from revolutionary and Third Worldist rhetoric. A language of "revolution" has been largely eclipsed by an idiom of "resistance," indicative of a crisis of totalizing narratives and a shifting vision of the emancipatory project. The idea of a vanguardist takeover of the state and the economy, associated with the politics of Lenin, has long since given way to the resistance to hegemony associated with Gramsci. Substantive nouns like "revolution" and "liberation" transmute into a largely adjectival opposition: "counter-hegemonic," "subversive," "adversarial." Instead of a macro-narrative of revolution, the focus is now on a decentered multiplicity of localized struggles. Though class and nation do not completely disappear from view, they lose their privileged position, being both supplemented and challenged by categories such as race, gender, and sexuality.

At the same time, political culture has to take into account the phenomena summed up in the term "postmodernism," which implies the global ubiquity of market culture, a new stage of capitalism in which culture and information become key terrains for struggle. A video performance by the Chicano group Culture Clash satirically stages the contradictory dynamics of the postmodern moment. It shows a radical Chicano and his Puerto Rican friend using Santeria to raise Che Guevara from the dead in order to solicit his political guidance. Miraculously reincarnated from the well-known poster, Che, in full guerilla regalia, asks for a briefing on world trends since his death, and is told of the decline of internationalism, the fall of communism, the capitalist cooptation of revolutionary symbols. Reading from a putative volume by James Michener, *The World since the Death of Che*, the Chicano (Chewy) gives Che the "good news" and the "bad news":

> CHE: What happened to Russia, the Communist Party?
> CHEWY: The party's over, Homes.
> CHE: Que malo! . . .
>
> CHE: Who won the Vietnam war?

CHEWY: The Vietnamese.
CHE: *(rifle upraised)* Que viva!
CHEWY: And then they moved to Orange County.

"Has the left accomplished anything?" asks the worried Che:

CHEWY: The left has made many strides since your death. Chile had a Marxist president.
CHE: *(rifle upraised)* Que bueno!
CHEWY: But the CIA killed him in 1973.
CHE: Que malo!
CHEWY: Grenada had a Marxist government.
CHE: La Victoria!
CHEWY: But now it's a Club Med.
CHE: Mierda!

Chewy then informs Che about life in the 1990s:

CHEWY: Comandante, these are crazy times. Communismo on the way down, capitalismo on the way up ...
CHE: ... Are you saying that the spirit of internationalism has died? That the philosophy, the ideology of los compañeros, Marx and Lenin, has faded? Then *(dramatically)* I died there in the mountains all in vain! *(Spreads his arms in a crucifix-like position.)*
CHEWY: *(in stereotypical Mexican accent)* Oooooy, co-mon-daaan-te, that's no reason to overact and spit on the fascist subscribers in the front row!

This transgenerational rendezvous illuminates the paradoxes of contemporary (Latino) radicalism in the dystopian 1990s. Now *las massas* have become *la raza* and the "Decade of the Hispanic" has turned out to be a "weekend sponsored by Coors." While Berkeley still hangs on as the "last communist stronghold in the quiché world," Chicanos (of whom Che had never heard) are now less interested in demonstrations than in *LA Law*. Cultural practices and political perspectives formerly proscribed or ignored by Marxist revolutionaries – Afro-diasporic religion, for example, and the sexual politics of lesbians of color – commingle with TV sports and sitcoms. Che is assassinated again, not in the mountains of Bolivia but in the urban jungles of California, while taking over a Domino's Pizza. His "domino" theory fails, and the Chicano radical returns to his TV, less concerned about the demise of his political hero than about the TV performance of his sports hero.

The gap between the deadly serious Che and the self-ironic Chewy is on one level the difference between the stereotypical *porteño* (Che speaks with an Argentinian accent and dances the tango) and the more tentative and self-mocking Chicano, but on another it reflects the divide between past revolutionaries fighting the imperialist monster from without and present-day radicals resisting within the belly of the by-now-postmodern beast. The historical abyss separating Che from the TV-addicted Chicano raises the question of oppositional strategies in the postmodern world. What would the Third World nationalist narrative entail for First World minoritarian struggles? Does resistance mean merely the reactive politics of protest? When a chant of *el Pueblo Unido* can be interrupted by a "49ers" cheer, and when revolutionary charisma is conjured up by Santeria, what does it mean to be politically radical? How can left politics be negotiated through the mass-mediated pleasures of the postmodern era? How does emancipatory cultural production traverse what Wahneema Lubiano calls the "slippery ground between reaching people and commodification?"[1] And finally, can popular culture be politically correct?[2]

POPULAR CULTURE AND POLITICAL CORRECTNESS

To begin to answer these questions we must clarify crucial terms, all of which come saturated with contested meanings. Within certain Marxist and Third Worldist discourses, "popular culture" evokes the culture of "the people" as a proleptic sign of inspirational cohesion and social transformation. "Mass-mediated culture," on the other hand, evokes capitalist consumerism and the machine of commodification for which "the people" are little more than an object of manipulation. While "mass culture" evokes Frankfurt School cultural pessimism and an atomized audience of narcoleptic monads, "popular culture" evokes cultural studies optimism and the insurgent energies of Bakhtin's carnival. But "popular" culture and "mass" culture are both far from being unitary sites. Do we refer "popular" to the point of consumption: to the box-office and Nielsen sense of culture consumed by the people? Or do we refer "popular" to its point of production, as culture produced by and for the people? The word "culture" itself, as Raymond Williams warned us, also embeds ideological minefields. Do we mean it in the honorific sense of monuments and masterpieces, or in the anthropological sense of how people live their lives? And do we equate "popular culture" with mass culture, or at least see the former as subsumed into the latter, or do we see popular culture in the Latin American and Middle Eastern sense as referring to non-hegemonic cultural production?

Mass and popular culture, in our view, are conceptually distinguishable but also mutually imbricated; it is the tense and lively dynamic between the two that defines the contemporary moment.[3] The appeal of the mass media derives, on a certain level, from their capacity to commodify the cultural memory or future hope of an egalitarian communitas. The media thus try to substitute the canned applause of simulacral festivities for the deep belly laugh of carnival. But popular culture no longer evokes agrarian nostalgia against modern machines, or sentimental replays of *bandera rossa* and *el pueblo unido*. Whatever its political orientation, whether created by people chanting "freedom" or consumed by couch-potato masses, popular culture is now fully enmeshed in transnational globalized technoculture. It makes sense, then, to see it as plural, as negotiating among diverse communities involved in a conflictual process of production and consumption.

340

The term "political correctness" (PC), meanwhile, buzzes with the polemics that have swirled around it. Do we mean it in the original leftist sense of a self-mocking apology for politically indefensible tastes, or in the right-wing sense of a broad-brush attack on a slew of ideological bogeymen? PC, in so far as it evokes a censorious attitude not toward behavior or language but rather toward cultural representations, is not a monolith; it operates in the name of diverse values. In the media, as we have seen, it can be text-centered, focussing on issues of realism and accuracy; or casting and institution-centered, concentrating on issues of chromatic self-representation; or character-centered, focussing on "positive images." Yet a correct left is not only a privileged left,[4] but also a losing left. We have tried to suggest the possibilities of a more dappled, antigrammatical beauty, an art that mobilizes social desires for community and alliance, that moves people, even physically, toward the passionately shared goal of a more egalitarian society. The relevant criterion then becomes: what actions and discourses push social life and representation in a more egalitarian direction along *all* the axes of oppression and liberation? The issue is not the correctness of the line or the identity of the speaker but the drift of the energy.

PC, as Michael Denning has pointed out, suggests a desire for a kind of standard etiquette or protocol to regulate relations between communities lacking sustained social connection, an impersonal code administering diplomacy between the disparate enclaves of a fractured left.[5] It is premised, then, on distance and a lack of intimacy. But in many cultures and communities, correctness and politeness are *themselves* markers of distance, while outrageous abuse and affectionate obscenity are signs of intimacy and camaraderie. While the laudatory goal behind PC is to stimulate respect and mutual answerability in a reciprocity that takes past oppressions into account, in practice it often degenerates into the sadomasochistic self-flagellations of guilty liberals and a competition for oppressed status among the subaltern – victimhood and "one-downs-personship" as cultural capital in a fluctuating identity stock market.

The PC phenomenon is more amorphous than the conceptual policing and cultural patrols associated with the term imply. Its meaning has shifted historically, from a reference to party-line internationalism and anticolonial solidarity to more localized modes of resistance coalescing around identity politics (race, gender, sexual orientation) and ecology. The real question, then, is less what constitutes the political correctness of specific products of mass-mediated popular culture than why we are asking this question now. The threshold encounter between Che and Chewy illuminates the dissonant modalities of popular culture confronted by contemporary cultural critics. Rather than taking cultural products and simply thumbing them up or down, cultural critique needs to see contemporary popular culture in a fissured, relational context, to ask who is producing and consuming what, for what purposes, in what situation, for whom, and by what means – always with an eye on the power constellations and the emancipatory projects at stake.

That the political correctness of popular culture is of concern at all indicates

341

crucial historical changes. PC language has its own momentum quite apart from hysterical right-wing denunciations. The general withdrawal from revolutionary euphoria and the shift into localized resistances have opened up a critical space in which the resistant instances already present in mass-mediated texts can be embraced. Even the concept of pleasure can be let out of the closet. This metamorphosis, associated with the rise of "cultural studies" as an academic discipline in the 1980s, has generated a proliferation of work that digs out "moments" of subversion. The popular culture/mass-media debate itself has acquired a less purist approach toward cultural products, one that reflects the entangled positioning of contemporary radicals themselves, who no longer boycott the system but rather work to various degrees within it.

These openings toward an uneasy working relation with establishment institutions, and the corollary adoption of a broader definition of subversion, including textual subversion, have brought with them the compensatory "closing" of PC politics. "PC" is in this sense more than the wailing of impotent radicals; it is a displaced attempt to control a leftist project in a context of postmodern multiplication of struggles, as well as in an intellectual environment where poststructuralist decenterings of the subject at times come close to a paralyzing dissolution of the "subjects of history." While the notion of revolution has been critiqued as a "totalization" that elides the contradictions of gender, race, and sexual orientation, the shift into a discourse of local resistances and multiple affiliations is ironically recentered through the PC "nudge." The hyperbolized PC often visible in the popular-culture debates is a partial symptom of the dissolution of a grand-macro project – revolution – into micro-struggles that on the one hand foster energy-wasting battles over turf but on the other open up the potential for emancipatory coalitions.

SELF-REPRESENTATION AND THE POLITICS OF IDENTITY

Today's PC is associated with a political atmosphere dominated by identity politics and issues of self-representation, issues fraught with personal and political tensions about who speaks, when, how, and in whose name. The politics of identity call for the "self-representation" of marginalized communities, for "speaking for oneself." And while poststructuralist feminist, gay/lesbian, and postcolonial theories have often rejected essentialist articulations of identity, and biologistic and transhistorical determinations of gender, race, and sexual orientation, they have at the same time supported "affirmative action" politics, implicitly premised on the very categories elsewhere rejected as essentialist,[6] leading to a paradoxical situation where theory deconstructs totalizing myths while activism nourishes them. Theory and practice, then, seem to pull in apparently opposite directions. The "constructionist" view has been instrumental in combating racism, sexism, and homophobia, but when stretched it seems to imply that no one can really speak for anyone (perhaps including even for oneself), or, conversely, that anyone can speak for anyone. Identity politics, on the other hand, suggest that people belong to recognizable social groups, and that delegated representatives can speak on their behalf. But is permission to represent a given community limited to card-carrying, epidermically suitable representatives of that community? Does the experience of oppression confer special jurisdiction over the right to speak about oppression? Could only an African-American have directed *Malcolm X*, as Spike Lee has argued? Should Paul Simon not have made "Graceland?" Would it have been better had Stevie Wonder made it? When does the fear of "appropriating" turn into a form of mental segregationism and the policing of racial borders, a refusal to recognize one's co-implication (Chandra Mohanty's term) with otherness? How can scholarly, curatorial, artistic, and pedagogical work "deal" with multiculturalism without defining it simplistically as a space where only Latinos would speak about Latinos, African-Americans about African-Americans and so forth,[7] with every group a prisoner of its own reified difference? To what extent can a member of one minoritarian group speak for another? How can we avoid the twin traps of "ethnic insiderism" (Paul Gilroy's phrase), in which only the Yoruba can speak for the Yoruba, and of facile appropriation in which any tourist who spends a week in Yorubaland can speak for the Yoruba? How do we not prolong the colonial legacy of misappropriation and insensitivity toward so-called minorities (including in the academic sense of the politics of prestige and citation) without silencing potential allies? Even talk of anti-essentialism and hybridity does not completely allay the anxiety concerning who speaks, about what, for whom, and to what end.[8]

Gayatri Spivak's celebrated question "Can the subaltern speak?," then, might be reversed to ask: "Can the non-subaltern speak?" To begin to answer, we may note that these anxieties about speaking are asymmetrical. Those who have been traditionally empowered to speak feel relativized simply by having to compete with other voices. Made aware of their own complicity in the silencing of others, they worry about losing a long taken-for-granted privilege. The disempowered or newly empowered, on the other hand, seek to affirm a precariously established right. "Disempowered" and "empowered," furthermore, are relational terms; people can occupy diverse positions, being empowered on one axis (say class), but not on another (say race and gender). Instead of a simple oppressor/oppressed dichotomy we find a wide spectrum of complex relationalities of domination, subordination, and collaboration. At the extreme ends of this continuum, certainly, are groups respectively empowered along all the axes and groups empowered along none of them. But even here there are no guarantees, for one's ancestral community does not necessarily dictate one's politics. Given the contradictory character of the socially situated psyche, individuals are traversed by dissonance and contradiction, existing within a constantly shifting cultural and psychic field in which the most varied discourses exist in evolving multivalenced relationships, constituting the subject, like the media, as the site of competing discourses and voices. Thus the individual may identify upward or downward; a person empowered on all the axes may identify with and, more importantly, affiliate with the disempowered, just as the disempowered may identify with the powerful and feel that the powerful represent their interests.[9] The self becomes a matrix of multiple discursive forms and identifications – which is in no way to deny realities of race, class, gender, nation but only to complicate and dialecticize them. That is why the recent academic fashion of identifying all speakers by their ethnicity – "Hopi artist . . ., white critic . . ." – is problematic. While on one level correcting the unilateral inscription of ethnicity and the surreptitious encoding of Whiteness as norm, on another level it does not go far enough because it encodes only the most superficial indices of ethnicity – color, origins – while eliding issues of ideology, discourse, identification, affiliation. Thus if one were really to pursue such labeling, one might produce interminable hybrid characterizations (such as "Chicano-identified feminist heterosexist, anarchist Anglo artist").

Given all this, should one expect an epidermically "incorrect" speaker whose community has not been directly marked by oppression, no matter how critical of the hegemonic system and how immersed in minoritarian perspectives and struggles, to dissolve into nothingness at the first appearance of a subaltern? (Such an idea might provoke a kind of subaltern envy.) No one should be ashamed of belonging to the identity categories into which they happen to have been born, but one is also accountable for one's active role or passive complicity in oppressive systems and discourses.[10] "It Ain't Where You're from," as Paul Gilroy, quoting the rap musician Rakim (W. Griffin) puts it; "It's Where You're at."[11] At the same time, it would be an act of bad faith to expect "minorities" to be color-blind toward the ethnically privileged, attentive only to their discourse and disregarding their affiliations. No one need perpetually apologize for the crimes of remote ancestors, but it would also be a crime to ignore benefits accrued over centuries, especially when those benefits "bleed into" contemporary situations of structured privilege. And although individuals may not for the most part fall neatly into oppressor/oppressed slots, there are also clear patterns of power and advantage. Discourses themselves are enunciated by persons bearing different community accents and intonations, ethnic codes of speech, body language, and self-presentation. To be conversant with the discourse of a community, and even to be able to defend it eloquently, is not commensurate with the "experiential authority" (in bell hooks' words) of those daily stigmatized by racial and colonial oppression.[12]

Antiracist and anti-Eurocentric pedagogy sometimes provokes a paralyzing guilt on the part of members of the dominant group. And while guilt is on one level a perfectly appropriate response to genocide, slavery, racism, and discrimination, it is on another level counter-productive. Guilt has a tendency to "curdle," to turn into a sour resentment toward those "provoking" the guilt. It leads to "compassion fatigue," premised on the self-flattering presumption of initial benevolence and the assumed luxury of a possible disengagement. Guilt can be narcissistic, leading to orgies of self-abuse. (Speak ill of me, goes the show-biz maxim, but speak of me.) We would therefore distinguish between a personalistic, neurotic guilt on the one hand, and a sense of collective and reciprocal answerability on the other. More productive than guilt, we would suggest, are anger, lucidity, self-awareness, outrage. For privileged participants in multi-cultural coalitions, the challenge is to be aware of social positioning, and to accomplish a "disaffiliation"[13] – an opting out of the country club of Euro-narcissism and privilege – that is neither a neurotic rejection of self nor an opportunistic appropriation of the other, and that is at the same time a reaffiliation. Relatively privileged people have many possible roles besides wallowing in self-regarding guilt: they can fight racism in their own milieu, work to restructure power, serve as spies and allies for marginalized people.

Speaking for oneself, by the same token, is not a simple act but a complex process, especially since women, minoritarian, and Third World peoples speak today in a theoretical context where the notion of a coherent subject identity, let alone a community identity, seems epistemologically suspect. (We find here the same process of poststructuralist dissolution that we found in relation to other categories such as "narrative" and "truth".) Third World feminist frustration with this (dis)articulation of the subject is eloquently summarized by Debra P. Amory:

> Doesn't it seem funny that at the very point when women and people of color are ready to sit down at the bargaining table with the white boys, that the table disappears? That is, suddenly there are no grounds for claims to truth and knowledge anymore and here we are, standing in the conference room making all sorts of claims to knowledge and truth but suddenly without a table upon which to put our papers and coffee cups, let alone to bang our fists.[14]

Amory denounces the arrogance with which metrocentric theory announces the demise of what others hold dear – nation, narrative, subjecthood.[15] In this sense, much of postmodern theory constitutes a sophisticated example of what Anwar Abdel Malek calls the "hegemonism of possessing minorities": its denial of the reality of marginalization is a luxury only those not marginalized can afford.[16] The center proclaims the end of its privileges, ironically, just when the periphery begins to lay claim to them. As Elizabeth Fox-Genovese writes:

> Surely it is no coincidence ... that the Western white male elite proclaimed the death of the subject at precisely the moment at which it might have had to share that status with the women and peoples of other races and classes who were beginning to challenge its supremacy.[17]

Thus thinkers from the center, blithely confident in national power and international projection, denounce non-metropolitan nationalisms as atavistic and passé. Metropolitan writers announce the "death of the author" just as "periph-eral" writers begin to win their Nobel Prizes. All these "divestitures" reflect a privilege available only to the already empowered, for the proclamation of the end of margins does not shortcircuit the mechanisms that effectively disappropriate peoples of their culture or nations of their power.

How, then, should the struggle to become subjects of history be articulated in an era of the "death of the subject"? Should Third Worldist notions of becoming "subjects" of history be dismissed as a pathetic lure and mystification? And does the decentering of identities mean that it is no longer possible to draw boundaries between privilege and disenfrachisement? At least provisionally, identities can be formulated as situated in geographical space and "riding" historical momentum. "Identities" are not fixed essences expressing a "natural" difference; they emerge from a fluid set of historically diverse experiences, within overlapping, poly-centric circles of identities. That identity and experience are mediated, narrated, constructed, caught up in the spiral of representation and intertextuality does not mean that all struggle has come to an end. Diana Fuss distinguishes between "deploying" or "activating" essentialism, and "falling into" or "lapsing into" essentialism. To insist that essentialism is always and everywhere reactionary is indirectly to buy into essentialism, to "act as if essentialism has an essence."[18] What Spivak calls "strategic essentialism" and what Hall refers to as "the fictional necessity of arbitrary closure," of "putting a period to the sentence," are crucial for any multicultural struggle that hopes to allow for communities of identifi-cation, even if those communities are multiple, discontinuous, and partly imaginary.

Attempting to avoid both falling into essentialist traps and being politically paralyzed by deconstructionist formulations, we would argue that it is precisely the overlapping of these circles that makes possible intercommunal coalitions based on historically shaped affinities. Rather than asking who can speak, then, we should ask about how to speak together, and more important, about how to move the plurilog forward. How might we interweave our voices, whether in chorus, in antiphony, in call and response, or in polyphony? What are the modes of collective speech? While it is dangerous to imagine that one can speak for others (that is, paradigmatically replace them), it is something else again to speak with or alongside others in the sense of forming alliances. In this sense we are less interested in identity as something one "has," than in identification as something one "does." The concept of crisscrossing identifications evokes the theoretical possibility and even the political necessity of sharing the critique of domination and the burden of representation. It even involves making representation less of a burden and more of a collective pleasure and responsibility. Coalitions are not conflict-free spaces, of course; alliances are often uneasy; dialog can be painful and polyphony can become cacaphony. But cultural polyphony would orchestrate a multifacted polylog among all those interested in restructuring power in more egalitarian ways. It would promote a mutually enriching proliferation of emancipatory discourses, transcending a mere coexistence of voices to foster a mutual adoption of other voices and accents, much as the members of a versatile jazz ensemble might exchange instruments and play the other's part. Thus strong voices can play off against one another; a flute becomes more of a flute when foiled by a guitar. In political terms this would imply the cultivation of what Charlotte Bunch has called "one-person coalitions"; that is, a situation in which not only Blacks but Whites would address issues of racism, where men as well as women would address issues of gender, where heterosexuals would speak against homophobia, the able-bodied about the disabled and so forth.[19] It would be an issue not of speaking "for" but rather "in relation," within intercommunal coalitions joined in shared struggles.

NEGOTIATING SPECTATORSHIP

Identity in the postmodern era is partially shaped by the media. By experiencing community with people never actually seen, consumers of electronic media can be affected by traditions to which they have no ancestral connection. Thus the media can normalize as well as exoticize other cultures, and can even fashion alternative communities and identities. Although film spectatorship can shape an imperial imaginary, as we saw earlier, there is nothing inherent in either celluloid or apparatus that makes spectatorship *necessarily* regressive. The strong "subject effects" produced by narrative cinema are not automatic or irresistible, nor can they be separated from the desire, experience, and knowledge of historically situated spectators, constituted outside the text and traversed by sets of power relations such as nation, race, class, gender, and sexuality. Media spectatorship forms a trialog between texts, readers, and communities existing in clear discursive and social relation to one another. It is thus a negotiable site of interaction and struggle, seen, for example, in the possibility of "aberrant" or resistant readings, as the consciousness or experience of a particular audience generates a counter-pressure to dominant representations.

In its quasi-exclusive focus on sexual as opposed to other kinds of difference, and in its privileging of the intrapsychic as opposed to the intersubjective and the discursive, film theory has often elided questions of racially and culturally inflected spectatorship. And although recent media theory has productively explored the sociologically differentiated modes of spectatorship, it has rarely done so through the grid of multiculturalism. The culturally variegated nature of spectatorship derives from the diverse locations in which films are received, from the temporal gaps of seeing films in different historical moments, and from the conflictual subject-positionings and community affiliations of the spectators themselves. The colonial situation in which colonized Africans and Asians went to European-owned theaters to watch European and Hollywood films, for example, encouraged a kind of spectatorial schizophrenia or ambivalence in the colonized subject, who might on the one hand internalize Europe as ideal ego and on the other resent (and often protest) offensive representations. Some of the major figures articulating anticolonial and postcolonial discourse symptomatically return in their writing to colonial spectatorship as a kind of primal scene. The "cinema stories of fabulous Hollywood," writes Kwame Nkrumah:

are loaded. One has only to listen to the cheers of an African audience as Hollywood's heroes slaughter red Indians or Asiatics to understand the effectiveness of this weapon. For in the developing continents, where the colonialist heritage has left a vast majority still illiterate, even the smallest child gets the message.[20]

The Martiniquian revolutionary theorist Frantz Fanon, the Ethiopian-American filmmaker Haile Gerima, and the Palestinian-American cultural critic Edward Said have all registered the impact of *Tarzan* on their impressionable young selves. Gerima recalls the "crisis of identity" provoked in an Ethiopian child applauding Johnny Weissmuller as he cleansed the "dark continent" of its inhabitants: "Whenever Africans sneaked up behind Tarzan, we would scream our heads off, trying to warn him that 'they' were coming."[21] In *Black Skin, White Masks*, Fanon too brings up *Tarzan* to point to a certain instability within cinematic identification:

> Attend showings of a Tarzan film in the Antilles and in Europe. In the Antilles, the young Negro identifies himself de facto with Tarzan against the Negroes. This is much more difficult for him in a European theatre, for the rest of the audience, which is white, automatically identifies him with the savages on the screen.[22]

Fanon's example points to the shifting, situational nature of colonized spectatorship: the colonial context of reception alters the very process of identification. The consciousness of the possible negative projections of other spectators triggers an anxious withdrawal from the film's programmed pleasures. The conventional self-denying identification with the White hero's gaze, the vicarious performance of a European selfhood, is shortcircuited through the awareness of being looked at in a certain way, as if one were being "screened" or "allegorized" by a colonial gaze within the movie theater. While feminist film theory has spoken of the "to-be-looked-at-ness" (Laura Mulvey's term) of female screen performance, Fanon's example calls attention to the "to-be-looked-at-ness" of spectators themselves, who become slaves, as Fanon puts it, of their own appearance: "Look, a Negro! . . . I am being dissected under white eyes. I am *fixed*."[23]

On the other hand, spectators can also return the gaze through critical comments or hostile looks. An active exchange of words and looks, whether in colonial Egypt or India, or in present-day Times Square movie theaters, turns public spectatorship into a discursive battle zone, where members of the audience actively negotiate "looking relations" (in Jane Gaines' phrase) between communities. In *Alexandria Why . . . ?* (1979) the movie theater literally becomes a space of ideological combat between an Australian soldier and Egyptian nationalists, while the Egyptian protagonist, lost in a Hollywood dream, watches a sequence (Helen Powell's "Red, White, and Blue" staged in front of battleship guns) that encodes its own nationalist agenda. Social contradiction, as such cases make clear, is alive not only in media texts but also within the audience. James Baldwin in the 1970s contrasted his own experience of watching Hollywood films, where almost no one looked like he did, with his attendance at Harlem performances of Orson Welles' all-Black *Macbeth* (1936), where Macbeth was "a nigger, just like me" and "where I saw the witches in church, every sunday."[24] Baldwin also recounts the racially differentiated reaction to *The Defiant Ones* (1958), a film that for him was rooted in a profound misunderstanding of the nature of racial hatred. Recounting the reaction of a Harlem audience, Baldwin wrote:

> It is this which black audiences resented about *The Defiant Ones*: that Sidney was in company far beneath him, and that the unmistakable truth of his performance was being placed at the mercy of a lie. Liberal white audiences applauded when Sidney, at the end of the film, jumped off the train in order not to abandon his white buddy. The Harlem audience was outraged, and yelled "Get back on the train, you fool! "[25]

Sidney jumps off the train, Baldwin concludes, in order to delude White people into thinking that they are not hated. The film's "liberal" gesture of inverting the imperial and masculinist rescue trope (here the Black man rescues the White), its proposal of a utopia of interracial male camaraderie, still maintains the Black in a subservient space. It fails to imagine the historical depths of a Black consciousness unimpressed by such "heroism." Audience reactions thus can divide along racial lines, as in cases where a historical film (such as *Ganga Zumba*, 1963) shows a Black rebel killing a slavedriver, where it is not uncommon for Black spectators to applaud, while Whites (even radical Whites) hold back. In such cases, the socially differentiated reactions of spectators become obvious. Applause, sighs, gasps, and other expressions of audience affectivity render palpable the visceral feelings that lurk behind abstract phrases like "spectatorial positioning."

Manthia Diawara argues that Black spectators cannot "buy into" the racism of a film like *Birth of a Nation* (1915). They disrupt the functioning of Griffith's film, rebelling against the "order" imposed by its narrative. For Black spectators, the character Gus, as a blackface incarnation of lust and violence, clearly cannot represent Blacks but only White prejudice toward Blacks.[26] bell hooks, meanwhile, speaks of the "oppositional gaze" of Black female spectators. That Blacks under slavery and segregation were punished for the very act of looking, hooks argues, generated a "traumatic relationship to the gaze." The existence of Black women within White supremacist culture, she continues, problematizes and complexifies the issue of female identity, representation, and spectatorship. Critical Black female spectators implicitly construct a theory of looking relations where "cinematic visual delight is the pleasure of interrogation."[27]

Neither text nor spectator is a static, preconstituted entity; spectators shape and are shaped by the cinematic experience within an endless dialogical process. Cinematic desire is not only intrapsychic; it is also social and ideological. In this sense, Stuart Hall's class- and ideology-based notion of "negotiated readings" might be extended to issues of race and ethnicity. We might thus speak of *racially* "dominant" readings, *racially* "negotiated" readings, and *racially* "resistant" readings.[28] We would add that a "resistant" reading on one axis (for example, class) might go hand in hand with a "dominant" reading on another axis (for instance, race), along all the permutations of social identity and affiliation. David Morley, complicating Hall's tripartite schema, argues for a discursive approach that would define spectatorship as the "moment when the discourses of the reader meet the discourse of the text."[29] Any comprehensive ethnography of spectatorship, we would argue, must distinguish multiple registers:

1. the spectator as fashioned by the text itself (through focalization, point-of-view conventions, narrative structuring, *mise-en-scène*);
2. the spectator as fashioned by the (diverse and evolving) technical apparatuses (movie theater, domestic VCR interactive technologies);
3. the spectator as fashioned by the institutional contexts of spectatorship (social ritual of movie-going, classroom analysis, cinémateque);
4. the spectator as constituted by ambient discourses and ideologies; and
5. the actual spectator as embodied, raced, gendered, and historically situated.

Text, apparatus, discourse, and history, in sum, are all in play and in motion. The analysis of spectatorship must therefore explore the tensions among the different levels, the diverse ways that text, apparatus, history, and discourse construct the spectator, and the ways that the spectator as subject/interlocutor shapes the encounter.

Nor is there a perfect match between alternative spectator and alternative text: here too there are tensions over class, gender, sexuality, ideology. Indeed, we would argue against the notion of any racially or culturally or even ideologically circumscribed essential spectator – *the* White spectator, *the* Black spectator, *the* Latino/a spectator, *the* resistant spectator. First, the categories themselves are sociologically imprecise, suppressing the heteroglossia characteristic of all communities. Is the "Latino/a spectator" a wealthy Cuban businessman, a Salvadorean refugee, or a Chicana domestic worker? Second, the categories repress the heteroglossia within spectators themselves. Spectators are involved in multiple identities (and identifications) having to do with gender, race, sexual preference, region, class, and age. Third, socially imposed epidermic identities do not strictly determine personal identifications and political allegiances. It is not only a question of what one is or where one is coming from, but also of what one desires to be, where one wants to go, and with whom one wants to go there. Within a complex *combinatoire* of spectatorial positions, members of an oppressed group might identify with the oppressing group (Native American children induced to root for the cowboys against the "Indians"; Africans identifying with Tarzan, Arabs with Indiana Jones), just as members of privileged groups might identify with the struggles of oppressed groups. Spectatorial positioning is relational: communities can identify with one another on the basis of a shared closeness or on the basis of a common antagonist. The spectator, in sum, inhabits a shifting realm of ramifying differences and contradictions.

Thus spectatorial positions are multiform, fissured, even schizophrenic. The view of spectatorial identification as culturally, discursively, and politically discontinuous suggests a series of gaps; the same person might be crossed by contradictory discourses and codes. The spectator comes to the cinema psychically disposed and historically positioned. The viewer of hegemonic cinema might consciously support one narrative or ideology, yet be subliminally seduced by the other fantasies proffered by the text. Thus we cannot posit a simple polarity between ceaselessly resistant, politically correct spectators on the one hand, and cultural dupes on the other. Even politically correct spectators are complex, contradictory, unevenly developed. On one level this "uneven development" has to do with the contradiction between the charismatic charm and power of the apparatus, of narrative, of performance, on the one hand, and the degree of the spectator's intellectual or political distance from that charm and power on the other. Bertolt Brecht's account of his reaction to a classic imperialist film, George Stevens' *Gunga Din* (1939), is revelatory in this regard:

> In the film *Gunga Din* ... I saw British occupation forces fighting a native population ... The Indians were primitive creatures, either comic or wicked: comic when loyal to the British, and wicked when hostile ... One of the Indians betrayed his compatriots to the British, sacrificed his life so that his fellow country-men should be defeated, and earned the audience's heart-felt applause. My heart was touched too: I felt like applauding and laughed in all the right places. Despite the fact that I knew all the time that there was something wrong, that the Indians are not primitive and uncultured people but have a magnificent age-old culture, and that this Gunga Din could also be seen ... as a traitor to his people.[30]

Even the theorist of distantiation, then, could not distance himself emotionally from the powerful myth-making machines of empire.

That the spectator is the scene of proliferating differences and contradictions does not mean that an opposite, agglutinative process of cross-racial identifications and alliance-imagining does not also take place. Amending Raymond Williams, we would argue for the existence, in movie theaters as well as outside of them, of *"analogical* structures of feeling,"* that is, for a structuring of filmic identification across social, political, and cultural situations, through strongly perceived or dimly felt affinities of social perception or historical experience. Spectatorship is not sociologically compartmentalized; diverse communities can resonate together. In a context where one's own community goes unrepresented, analogical identifications become a compensatory outlet. A member of a minoritarian group might look for him/herself on the screen, but, failing that, might identify with the next closest category, much as one transfers allegiance to another sports team after one's own team has been eliminated from the competition. Larry Peerce's *One Potato, Two Potato* (1964), a film about interracial marriage, offers a poignant narrative example of this analogical process. The Black husband in the film, enraged by a series of racially motivated slights, attends a western in a drive-in movie theater. Projecting his anger, he screams out his support for the Indians, whom he sees as his analogs in suffering, and his hatred for the cowboys. Reading "against the grain" of the western's colonialist discourse, he is thrown into the imaginative space of alliance.

Far from being essentially regressive and alienating, the space of media spectatorship is politically ambivalent. The theories of the apparatus and of dominant cinema first developed in the 1970s were rightly critiqued as being monolithic, even paranoid, failing to allow for progressive deployment of the apparatus, or for resistant texts, or for "aberrant readings." The very word "apparatus" evokes an overwhelming cinema-machine, imagined as a monstrous operation or *engrenage*, in which the spectator is denied even a Chaplinesque *Modern Times*-style subterfuge. But everyday spectatorship is more complex and overdetermined. Anyone who has been part of or witnessed a combative audience given to hisses, insults, ironic laughter, and satiric repartee is unlikely to portray spectators as the passive objects of an all-powerful apparatus. In communities given to impromptu verbal improvisation, the audience comments to the screen (and to each other), affirming the existence of the community itself.[31] At times a full-scale dialog breaks out; the film loses its diegetic hold as the spectacle is displaced from screen to audience. Paralinguistic expressions, such as hisses or applause, create a distantiating effect; audience participation modifies the experience of the film.

Furthermore, the same cinematic apparatus that creates blockbusters can also provide alternative films to audiences. While adventure films can nourish imperial narcissism, other films flatter the subjects of less retrograde ideologies. Nor are Hollywood films monolithically reactionary. Even hegemonic texts have to negotiate diverse community desires – Hollywood calls it "market research." As Fredric Jameson, Hans Magnus Enzensberger, Richard Dyer, and Jane Feuer have all argued, to explain the public's attraction to a text or medium one must look not only for the "ideological effect" that manipulates people into complicity with existing social relations, but also for the kernel of utopian fantasy reaching beyond these relations, whereby the medium constitutes itself as a projected fulfillment of what is desired and absent within the status quo. Symptomatically, even imperialist heroes like Indiana Jones and Rambo are posited not as the oppressors but as the liberators of subject peoples. Films can nourish dreams of upward mobility or encourage struggle for social transformation. Altered contexts, meanwhile (for example, alternative films screened in hospitals, union halls, and community centers), also generate altered readings. The confrontation is not simply between individual spectator and individual author/film – a formulation that recapitulates the individual-versus-society trope – but between and among diverse communities within diverse contexts viewing diverse films in diverse ways.

A scene in Spike Lee's *Malcolm X* (1992) illustrates this diversification within spectatorship. The scene takes place on a train, a chronotope evoking for Blacks both subordinate service roles and an opportunity for travel.[32] Three elderly Black waiters and young Malcolm Little, all dressed in "sandwichman" uniforms, are listening to the Joe Louis–Billy Conn fight on the radio. The waiters mimic Louis' moves, acting as if they were at the ringside themselves. When the White boss stops by, they quickly resume their customary subservient roles. Like Louis himself, they "play possum," waiting for an opening. They vicariously savor the physical victory of a Black man over a White man, enjoying a moment of symbolic revenge for the Black community. (Historically, such moments had more than a "safety valve" function; in the flush of jubilation after such victories, Blacks often became more assertive. After the 1910 Jack Johnson–Jim Jeffries fight, for example, racial fights broke out in every state in the south and in much of the north.) It is significant that the waiter-"viewers" in *Malcolm X* are not solitary observers; they react, move, gesticulate, in concert. We are far from the model of the passive voyeur, like the wheelchair-bound L.B. Jeffries at the beginning of *Rear Window* (1954), drinking in the spectacle with lonely eyes. We are also far from the social isolation that makes Jeffries-style voyeurism, and voyeuristic cinema, the "normal" condition. The atomization of consuming solitudes forecloses, as it were, all forms of non-consumerist participation. But even in *Rear Window*, the initially apathetic Jeff "comes alive" through what he sees and shares his experience with other "spectators" (Lisa and Stella) in a kind of ephemeral communitas of spectatorship. To this general phenomenon of spectatorial awakening and identification the Spike Lee film brings an added dimension of anger and social oppression. The Black waiters transform their working galley into a temporary liberated zone, an alternative space of discursive freedom where they can articulate their hidden hopes and transcripts. And by actively miming a (physical) struggle, they begin to move from individual, internal resistance to the socialization of resistant practices.

A purely cognitive approach to film reception allows little space for such differences. It does not explore how spectators can be made to identify with tales told against themselves. Privileging denotation over connotation, a cognitive model has little room for what one might call *racialized schemata* or *ethnically inflected cognition* – that is, the fact that the appearance of a White policeman in a film, for example, might trigger feelings of ease and protectedness in some "interpretive communities" and bitter memories and feelings of menace in others. Different reactions to films are symptomatic of different historical experiences and social desires. How do we account for orientalist films screened in the Middle East, where the spectator is simultaneously pleasured by luxuriant Western fantasies and irritated by a distorting specularity? And through what displacements of identification was *Rambo* sometimes received in anti-US Lebanon not as a product of American imperialism but as an exemplum of soldierly courage?

Perception itself is embedded in history. The same filmic images or sounds provoke distinct reverberations for different communities. For the Euro-American, shots of Mount Rushmore (in *North by Northwest*, for example) might evoke fond memories of patriotic father figures; for the Native American they might evoke feelings of dispossession and injustice. What does it mean, for a reservation-based Native American, to hear the lyrics from the theme song to *Oklahoma!* – "We know we belong to the land/and the land we belong to is grand"? A shot of a familial visit to church, a character crossing himself, or the sound of church bells to announce a marriage or a death, similarly, all address themselves to an interlocutor presumed to be, if not Christian, at least familiar with Christian culture. But images which for one spectator evoke a reassuring norm, for another might just as easily provoke a sense of exclusion, and in the specific case of Jewish culture even come burdened with overtones of oppression. (In Eastern European Jewish poetry, for example, church bells often signify danger.)[33] If communities respond differently to symbolically charged events like national holidays ("Thanksgiving" for Native Americans) and religious rituals (Christmas for Jews, Muslims, Buddhists), they also respond diversely to mediated representations. A multicultural audio-visual pedagogy, in this sense, would render explicit hidden assumptions about address, problematizing the text's "universal" norms.

Resistant readings, for their part, depend on a certain cultural or political preparation that "primes" the spectator to read critically. In this sense we would question the more euphoric claims of theorists, such as John Fiske, who see TV viewers as mischievously working out "subversive" readings based on their own popular memory. Fiske rightly rejects the "hypodermic-needle" view that sees TV viewers as passive drugged patients getting their nightly fix, reduced to "couch potatoes" and "cultural dupes." He suggests that minorities, for example, "see through" the racism of the dominant media. But while disempowered communities can decode dominant programming through a resistant perspective, they can do so only to the extent that their collective life and historical memory have provided an alternative framework of understanding. In the case of the Persian Gulf war, for example, the majority of American viewers, including many people of color, lacked any alternative grid to help them interpret events, specifically a view rooted in an understanding of the legacy of colonialism and its particular complexities in the Middle East. Primed by orientalist discourse and by the sheer inertia of the imperializing imaginary, they gave credence to whatever views the administration chose to present. Thus even some victims of racism within the US were persuaded by the media to buy into an imperialist narrative, made to forget the linked analogies between colonial/international and domestic/national forms of oppression.

In an increasingly transnational world, media spectatorship impacts complexly on national identity, communal belonging, and political affiliation. To a certain extent, a negotiation with diverse national desires is built into cinema, in that most film industries, especially those without strong domestic markets, have to take into account the possible reactions of other nationalities. At times, collective memories and desires encounter one another in a kind of transcultural rendezvous. Films, TV, and VCRs allow immigrants, refugees, and exiles to luxuriate in the landscapes of their lost homeland, to bathe in the sounds of their childhood language. The media and exile interact in what Hamid Naficy calls a space of "liminality" involving "ambivalences, resistances, slippages, dissimulations, doubling, and even subversions of the cultural codes of *both* the home and host societies."[34] Arabic, Hindi, and Farsi video tapes (unsubtitled) are sold in local

354

grocery stores in the US, reinforcing an imaginary community and sometimes suggesting a desire for insularity, a denial of "being here." Iranian exile TV programs such as *Parandush* nourish nostalgia for the homeland through maps, landscapes, and poetry, invoking the paradigm of exile as it has traditionally functioned within Iranian culture. The viewer's glance takes in TV programming from the standpoint of an interior crowded with ethnically coded souvenirs, carpets, flags, aromas, and handicrafts.[35] For Arab Jews (Mizrahim) in Israel, marginalized by official hostility toward the "orient," watching Egyptian, Turkish, Indian, and Iranian films releases a communal nostalgia, disallowed in the public sphere, for their Middle Eastern and North African countries of origin. Transnational spectatorship can also mold a space of future-oriented desire, nourishing the imaginary of "internal emigrés," actively crystallizing a sense of a viable "elsewhere," giving it a local habitation and a name, evoking a possible "happy end" in another nation. Given the inequitable distribution of power among nations and peoples, such movements are often one-directional, and the desire for an elsewhere is often frustrated by the law of green cards and border patrols. Cross-cultural spectatorship, in other words, is not simply a utopian exchange between communities, but a dialog deeply embedded in the asymmetries of power.

The ethnically hybrid character of most world metropolises, meanwhile, turns cinema-going into a revealing multicultural experience: screenings of "foreign" films for mixed audiences in New York or London or Paris, for example, can create a gap between cultural "insiders" who laugh at the jokes and recognize the references, and the "outsiders" who experience an abrupt dislocation. Not conversant with the culture or language in question, they are reminded of the limits of their own knowledge and indirectly of their own potential status as foreigners. Thus First Worlders in their own countries come to share an experience common to dislocated Third World and minoritarian audiences; the feeling that "this film was not made for us."

If spectatorship is on one level structured and determined, on another it is open and polymorphous. The cinematic experience has a ludic and adventurous side as well as an imperious one; it fashions a plural, "mutant" self, occupying a range of subject positions.[36] One is "doubled" by the cinematic apparatus, at once in the movie theater and with the camera/projector and the action on screen. And one is further dispersed through the multiplicity of perspectives provided by even the most conventional montage. Cinema's "polymorphous projection-identifications" (Edgar Morin's term) on a certain level transcend the determinations of local morality, social milieu, and ethnic affiliation.[37] Spectatorship can become a liminal space of dreams and self-fashioning. Through its psychic chameleonism, ordinary social positions, as in carnival, are temporarily bracketed.

Contemporary spectatorship and media pedagogy must also be considered in the light of changing audio-visual technologies. These technologies make it possible to bypass the search for a pro-filmic model in the world; one can give visible form to abstract ideas and improbable dreams. The image is no longer a copy but rather acquires its own life and dynamism within an interactive circuit. Electronic mail, meanwhile, makes it possible for a community of strangers to exchange texts, images, video sequences, thus enabling a new kind of international pedagogy. Computer graphics, interactive technologies, and "virtual reality" carry the "bracketing" of social positions to unprecedented lengths. Within cybernetic paraspace, the flesh-and-blood body lingers in the real world while computer technology projects the cybersubject into a terminal world of simulations. Such technologies expand the reality effect exponentially by switching the viewer from a passive to a more interactive position, so that the raced, gendered, sensorial body can be implanted, theoretically, with a constructed virtual gaze, becoming a launching site for identity travel. Might virtual reality or computer simulation be harnessed, one wonders, for the purposes of multicultural pedagogy, in order to communicate, for example, what it feels like to be an "illegal alien" pursued by the border police, or a civil rights demonstrator feeling the lash of police brutality in the early 1960s? Yet it would be naive to place exaggerated faith in these new technologies, for their expense makes them exploitable mainly by corporations and the military. As ever, the power largely resides with those who build, disseminate, and commercialize the systems.[38] All the technological sophistication in the world, furthermore, does not guarantee empathy or trigger political commitment. The historical inertia of race, class, and gender stratification is not so easily erased. Nor should an antiracist pedagogy rely on empathy alone. A person might "sample" oppression and conclude nothing more than: "C'est la vie" or "Thank God it wasn't me!" The point is not merely to communicate sensations but rather to advance structural understanding and engagement in change.

Within postmodern culture, the media not only set agendas and frame debates but also inflect desire, memory, fantasy. By controling popular memory, they can contain or stimulate popular dynamism. The challenge, then, is to develop a media practice and pedagogy by which subjectivities may be lived and analyzed as part of a transformative, emancipatory praxis.[39] The question of the correctness of texts, we have argued, is less important than the question of mobilizing desire in empowering directions. PC ignores desire, the intersubjective relations between people, and between text and audience. The question then becomes: given the libidinal economy of media reception, how do we crystallize individual and collective desire for emancipatory purposes? An anti-Eurocentric pedagogy, in this sense, must pay attention to what Guattari calls the "production machines" and "collective mutations" of subjectivity. As right-wing forces attempt to promote a superegoish "conservative reterritorialization" of subjectivity, those seeking change in an egalitarian direction must know how to crystallize individual and collective desire.

A radical pedagogy of the mass media would heighten awareness of all the cultural voices they relay. It would point both to the "off-screen" voices of hegemony and to those voices muffled or suppressed. The goal would be to discern the often distorted undertones of utopia in the mass media, while pointing to the structural obstacles that make utopia less realizable and at times even less imaginable. (By "utopia," again, we refer not to totalizing "progressive" metanarratives, but rather to "critical utopias" generated by the dissatisfactions of everyday life and aiming at a reimagining of the possible.)[40] Such an approach would combat the selectivity of hearing promoted by mass culture. It would recover the critical and utopian potential of mass-mediated texts, even when this potential is half-denied or repressed within the text itself. The issue is not one of imposing an interpretation, but rather of bringing out the text's muffled voices, rather like the work of a sound-studio mixer who reelaborates a recording to tease out the bass, or clarify the treble, or amplify the instrumentation.

We would also argue for a kind of pedagogic jujitsu, in the form of the classroom hijacking or *détournement* of media texts. With the help of a VCR, teachers and students can raid the mass-media archive. Eurocentric texts can be snapped out of their original context to be reread and even rewritten by teachers and students. Rather than remaining passive spectators, students can "decanon-ize" the classics, rescripting or reediting films according to alternative perspectives. Students might write a paper or produce a video imagining *Imitation of Life* (1934), for example, from the perspective of the Louise Beavers or the Freddi Washington character, rather than that of the White character played by Claudette Colbert. They might imagine a film from the perspective of an apparently minor subaltern character; for instance, the "squaw" in *The Searchers* (1956). Whole genres could be revised: the western could be rewritten from a Hopi or Cheyenne perspective, the Hollywood musical from an African-American perspective, the "Raj nostalgia" film from an anticolonialist perspective. Video-editing techniques – split frame, voice-over against image, freeze-frame, new voice-overs, changed music – could stage, on an audio-visual level, the clash of perspectives.

The techniques of Augusto Boal could also be adopted for a mixed-mode pedagogy. In *Theater of the Oppressed*, Boal distinguishes between three models of theater: an Aristotelian model where the spectator delegates power to the character, who thinks and acts in his or her place; a Brechtian model, where the spectator retains the power to think but relinquishes the power to act; and Boal's model, where the spectator exercises the power both to think and to act. The goal is to turn spectators into "spect-actors." The classroom can become a theatrical space, where students can interrupt film clips to act out their suggestions of how one of the characters might better have dealt with socially generated oppression. (It doesn't matter that the action is fictional, Boal stresses; what matters is that it is action.)[41]

Film and media pedagogy can also deploy the social heteroglossia of the classroom itself to call attention to the students' own ideological assumptions and affective investments. Rather than an act of self-indulgence, spectatorship might become an act of self-confrontation. One of Adrian Piper's videos, for example, informs the "White" spectator that he/she is in all probability part Black, since after 400 years "there are no genetically distinguishable white people in this country." And "Now that you know you're black," she asks provocatively, "aren't you eager to enjoy the benefits that blackness brings?" and "If racism isn't just 'our' problem, but equally 'yours,' how are you going to solve it?"[42] By coaxing Whites into a realization both of their hybridity and of their privilege, as Judith Wilson puts it, "Piper exposes the actual flimsiness of the categories that preserve white power."[43] At the same time, Piper undercuts the comfortably voyeuristic premises of the classic scene of "Whites" watching "Black" performance.

A media-based pedagogy could at the same time empower "minorities" and build on privileged students' minimal experience of otherization to help them imagine alternative subject positions and divergent social desires.[44] An experimental pedagogy could thus embody multicultural ideals in symbolic form. Since cultural identity, as Stuart Hall has pointed out, is a matter of "becoming" as well as "being," belonging to the future as well as the past,[45] multicultural media studies could provide a nurturing space for the playing out of the secret hopes of social life, a laboratory for the safe articulation of identity oppressions and utopias, a space of community fantasies and imagined alliances. Media pedagogy of this kind parallels the realm of "indigenous media." Faye Ginsburg speaks of "indigenous media" as a means for "reproducing and transforming cultural identity among people who have experienced massive political, geographic, and economic disruption."[46] Alex Juhasz, extending Ginsburg's conception to First World alternative media, sees AIDS activist video as a form of "indigenous media," where victims of "massive disruption" counter their oppression.[47] Speaking of the camcorder activism of the Kayapo in Brazil, Terence Turner stresses how their video work concentrates not on the retrieval of an idealized pre-contact past but on the processes of identity construction in the present. The Kayapo use video to communicate between villages, to record and thus perpetuate their own ceremonies and rituals, to record the official promises of Euro-Brazilian politicians (and thus hold them accountable), and to disseminate their cause around the world, in a "synergy between video media, Kayapo self-representation, and Kayapo ethnic self-consciousness."[48] Just as people all over the world have turned to cultural identity as a means of mobilizing the defense of their social, political, and economic interests, multicultural media activism and pedagogy might serve to protect threatened identities or even to create new identities, a catalyst not only for the public-sphere assertion of particular cultures but also for fostering the "collective human capacity for self-production."[49] We might see media in this sense as exercising a tribalizing power, as potentially increasing the aché (Yoruba for "power of realization") of an emergent community or coalition.

A radical, polycentric multiculturalism, we have tried to suggest, cannot simply be "nice," like a suburban barbecue to which a few token people of color are invited. Any substantive multiculturalism has to recognize the existential realities of pain, anger, and resentment, since the multiple cultures invoked by the term "multiculturalism" have not historically coexisted in relations of equality and mutual respect. It is therefore not merely a question of communicating across borders but of discerning the forces which generate the borders in the first place. Multiculturalism has to recognize not only difference but even bitter, irreconcilable difference. The Native American view of the land as a sacred and communal trust, as Vine Deloria points out, is simply not reconcilable with a view of land as alienable property.[50] The descendants of the slave ships and the descendants of the immigrant ships cannot look at the Washington Monument, or Ellis Island, through exactly the same viewfinder. But these historical gaps in perception do not preclude alliances, dialogical coalitions, intercommunal identifications and affinities. Multiculturalism and the critique of Eurocentrism, we have tried to show, are inseparable concepts; each becomes impoverished without the other. Multiculturalism without the critique of Eurocentrism runs the risk of being merely accretive – a shopping mall boutique summa of the world's cultures – while the critique of Eurocentrism without multiculturalism runs the risk of simply inverting existing hierarchies rather than profoundly rethinking and unsettling them.

Central to multiculturalism is the notion of *mutual and reciprocal relativization*, the idea that the diverse cultures placed in play should come to perceive the limitations of their own social and cultural perspective. Fanon speaks of the necessary decision to accept "the reciprocal relativism of different cultures, once colonialism is excluded."[51] Each group offers its own exotopy (according to Bakhtin), its own "excess seeing," hopefully coming not only to "see" other groups, but also, through a salutary estrangement, to see how it is itself seen. The point is not to embrace the other perspective completely but at least to recognize it, acknowledge it, take it into account, be ready to be transformed by it. By counterpointing cultural perspectives we practice what George Marcus and Michael Fischer call "defamiliarization by cross-cultural juxtaposition."[52]

At the same time, historical configurations of power and knowledge generate a clear asymmetry within this relativization. The powerful are not accustomed to being relativized; the world's institutions and representations are tailored to the measure of their narcissism. Thus a sudden relativization by a less flattering perspective is experienced as a shock, an outrage, giving rise to a hysterical discourse of besieged civility and reverse victimization. Disempowered groups, in contrast, are not only historically accustomed to being relativized, they often display a highly relativizing, even disdainful attitude toward the dominant cultures. Those who have known in their bodies the violence of the system are less inclined to be deluded by its idealizations and rationalizations. But what we have been calling polycentric multiculturalism is not a favor, something intended to make other people feel good about themselves; it also makes a cognitive, epistemological contribution. More than a response to a demographic challenge, it is a long-overdue gesture toward historical lucidity, a matter not of charity but of justice. An answer to the stale, flat, and unprofitable complacencies of monoculturalism, it is part of an indispensable reenvisioning of the global politics of culture.

NOTES

1 Wahneema Lubiano's intervention in "A Symposium on Popular Culture," *Social Text*, No. 36 (Fall 1993), p. 14.

2 This question is based on a three-part MLA panel (New York, 1992), organized by Andrew Ross, in which we participated; see *Social Text*, No. 36 (Fall 1993).

3 This view is of course shared with many others, such as Andrew Ross, Stanley Aronowitz, Juan Flores. See, for example, Juan Flores, "Reinstating Popular Culture: Responses to Christopher Lasch," *Social Text*, No. 12 (Fall 1985), pp. 113–23.

4 Jane Gaines makes this point in "Women and Representation: Can We Enjoy Alternative Pleasure?," in Patricia Erens, ed., *Issues in Feminist Film Criticism* (Bloomington: Indiana University Press, 1990).

5 See Michael Denning, "The Academic Left and the Rise of Cultural Studies," in *Radical History Review*, No. 54 (Fall 1992).

6 Among the concerns of the Society for Cinema Studies Taskforce on "Race," established in 1988, for example, was not only to engage in minoritarian discourse but also to promote "minority" participation in the discipline.

7 Trinh T. Minh-ha makes a similar point in "Outside In Inside Out," included in her *When the Moon Waxes Red: Representation, Gender and Cultural Politics* (New York: Routledge, 1991).

8 In art, it is not always clear who is speaking. Countless cases of artistic reception contradict the view of literary texts as transparently conveying the unmediated experience of an originary identity. Often, Henry Louis Gates Jr argues, readers and critics have been fooled, attributing "authenticity" where it was not, and damning "inauthenticity" where it did not exist. The bestseller *Education of Little Tree*, the "true" story of a Native American, orphaned at the age of ten, who learns Indian ways from his Cherokee grandparents, was hailed by critics as "deeply felt" and "one of the finest American autobiographies ever written." Yet in fact the book was written under a pseudonym by Asa Ear Carter, a Ku Klux Klan terrorist and anti-Semite who actually penned Governor George Wallace's notorious 1963 "Segregation Forever" speech. But *Little Tree* was just the latest in a long chain of ventriloqual racial narratives (for instance, *Confessions of Nat Turner*), racial impersonations, and ersatz slave narratives. Readers of Frank Yerby's historical romances or Samuel R. Delaney's science fictions, conversely, rarely imagine that both authors are Black.

9 The White male Jewish lawyer William Kunstler, for example, is affiliated with disenfranchised communities and strives to empower them, whereas it can be argued that the Black male judge Clarence Thomas often seems to work against the interests of his own people.

10 A number of feminist writers have argued against the idea that correct politics "flow" from identity. See Chandra Talpade Mohanty's Introduction to Chandra Talpade Mohanty, Ann Russo, and Lourdes Torres, eds, *Third World Women and the Politics of Feminism* (Bloomington: Indiana University Press, 1991). Kathryn Harris refers to the practice of fixing "a woman along a pre-determined hierarchy of oppressions in order to justify or contest a political opinion by reference to a speaker's identity." See her "New Alliances: Socialist Feminism in the Eighties," in *Feminist Review*, No. 31 (1989). See also Linda Briskin, "Identity Politics and the Hierarchy of Oppression," *Feminist Review*, No. 35 (Summer 1990).

11 Paul Gilroy uses Rakim's lyrics as the title of his essay on "The Dialectics of Diasporic Identification." See *Third Text*, No. 13 (Winter 1990–1).

12 Just as feminist theory has de-essentialized the gendered subject, postcolonial discourse has placed race in "quotation marks" to see it as a socially constructed trope. Nevertheless, "male bonding," as feminist theorists like Elaine Showalter and Jane Marcus point out, can at times exercise a cohesive force stronger than theoretical

enmities, a point that applies by extension to the possible "ethnic bonding" of Euro-American filmmakers and academicians. (The Old Boys' Network criticized in feminist and gay/lesbian writings is not less an ethnic/racial network.)

13 We are indebted to Caren Kaplan for the term "disaffiliation," and for her very precise formulation on these questions in her presentation on Whiteness at "Cross Talk: A Multicultural Feminist Symposium," organized by Ella Shohat and the New Museum of Contemporary Art's Education Department (directed by Susan Cahn), New York City (June 1993). A selection from the papers is edited for *Social Text* by Ella Shohat, forthcoming Spring 1996.

14 Debra P. Amory, "Watching the Table Disappear: Identity and Politics in Africa and the Academy," a paper given at the African Studies Association (1990).

15 Henry Louis Gates Jr, in a similar vein, argues that the Western male subject has long been constituted historically, while the subaltern have to explore and reclaim identity before critiquing it. Henry Louis Gates Jr, "Canon Formation and African-American Tradition," in Dominick LaCapra, ed., *The Bounds of Race* (Ithaca, NY: Cornell University Press, 1991).

16 Anwar Abdel Malek, "Orientalism in Crisis," *Diogenes*, No. 44 (Winter 1963), pp. 107–8.

17 Elizabeth Fox-Genovese, "The Claims of a Common Culture: Gender, Race, Class and the Canon," *Salmagundi*, No. 72 (Fall 1986), p. 121.

18 See Diana Fuss, *Essentially Speaking* (London: Routledge, 1989), pp. 20–1.

19 See Charlotte Bunch, "Making Common Cause: Diversity and Coalitions," in *Ikon*, No. 7 (Spring/Summer 1987).

20 Kwame Nkrumah, *Neo-Colonialism: The Last Stage of Imperialism* (London: Nelson, 1965), p. 246.

21 Haile Gerima, interview with Paul Willemen, *Framework*, Nos 7–8 (Spring 1978), p. 32.

22 Frantz Fanon, *Black Skin, White Masks* (New York: Grove Press, 1967), pp. 152–3.

23 Ibid., p. 112–16.

24 James Baldwin, *The Devil Finds Work* (New York: Dial Press, 1976), p. 34.

25 Ibid., p. 62.

26 See Manthia Diawara, "Le Spectateur Noir Face au Cinéma Dominant: Tours et Détours de l'Identification," *CinemAction*, No. 46 (1988).

27 bell hooks, *Black Looks: Race and Representation* (Boston: South End Press, 1992), pp. 115–31. Jane Gaines had pursued similar lines of questioning in her essay "White Privilege and Looking Relations: Race and Gender in Feminist Film Theory," in Erens, ed., *Issues in Feminist Film Criticism*. For more on the issue, see also E. Deidre Pribram, ed., *Female Spectators* (London: Verso, 1988).

28 Stuart Hall, "Encoding/decoding," in Hall *et al.*, eds, *Culture, Media, Language: Working Papers in Cultural Studies* (London: Methuen, 1979), p. 136.

29 See David Morley, *The "Nationwide Audience": Structure and Decoding* (London: BFI, 1980).

30 John Willet, ed., *Brecht on Theatre* (London: Hill and Wang, 1964), p. 151.

31 Christian Metz makes a similar point about audiences in provincial Spain. See Metz, *The Imaginary Signifier* (Bloomington: Indiana University Press, 1982).

32 Paul Gilroy elaborates on the chronotope of the train in *The Black Atlantic* (Harvard: Harvard University Press, 1993), p. 33.

33 In *Singin' in the Rain* (1952), to take a counter-example, Gene Kelly and Donald O'Connor, as they sing "Moses," wrap themselves with lined curtains reminiscent of Jewish prayer shawls (*talith*), a visual allusion that Jewish spectators are more likely to appreciate.

34 Hamid Naficy, *The Making of Exile Cultures: Iranian Television in Los Angeles*

(Minneapolis: University of Minnesota, 1993), p. xvi.

35 Ibid., p. 106.

36 See Jean-Louis Schefer, *L'Homme Ordinaire du Cinéma* (Paris: Gallimard, 1980).

37 See Edgar Morin, *Le Cinéma ou L'Homme Imaginaire* (Paris: Gonthier, 1958).

38 Anne Friedberg, *Window Shopping: Cinema and the Postmodern Condition* (Berkeley: University of California Press, 1992).

39 See Rhonda Hammer and Peter McLaren, "The Spectacularization of Subjectivity: Media Knowledges, Global Citizenry and the New World Order," *Polygraph*, No. 5 (1992).

40 Tom Moylan, *Demand the Impossible: Science Fiction and the Utopian Imagination* (New York: Methuen, 1986), p. 213.

41 Augusto Boal, *Theatre of the Oppressed* (New York: Theatre Communications Group, 1979).

42 See Maurice Berger, "The Critique of Pure Racism: An Interview with Adrian Piper," *Afterimage* (October 1990), p. 5.

43 See Judith Wilson's brilliant discussion of Piper's work: "In Memory of the News and of Our Selves: The Art of Adrian Piper," *Third Text*, Nos 16/17 (Autumn/Winter 1991). The University of Washington Press will be publishing a book on Piper, featuring essays on her work along with a set of audio and videotape works.

44 Charles Ramirez Berg makes this suggestion in his extremely useful essay "Analyzing Latino Stereotypes," in Lester Friedman and Diane Carson, eds, *Multicultural Media in the Classroom* (Urbana: University of Illinois Press, 1995).

45 Stuart Hall, "Cultural Identity and Cinematic Representation," *Framework*, No. 36 (1989).

46 Faye Ginsburg, "Indigenous Media: Faustian Contract or Global Village?," *Cultural Anthropology*, Vol. 6, No. 1, p. 94.

47 Alexandra Juhasz, "Re-Mediating Aids: The Politics of Community Produced Video," Ph.D. dissertation, New York University (1991); forthcoming from Duke University Press.

48 Terence Turner, "Defiant Images: The Kayapo Appropriation of Video," Forman Lecture, RAI Festival of Film and Video, Manchester 1992.

49 Terence Turner, "What is Anthropology that Multiculturalists Should Be Mindful of it?" Paper presented at the American Anthropological Association, San Francisco, 1992.

50 Interview with Vine Deloria in the film *Savagery and the American Indian* (1989).

51 See Frantz Fanon, *Toward the African Revolution* (New York: Monthly Review Press, 1967), p. 447.

52 George Marcus and Michael M.J. Fischer, *Anthropology as Cultural Critique: An Experimental Moment in the Human Sciences* (Chicago: University of Chicago Press, 1986), p. 157.

SELECT BIBLIOGRAPHY

What follows is a recommended bibliography of books centered on issues of Eurocentrism and multiculturalism. For reasons of space, we have not included every title cited in the text. For these, consult the notes at the end of each chapter.

Abrash, Barbara and Catherine Egan, eds. *Mediating History: The MAP Guide to Independent Video*. New York: New York University Press, 1992.

Abu-Lughod, Janet L. *Before European Hegemony: The World System A.D. 1250–1350*. New York: Oxford University Press, 1989.

Abu-Lughod, Lila. *Veiled Sentiments: Honor and Poetry in a Bedouin Society*. Berkeley: University of California Press, 1986.

———. *Writing Women's Worlds: Bedouin Stories*. Berkeley: University of California Press, 1993.

Ahmad, Aijaz. *In Theory: Classes, Nations, Literatures*. London: Verso, 1992.

Ahmed, Leila. *Women and Gender in Islam: Historical Roots of a Modern Debate*. New Haven, Conn.: Yale University Press, 1992.

Alcalay, Ammiel. *After Jews and Arabs: Remaking Levantine Culture*. Minneapolis: University of Minnesota Press, 1993.

Alea, Tomas Gutierrez. *Dialectica del Espectador*. La Habana: Ediciones Union, 1982.

———. *Memories of Underdevelopment*. New Brunswick, NJ: Rutgers University Press, 1990.

Allen, Paula Gunn. *The Sacred Hoop*. Boston: Beacon Press, 1986.

———, ed. *Spider Woman's Granddaughters: Traditional Tales and Contemporary Writing by Native American Women*. Boston: Beacon Press, 1989.

Alloula, Malek. *The Colonial Harem*, trans. Myrna Godzich and Wlad Godzich. Minneapolis: University of Minnesota Press, 1986.

Alvarez, Santiago, *et al. Cine y Revolucion en Cuba*. Barcelona: Editora Fontamara, 1975.

Amin, Samir. *Delinking: Towards a Polycentric World*, trans. Michael Wolfers. London: Zed, 1985.

——— *Eurocentrism*. New York: Monthly Review Press, 1989.

Anderson, Benedict. *Imagined Communities: Reflections on the Origins and Spread of Nationalism*. London: Verso, 1983.

Anzaldúa, Gloria. *Borderlands: La Frontera*. San Francisco: Spinsters/Aunt Lute Foundation, 1987.

———, ed. *Making Face, Making Soul, Haciendo Caras*. San Francisco: Aunt Lute Foundation, 1990.

Armes, Roy. *Third World Filmmaking and the West*. Berkeley: University of California Press, 1987.

Aronowitz, Stanley. *Roll over Beethoven: The Return of Cultural Strife.* Hanover and London: Weleyan, 1993.

Asad, Talal, ed. *Anthropology and the Colonial Encounter.* London: Ithaca Press, 1975.

Asante, Molefi Kete. *The Afrocentric Idea.* Philadelphia: Temple University Press, 1987.

———. *Afrocentricity.* Trenton, NJ: Africa World Press, 1988.

———, and Kariamu Welsh Asante. *African Culture: The Rhythms of Unity.* Trenton, NJ: Africa World Press, 1990.

Axtell, James. *The European and the Indian: Essays in the Ethnohistory of Colonial North America.* Oxford: Oxford University Press, 1982.

Ayala Blanco, Jorge. *La Aventura del Cine Mexicano.* Mexico City: Ediciones Era, 1968.

———. *La Busqueda del Cine Mexicano: 1968–1972.* Mexico City: UNAM, 1974.

Bachy, Victor. *Le Cinéma de Tunisie.* Tunis: Société Tunisienne de Diffusion, 1976.

———. *Le Cinéma au Mali.* Brussels: OCIC, 1982.

———. *Le Cinéma en Côte d'Ivoire.* Brussels: OCIC, 1982.

———. *La Haute Volta et le Cinéma.* Brussels : OCIC, 1982.

Baker Jr, Houston A. *The Journey Back: Issues in Black Literature and Criticism.* Chicago: University of Chicago Press, 1980.

———. *Blues, Ideology and Afro-American Literature.* Chicago: University of Chicago Press, 1984.

———. *Modernism and the Harlem Renaissance.* Chicago: University of Chicago Press, 1984.

———. *Long Black Song.* Charlottesville: University Press of Virginia, 1990.

———. *Black Studies, Rap and the Academy.* Chicago: University of Chicago Press, 1993.

Baldwin, James. *The Devil Finds Work: An Essay.* New York: Dial Press, 1976.

Balibar, Etienne and Immanuel Wallerstein. *Race, Nation and Class: Ambiguous Identities.* London: Verso, 1991.

Balogun, Françoise. *Le Cinéma au Nigeria.* Brussels/Paris: OCIC/L'Harmattan, 1984.

Banerjee, Shampa, ed. *New Indian Cinema.* Delhi: Vikas, 1977.

Barker, Francis, Peter Hulme, Margaret Iversen, and Diana Loxley, eds. *Europe and Its Others.* Vols 1 and 2. Colchester: University of Essex, 1984.

Barnouw, Erik, and S. Krishnaswamy. *Indian Film.* New York: Columbia University Press, 1963; 2nd edn: New York: Oxford University Press, 1980.

Bataille, Gretchen M., and Kathleen Mullen Sands. *American Indian Women: Telling Their Lives.* Lincoln: University of Nebraska Press, 1984.

Benitez-Rojo, Antonio. *The Repeating Island: The Caribbean and the Postmodern Perspective,* trans. James E. Maraniss. Durham, NC: Duke University Press, 1992.

Berg, Charles Ramirez. *Cinema of Solitude: A Critical Study of Mexican Film, 1967–1983.* Austin: University of Texas Press, 1992.

Berger, Maurice, *et al. Race and Representation.* Hunter College of the City University of New York. Exhibition January 26–March 6, 1987.

Bergeron, Regis. *Le Cinéma Chinois,* Vol. 1: *1905–1949.* Lausanne: Alfred Eibel, 1977.

———. *Le Cinéma Chinois,* Vol. 2: *1949–1983.* 3 Vols. Paris: L'Harmattan, 1983.

Berkhofer, Robert F. *The White Man's Indian.* New York: Vintage, 1979.

Bernal, Martin. *Black Athena.* New Brunswick, NJ: Rutgers University Press, 1987. Vols I and II.

Berrah, Mouny, *et al. Cinémas du Maghreb.* Paris: *CinemAction,* No. 14/Papyrus Editions, 1981.

Berry, Chris, ed. *Perspectives on Chinese Cinema.* London: BFI, 1991.

Bestman, Martin T. *Sembene Ousmane et l'Esthétique du Roman Négro-africain.* Sherbrooke, Quebec: Editions Naarman, 1981.

Bhabha, Homi K., ed. *Nation and Narration.* London: Routledge, 1990.

Binet, Jacques, Ferid Boughedir, and Victor Bachy, eds. *Cinémas Noirs d'Afrique.* Paris:

CinemAction, No. 26/L'Harmattan, 1983.

"Black British Cinema." ICA Documents No. 7. London: ICA, 1988.

"Black Film Issue." Smith, Valery, Camille Billops, and Ada Griffin, eds. *Black American Literature Forum*, Vol. 25, No. 2 (Summer 1991).

Blaut, J.M. *The Colonizer's Model of the World: Geographical Diffusionism and Eurocentric History*. New York and London: Guilford Press, 1993.

Bloom, Lisa. *Gender on Ice*. Minneapolis: University of Minnesota Press, 1993.

Boal, Augusto. *Theatre of the Oppressed*, trans. Charles A. and Mari-Odilia Leal McBride. New York: Theatre Communications Group, 1979.

Bodley, John H. *Victims of Progress*. Mountain View, Calif.: Mayfield, 1990.

Bogle, Donald. *Blacks in American Films and Television: An Illustrated Encyclopedia*. New York: Simon and Schuster, 1988.

———. *Toms, Coons, Mulattoes, Mammies, and Bucks: An Interpretive History of Blacks in American Films*. New York: Continuum, 1989.

Bosi, Alfredo. *Dialectica da Colonização*. São Paulo: Companhia das Letras, 1992.

Boskin, Joseph. *Sambo: The Rise and Demise of an American Jester*. New York: Oxford University Press, 1986.

Bosseno, Christian, ed. *Youssef Chahine l'Alexandrin*. Paris: *CinemAction*, No. 33/Cerf, 1985.

Boujedra, Rachid. *Naissance du Cinéma Algérien*. Paris: François Maspero, 1971.

Boulanger, Pierre. *Le Cinéma Colonial*. Paris: Editions Seghers, 1975.

Bourdieu, Pierre, ed. *La Misère du Monde*. Paris: Editions du Seuil, 1993.

Bowser, Pearl, ed. *In Color: Sixty Years of Images of Minority Women in the Media: 1921–1981*. New York: Third World Newsreel, 1983.

———, and Renee Tajima. *Journey across Three Continents*. New York: Third World Newsreel, 1985.

Brantlinger, Patrick. *Rule of Darkness: British Literature and Imperialism, 1830–1914*. Ithaca, NY: Cornell University Press, 1988.

———. *Crusoe's Footprints*. New York: Routledge, 1990.

Bridges, George and Rosalind Brundt, eds. *Silver Linings: Some Strategies for the Eighties*. London: Lawrence and Wishart, 1981.

Bristow, Joseph. *Empire Boys: Adventures in a Man's World*. London: HarperCollins, 1991.

Brossard, Jean-Pierre. *L'Algérie vue par son Cinéma*. Documentation for the International Film Festival, Locarno, 1981.

Brotherston, Gordon. *Image of the New World: The American Continent Portrayed in Native Texts*. London: Thames and Hudson, 1979.

———. *Book of the Fourth World: Reading the Native Americas through Their Literature*. Cambridge: Cambridge University Press, 1992.

Bruner, Charlotte H., ed. *Unwinding Threads: Writing by Women of Africa*. London: Heinemann, 1983.

Burger, Julian. *The Gaia Atlas of First Peoples*. New York: Doubleday, 1990.

Burton, Julianne, ed. *Cinema and Social Change in Latin America: Conversations with Filmmakers*. Austin: University of Texas, 1986.

———, ed. *The Social Documentary in Latin America*. Pittsburg, Penn.: University of Pittsburg Press, 1990.

Buscombe, Edward, ed. *The BFI Companion to the Western*. New York: Da Capo, 1988.

Cabral, Amilcar. *National Liberation and Culture*. Syracuse, NY: Syracuse University Program of Eastern African Studies, 1970.

Calder, Angus, *et al. African Fiction and Film: Three Short Case Studies*. Milton Keynes: Open University Press, 1983.

Callaway, Helen. *Gender, Culture and Empire*. Chicago: University of Illinois Press, 1987.

Carby, Hazel. *Reconstructing Womanhood: The Emergence of the Afro American Woman Novelist*. New York: Oxford University Press, 1987.

Carew, Jan. *Fulcrums of Change*. Trenton, NJ: Africa World Press, 1988.

Center for Contemporary Cultural Studies, ed. *The Empire Strikes Back*. London: Routledge and Kegan Paul, 1983.

Césaire, Aimé. *Discourse on Colonialism*. New York: Monthly Review Press, 1972.

Chakravarty, Sumita. *National Identity in Indian Popular Cinema*. Austin: University of Texas Press, 1993.

Chaliand, Gerard. *Revolution in the Third World*. Harmondsworth: Penguin, 1978.

Cham, Mbye B. *Ex-Iles: Caribbean Cinema*. Trenton, NJ: Africa World Press, 1991.

────── and Claire Andrade-Watkins, eds. *Blackframes: Critical Perspectives on Black Independent Cinema*. Cambridge, Mass.: MIT Press, 1988.

Chanan, Michael, ed. *Chilean Cinema*. London: BFI, 1976.

──────. *Santiago Alvarez*. London: BFI, 1980.

──────. *Twenty-five Years of the New Latin American Cinema*. London: BFI/ Channel Four Television, 1983.

──────. *The Cuban Image*. London: BFI, 1985.

Chatterjee, Partha. *Nationalist Thought and the Colonial World*. Minneapolis: University of Minnesota Press, 1993.

Chaudhuri, Nupur, and Margaret Strobel, eds. *Western Women and Imperialism: Complicity and Resistance*. Bloomington: Indiana University Press, 1992.

Cheyfitz, Eric. *The Poetics of Imperialism*. New York: Oxford University Press, 1991.

Chinweizu. *Voices from Twentieth Century Africa*. Boston: Faber and Faber, 1988.

Chomsky, Noam. *Year 501: The Conquest Continues*. Boston: South End Press, 1993.

Chow, Rey. *Writing Diaspora: Tactics of Intervention in Contemporary Cultural Studies*. Bloomington: Indiana University Press, 1993.

Churchill, Ward, ed. *Marxism and Native Americans*. Boston: South End Press, 1983.

──────. *Fantasies of the Master Race*, ed. M. Annette Jaimes. Monroe, Maine: Common Courage Press, 1992.

──────. *Struggle for the Land*. Monroe, Maine: Common Courage Press, 1993.

Clifford, James. *The Predicament of Culture*. Cambridge, Mass.: Harvard University Press, 1988.

──────, and George Marcus, eds. *Writing Culture: The Poetics and Politics of Ethnography*. Berkeley: University of California Press, 1986.

Cluny, Claude-Michel. *Dictionnaire des Nouveaux Cinémas Arabes*. Paris: Sinbad, 1978.

Contreras Torres, Miguel. *El Libro Negro del Cine Mexicano*. Mexico City: Editora Hispano-Continental Films, 1960.

Cortes, Carlos E., and Leon G. Campbell, eds. *Race and Ethnicity in the History of the Americas: A Filmic Approach*. Riverside, Calif.: University of California, Latin American Studies Program Film Series, No. 4, 1979.

Crawford, Ian Peter and David Turton. *Film as Ethnography*. Manchester: Manchester University Press, 1992.

Cripps, Thomas. *Slow Fade to Black*. New York: Oxford University Press, 1977.

──────. *Black Film as Genre*. Bloomington: Indiana University Press, 1979.

──────. *Making Movies Black: The Hollywood Message Movie from World War II to the Civil Rights Era*. New York: Oxford University Press, 1993.

Custen, George. *Bio/Pics*. New Brunswick, NJ: Rutgers University Press, 1992.

Cyr, Helen W. *A Filmography of the Third World*. Metuchen, NJ: Scarecrow Press, 1986.

Dangerous Memories: Invasion and Resistance Since 1492. Chicago: Chicago Religious Task Force on Central America, 1991.

Daniels, Thérèse, and Jane Gerson, eds. *The Color Black*. London: BFI, 1989.

Das Gupta, Chidananda. *Talking about Films*. New Delhi: Orient Longman, 1981.

Davies, Miranda, ed. *Third World–Second Sex.* London: Zed, 1983.

Davis, Angela. *Women, Race, and Class.* New York: Vintage, 1983.

Davis, Charles D. *Black is the Color of the Cosmos*, ed. Henry Louis Gates Jr. Washington, DC: Howard University Press, 1989.

Deloria, Vine, Jr. *Custer Died for Your Sins.* New York: Avon Books, 1969.

Dent, Gina, ed. for a project by Michele Wallace, *Black Popular Culture.* Seattle, Wash.: Bay Press, 1992.

Diawara, Manthia. *African Cinema.* Bloomington: Indiana University Press, 1992.

——, ed. *Black American Cinema: Aesthetics and Spectatorship.* London: Routledge, 1993.

van Dijk, Teun A. *Racism and the Press.* New York: Routledge, 1991.

Dorfman, Ariel. *The Empire's Old Clothes: What the Lone Ranger, Babar, and Other Innocent Heroes Do to Our Minds.* New York: Pantheon Books, 1983.

——, and Armand Mattelart. *How to Read Donald Duck.* New York: International General, 1975.

Downing, John D.H., ed. *Film and Politics in the Third World.* New York: Autonomedia, 1987.

Drinnon, Richard. *Facing West: The Metaphysics of Indian-Hating and Empire-Building.* New York: Schocken, 1980.

DuBois, Ellen Carol, and Vicki L. Ruiz, eds. *Unequal Sisters: A Multi-Cultural Reader in U.S. Women's History.* New York: Routledge, 1990.

Enloe, Cynthia. *Bananas, Beaches, and Bases: Making Feminist Sense of International Politics.* Berkeley: University of California Press, 1989.

Essed, Philomena. *Understanding Everyday Racism.* London: Sage, 1991.

Etienne, Mona and Eleanor Leacock, eds. *Woman and Colonization: Anthropological Perspectives.* New York: Praeger, 1980.

Fabian, Johannes. *Time and the Other: How Anthropology Makes Its Object.* New York: Columbia University Press, 1983.

Fanon, Frantz. *The Wretched of the Earth.* New York: Grove Press, 1964.

——. *A Dying Colonialism.* New York: Grove Press, 1967.

——. *Black Skin, White Masks.* New York: Grove Press, 1967.

——. *Toward the African Revolution.* New York: Monthly Review Press, 1967.

Farid, Samir. *Arab Cinema Guide.* Cairo: Arab Cinema Guide, 1979.

Ferguson, Russell, Martha Gever, Trihn T. Minh-ha, and Cornel West, eds. *Out There: Marginalization and Contemporary Cultures.* Cambridge, Mass.: MIT Press, 1990.

Fischer, Lucy, ed. *Imitation of Life* (Script and Essays). New Brunswick, NJ: Rutgers, 1992.

Fisher, Dexter. *The Third Woman: Minority Women Writers of the United States.* Boston: Houghton-Mifflin, 1980.

Fitz, Earl E. *Redicovering the New World: Inter-American Literature in a Comparative Context.* Iowa City: University of Iowa Press, 1991.

Flores, Juan. *Divided Borders: Essays on Puerto Rican Identity.* Houston, Tex.: Arte Publico, 1993.

Forbes, Jack. *Columbus and Other Cannibals.* New York: Autonomedia, 1992.

Fowler, Carolyn. *Black Arts and Black Aesthetics: A Bibliography.* Atlanta, Ga.: Atlanta University Press, 1976.

Franco, Jean. *Plotting Women: Gender and Representation in Mexico.* New York: Columbia University Press, 1989.

Frank, Andre Gunder. *Capitalism and Underdevelopment in Latin America.* Harmondsworth: Penguin, 1971.

Fregoso, Rosa Linda. *The Bronze Screen: Chicana and Chicano Film Culture.* Minneapolis: University of Minnesota Press, 1993.

Freire, Paulo. *Pedagogy of the Oppressed*. New York: Continuum, 1982.

Friar, Ralph, and Natasha Friar. *The Only Good Indian: The Hollywood Gospel*. New York: Drama Book Specialists, 1972.

Friedman, Lester, ed. *Unspeakable Images: Ethnicity and the American Cinema*. Urbana, Ill: University of Illinois Press, 1991.

Fusco, Coco. *Reviewing Histories: Selections from New Latin American Cinema*. Buffalo, NY: Hallwalls, 1987.

———. *Young British and Black*. Buffalo, NY: Hallwalls, 1988.

Gabriel, Teshome H. *Third Cinema in the Third World: The Aesthetics of Liberation*. Ann Arbor, Mich.: UMI Research Press, 1982.

Gaffary, Farrokh. *Le Cinéma en Iran*. Teheran: High Council of Culture and Art, Center for Research and Cultural Coordination, 1973.

Galeano, Eduard. *The Open Veins of Latin America*. New York: Monthly Review Press, 1973.

Garaudy, Roger. *O Ocidente é um Acidente*. Rio de Janeiro: Forense-Universitaria, 1976.

Garcia Riera, Emilio. *El Cine Mexicano*. Mexico City: Ediciones Era, 1963.

———. *Historia Documental del Cine Mexicano*. 8 Vols. Mexico City: Ediciones Era, 1969–74.

Gardies, André. *Cinéma d'Afrique Noire Francophone*. Paris: L'Harmattan, 1989.

Gates Jr, Henry Louis *Black Literature and Literary Theory*. London and New York: Methuen, 1984.

———, ed. *"Race," Writing, and Difference*. Chicago: University of Chicago Press, 1986.

———. *Figures in Black*. New York: Oxford University Press, 1987.

———. *The Signifying Monkey*. New York: Oxford University Press, 1988.

Gaur, Madan. *The Other Side of the Coin: An Intimate Study of Indian Film Industry*. Bombay: Trimurti Prakashan, 1973.

Gayle Jr, Addison. *The Black Aesthetic*. New York: Doubleday, 1972.

Genovese, Eugene D. *From Rebellion to Revolution*. New York: Vintage Books, 1981.

———. *In Red and Black: Marxian Explorations in Southern and Afro-American History*. Knoxvill: University of Tennessee Press, 1984.

Getino, Octavio. *Cine y Dependencia: El Cine en la Argentina*. Buenos Aires/Lima: Cine-Liberacion 1976–8.

Ghareeb, Edmund, ed. *Split Vision: The Portrayal of Arabs in the American Media*. Washington, DC: American-Arab Affairs Council, 1983.

Gilman, Sander L. *Difference and Pathology*. Ithaca, NY: Cornell University Press, 1985.

———. *The Jew's Body*. New York: Routledge, 1991.

Gilroy, Paul. *There Ain't No Black in the Union Jack*. London: Hutchinson, 1987.

———. *The Black Atlantic: Modernity and Double Consciousness*. Cambridge, Mass.: Harvard University Press, 1993.

Giroux, Henry A. *Border Crossings: Cultural Workers and the Politics of Education*. London: Routledge, 1992.

———, and Peter McLaren. *Between Borders: Pedagogy and the Politics of Cultural Studies*. New York: Routledge, 1994.

Giudici, Alberto. *El Cine Argentino; Hollywood: Del Esplendor al Ocaso*. Buenos Aires: Accion, 1976.

Gladwin, T. and A. Saidin. *Slaves of the White Myth: The Psychology of Neocolonialism*. Atlantic Highlands, NJ: Humanities Press, 1981.

Glissant, Edouard. *Caribbean Discourse*. Charlottesville: University Press of Virginia, 1989.

Godoy Quesada, Mario. *Historia del Cine Chileno*. Santiago: no publisher given, 1966.

Goldberg, David Theo, ed. *Anatomy of Racism*. Minneapolis: University of Minnesota Press, 1990.

———. *Racist Culture: Philosophy and the Politics of Meaning.* Oxford: Blackwell,1993.

Gomez-Peña, Guillermo. *Warrior for* Gringstroika. St Paul, Minn.: Graywolf, 1993.

Gould, Stephen Jay. *The Mismeasure of Man.* New York: W.W. Norton, 1981.

———. *The Flamingo's Smile.* New York: W.W. Norton, 1985.

Greenblatt, Stephen J. *Learning to Curse.* New York: Routledge, 1990.

———. *Marvelous Possessions: The Wonder of the New World.* Chicago: University of Chicago Press, 1991.

Grewal, Inderpal and Caren Kaplan, eds. *Scattered Hegemonies: Postmodernity and Transnational Feminist Practices.* Minneapolis: University of Minnesota Press, 1994.

Grinde Jr, Donald A., and Bruce E. Johansen. *Exemplar of Liberty: Native America and the Evolution of Democracy.* Los Angeles: American Indian Studies Center, University of California, 1991.

Guerrero, Ed. *Framing Blackness.* Philadelphia: Temple University Press, 1993.

Gumucio-Dragon, Alfonso, ed. *Cine, Censurio y Exilio en America Latina.* La Paz: Ediciones Film/Historia, 1979.

———. "*Chuquiago*: X-Ray of a City." *Jump Cut,* No. 23 (October 1980), pp. 6–8.

———. *El cine de los trabajadores.* Managua: Colección Textos, 1981.

Gutierrez-Alea, Tomas. "The Viewer's Dialectic." Parts 1 and 2. *Jump Cut,* No. 29 (February 1984), pp. 18–21, and No. 30 (March 1985), pp. 48–53.

Guzman, Patricio, and Pedro Sempere. *Chile: El Cine contra el Fascismo.* Valencia: Fernando Torres, 1977.

Haffner, Pierre. *Essais sur les Fondements du Cinéma Africain.* Paris: Nouvelles Editions Africaines, 1978.

Hall, Doug, and Sally Jo Fifer. *Illuminating Video: An Essential Guide to Video Art.* Aperture in association with the Bay Area Video Coalition, 1990.

Hall, Stuart. *Race and Class in Post-Colonial Society.* New York: UNESCO, 1977.

———, *et al. Policing the Crisis.* London: Macmillan, 1978.

Haraway, Donna J. *Primate Visions.* New York: Routledge, 1989.

———. *Simians, Cyborgs, and Women: The Reinvention of Nature.* New York: Routledge, 1991.

Harding, Sandra, ed. *"Racial" Economy of Science: Toward a Democratic Future.* Bloomington: Indiana University Press, 1993.

Harlow, Barbara. *Resistance Literature.* New York: Methuen, 1987.

Harris, J.E. ed. *Global Dimensions of the African Diaspora.* Washington, DC: Howard University Press, 1982.

Hawk, Beverly G., ed. *Africa's Media Image.* Westport, Conn.: Greenwood, 1993.

Hebdige, Dick. *Subculture: The Meaning of Style.* London: Methuen, 1979.

———. *Cut 'n Mix: Culture, Identity and Caribbean Music.* London: Methuen, 1987.

Hennebelle, Guy, ed. *Les Cinémas Africains en 1972.* Paris: *L'Afrique Littéraire et Artistique,* No. 20/Société Africaine d'Edition, 1972.

———. *Le Tiers-Monde en Films.* Paris: CinemAction/Tricontinental, 1982.

———, and Alfonso Gumucio-Dragon, eds. *Les Cinémas de l'Amerique Latine.* Paris: Lherminier, 1981.

Hernton, Calvin C. *Sex and Racism in America.* New York: Grove Press, 1965.

———. *The Sexual Mountain and Black Women Writers.* New York: Doubleday, 1987.

Hicks, Emily D. *Border Writing.* Minneapolis: University of Minnesota Press, 1991.

Hijar, Alberto, ed. *Hacia un Tercer Cine.* Mexico City: UNAM, 1972.

Hobsbawm, Eric, and Terence Ranger, eds. *The Invention of Tradition.* Cambridge: Cambridge University Press, 1983.

Hoch, Paul. *White Hero, Black Beast: Racism, Sexism and the Mask of Masculinity.* London: Pluto Press, 1979.

Hockings, Paul, ed. *Principles of Visual Anthropology.* The Hague: Mouton, 1975.

Hodge, John L., Donald K. Struckmann, and Lynn Dorland Trost. *Cultural Bases of*

Racism and Group Oppression. Berkeley, Calif.: Two Riders Press, 1975.

Hojas de Cine: Testimonis y Documentos del Nuevo Cine Latinoamericano, Vols I, II, III: *Centroamerica y el Caribe*. Mexico City: Fundación Mexicana de Cineastas, 1988.

Holloway, Joseph E., ed. *Africanisms in American Culture*. Bloomington: University of Indiana Press, 1990.

Honour, Hugh. *The Image of the Black in Western Art*. 4 Vols. Cambridge, Mass.: Harvard University Press, 1989.

hooks, bell. *And There We Wept*. Privately published, 1978.

———. *Ain't I A Woman? Black Women and Feminism*. Boston: South End Press, 1981.

———. *Feminist Theory. From Margin to Center*. Boston: South End Press, 1984.

———. *Talking Back*. Boston: South End Press, 1989.

———. *Yearning: Race, Gender, and Cultural Politics*. Boston: South End Press, 1990.

———. *Black Looks: Race and Representation*. Boston: South End Press, 1992.

———. *Sisters of the Yam: Black Women and Self-Recovery*. Boston: South End Press, 1993.

———, and Cornel West. *Breaking Bread*. Boston: South End Press, 1991.

Hull, Gloria T., Patricia Bell Scott, and Barbara Smith, eds. *But Some of Us Are Brave*. Old Westbury, NY: Feminist Press, 1982.

Hulme, Peter. *Colonial Encounters: Europe and the Native Caribbean 1492–1797*. London: Methuen, 1986.

———, and Neil L. Whitehead, eds. *Wild Majesty: Encounters with Caribs from Columbus to the Present Day*. Oxford: Clarendon, 1992.

"Identity." ICA Documents No. 6. London: ICA, 1987.

The Independent Commission on International Humanitarian Issues. *Indigenous Peoples: A Global Quest for Justice*. London: Zed, 1987.

Introduction to Korean Motion Pictures. Seoul: Motion Picture Production Corporation, 1980.

Jacobs, Paul, and Saul Landau, with Eve Pell. *To Serve The Devil*, Vol. 1: *Natives and Slaves*. New York: Vintage Books, 1971.

Jaimes, Annette M., ed. *The State of Native America*. Boston: South End Press, 1992.

Jalée, Pierre. *The Pillage of the Third World*. New York: Monthly Review Press, 1968.

James, C.L.R. *The Black Jacobins*. New York: Vintage Books, 1989.

James, David E. *Allegories of Cinema: American Film in the Sixties*. Princeton, NJ: Princeton University Press, 1989.

Jameson, Fredric. *The Geopolitical Aesthetic: Cinema and Space in the World System*. Bloomington and London: Indiana University Press and BFI, 1992.

JanMohamed, Abdul R. *Manichean Aesthetics: The Politics of Literature in Colonial Africa*. Amherst: University of Massachusetts Press, 1983.

———, and David Lloyd, eds. *The Nature and Context of Minority Discourse*. New York: Oxford University Press, 1990.

Jarvie, I.C. *Window on Hong Kong: A Sociological Study of the Hong Kong Film Industry and Its Audience*. Hong Kong: University of Hong Kong Centre for Asian Studies, 1977.

Jayawardena, Kumari. *Feminism and Nationalism in the Third World*. London: Zed, 1986.

Jefferson, Tony, and Stuart Hall, eds. *Resistance through Rituals*. London, Hutchinson, 1975.

Jennings, Francis. *The Invasion of America: Indians, Colonialism and the Cant of Conquest*. New York: W.W. Norton, 1975.

Jhally, Sut, and Justin Lewis. *Enlightened Racism: The Cosby Show, Audiences and the Myth of the American Dream*. Boulder, Colo.: Westview Press, 1992.

Johansen, Bruce E. *Forgotten Founders: How the American Indian Helped Shape Democracy*. Boston: Harvard Common Press, 1982.

Johnson, Charles. *Being and Race: Black Writing since 1970.* Bloomington: Indiana University Press, 1990.

Johnson, Randal. *Cinema Novo X 5: Masters of Contemporary Brazilian Film.* Austin: University of Texas Press, 1984.

———, and Robert Stam, eds. *Brazilian Cinema.* Rutherford, NJ: Fairleigh Dickinson University Press, 1982; republished Austin: University of Texas Press, 1987.

Jordan, Winthrop D. *White over Black.* Baltimore, MD.: Penguin, 1968.

Josephy Jr, Alvin M. *America in 1492.* New York: Alfred A. Knopf, 1992.

Joshi, Svati, ed. *Rethinking English.* New Delhi: Trianka, 1991.

Kabbani, Rana. *Europe's Myth of the Orient.* Bloomington: Indiana University Press, 1986.

Kabir, Nasreen. *Les Stars du Cinéma Indien.* Paris: Centre Georges Pompidou/Centre National de la Cinématographie, 1985.

Katz, Judith H. *White Awareness: Handbook for Anti-Racism Training.* Norman: University of Oklahoma Press, 1978.

Keller, Gary D., ed. *Cine Chicano.* Mexico City: Cineteca Nacional, 1988.

Khan, Aga Saddruddin and Hassan bin Talal, *Indigenous Peoples: A Global Quest for Justice.* London: Zed, 1987.

Khan, M. *An Introduction to the Egyptian Cinema.* London: Informatics, 1969.

Khlifi, Omar. *L'Histoire du Cinéma en Tunisie.* Tunis: Société Tunisienne de Diffusion, 1970.

Killingray, David. *A Plague of Europeans.* Harmondsworth: Penguin, 1973.

King, John, Ana M. Lopez, and Manuel Alvarado, eds. *Mediating Two Worlds: Cinematic Encounters in the Americas.* London: BFI, 1993.

Kipnis, Laura. *Ecstasy Unlimited: On Sex, Capital, Gender and Aesthetics.* Minneapolis: University of Minnesota Press, 1993.

Klotman, Phyllis Rauch, ed. *Screenplays of the African American Experience.* Bloomington: Indiana University Press, 1991.

Kochman, Thomas. *Black and White Styles in Conflict.* Chicago: University of Chicago Press, 1981.

Korzenny, Felipe and Stella Ting-Toomey, eds. *Mass-Media Effects across Cultures.* London: Sage, 1992.

Kovel, Joel. *White Racism: A Psychohistory.* New York: Columbia University Press, 1984.

Kruger, Barbara, and Phil Mariani, eds. *Remaking History.* Seattle, Wash.: Bay Press, 1989.

Krupat, Arnold. *For Those Who Come After.* Berkeley: University of California Press, 1985.

———. *The Voice in the Margin: Native American Literature and the Canon.* Berkeley: University of California Press, 1989.

LaCapra, Dominick, ed. *The Bounds of Race.* Ithaca, NY: Cornell University Press, 1991.

Lakoff, Robin. *Language and Woman's Place.* New York: Harper and Row, 1975.

Lambropoulos, Vassilis. *The Rise of Eurocentrism: Anatomy of Interpretation.* Princeton, NJ: Princeton University Press, 1993.

Laroui, Abdallah. *L'Idéologie Arabe Contemporaine.* Paris: François Maspero, 1967.

———. *The Crisis of the Arab Intellectual: Traditionalism or Historicism?*, trans. from the French by Diarmid Cammell. Berkeley: University of California Press, 1976.

Lash, Scott, and Jonathan Friedman. *Modernity and Identity.* Oxford: Blackwell, 1992.

"The Last 'Special Issue' on Race?" *Screen*, Vol. 29, No. 4 (Autumn 1988).

"Latin American Dossier." Parts 1 and 2. *Framework*, No. 10 (Spring 1979), pp. 11–38, and No. 11 (Autumn 1979), pp. 18–27.

"Latin American Film." Dossier. *Jump Cut*, No. 30 (March 1985), pp. 44–61.

"Latin American Militant Cinema." Special issue. *Cineaste 4*, No. 3 (1970–1).

Lavie, Smadar. *The Poetics of Military Occupation: Mzeina Allegories of Bedouin Identity under Israeli and Egyptian Rule.* Berkeley: University of California Press, 1990.

Leab, Daniel J. *From Sambo to Superspade: The Black Experience in Motion Pictures.* Boston: Houghton-Mifflin, 1976.

Lee, Spike, with Lisa Jones. *Uplift the Race: The Construction of School Daze.* New York: Simon and Schuster, 1988.

——. *Do The Right Thing.* New York: Simon and Schuster, 1989.

——. *Mo' Better Blues.* New York: Simon and Schuster, 1990.

——. *By Any Means Necessary.* New York: Hyperion, 1992.

Lent, John A. *The Asian Film Industry.* Austin: University of Texas Press, 1990.

Leon-Portilla, Miguel, ed. *The Broken Spears: The Aztec Account of the Conquest of Mexico.* Boston: Beacon Press, 1962.

Leyda, Jay. *Dianying: Electric Shadows – An Account of Films and Film Audience in China.* Cambridge, Mass.: MIT Press, 1972.

Li Cheuk-to, ed. *A Study of Hong Kong Cinema in the Seventies.* Hong Kong: Eighth International Film Festival, 1984.

Liauzu, Claude. *Aux Origines des Tiers-Mondismes: Colonistes et Anticolonialistes en France 1919–1939.* Paris: Editions l'Harmattan, 1982.

Lin Niantong, ed. *Cantonese Cinema Retrospective, 1950–59.* Hong Kong: Second International Film Festival, 1978.

——. *Hong Kong Cinema Survey, 1946–68.* Hong Kong: Third International Film Festival, 1979.

Lippard, Lucy R. *Mixed Blessings: New Art in a Multicultural America.* New York: Pantheon Books, 1990.

Lipsitz, George. *Time Passages: Collective Memory and American Popular Culture.* Minneapolis: University of Minnesota Press, 1990.

Littin, Miguel. *Cine Chileno: La Tierra Prometida.* Caracas: Rocinante, 1974.

Lloyd, David. *Nationalism and Minor Literature.* Berkeley: University of California Press, 1987.

Long, Daniel. *The Power within Us: Cabeza de Vaca's Relation of His Journey from Florida to the Pacific, 1528–1536.* New York: Duell, Sloan and Pearce, 1944.

Lowe, Lisa. *Critical Terrains: French and British Orientalisms.* Ithaca, NY: Cornell University Press, 1991.

Lunenfeld, Marvin, ed. *1492: Discovery/Invasion/Encounter.* Chicago: Newberry Library, 1989.

Lyons, Oren, John Mohawk, Vine Deloria Jr., Laurence Hauptman, Howard Berman, Donald Grinde Jr., Curtis Berkey, and Robert Venables. *Exiled in the Land of the Free: Democracy, Indian Nations, and the U.S. Constitution.* Santa Fe, Calif.: Clear Light, 1992.

Maarek, Philippe J., ed. *Afrique Noire: Quel Cinéma?* Paris: Association du Ciné-Club de l'Université Paris X, 1983.

MacCannell, Dean. *Empty Meeting Grounds: The Tourist Papers.* London: Routledge, 1992.

MacKenzie, John M., ed. *Imperialism and Popular Culture.* Manchester: Manchester University Press, 1986.

al-Mafraji, Ahmed Fayadh. *The Cinema in Iraq.* Baghdad: Research and Studies Center, General Establishment for Cinema and Theatre, Ministry of Culture and Information, 1978.

Magdoff, H. *Imperialism: From the Colonial Age to the Present.* NY: Monthly Review Press, 1978.

Maherzi, Lofti. *Le Cinéma Algérien: Institutions, Imaginaire, Idéologie.* Algiers: Société Nationale d'Edition et de Diffusion, 1980.

Mahieu, Jose Agustin. *Breve Historia del Cine Argentino.* Buenos Aires: EUDEBA, 1966.

Malkmus, Lizbeth, and Roy Armes. *Arab and African Filmmaking.* London: Zed, 1991.

Mannix, Daniel P., with Malcolm Cowley. *Black Cargoes.* New York: Viking, 1962.

Mapping Colonialism. Berkeley: Group for the Critical Study of Colonialism, University of California, 1988.

Marable, Manning. *How Capitalism Underdeveloped Black America.* Boston: South End Press, 1983.

———. *Black America.* Westfield, NJ: Open Magazine, pamphlet series, 1992.

Marcus, George E. and Michael M.J. Fischer, *Anthropology as Cultural Critique: An Experimental Moment in the Human Sciences.* Chicago: University of Chicago Press, 1986.

Marshall, P. and G. Williams. *The Great Map of Mankind: British Perceptions of the World in the Age of Enlightenment.* London: Dent, 1982.

Martin, Angela, ed. *African Films: The Context of Production.* BFI Dossier No. 6, British Film Institute, 1982.

Martinez Pardo, Hernando. *Historia del Cine Colombiano.* Bogota: Guadalupe, 1978.

Martinez Torres, Augusto, and Manuel Perz Estremera. *Nuevo Cine Latinoamericano.* Barcelona: Editorial Anagrama, 1973.

Mattelart, Armand. *La Cultura Como Empresa Multinacional.* Mexico City: Ediciones Era, 1974.

———. *Multinational Corporations and the Control of Culture.* Brighton: Harvester Press, 1979.

———, and Seth Siegelaub, eds. *Communication and Class Struggle,* Vol 1: *Capitalism, Imperialism.* New York: International General, 1979, and Vol. 2: *Liberation, Socialism.* New York: International General, 1983.

Mauduy, Jacques, and Gerard Henriet. *Géographies du Western.* Paris: Nathan, 1989.

Maynard, Richard A. *Africa on Film: Myth and Reality.* Rochelle Park, NJ: Hayden Book Co., 1974.

———. *The Black Man on Film: Racial Stereotyping.* Rochelle Park, NJ: Hayden Books, 1974.

Mazrui, Ali A. *The Africans.* Boston: Little, Brown, 1986.

McCarthy, Cameron and Warren Crichlow, eds. *Race and Representation in Education.* New York: Routledge, 1993.

McClure, John. *Late Imperial Romance: Literature and Globalization from Conrad to Pynchon.* London: Verso, 1994.

McCulloch, J. *Black Soul, White Artifact.* New York: Cambridge University Press, 1983.

McGrave, Bernard. *Beyond Anthropology.* New York: Columbia University Press, 1989.

Megherbi, Abdelghani. *Les Algériens au Miroir du Cinéma Colonial.* Algiers: Editions SNED, 1982.

Mellencamp, Patricia and Philip Rosen. *Cinema Histories/Cinema Practices.* Fredericksburg, Md.: University Publications of America, 1984.

Memmi, Albert. *Dominated Man.* Boston: Beacon Press, 1968.

———. *The Colonizer and the Colonized.* London: Souvenir Press, 1974.

Merchant, Carolyn. *Ecological Revolutions: Nature, Gender and Science in New England.* Chapel Hill: University of North Carolina Press, 1989.

Merle, Marcel, ed. *L'Anti-colonialisme Européen de las Casas à Karl Marx.* Paris: Armand Colin, 1969.

Mernissi, Fatima. *Le Harem Politique: Le Prophète et les Femmes.* Paris: Editions Albin Michel, 1987.

———. *The Forgotten Queens of Islam.* Minneapolis: University of Minnesota Press, 1993.

Mesa, Carlos D. *El Cine en Bolivia.* La Paz: Don Bosco de la Laz, 1976.

——, Beatriz Palacios, Jorge Sanjines, Arturo Von Vacano, *et al. Cine Boliviano: Del Realizador al Critico*. La Paz: Gisbert, 1979.

Meyerson, Michael, ed. *Memories of Underdevelopment – The Revolutionary Films of Cuba*. New York: Grossman, 1973.

Mikhail, Mona N. *Images of Arab Women: Fact and Fiction*. Washington, DC: Three Continents Press, 1981.

Miles, Robert. *Racism*. New York: Routledge, 1989.

Miller, Christopher. *Blank Darkness: Africanist Discourse in French*. Chicago: University of Chicago Press, 1985.

——. *Theories of Africans*. Chicago: University of Chicago Press, 1990.

Miller, Randall M., ed. *The Kaleidoscopic Lens: How Hollywood Views Ethnic Groups*. Englewood, NJ: Jerome S. Ozer, 1980.

Mitchell, Timothy. *Colonizing Egypt*. Berkeley: University of California Press, 1991.

Mohanty, Chandra Talpade, Ann Russo, Lourdes Torres, eds. *Third World Women and the Politics of Feminism*. Bloomington: Indiana University Press, 1991.

Mora, Carl J. *Mexican Cinema: Reflections of a Society 1896–1988*. Berkeley: University of California Press, 1988.

Moraga, Cherríe, and Gloria Anzaldúa, eds. *This Bridge Called My Back: Writings by Radical Women of Color*. Watertown, Mass.: Persephone Press, 1981.

Morrison, Toni, ed., *Race-ing Justice, En-gendering Power: Essays on Anita Hill, Clarence Thomas and the Construction of Social Reality*. New York: Pantheon, 1992.

——. *Playing in the Dark: Whiteness and the Literary Imagination* (New York: Vintage Books, 1993).

Mosse, George L. *Toward the Final Solution: A History of European Racism*. London: Dent, 1978.

Mphahlele, Ezekiel. *The African Image*. New York: Praeger, 1962.

Mudimbe, V.Y. *The Invention of Africa: Gnosis, Philosophy, and the Order of Knowledge*. Bloomington: Indiana University Press, 1988.

Murray, James P. *To Find an Image: Black Films from Uncle Tom to Superfly*. Indianapolis: Bobbs-Merrill, 1973.

Nabokov, Peter, ed. *Native American Testimony*. New York: Viking, 1991.

Naficy, Hamid. *The Making of Exile Cultures: Iranian Television in Los Angeles*. Minneapolis: University of Minnesota Press, 1993.

——. and Teshome H. Gabriel, eds. *Otherness and the Media: Ethnography of the Imagined and the Imaged*. Langhorne, Penn.: Harwood, 1993.

Nah, June and Maria Patricia Fernandez-Kelly. *Women, Men and the International Division of Labor*. Albany, NY: SUNY Press, 1983.

Nandy, Ashis. *The Intimate Enemy: Loss and Recovery of Self under Colonialism*. Delhi: Oxford University Press, 1991.

Nelson, Cary, Paula A. Treichler and Lawrence Grossberg, eds. *Cultural Studies*. New York: Routledge, 1992.

Nesteby, James. *Black Images in American Films, 1896–1954*. Washington, DC: University Press of America, 1982.

Nevares, Beatriz Reyes. *The Mexican Cinema – Interviews with Thirteen Directors*. Albuquerque: University of New Mexico Press, 1976.

Ngũgĩ wa Thiong'o. *Writers in Politics*. London: Heinemann, 1981.

——. *Decolonizing the Mind*. London and Nairobi: James Currey/Heinemann Kenya, 1986.

Nichols, Bill. *Representing Reality: Issues and Concepts in Documentary*. Bloomington: Indiana University Press, 1991.

The 1989 Guide to Multicultural Resources. Madison, Wisc.: Praxis Publications, 1989.

Nixon, Rob. *London Calling: V.S. Naipaul, Postcolonial Mandarin*. New York: Oxford

University Press, 1992.

Nkrumah, Kwame. *Neo-Colonialism: The Last Stage of Imperialism*. London: Nelson, 1965.

Noble, Gil. *The Negro in Films*. London: Skelton Robinson, 1948.

———. *Black Is the Color of My TV Tube*. Secaucus, NJ: Lyle Stuart, 1981.

Noriega, Chon, ed. *Chicanos and Film: Essays on Chicano Representation and Resistance*. New York: Garland, 1991. Reprinted University of Minnesota Press, 1992.

Norris, Christopher. *Uncritical Theory: Postmodernism, Intellectuals and the Gulf War*. Amherst: University of Massachusetts, 1992.

Nouri, Shakir. *À la recherche du cinéma irakien*. Paris: Editions l'Harmattan, 1986.

Null, Gary. *Black Hollywood: The Negro in Motion Pictures*. Secaucus, NJ: Citadel Press, 1975.

Ong, Aihwa, *Spirits of Resistance and Capitalist Discipline*. Albany, NY: SUNY Press, 1987.

"Other Cinemas, Other Criticisms." Special issue. *Screen 26*, Nos 3–4 (1985).

Otten, Rik. *Le Cinéma au Zaire, au Rwanda et au Burundi*. Brussels/Paris: OCCIC/L'Harmattan, 1984.

Pagden, Anthony. *Spanish Imperialism and the Political Imagination*. New Haven, Conn.: Yale University Press, 1990.

Palacios More, René, and Daniel Mateus. *El Cine Latinoamericano*. Madrid: Sedmany, 1976.

Paranagua, Paulo Antonio. *Cinéma na America Latina*. Porto Alegre, Brazil: L and PM, 1984.

———, and José Carlos Avellar, eds. *Cinema Bresilien 1970–1980*. Documentation for the International Film Festival, Locarno, 1983.

Parker, Andrew, Mary Russo, Doris Sommer, and Patricia Yaeger. *Nationalisms and Sexualities*. New York: Routledge, 1992.

Parrain, Pierre. *Regards sur le Cinéma Indien*. Paris: Cerf, 1969.

Parry, Benita. *Delusions and Discoveries: Studies on India in the British Imagination 1880–1930*. Berkeley: University of California Press, 1972.

Passek, Jean-Loup, ed. *Le Cinéma Indien*. Paris: Centre Georges Pompidou/L'Equerre, 1983.

Patterson, Lindsay, ed. *Black Films and Filmmakers*. New York: Dodd, Mead and Co., 1975.

Pearce, Roy Harvey. *Savagism and Civilization*. Berkeley: University of California Press, 1988.

Penley, Constance and Andrew Ross, eds. for the *Social Text* Collective. *Technoculture*. Minneapolis: University of Minnesota Press, 1991.

Peterson, Scott. *Native American Prophecies: Examining the History, Wisdom, and Startling Predictions of Visionary Native Americans*. New York: Paragon House, 1990.

Petrie, Duncan, ed. *Screening Europe: Image and Identity in Contemporary European Cinema*. London: BFI, 1992.

Pettit, Arthur G. *Images of the Mexican American in Fiction and Film*. College Station: Texas A and M University Press, 1980.

Pick, Zuzana M., ed. *Latin American Filmmakers and the Third Cinema*. Ottawa: Carleton University Press, 1978.

———. *The New Latin American Cinema: A Continental Project*. Austin: University of Texas, 1993.

Pieterse, Jan Nederveen. *Empire and Emancipation*. London: Pluto Press, 1990.

———. *White on Black: Images of Africa and Blacks in Western Popular Culture*. New Haven, Conn.: Yale University Press, 1992.

Pines, Jim. *Blacks in Films: A Survey of Racial Themes and Images in the American Film*.

London: Studio Vista, 1975.

——, and Paul Willemen, eds. *Questions of Third Cinema*. London: BFI, 1989.

Pommier, Pierre. *Cinéma et Développement en Afrique Noir Francophone*. Paris: Pedone, 1974.

Post-Revolutionary Iranian Cinema. Teheran: General Department of Cinematic Research and Relations, 1982.

Pratt, Mary-Louise. *Imperial Eyes: Travel Writing and Transculturation*. New York: Routledge, 1992.

Pribram, Deidre, ed. *Female Spectators: Looking at Film and Television*. London: Verso, 1988.

Price, Richard, ed. *Maroon Societies: Rebel Slave Communities in the Americas*. New York: Anchor Books, 1973.

Price, Sally. *Primitive Art in Civilized Places*. Chicago: University of Chicago Press, 1989.

Quiquemelle, Marie-Claire, and Jean-Loup Passek, eds. *Le cinéma Chinois*. Paris: Centre Georges Pompidou, 1985.

Raboteau, Albert J. *Slave Religion*. New York: Oxford University Press, 1978.

"Racism, Colonialism, and Cinema." Special issue. *Screen 24*, No. 2 (1983)

Raha, Kiranmoy, ed. *Indian Cinema 81/82*. New Delhi: Indian Directorate of Film Festivals, 1982.

Ramachandran, T.M., ed. *Seventy Years of Indian Cinema (1913–1983)*. Bombay: Cinema India International, 1985.

Ramos, Juanita, ed. *Compañeras: Latina Lesbians*. New York: Latina Lesbian History Project, 1987.

Rangoonwalla, Firoze. *Satyajit Ray's Art*. Delhi: Clarion Books, 1980.

——. *Indian Cinema: Past and Present*. New Delhi: Clarion Books, 1983.

Ranucci, Karen. *Directory of Film and Video Production Resources in Latin America and the Caribbean*. New York: Foundation for Independent Video and Film, 1989.

Rashad, Adib (James Miller). *Aspects of Euro-Centric Thought*. Hampton, Va.: United Brothers and Sisters Communications Systems, 1991.

Raskin, Jonah. *The Mythology of Imperialism*. New York: Delta, 1971.

Ray, Satyajit. *Our Films, Their Films*. New Delhi: Orient Longman, 1986.

Rayns, Tony, and Scott Meek. *Electric Shadows: Forty-five Years of Chinese Cinema*. London: BFI, 1980.

Reeves, Geoffrey. *Communications and the "Third World."* London: Routledge, 1993.

Reid, Mark A., *Redefining Black Film*. Berkeley: University of California Press, 1992.

Retamar, Roberto Fernandez. *Caliban and Other Essays*. Minneapolis: University of Minnesota Press, 1989.

Reyes, Aurelio de los. *Los Origenes del Cine en Mexico*. Mexico City: UNAM, 1973.

——, et al. *80 Anos de Cine en Mexico*. Mexico City: Imprensa Madero, 1977.

Richards, Jeffrey. *Visions of Yesterday*. London: Routledge and Kegan Paul, 1973.

Robbins, Bruce. *Secular Vocations: Intellectuals, Professionalism, Culture*. London: Verso, 1993.

Rocha, Glauber. *Revisão Critica do Cinema Brasileiro*. Rio de Janeiro: Editora Civil-azação Brasileira, 1963.

——. *O Seculo do Cinema*. Rio de Janeiro: Editora Alhambra, 1983.

Rodney, Walter. *How Europe Underdeveloped Africa*. London: Bogle-L'Ouverture, 1972.

Roediger, David R. *The Wages of Whiteness: Race and the Making of the American Working Class*. London: Verso, 1991.

Rogin, Michael. *Ronald Reagan, the Movie*. Berkeley: University of California Press, 1987.

Rosaldo, Renato. *Culture and Truth: The Remaking of Social Analysis*. Boston: Beacon Press, 1989.

Rose, Phyllis. *Jazz Cleopatra*. New York: Random House, 1989.

Rose, Tricia. *Black Noise*. Middletown, Conn.: Wesleyan University Press, 1994.

Ross, Andrew. *No Respect: Intellectuals and Popular Culture*. New York: Routledge, 1989.

Rowe, William, and Vivian Schelling. *Memory and Modernity: Popular Culture in Latin America*. New York: Verso, 1991.

Rubin, Bernard, ed. *Small Voices and Great Trumpets: Minorities in the Media*. New York: Praeger, 1980.

Ryan, Michael, and Douglas Kellner. *Camera Politica*. Bloomington: Indiana University Press, 1988.

Saadawi, Nawal El. *The Hidden Face of Eve: Women in the Arab World*. London: Zed, 1980.

Sadoul, Georges, ed. *The Cinema in Arab Countries*. Beirut: Interarab Center for Cinema and Television/UNESCO, 1966.

Said, Edward W. *Orientalism*. New York: Pantheon, 1978.

———. *The Question of Palestine*. New York: Times Books, 1979.

———. *Covering Islam: How the Media and the Experts Determine How We See the Rest of the World*. New York: Pantheon Books, 1981.

———. *The World, The Text and the Critic*. Cambridge, Mass.: Harvard University Press, 1983.

———. *After the Last Sky*. New York: Pantheon, 1986.

———. *Culture and Imperialism*. New York: Knopf, 1992.

———, and Christopher Hitchens, eds. *Blaming the Victims: Spurious Scholarship and the Palestinian Question*. London: Verso, 1988.

Saldivar, José David. *The Dialectics of Our America*. Durham, NC: Duke University Press, 1991.

Sale, Kirkpatrick. *The Conquest of Paradise*. New York: Alfred A. Knopf, 1990.

Salles, Gomes, and Paulo Emilio. *Cinema: Trajetoria no Subdesenvolvimento*. Rio de Janeiro: Paz e Terra/Embrafilme, 1980.

Salmane, Hala, *et al. Algerian Cinema*. London: BFI, 1976.

Sanchez, Alberto Ruy. *Mitologia de un Ciné en Crisis*. Mexico City, Premia Editora, 1981.

Sangari, Kumkum, and Sudesh Vaid, eds. *Recasting Women: Essays in Colonial History*. New Delhi: Kali for Women Press, 1989.

Sarkar, Kobita. *Indian Cinema Today*. Delhi: Sterling Publishers, 1975.

Schiller, Herbert I. *Mass Communications and American Empire*. New York: Augustus M. Kelley, 1970.

———. *Communication and Cultural Domination*. New York: M.E. Sharpe, 1976.

Schneider, Cynthia, and Brian Wallis, eds. *Global Television*. New York: Wedge Press, 1988.

Schnitman, Jorge A. *Film Industries in Latin America: Dependency and Development*. Norwood, NJ: Ablex, 1984.

Scognamillo, Giovanni, *et al. The Turkish Cinema*. Istanbul: IDGSA, 1979.

Scott, James C. *Domination and the Arts of Resistance*. New Haven, Conn.: Yale University Press, 1990.

Sen, Mrinal. *Views on Cinema*. Calcutta: Ishan Publications, 1977.

Sertima, Ivan van. *They Came before Columbus*. New York: Random House, 1975.

Shah, Panna. *The Indian Film*. Bombay: Motion Picture Society, 1950.

Shaheen, Jack. *The TV Arab*. Bowling Green, Ohio: Bowling Green State University Popular Culture Press, 1984.

Sharpe, Jenny. *Allegories of Empire: The Figure of the Woman in the Colonial Text*. Minneapolis: University of Minnesota Press, 1993.

Shohat, Ella. *Israeli Cinema: East/West and the Politics of Representation*. Austin:

University of Texas Press, 1989.

Sidran, Ben. *Black Talk.* New York: Da Capo, 1983.

da Silva, Janice Theodoro. *Descobrimentos e colonização.* São Paulo: Editora Atica, 1987.

Simone, Timothy Maliqalim. *About Face: Race in Postmodern America.* New York: Autonomedia, 1989.

Simonson, Rick, and Scott Walter, eds. *The Graywolf Annual Five: Multi-Cultural Literacy.* St Paul, Minn.: Graywolf Press, 1988.

Singh, K.S., ed. *Visual Anthropology and India.* Calcutta: Seagull Books, 1992.

Sleeter, Christine E., *Empowerment through Multicultural Education.* Albany: State University of New York Press, 1991.

Sklar, Robert, and Charles Musser, eds. *Resisting Images: Essays on Cinema and History.* Philadelphia: Temple University Press, 1990.

Slotkin, Richard. *Regeneration through Violence: The Mythology of the American Frontier, 1600–1860.* Middletown, Conn.: Wesleyan University Press, 1973.

———. *The Fatal Environment: The Myth of the Frontier in the Age of Industrialization, 1800–1890.* Middletown, Conn.: Wesleyan University Press, 1985.

———. *Gunfighter Nation: The Myth of the Frontier in Twentieth Century America.* New York: Atheneum, 1992.

Smith, Anthony. *The Geopolitics of Information: How Western Politics Dominates the World.* New York: Oxford University Press, 1980.

Smith, Barbara. *Home Girls: A Black Feminist Anthology.* New York: Kitchen Table Women of Color Press, 1983.

Smith, Valery. *Self-Discovery and Authority in Afro-American Narrative.* Cambridge, Mass.: Harvard University Press, 1987.

Smitherman-Donaldson, Geneva, and Teun A. van Dijk. *Discourse and Discrimination.* Detroit: Wayne State University Press, 1988.

Solanas, Fernando E., and Octavoi Getino. *Ciné, Cultura y Descolonización.* Mexico City: Siglo Veintiuno Editores, 1973.

Sollors, Werner. *Beyond Ethnicity.* New York: Oxford University Press, 1986.

———. *The Invention of Ethnicity.* New York: Oxford University Press, 1989.

Social Text. Special Issue on Postcolonialism (with an introduction by John McClure and Aamir Mufti), Vols 31–2. Durham, NC: Duke University Press, 1992.

Soyinka, Wole. *Myth, Literature and the African World.* New York: Cambridge University Press, 1976.

Spillers, Hortense J. *Comparative American Identities.* New York: Routledge, 1991.

Spivak, Gayatri Chakravorty. *In Other Worlds.* New York: Methuen, 1987.

———. *The Post-Colonial Critic: Interviews, Strategies, Dialogues,* ed. Sarah Harasym. New York: Routledge, 1990.

Sprinker, Michael, ed. *Edward Said: A Critical Reader.* Oxford: Blackwell, 1992.

Spurr, David. *The Rhetoric of Empire: Colonial Discourse in Journalism, Travel Writing and Imperial Administration.* Durham, NC: Duke University Press, 1993.

Stam, Robert. *Reflexivity in Film and Literature: From Don Quixote to Jean-Luc Godard.* Ann Arbor: University of Michigan Press, 1985; republished New York: Columbia University Press, 1992.

———. *Subversive Pleasures: Bakhtin, Cultural Criticism, and Film.* Baltimore, Md.: Johns Hopkins University Press, 1989.

Standly, Fred L., and Lois H. Pratt, eds. *Conversations with James Baldwin.* Jackson: University Press of Mississippi, 1989.

Stannard, David E. *American Holocaust: Columbus and the Conquest of the New World.* New York: Oxford University Press, 1992.

Stedman, Raymond William. *Shadows of the Indian.* Norman: University of Oklahoma Press, 1982.

Stein, Stanley J., and Barbara H. Stein. *The Colonial Heritage of Latin America*. New York: Oxford University Press, 1970.

Steinberg, Stephen. *The Ethnic Myth: Race, Ethnicity and Class in America*. Boston: Beacon Press, 1981.

Stember, C.H. *Sexual Racism*. New York: Elsevier, 1976.

Street, Brian. *The Savage in Literature: Representations of "Primitive" Society in English Fiction 1858–1920*. London: Routledge and Kegan Paul, 1975.

Strobel, Margaret. *European Women in British Africa and Asia*. Bloomington: Indiana University Press, 1990.

Suleiri Sara. *The Rhetoric of English India*. Chicago: University of Chicago Press, 1992.

Sussekind, Flora. *O Brasil não é longe dàqui*. São Paulo: Companhia das Letras, 1990.

Swann, Brian, and Arnold Krupit, eds. *I Tell You Now: Autobiographical Essays by Native American Writers*. Lincoln: University of Nebraska Press, 1987.

Symposium on Cinema in Developing Countries. New Delhi: Ministry of Information and Broadcasting, 1979.

Taguieff, P.A. *La Force du Préjugé*. Paris: Editions la Découverte, 1987.

Takaki, Ronald T. *From Different Shores: Perspectives on Race and Ethnicity in America*. New York: Oxford University Press, 1988.

Taussig, Michael. *Shamanism, Colonialism, and the Wild Man: A Study in Terror and Healing*. Chicago: University of Chicago Press, 1987.

———. *Mimesis and Alterity: A Particular History of the Senses*. New York: Routledge, 1993.

"Third World Film." *Jump Cut*, No. 27 (July 1982), pp. 14–40.

Thompson, Robert Farris. *Flash of the Spirit*. New York: Random House, 1983.

Thoraval, Yves. *Regards sur le Cinéma Egyptien*. Beirut: Dar el-Machreq, 1976.

Todorov, Tzvetan. *The Conquest of America*. New York: Harper and Row, 1984.

———. *On Human Diversity: Nationalism, Racism and Exoticism in French Thought*, trans. Catherine Porter. Cambridge, Mass.: Harvard University Press, 1993.

Tomlinson, John. *Cultural Imperialism*. Baltimore, Md.: Johns Hopkins University Press, 1991.

Tompkins, Jane. *West of Everything: The Inner Life of Westerns*. New York: Oxford University Press, 1992.

Torgovnick, Marianna. *Gone Primitive*. Chicago: University of Chicago Press, 1990.

Trask, Haunani-Kay. *From a Native Daughter: Colonialism & Sovereignty in Hawaii*. Monroe, Maine: Common Courage Press, 1993.

Trinh T. Minh-ha. *Woman, Native, Other*. Bloomington: Indiana University Press, 1989.

———. *When the Moon Waxes Red: Representation, Gender and Cultural Politics*. New York: Routledge, 1991.

———. *Framer Framed*. London: Routledge, 1992.

Troupe, Quincy. *James Baldwin: The Legacy*. New York: Simon and Schuster, 1989.

U.S. Commission on Civil Rights. *Window Dressing on the Set: Women and Minorities in Television*. Washington, DC: U.S. Commission on Civil Rights, 1977.

de Usabel, Gaizka S. *The High Noon of American Films in Latin America*. Ann Arbor: University of Michigan Press Research Press, 1982.

Valverde, Umberto. *Reportaje Critico al Cine Colombiano*. Bogota: Toronuevo, 1978.

Vasudev, Aruna. *Liberty and Licence in the Indian Cinema*. New Delhi: Vikas, 1978.

———. *The Role of the Cinema in Promoting Popular Participation in Cultural Life in India*. Paris: UNESCO, 1981.

———. *The Film Industry's Use of Traditional and Contemporary Arts*. Paris: UNESCO, 1982.

———. *Indian Cinema 82/83*. New Delhi: Indian Directorate of Film Festivals, 1983.

———, and Philippe Lenglet, eds. *Indian Cinema Superbazaar*. New Delhi: Vikas, 1983.

379

Vega, Alicia, ed. *Re-vision del Cine Chileno*. Santiago: Aconcagua, 1979.

Vieyra, Paulin Soumanou. *Le Cinema et l'Afrique*. Paris: Présence Africaine, 1969.

———. *Le Cinéma Africain des Origines à 1973*. Paris: Présence Africaine, 1975.

———. *Le Cinéma au Senegal*. Brussels/Paris: OCIC/L'Harmattan, 1983.

Viswanathan, Gauri. *The Masks of Conquest: Literary Study and British Rule in India*. New York: Columbia University Press, 1989.

Wall, Cheryl A., ed. *Changing Our Own Words*. New Brunswick, NJ: Rutgers University Press, 1989.

Wallace, Michele. *Black Macho and the Myth of the Superwoman*. New York: Dial Press, 1979.

———. *Invisibility Blues*. London: Verso, 1990.

Wallerstein, Immanuel. *The Modern World System*. New York: Academic Press, 1974.

Ware, Vron. *Beyond the Pale: White Women, Racism and History*. London: Verso, 1992.

Weatherford, Jack. *Indian Givers: How the Indians of the Americas Transformed the World*. New York, Fawcett, 1988.

———. *Native Roots: How the Indians Enriched America*. New York: Fawcett, 1991.

West, Cornel. *Beyond Eurocentrism and Multiculturalism*. Vols I and II. Monroe, Maine: Common Courage Press, 1992.

———. *Keeping Faith: Philosophy and Race in America*. London: Routledge, 1993.

Willemen, Paul, and Behroze Gandhi, eds. *Indian Cinema*. BFI Dossier No. 5, London: BFI, 1982.

Williams, Eric. *From Columbus to Castro: The History of the Caribbean, 1492–1969*. New York: Vintage Books, 1984.

Williams, Patricia J. *The Alchemy of Race and Rights*. Cambridge, Mass.: Harvard University Press, 1991.

Williams, Walter W. *The Spirit and the Flesh: Sexual Diversity in American Indian Culture*. Boston: Beacon Press, 1992.

Willis, Susan. *Specifying: Black Women Writing the American Experience*. Madison: University of Wisconsin Press, 1987.

Woll, Allen L. *The Latin Image in American Film*. Los Angeles: University of California Latin American Center Publications, 1980.

———, and Randall M. Miller. *Ethnic and Racial Images in American Film and Television*. New York: Garland, 1987.

Wright, Ronald. *Stolen Continents: The Americans through Indian Eyes since 1492*. Boston: Houghton-Mifflin, 1992.

Wunenburger, Jean-Jacques, ed. *La Recontre des Imaginaires: entre Europe et Amériques*. Paris: L'Harmattan, 1993.

X, Malcolm. *The Autobiography of Malcolm X*. Harmondsworth: Penguin, 1968.

Xavier, Ismail. *Sertão Mar: Glauber Rocha e a estetica da Fome*. São Paulo: Editora Brasiliense, 1983.

———. *Alegorias do Subdesenvolvimento: Cinema Novo, Tropicalismo, Cinema Marginal*. São Paulo, Brazil: Editoria Brasiliense, 1993.

Yeboah, Samuel Kennedy. *The Ideology of Racism*. London: Hansib, 1988.

Young, Robert. *White Mythologies: Writing History and the West*. New York: Routledge, 1990.

INDEX

381